INTRODUCTION TO BUSINESS

THIRD EDITION

INTRODUCTION

John A. Reinecke

University of New Orleans

TO BUSINESS

A Contemporary View

William F. Schoell
University of Southern Mississippi

ALLYN AND BACON, INC.
Boston, London, Sydney, Toronto

Production Editor: David Dahlbacka
Designer: Dorothy Thompson
Art Editor: Armen Kojoyian
Cover Designer: Christy Rosso
Preparation Buyer: Patricia Hart
Manufacturing Buyer: Linda Jackson
Series Editor: Jack B. Rochester
Managing Editor: Michael E. Meehan

Library of Congress Cataloging in Publication Data

Reinecke, John A   1931–
   Introduction to business.

   Includes index.
   1. Business.   I. Schoell, William F., joint author.
II. Title.
HF5351.R44   1980   658.4   79–20564
ISBN 0–205–06879–0

Printed in the United States of America

Credits

Four-Color insert: p. 1—Printed with the permission of Gerber Products Company. p. 2—© Johnson & Johnson. p. 3 top—Baccarat, Inc.,
55 East 57th St., New York, NY 10022. p. 3 right—Advertisement
courtesy of Danskin, Inc. p. 4—Courtesy of Wells Fargo Bank.
Section One: facing p. 1 (top)—Daniel S. Brody/Stock, Boston. facing p. 1 (bottom)—Patricia Hollander Gross/Stock, Boston.
Chapter 1: p. 2, 3—Patricia Hollander Gross/Stock, Boston. p. 9—
Economic Indicators (Washington, D.C.: U.S. Government Printing
Office, March 1979), p. 1. p. 10—Reprinted from *U. S. News & World
Report*, February 20, 1978, p. 66. Copyright 1978 U. S. News & World
Report, Inc. p. 11 (top)—*Dunagin's People* by Ralph Dunagin. Cour-
tesy Field Newspaper Syndicate. p. 11 (bottom)—Prepared from *Statistical Yearbook*. Copyright, United Nations (1977). Reproduced by
permission. p. 12—*Federal Reserve Bulletin*, February 1976, p. A-55;
and March 1979, pp. A-52, A-53. p. 13—"Paying a Price," *Time*, June
5, 1978, p. 76. Reprinted by permission from *Time*, The Weekly
Newsmagazine; Copyright Time Inc. 1978. p. 15—Courtesy Joy Manufacturing Company, Pittsburgh, PA 15222. p. 17—"Rural Luddites:
Continued on Index p. I-13.

For Gladys and Rosie

Short Contents

Contents

Preface

Introduction to Business: A Contemporary View, Third Edition, reveals the excitement, the meaning, and the challenge that is found in business. It displays the variety of life in the business world as it really is—with a large dose of humanity.

The language of the book is concrete and is within the grasp of the average reader. Complicated, abstract terminology is avoided. The interest level is kept high by providing even more real-world examples than the preceding edition.

Many concepts will be new to you. The new concepts—especially those that are important to the understanding of business—are given special treatment. These key concepts are introduced at the beginning of each chapter in the order of their appearance and appear in boldface print in the text discussion. They are highlighted in the margins of the text and listed alphabetically, with definitions, at the end of each chapter. In this way, you become thoroughly acquainted with common business terms.

Review and discussion are aided by setting clear learning objectives at the start of each chapter and by providing review and discussion questions and brief incidents or cases at the end of each chapter. Throughout the book there are discussion-stimulating materials boxed in blue. They may present, for example, two opposing points of view or ask you to reach a conclusion on a tough contemporary issue. These questions, incidents, and "blue boxes" keep you interested.

This book uses two means of linking the chapters together. First, it arranges the chapters in logical groups and sequence. Five sections, or chapter groups, are set apart. Each has a goal and each one builds on the previous one. Second, it uses the continuing case history of the Rocketoy Company to tie the learning together. The ongoing case pictures the birth, development, and growing pains of a toy manufacturer. It shows how many of the concepts in the preceding chapters enter the life of Rocketoy.

The book starts with the basic economic ideas that explain business activity. Next, you learn about the forms of business ownership, the organization of a firm, and basic management. Then the book "tours" the functional areas—production, marketing, and finance—and looks at accounting, personnel activities, labor relations, and computers. Here you see the types of decisions faced by managers. The last two sections introduce the areas of small business and international business and, finally, the interaction of business and society is explored.

In every chapter, particularly the last one, there is special insight into business careers. The effect of this career orientation is to develop a taste for business and to help clarify a career choice.

We have prepared a teaching package both the seasoned teacher and those who are beginning their teaching career will hopefully find useful. It includes a comprehensive Instructor's Manual, Test Bank Manual, Annual Newsletter (which updates the text), and Transparency Masters. Students will find the Study Guide helpful in sharpening their understanding of the text and business terminology.

Many changes from the previous edition were inspired by its readers. We want to continue to learn from our readers as they are the best possible critics.

We owe special thanks to Jack Rochester, our editor, Renee Burke and David Dahlbacka, our production editors, Dorothy Thompson, our designer, and Pam Rockwell, our copyeditor. We are indebted for their effort to make the book lively, interesting, and current. We would also like to thank Vicky Prescott, Lisa Leveroni, and Armen Kojoyian for their fine work in preparing the Annual Reports for the previous edition.

For clerical, research, typing, proofreading, and other supportive assistance, we wish to thank Susan Middleton, Karen Crooke, Kathleen Kinberger, Ute Wittorf, Eunice Ching, and Linda Varnado.

Finally, to our families, we owe special personal thanks for their patience and understanding.

John A. Reinecke

William F. Schoell

Acknowledgments

We are grateful to the following reviewers for their thoughtful suggestions during the development of this manuscript:

Nancy Carr
Community College of Philadelphia

John D. Christensen
Westchester Community College

William Cleary
Bradley University

Benjamin M. Compaine
Community College of Philadelphia

Garland Holt
Tarrant County Junior College, NE Campus

Karl J. Killman
Davenport College of Business

Alexander Langerfelder
Middlesex Community College

Jim Lee Morgan
West Los Angeles College

Ron Rath
Kirkwood Community College

David Sellers
Davenport College

Ralph Wilcox
Kirkwood Community College

In addition, we would like to thank the following people who graciously offered suggestions for improvement in the form of comments to Allyn and Bacon sales representatives, in personal letters and on comment cards. Their remarks were carefully read and analyzed by the authors and editorial staff, and implemented wherever possible.

Paul Caruso
Bluefield State College

Gerry Conner
Linn-Benton Community College

Ralph Wilcox
Kirkwood Community College

Enrique J. Arroyo
Catholic University of Puerto Rico

Gordon Broderson
Centralia College

S. Bowdidge
Southwest Missouri State University

Edward Atzehoefer
Clark Technical College

Maurice M. Sampson
Community College of Philadelphia

Joseph Trebes
Catonsville Community College

Lee Kilbourne
University of Wisconsin

Mary Helen Casey
Nash Technical Institute

Russell W. Lott
Northwest Mississippi Junior College

Richard Stone
Cuesta College

James A. Albanese
Rio Hondo College

Dennis Bradley
Keuka College

Evan Thompson
Cleveland County Tech

Herbert A. Schloo, Jr.
Hampton Institute

E. Reber Casstevens
Southern Illinois University

Jim Lee Morgan
West Los Angeles College

Nancy Carr
Community College of Philadelphia

H. Russell Heritage
Treasure Valley Community College

Milt Josephs
NYS Community College

William Clarey
Bradley University

A. M. Nilsen
Phillips College

Minnie Battle
Utica Junior College

Donnie McGahee
West Georgia College

Barbara L. Piasta
Somerset County College

Garland E. Holt
Tarrant County Junior College

Laurence L. Kogut
Hillsborough Community College

Betty J. Brown
University of Tennessee

Hank Ruelas
Foothill College

Edward P. Freedman
Northern Virginia Community College

G. Rieder
*Minneapolis Vocational and
Technical Institute*

D. Tully
Waukesha County Tech

Leo A. Erlon
Rockland Community College

Paul Doran
Jefferson State Junior College

J. H. Foegen
Winona State University

Robert Close
American River College

We would like to give special thanks to Robert Googins of Southern Oregon State College for the idea of career symbols applied to problems and exercises in the Study Guide.

INTRODUCTION TO BUSINESS

OUR STUDY of business begins with a discussion of its economic setting and the reasons why business firms exist.

In Chapter 1 we examine what an economic system is and why it exists. The main purpose of any economic system is to enable people to cope with the economic problem—how to satisfy their unlimited wants with their limited resources. This is the overall economic problem that confronts all people. Two vastly different types of economic systems are collectivism and capitalism. We compare and contrast them both in their "pure forms" and in their "real-world forms."

In Chapter 2, we take a look at the reasons why business firms exist. The business firm is the basic building block for organizing production activity in a capitalist economic system. Most economic activity is channeled through business firms in a capitalist nation such as the United States.

Photos: top—Stock, Boston; bottom—Stock Boston.

SECTION ONE

Introduction

Economic Ideas for Business

CHAPTER 1

Objectives: After reading this chapter, you should be able to

1. Define the economic problem and discuss how we cope with it.
2. Describe ways in which the performance of an economic system is measured.
3. Compare the quantity and the quality of life approaches to measuring the performance of an economic system.
4. List and define the factors of production.
5. State the basic purpose of an economic system.
6. Compare and contrast the collectivist and capitalist economic systems.
7. List and discuss the chief characteristics of a capitalist economic system.
8. Explain why real-world economic systems are not pure and give examples.
9. Define business and discuss the role of profit in business activity.

Key Concepts: Look for these terms as you read the chapter

the economic problem	entrepreneur
specialization	mercantilism
exchange	laissez faire
standard of living	capitalism
Gross National Product (GNP)	private enterprise
	collectivism
inflation	central planning
Disposable Personal Income (DPI)	individualism
	the Protestant ethic
utility	capital formation
value in exchange	consumer power
factors of production	consumerism
land	business
labor	profit
capital	
entrepreneurship	

Human beings have always been "wanting" animals. The early cave dwellers' unlimited needs and wants had to be satisfied with the limited resources available to them. This is what the economic problem is all about—satisfying unlimited wants with limited resources.

Although the cave people lived in small, independent groups, modern people live with others in large, interdependent social and economic systems. In advanced systems we learn even more wants—we learn to want many more things than we really need in order to survive. Our natural resources, however, have not increased to the same degree as our wants. Thus the economic problem has been brought into sharper focus.

By specializing and exchanging, we can satisfy more wants with our limited resources. This raises our standard of living because we have more products and services to consume. But recently more people have been questioning whether we really are better off. They question whether a greater output of products and services really improves the quality of life.

An economic system is a framework for satisfying human wants. Two vastly different types of systems are the collectivist and the capitalist systems. We will discuss both in their pure and real world forms. One major difference between these systems is the role played in the economy by profit-seeking business firms. One major similarity between the two systems is that both must cope with general economic problems.

The Economic Problem

Because human wants are unlimited while productive resources are limited, we face a problem. It is **the economic problem—how to satisfy these unlimited wants with limited resources.** This problem exists for nations, individual consumers, business firms, and charitable organizations.

the economic problem

For example, should Congress provide for more spending on space exploration or more for medical research and education? Should the defense budget be cut in order to shift more funds to social welfare programs such as public housing? The Department of Health, Education, and Welfare (HEW) spends billions of dollars every year for social programs. Is HEW using this money in the best way possible or should it expand some programs and cut back on some others?

What about individual consumers who are faced with an almost endless variety of products and services to buy? Since their buying power is limited, they cannot have them all. Like Congress, consumers also must make choices about how they will spend their funds.

Business firms also face the economic problem. Should a company increase spending on advertising its present products or should it spend more on research and development to come up with new products? Charitable organizations also have to decide how they will use their resources. For example, should the American Cancer Society invest more in research to find a cure for cancer or spend more to educate people about self-detection of cancer?

But what are "scarce resources"? One example is natural resources. Some of these are renewable (forests) but some are not renewable (petroleum). With proper forest management, timber is a renewable natural resource. But no matter how well petroleum resources are "managed," they eventually will run out. Critical decisions must be made about how increasingly scarce natural resources will be used, for example, to meet our energy needs. We must decide the roles that coal, petroleum, solar power, geothermal power, and nuclear power will play.

The concept of resources does not mean just natural resources, however. It includes all productive resources, as we will see later in the discussion of the factors of production.

The economic problem has always existed and will continue to exist. The early cave people faced many problems in their struggle to survive. They had to satisfy basic needs for food, clothing, and shelter by finding and preparing food, making clothing, and finding a cave. Each cave dweller was independent, or *self-sufficient*. If a man and a woman shared these tasks, each one's economic fate as a producer and a consumer became tied to that of the other. They still faced the same economic problem, but the number of options for solving it increased. In other words, the family unit made it easier for them to cope with the economic problem because of specialization and exchange.

Specialization

Sharing in the task of providing their basic needs meant that neither person had to provide for all his or her needs alone. Before the formation of the family units, each person had to hunt and cook alone. After, each one had more freedom to do only one task—either to hunt or to cook. This is an example of specialization in a simple economic system.

specialization **Specialization means giving more effort to a specific (specialized) task instead of giving less effort to a greater number of tasks. Each person can make better use of his or her limited time and talents (that is, become more efficient in performing a specialized task) when there is specialization.** For the cave dwellers this meant one person would specialize in hunting and the other would specialize in cooking.

A modern example of specialization is the assembly line in an automobile plant. Each worker on the assembly line performs a highly specialized task. In extreme cases a worker may tighten only one or two bolts. As we will see in several later chapters, very simple and routine tasks or chores can cause workers to become bored and less productive.

Humanizing the assembly line has become a big challenge for management in a wide variety of businesses. In some types of businesses computerized robots are used to perform many tasks that humans would consider dull and boring.

Exchange

Specialization is pointless, however, unless specialists can exchange. **Exchange means trade, or giving up one thing to get another thing.**　　　　exchange

　　Let's assume that our caveman specializes in hunting and the woman specializes in cooking. The man exchanges part of his hunt for part of the meal prepared by the woman. Specialization and exchange, of course, are extended beyond the family unit in modern economies. Over time we have come to live in larger groups. From the single family, we have evolved to more complex groups such as tribes, villages, towns, cities, and nations with increasing dependence on specialization and exchange.

　　Production has become organized in shops, stores, and factories. Even your local McDonald's or Burger King restaurants practice specialization. The fast service you are used to would not be possible if one person had to raise, harvest, and deliver the beef, lettuce, and tomatoes, take your order, prepare the food, package it, and collect payment for it.

　　The specialization and exchange process, therefore, now includes a great many people. It is a fact of life in modern economic systems. Each person is dependent on more people to satisfy his or her wants. In other words, there is *economic interdependence* among specialists. The process of exchange organizes people into groups and an economic system is the result. Although there are many different types of economic systems, all have one element in common—they exist to satisfy human wants.

Needs and Wants

An isolated person has basic needs such as food, clothing, and shelter that must be satisfied for survival. Once the person relates to other people, specialization and exchange begin and the individual learns new wants. Satisfaction of needs is necessary for survival. Satisfaction of wants helps to make life more enjoyable.

　　A person's need for food may be satisfied by eating wild berries. But he or she may learn, as a result of coming into contact with other people, to want fancy cuts of meat and pastries. No one really needs a TV, a trash compactor, or a backyard swimming pool for survival, but life would be rather dull if we focused only on satisfying our most basic survival needs. As we will see, some people question how far we should go in creating new wants and how important consumption should be in our lives as total human beings. Some people say many business firms devote too much effort to making consumers feel left out if they don't have the latest products on the market. One of the tools firms use to make us want more is advertising, which often is attacked for contributing to what critics call our overly materialistic lifestyle. In other words, some people believe that we are using up our scarce resources to cater to questionable wants.

In some cases conflict arises over *who* is the best judge of what is good for us. How far should individuals be permitted to go in satisfying their own wants regardless of the effects of their consumption on the rest of society? A good example is the gas-guzzling car. Even after gasoline prices skyrocketed, some people still wanted big cars that got few miles per gallon of gas; and car makers were willing to cater to their desire. Congress responded by passing laws that require new cars to meet certain miles-per-gallon standards.

Advances in transportation and communications have led to even wider contact among people. In a real sense, our world is shrinking. The most remote cities of the world are seconds away by phone and only hours away by jet. Communications satellites help broadcast live TV specials and news programs to hundreds of millions of people around the world. Not only does such contact increase the number of people to whom sellers can sell their products but it also encourages greater specialization. It has led too, to the learning of still more wants. Who would have thought that McDonald's restaurants would be a big hit in Paris, that Pizza Hut would be so successful in Tokyo, or that so many Americans would take up eating yogurt?

Measuring an Economy's Performance

As we have said, the purpose of an economic system is to satisfy human wants. It is, therefore, desirable to measure its performance. Comparisons of different systems may be made by a measure called the standard of living. **The standard of living is a relative measure of economic well-being that helps us compare the well-being of one society with that of another society and to observe change in well-being over time.**

standard of living

There are several approaches to measuring the standard of living. **One measure is Gross National Product (GNP). This is the sum of the market values of all final products and services produced in a nation during a given year.** (See Figure 1–1.) Dividing GNP by population gives

Gross National Product (GNP)

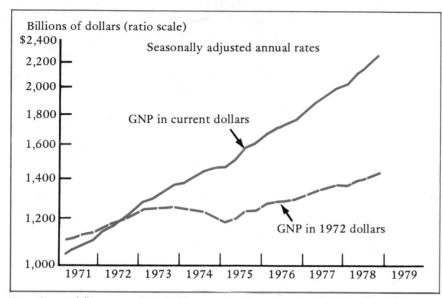

FIGURE 1–1

Gross National Product of the United States

NOTE: Current dollars are unadjusted with respect to prices over a period of time. The dollars shown are in terms of the level of prices prevailing for each of the years shown. The effects of price changes are adjusted for by using constant dollars, in this case, 1972 dollars.

Source: *Economic Indicators.*

us a measure of the economic well-being of an average person in that country (per capita GNP).

The GNP of the United States is measured in trillions of dollars. It took only 200 years for our GNP to reach the trillion dollar mark and a little more than 7 years to reach the second trillion dollar mark in 1978. It is projected to cross the $4 trillion mark in 1985.

The numbers themselves are staggering but much of the increase in dollar GNP is due to inflation. **Inflation means an increase in the prices of products and services over a period of time.** It has been a very serious problem in the United States and in most other countries during recent years. Inflation is one reason that the prices of new homes and new cars are so high. In short, the dollar is worth less and less (will buy less and less) as inflation continues. During recent years, price increases have accounted for a huge part of the increase in our GNP.

inflation

To measure the actual growth in GNP undistorted by inflation, we can express GNP in *real terms*. We do this by setting prices in terms of a base year. For example, we could express the current GNP in terms of the purchasing power of the dollar in 1967. Stated in real terms, our per capita GNP has increased at an average rate of 1.9 percent per year over the last 100 years.

Figure 1–2 compares our GNP with that of several other countries. It shows per capita GNP for each of the countries in American dollars.

How Much Is 1 Trillion Dollars?

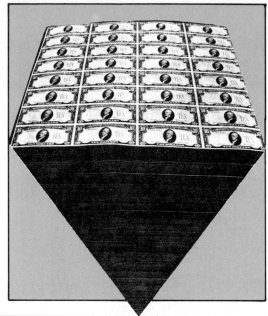

It's a trillion-dollar world for Americans now.

The U.S. economy will churn out goods and services at the rate of 2 trillion dollars a year before 1978 is over.

Public debt of the U.S. government is approaching 1 trillion dollars.

Spending by Washington will top 500 billion—a half trillion—dollars during the year that starts October 1 if President Carter's plans are carried out.

For a look at what 1 trillion dollars amounts to, here are six measures—

PICTOGRAM® **1 trillion dollars would buy . . .**

172,414,000 Autos

18.7 years of U.S. output, at 1977's rate and average price

18,416,000 New Houses

12.7 years of U.S. production, at 1977's rate and average price for single-family homes

A shopper buying goods 24 hours a day, seven days a week, would have to spend—

$100,000 a minute for 19 years

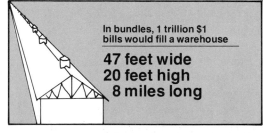

In bundles, 1 trillion $1 bills would fill a warehouse

**47 feet wide
20 feet high
8 miles long**

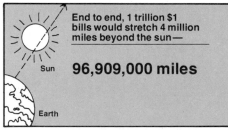

End to end, 1 trillion $1 bills would stretch 4 million miles beyond the sun—

96,909,000 miles

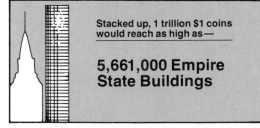

Stacked up, 1 trillion $1 coins would reach as high as—

5,661,000 Empire State Buildings

Source: U.S. Depts. of the Treasury, Commerce: Federal Home Loan Bank Board: Ward's Automotive Reports: *USN & WR* Economic Unit.

Source: *U.S. News and World Report.*

"We can still beat inflation, gentlemen, but it's going to cost more to do it."

SOURCE: *Dunagin's People,* Field Newspaper Syndicate.

FIGURE 1–2

Gross National Product per capita for selected countries (in U.S. dollars)

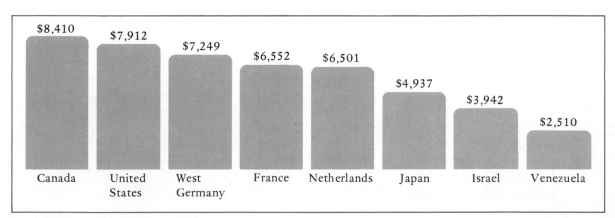

NOTE: GNP per capita is a country's total GNP divided by its population.

Source: *Federal Reserve Bulletin.*

INFLATION

In October, 1978, it cost $200.90 to buy what $100.00 would have bought in 1967. The percentages following each of the groups of products and services below show how much prices went up between 1967 and 1978.

- food—116%
- housing—109%
- fuel—120%
- clothing—63%
- medical care—89%

Disposable Personal Income (DPI)

Some people think that **Disposable Personal Income (DPI)** is a better measure of the people's welfare. DPI is a smaller amount than GNP. **DPI is what remains of our current incomes after we have paid our taxes.** (See Table 1–1.)

Measures such as GNP and DPI, however, do not indicate the *quality of life* in a nation. There are side effects of high productivity that are not measured by GNP—pollution, congested cities, rapid depletion of basic natural resources, and so on. These factors may have a strong negative effect on the enjoyment of productive efforts. In other words, the value of things is subjective—it depends on the judgment of the people who possess or consume them. We will return several times to this basic problem in measuring our total well-being. Are we really better off simply because we produce more products and services or do we also have to look beyond quantity and consider the overall quality of our lives?

There is some evidence that some of us are becoming more conscious of and concerned with the quality of life. Some businesses, for example,

TABLE 1-1

Gross National Product, personal income, disposable personal income, and personal saving for selected years

		1950	1970	1978
	GROSS NATIONAL PRODUCT[1]	286.2	982.4	2,106.9
	PERSONAL INCOME	226.1	801.3	1,707.6
Less:	Personal tax and nontax payments	−20.6	−115.3	−256.2
Equals:	DISPOSABLE PERSONAL INCOME	205.5	686.0	1,451.4
Less:	Personal outlays	−194.7	−635.4	−1,375.2
Equals:	PERSONAL SAVING	10.8	50.6	76.2

[1] All amounts given in billions of dollars

Source: *Statistical Yearbook.*

are finding it harder to transfer employees to less desirable areas even if it means a promotion and a pay raise. Some labor unions are fighting against compulsory overtime and an unhealthful job environment. Consumers are demanding safer products and some states are passing laws to help protect the environment.

PAYING A PRICE

The U.S. quest for a cleaner, safer environment has forced companies to adhere to thousands of dizzying—and expensive—Government regulations. General Motors has figured out exactly just how high the cost is running for itself.

The research, development and administrative expenses of meeting Government regulations at GM came to $1,258,000,000 [in 1977], or an average of $200 for every car and truck the company sold in the U.S. The work involved the equivalent of 23,700 employees. It included everything from putting in new production machinery to the cost of designing cars to meet federal pollution, safety, health, noise and other regulations. But it did not include installation of federally mandated parts, such as emissions-control systems and safety bumpers, on the cars. These costs also become part of the price the consumer must pay, but GM did not give out the figures. In addition, says Chairman Thomas Murphy, the fuel-economy standards coming into effect between now and the early 1980s "could add another $800 or more to the average retail price of our cars."

Source: *Time.*

Satisfaction of Wants

A want is satisfied by consuming a product or a service that is useful in relation to the want. If a product or a service can satisfy a certain want, then it has **utility. Utility means usefulness in satisfying wants.**   utility

Wants are very specific to individuals. If you drew up a list of your wants it probably would be similar in certain ways to somebody else's. Basic needs like food would appear in both lists. Beyond these, however, there would be many differences in the types of wants.

Since people have different wants, different products have different degrees of utility for different persons. Even if two people have the same want, we cannot assume that a certain product that satisfies the want would have the same utility to both people. But if a product has utility for someone, it is valuable to that person. The concept of value is very important.

value in exchange

Since all of us must breathe, air has value to all of us. But people ordinarily will not pay anything for it because it is too plentiful. It has *value in use* but no value in exchange. **Something has value in exchange when it can command something else in return for it. It can be swapped for something else.**

An example will help to illustrate the meaning of value in exchange. Mr. App has some apples and Mr. Oran has some oranges. Suppose both men want apples and oranges. Mr. App can exchange some apples for some oranges. Mr. Oran can exchange some oranges for some apples. Exchange would occur if both men thought that they would benefit from it. Mr. App, since he already has apples, values apples less than Mr. Oran, who has none. Mr. Oran, since he already has oranges, values oranges less than Mr. App, who has none.

The exchange does *not* involve things of equal value. Mr. App's apples are worth less to him than the oranges he gets in return. Mr. Oran's oranges are worth less to him than the apples he gets in return. In other words, how much anything is worth to you depends partly on how much of it you already have. The more you have of it, the less you want (and the less you are willing to pay) to get more units. This is the principle of *diminishing marginal utility.*

The Factors of Production

factors of production

Limited resources must be used wisely to achieve a high level of production. **The following limited resources are the factors of production:**

- **land**
- **labor**
- **capital**
- **entrepreneurship**

The factors of production are the *inputs* of the productive system. The products and services produced in order to satisfy human wants are the *outputs* of the system. (See Figure 1–3.)

FIGURE 1–3

The productive system's inputs and outputs

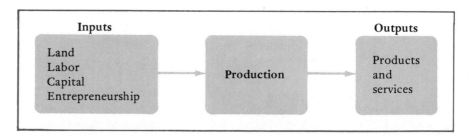

If you liked the Stone Age, you're going to love the day the oil runs out.

Things will be a lot quieter, because all the motors will have stopped. Without traffic on the freeway you'll be able to walk to work. Except there won't be much work to walk to.

There won't be any plastics or vinyls or man-made fibers or fertilizers. The thousands of everyday products that are made from petroleum will have vanished from our lives. Life will become, let us say, simpler.

Of course, it doesn't have to be this way. But today, while we have the lead time necessary to develop nuclear power, or to switch our industries from oil and gas to coal, we are doing nothing. We are waiting. Waiting for "someone else" to solve our energy problem. If we wait long enough, we'll all be waiting in the dark, won't we?

We think it's time this country had a strong, reasoned energy policy. If you feel the same way, speak out now. Demand that your elected representatives support intelligent energy legislation.

 **JOY MANUFACTURING COMPANY**
OLIVER BLDG. PITTSBURGH, PA 15222
TM

MANUFACTURERS OF MACHINERY AND EQUIPMENT FOR THE ENERGY INDUSTRIES
COAL MINING, MINERAL MINING, URANIUM EXTRACTION, AIR HANDLING, OIL AND GAS WELL DRILLING, POLLUTION CONTROL

Source: Joy Manufacturing Company.

Land

land

Land as a factor of production means all natural resources. Examples are petroleum, iron ore, and farm land. In the long run, all natural resources can run out. But, as we said earlier, with proper management some will last for a very long time (air, water, forests). Others, however, will run out (petroleum, uranium, other metals). Physical land is limited, too. We have a choice between thoughtless and rapid use of our resources and carefully planned use.

During our frontier days, as settlers used up the natural resources in one area, they moved westward to new areas where the resources were plentiful. This type of resource use has been called a "cowboy economy." During the last several decades, however, we have realized that we could run out of natural resources. The "cowboy economy" has become the "spaceship economy." A crew on a spaceship must conserve and recycle the resources on board. We must do the same for the natural resources here on earth!

The United States does have a large share of many of the most important resources. But we also are the greatest user of natural resources in the world. In the case of oil and some other materials, we are becoming more and more dependent on other nations for supplies. For example, we are importing about half of the oil we consume. As we will see in Chapter 16, this fact is having some serious effects on our nation's foreign trade.

Labor

labor

Labor means human mental and physical effort. Much of our economic progress is the result of substituting mental effort for physical effort. Mental effort leads to technological "breakthroughs" that result in greater output from the same or less physical effort. This enables us to get more satisfaction from a given quantity of natural resources. For example, if such progress enables us to get 10 percent more energy from a ton of coal, the effect is the same as increasing the coal supply by 10 percent.

As we will see later in our book, one of the major challenges in businesses today is increasing the productivity of labor. When labor productivity remains stable or decreases while wages go up, consumers must pay more for the products they buy. There is also a lot of talk about declining American productivity as a reason why some American firms have started producing in foreign countries. This trend is having many kinds of effects on American business, as we will see in Chapter 16.

Capital

**Capital as a factor of production means tools and machinery or any-
thing made by humans that aids in producing and distributing products and services. It is human-made productive capacity.**   capital

   There is a close relationship between capital and labor. Machinery
can help make labor more productive. In some cases, machinery dis-
places labor—machines take over the jobs of human workers. Although
this is a major reason for increased productivity, it also has been a major
issue in some strikes by labor unions.

**OPPOSING FARM
MECHANIZATION**

> The 19th century English Luddites smashed machines in a
> doomed effort to preserve the jobs of textile workers. Califor-
> nia Rural Legal Assistance, a federally subsidized antipoverty
> group, does not go quite that far. But [in January, 1979] it
> filed suit in a state court in Oakland seeking to enjoin the Uni-
> versity of California from using state money to develop farm
> machines. The C.R.L.A. charges that the introduction of more
> modern mechanical tomato, grape and lettuce pickers will pri-
> marily benefit large growers and will cost 120,000 California
> farm laborers their jobs.

Source: *Time.*

   An economy must produce more than it currently consumes in order
to add to its capital equipment. It must have some savings to finance
new investment, such as the construction of new factories. How much
of its output a country can devote to its productive facilities depends
heavily on the willingness and ability of its people to postpone consumption, or save. This is a major problem in the world's poorer countries because most of the output must be consumed by the citizens.
These countries can ill afford to invest in new plants and equipment
when, for example, people are starving.

Entrepreneurship

**Entrepreneurship occurs when a person or a business firm assumes   entrepreneurship
risk in the hope of making a profit. Bringing land, labor, and capital
together and managing them productively to produce a product or
service is entrepreneurship. An entrepreneur is a person who assumes   entrepreneur
the risk of organizing and managing a business in the hope of making a**

profit. He or she takes the risk of not making a profit. If a profit is earned, it is received by the entrepreneur.

People who go into business have no guarantee of earning a profit. They assume the risk of losing what they invest in their firms. Their willingness to assume the risk depends a lot on how healthy they think the economy will be in the future, the past political stability of the country, and their expected profit from undertaking the risk.

The factors of production can be combined and used in many ways to produce many different things. The amount and variety of products and services produced depend mainly on the way economic life is organized.

**WHAT DO
YOU THINK?**

**How Do We Deal
with Limited
Natural Resources?**

Two ways of dealing with the growing scarcity of natural resources (land as a factor of production) are to limit wants and/or to increase the capacity of natural resources to satisfy our wants.

Government can adopt policies to limit consumption. For example, to discourage consumption of gasoline, it could be rationed.

Another approach is to use the other factors of production to help us to expand the want-satisfying capacity of our natural resource base. Human mental effort (labor) leads to new technology. Entrepreneurs put this technology to work by building new plants and equipment (capital) based on that technology. To get more miles per gallon from gasoline, for example, technological advances are made in engineering and producing cars. Which approach is better? WHAT DO YOU THINK?

The Purpose of an Economic System

The purpose of an economic system is to provide a framework for satisfying human wants. In our system, most of the productive economic activities (producing and selling products and services) are channeled through business firms which operate in a *market* system. But there are other types of economic systems in which business firms play a lesser role in satisfying human wants.

In ancient Greece, for example, producing products for sale was not common. Agriculture was the main economic activity. Business activity and the seeking of profit were considered acceptable but lowly activities.

During the Middle Ages, the Church taught that people should not seek economic betterment but should concentrate on salvation. Although there was a great deal of business activity, it was looked upon as worldly, and often sinful.

The next major "age," as far as economic philosophy is concerned, was the age of mercantilism. **Mercantilism was an economic philosophy that advocated building strong national states (nations) from warring feudal kingdoms. A major goal was to increase the government's holdings of precious metals such as gold and silver.** The nation with the greatest supply of precious metals was considered the most powerful. This is why mercantilist nations favored building their export trade. The greater the volume of products a country sells to people in other countries, the more gold and silver it receives in payment from the buying countries. The citizens could be poor but as long as gold is in the state treasury, the state is considered wealthy.

Mercantilism was followed by a period of laissez-faire economics in Europe and, later, in the United States. **Laissez faire means let people do as they please. When applied to business, it means let the owners of business set the rules of competition without any government regulation or control.**

This new economic philosophy began in France. But it was first presented in complete form by the Englishman Adam Smith in his book *The Wealth of Nations* (1776). Smith believed in free competition and capitalism. If each person sought to improve his or her economic well-being, Smith believed, the economic well-being of the entire nation would be improved. He believed that government should interfere with the operation of individual self-interest only when it is necessary to protect society. Even today, there is a great deal of controversy in capitalist countries about government "interference" in business affairs.

Capitalism is an economic system based on private ownership of the factors of production. The major features of capitalism are

- individualism
- private property
- profit incentive
- consumer power
- freedom to compete
- occupational freedom
- freedom of contract
- limited role of government

Our economic system essentially is a capitalist system based on private enterprise. **Private enterprise means private ownership of firms**

mercantilism

laissez faire

capitalism

private enterprise

that make and sell products and services. But we do *not* have a purely capitalistic system or a purely private enterprise system. Our economic system has changed over time. It contains many of the ideas of capitalism and also certain concepts borrowed from collectivist systems. Perhaps it can be described best as a *mixed economy*. On the other hand, the Soviet Union's economic system also can be described as a mixture of collectivism and capitalism. Let's discuss the pure collectivist system first.

Collectivism

collectivism

In any economic system decisions must be made about the best uses of resources and how the products produced from them will be distributed. In a purely collectivist system, the government controls social and economic decision making. **Collectivism means government ownership of the factors of production and government control of all economic activities.** There is little or no private property. The government determines the economy's rate of growth, the amount of investment, how resources will be used, and how the output of products and services will be divided among the people.

THE DISAPPEARANCE OF INDIVIDUAL FREEDOMS

In April 1975, Cambodia fell to the Communist Khmer Rouge and individual freedoms began to disappear in Democratic Kampuchea, the new name given to Cambodia. As part of the revolution, middle- and upper-class city dwellers were forced to leave the cities to work on farms. For the first time since the communist takeover, two Western news correspondents were allowed to visit Cambodia in late 1978. One of the reporters gave the following account after returning to the United States:

> The Cambodian revolution evidently has forced [those city dwellers] to conform to an austere standard of hard manual labor: no money, no mail system, no telephone service, no books, almost no individual property, no advanced education, little or no religion, and none of the freedoms accepted or at least professed by most of the rest of the world.

Source: *Time.*

The government also uses direct means to achieve the desired results. For example, if it is decided that the output of military equipment should be increased, the government could order a reduction in the output of consumer products such as refrigerators and cars. The resources that were used in producing these products are shifted to producing military equipment. Wage rates and prices of products also are set by the government.

Governments in collectivist countries also practice central planning. **Central planning means that the government drafts a master plan of what it wants to accomplish and directly manages the economy to achieve the plan's goals.** Government fixes the total supply of products and services available for household consumption and distributes them in limited amounts and at fixed prices to households. There is no guarantee that the products and services produced are what consumers want. Consumers, therefore, spend their fixed incomes on fixed amounts of products and services at fixed prices.

central planning

TWO POINTS OF VIEW

Egalitarianism in the United States

Collectivist systems are egalitarian in that they seek to equalize incomes and to achieve a uniform standard of living for their people.

Egalitarians in the United States want to do the same. They denounce laissez-faire economics and are strongly critical of business. They see the government's social programs as the equalizing and leveling force in society. Through those programs, they believe, the "have nots" will have more and the "haves" will have less. This redistribution of income and wealth would continue until there is total equality. Although egalitarians are in the minority in the United States, the egalitarian movement does have a lot of appeal to some groups in our society.

Critics of egalitarianism argue that an egalitarian system cannot exist in a capitalist economy because equal wealth would destroy the profit incentive. In a political democracy each person has an equal voice in choosing elected officials because each person has one vote. But in a capitalist system, incomes among people are not equal. The critics of egalitarianism question whether the voters will elect politicians who favor laws to equalize incomes. These critics wonder if the United States can have a political democracy while also having a capitalist economic system.

Collectivism often is accompanied by a totalitarian government (there is only one political party) that allows very little individual freedom to its people. The system seeks to achieve what it alleges to be the "greatest good for the greatest number of people." People contribute to the system on the basis of their abilities and they receive from it on the basis of their needs. The individual is less important than the system, and the government determines each person's role in the system.

Collectivist systems, however, stress social and economic equality among their citizens. They seek to eliminate differences in economic welfare among people of different occupations, races, and backgrounds. A uniform standard of living is sought in order to eliminate friction among the various classes of people. In other words, collectivist systems *in their pure form* are egalitarian systems.

Capitalism

Individualism

individualism

The basic idea underlying capitalism is individualism. **Individualism is the idea that the group, the society, and the government are necessary but are less important than the individual's self-determination.** The ancient Greeks valued the dignity and uniqueness of the individual. Although people lost sight of this value during some of the darker periods of history since ancient Greece, the idea of individualism remains a cornerstone of most of the Western democracies. It stands at the center of the Constitution of the United States.

Capitalism, as we have seen, recognizes the strength of individual self-interest. A person will, if left alone, seek his or her own economic betterment. Given certain political conditions, this leads to the efficient and economical use of resources.

Protestant ethic

The full development of individual initiative and some other basic ideas of capitalism required a shift in Christian philosophy from the medieval stress on spiritual matters and distrust for business to the more practical Protestant ethic. **The Protestant ethic is a tradition that stresses the value of hard work, accumulation of property, and self-reliance. Wealth, in itself, is not sinful.** The most extreme form of the Protestant ethic existed in the United States during the nineteenth century, when the notion of the survival of the economically fittest was added to it. Thus the seal of Christian respectability was given to the rugged individualists who dominated America's economic growth in the latter half of the nineteenth century.

Private Property

Related to individualism is the right of *private property*. This is a person's right to acquire, to use, to accumulate, and to dispose of things of value. Individual initiative would be greatly limited if a person could not own and accumulate property. Consider the passage of California's "Proposition 13" in 1978 and the rapid spread of similar laws to other states. These laws seek to limit the amount of property tax that homeowners have to pay on their houses and to help ease the feeling among homeowners that taxes would rise to the point where they could no longer afford to pay them.

Private property has existed in most cultures. The English settlers brought this tradition with them to America. It has a prominent place in our Constitution and Bill of Rights. Although our legal system strongly defends the right of private property, it cannot be an absolute right. In any society, certain limits must be placed on the right of ownership. For example, a person who owns a house cannot use it to conduct illegal acts. Nor can the owner set fire to it if that would endanger other people. Society places certain limits on property rights so that one person's property cannot be used to hurt others. A balance is struck between the individual's private property rights and the society's common good. Federal, state, and local governments, for example, can use eminent domain proceedings to force property owners to sell their property when it is needed for highways or other public uses. Even in these cases the owner has the right to challenge the government's proposed action in court.

A basic aspect of private property is that a person can accumulate it and use it as he or she pleases within the very broad limits set by society. This concept is at the heart of the profit incentive.

Profit Incentive

One reason for our high standard of living is that many people use their private property to generate more property. They invest it to make a profit. The incentive to invest lies in the chance of getting a return—*making a profit*—from it. If people could not profit, they would have little reason to use their property in such a way. Instead, they would use up, or consume, their property. If they were not permitted to make a profit from investing or going into business, they simply would not bother to accumulate property.

The right to pursue profit involves *risk*. The degree of risk depends mainly on the use to which the property is put. As we'll see in Chapter 15, every year thousands of Americans go into business for themselves.

Many risk their accumulated savings, sell their homes, and go into debt in order to get started. They do so to try to make a profit. This process of putting money into business firms in order to try to make more money is called *investment*.

Investment is necessary for a nation's economic growth. It makes possible all the new products and services that appear on the market every year. It also creates jobs and provides tax revenues for governments. The more complex forms of productive business activity require large amounts of equipment, tools, land, and other things that easily can cost hundreds of millions of dollars. **Capital formation is another way to describe the process of investment. Capital formation is the process of adding to the productive capacity of an economy.**

capital formation

Certain institutions have been developed to help this process of capital formation. The corporation, which is discussed in Chapter 3, helps to make possible capital formation on a large scale. IBM, General Motors, General Electric, and American Telephone and Telegraph are examples of multibillion dollar corporations. Chapter 10 discusses banks and other financial institutions that help in this process. As we also will see in Chapter 10, there has been a shortage of savings in the United States in recent years and this is slowing new investment by businesses.

Consumer Power

TABLE 1-2

Government versus consumer control over economic decision making

Unless a firm can cultivate a group of customers, it will not survive. It must have buyers for its products or services. In our system the consumer enjoys a position of great influence. No one guarantees success to a firm. **Consumer power means the consumer is free to do business**

Collectivism	Capitalism
1. Government practices central planning.	1. Individual consumers make independent choices by exercising their consumer power.
2. Central planning determines how resources will be used.	2. Consumer choices determine how resources will be used.
3. Resources are allocated to achieve the goals set by government planners.	3. Resources are allocated in response to decisions made by individual consumers.
4. Government planners determine • what will be produced • how it will be produced • how much will be produced • how the products and services will be distributed	4. Consumers influence • what will be produced • how it will be produced • how much will be produced • how the products and services will be distributed

with whomever he or she chooses. Business firms, according to this concept, are in business to serve consumers, to provide them with want-satisfying products and services. By doing this, businesses may earn a profit. Consumers, therefore, decide the economic fate of a firm through their individual decisions to buy from one firm or another. This is another way in which individualism is so important in our economic system. (See Table 1–2.)

As we will see later, questions have been raised about the degree of

consumer power

A NEW APPROACH TO REMEDYING CUSTOMER COMPLAINTS

General Motors (GM) began testing a new concept in remedying customer complaints in 1978—a binding arbitration program. The test was conducted in the Minneapolis–St. Paul area.

The auto maker chose Minnesota to test the program because it considers the area a typical auto market, and selected the state's Better Business Bureau to run it because the organization has an activist reputation. GM is vague on the details, but apparently it is seeking ways to resolve complaints of auto defects that crop up after the company's 12,000-mi./12-month warranty expires. In such cases, dealers often balk at providing free repairs because they are not reimbursed by the corporation.

The program is intended to help GM to deal with customer complaints in a positive manner.

Under the Minnesota program, GM agrees to abide by an arbitrator's decision in disputes between dealers and customers and will reimburse full costs to dealers if the arbitrator finds for the customer.

We probably will see greater use of arbitration in the future as an approach to resolving customer complaints.

The increasing success of auto buyers in raising complaints about defects clearly moved GM to try the Minnesota experiment, which the company says was first devised several years ago. There is also evidence that Detroit worries that if it does not move to curtail consumer complaints, government will step in. Robert B. Reich, director of policy planning at the Federal Trade Commission, says the agency is "very interested" in arbitration as a means of handling the increasing volume of consumer complaints.

Source: *Business Week.*

consumerism

power consumers really have. **Consumerism** has become a deep-seated force in our business system. **Basically, this movement is concerned with enhancing consumers' power relative to that of sellers.** Examples of consumerist concerns are product safety, disclosure of product ingredients, precautions for product use, and truth in advertising. Several government agencies have been set up to protect consumers. Examples are the Consumer Product Safety Commission, the National Highway Traffic Safety Administration, the Food and Drug Administration, and the Office of Consumer Affairs in the Department of Health, Education, and Welfare.

Perhaps you have heard the concept of consumer power expressed in terms of "casting dollar votes in the marketplace." Firms that do not provide want-satisfying products and services will not receive any "dollar votes" from consumers. Consumers will not buy what these firms offer for sale and they will lose out in the competitive struggle for customers.

Businesses, of course, do what they can to influence our buying decisions. American firms, for example, spend billions of dollars every year on advertising to inform us about their products and to persuade us to buy them.

Freedom to Compete

People who are free to compete can risk their private property in the hope of earning a profit. Within very broad limits, a person can go into any business, no matter how much the existing competitors would like to keep the field to themselves.

Competition among firms benefits consumers and firms. For consumers, it usually results in higher-quality products, greater variety, better service, and lower prices. For firms, it provides an incentive to remain efficient and please their customers. If a firm does not, it may lose customers to rival firms that can do a better job of catering to customer wants. (See Figure 1–4.)

Occupational Freedom

Still another example of individual freedom is the freedom of occupational choice. You are free to start up a new firm—go into business for yourself—or to work for someone else. The choice of occupation is a highly personal one. Individuals make this choice guided by their own best economic interests and within the limits of their talents and education.

In some economic systems, however, central planning determines the

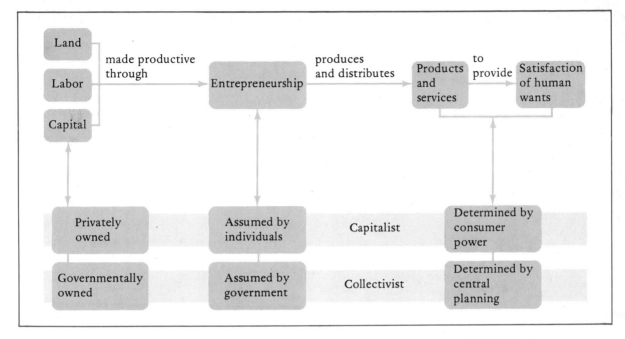

FIGURE 1–4

The purpose of an economic system

need for persons to fill various job categories. People are trained for and assigned to those jobs. The choice of a job is made by the government, not the individual.

Freedom of Contract

One of the most important freedoms is freedom of contract. This freedom enables a person to enter into contracts with other people. Examples of contracts include installment contracts such as those involved in financing the purchase of a new car by making monthly payments; insurance policies; apartment leases; employment contracts; and partnership agreements. As long as the contract is legal, it is protected by law and is legally enforceable in court. We will discuss contracts in greater detail in Chapter 3.

Limited Role of Government

Americans generally dislike excessive government interference in their personal and business lives. Although what is considered to be government interference has changed over the years, the basic tradition of economic freedom still is very much a part of our system.

In general, the government is permitted to step in only when the welfare of citizens is threatened by business action or by the failure of

TABLE 1-3

Basic ideas underlying capitalism and collectivism

Capitalism

1. The individual is of primary importance
2. Private property
3. Profit incentive
4. Consumer power
5. Freedom to compete
6. Occupational freedom
7. Freedom of contract
8. Limited role of government

Collectivism

1. The individual is less important than the system, which seeks equality for all of its citizens
2. No private property
3. No recognition of profit
4. Central control over social and economic decision making
5. Competition results in economic waste
6. Central planning determines the need for various types of occupations
7. Little freedom of contract
8. The government is the primary decision maker

business to act. We generally accept this regulatory role of government in the economy, but there is a difference of opinion over the manner in which government should exercise its regulatory role. Examples from recent years include government action in dealing with inflation, unemployment, energy, and health insurance.

Closely related to the concept of the limited role of government is a belief that price is the basic regulator of the economic system. These, and related ideas, are discussed in the next chapter.

Table 1–3 compares some of the basic ideas that underlie capitalism and collectivism.

Modern Collectivism

Just as our economic system is not purely capitalist, neither are the economic systems of all the communist countries purely collectivist.

TABLE 1-4

Three varieties of collectivism

Variety	Major characteristics	Examples
1. Marxism-Leninism (Communism)	"The most repressive variant of socialism, . . . (it) is a kind of secular religion, preaching the necessity of class warfare, the dictatorship of the proletariat and the concentration of near total power in a tightly structured party that is supposedly the vanguard of the revolutionary masses. Communism is dogmatic in its determination to abolish private property and nationalize the means of production as the first steps toward achieving its ultimate goal, the classless society."	The Soviet Union and its East bloc satellites, China, Mongolia, North Korea, Viet Nam, Laos, Cambodia, Cuba, Albania, Yugoslavia
2. Social Democracy	"The most liberal version of socialism. . . . [It] accepts a multiparty political system and believes in gradual, peaceful means of reaching its socialist goals. In practical terms, this has meant that social democrats have concentrated more on alleviating what they regard as hardships created by capitalist economies (unemployment, salary and wage inequities) than on directly restructuring societies according to a collectivist blueprint."	West Germany, Austria, Belgium, Denmark, Finland, Luxembourg, Norway, The Netherlands, Portugal
3. Third World Socialism	"Despite their great differences, these socialisms have several things in common. First, all these societies call themselves socialists, although their beliefs may be rooted less in Marxism than in nationalism or an indigenous phenomenon like the communalism of tribal Africa. Second, largely because of their experience with colonialism, they reject capitalism as identifiable with imperialism and exploitation. Third, they pursue policies aimed at decreasing the role of private property in the economy and sharply curbing investment by private foreign firms."	Algeria, Libya, Syria, Iraq, Tanzania, Guyana

Source: *Time.*

(See Table 1-4.) Pure collectivism involves setting exact rates of growth, exact allocations of capital, and exact prices.

In some forms of collectivism, instead of setting an exact wage rate or the exact price at which a product will sell, planners set minimum and maximum levels of wages and prices. Market forces, such as supply and demand, determine the exact level of prices within the range set by the minimum and maximum.

In some collectivist countries managers do have some freedom in running factories but they are responsible for meeting the production targets set for them by government planners. There also may be some private enterprise. Collective farmers in the Soviet Union, for example, are allowed to farm small plots of land in their spare time and to sell the output. If they make a profit, they can keep it. Permission to make private profit is, of course, very unusual in the Soviet Union.

Modern Capitalism

The socioeconomic systems of some Western European nations can be classified as social democracies. These nations have adopted some rather severe restrictions of the classic capitalist freedoms. In Great Britain the practice of medicine and ownership of certain basic industries such as coal and steel are in the hands of the government. The French and Italian governments own auto manufacturing companies. Other economic activities also are highly regulated by government in many social democracies. Advertising may be severely restricted and consumption of some products is controlled by rationing. Taxation is much heavier than it is in the United States.

Even in the United States, we are far from the classical ideal of capitalism. The basic belief in individualism has probably eroded somewhat during the past four or five decades. The Great Depression of the 1930s caused many Americans to rethink their basic distrust of "big government." As we will see later in our book, many laws were passed during the 1930s that placed limits on what businesses can do. Labor legislation made it illegal for employers to fire or threaten to fire employees who try to organize a labor union and it also set the normal working week of 40 hours. Other legislation of the thirties was aimed at helping small business to survive in the competitive struggle with big businesses, notably small grocery stores and huge supermarket chains. The notion that every American has a right to a job was born during the 1930s. Unemployment benefits and the entire social security program sprang from the depression era.

Private property still is at the heart of our economic system but there

"The cities need help, the poor need help, the third world needs help, and you're the helpers!"

Source: *Dunagin's People*, Field Newspaper Syndicate.

are many laws that pertain to the use of private property. A firm that serves the general public, such as a restaurant, cannot refuse, for example, to serve a customer because of race or national origin. Zoning laws are another form of regulation of the use of private property.

There are many other issues still unresolved in the modern capitalist system. For example, some people question whether the progressive federal income tax has damaged our individual initiative. Under the taxation system, your tax rate goes up as your income goes up. Has that reduced the willingness of some people to work overtime or to invest their money in the hope of earning a profit? Has our welfare system reduced the incentive of some people to work? What of the effects of inheritance and estate taxes on the incentive to accumulate property?

If consumers have so much power, would consumerism be such an issue in our system? Would government agencies and commissions have to be in the business of consumer protection?

What about the freedom to compete? Even more basic, what is competition? We have laws that prevent large and powerful firms from running small and less powerful firms out of business, even if they are less efficient than the larger firms.

The Small Business Administration (SBA) was set up by the federal government to give various types of financial and management assistance to small firms. Should our government be in the business of helping people go into business? Should the biggest customer in the world, the United States government, limit its choice of suppliers in some buying situations to only small firms?

What about occupational freedom? Our government and private businesses sponsor many programs to develop our nation's human resources. Although often criticized, these programs probably have broadened the range of career choices for many people. Examples of these programs are financial assistance to needy students and funding on-the-job training in private businesses. Job safety and health also have become major concerns of government.

Freedom of contract also has come under more government regulation. Does the federal minimum wage increase unemployment of marginally qualified workers? Does the minimum wage make it harder for a teenager to find a part-time job? In some states new employees are required to join a labor union if there is one representing the employer's workforce whether or not the new employee wants to join the union.

Finally how limited is the role of government in our economy today? Some of the biggest economic problems facing us in recent years have been inflation and unemployment. The government's role in seeking solutions to these problems is, of course, dictated by the voters but it is a major one. Over the past several decades, Americans have tended to look more and more to the government as a solver of our economic problems. Even business firms look to Washington for help. And they, along with other special interest groups, spend millions of dollars a year on lobbying efforts. In many cases, whether a particular program or law is regarded as interference or assistance depends on the observer's point of view.

At any rate, there is little doubt that many forms of government regulation and taxation further distinguish the United States today from the capitalist ideal. Capitalism has been modified at least as much as collectivism since 1930. You may wonder where this borrowing of elements from other systems may lead us. In the United States that depends on the voting public. In the Soviet Union it depends on the will of the leaders.

What Is Business?

We purposely have put off defining *business* until we had developed some of the basic ideas that underlie our type of economic system. **In**

our economic system, business is all profit-directed economic activi-   business
ties that are organized and directed to provide products and services.

Notice the term *profit* in our definition. Profit is the basic motivator of
business activities in our system. It is the major driving force. **To busi-**   profit
ness people, profit is what remains of the sales revenues they receive
from selling their products or services after they deduct the costs in-
curred in producing and selling those products and services.

Sales Revenues	$150,000
— Expenses	− 125,000
Profit (before tax)	$ 25,000

Businesses earn sales revenues by selling want-satisfying products
and services to their customers. A firm can survive over the long run
only if it continues to satisfy and serve its customers. This makes it
possible for the firm to make a profit while serving its customers. Meanwhile, the firm also is serving society. For example, profitable firms pay
taxes that help to support public education and county hospitals. As we
will see later in the book, businesses must be *managed effectively* to
survive the competition of rival firms.

Many businesses produce and sell tangible (physical) products like
cameras, cars, furniture, trucks, and farm machinery. Some firms, however, provide intangible services. Examples are the Metropolitan Life
Insurance Company, Holiday Inns, Hertz, and United Air Lines. The
services sector of our economy has been growing rapidly during recent
decades.

Finally there are many organizations in our economy that engage in
activities very similar to those of business firms. The big difference
between them and business firms is that they are not seeking to earn a
profit for owners. Examples of these nonprofit organizations are chari-
ties, political parties, state universities and colleges, and government
units, such as police and fire departments and the Department of Defense.

The Postindustrial Services Economy

During the 1950s and 1960s, the United States economy began undergoing a basic change from an industrial economy based on the man-

ufacture of tangible products to a *postindustrial economy* based on the creation of intangible services. The effects of this change still are being felt in our economy.

The tremendous growth of our economy during the 1950s and 1960s contributed to record high levels of disposable personal income, and American consumers began buying huge amounts of intangible services. Recreation, entertainment, travel, and other service industries began growing faster than many of our manufacturing industries. One of the most dramatic examples of this growth in service industries is the fantastic spread of fast-food restaurants, such as McDonald's, Burger King, Kentucky Fried Chicken, and Pizza Hut.

We will discuss the implications of this shift from an industrial to a postindustrial economy at several places in this book.

Summary and Look Ahead

Economic systems help us to satisfy our unlimited wants with our limited resources. Because our wants are so varied and because our resources in many instances have become more scarce, the economic problem today is more complex than it was in the past.

Several elementary concepts (utility, value, specialization, exchange, standard of living, diminishing marginal utility, and the factors of production) are relevant in any type of economic system, whether it is a capitalist or a collectivist economic system.

The major ideas underlying the U.S. private-enterprise system are individualism, private property, profit incentive, consumer power, freedom to compete, occupational freedom, freedom of contract, and the limited role of government.

The type of economic system most unlike the private-enterprise, or capitalist, system is the collectivist system. In this type of system, private property and the other institutions and ideas of the private enterprise system are largely absent. Central planning by the government replaces individual freedoms and initiative.

Most economic systems in the world today fall somewhere between the two extremes of pure capitalism and pure collectivism. Our system has adopted some collectivist ideas. Our social security system, for example, would not exist in a purely capitalist system. However, collectivist systems also have adopted some capitalist ideas. The use of the profit incentive to get more production from the Soviet farmer is an example.

Business, in our economy, includes all profit-directed economic activities that are organized and directed to provide the products and services that contribute to our standard of living.

In the next chapter we will see how people use the freedoms provided by our economic system to form business firms, and we will discuss why business firms exist.

CAREERS IN BUSINESS

It is never too early to start planning a career. The dizzy pace at which the world is changing makes nearly all choices of occupation somewhat risky, which underlines the importance of choosing carefully. It also brings home the idea that the more hectic the competition for jobs becomes, the more important your preparation becomes. You face the double challenge of being well prepared for a first job and also being prepared to change jobs.

Your education at this time, then, must teach you how to learn and how to adjust to change. This book can help, especially if your career is in the business world. It will give you some ideas about the whys of business.

Beginning with Chapter 6 and in most of the chapters that follow it, there is a Career Profile. Each of these Career Profiles features a young person who is in the business world. Each one of these people will have several interesting and informative comments about the business world, especially about their jobs—what they do.

These profiles will give you an opportunity to "put yourself in the shoes" of people who are involved in a wide variety of business careers. We hope this will start you thinking about career opportunities. We wish you good luck in the greatest adventure of a lifetime—the search for a career. We hope that your choice will be a career in the business world!

Key Concepts

business All profit-directed economic activities that are organized and directed to provide products and services.

capital A factor of production. Tools and machinery or anything made by humans that aids in producing and distributing products and services. Human-made productive capacity.

capital formation The process of adding to the productive capacity of an economy.

capitalism An economic system based on private ownership of the factors of production. The bulk of economic decision making is in the hands of individuals and privately owned business firms.

central planning Practiced in collectivist economic systems. The government decides how productive resources will be used and how output will be distributed.

collectivism   An economic system in which the factors of production are owned by the government. It controls social and economic decision making.

consumerism   A movement to enhance the power of consumers relative to that of business firms. Any action taken or legislation enacted that shows concern for the welfare of consumers.

consumer power   The concept that the consumer influences the quality, style, etc. of products produced by business firms and determines the success of those firms.

Disposable Personal Income (DPI)   The incomes of people minus taxes paid by them.

the economic problem   The problem of trying to satisfy our unlimited wants with limited resources.

entrepreneur   A person who assumes the risk of organizing and managing a business in the hope of making a profit.

entrepreneurship   A factor of production. Occurs when a person or firm assumes risk in the hope of making a profit. Bringing land, labor, and capital together and managing them productively to produce a product or service.

exchange   Makes specialization, or division of labor, possible. A specialist trades part of his or her output for part of the output of other specialists. Trading one thing for another thing.

factors of production   The elements needed for producing products and services. The inputs of the productive system: land, labor, capital, and entrepreneurship.

Gross National Product (GNP)   The market value of all final products and services produced in a nation during a given year.

individualism   The idea that the group, the society, and the government are necessary but are of less importance than the individual's self-determination. A characteristic of a free enterprise, or capitalist, economic system.

inflation   An increase in the prices of products and services over a period of time that has the effect of reducing the purchasing power of a nation's currency.

labor   A factor of production. Human mental and physical effort needed to produce products and services.

laissez faire   Let people do as they please. As an economic philosophy, it means let the owners of business set the rules of competition without any governmental regulation or control.

land   A factor or production. Includes all natural resources.

mercantilism   An economic philosophy that advocated building strong national states and that viewed the strength of a nation to be in its supply of precious metals, such as gold and silver.

private enterprise   Private ownership of business firms.

profit   What remains after a business deducts its costs of doing business (expenditures) from the sales revenues (receipts) it receives from selling its products or services.

the Protestant ethic   A tradition stressing the values of hard work, accumulation of property, and self-reliance.

specialization   Giving more effort to a specific task instead of giving less effort to a greater number of tasks. Dividing work into several tasks and having one person perform only a limited number of those tasks. Each person can make better use of his or her limited time and talents and become more efficient in performing a specialized task.

standard of living   A measure of economic well-being; often expressed as per capita Gross National Product.

utility   The ability of a product or a service to satisfy a human want; usefulness.

value in exchange   The ability of one product or service to command another product or service in an exchange.

For Review . . .

1. Has the economic problem become more complex in modern times than it was in earlier times? Explain.
2. Discuss the processes of specialization and exchange and their relationship to the economic problem.
3. Distinguish between needs and wants.
4. Should comparisons of the standards of living in different countries be based on per capita GNP? Explain.
5. What is the basic purpose of a) a capitalist economic system and b) a collectivist economic system?
6. List and define the factors of production.
7. List and discuss the major features of capitalism.
8. In what ways does pure capitalism differ from pure collectivism?
9. In what ways has our economic system changed over the last century?
10. Capital formation is necessary for fuller economic development. How does it occur in the absence of private property and profit incentive?
11. What is the basic motivation for business firms to produce want-satisfying products and services for consumers?

. . . For Discussion

1. How do you as an individual cope with the economic problem?
2. Should future generations of people be considered when we cope with the economic problem?
3. Individual initiative is important in our system. What factors determine a person's initiative?
4. Does consumer power guarantee that consumer welfare is maximized?
5. One of the features of capitalism is freedom to compete. When should limitations be placed on this freedom?
6. What is profit? What determines how much profit a business firm will make?

Incidents

The Economic Problem—Still with Us

"Oil will power Mexico's proclaimed social and industrial revolution. With crude reserves possibly second only to those of Saudi Arabia, Petróleos Mexicanos (Pemex), the state oil company, claims to be far ahead of its development schedule and promises a $10 billion profit by 1982. But despite these new found riches, a political consensus is lacking. Mexico cannot decide how to spend the bonanza or who should be first to benefit from it. Broadly, how can the oil money help the poor and develop the country at the same time, without firing up inflation and overturning traditional social structures?"

Thus, the economic problem still exists.

"Some would concentrate on agriculture, which could ease the lot of the two of every five Mexicans who are looking for a job. Others believe that expanding industry should be top priority; that could help disperse the burgeoning urban population and more directly improve the quality of life. 'Unfortunately,' says a foreign consultant based in Mexico City, 'the government hasn't decided which road to take.' He says that any large investment in rural areas would depend on 'legal changes in land ownership rules,' and that could prove a very tough political nut."

Questions

1. Describe the economic problem in Mexico.
2. Will the oil profits solve Mexico's economic problem? Explain.
3. If you were making the decision for the Mexican government, what use would you recommend for the oil profits? Explain your reasons.

Source: *Business Week.*

A Russian Capitalist?

Government-run stores in Russia experienced a big shortage of cosmetics in 1978 because Russian cosmetics plants met only half their production quota for lipstick, one-third of their quota for mascara, and one-eighth of their quota for eyeshadow. The problem was recognized by the government planners in 1977 but they were unable to correct it during 1978.

As a result of the shortage of cosmetics, a huge black market for cosmetics developed in Russia. One of the first "entrepreneurs" who tried to fill the black market demand was a Russian plumber. The plumber manufactured his own cosmetics and sold them at prices that were three times higher than the prices set by the government. He ground different colors of children's chalk to make eyeshadow, made nail polish from furniture lacquer sprinkled with metal filings for sparkle, and made mascara from black ink and shoe polish. For packaging, he relied on help from a "partner" who worked for a government fountain pen plant.

The plumber had a very profitable business going until he was arrested in October 1978 for "profiteering."

Questions

1. How would you explain the failure of the central planners to correct the shortage situation?
2. How would you explain the existence of a black market for the cosmetics?
3. Was the plumber an entrepreneur? Why or why not?

Source: *The Times-Picayune.*

ROCKETOY COMPANY 1

In this chapter and in nine others we will use the Rocketoy Company to illustrate how the ideas in the text fit into the life of a firm. In each of the ten episodes the history of Rocketoy will unfold, revealing the variety of problems faced by its management. This will give the concepts you learn in the book greater meaning.

The Rocketoy Company episodes illustrate the use of the case method. The case method can be exciting. It shows that "real-world" solutions to problems require more from a manager than can be found in textbooks. Your judgment of the personalities that will appear in the Rocketoy episodes will affect the responses you make to the questions we raise. It is important to "hash it all out" with the others in your class. Let's get on with the facts!

While Terry Phillips was growing up in Milwaukee, he spent a lot of time tinkering in his father's workshop. As a result, he developed great skill in woodworking, carpentry, and whittling. At age 10, he sold his first wooden toy. By the time he was 16, Terry was making and selling 50 items per month to friends and relatives.

After he graduated from high school, Terry borrowed $2,000 from his uncle, Joe Phillips, who had faith in Terry's creativity and good business sense. This interest-free loan enabled Terry to rent a garage in his neighborhood. It also enabled him to buy the basic equipment he needed to make up to 500 toys per month in five basic models. He sold these to stores in Milwaukee—three variety stores, a novelty shop, and a large toy store.

Terry's sister, Pam, had recently graduated from junior college where she studied accounting. She agreed to keep Terry's financial records on a part-time basis for a wage of $5 per hour. She became his first employee.

Terry also got help from a lawyer he hired to check sales contracts. A local banker helped Terry to set up a checking account for the business and arranged for a short-term loan at a reasonable interest rate. The bank loan made it possible for Terry to buy wood and paint in larger quantities and to hire a shop assistant.

In the first year, after expanding the shop, sales grew a little and, despite the added wages and interest cost, Terry was able to pay his uncle back one-fourth of his original loan. By the end of the year, Terry got a year-long trial contract with a national toy distributor (Toyco) to supply them with 2,000 units of his "Rocketoy." The Rocketoy is a simple, durable toy space rocket that appeals to children 8–10 years old. At this stage, the Rocketoy Company seemed to be a fantastic success.

Questions

1. How does the Rocketoy Company illustrate the principles of specialization and exchange?

2. Describe the factors of production used by Terry.

3. Could the Rocketoy Company have come about under a collectivist economic system? Why or why not?

4. Why are Uncle Joe and the bank willing to lend Terry money? Are they taking a risk? Why?

The Business Firm

Objectives: After reading this chapter, you should be able to

1. Explain what a market economy is and how it works.
2. Define the law of demand and explain why it is valid.
3. Identify and describe the major factors that influence the overall demand for products and services in an economy.
4. Define the law of supply and explain why it is valid.
5. Explain the major factors that influence the overall supply of products and services in an economy.
6. Draw a demand curve and a supply curve and explain the significance of their intersection on a graph.
7. Distinguish between a change in demand and a change in quantity demanded.
8. Distinguish between a change in supply and a change in quantity supplied.
9. Discuss the reasons why people form business firms.
10. Give examples of ways firms try to increase their profits.
11. Explain why business owners assume risk.

Key concepts: Look for these terms as you read the chapter

market economy	supply
price	law of supply
demand	demand curve
law of demand	supply curve
discretionary income	business opportunity
real income	risk

Because there are not enough resources to satisfy our unlimited wants, we must choose what will and what will not be produced. These choices determine how resources will be used. Under our economic system, independent decisions made by consumers and producers guided by the price system determine how resources are allocated.

The business firm is the basic building block for the production of products and services in our system. Most economic activity is channeled through business firms, which gather and organize resources for production. They do so in the hope of making a profit.

The Market Economy

The term *market* has many meanings. To some people it might mean the place where they shop for groceries. To other people it might mean the stock market. To a manufacturer of women's dresses it might mean the current level of demand for dresses.

In this chapter we will think of a market as a set of economic forces (supply and demand) which together form a price. Supply forces tend to bring products and services into production. Demand forces tend to result in consumption of those products and services. Supply and demand interact to form a price. Since markets play a large role in our economy, we say we have a market economy.

A market economy is an economic system in which prices determine how resources will be allocated and how the products and services produced will be distributed. Markets exist to form prices.

market economy

Prices

Prices induce or limit production and consumption. Were it not for the price consumers have to pay to get things, they could consume as much as they want. Since consumers have limited income and limited buying power, however, they must limit the amount they buy. The supplier of an item, on the other hand, would have no incentive to supply it without being paid for it. Price, therefore, must be at a level such that some producers are willing to produce products and services for sale and some consumers are willing to buy them for consumption.

In a very simple economy, prices as we know them would not exist. One person might trade potatoes for oranges produced by someone else. The two traders would agree on a rate of exchange of potatoes for oranges. This simple type of trading is called *barter*. Products and services are exchanged directly for other products and services. Barter still exists, especially in international business dealings. PepsiCo, for example, swaps Pepsi syrup for Russian vodka. General Motors bartered earth-moving equipment in return for Russian timber. Although GM had no direct use for timber, it found cash buyers for the timber elsewhere. Without the barter arrangement GM's timber sale might not have been possible because the Soviets do not like their currency to leave the country.

price

Money facilitates or simplifies exchange. It serves as a medium of exchange; it is the common measure of value for potatoes and oranges and thousands of other products and services. **Price, therefore, is the quantity of money (or other products and services) that is paid in exchange for something else.**

All economic systems must have a way of determining

- which products and services will be produced
- how much of each will be produced
- the methods of producing them
- how they will be divided among the people

In a market economy these decisions are made through a price-making process in markets. The prices of different products and services determine how resources will be allocated among alternative ends. Those prices also determine the kinds of products and services that will be produced, their quantities, and the amounts that are made available to customers. A market economy, therefore, also can be called a *price system*. To understand how all this works, let's study the forces of demand and supply.

Demand

As we have seen, the basic human needs are for food, clothing, and shelter. We express these needs when we demand to buy a can of Green Giant peas, a red coat, or a new house.

Because our incomes are limited, each of us has some wants that will not be fully satisfied. You have to choose, therefore, which wants you will try to satisfy. Price helps you choose. By comparing prices of different things, you decide how much of item A must be given up to get one unit of item B. Price is the yardstick for comparisons. It is a major guide to production and consumption decisions.

In a modern economy new wants are always appearing and new products and services are always being offered to satisfy those wants. The suppliers of these products and services try to get consumers to spend money on them. In this way the consumer's desire for want satisfaction and the supplier's desire for profit are supposed to be satisfied.

In business demand means much more than desire on the part of a would-be buyer. For example, perhaps everyone in your class would like to own a new Corvette. But General Motors will not rush into the production of Corvettes for you and your classmates, because GM is concerned with demand in the economic sense, not desire by itself.

Demand for a product or a service exists when there are people who   demand

- **desire the product or service**
- **have the buying power to purchase it**
- **are willing to part with some buying power in order to buy it**

Each of these requirements must be met in order for effective demand (or a market) to exist for a product or a service.

As we will see in our marketing chapters, firms do what they can to increase the demand for their products and services. For example, they use advertising to build desire and willingness to spend. They often offer credit to increase consumer buying power.

For most products a greater number of units are demanded at a lower price than at a higher price. One of the reasons for this is the principle of diminishing marginal utility, mentioned in Chapter 1. A fourth shirt, for example, gives you less additional satisfaction than the first one did. You may be better off with four shirts than with only one, but you probably are not four times better off. As additional units lose something (mar-

Source: *Dunagin's People*, Field Newspaper Syndicate.

law of demand

ginal utility, or usefulness), you are willing to pay less and less to get them. One reason is that your buying power is limited. **The inverse relationship between price and quantity demanded is the "law of demand"—as price goes up, the quantity demanded goes down.**

We can talk about demand from different points of view. The overall demand for all products and services in an economy is called *aggregate demand.* We also can refer to the total demand for a specific product class, such as the demand for cars. Narrowing it further, we could discuss the demand for a specific brand, such as Chevrolet Corvettes. An especially important distinction is *industry* and *firm demand.* The demand for cars is an example of industry demand, and the demand for GM cars is an example of firm demand.

The concept of demand, however, involves more than a relationship between quantity and price. Among the many nonprice factors that underlie demand are

- buying power
- willingness to spend
- population changes
- population shifts
- changes in tastes and cultural values
- presence of substitute products and services and their prices

Buying Power

Buying power comes from

- current income
- accumulated wealth
- credit

discretionary income

real income

Current income is the major source of buying power for Americans. Your current income is your salary or wages plus interest on savings accounts, rental income, dividends on stock, and interest on bonds. But you cannot spend it all because you have to pay taxes. Disposable income is your current income minus the taxes you pay. **Discretionary income is what remains of your disposable income after you have bought your necessities.** It is available to spend on "luxuries." **Finally your real income is your income expressed in terms of buying power; it is your income adjusted for the decline in buying power due to inflation.** Suppose your income doubles over a 10-year period. Unless you could buy twice as much at the end of the period as you could at the beginning, your real income did not really double. (See Figure 2–1.)

Our federal income tax has a big effect on the way income is *distributed* in our country. The income tax takes money from higher-income people and redistributes it, through government spending, to lower-in-

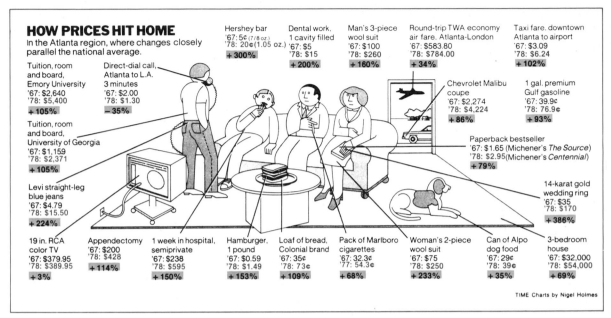

HOW PRICES HIT HOME
In the Atlanta region, where changes closely parallel the national average.

Tuition, room and board, Emory University
'67: $2,640
'78: $5,400
+105%

Tuition, room and board, University of Georgia
'67: $1,159
'78: $2,371
+105%

Levi straight-leg blue jeans
'67: $4.79
'78: $15.50
+224%

Direct-dial call, Atlanta to L.A. 3 minutes
'67: $2.00
'78: $1.30
−35%

Hershey bar
'67: 5¢ (7/8 oz.)
'78: 20¢ (1.05 oz.)
+300%

Dental work, 1 cavity filled
'67: $5
'78: $15
+200%

Man's 3-piece wool suit
'67: $100
'78: $260
+160%

Round-trip TWA economy air fare, Atlanta-London
'67: $583.80
'78: $784.00
+34%

Chevrolet Malibu coupe
'67: $2,274
'78: $4,224
+86%

Taxi fare, downtown Atlanta to airport
'67: $3.09
'78: $6.24
+102%

1 gal. premium Gulf gasoline
'67: 39.9¢
'78: 76.9¢
+93%

Paperback bestseller
'67: $1.65 (Michener's *The Source*)
'78: $2.95 (Michener's *Centennial*)
+79%

14-karat gold wedding ring
'67: $35
'78: $170
+386%

19 in. RCA color TV
'67: $379.95
'78: $389.95
+3%

Appendectomy
'67: $200
'78: $428
+114%

1 week in hospital, semiprivate
'67: $238
'78: $595
+150%

Hamburger, 1 pound
'67: $0.59
'78: $1.49
+153%

Loaf of bread, Colonial brand
'67: 35¢
'78: 73¢
+109%

Pack of Marlboro cigarettes
'67: 32.3¢
'77: 54.3¢
+68%

Woman's 2-piece wool suit
'67: $75
'78: $250
+233%

Can of Alpo dog food
'67: 29¢
'78: 39¢
+35%

3-bedroom house
'67: $32,000
'78: $54,000
+69%

TIME Charts by Nigel Holmes

Percentage figures show changes in retail prices from base year of 1967.
Source: *Time.*

FIGURE 2–1

How prices hit home

come people. This results in less demand for luxuries and more demand for basic food, clothing, and shelter. Aggregate consumer demand, however, increases because people with lower incomes tend to spend a greater proportion of their income than people with higher incomes. People with higher incomes tend to save a greater proportion of their income.

Accumulated wealth can be liquid or nonliquid. Liquid wealth can be converted quickly into a known amount of cash for making purchases. Money in regular savings accounts is an example. It can be withdrawn easily and quickly to buy or make down payments on major purchases such as homes, cars, and home appliances. United States savings bonds are another example of liquid wealth.

An example of nonliquid wealth is a family's equity in their home, the difference between its current market value and what they owe on the mortgage. You can look at your bank book and determine how much money you have on deposit. It is much harder to put a dollar value on the equity in a house because its true current market value must be determined. Loan companies, banks, and savings and loan associations often are willing to grant loans to people on the basis of their equity in their homes. This frees this nonliquid wealth for current use.

There are two basic types of credit. *Installment credit* involves making regular monthly payments (installments) on credit purchases. It is very

INDEXING
FEDERAL
INCOME TAXES

Because of rising concern among Americans about inflation, there have been several proposals to index federal income taxes. Without indexing, people who receive pay increases to keep up with inflated prices end up in higher tax brackets.

Suppose a household of four people earned $10,000 in 1975 and paid $709 in federal income taxes. That is 7.1 percent of the household's income. Let's assume that between 1975 and 1980, prices rise each year by 7 percent. Now, suppose that the household receives a 7 percent pay increase each year to offset rising prices. In 1980 the household would pay $1,433 (10.2 percent of its income) in federal income taxes even though its real buying power did not increase at all.

One way to avoid this "inflation tax" is to raise the personal exemption each year by the same percentage as the inflation rate for each year. Thus if the personal exemption is $750 one year and the inflation rate is 10 percent for that year, next year's personal exemption would be raised by 10 percent to $825. Each tax bracket also would be raised by the same percentage. A household that receives a 10 percent increase in income over that year, therefore, would stay in the same tax bracket.

important in the purchase of consumer durables such as cars. *Noninstallment credit* involves paying in full for your charge purchases at the end of the credit period, usually 30 days. Both types of credit have expanded greatly in our economy during recent years, especially installment credit. In fact, ours often is referred to as a credit economy. Without credit, millions of Americans would have a much lower standard of living. We buy and use products today and pay for them in the future. In the case of a home, the credit period may be 30 years.

CONSUMER
DEBT

Total consumer debt, including home mortgages, now stands at $1 trillion—equal to about $4,600 for every man, woman, and child in the land. After consumers have paid their taxes, another 21¢ of every dollar they earn must go to pay off existing debts, an unprecedented burden on the consumer.

The above figures pertain to the second quarter of 1978.

Source: *Business Week.*

Willingness to Spend

How much income and other types of buying power people have affects their ability to buy. But we also have to consider their willingness to buy. Business people are concerned about consumer confidence in the economy. The Survey Research Center at the University of Michigan, for example, conducts consumer polls to gauge consumer confidence in the economy. In general, consumers are more willing to spend when they have confidence in the economy. When they lack confidence, they tend to spend less and to save more. But during some recent years, this general pattern has not always held true.

Periods of low consumer confidence have been accompanied by high levels of consumer spending. Part of the explanation for this is the very high rate of inflation during recent years. When consumers expect inflation to continue, they reason that tomorrow's prices will be even higher than today's. This is called *inflationary psychology*. Saving money loses much of its appeal. Since the buying power of the dollar declines, many consumers prefer to buy products they hope will increase in value. This is why many consumers have recently been buying jewelry, furs, silverware, antiques, and fine china. They look upon these purchases as investments that will increase in value. Even clothing retailers have used the appeal of "investment dressing" to help sell more expensive types of clothing. The appeal of saving for a rainy day also probably has declined because of social security, pension plans, and unemployment compensation.

Population Changes

Population changes also affect demand. Sellers of necessary products and services tend to experience increased demand when the population increases. A decline in the number of births, on the other hand, means a decline in the demand for baby food. Changes in the age distribution and ethnic makeup of the population also affect demand. For example, the proportion of children and teenagers in our population will decline during the coming decades. This means a decline in demand for child-oriented toys and elementary and secondary education. But the proportion of people 65 years old and older will increase. This means increased demand for digestive aids, decaffeinated coffee, and bran cereals. By the year 2000 the median age of Americans is projected to be 35, up from 28 in 1970 and 30 in 1980. (The median is the middle number of a group of numbers ranked from the smallest to the largest. This concept is discussed in Chapter 14.) The increasing number of Spanish-surnamed Americans in the population has increased the demand for Spanish-oriented products and services.

Population Shifts

Population shifts also can affect demand. During recent years there has been some movement of people and industry from the older industrialized East-North Central and Mid-Atlantic states to the Sunbelt states in the South and Southwest. This regional shift is increasing the demand for outdoor recreation equipment and housing in the Sunbelt states. There also are major shifts within our Standard Metropolitan Statistical Areas (SMSAs). An SMSA is an area that includes a central city (or twin cities) with a population of 50,000 or more and the surrounding counties that are economically and socially integrated with it.

In many SMSAs, the central cities are losing population to their suburbs. In fact over half of the people in our SMSAs now live in the suburbs. This trend has increased the demand for lawn-care products, outdoor swimming pools, tennis courts, and private cars. At the same time it has decreased sales for the merchants in downtown shopping areas. In very recent years, however, there is evidence that some people, especially older persons, are moving back into our central cities, many of which are experiencing increased demand for medical services, nursing homes, and apartment buildings as a result. Some younger people also are buying and modernizing older homes in central cities. The high price of new houses is a factor here. The increase in demand for do-it-yourself books, tools, and clinics is due, in part, to this shift. Finally some SMSA dwellers are moving to smaller towns and rural areas to escape big-city problems such as high taxes, congestion, crime, and

"My husband fancies himself as an expert repairman. Do you have any 'UNDO-IT yourself books'?"

Source: *The Better Half,* The Register and Tribune Syndicate.

pollution. The demand for home canning equipment, rural land, and pick-up trucks has increased as a result.

Changes in Tastes and Cultural Values

Changes in consumer tastes and cultural values also can affect demand. The demand for unfiltered cigarettes, big cars, and fountain pens decreased because of a change in taste to filtered cigarettes, economy cars, and ball-point and felt-tipped pens. The growing acceptance of a singles life style has increased the demand for products and services for the "singles market." The rising divorce rate creates two households in place of one and increases the demand for housing and household appliances. The women's rights movement has increased the demand for child-care centers, business clothing, and convenience foods. We will discuss other changes in our cultural values and how they affect business in Chapter 17.

Presence and Prices of Substitutes

Finally the presence of substitute products and services and their prices can affect the demand for a product or a service. The demand for dry cleaning, butter, ocean cruises, train tickets, tooth powder, and shaving soap declined when new clothing fabrics, margarine, air travel, toothpaste, and electric shavers were introduced. There have been some big shifts in demand for some products and services in recent years due to shortages of some basic resources and big price jumps. The high cost of electricity and natural gas has increased the demand for wood-burning heaters and home-insulation materials. In some cases, firms that market products that are in short supply have to, in effect, ration them among their customers in an effort to reduce demand for them.

Supply

The other half of the price system is supply. **The supply of a product or a service results from the effort of producers. The quantity supplied is the number of units of a product or a service that producers will offer for sale at a certain price.**

supply

In most cases, a greater number of units will be offered for sale at a higher price than at a lower price. A higher price leads producers to supply more units than a lower price would because they perceive more profit potential. Price and quantity vary in the same direction. **This is the "law of supply"—as price goes up, the quantity supplied goes up.**

law of supply

Like the concept of demand, the concept of supply involves much more than a relationship between quantity and price. Among the many factors that underlie supply are

- the outlook for the economy
- the outlook for the industry
- the firm's objectives
- technological progress
- expected profitability of producing other products and services
- the nature of competition
- government spending policies and regulations
- other environmental factors

The Outlook for the Economy

The aggregate supply of all products and services is affected by many of the same things that affect overall demand. For example, producers who expect consumer buying power to increase may step up production in order to satisfy the expected increase in demand. When economic forecasters predict good times ahead, producers are optimistic and are willing to produce in anticipation of orders from customers.

The Outlook for the Industry

The outlook for a particular industry affects supply in that industry. For example, if September and October car sales indicate that consumers are not in a buying mood, car makers will cut back on production. They will not produce as many units as they would have if the buying response were greater. When car makers cut back on production, they cut back on their orders for steel and the many other products that are used to make cars.

The Firm's Objectives

A firm's objectives also affect how much it is willing to supply. A firm's market share is the percentage of total sales it has in its industry. Some firms have an objective of increasing their market share by producing and selling in large volumes, often at prices that are lower than those charged by their competitors. On the other hand, some firms are more concerned with building an image among consumers for providing high-quality products. They may offer fewer units for sale in order to help build a reputation for "quality rather than quantity."

Technological Progress

Technological progress also affects supply. From both a cost and a quality standpoint, color TVs can be made more efficiently today than 15 years ago. The same is true for computers, pocket calculators, and photocopying machines. This induces suppliers to supply more.

Expected Profitability of Producing Other Products and Services

The supply of a product will decrease when a firm thinks it can make more profit by shifting its resources to another product. This is especially true when a firm can easily switch from making one product to making another. General Electric stopped making many types of small appliances and RCA, Xerox, and General Electric stopped making computers because they believed they could make more profit by making other products.

The Nature of Competition

The nature of competition in an industry also affects supply. When only three or four firms produce essentially the same product, the firms tend to recognize their interdependence. They know if they flood the market, all of them could end up with less profit because price will tend to fall due to excess supply.

Government Spending Policies and Regulations

Government spending policies and regulations also can stimulate or depress the supplies of some products and services. Tax incentives might induce oil companies to search harder for new oil reserves and steel companies to build new plants that are more efficient. At any given price, these firms might be willing to supply more than if the tax incentives were absent. Many home insulation producers expanded their production capacity when Congress started talking about tax credits for homeowners who added insulation to their houses.

Other Environmental Factors

Other environmental factors can also affect supply. Mounting product liability risk, for example, has led some drug manufacturers to stop producing certain types of live virus for diseases like measles and mumps. The cost of product liability insurance is high and, in some cases, potential suppliers of high-risk products prefer not to offer them for sale.

The Determination of Market Prices

To see how supply and demand determine prices, let us study the supply and demand for plastic rulers. Table 2–1 shows the relationship between price and quantity supplied. Table 2–2 shows the relationship between price and quantity demanded. Putting the law of supply and the law of demand into graphical form gives us Figure 2–2.

TABLE 2-1

Price and quantity supplied

Price (cents per unit)	Quantity supplied (units)
6	100
28	200
50	300
67	400
89	500
As price increases . . .	*. . . quantity supplied increases*

TABLE 2-2

Price and quantity demanded

Price (cents per unit)	Quantity demanded (units)
75	100
62	200
50	300
37	400
25	500
As price decreases . . .	*. . . quantity demanded increases*

demand curve

supply curve

The demand curve (D) shows how many units are demanded at various prices. **A demand curve is a line that shows the number of units that will be demanded (bought) at each price at a given point in time. Fewer units are demanded at higher prices than at lower prices.**

The supply curve (S) shows how many units are supplied at various prices. **A supply curve is a line that shows the number of units that will be supplied (offered for sale) at each price at a given point in time. Fewer units are supplied at lower prices than at higher prices.**

The supply and demand curves in Figure 2–2 cross at a price of $.50 per unit. Only at this price is the quantity suppliers are willing to offer exactly equal to the quantity buyers are willing to buy. The market is cleared at this price. At higher prices, suppliers would be willing to supply more units than buyers would be willing to buy. At lower prices, buyers would be willing to buy more units than suppliers would be willing to supply.

The situation shown in Figure 2–2 is oversimplified, however. For example, the amount of money available in an economy (the money supply) also affects prices. If there is too much money in relation to products and services, prices will rise. Such price inflation is due to too much money chasing too few products and services.

Government regulations and policies also can interfere with the forces of supply and demand. For example, government policy makers have debated for years the effect of price controls on the supply and

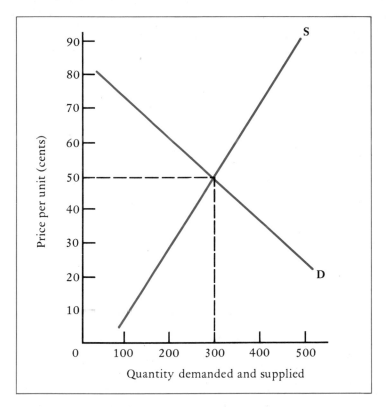

The point where the supply and demand curves cross indicates a market price of 50 cents per unit. The quantity demanded is 300 units and the quantity supplied is 300 units. At the price of 50 cents per unit, the quantity consumers wish to buy is exactly the same as the quantity producers wish to sell. We call this the *equilibrium* price because the quantity demanded and the quantity supplied are in balance at this price, and the market is cleared.

FIGURE 2–2

Determination of market price

demand for natural gas and crude petroleum. When the Organization of Petroleum Exporting Countries (OPEC) raised the price of their oil, the government did not allow American oil producers to follow suit. The price of American oil from old wells was kept below the OPEC price. Some people say this reduced the incentive for American oil producers to pump more oil, which led to efforts to deregulate oil prices. The government's various attempts at price supports for farmers also interfere with the natural workings of the forces of supply and demand. The same is true when city governments practice rent control.

Nevertheless, Figure 2–2 does give us a basic insight into the nature of price. Whether we are talking about the price we pay for hamburgers or cars, the price we get for our labor (wage), or the price we pay to borrow money (interest), the forces of supply and demand are at work.

Figure 2–3 shows changes (or shifts) in the demand and supply curves. The shifts are due to changes in the underlying forces of supply and demand. A shift from D_0 to D_1 means that, at any given price, demand is *greater* than it was before the shift. One of the reasons a firm advertises its product or service is the hope that it will shift its demand curve up and to the right. More units will be demanded at any given price.

A shift from D_0 to D_2 means that, at any given price, demand is *smaller* than it was before the shift. Over the years, the demand curves for men's hats, 78-RPM records, dial telephones, and toothpowder have shifted to the left. Fewer units are demanded at any given price.

A shift from S_0 to S_1 means that, at any given price, supply is *greater* than it was before the shift. More units are supplied at any given price. The entry of so many firms, especially Japanese producers, into the market for CB radios and pocket calculators has caused more CB units and pocket calculators to be for sale at any given price than were available when these products were first introduced to consumers.

A shift from S_0 to S_2 means that, at any given price, supply is *smaller* than it was before the shift. Fewer units are supplied at any given price. The great increase in antique collecting probably has caused the supply curves for many types of antiques to shift to the left.

Study Table 2–3 carefully. A change in demand or a change in supply involves shifts in demand or supply curves. New curves have to be drawn to show the shifts. A change in quantity demanded or a change in

FIGURE 2–3

Changes (or shifts) in demand and supply curves

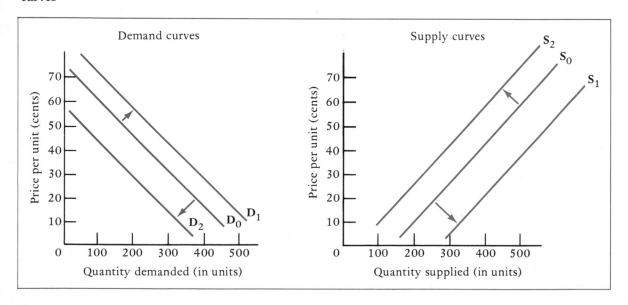

TABLE 2-3

**Demand and supply
concepts**

Change in demand   Means that a greater or lesser number of units is bought without changing price. This means a *shift* in the demand curve. If it shifts up and to the right, a greater number of units is demanded at any given price. If it shifts down and to the left, a lesser number of units is demanded at any given price.

Change in supply   Means that a greater or lesser number of units is supplied without changing price. This means a *shift* in the supply curve. If it shifts up and to the left, a lesser number of units is supplied at any given price. If it shifts down and to the right, a greater number of units is supplied at any given price.

Change in quantity demanded   Means that a greater or lesser number of units is bought because of a change in price. An increase in quantity demanded means that a greater number of units is bought because the price has been lowered. We are moving down a *particular demand curve*. A decrease in quantity demanded means that a lesser number of units is bought because the price has been raised. We are moving up a particular demand curve.

Change in quantity supplied   Means that a greater or lesser number of units is supplied because of a change in price. An increase in quantity supplied means that a greater number of units is supplied because the price has been raised. We are moving up a *particular supply curve*. A decrease in quantity supplied means that a lesser number of units is supplied because the price has been lowered. We are moving down a particular supply curve.

quantity supplied does not involve any shifts in demand or supply curves. These changes can be shown without having to draw new curves.

The Business Firm

Demand gives a firm an opportunity to provide want-satisfying products and services. Supply results from efforts by business firms to profit from this demand.

The business firm is the basic building block for organizing production in our system. Through it, resources are organized for production. Land, labor, and capital must be gathered and converted into products and services that can be sold. This business activity must be directed and guided by the management of business firms.

Business activity requires decision making to produce and sell products and services. It requires buying as well as selling. Thus the market plays a role. How resources are used depends basically on choices made by firms and consumers. Both are guided by market prices. The firm is the key to the market's operation. It guides the flow of resources

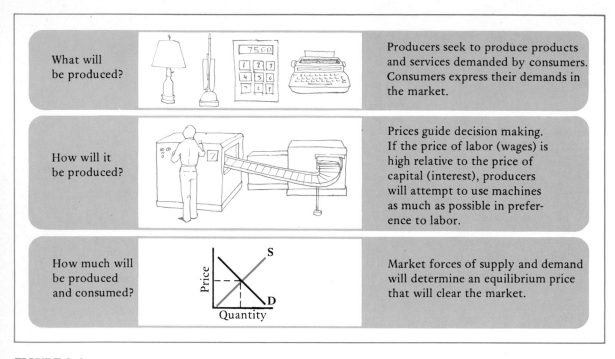

What will be produced?		Producers seek to produce products and services demanded by consumers. Consumers express their demands in the market.
How will it be produced?		Prices guide decision making. If the price of labor (wages) is high relative to the price of capital (interest), producers will attempt to use machines as much as possible in preference to labor.
How much will be produced and consumed?		Market forces of supply and demand will determine an equilibrium price that will clear the market.

FIGURE 2–4

Economic decision making in capitalist economic systems is guided by price

through the marketplace. The firm is an input-output system. The inputs are productive resources that the firm buys in the marketplace. The outputs are the products and services it produces and sells in the marketplace. Both input and output depend on market prices. (See Figure 2–4.)

Resources and the products and services produced from them are all scarce, which is why they command prices. The firm's costs of doing business (converting resources from one form to another) must be less than the sales revenues it receives from selling its output if it is to earn a profit. To determine how profitable it is, a firm must keep records of its costs and sales. The process of accounting traces the effects of resource flows on its profits. We will discuss this in detail in Chapter 9.

Although it is hard to define some of the terms used in modern business, the following statements summarize some key points:

- A business firm is an entity (thing) that seeks to make a profit by gathering and allocating productive resources to satisfy demand.
- Most economic activity in our system is channeled through privately owned business firms.
- Business activity involves gathering and allocating resources in the hope for profit.
- Since resources are scarce and choices must be made, business activity requires that costs be recognized.

Effort	is exerted to exploit	Opportunity
Supply	is created to satisfy	Demand
Prices	are determined in	Markets
Entrepreneurship	is concerned with	Risk assumption
Risk	is assumed in the hope of	Profit
Profit	involves a recognition of	Costs
Decision making	is necessary because of the	Choice process
Production activity	is guided by the	Price system
Land ⎫ Labor ⎬ Capital ⎭	are made productive through	Entrepreneurship
Factors of production (inputs)	are converted to	Marketable products and services (outputs)
Marketing activity	is guided by the	Price system
Markets	exist because of	Specialization and exchange

- Producer and consumer choices are guided by prices.
- Prices are determined by the price system.
- Business activity requires that demand is present and salable products and services can be supplied to satisfy buyers.

You might find it helpful to study Figure 2–5.

FIGURE 2–5

The nature of business activity

The Motivation of the Firm

People form business firms to produce and sell want-satisfying products and services in the hope for profit. Profit, however, does not appear until it is earned. In our system there is no guarantee that a firm will make a profit. It is the hope for profit that leads people to start and operate businesses. By providing products and services that satisfy customers, a firm may make a profit.

Suppose Tommy Fields, age seven, opens a lemonade stand because he hopes to make a profit. During the first week he sells 20 cups of lemonade at five cents per cup. Is his profit for the week one dollar?

The answer depends on many things. If the cost of sugar, lemons, and cups is two cents per cup, Tommy's profit is not one dollar but sixty cents—the difference between one dollar in sales revenues and forty cents in costs (two cents per cup times 20 cups). If his parents wanted to be paid for the things they supplied him, Tommy would realize that his supplies are scarce resources. His profit is sales revenues minus the cost of doing business.

If sales revenues are greater than costs, a profit is earned. A firm may increase its profit by raising prices, lowering costs, or selling more units. But most firms cannot raise prices very much without reducing sales.

THINK ABOUT IT!

The Importance of Profit to You

Samuel Gompers, head of the American Federation of Labor from 1886 to 1924, recognized the vital role of profit to American workers when he said, "The worst crime against working people is a company that fails to make a profit."

The profits earned by business are important to you in many ways. Profits reinvested in firms for growth create jobs. Profit not only rewards a firm's current owners, but it also attracts new investors. This stimulates investment, creates more jobs, and raises our standard of living.

Business profits also are a major source of federal, state, and local government tax revenues. These tax payments by businesses help to pay for schools, hospitals, and other social services.

Profitable firms can afford to set up programs to train people who want to work but cannot find jobs because they lack job skills. Profitable firms can afford to invest in costly pollution control devices, support the arts, participate in efforts to rebuild our deteriorating cities, and so on. Unprofitable firms cannot afford this.

But in recent years the word *profit* to some people has come to mean something ugly—like greed. There is a lot of misunderstanding of profit in our country. In public polls, the average American tends to overestimate the profits that the average company makes. Below are figures for manufacturing corporations that show the relation of profits after taxes to stockholders' equity (the financial interest of the owners of the corporation) and to sales for selected years:

Year	Ratio of profits after taxes to stockholders' equity (percent)	Profits after taxes per dollar of sales (cents)
1975	11.6	4.6
1976	14.0	5.4
1977	14.2	5.3

How important are profits in our business system?
THINK ABOUT IT!

Source: *Statistical Abstract of the United States.*

Most of them try to increase profit by cutting costs and/or increasing the number of units sold.

If a firm's sales revenues and costs are equal, it earns no profit. It only breaks even. Very few people go into business to break even. This is especially true if there is no "owner's salary" included in the firm's list of expenses. Firms that only break even give their owners no economic return for being in business.

Any *after-tax profit* that is earned by the firm is reinvested in the firm and/or is distributed to the owners. For many firms, reinvested profit is the major source of funds to finance their growth. The owners, in effect, are willing to reinvest their profit in the firm rather than take it out for personal use.

That firms seek profit is an accepted fact in capitalist economies. There is some argument, however, whether profit should be their *only* objective. Do businesses owe something to people other than their owners and their customers? Is it enough for a firm to earn profit for its owners by providing want-satisfying products and services for its customers?

Businesses do pay federal, state, and sometimes city taxes on their profits. They also pay property taxes and licensing fees. Governments use these tax revenues to provide useful services to society, such as public education, police and fire protection, and trash collection. Businesses also hire employees who earn wages and salaries. They provide jobs to our people. Some people believe that as long as businesses provide jobs and want-satisfying products and services to their customers and pay taxes, the firms are contributing to society's well-being.

Some other people, however, believe that businesses owe more to society. For example, a firm may be providing products and services that satisfy its customers but in the process it may be creating problems for the rest of society. Soft drinks and beer may be packaged in aluminum cans to satisfy drinkers who want this convenience, but society in general has to pay for cleaning up the litter that some users of these cans create. Thus, aluminum can producers are spending money to educate consumers about the need for proper disposal of used cans. Cigarette makers give their customers what they want, but nonsmokers are becoming more active in promoting laws that prohibit smoking in public buildings. In other words, some people believe that firms are accountable to society in general, not only to their customers and owners.

This concept of the *social responsibility of business* is discussed at several places in this book. The issue of the social responsibility of business arises in such areas as the hiring of the handicapped, job-training for other disadvantaged people, cleaning up pollution, helping in the battle against inflation, supporting community projects, and establishing affirmative action programs to recruit and hire women and minorities.

Profit Opportunity and Organized Effort

One fact remains, however. A firm cannot survive over the long run if it does not earn a profit from its operations. It must find a way to use its scarce resources and convert them into salable products and services. It must both identify an opportunity for profit and use its resources to try to make that profit.

PROFIT IN WASTE CONVERSION

> As we'll see throughout this book, no firm exists in a vacuum. Businesses must be alert to changes in their environment because those changes can create opportunities for them to profit by serving new needs. During recent years, for example, conservation and pollution controls have created challenging opportunities for many firms. These are two especially important concerns of petroleum refineries in managing their waste disposal.
>
> Several years ago a firm in Houston, Texas, saw an opportunity to make a profit and provide a useful service to petroleum refineries, the firm's own customers, and society in general. The firm, Merichem Company, accumulates waste products from petroleum refineries and reprocesses them into a variety of industrial chemicals for sale to its customers.
>
> Whether Merichem pays a supplier (refinery) a price for its waste material or charges that supplier a waste disposal fee depends largely on transportation costs and the relative volume of waste at each refinery. Careful attention to costs and good management enables Merichem to make a profit while, at the same time, serving its suppliers, customers, and society in general.

Source: *Traffic Management.*

business opportunity

Before an opportunity can be exploited, it must exist and be recognized. **A business opportunity exists where there is a set of circumstances that may enable a firm to make a profit.** This set of circumstances can be the result of decisions made by persons inside or outside the firm or it can be mostly good luck.

Dr. E. H. Land's dedication to research and development enabled him to enter an industry that had been dominated for years by Kodak. He created the instant photography industry. IBM's dedication to research and development enabled it to become the dominant firm in the computer industry. Opportunity for these firms resulted from their decision to invest money and time in research and development.

Volkswagen's decision to begin manufacturing Volkswagens in New Stanton, Pennsylvania, created opportunity for many firms. Some firms, for example, built houses for the new residents who moved there to work in the plant. Their opportunity was the result of a decision made by Volkswagen.

A lot of opportunity is the result of being in the "right place at the right time." This is as true for businesses as it is for individuals. Probably thousands of Americans have struck it rich because the land they had owned for years happened to be in the growth path of a nearby city. How many health food stores struggled to survive for years serving a handful of customers before eating health foods became a nationwide fad for thousands of Americans? How much opportunity have other fads like jogging created for sporting goods manufacturers?

At any rate, the framework for evaluating opportunity is the *marketplace*. A firm searches the marketplace for unsatisfied wants that could be satisfied at a profit to the firm with its resources and capabilities. If it can accomplish this, it creates customers for the product or service it offers.

Gillette, for example, introduced its Ultra Max shampoo after searching the marketplace for unsatisfied wants. Gillette's research showed that 75 million Americans were using blow dryers and they wanted a shampoo that was especially made for them. Gillette's financial resources and its marketing capability enabled it to capitalize on the opportunity it had identified.

Exploiting opportunity need not involve developing new products. A grocer is exploiting opportunity simply by staying open an hour longer than the competitors in order to satisfy late-night shoppers. Today the fastest-growing part of the retail food industry is convenience stores. Minit Markets, Li'l General, and 7-Eleven stores recognized an opportunity to profit from serving the wants of people who want the ultimate in shopping convenience (nearby stores with extended shopping hours, easy parking, no long lines) and are willing to pay prices that are above those in supermarkets.

Exploiting opportunity, however, requires a keen ability to stay in tune with customer wants. Abercrombie and Fitch, for example, opened its doors in 1892 in Manhattan to serve the upper-class sports enthusiasts and adventurers. The store outfitted Theodore Roosevelt's African safaris and Admiral Byrd's Antarctica expedition. But the firm went bankrupt in 1977. One of the main reasons was its failure to adjust to a younger generation of sports activists who were more budget conscious and wanted to buy from department stores and discount stores.

Finally exploiting opportunity also requires an ability to meet it with organized effort and productive resources. In other words, the firm must have the resources and the capability to exploit the opportunity. Since a firm's resources and capabilities are limited, they must be used to best advantage. Even if two firms have the same kind and amount of resources, one may be able to develop more capability than the other through better management. Superior strength in resources and capabilities enables a firm to take a broader view of what constitutes market opportunity.

The Role of Risk

risk

It is the hope for profit that motivates people to go into business. Since hopes are not always realized, risk is present. **Risk is the chance of loss.** The hope for profit explains risk-assumption. The person thinks the expected profit is worth the risk involved. The greater the reward a business owner expects, the more risk he or she is likely to take.

People, however, see risk differently. What one person sees as a very risky investment, another may see as quite safe. This perception of risk is important in understanding why people are willing to risk their money in the hope for profit. Each year thousands of new firms are started in the United States. Their owners willingly invest their money in them in the hope of making a profit from serving customer wants. As we will see in Chapter 15, many of these new firms fail.

Much of our material progress is due to our highly stable political and economic systems. That stability helps to reduce the risk seen in a possible investment. Thus a person is more likely to invest in the United States than in a foreign country where frequent and violent revolutions occur. This is one reason that in recent years there has been a great increase in foreign investment in our country. Business people and individual investors overseas are setting up firms here and buying stocks and bonds in American corporations.

The nature of risk and how businesses handle it are discussed at several places in this book. For now, it is enough to know that risk is *always* present in business and any other type of human activity.

Summary and Look Ahead

Ours is a market economy in which relative prices determine how limited resources will be used to satisfy unlimited wants. Because resources are limited, choices must be made about what will be produced. These choices are made by consumers and producers working through the price system.

Prices induce or limit production and consumption. The price system helps firms decide which products and services will be produced, how much will be produced, how they will be produced, and how they will be distributed. These decisions are not made by a central planning agency. They are made by millions of consumers and many producers through the price-formulating process of a market.

The law of demand means that more of a given product or service is demanded at lower prices than at higher prices. The law of supply means that more of a given product or service is offered for sale at higher prices than at lower prices. These forces of supply and demand work to determine prices.

The business firm is the basic building block for organizing production in our economy. It gathers productive resources (inputs) and converts them into salable products or services (outputs). Both input and output depend on the price system.

The hope of profit motivates people to go into business. They earn profit from identifying business opportunity and exploiting it through organized effort. But risk is always present.

Now that we know what a firm is and why it exists, we can go on to discuss the different forms of ownership of business firms.

A HEALTHY ATTITUDE TOWARD BUSINESS

Most people who have attended college work for businesses. Some are there because they couldn't find anything else and needed to earn a living. Some are very unhappy because their only reason for staying in their jobs is to earn a living. This situation is unfortunate because these people are not nearly as productive or happy as they would be if they were doing work that really gave them satisfaction.

If you're going to work in business, it helps to start with the right attitude toward business itself and toward your particular job and employer. Most people who are taking this course in business administration already have a generally favorable attitude toward business. They know that it is a worthwhile activity. They know that: (1) business is the chief provider of goods and services to our nation; (2) business is working hard now to improve opportunities for all and to eliminate discrimination among workers and managers; (3) business has to be flexible, inventive, and open to new ideas if it is to grow; and (4) business holds the key to economic growth and technological development. In short, business can be exciting and satisfying for most people.

If you are going to be motivated in the specific firm and job you choose, however, you must examine your own values and attitudes. In some cases, values and attitudes are only loosely held, that is, you don't have a very strong basis for holding them. If this is true about some of your presently held reasons for accepting or rejecting a career, you'd better get informed. There is nothing like facts to repair distorted or biased attitudes and values. A good example is the female graduate of a fine Eastern college. She nearly turned down a job offer in Texas because she had some very bad impressions of Texans. This was due to her exposure to an obnoxious fellow student who was from Texas, and her attitude also reflected a touch of "Ivy League snobbery" on the part of her classmates. After flying down for one interview in Dallas, she found out how wrong her previous impressions were. She took the job and found a rewarding career as a director of personnel for a large electronics firm.

You may need to get more facts, too, so that the values you employ in choosing a job are reasonable ones. Don't assume that all advertising people are phonies or that all accountants are dull. Don't believe any of the clichés about occupations. Get the facts. They will strengthen your system for evaluation.

Key Concepts

business opportunity Exists when a set of circumstances may enable a person or firm who exploits it to reap some benefit or profit.

demand Exists when there are people who desire a product or a service, they have the buying power to purchase it, and they are willing to part with some buying power in order to buy it. The quantity demanded is the number of units of a product or service that people will buy at a certain price at a given point in time.

demand curve A curve showing the number of units of a product or a service that will be demanded (bought) at each price at a given point in time. Usually slopes down and to the right.

discretionary income The amount of income a household has left after paying taxes and making expenditures for necessary products and services.

law of demand More of a product or service is demanded (will be bought) at a lower price than at a higher price. Graphically depicted as a demand curve.

law of supply More of a product or service is supplied (offered for sale) at a higher price than at a lower price. Graphically depicted as a supply curve.

market economy An economic system in which relative prices determine how productive resources (the factors of production) will be allocated and how the products and services produced will be distributed. These prices are determined in markets through the interaction of supply and demand.

price The quantity of money (or other products and services) that is paid in exchange for something else.

real income Current income expressed in terms of buying power; current income adjusted for the decline in buying power due to inflation.

risk The chance of loss. All business activity involves risk.

supply The quantity of a product or a service that is made available for sale as the result of effort by producers. Price induces supply. The quantity supplied is the number of units of a product or service that sellers are willing to offer for sale at a certain price at a given point in time.

supply curve A curve that shows the number of units of a product or a service that will be supplied (offered for sale) at each price at a given point in time. Usually slopes up and to the right.

For Review . . .

1. What is a market economy? Is it the same as a price system? Explain.
2. Contrast demand and quantity demanded, state the "law of demand," and draw a demand curve.
3. What are the three main sources of buying power?
4. Contrast disposable income, discretionary income, and real income.
5. Contrast supply and quantity supplied, state the "law of supply," and draw a supply curve.
6. What is the significance of (*a*) the intersection of a supply curve and a demand curve on a graph, and (*b*) shifts in demand and supply curves?
7. Are supply and demand forces the only ones that affect prices? Explain.
8. What can a firm do to increase its profits?
9. In what two basic ways can a firm use its after-tax profit?

10. What is "business opportunity"?
11. Why is risk present in business activity?

. . . For Discussion

1. Can products or services really be overpriced?
2. Is the concept of the social responsibility of business at odds with its need to make a profit?
3. What is a "favorable business climate"?
4. The chapter said that the hope for profit is the main reason why business people undertake risk. What other reasons for going into business can you identify?
5. Are there any types of business opportunity in your community that are not being exploited? If there are, why are they not being exploited?
6. Why do people perceive risk differently?
7. Is it true that all businesses must serve their customers if they are to survive?

Incidents

Supply and Demand and CB Radios

"Once limited to truckers and their Smokey Bear antagonists on highway patrols, Citizens Band radio has grown to the point where about 20 million American "good buddies" have CB rigs in their cars or homes. Yet despite the boom in the industry, a lot of firms that tried to capitalize on the craze are going bust. A case in point: Hy-Gain Electronics Corp. of Lincoln, Neb., one of the largest U.S. makers of ham radio and CB gear. Burdened by $31 million in debts and a $24 million earnings loss in fiscal '77, Hy-Gain has filed for bankruptcy and told 1,000 employees at its plants in Lincoln and Puerto Rico to go home. . . .

"What did the company in was the CB craze, and a bit of incredibly bad timing. Hy-Gain began making the compact communications units [in 1974], and raced to sales of $96.8 million in 1976. Responding to public interest in CB, the Federal Communications Commission in July of that year authorized new 40-channel sets that could be sold after Jan. 1, 1977. Hy-Gain and other makers slashed prices on the old 23-channel sets, but the public preferred to wait for the new models. Result: Hy-Gain had to buy back from dealers $12 million to $14 million worth of 23-channel equipment. It converted many of those to 40 channels,

. . . but by that time the market was saturated. Hy-Gain's sales were cut in half, to $50.4 million, and the company's stock—a record $28 in 1976—plummeted to about 50¢."

Questions

1. Were the price cuts on 23-channel CBs an attempt by CB makers to increase demand or an attempt to increase quantity demanded? Explain.
2. Why did the market become over-saturated with CB radios?
3. Is risk always present in business activity? Discuss.

Source: *Time.*

Demand Outlook in the Furniture Industry

In 1979 American furniture manufacturers were looking forward to record demand during the 1980s.

"Just ahead of them, starting next year, they see their most prosperous decade ever. The biggest reason: During the next 10 years, the 30-to-39-year-old age group, which spends more money per capita on furniture than any other, will emerge as the largest segment of the U.S. population, increasing 26.2% to 39.5 million persons. Last year this age group spent about $260 per household on furniture, compared with only $219 by people in their twenties."

There were other reasons for optimism among furniture manufacturers.

"Oil shortages also will be a boon to furniture sales, manufacturers believe. They figure that the uncertainty over availability of gasoline and its

soaring price has already started to redirect much of people's leisure time to activities at home. This will result in increased furniture expenditures, and the continuing trend to two incomes per household will enable families to make more expensive purchases."

Questions

1. How would you describe the outlook for the furniture industry?
2. Were the furniture manufacturers expecting a change in demand or a change in quantity demanded? Explain.
3. Are changes in consumer tastes important to furniture manufacturers? Explain.
4. Which source of buying power was causing optimism among the furniture manufacturers? Explain.

Source: *Business Week.*

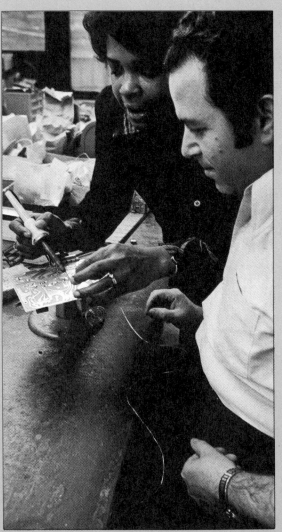

IN THIS section we place the business firm under a microscope in order to get a sharper focus on its nature and workings.

Chapter 3 describes the forms of business ownership and the law. Although many people think mainly of corporations when they think of business firms, there are other forms of ownership. In fact, the vast majority of American firms are not corporations. But corporations do conduct most of the business activity in the United States.

Chapter 4 studies the firm as an organization. Its goals can be achieved only if its human, financial, and physical resources are meaningfully related to each other. This is why organization is so important. We discuss the formal and informal organizational aspects of the business firm.

It is within the organization that managers perform functions that enable a firm to reach its goals. Chapter 5, therefore, looks at the nature and functions of management.

SECTION TWO

Business Basics

Ownership

CHAPTER
3

Objectives: After reading this chapter, you should be able to

1. Identify the reasons for and give examples of the growth of public ownership in the United States.
2. Tell what is included in a partnership agreement.
3. List and compare the relative advantages and disadvantages of the three major forms of ownership of business firms.
4. Tell what information usually is required in an application for a corporate charter.
5. Distinguish between common and preferred stock.
6. Diagram the relationships among stockholders, the board of directors, and the officers of a corporation.
7. Discuss the relative importance of the three major forms of ownership in terms of the number of firms, sales revenues received, and profit earned.
8. Identify and discuss the relative advantages and disadvantages of large-scale operations.
9. Explain the concept of countervailing power.
10. List and discuss other forms of business ownership that are modifications of the three basic forms of ownership.
11. List and define the parts of a valid contract.
12. Give examples of the agency-principal relationship.
13. Distinguish between real and personal property.
14. Explain the significance of the Uniform Commercial Code to business.

Key concepts: Look for these terms as you read the chapter

sole proprietorship	countervailing power
unlimited liability	limited partnership
partnership	joint venture
partnership agreement	business trust
corporation	cooperative association
stockholders	mutual company
Subchapter S Corporation	contract
corporate charter	agency-principal relationship
common stock	
preferred stock	bailor-bailee relationship
board of directors	real property
cumulative voting	personal property
proxy	warranty
corporation bylaws	Uniform Commercial Code (UCC)
professional managers	

Our government sometimes undertakes ownership of organizations that provide products and services to consumers. For example, some cities are served by publicly owned transit companies. Government ownership, however, is the exception; private ownership is the rule. There are three basic forms of private ownership of business firms: sole proprietorships, partnerships, and corporations.

Regardless of their form of ownership, business firms vary in size from the very small to the very large. We usually think of one-owner firms as being small firms and of corporations as being large firms. But there are some large one-owner firms and some relatively small corporations. For the most part, when we talk about "big business," we are talking about corporations.

There are several basic business law concepts and institutions that help us to understand why these different forms of ownership exist. Knowledge of the different forms of ownership also will prove helpful in understanding several of the later chapters.

Public versus Private Ownership

In the capitalist system a person has the right to save and to invest money to make more money. The same right holds for a group of people. Persons, alone or in groups, can risk their money by going into business to try to make a profit. Private ownership of business firms is a basic part of the capitalist system.

Private ownership is not the only form of ownership in our business system. Public, or government, ownership has become important, especially in recent decades. If we compared the growth rates of the private and public sectors of our economy, we would find that the public sector has grown faster in the years since 1930. Governments buy about 20 percent of our Gross National Product and the federal government owns about one-third of the land in the United States.

Because the founders of our country feared too much government interference and control, they resisted public ownership. As we saw in Chapter 1, laissez-faire economics is at the heart of capitalism. The Great Depression that started in 1929 caused us to re-examine the basic reasons for fearing "big government." During the depression, many people questioned the ability of the capitalist system to survive. We became much more agreeable to the idea that government can and should play a role in the economy. Over the years that role has included government acting as a regulator of business activity and, in some cases, as a competitor of privately owned firms.

Why Public Ownership?

Public ownership may be undertaken for many reasons:

- The investment required may be too great for private investors, or the potential payoff may be too far off and intangible, making private investors unwilling to assume the risk.
- Public ownership may be the only option left when privately owned firms fail.
- Public ownership may be needed to stimulate competition among privately owned firms.
- Services are believed to be too important to society's welfare to be left up to private businesses.

In some cases the investment required may be too great for private investors. As we will see in Chapter 10, the Federal Deposit Insurance Corporation (FDIC) and the Federal Savings and Loan Insurance Corporation (FSLIC) are government agencies that insure the deposits in banks and savings and loan associations (S&LAs) that meet the FDIC's and the FSLIC's requirement for coverage. Some banks and S&LAs that are nonmembers have insurance with private firms but, in some cases, these firms have been unable to pay off depositors when the banks or S&LAs have failed.

When the United States entered the space race, the government set up the National Aeronautics and Space Administration (NASA). The amount of the required investment was too great and the potential payoff on the investment was too far off and intangible for private investors to assume the risk alone.

Several years ago a swine flu epidemic threatened the United States and drug makers rushed into the production of vaccines. Privately owned insurance companies were unwilling to provide liability insurance to these manufacturers because of the great risk involved. As a result the federal government had to provide it.

Privately owned businesses that provide needed services sometimes do fail, and government may step in to ensure that the services are still provided. Thus, the federal government has set up the National Railroad Passenger Corporation (Amtrak) and the Consolidated Rail Corporation (Conrail).

Public ownership also may be undertaken to stimulate competition among firms in an industry. Canada's government-owned Canadian National Railroad competes with the privately owned Canadian Pacific Railroad. Some people believe that the United States government should own and operate shipyards to compete with privately owned shipyards.

Finally the federal government is in the mail and the social security

CONRAIL

> Consolidated Rail Corp. was created by Congress in 1976—and given $2 billion in taxpayers' money—to replace Penn Central Transportation Co. and six other bankrupt railroads in the Northeast. After such an infusion of federal money to upgrade its facilities, Conrail was expected to be well on its way toward profitability by 1978.
>
> Instead, government officials are beginning to conclude that Conrail will never become self-sufficient. It is losing more money than the railroads it replaced. Service has deteriorated, not improved.

Source: *Business Week.*

"businesses" and local governments are in the water, sewage, and garbage collection "businesses" because these services are felt to be too important to the public welfare to be left to private firms. In recent years many people have argued that even these public services should be turned over to private firms, especially in states and cities where the voters have turned down proposals for property tax increases.

Private ownership is the main type of ownership in the United States. The three most common forms of ownership are

- the sole proprietorship
- the partnership
- the corporation

The Sole Proprietorship

The sole proprietorship is the oldest and is still the most common form of ownership in the United States. **A sole proprietorship is a business owned and managed by one person. That person, however, may have help from others in running the business.** The sole proprietor is the classic example of the entrepreneur. Only a sole proprietor can say, "I am the company" or "This is my business."

sole proprietorship

Advantages of the Sole Proprietorship

Suppose Alice Stone wanted to go into the florist business. She might find that the sole proprietorship is the easiest way for her to start. There are no general laws that regulate the setting up of a sole proprietorship. Of course, the business activity must be legal and there may be local and state laws that require licenses and permits. Usually the sole proprietor is required to register the firm's name at the county courthouse. This prohibits two firms from operating under the same name. Other license and permit requirements are discussed in Chapter 15. Otherwise, Alice can go into business any time she pleases. Simplicity in starting the business is a major advantage of the sole proprietorship.

As sole owner, Alice owns the firm outright. She is the sole owner of any profits (or losses). Alice also may get personal satisfaction out of seeing her firm grow under her direct guidance. She does what she believes is best for her firm and makes decisions without required approval from anyone else.

Because Alice is the firm, she pays only personal income taxes on the firm's profits. There is no income tax on the firm as a separate entity. If Alice wants to go out of business, she simply sells her inventory and equipment. She needs permission from no one. A sole proprietorship is easy to dissolve.

The sole proprietorship's major advantages, therefore, are

- simplicity in starting the business
- ownership of all the profits
- enjoyment gained from a great deal of personal involvement and satisfaction from being one's own boss
- the ability to make management decisions without required approval from anyone else
- no tax on profits of the business as a separate entity, only on the owner's personal income
- simplicity in dissolving the business

Disadvantages of the Sole Proprietorship

unlimited liability

Since Alice is the firm, she is legally liable for all its debts. She has unlimited liability. **Unlimited liability means that a proprietor is liable for claims against the business that go beyond the value of his or her ownership in the firm. The liability extends to his or her personal property (furniture, car, and personal savings) and, in some cases, real property (home and other real estate).** If Alice goes out of business and still owes her business creditors $10,000 after selling her inventory, equipment, and other business property, those creditors can legally lay claim to Alice's nonbusiness property.

The amount of money Alice is able to invest in the firm is limited to what she has and what she can borrow. In many cases the difficulty of raising more money discourages this type of ownership.

As the firm grows Alice may find that she is spreading herself too thin. A sole proprietor usually takes on the entire task of running the business. The entire burden of management is borne by the owner.

If a sole proprietor cannot pay off his or her business debts with business property, business creditors can force the proprietor to withdraw money from his or her personal savings account, sell his or her car and other personal property, and (in some states) sell his or her home to pay off the creditors. This unlimited liability exists because there is no legal distinction between the sole proprietor and the sole proprietor's business. Sole proprietors run the risk of losing everything they own. There is no limit to their financial liability. THINK ABOUT IT!

If Alice were to die, go to prison, or go insane, the business would be legally terminated. The business may be passed on to a son or daughter, but when this occurs a new proprietorship is formed. The built-in impermanence of a sole proprietorship makes it hard for the firm to grow and to attract employees who want a permanent job.

The sole proprietorship's major disadvantages, therefore, are

- unlimited financial liability for business debts
- difficulty in raising funds for expansion
- no sharing of the burden of management
- impermanence of the business firm

The Partnership

Most states have adopted the Uniform Partnership Act. **It defines a partnership as "an association of two or more persons to carry on as co-owners of a business for profit."** Instead of one owner, there are at least two. The partnership form of ownership came about to overcome some of the more serious disadvantages of the sole proprietorship. It also dates back to ancient times.

partnership

Advantages of the Partnership

Instead of a sole proprietorship, suppose Alice decided to form a partnership with Joe Gunn. Getting started requires the partners to comply with the same general types of licensing and permit requirements that proprietorships have to comply with. But Alice and Joe also will have to enter into a partnership agreement, also called Articles of Partnership or Articles of Copartnership. **A partnership agreement usually states**

- **the name, location, and business of the partnership**
- **the names of the partners**
- **each partner's contribution of money, skills, and participation in managing the business**
- **the other duties of each partner**
- **how profits and losses will be shared**
- **the procedure for the withdrawal of one or more partners**
- **the procedure for dissolving the partnership**

The partnership agreement can be oral or written, but it is wise to put it in writing to help avoid future disagreements between the partners. Other than setting up this agreement, getting started is as simple as it is for the sole proprietorship.

Since Alice and Joe are in business together, they can pool their funds and talents. They can invest more than either one could invest alone; and they have a greater ability to borrow money, since their combined personal and real property (in most states) are available to creditors. By pooling their talents, they can divide the tasks of the business and enjoy the benefits of specialization.

Like a sole proprietorship, a partnership is not taxed as a business separate from its owners. The owners, not the firm, are taxed.

The partnership's major advantages, therefore, are

- simplicity in starting the business
- the pooling of funds and talents of the partners
- greater borrowing power than a sole proprietorship
- more opportunity for specialization than a sole proprietorship
- like the sole proprietor, the partners' enjoyment of personal involvement and satisfaction in running the business
- no tax on profits of the business as a separate entity, only on the owners' personal incomes

Disadvantages of the Partnership

Partners, like sole proprietors, have unlimited financial liability for the partnership's debts. It is a *joint liability*. This means that Alice is responsible for business debts incurred by Joe and vice versa.

Suppose Alice and Joe's business fails and they still owe creditors $50,000 after selling the partnership's property to pay off the creditors. The partnership agreement in Figure 3–1 shows that Alice and Joe each contributed $15,000 in cash (see #5) to start the business and they agreed to equally bear any losses (see #7). But suppose after selling off

PARTNERSHIP AGREEMENT

THIS PARTNERSHIP AGREEMENT made and entered into this first day of January 1980 by and between Alice Stone of San Francisco, California and Joseph Gunn of San Francisco, California.

WITNESSETH:

1. The parties hereby agree to form a partnership.
2. The name of the partnership shall be S & G Florists.
3. The business to be conducted shall be a florist business.
4. The principal place of business of the partnership shall be at 807 East Main Avenue, San Francisco, California.
5. The capital of the partnership is to consist of the sum of $30,000. Alice Stone is to contribute $15,000 in cash and Joseph Gunn is to contribute $15,000 in cash. No interest shall be paid to the partners on any contributions to capital.
6. Whenever required, additional capital shall be contributed by the partners in the proportion of the initial capital contribution.
7. The net profits of the partnership shall be divided equally and the partners shall equally bear the net losses.
8. Each partner shall be entitled to a drawing account as may be mutually agreed upon.
9. Neither partner shall receive a salary.
10. Each partner shall have an equal right in the management of the partnership.
11. Alice Stone shall devote her entire time and attention to the business. Joseph Gunn shall devote his entire time and attention to the business.
12. Either partner may retire from the partnership after giving the other partner at least 90 days written notice of his or her intention so to do. The remaining partner shall have the option of purchasing the retiring partner's interest or to terminate and liquidate the business. The purchase price shall be the balance in the retiring partner's capital account based upon an audit by an independent public accountant to the date of retirement. The purchase price shall be payable 50 percent in cash and the balance in 36 equal monthly installments and shall not bear interest.
13. Upon the death of a partner, the surviving partner shall have the option to either purchase the interest of the decedent or to terminate and liquidate the business. The purchase price and payment shall be the same as above set forth.
14. The partnership shall begin the tenth day of January 1980, and shall continue until dissolved by retirement or death of a partner or by mutual agreement of the partners.

IN WITNESS WHEREOF, the parties have signed this agreement.

Witnesses:

Roger Allen   *Alice Stone* (SEAL)

Vernon Collins   *Joseph Gunn* (SEAL)

FIGURE 3–1

A partnership agreement

all his personal and real property, Joe can pay off only $20,000 of his $25,000 share of the unpaid debt. Alice will be liable for paying her $25,000 share plus the $5,000 that Joe is unable to pay.

In forming a partnership, one must choose a partner(s) with great care. Personal disagreements have caused many failures. For example, disagreement can occur over how long the partners intend to be in business; the amount of money each is to invest; their salaries; how profits or losses will be shared; the duties of each; the procedure for admitting new partners; and the procedure for dissolving the partnership. This is why the partnership agreement should be in writing.

A partnership is legally terminated upon the death, withdrawal, or insanity of a partner. Although an heir of a deceased partner might step in and help run the business, this is not the same partnership. In some cases partners will buy partnership insurance and enter into a buy-and-sell agreement. This ensures that money will be available upon the death of one partner so that the other(s) will be able to buy out his or her share from the deceased partner's estate. The buy-and-sell agreement spells out the value of the partnership shares and preserves the business for surviving partners.

Furthermore, a partner cannot simply withdraw his or her investment in the business. He or she must find an outsider (or a present partner) who is willing to buy in and that person must be acceptable to the remaining partner(s). In a sense each partner's investment is frozen in the business.

The partnership's major disadvantages, therefore, are

- unlimited and joint financial liability
- the potential for personal disagreements between the partners
- impermanence of the business firm
- the freezing of each partner's investment in the business

The Corporation

The corporation form of ownership was created to overcome some of the disadvantages of sole proprietorships and partnerships. Originally the corporate form of ownership was restricted to firms owned or controlled by the government or to those formed to serve a public purpose, such as railroads and banks. A charter was required from either the federal or state government in order to incorporate. The corporation is *legally separate from its owners.* It is a creation of government authority.

Prior to the Civil War corporations were somewhat rare. After the Civil War many states passed incorporation laws that made it easy for firms to become corporations.

corporation

In 1819 John Marshall, Chief Justice of the United States Supreme Court, defined a **corporation** as **"an artificial being, invisible, intangible, and existing only in contemplation of law."** **A corporation is a separate and legal entity apart from its owners.** It can buy, hold, and sell property in its own name.

There are several types of corporations based on ownership:

- Private corporations such as Ford Motor Company are organized, owned, and operated by private investors.

· Public corporations such as the FDIC and the FSLIC are organized, owned, and operated by the government.
· Quasi-public corporations such as Amtrak are organized, owned,
and operated jointly by private investors and the government.

It is important to recognize the difference between a public corporation and the phrase "going public." A public corporation, as we have
seen, is a corporation that is organized, owned, and operated by the
government. The phrase "going public" usually refers to a small private
corporation that is preparing to offer its shares of ownership (stock) for
sale to the general public.

Private corporations are profit-seeking organizations. Public and
quasi-public corporations may seek to earn a profit or may be operated
solely as a public service and not seek to earn a profit.

Finally, some corporations are nonprofit corporations. Examples are
municipalities, charitable organizations, churches, and political parties.
Among the reasons nonprofit organizations incorporate are to qualify as
a nontaxable entity and to provide legal protection for members of the
organization.

Advantages of the Corporation

The owners of a corporation are its shareholders, or stockholders.   stockholders
Stockholders are persons who own the common and/or preferred
stock of a corporation. Stock certificates are certificates of ownership in
a corporation. (See Figure 3–2.)

A stockholder owns a partial interest in the whole corporation. Suppose you own one share of stock in American Telephone and Telegraph
(AT&T). You are not entitled to walk into the corporation's headquarters
and demand to see the "property" that you own. The property is owned
by the corporation. What you own is a fractional part of the entire
corporation. The value of that part varies with changes in the value of

Under the law a corporation is separate from its owners. The
corporation itself is a legal entity. Although the owners of
a corporation have only limited financial liability, the corporation itself has unlimited liability. For example, a corporation
that owns another firm (a subsidiary) and is unable to pay off
its debts can be forced to sell its subsidiary in order to get
money with which to pay its debts. THINK ABOUT IT!

THINK ABOUT IT!

**Corporations Are
Separate from
Their Owners**

007-3600-69

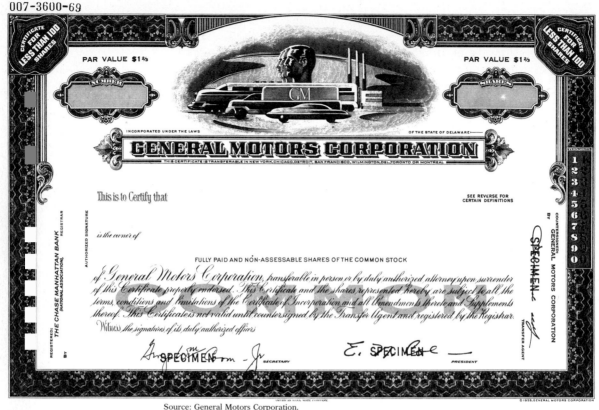

Source: General Motors Corporation.

FIGURE 3–2

Ownership in General Motors Corporation is shown by stock certificates

the shares of stock that you own. This is determined by the supply of and demand for the shares on the market.

A corporation's stockholders are not the corporation because the corporation is a separate and legal entity. The stockholders, therefore, have only *limited financial liability*. This is the corporation's major advantage over sole proprietorships and partnerships. If you bought stock in a corporation, the most you could lose is what you paid for your shares of stock. This is true regardless of how much the firm owes to its creditors.

Let's return to Alice and Joe's business. Suppose the partnership is doing a good business and the owners want to expand by opening three new shops. Alice and Joe, however, have little money to put into expanding the firm and they have borrowed up to their credit limit.

A logical step would be for them to incorporate. Incorporation would give them access to people who might want to buy shares in the new corporation. Suppose Joe and Alice need $500,000 to expand. They might find it easier to get 1,000 persons to invest $500 each than it would be for them to borrow a lump sum of $500,000 or to find another partner willing to put up the entire $500,000. Corporations, therefore, usually find it easier to get money for expansion.

A corporation, for all practical purposes, can exist forever. The death, insanity, or imprisonment of a stockholder has no direct effect on the corporation's existence since it is separate from its owners.

A proprietor may have trouble selling his or her business, and selling one's interest in a partnership requires the approval of the other partners. But transfer of ownership is simple in a corporation. Stockholders just sell their shares of stock. They don't need permission from anyone else. All that is needed is a buyer and a seller.

Organized stock exchanges such as the New York Stock Exchange make it easy for buyers and sellers to get together. Every day millions of shares in hundreds of corporations are traded. In most cases the actual seller and buyer never see each other because they deal through middlemen who buy and sell for them. We'll discuss the operation of stock exchanges in Chapter 10.

The corporation's major advantages, therefore, are

- its existence as a separate legal entity
- the limited financial liability of the owners
- the long life of the business
- easy transfer of ownership
- greater financial capability

Disadvantages of the Corporation

A major disadvantage is that a corporation is subject to special taxation. As an entity separate from its owners, a corporation pays federal and state taxes on its profits. Furthermore, corporations pay franchise taxes to states in which they do business.

The federal income tax rate for corporations is 17 percent on the first $25,000 of profit, 20 percent on the next $25,000, 30 percent on the next $25,000, 40 percent on the next $25,000, and 46 percent on profit above $100,000. The corporation pays this tax. If it pays dividends to stockholders from its after-tax profits, the stockholders pay personal income taxes on the dividends. Thus corporate profits are taxed twice. A stockholder can exclude only $100 of dividends from domestic corporations from his or her taxable income each year.

A small corporation with no more than 15 stockholders has the option of being taxed somewhat like a partnership. These corporations are called Subchapter S Corporations. Tax laws can and do affect the   **Subchapter S Corporation**

relative attractiveness of the corporate form in comparison to the partnership form of ownership. (See Table 3–1.)

Corporations also must conform to precise legal requirements to be granted a charter. Each state has its own incorporation laws, and some of these laws are complex. It often is necessary to hire a lawyer to set up a corporation. In addition to the lawyer's fees, the organizers also have to pay state incorporation fees. In other words, corporations are more complicated to form than sole proprietorships and partnerships.

Corporations also are subject to more state and federal regulation. The corporation's charter restricts the type of business activity in which it can engage. If a corporation wants to sell its shares of stock nationally, it must get prior approval from a federal regulatory agency, the Securities and Exchange Commission (SEC). A new corporation that wants to sell its shares of stock only in the state where it is incorporated must get prior approval from the appropriate state agency, usually the secretary of state. Corporations also have to file numerous reports to state and federal government agencies concerning their operations, which means that they lack some degree of secrecy. The paperwork involved in complying with these requirements can be very costly.

TABLE 3-1

Federal income taxes and the form of ownership

	Proprietorship or partnership	Large corporation (no dividends to owners)	Large corporation (all earnings paid to owners)	Small corporation (15 or fewer owners)*
Sales	$1,000,000	$1,000,000	$1,000,000	$1,000,000
Expenses	$700,000	$700,000	$700,000	$700,000
Before-tax profit	$300,000	$300,000	$300,000	$300,000
Tax on firm†	0	$118,750	$118,750	0
After-tax profit	$300,000	$181,250	$181,250	$300,000
Tax on owners‡	$135,000	__**	$81,563	$135,000
After-tax owners' earnings	$165,000	__**	$99,687	$165,000

* Taxed similar to a partnership.

† 17 percent on first $25,000 of profit, 20 percent on next $25,000, 30 percent on next $25,000, 40 percent on next $25,000, and 46 percent on profit above $100,000 for corporations.

‡ Assuming 45 percent tax rate on income.

** No taxes paid by owners since dividends are not received by them.

The corporation's major disadvantages, therefore, are

- special and double taxation
- complicated and costly formation
- considerable government regulation and reporting requirements
- lack of secrecy in operations

Table 3–2 summarizes the relative advantages and disadvantages of the three forms of private ownership.

Forming and Operating a Corporation

Suppose you and several other people decide to go into business. After a careful analysis of the relative advantages of the three forms of ownership, you decide to form a corporation. It's a good idea to start by talking

TABLE 3-2

Relative advantages and disadvantages of the sole proprietorship, partnership, and corporate forms of ownership

Sole proprietorship	Partnership	Corporation
Advantages		
Simplest to start	Few restrictions on starting	Separate and legal entity
Proprietor owns all profits	Pooling of funds and talents of partners	Limited financial liability of owners
Personal involvement	Greater borrowing power than sole proprietorship	Long life
Sole decision maker	More opportunity for specialization than sole proprietorship	Easy transfer of ownership
No tax on the business as distinct from owner	Personal involvement	Greater financial capability
Easy to dissolve	No tax on the business as distinct from owners	
Disadvantages		
Unlimited financial liability	Unlimited and joint financial liability	Special and double taxation
Difficulty in raising funds for expansion	Potential for personal disagreements	Complicated and costly to form
Proprietor assumes entire burden of management	Relative impermanence	Government regulation and reporting requirements
Impermanence	Frozen investment	Lack of secrecy in operations

to a lawyer. Although nonlawyers can set up a corporation, there is a danger that you may overlook some of the important legal requirements.

The choice of a state in which you incorporate is another major

FIGURE 3–3

Articles of Incorporation (corporate charter) for the state of Mississippi

(TO BE EXECUTED IN DUPLICATE)
ARTICLES OF INCORPORATION
OF

_____

We, the undersigned natural persons of the age of twenty-one years or more, acting as incorporators of a corporation under the Mississippi Business Corporation Act, adopt the following Articles of Incorporation for such corporation:

FIRST: The name of the corporation is_____

SECOND: The period of its duration is_____
(May not exceed 99 years)

THIRD: The specific purpose or purposes for which the corporation is organized stated in general terms are:

(It is not necessary to set forth in the Articles of Incorporation any of the powers set forth in section 4 of the Mississippi Business Corporation Act).

(Use the following if the shares are to consist of one class only)
FOURTH: The aggregate number of shares which the corporation shall have authority to issue

is_____of the par value of_____Dollars

($_____) each (or without par value) (par value or sales price shall not be less than $1.00 per share) (If no par shares are set out, then the sales price per share, if desired)

(Use the following if the shares are divided into classes)
FOURTH: The aggregate number of shares which the corporation is authorized to issue is

_____, divided into_____classes. The designation of each class, the number of shares of each class and the par value, if any, of the shares of each class, or a statement that the shares of any class are without par value, are as follows:

Number of Shares	Class	Series (If any)	Par Value per Share or Statement That Shares are Without Par Value

Source: State of Mississippi.

decision you will have to make, because legal requirements and incorporation costs vary from state to state. But the choice of a state must be made only after careful research. It often is wise to incorporate in the state where the firm plans to conduct most of its business. This makes incorporation more convenient and it also offers other advantages, such as preferences when state contracts are awarded.

Several terms are used in describing corporations based on their state of incorporation:

- A *domestic corporation* is one that operates in the state in which it was chartered.
- A *foreign corporation* is one that operates in other states besides the one in which it was chartered.
- An *alien corporation* is one that operates in other countries besides the one in which it was chartered.

A corporate charter is a contract between the people setting up a corporation and the government of the state in which it is being incorporated. The charter authorizes formation of the corporation. Figure 3–3 shows the Articles of Incorporation, or corporate charter, for the state of Mississippi.

corporate charter

The incorporators apply for a charter to the secretary of state (or other designated state official or agency) in which the corporation is being formed by filling out application forms and paying the required fees. Typically, the incorporators are required to provide or state

- the names of the incorporators
- the name of the corporation
- the business in which the firm will engage
- the purposes of the corporation
- the address and county in which the headquarters will be located

If the application is approved, the secretary of state issues the charter. In most states the charter is sent to the clerk of the county in which the corporate headquarters is to be located. The charter is notarized (certified, or made legally effective) by the county clerk and recorded.

The Stockholders

As we said earlier, the stockholders are the owners of a corporation. In very small corporations a relatively few stockholders may own all the stock, and it is not actively traded. These are called *close corporations*. Professional football teams and family businesses that have been incorporated usually are close corporations.

IBM, GM, and AT&T are examples of widely held corporations. This means they have many stockholders, perhaps numbering in the tens of thousands. Stock in these corporations is actively traded. They are called *open corporations.*

Corporations usually hold annual stockholders' meetings. The officers who run the corporation present reports on the firm's activities, and any proposed activities that require stockholder approval are voted on at the meeting. Examples are the election of new members to the board of directors, the choice of an independent auditor, and a proposal to change the corporation's name. In recent years some stockholders have raised thorny questions about the social responsibility of their corporations. Examples of these stockholder concerns are hiring and promotion policies for women and minorities, conservation, pollution, and doing business in countries that allegedly violate the human rights of their citizens.

There are two basic types of stock, common stock and preferred stock. **Common stock is a certificate showing ownership in a corporation. All shares of common stock are equal in value and all common stockholders enjoy the same rights. Common stock is voting stock and common stockholders have a residual right to the corporation's earnings.** They have a right to earnings that remain (residual earnings) after the corporation has met the prior claims of bondholders and preferred stockholders. The actual payment of a common stock dividend from these residual earnings does not occur until the board of directors declares a common stock dividend. If the corporation goes bankrupt, the common stockholders are the last to receive any proceeds from the sale of the corporation's property. Creditors, bondholders, and preferred stockholders share in the proceeds before the common stockholders. Thus common stockholders are the residual owners of a corporation.

Preferred stock is a certificate that also shows ownership in a corporation. Preferred stockholders usually cannot vote their shares. But they do enjoy certain preferences. As we have seen, they have a right to receive the dividend indicated on their stock certificates before common stockholders receive any dividends. This dividend also is not owed until declared by the corporation's board of directors.

The Board of Directors and Corporate Officers

A corporation's board of directors is elected by its stockholders. (See Figure 3–4.) **The board of directors is a group of people who are given the power to govern the corporation's affairs and to make general policy. This power comes from the corporate charter and the corporation's stockholders.** In small corporations the major stockholders often manage the business. But in larger corporations, with thousands of stockholders, the board of directors is accountable for guiding the affairs of the business.

The number of votes a stockholder has in elections of board members

<!-- margin glossary terms -->
common stock

preferred stock

board of directors

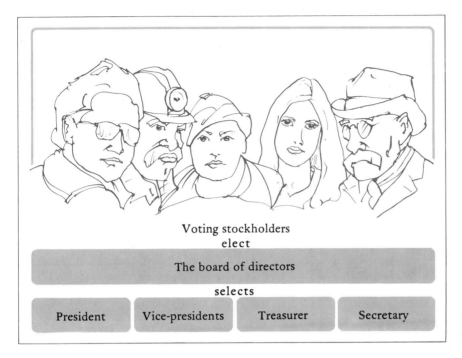

Voting stockholders
elect

The board of directors

selects

| President | Vice-presidents | Treasurer | Secretary |

FIGURE 3–4

The corporate structure

and other business brought up for a vote in stockholders' meetings depends on the number of shares he or she owns. It is not a case of "one person, one vote," which is why many small stockholders in widely held (open) corporations do not bother to vote their shares at stockholders' meetings.

For example, a person who owns 10 shares of IBM stock may choose not to vote. But attempts to control such a corporation can be effective if a group of stockholders pool their votes to get a voting majority. To give small stockholders more power in electing the board, some states require cumulative voting. **With cumulative voting, the number of votes a stockholder has is the number of shares he or she owns times the number of directors to be elected.** A person who owns 10 shares would have only 10 votes regardless of the number of directors being elected if there were no cumulative voting. If five board members were being elected, that same person would have 50 votes with cumulative voting. All 50 votes could be cast for one director. Cumulative voting thus gives more voting power to small stockholders.

There are many small investors who buy shares in several corporations. They are more interested in dividend performance or increases in the selling prices of the stocks than they are in voting. They have neither the interest nor ability to keep up with company affairs. The board currently in power can stay there by seeking votes from enough people who actually vote.

cumulative voting

**YOU BE THE
JUDGE!**

**Do We Need a
Codetermination
Act in the United
States?**

In July 1976 West Germany passed a "codetermination" law, which gave workers in about 600–650 major companies a nearly equal voice with stockholders in running the companies. The idea was to extend political democracy to economic life. Other terms for this type of legislation are *worker participation* and *industrial democracy.*

Worker participation in company decision making exists at two levels in West Germany. At the top, workers are represented on supervisory boards that are similar to boards of directors in American firms. At the bottom, there is worker representation on the plant level in works councils. These councils have an equal voice with management in decisions about hiring, firing, and working conditions. The basic idea of worker participation has existed for a number of years. The West German coal and steel industries have operated under worker participation since 1951, and big firms in other industries have been required since 1952 to allot one-third of supervisory seats to labor. The 1976 law raises the percentage to half for the largest firms.

In 1976 the United Auto Workers (UAW) asked Chrysler Corporation to give the union two seats on Chrysler's board but dropped the idea when Chrysler resisted. Except for the UAW, most American unions oppose the idea for a number of reasons. Some union people see worker participation as a threat to union strength because board members representing labor might be independent of unionized labor. Some unionists also contend that American union workers already enjoy enough participation through the collective bargaining process. Do we need a codetermination act in the United States? YOU BE THE JUDGE!

Source: Furlong, *Labor in the Boardroom.*

proxy

Stockholders must be notified of the date, time, and place of stockholder meetings. Since many of them are unable or unwilling to attend, a proxy form usually is included along with the meeting notice. (See Figure 3–5.) **A proxy is a person who is appointed to represent another person. By signing a proxy form, a stockholder transfers his or her right to vote at a stockholders' meeting to someone else.** A stockholder who does not attend the meeting or does not return the proxy form loses voting rights in that meeting.

By gaining enough proxy forms, current directors can keep their seats on the board. The job of soliciting proxies is easy for current board members. They can get the names and addresses of stockholders, and

JACLYN, INC.

NOTICE OF ANNUAL MEETING OF STOCKHOLDERS

To the Stockholders of
JACLYN, INC.

The annual meeting of stockholders of JACLYN, INC. will be held at the offices of the Company, 635 59th Street, West New York, New Jersey, on Monday, November 13, 1978 at 9:30 o'clock A.M., prevailing local time, for the following purposes:

1. To elect directors to serve until the next annual meeting and until their successors are duly elected and qualify;

2. To ratify the appointment of Touche Ross & Co. to serve as the auditors of the Company for the fiscal year begun July 1, 1978; and

3. To transact such other business as may properly be brought before the meeting or any adjournments thereof.

Only stockholders of record at the close of business on October 13, 1978 are entitled to notice of and to vote at the annual meeting or at any adjournments thereof.

Your attention is called to the Proxy Statement on the following pages. We hope that you will attend the meeting. If you do not plan to attend, please fill in, sign, date and mail the enclosed proxy in the enclosed envelope, which requires no postage if mailed in the United States.

By Order of the Board of Directors

ALEX CHESTNOV,
Secretary

FIGURE 3–5

Notice of annual meeting of stockholders and proxy form

JACLYN, INC.

PROXY—ANNUAL MEETING STOCKHOLDERS—NOVEMBER 13, 1978

The undersigned hereby appoints ALEX CHESTNOV and PETER S. KOLEVZON and each of them, as proxies, with power of substitution, to vote all shares of stock the undersigned is entitled to vote at the annual meeting of stockholders of JACLYN, INC. to be held at the offices of the Company, 635 59th Street, West New York, New Jersey, on November 13, 1978 at 9:30 A.M., prevailing local time, and at any adjournments thereof.

(a) **WITH** ☐ **WITHOUT** ☐ authority to vote for the election of directors;

(b) **FOR** ☐ **AGAINST** ☐ ratification of the appointment of Touche Ross & Co. as auditors of the Company; and

(c) upon such other matters as may properly come before the meeting or any adjournments thereof.

This proxy will be voted as specified. If not otherwise specified, it will be voted for the election of six directors as described in the Proxy Statement and for ratification of the appointment of Touche Ross & Co. as auditors of the Company.

This proxy is solicited by management.

Dated: , 1978

....
(Signature of Stockholder)

Signature should agree with name stenciled hereon. Please correct any errors in address shown. If signing in representative capacity include full title. Proxies by a corporation should be signed in its name by an authorized officer. Where stock stands in more than one name, all holders of record should sign.

Source: Jaclyn, Inc.

Source: *Agatha Crumm,* King Features Syndicate.

the corporation pays the cost of solicitation. Thus it's easy for a board to keep itself in power as long as it does a good job in the opinion of voting stockholders. Unseating a board member can be tough.

Institutional investors, such as mutual funds, pension funds, investment clubs, and insurance companies, are professionally managed investors. They usually do not seek to exercise control of the corporations whose stock they hold. They buy and sell those shares mainly to make profits. But they may enjoy some degree of control because of their tremendous capacity to invest.

The board of directors also elects its own officers. These *board officers* usually include a chairperson of the board, a vice-chairperson, and a secretary. The board also holds periodic meetings.

Although the stockholders have the authority to draw up the corporation's bylaws, they usually leave it up to the board. **Corporation bylaws are the rules by which the corporation will operate. They include**

corporation bylaws

- **place and time of meetings**
- **procedure for calling meetings**
- **directors' pay**
- **duties of the corporate officers**
- **regulations for new stock issues**
- **procedure for changing the bylaws**

Another task of the board is selecting the *corporation's officers,* or its top managers, who include the president, vice-president(s), secretary, and treasurer. The corporation's officers are employees of the board and they also are the corporation's top management. These officers, in turn, hire other, lower-level managers to help in running the corporation. In actual practice boards sometimes select only the president, or chief executive officer (CEO), and he or she then selects the other corporate officers.

The board also is accountable to the stockholders for the actions of the corporate officers. In other words, the board performs the function of a "watchdog." As such, the board usually has the authority to accept or reject the officers' actions in managing the corporation.

In some corporations the board plays a very active role in managing the corporation. It holds frequent meetings and has a lot of say about the firm's day-to-day management. This is especially likely to be the case in small, closely held corporations.

On the other hand, some boards are content to select the company president. The president then selects other corporate officers and the board merely acts as a "review board" for the president and the other officers' decisions. In fact, the president pretty much runs the entire corporation subject to "rubber stamp" approval by the board.

Thus the distinctions between the board and the corporate officers often are blurred. In some corporations the chairperson of the board is also the company's president. The corporation's other top managers also may be on the board. In such a case the board members who are not corporate officers are called *outside directors.*

Board members do have certain legal obligations. They must act in the best interests of the stockholders and be reasonable and prudent in doing their jobs. They must be as careful in managing the corporation's affairs as they are in managing their personal affairs. In the past, board members have been held liable for illegal acts and fraud, but not for poor judgment. More recently, however, some courts have held directors liable for using what the courts consider to be poor judgment.

TABLE 3-3

Number of businesses operating in principal industries in the United States

Industry	Number of firms (in thousands)		
	Proprietorships	Active partnerships	Active corporations
Agriculture, forestry, and fisheries	3,367	123	56
Mining	56	16	14
Construction	892	61	191
Manufacturing	222	29	217
Transportation, communication, and public utilities	355	17	81
Trade:	2,193	193	615
Wholesale	336	31	220
Retail	1,765	162	395
Finance, insurance, and real estate	744	434	412
Services	3,034	199	436
All industries	10,881	1,073	2,024

Source: *Statistical Abstract of the United States.*

American Business by Form of Ownership

As has been true since the founding of our country, most American business firms are sole proprietorships. Close to 80 percent of our business firms take this form of ownership, including the vast majority of small retailers and service establishments. Typical examples are beauty salons, barber shops, car repair shops, and bicycle shops. Table 3–3 and Figure 3–6 indicate that

- there are nearly 11 million sole proprietorships in the United States
- sole proprietorships receive about 10 percent of all sales revenues of American firms
- sole proprietorships receive about 23 percent of all net profit of American firms

Sole proprietorships and partnerships combined account for about 86 percent of the total number of firms, excluding farms, in the United States.

Partnerships account for only 8 percent of American business firms, the smallest percentage among the three forms of ownership. The partnership form has declined in popularity over the years. Many physicians who were associated in partnerships, for example, are now members of professional corporations. Partnerships still are popular, however,

FIGURE 3–6

Number, revenues, and net profit of American business firms according to form of ownership

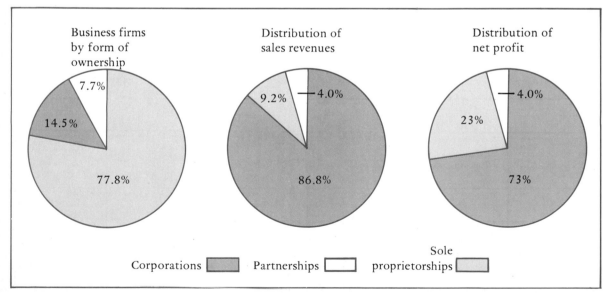

Source: *Statistical Abstract of the United States.*

TABLE 3-4

The twenty-five largest
industrial corporations
in the United States
ranked by sales, 1978

Rank	Company	Sales ($000)	Assets ($000)	Net income ($000)	Employees (number)	Net income as percent of sales
1	General Motors (Detroit)	63,221,100	30,598,300	3,508,000	839,000	5.5
2	Exxon (New York)	60,334,527	41,530,804	2,763,000	130,000	4.6
3	Ford Motor (Dearborn, Mich.)	42,784,100	22,101,400	1,588,900	506,531	3.7
4	Mobil (New York)	34,736,045	22,611,479	1,125,638	207,700	3.2
5	Texaco (Harrison, N.Y.)	28,607,521	20,249,143	852,461	67,841	3.0
6	Standard Oil of California (San Francisco)	23,232,413	16,761,021	1,105,881	37,575	4.8
7	International Business Machines (Armonk, N.Y.)	21,076,089	20,771,374	3,110,568	325,517	14.8
8	General Electric (Fairfield, Conn.)	19,653,800	15,036,000	1,229,700	401,000	6.3
9	Gulf Oil (Pittsburgh)	18,069,000	15,036,000	791,000	58,300	4.4
10	Chrysler (Highland Park, Mich.)	16,340,700	6,981,200	(204,600)	157,958	—
11	International Tel. & Tel. (New York)	15,261,178	14,034,866	661,807	379,000	4.3
12	Standard Oil (Ind.) (Chicago)	14,961,489	14,109,264	1,076,412	47,011	7.2
13	Atlantic Richfield (Los Angeles)	12,298,403	12,060,210	804,325	50,716	6.5
14	Shell Oil (Houston)	11,062,883	10,453,358	813,623	34,974	7.4
15	U.S. Steel (Pittsburgh)	11,049,500	10,536,300	242,000	166,848	2.2
16	E. I. du Pont de Nemours (Wilmington, Del.)	10,584,200	8,070,300	787,000	132,140	7.4
17	Western Electric (New York)	9,521,835	6,133,617	561,200	161,000	5.9
18	Continental Oil (Stamford, Conn.)	9,455,241	7,445,165	451,340	42,780	4.7
19	Tenneco (Houston)	8,762,000	10,134,000	466,000	104,000	5.3
20	Procter & Gamble (Cincinnati)	8,099,687	4,983,817	511,668	55,600	6.3
21	Union Carbide (New York)	7,869,700	7,866,200	394,300	113,371	5.0
22	Goodyear Tire & Rubber (Akron, Ohio)	7,489,102	5,231,103	226,127	154,013	3.0
23	Sun (Radnor, Pa.)	7,428,238	5,497,826	365,393	33,721	4.9
24	Caterpillar Tractor (Peoria, Ill.)	7,219,200	5,031,100	566,300	84,004	7.8
25	Eastman Kodak (Rochester, N.Y.)	7,012,923	6,801,067	902,284	124,800	12.9

Source: *Fortune.*

among ad agencies, public accounting firms, retail stores, and law firms. Table 3–3 and Figure 3–6 indicate that

- there are roughly one million partnerships in the United States
- partnerships receive about 4 percent of all sales revenues of American firms
- partnerships receive about 4 percent of all net profit of American firms

Only about 14 percent of our nonfarm businesses are corporations. They, however, receive the largest shares of total sales revenues and net profit of American businesses. Corporations conduct most of the business activity in our system. Some have more employees than some state governments and some have sales revenues that exceed the GNP of many small nations. (See Table 3–4.) Table 3–3 and Figure 3–6 indicate that

- there are roughly 2 million corporations in the United States
- corporations receive about 86 percent of all sales revenues of American firms
- corporations receive about 73 percent of all net profit of American firms

In Chapter 16 we will study the supergiants among corporations—the multinational corporations.

The Effects of Size

The relative advantages of the three forms of ownership we have discussed relate basically to the form of ownership. While we usually think of sole proprietorships as very small firms and corporations as very large firms, this is not always accurate. Some sole proprietorships, for example, are as large as or larger than some small corporations. In other words, the *size* of a business firm has no necessary relationship to its form of ownership.

It is also true that when we talk about "big business," we are talking about big corporations. Some of our biggest corporations, however, have very little in common with small corporations. Small, locally owned corporations have more in common with sole proprietorships and partnerships than they have in common with Exxon, General Electric, and other huge corporations. In fact, in discussing "business interests" we often find vast differences of opinion between big corporations, medium-sized corporations, and small corporations, sole proprietorships, and partnerships regarding what is "good" for business.

There is nothing gross about profit.

When a large corporation reports a profit, it's fashionable in some circles to blame the corporation and the profit for all the ills of our economy.

Yet, when people prosper from their own hard work, that's lauded as a guarantee of our democratic society.

But after all, what are corporations? They are businesses (groups of people) owned by stockholders (more people).

And what happens to that profit? First off, as much as half goes out as taxes. Which eventually end up benefiting the public (people).

About forty per cent of what's left is paid directly to stockholders (more people) as dividends.

And those "retained" profits (which average 3¢ on a dollar of sales) are used to buy new machinery, build new plants and make more jobs for (you guessed it!) people.

If there is anything "gross" about profit, it is the notion that, somehow, the people don't benefit from it.

The Grinding Machine Division's Stepmaster™ computer-controlled grinder automatically grinds multiple shaft diameters, a big improvement in grinding technology.

 WARNER & SWASEY
Productivity equipment and systems in machine tools, textile and construction machinery

© 1979 THE WARNER & SWASEY COMPANY   Executive Offices: 11000 Cedar Avenue, Cleveland, Ohio 44106

Source: Warner & Swasey, Inc.

Advantages of Large-Scale Operation

The larger a firm's size, the more likely it can afford to set up research and development, product testing, marketing research, and advertising departments and hire specialists such as engineers, chemists, market researchers, and advertising copywriters to staff them. A small firm usually cannot afford this degree of specialization. It may have one manager in charge of all production operations instead of separate managers for warehousing, traffic, production scheduling, and product quality control.

Large firms also are often able to borrow more money and get favorable interest rates. The prime interest rate that often is reported in the news is the rate banks charge their most credit-worthy customers—the big corporations. It is lower than the rate most smaller firms pay to borrow money.

professional managers

Large firms tend to be more permanent, which helps them in hiring managers and workers who value permanence in employment. **Professional managers are people whose profession or career is management. Such a person participates in managing a firm in which he or she is not a major owner.** Sole proprietors, partners, and the owners of small corporations usually are *owner-managers*. Only the larger firms can afford to hire professional managers. Partners in successful partnerships, however, can attract high-quality personnel who might expect to be offered a chance to buy into the firm. This practice is common in law and accounting firms.

Although stockholders are the direct owners of a corporation, there are millions of other people who have an indirect ownership in some large corporations. For example, some of the money in union pension funds is used to buy stock in large corporations. The union members are *indirect* owners of stock. This practice, of course, gives large corporations access to hundreds of millions of investment dollars.

The advantages of large-scale operation, regardless of the form of ownership, are

- greater opportunity for specialization by workers and managers
- greater borrowing power
- greater availability of managerial talent
- greater access to investment money

Disadvantages of Large-Scale Operation

Some economists, government regulators, small business owners, politicians, and labor leaders believe that businesses can be too big. Large size can result in reduced competition and greater concentration of economic power in certain sectors of the economy. Some people would like to see giant corporations like AT&T and GM broken up.

countervailing power

Big labor and government also are part of our business system. **The overall balancing of power between big business, big labor, and gov-**

ernment is called countervailing power. The offsetting size and power of each of these three supposedly will prevent any one of them from becoming too powerful and dominant in our society.

The corporation is one of our most basic business institutions. Without it, business activity as we know it would be impossible.

Large corporations can afford to invest in costly research and development. This leads to new manufacturing techniques, improvements to established products, and the introduction of new products. Large-scale operations also are economical. The classic example is the modern assembly line in manufacturing. As a greater number of units are produced, the manufacturing cost per unit tends to decline, which can lead to lower prices for consumers.

However, some people believe that corporations can be too big. They argue that the tremendous size of some corporations contributes to reduced management efficiency, which, in turn, leads to lower profits and higher prices to consumers.

Other people are critical of big corporations from a different point of view. Bigness, to them, is "badness." Many of these critics believe that the huge size and economic power of some corporations lead to reduced competition among firms and greater concentration of economic power. When is a corporation too big? WHAT DO YOU THINK?

In any large organization there is some tendency toward impersonality. In some of our largest corporations, for example, the lack of personal contact between workers and managers tends to make the workers feel uninvolved with the business. They have trouble identifying with the corporation, its owners, and its managers. There is more personal contact in small firms.

The sole proprietor who assumes risk stands to gain all the rewards. In smaller corporations the accomplishments of managers can be observed more easily than in large corporations, where there are many levels of managers. These hired managers stand to gain fewer of the rewards from risk assumption. Some may become overly conservative and avoid taking risks, even when that may be best for the firm.

The disadvantages of large-scale operation, regardless of the form of ownership, are

- the potential for too much concentration of economic power
- the potential for reduced management efficiency
- some tendency toward impersonality
- the potential for overconservatism in management

Other Forms of Business Ownership

The sole proprietorship, the partnership, and the corporation are the three major forms of ownership of business firms. But over the years some modifications of these three basic forms have been made in order to overcome some of their disadvantages. Examples are

- limited partnerships
- joint ventures
- business trusts
- cooperative associations
- mutual companies

Limited Partnerships

The previous discussion of the partnership focused on the general partnership in which all partners are co-owners and each has unlimited liability for the firm's debts. This liability also is a joint liability.

JUNIOR PARTNERS AND SENIOR PARTNERS

In some large, well-established partnerships, such as some certified public accountant firms, a small number of the partners in the firm are senior partners. They make all the policy decisions in the firm. Often they are called managing partners.

Some of the firm's promising employees may be invited to become junior partners. They agree to allow the senior partners to make policy decisions. The junior partner buys shares in the firm and, in return, he or she is given a percentage of the firm's profits. As the junior partner gains experience and becomes more valuable to the firm, he or she may be invited to buy more shares and may be elected a senior partner.

In a limited partnership there is at least one general partner and one limited partnership
or more limited partners. A limited partner's liability is limited to his or
her financial investment in the firm. This feature helps general partners
to attract investment dollars from people who do not want to assume
unlimited financial liability or participate in managing the firm. Under
the law, partners are assumed to be general partners unless it is made
known that they are limited partners. If a limited partner does participate in managing the firm, that person's limited liability must be disclosed to the firm's creditors.

The following are several types of partners:

- silent partner—a partner who does not actively participate in
  managing the firm but whose name is identified with the firm.
- secret partner—a partner who actively participates in managing
  the firm but whose identity is not disclosed to the public.
- dormant (sleeping) partner—a partner who does not actively participate in managing the firm and whose identity is not disclosed
  to the public.
- nominal partner—a person who is not an actual partner but
  whose name is identified with the firm because he or she is a
  well-known personality. Use of the name gives the firm promotional benefits and the person usually is paid a fee for the use of
  his or her name.

These partners can be general or limited partners but the dormant partner most often is a limited partner.

Joint Ventures

The joint venture is a special type of temporary partnership arrange- joint venture
ment. It is set up for a specific purpose and it ends when that purpose is
accomplished. A partner's death or withdrawal does not end the joint
venture. Usually, one general partner manages the venture and the
others have limited financial liability.

This arrangement has been popular in real estate during recent years.
Several persons may pool their funds and talents to buy an older home,
remodel it, and sell it. They divide the profit they make and the joint
venture ends. Another example is a group of brokerage firms that get
together to sell a new stock issue for a corporate client. These firms
make up an underwriting syndicate.

Business Trusts

In a business trust the trustee holds the property, runs the business, business trust
and accepts funds from investors. The trustee makes all management

decisions, including how any profit will be divided. The investors have no say in management but they do have limited financial liability. They receive trust shares but they do not vote for the people who manage the trust. An example is a mutual fund that accepts funds from investors. The trustee pools their investment dollars and uses them to buy stock in other firms.

Cooperative Associations

cooperative association

A cooperative association (or, simply, a co-op) is a group of persons who act together to accomplish some purpose. They are incorporated and the members elect a board of directors. Each member has only one vote. Co-ops do not seek to earn a profit in the usual sense of the term. They are set up to help their members. Any revenues that they earn in excess of their cost of doing business are returned to the owners. Examples of co-ops include

- employee credit unions—accept savings deposits from members who own shares in the co-op. Members also can borrow from the co-op. Savers receive interest and borrowers pay interest to the credit union.
- agricultural co-ops—help member farmers to market their products. The Florida Orange Growers Association is an example.
- buying co-ops—help members to buy their products at lower prices. Farmers may get together and set up a co-op to buy seed, fertilizer, and so on.
- consumer co-ops—customer-owned retail facilities. Consumers get together and form a buying pool in order to get quantity discounts and to eliminate independently owned middleman firms like wholesalers and retailers. Owner-members in many rural areas also set up consumer co-ops for selling electricity.

Mutual Companies

mutual company

A mutual company is similar to a cooperative because the users are the owners. They have a board of directors like a corporation, but the vast majority of members typically do not vote. Many life insurance companies and savings and loan associations (S&LAs) are mutual companies. When you buy an insurance policy from Massachusetts Mutual, you become an owner and you receive a "dividend" on your policy. Unlike a dividend from a corporation, it is not taxable. When you deposit savings in a mutual S&LA, you also become an owner. You receive "dividends" on your savings, but the "dividends" are considered to be interest for income tax purposes, and you pay income tax on them.

Business Law Concepts and Institutions

Several basic legal concepts and institutions are related to the form of ownership of a business. These are

- the law of contracts
- the law of agency and bailments
- the law of property
- the Uniform Commercial Code

The Law of Contracts

The interdependence of people in an advanced economy requires a great number of transactions and agreements among them. Sales transactions, for example, often are based on formal sales contracts. A partnership agreement is a contract that spells out responsibilities and rights of each of the partners. The law of contracts is basic to the right to own property.

A contract is a mutual agreement between two or more people to   contract
perform or not perform certain acts. In order to be valid, a contract must include

- an agreement—an offer seriously and clearly made by one party (the offeror) to another party (the offeree) who must accept it seriously and clearly.
- consideration—the value that each party gets or gives. With few exceptions, it must be shown that both parties intended to bargain and have actually exchanged something for a contract to be enforceable by a court.
- competence—the ability to incur liability (debt) or to gain legal rights. A person who is insane or below a certain age (it varies from state to state) may not be legally competent to make a contract.
- a legal objective—what a legal objective is depends on the law in the jurisdiction where the contract is made.

Businesses enter into contracts with suppliers for materials, customers for purchases, employees for employment, and with other persons and firms. A court will enforce a contract if it meets the requirements discussed above.

The Law of Agency and Bailments

An agency-principal relationship exists when one party (the agent) is   agency-principal
authorized and consents to act on behalf of another (the principal). An   relationship

agent must always act for the benefit of and under the control of the principal. The principal usually is liable for acts of the agent that come within the scope of the agent's authority.

A common example of this relationship occurs when a firm sells some of its products through a manufacturer's agent. This person is not on the firm's payroll as a salesperson. He or she is an independent agent middleman. Suppose Paula Smith is a manufacturer's agent who sells $20,000 of auto parts to a garage on behalf of her principal, Acme Steel. Acme must deliver the parts as long as the contract between Smith and Acme is valid and it does not prohibit the action taken by Smith.

bailor-bailee relationship   **Another common business relationship is the bailor-bailee relationship. A bailor gives possession and control of his or her property to a bailee. The bailor, however, still owns the property.** An example is a public warehouse that leases space to firms for storing their inventories. A bailment, therefore, is a transfer of possession without sale.

The Law of Property

In law, property means ownership of a thing, including the right to possess, use, or dispose of that thing. In one sense, it means the same thing as *title*. There are two main types of property:

real property
- **real property—land and its permanent attachments, such as houses, garages, and office buildings.** Table 3–5 discusses several types of ownership of real property.

personal property
- **personal property—all property other than real property, such as furniture, clothing, cars, and bank accounts.**

warranty
In the sale of property, the question of warranty may become important. **A warranty is a representation, or a legal promise, made by the seller of a product that assures the buyer that the product is or shall be as represented by the seller.**

There are two kinds of warranty: express warranty and implied warranty. An *express warranty* is a specific representation about the product that is made by the seller. For example, a label on a shirt that says "This garment is 50 percent cotton and 50 percent nylon" is an express warranty. An *implied warranty* does not state but suggests that all merchandise will perform satisfactorily. Suppose you buy a food blender and the motor burns out after one week's normal use. You could return the blender or keep it and sue for damages (legally demand payment for loss), even though no specific warranty had been made.

In recent years, the Federal Trade Commission (FTC), a federal regulatory agency, has been given authority to require sellers of products to provide clear and unambiguous warranties, for example, to specify the time period covered by the warranty and to spell out the meaning of the warranty. For most products you see today, the manufacturers offer limited warranties. Some guarantee their products against "defects of material or workmanship" for 30 or 90 days. Some others go a lot further. Sears, for example, offers a one-year replacement guarantee (not just repair) on some of its appliances.

The Uniform Commercial Code

A firm that does business in only one state engages in intrastate commerce. A firm that does business in two or more states engages in interstate commerce. Most firms engaged only in intrastate commerce during our early history, but many today engage in interstate commerce.

Many of the laws that pertain to business are state laws. A firm in interstate commerce must understand and conform to the laws of different states. If these laws were all uniform in content, coverage, enforcement, and so on, there would be little problem. But they are not uniform.

TABLE 3-5

Types of real property ownership

Joint tenancy	Two or more persons share title. Each has equal rights to use and enjoy the property during their lives. When one owner dies, the entire estate goes to the survivors, not to that owner's heirs. The last survivor is the full owner of the estate. Today, a joint tenancy also can be created in personal property. An example is a savings account in a bank.
Fee simple	A person is the owner in fee simple of real property when he or she owns the entire estate. The last survivor in joint tenancy has an estate in fee simple.
Tenancy in common	Two or more persons share title. Each tenant's share passes to his or her heirs at the tenant's death.
Tenants by the entirety	A form of joint tenancy. It can be ended only by death of one party. The other partner becomes sole owner. Only a wife and husband can be tenants by the entirety.
Community property	Property husbands and wives own together under the laws of community property states. In general, any property obtained through the efforts of both husband and wife becomes community property. Excluded are gifts and legacies to only one partner or property a husband or a wife owned before marriage. When a husband or wife dies, half of the property belongs to the survivor. Only the other half can be willed to others.
Life estate	An interest in property that is granted to or willed to a person that lasts only during the possessor's lifetime.
Future estate	Property owned but which cannot be enjoyed until some future time. A wife owns a future estate in property that her husband owns but that will go to her upon his death.

Efforts to bring some degree of uniformity to state business laws began in the 1890s. By the 1950s these efforts resulted in the establishment of uniform laws pertaining to such things as sales, bills of lading, partnerships, and negotiable instruments. Thus we had the Uniform Sales Act, the Uniform Bills of Lading Act, the Uniform Partnership Act, and the Uniform Negotiable Instruments Act. The problem was that not all states adopted all of these uniform statutes.

Uniform Commercial Code (UCC)

Effort, therefore, was directed to developing a uniform statute that would encompass all the various individual uniform acts. **The result was the Uniform Commercial Code (UCC). The UCC is a statute that combines and coordinates uniform acts into a single commercial code.** All states except Louisiana have adopted the UCC, which has reduced the problems firms face in interstate commerce.

The UCC, however, does not cover all areas of commercial law. The various states still do rely on precedent (common law) in solving some commercial disputes. For example, the code provides that it shall be supplemented by the principles of law that pertain to capacity to contract and fraud.

Summary and Look Ahead

The three major forms of ownership of business are the sole proprietorship, the partnership, and the corporation. These are all forms of private ownership in contrast to public ownership. Private ownership is the most common form of ownership in the United States. But there is more public ownership today than there was fifty years ago.

Most privately owned firms are sole proprietorships. Most of these are small and employ only a handful of people. In many, the owner is the only employee.

A partnership is a firm owned by two or more persons who voluntarily go into business together. Like the proprietorship, this form of ownership also dates back to ancient times.

A corporation is something separate and distinct from its owners. It is a creation of government authority. It comes into existence when its owners are granted a corporate charter by the state in which it is formed. Ownership is gained by the purchase of shares of stock.

What form of ownership is "best" depends on the circumstances in each situation. In no sense is one form of ownership always better than another.

The law of contracts, the law of agency and bailments, and the law of property are basic to our type of business system. The Uniform Commercial Code (UCC) helps firms that engage in interstate commerce by bringing some "order" and uniformity to state laws that affect business.

In the next chapter, we view the firm as an organization. As we will see, a firm has both formal and informal dimensions.

To listen to a lot of people these days—and that includes some business teachers and textbook writers—you'd think everybody works for a big corporation. Of course, a lot of people do. But many people find it much better working for themselves—running their own businesses.

Why not ask yourself this question: "Am I better equipped to work for somebody else or to be my own boss?" Weigh the points on each side. Can you handle a lot of uncertainty? Can you come up with enough money to start a business? Do you have something to sell? If the answer is yes to all of these, then maybe you should start out on your own. If you value security, if you have a small bank account and no one to back you financially, if you don't have a strong, clearly defined service or product to offer, then go to work for an established firm.

Maybe you have only some of the things you need. In that case it might be a good idea to go to work for a small business. In this way you may learn a lot and earn enough to overcome your handicaps. Later you can start your own business—older, wiser, and richer. As somebody with a lot of sense once said, "Making mistakes with somebody else's money is much easier to take than making mistakes with your own money!"

WOULD YOU LIKE TO BE YOUR OWN BOSS?

Key Concepts

agency-principal relationship Exists when one party (the agent) is authorized and consents to act on behalf of another (the principal).

bailor-bailee relationship A common occurrence in business. A bailor gives possession and control of his or her property to a bailee. The bailor still owns the property but the bailee holds it in trust. In bailment, the bailor is the person who delivers goods in trust to a bailee, who is the person to whom the goods are committed in trust. A bailment is a transfer of possession without sale.

board of directors The group of persons, elected by a corporation's stockholders, that is ultimately responsible for the management of that corporation.

business trust A business arrangement, created by an agreement, in which a trustee holds the property, runs the business, and accepts funds from investors. These investors receive trust shares, have limited liability, but do not vote for the trustee. A mutual fund is an example.

common stock A certificate showing ownership in a corporation. All shares are equal in value and all common stockholders enjoy the same rights. Common stockholders are the residual owners of a corporation.

contract A mutual agreement between two or more people to perform or not perform certain acts. Consists of an offer seriously and clearly made by one party (the offeror) to another party (the offeree) who must accept it in a serious and unambiguous manner. To be valid a contract must include an agreement, consideration, competence of parties, and a legal objective.

cooperative association Also called a co-op. An association formed and owned by a group of persons who act together to accomplish some purpose. It is a collective undertaking, and any revenues in excess of costs are returned to the owner-member. A co-op is incorporated and the members elect a board of directors. Each member has only one vote. Employee credit unions and consumer co-ops are examples.

corporate charter A document that states the purpose for which a corporation is being formed, the nature of its business, its founders, and the number of shares of stock it can issue. Granted by the state in which it is being formed, or incorporated. Authorizes the formation of a corporation.

corporation The legal entity (thing) created by law that is granted rights set out in the corporate charter. A separate and legal entity apart from its owners. "An artificial person."

corporation bylaws The rules by which a corporation will operate. Usually state place and time of stockholders' meetings, procedure for calling those meetings, duties of the corporate officers, procedure for changing the bylaws, etc.

countervailing power The term used to describe the balance of power between big labor, big business, and government. The theory is that each is large and powerful enough to prevent any one of them from becoming too powerful and dominant in our society.

cumulative voting A requirement in some states that the number of votes a stockholder has is the number of shares owned times the number of directors to be elected.

joint venture A special type of temporary partnership arrangement that is set up for a specific

purpose and ends when that purpose is accomplished.

limited partnership A type of partnership in which there is at least one general partner and one or more others (limited partners) whose financial liability is limited to their financial investment in the firm.

mutual company A firm that is owned by its user members. An example is a life insurance company that is owned by its policyholders.

partnership Defined by the Uniform Partnership Act as "an association of two or more persons to carry on as co-owners of a business for profit."

partnership agreement Also called Articles of Partnership or Articles of Copartnership. An oral, but preferably written, contract between the owners of a partnership that states the name, location, and business of the firm and the names of the partners along with their duties, obligations, and rights in running the business and sharing in the profits.

personal property All property except land and its permanent attachments. Examples are cars, furniture, and office machines.

preferred stock A certificate showing ownership in a corporation. It has preference over common stock in dividends and liquidation of the corporation's assets. Preferred stockholders may or may not have the right to vote.

professional managers Hired managers. Most often used when there is a separation of ownership and management in a firm. Persons whose career is management.

proxy A person appointed to represent another person. A stockholder transfers his or her right to vote at a stockholders' meeting to a proxy by signing a proxy form.

real property Land and its permanent attachments.

sole proprietorship A business firm owned by one person. The firm and the proprietor are the same.

stockholders Also called shareholders. A corporation's stockholders are the persons who own it. The owners of the entity that is the corporation.

subchapter S corporation A small corporation with no more than 15 stockholders that can choose to be taxed as a partnership and still enjoy the advantages of incorporation.

Uniform Commercial Code (UCC) A statute that combines and coordinates uniform acts into a single commercial code. Helps bring uniformity among state laws that regulate business activity.

unlimited liability Proprietors and general partners are liable for claims against their firms that are not limited to the value of their ownership in those firms. Liability extends to their personal property and, possibly, real property.

warranty A representation, either express or implied, made by the seller of a product that assures the buyer that the product is or shall be as represented by the seller.

For Review . . .

1. List and discuss four reasons for public ownership of the means of production in our economic system.
2. List, define, and discuss the relative advantages and disadvantages of the three most common forms of ownership of business firms.
3. Is there any necessary relationship between a firm's size and its form of ownership? Discuss.
4. What are the relative advantages and disadvantages of large-scale operation to a firm?
5. Contrast "owner-managers" and "professional managers."
6. Compare the three forms of ownership of business firms in terms of (a) numbers; (b) revenues received; and (c) profit earned.
7. Define (a) domestic corporation; (b) foreign corporation; (c) alien corporation; (d) public corporation; (e) private corporation; (f) close corporation; and (g) open corporation.
8. Discuss the corporate structure in terms of stockholders, the board of directors, and the corporate officers.
9. List and discuss five modifications of the three major firms of ownership of business firms.
10. List and discuss the requirements of a valid contract.
11. What is an agency-principal relationship?
12. Distinguish between real property and personal property.

. . . For Discussion

1. Does the president of General Electric get less personal satisfaction from his job than the proprietor of a small business?
2. What is the most serious disadvantage of the partnership form of ownership?
3. Which form of business ownership is "best"?
4. Who or what really controls a corporation?
5. Are the professional managers in a large corporation more likely to assume more social responsibility than a sole proprietor or partners in a small firm?
6. Is the profit incentive that we discussed in Chapter 2 as important to professional managers in a large corporation as it is to the sole proprietor of a small business?
7. Do owners of small businesses have any "countervailing power"?

Incidents

Conrad Hilton: Innkeeper to the World

"He attributed his success to his rather square and old-fashioned philosophy that 'man with God's help and personal dedication is capable of anything he can dream.' But who could argue with the shrewdly audacious small-town boy who put together the world's foremost chain of luxury hotels and became a multiple millionaire and one of the most colorful American businessmen? From New York to Istanbul and from Las Vegas to Addis Ababa, the name of Conrad Nicholson Hilton was synonymous with hotel, as in 'I'm staying at the Hilton.'

"When he died of pneumonia [in 1979] at a wizened 91, his perenially profitable Hilton Hotels Corp. owned, managed or franchised 185 hostelries in the U.S. with revenues of $372 million in 1977. (The overseas subsidiary, Hilton International, was sold to Trans World Airlines in 1967.) Though Hilton's son Barron, 51, took over as chief executive more than a decade ago, Papa kept the title of chairman and continued to turn up daily at his Beverly Hills office to answer fan mail and assist charities. . . .

"Hilton was born in San Antonio, N. Mex., on Christmas Day, 1887, when the state was still a territory. In 1919 he plunked down his entire savings of $5,000 to buy a small hotel in oil-rich Cisco, Texas, and eventually put together a small chain before the Depression wiped him out. With borrowed money he bounced back and bought up hotels at distress prices before and during World War II. He acquired a prestigious lineup: Los An-geles' Town House, Chicago's Palmer House, New York's Waldorf-Astoria and in 1954, the entire Statler chain.

"At the same time, Hilton led the way overseas for other U.S. chains by opening hotels and widely introducing such novelties as coffee shops, self-service elevators, health clubs and swimming pools in Europe, the Caribbean and the Far East. He once wrote: 'I like the tumult of life. I like its problems, its ever changing stresses.' It was a zest that was reflected almost daily in Conrad Hilton's long, full and useful life."

Questions

1. How important do you think personal involvement and satisfaction were to Mr. Hilton when he started out?
2. Why do you think the company became a corporation?

Source: *Time.*

The Importance of Small Business

For most Americans, the word 'business' connotes thoughts of large, multi-faceted operations, automobile manufacturers, the aerospace industry, oil conglomerates, and utility companies.

Of the 13.9 million businesses in the United States, 10.7 million non-farm enterprises are considered small businesses. Additionally, 99 percent of the 3.3 million American farms fall into the small business category.

This image problem of the small business community, a general lack of awareness on the part of the public, the media, and many in government that small business is the largest and most important sector of the American economy, is prevalent throughout the country.

Yet small business accounts for 43 percent of the U.S. Gross National Product. Small businesses are responsible for nearly 8 of every 10 dollars earned by the construction industry, 7 of every 10 dollars in sales made by retailers and wholesalers, and 6 of every 10 dollars generated by service firms.

Small businesses provide 58 percent of total U.S. business employment, and they directly or indirectly provide the livelihood for over 100 million Americans.

Questions

1. Are most of the 10.7 million non-farm small businesses sole proprietorships, partnerships, or corporations?
2. Explain why most Americans think of big corporations when they hear the word *business.*
3. What would you recommend that the small business community do to show the American public the importance to our business system of small business?

Source: *Business America.*

ROCKETOY COMPANY 2

The large toy distributor (Toyco) that signed a trial contract for 2,000 Rocketoys negotiated with Terry for a longer-term contract for 10,000 units each of three of Terry's most popular toys. Terry recognized the opportunity here and he wanted to close the deal.

Terry's only problem was his shortage of funds. This is common in many sole proprietorships like Terry's. Terry could not afford to buy the additional equipment and materials needed to meet the production requirements called for in the proposed contract. Although he reinvested all his profit in his business, Terry still needed more money for expansion.

Furthermore, Terry found that he needed more employees. Although he had three full-time production workers, he knew that the new contract would require the hiring of at least five more workers.

Toyco offered Terry a $25,000 loan if he would agree to sign the proposed contract. Terry figured the loan would be adequate to enable him to "tool up" for the new order. Because Toyco was convinced that it could make a large profit from sales of Rocketoy's products, Toyco was willing to lend the money at a very low rate of interest. Terry is seriously considering the offer.

Meanwhile, Joe Phillips approached Terry with a proposal to take him in as a general partner. Since Joe is quite wealthy, the new partnership would have no financial problems. Besides what Joe could contribute in cash, his being a partner would make Rocketoy a much better credit risk for any potential creditors.

Finally, Terry was also approached by three Milwaukee investors who wanted to make Rocketoy a corporation. They assured Terry that they were seriously interested investors who would gladly invest in the firm as stockholders.

Questions

1. Why do you think Toyco was willing to lend Terry $25,000?
2. Why did Terry reinvest all his profit in his firm?
3. What are the relative advantages and disadvantages of the sole proprietorship, partnership, and corporation in Terry's case?
4. Would you advise Terry to take Uncle Joe in as a general partner, to form a corporation, or to take the loan from Toyco? Explain the reasons for your recommendation.

CHAPTER 4

Organization

Objectives: After reading this chapter, you should be able to

1. Tell the difference between personal and organizational objectives and explain how they are integrated.
2. Draw a figure that illustrates the hierarchy of organizational objectives.
3. List and give an example of the different bases for departmentation.
4. Relate the span-of-management concept to the echelons of management.
5. List and explain the factors that affect a manager's optimum span of management.
6. List and explain the three actions involved in the delegation process.
7. Relate the delegation process to the degree to which a firm is centralized or decentralized.
8. Compare the line, line and staff, and committee organization structures.
9. Tell the difference between line function and staff function and give an example of each.
10. Identify several sources of line-staff conflict.
11. Draw an organization chart and tell what it indicates and does not indicate.
12. Draw a figure that illustrates the hierarchy of human needs and discuss those needs.
13. Compare formal and informal organizations.
14. Explain why informal groups arise and discuss their basic characteristics.

Key concepts: Look for these terms as you read the chapter

organization	decentralization
hierarchy of organizational objectives	line authority
	line functions
departmentation	staff functions
span of management	staff
echelons of management	functional authority
delegation	organization chart
responsibility	hierarchy of needs
authority	informal groups
accountability	informal organization
centralization	

An organization is a logical combination of human, financial, and physical resources put together by management so that certain goals can be accomplished. All firms have goals that can be reached only if their human, financial, and physical resources are tied together logically. This is why businesses are formally structured.

Individuals can accomplish their own personal objectives and help to achieve company objectives if both types of objectives are carefully integrated. Otherwise, a person will not get much satisfaction from the organization. The formal organization, therefore, is the structure that helps a firm and its employees to achieve their goals.

People are the most important resource of any organization. An organization also can be viewed in terms of how these people behave. A firm, or any other type of organization, contains a collection of smaller, informal groups. These informal groups are not created by management but by the group members themselves to satisfy some of their needs. The entire set of these small groups is the informal organization of a firm. It is separate and distinct from the formal organization.

What Is an Organization?

Imagine two cars traveling in opposite directions on the same street. They approach an intersection with four stop signs. Both cars stop. No other cars are present. Suppose driver A signals for a turn that will put his car in the path of driver B. Both drivers must interact to avoid a wreck. Avoiding a wreck is an objective of both drivers. Traffic signals and rules lend structure so that one driver will always let the other pass first.

Now consider a business firm whose objective is to make a profit by providing want-satisfying products to customers. The employees' objective is to earn a living. Workers interact with one another and with the tools of production. They perform those tasks necessary for the firm to make a profit and for the employees to earn a living. People, tasks, and physical resources must be combined into a structure that enables the firm and its employees to achieve their goals.

We have seen two examples of organization. They are very different types because they vary in size, length of life, complexity, and formality. The two drivers interact briefly and informally. The greater number of employees interact over a longer period of time on the basis of work rules and procedures. There is more formal structuring of the relationships among people, activities, and physical resources than there is between the two drivers.

Both, however, are examples of organization. Notice that three key elements of organization are present:

- human interaction
- actions toward an objective (goal-directed activity)
- structure

An organization, therefore, is something that is structured so that human activity can be coordinated to accomplish objectives.   organization

Why Do People Join Organizations?

People belong to organizations because they believe that they can achieve their goals better within them than they could outside. You might join a fraternity or a sorority because you expect it will help you to have a satisfying social life at college. You might figure that you would have more social functions to attend than if you were not a member. Most of us belong to many organizations because we have so many different goals. No one organization could satisfy them all.

In a business firm people's needs are similar enough to enable them to satisfy some of their needs through the firm. Employees can earn a living and perhaps receive bonuses for doing exceptionally good work. But, as we'll see, people on the job have other social needs that may not be satisfied by the firm. An assembly-line worker may be earning a living on the job by doing the tasks assigned to him or her by the boss. But this person also may want to "feel important" and be well liked by coworkers. As a result people on the job often form informal groups that help them to satisfy wants that may not be satisfied by the formal structure of the firm. People tend to remain in an organization only if it helps them to satisfy their goals.

Personal and Organizational Objectives

People contribute to an organization if they think it helps to satisfy their personal objectives. Integrating various personal objectives into a unified statement of the firm's objectives is not easy. For example, an employee may easily accept a company's objective "to make a profit." Doing so may provide money to be shared in the firm's profit-sharing plan. But that same employee may not accept a company objective "to be a good community citizen." Doing so, for example, could cause the firm to invest large sums of money in pollution control equipment and to make company contributions to the local symphony orchestra. These "extra costs" might leave less money for pay raises.

Ideally an organization would meet all the personal objectives of all the people associated with it. Personal goals, however, often are in conflict. As a result a firm's objectives usually are something other than the sum of the personal objectives of its different publics (employees, suppliers, owners, creditors, customers, etc.).

Formal organizations like business firms *suboptimize* objectives. This means they settle for less than the total achievement of all the objectives of their publics. Not all the personal goals of all of a firm's publics will be fully satisfied. Nor will company goals be completely achieved. For example, an employee may want to grow on the job—to be given the opportunity to learn new skills and be promoted to a higher-level job. But the firm may need his or her services in a very specialized job. The worker's desire for more varied tasks conflicts with the firm's objectives. The reason that every employee is never totally satisfied with their em-

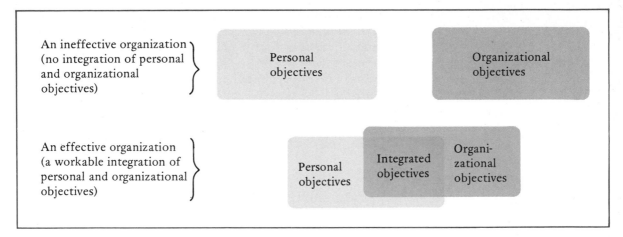

ployer is that the personal and organizational objectives never are in total harmony. There always is some degree of conflict. (See Figure 4–1.)

A *tradeoff* is necessary. Neither the worker's objective nor the firm's objective will be achieved 100 percent. A compromise is worked out whereby the firm and the worker each get something, but not all that each might want. The employee's job might be broadened to include a greater variety of tasks. This increases his or her job satisfaction and the employee may become more productive; and the firm, of course, benefits.

FIGURE 4–1

Personal objectives, organizational objectives, and organizational effectiveness

Organization as Structure

All firms are structured to help achieve company and personal goals. How complex and formal this structure is depends on many things. Firms that have only a handful of employees, for example, require less formal structure than firms with many employees. Thousands of small owner-manager firms do not have very formalized structures. The owner often works beside the firm's few employees and directs the activities which he or she assigns to them. But large firms require more attention to structure because there are more workers, greater specialization of labor, and a greater number of levels of managers.

For example, an owner-manager of a women's dress shop selects and orders merchandise from dress manufacturers, determines prices, and sets credit policies. He or she may have several salespersons, a bookkeeper, and perhaps a credit manager and a delivery driver. These people are in face-to-face contact, and the owner personally runs the business. But in a large department store, there are many more salespersons, several delivery drivers, an entire credit department, an accounting department, and managers (buyers) for each separate department. It's almost impossible for one person to run such a large business alone.

In the case of a giant retailing firm like Sears, the need for formal structure is obvious. The owner-manager of a women's dress shop can place orders with the manufacturers, but it takes many, many employees just to deal with Sears' more than 12,000 suppliers in the United States. Formal organization is clearly needed.

What Is Being Structured?

An organizational structure is created to help achieve goals. Within that structure, activities are performed to help achieve those goals. Organizational "structuring," therefore, focuses first on those activities.

A primary goal of your school is to educate students. One of your goals is a good education. Relationships among the activities needed to reach these goals must be structured. The two essential activities here are teaching and learning; and they require people, books, and classrooms for their performance.

Teachers must be assigned to courses, textbooks must be related to courses, and classrooms must be assigned. Of course, students also must be assigned to teachers and courses. In other words, three basic components must be related to each other through the process of organizing:

- people
- activities
- physical resources

Objectives: The Underlying Reason for Organization

Objectives are the ends that we want to accomplish in an organization. In order to accomplish them, certain activities must be performed by people working with other resources. These activities are the means for accomplishing the organization's objectives. Activities are the connecting link between an organization's objectives and its structure. It is through the organizational structure that management coordinates the activities of workers that are required to reach the organization's objectives.

But what objective tells Harry the janitor to sweep the floor? The overall company objective "to supply customers with a quality product

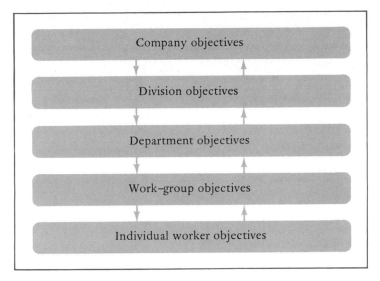

FIGURE 4–2

The hierarchy of organizational objectives

at a reasonable price" does not tell Harry what he should do to help the firm reach its goals. The company objective is too broad to provide a specific objective for Harry.

Figure 4–2 shows a hierarchy of organizational objectives. This concept involves breaking down broad company goals into specific goals
for each person in the organization. Broad organizational goals are broken down successively into goals for company divisions, depart-
ments, work-groups, and individual workers. This process tells Harry that his job (activity) is sweeping the floor. The number of levels of objectives depends on the firm's size and complexity. There are fewer levels in very small firms than in very large ones.

hierarchy of organizational objectives

Identifying, Grouping, and Assigning Activities

The first step in building an organizational structure is to analyze the major activities that must be performed to help the organization reach its objectives. For a manufacturer these activities usually are production, marketing, and finance. Each activity is assigned to a separate department within the firm.

Firms are broken down into departments through the process of departmentation. Departmentation means identifying, grouping, and
assigning activities to specialized departments within an organization.

departmentation

There are two basic approaches to identifying activities. First, we could observe workers and classify their activities such as assembling parts, buying raw materials, and pricing products. The other approach is to start with company goals and determine what activities are needed to reach those goals. This method is the only one available to a brand-new firm.

Next, activities are grouped and assigned. There are six major bases upon which an organization could be departmented:

- function
- geography
- product
- customers
- process
- time

An example of departmentation by *function* is a charitable organization that has solicitation, collecting, and disbursing departments. Many oil companies are departmented by functions: exploration, production, refining, marketing, and finance.

The Bell Telephone System and the U.S. Internal Revenue Service (IRS) are departmentalized partly on a *geographical* basis. Depending on where you live, the name of your phone company will differ even though all of them may be part of the Bell System. Where you live also determines where you send your tax return and where your refund will be mailed from.

General Motors divides along *product* lines. There are separate divisions for Pontiac, Oldsmobile, Chevrolet, Buick, and Cadillac.

Many firms use a *customer* basis. Some electronics firms have one division serving defense customers and another serving nondefense customers.

An example of *process-based* departmentation is a brewery that has a cooking and an aging department.

Finally, some firms use *time* as a basis for departmentation. Some employees might work the day shift and others work the night shift. Some colleges operate regular day classes and also have an evening division.

Many firms use several bases for departmentalizing. A firm might be divided by function into production, marketing, and finance departments. The marketing department could be divided into a domestic sales organization and a foreign sales organization (geography). Decisions of this type are influenced by the relative advantages of the different approaches and the experience, preferences, and judgment of top management.

Activities are departmentalized to make work more efficient and to provide a means for controlling operations. Modern technology also leads to greater departmentation. For example, the increasing importance of computer technology in business has led many firms to set up data processing departments. The faster pace of technological change has led many firms to also set up research and development departments.

Another reason for departmentation is the simple fact that the number of subordinates a manager can manage is limited. Without departmentation a firm's size would be limited to the number of persons the top manager could supervise directly. We'll discuss this later in the chapter.

Departmentation, however, is not intended to create "walls" around departments. For example, when problems arise that involve two or more departments, personnel from the departments involved are combined to solve them. Engineering, production, finance, and marketing personnel, for example, might work together in an effort to modify a product that, due to faulty design, is causing customer complaints. After the problem is solved, the work group is dissolved.

The Span of Management

As we have seen, one reason for departmentation is that there are limits to a manager's ability to supervise subordinates effectively and directly. **Span of management refers to the number of persons an individual manager supervises.** The wider the span of management, the more subordinates are directly managed by a manager. It is generally believed that wider spans are more practical at lower levels in the firm.

span of management

Assembly-line foremen are lower-level managers who supervise workers who perform very similar and routine tasks. Modern production technology reduces complex tasks to more easily learned routine tasks. Assembly-line foremen, therefore, do not have to spend much time supervising any one subordinate.

Top-level managers manage other managers, and their work is not routine. Such a manager spends a considerable amount of time managing each subordinate. This means that the span of management is narrow. **This is why large firms usually have several echelons (layers or levels) of management.**

echelons of management

New technology is having an effect on the span of management. For example, large retail chain stores use computers to record sales of various products in each outlet. Computer use simplifies store managers' decisions about what to buy for their stores and makes it possible for a district manager to supervise a greater number of store managers.

There is no single generally accepted formula for determining the optimum span of management. But there are several factors that managers should consider in determining what their optimum span of management is. These include

- how well-defined the subordinates' jobs are and the complexity of their work
- the subordinates' training and ability to work with others
- the subordinates' motivation
- the pace of technological change in the industry
- ability of the manager and subordinate to communicate effectively with each other
- the manager's capability
- the manager's willingness and ability to plan, to delegate, and to evaluate subordinates' job performance

The Delegation Process

delegation

Without delegation, a firm could not be departmented. **Delegation means the entrusting of part of a superior's job (or activities) to a subordinate. Three actions are involved in the delegation process:**

- **assigning responsibility**
- **granting authority**
- **establishing accountability**

responsibility

Responsibility is the obligation of a subordinate to perform an assigned task. In delegating activities the superior assigns a responsibility to subordinates to carry out their assigned tasks.

authority

Authority is the counterpart of responsibility. **Authority is the right to take the action necessary to accomplish an assigned task.** Authority and responsibility must be balanced to enable subordinates to perform their assigned tasks.

accountability

Accountability is the act of holding subordinates, delegated adequate authority to fulfill their responsibilities, liable for performing their assigned tasks and for reporting results to their superiors. The subordinates are accountable to their superiors.

Roy manages a car tire shop. Sam removes old tires, Tom switches them on the rims, and Bill balances and remounts them. Roy assigned responsibility to them for performing these tasks and he also granted authority to them to use the necessary tools to accomplish their tasks. Roy also established accountability because the subordinates are answerable to him for results.

Delegation, however, does *not* relieve Roy of the responsibility for seeing to it that his subordinates do their jobs. If a customer's tires wear out because of faulty balancing, it is Roy's responsibility. In other words, the final responsibility rests with the person who is delegating. Roy is careful to delegate the proper amount of authority to the right subordinates but, in the final analysis, he is responsible for seeing to it that his subordinates actually carry out the tasks that are assigned to them.

The fact that delegation does not relieve a manager of responsibility makes some managers afraid to delegate. To delegate effectively managers must have faith in their subordinates' abilities, be willing to let them learn by their mistakes, and be willing to follow up on how well they are doing their jobs. Managers, therefore, should select qualified subordinates who are capable of performing their assigned tasks.

Span of management and delegation are closely related. Except for very small firms, no firm could function effectively without some delegation. Managers who are afraid to delegate do everything themselves. Their span of management is likely to be very narrow. A sole proprietor, for example, who refuses to delegate limits the size of his or her firm. It cannot expand beyond what the proprietor is capable of doing alone.

Centralization versus Decentralization of Authority

The amount of delegation in a firm determines how much the power to decide (authority) is concentrated. **Centralization of authority means that decision-making authority is concentrated in the hands of a few people at the top level of a firm. Such a firm is said to be relatively centralized.** Its managers believe that this centralization makes it easier to coordinate and control the firm's activities.

centralization

Decentralization of authority means that decision-making authority is spread throughout the firm. Such a firm is said to be relatively decentralized. Middle- and lower-level managers have more decision-making authority than in more centralized firms. This frees top-level managers to devote more time and effort to long-range planning.

decentralization

Centralization and decentralization of authority have nothing necessarily to do with geography. A firm with plants in many cities is not decentralized if decision-making power is concentrated at headquarters.

Types of Organizational Structures

There are three basic types of organizational structures:

- the line organization
- the line and staff organization
- the committee organization

The Line Organization

The line organization is the oldest and simplest type of organizational structure. It has been used by military organizations and the Roman Catholic Church and by business firms. In the military the general gives orders to the colonel, the colonel gives orders to the major, the major gives orders to the captain, the captain gives orders to the lieutenant, the lieutenant gives orders to the sergeant, the sergeant gives orders to the corporal, and the corporal gives orders to the private. The Pope is the head of the Roman Catholic Church and the chain of command extends downward through cardinals, archbishops, bishops, and priests.

line authority

From one point of view, line authority is the authority relationship that exists between superiors and subordinates. **Line authority is the right to direct subordinates' work.** In the line organization, as we have seen, the chain of command extends from the top to the bottom of the organization. At any given position in the chain, a person takes orders from people higher in the chain and gives orders to people lower in the chain.

Each superior has direct line authority over his or her subordinates, and each person in the organization reports directly to one boss. Each superior also has total authority over his or her assigned tasks. The major advantages of the line organization are

- the organizational structure is easy to understand
- each person has only one direct supervisor
- decisions may be made faster because each supervisor is accountable to only one immediate supervisor
- authority, responsibility, and accountability are defined clearly and exactly, which makes it hard to "pass the buck" to someone else

Despite its advantages the line organization suffers from some disadvantages that restrict its use in modern business to very small firms. The major disadvantages are

- each supervisor must be an expert in all aspects of his or her subordinates' work because there are no "specialists" or advisors to turn to
- the paperwork required in directly supervising each subordinate is a burden on each supervisor's time
- the organization has the potential of becoming too inflexible and too bureaucratic

The Line and Staff Organization

line functions

Another view of authority involves the distinction between line functions and staff functions. **Line functions contribute directly to reaching**

primary firm goals. For example, consider the case of a manufacturing firm whose primary goal is "to make a quality product and sell it at a fair price." The line functions are "production" and "marketing." For a retailer, "purchasing" and "selling" are the line functions. They are most directly concerned with achieving company goals. In a personal finance company, "lending" and "collecting" are the line functions.

Staff functions help the line to achieve primary firm goals. In the manufacturing firm above, "quality control" and "market research" are staff functions. Quality control helps the production manager to produce a quality product. Market research helps the marketing manager to sell it.

staff functions

The use of staff is one way to divide up the work of line managers. **Staff are people who advise and assist line managers to achieve company objectives.**

staff

The *personal staff* perform duties at the request of his or her line boss. The duties can range from opening the line manager's mail to representing the line manager at company meetings. Personal staff usually have the title of "assistant to."

Specialized staff serve the entire firm, not just one line manager. They have a high degree of expertise in their area of specialization. The marketing manager (a line executive) seeks advice from the director of marketing research (a staff executive) concerning whether or not to introduce a new product. The director of marketing research might also supply information to the production manager (a line executive) concerning sales forecasts so that production scheduling might be more efficient.

Staff people *serve* and *advise* line managers. In recent years there has been a tendency in many firms to add new staff positions. Computer specialists, tax-law experts, and other advisers and analysts are examples. These staff people cannot issue orders to line managers. They can only give line managers advice and assistance. But the head of a staff department, such as the director of marketing research, does have the necessary line authority to run the marketing research department.

As you might suspect from the above discussion, there is a lot of potential for line-staff conflict in a business firm. Figure 4–3 discusses the nature of this conflict. There are several ways to reduce this conflict. Some firms require line managers to consult staff people before making decisions on matters in the staff's area of expertise. In some cases the line manager need only discuss the matter and is not required to follow the staff's advice. In other cases the line manager must get the approval of the staff before making certain types of decisions. Thus a production manager has to clear new recruits with the personnel department before hiring them.

In still other cases the staff have authority to issue orders directly to line personnel. This is functional authority. It is granted only in the

functional authority

How staff sees line:

1. They get all the credit when things go right—we get the blame when things go wrong.
2. They have the final word, although we're trained experts in our fields.
3. They don't even want to try to see things from our point of view.
4. We may spend months developing recommendations, but they refuse even to listen to our advice, much less accept it.
5. They're older people who have been with the company so long that they're afraid to try new methods.
6. They resist change no matter what.

How line sees staff:

1. After all, I am the one who has the final word—they only give out advice.
2. There's only one right way—their way.
3. They can't even talk in English—it's always technical talk.
4. What he's doing now used to be part of my job.
5. They're know-it-all young college graduates who are always trying to change the way we do things around here.
6. They want to jump the gun without thinking through their ideas and recommendations.

FIGURE 4–3

Some potential sources of line-staff conflict

staff's area of expertise and only if it will benefit the firm. Thus a plant manager's authority over safety matters may be removed by superiors and given to a safety inspector who has authority to shut down the plant if dangerous working conditions exist.

Automation and computers enable some firms to eliminate some lower-level management jobs. Suppose a computer can do the same tasks as a lower-level manager at a lower cost. Chances are that the manager will be replaced. But since top managers often lack the technical know-how for using computers, they hire specialists (staff) to advise them. Thus instead of starting at the bottom of the line organization, many young technicians start in a staff position directly advising top management.

Staff status does *not* mean inferior status. Many staff specialists enjoy more pay and prestige than line managers. And, as we said earlier, staff executives do have line authority in their own departments.

The line and staff organization's major advantages are

- staff specialists are available to advise, support, and serve line executives
- line executives need not get bogged down in technical matters and can devote more time and energy to their line functions

The line and staff organization is the most widely used form of organization in contemporary business, especially among middle-sized and larger firms. But it does have several potential disadvantages:

- the potential for line-staff conflict
- the potential for going overboard in creating and filling unnecessary staff positions

PARKINSON'S LAW

As we have seen, one of the disadvantages of the line and staff organization is the potential for creating staff positions with little or no consideration to the need for those positions or the costs of staffing them.

Some managers tend to measure their own importance in the organization in terms of the number of staff specialists reporting to them, the amount of paperwork they can generate and receive, and the amount of increase in their budgets they can get approval for.

Paraphrasing two of Professor C. Northcote Parkinson's "laws" on bureaucracy

- work expands to fill the time allowed for completing it
- as budgets increase, work expands to fit them

Source: Parkinson, *Parkinson's Law.*

The Committee Organization

In the committee organizational structure, several persons share authority and responsibility for accomplishing an objective. Instead of reporting to one manager, subordinates may report to several. This form of organization, where it does exist, usually exists *within* the overall line and staff organization. Other names for committee organization are project management, program management, team management, and group management.

Some committees, such as company policy committees, are standing, or permanent, committees. Others are ad hoc committees that are formed to accomplish a particular objective and are disbanded after accomplishing it. An example is a committee formed to select the site for a new plant.

Many manufacturing firms have new product committees. Such a committee is made up of line and staff executives from various departments within the firm—accounting, finance, production, marketing, and engineering. The committee's job is to come up with new product ideas and develop them into marketable new products.

The major advantages of the committee form of organization are

- decisions are based on the combined expertise and judgment of committee members
- participation by persons in different departments may increase their commitment to committee decisions
- there is less chance of one person's biases affecting committee decisions

The major disadvantages of the committee form of organization are

- there is greater potential for buck-passing
- there is a tendency to take a long time in making a decision
- decisions often represent a compromise among the members rather than what might be best for the firm

The Organization Chart

organization chart

A firm's structure can be quite complex. **An organization chart helps us to understand a firm's structure. It graphically depicts a firm's formal structure at a given point in time.** It indicates

- the tasks that must be performed if the firm is to achieve its goals
- the lines of authority (chain of command)
- how the firm is departmented
- how the departments relate to each other
- the various positions and standing committees in the firm
- the titles of those positions

How complex these charts are depends on what management wants them to show. Generally, the larger the firm, the more complex the chart will be.

Figure 4–4 is an organization chart of a manufacturer. The top box shows the person who has final responsibility for the firm's management. In this case it is the president. But it could have been the chairperson of the board of directors. The vice-presidents of production and marketing report directly to the president. Plant superintendents A and B report directly to the vice-president of production. The other reporting relationships (the chain of command, or line authority) are indicated by the solid line. Notice the different echelons (levels) of management and the wider spans of management as we move down from the top.

FIGURE 4–4

The line and staff organization

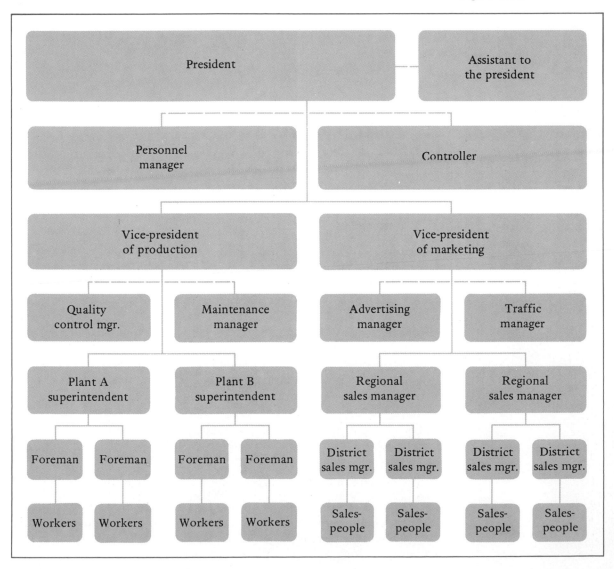

The staff organization is described by means of a broken line. The assistant to the president is personal staff. That assistant serves only the president. The personnel manager and the controller are specialized staff. They serve the entire firm. There is no functional authority in this firm. If the quality control manager did have functional authority over the plant superintendents, it would be shown on the chart by a dotted line.

From the chart we can infer something about the top-down delegation of authority. The president delegates to the vice-presidents of production and marketing who, in turn, delegate to the plant superintendents and regional sales managers.

An organization chart by itself does not tell the degree to which authority is delegated. A manager might be a manager in name only. Nor does it tell us anything about the *informal organization,* which we will discuss shortly.

The Dynamics of Organization

Organizations are dynamic, ever-changing structures. We hinted at this when we said that an organization chart depicts an organization's formal structure at a *given point in time.*

Some critics of the traditional line and staff organization say that it often is too inflexible. It is built on hierarchies of power in which orders are passed down the chain of command. People at the lower levels have to wait for "orders" from people at the higher levels, which may tend to reduce their initiative on the job. Meanwhile, rapid changes in technology, market conditions, and government regulations are taking an increasing amount of top management's time, which slows down their passing of "orders" down the chain of command.

One of the newer approaches to organization that still is evolving is the matrix structure, or matrix management. Firms like Shell Oil and General Electric are using it to regain some of the flexibility of smaller firms. They are pushing decision-making power down in the organization by structuring their organizations around *objectives* rather than authority relationships and by placing emphasis on teamwork.

For example, a firm that builds engineering equipment may have a production manager, a research and development (R&D) manager, and an engineering manager. (See Figure 4–5.) These are permanent functional departments and under these managers are production specialists, research scientists, and engineers, respectively. Suppose the firm has two projects under way. Project A requires the services of two engineers and a research scientist. These people are transferred temporarily from their functional departments to Project Manager A until the

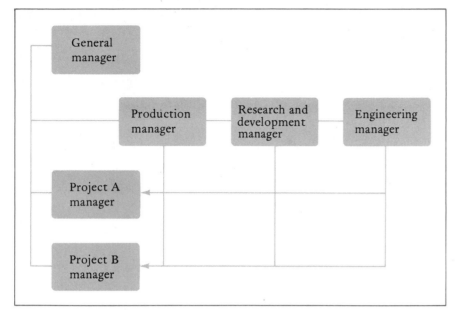

FIGURE 4–5

A matrix structure

project is completed. They are under Project Manager A's direction while they are assigned there.

Project B requires the services of two production specialists and one engineer. These people are transferred temporarily from their functional departments to Project Manager B until the project is completed. They are under Project Manager B's direction while they are assigned there.

By being able to reassign personnel based on task needs, the firm is able to make better use of its personnel. But the matrix structure can cause conflict and uncertainty because there may be dual and even triple lines of authority. In other words, a subordinate may be accountable to two or three superiors.

As we have seen, the traditional line and staff organization chart depicts the chain of command. Rensis Likert, a management theorist, has suggested the concept of "linking pins" in structuring an organization.[1] (See Figure 4–6.) Every manager, in reality, is a member of two groups. In one group, he or she interacts with superiors. In the other group, he or she interacts with subordinates. The manager can serve as a linking pin between these groups. The goal is to reduce the impersonality of hierarchical relationships among people in an organization and to integrate the work of people on different levels.

[1] Rensis Likert, *The Human Organization* (New York: McGraw-Hill Book Co., 1967), pp. 113–115.

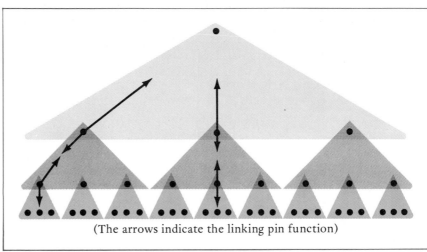

(The arrows indicate the linking pin function)

FIGURE 4–6

The linking pin

Source: Likert, *New Patterns of Management.*

Some of the newer ideas on organization have led to some modifications of the traditional line and staff organization. Typical examples of these modifications are

- wider spans of management
- greater decentralization
- less rigid chains of command
- authority based on knowledge instead of position

The Human Dimension of Organization

Psychologists tell us that a person is a unique being with a unique personality. No two people are exactly alike in terms of needs, wants, beliefs, values, and attitudes.

Although people are different, they all have certain basic needs. **Abraham H. Maslow arranged these needs in a hierarchy of needs.** (See Figure 4–7.) **The hierarchy is based on the prepotency (superiority) of needs.** They emerge in the following order:

hierarchy of needs

- **physiological needs**
- **safety needs**
- **belonging needs**
- **esteem needs**
- **self-actualization needs**[2]

[2] A. H. Maslow, "A Theory of Human Motivation," *Psychological Review*, 50 (1943), 370–396.

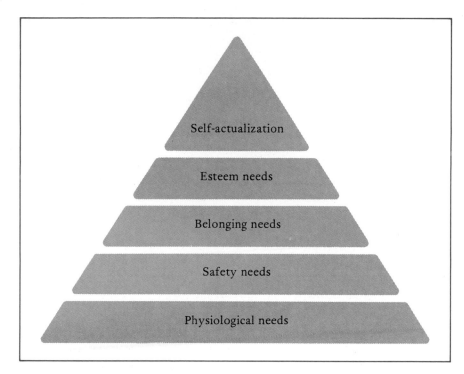

FIGURE 4–7

The hierarchy of human needs

The physiological needs (food, clothing, shelter, and sex) are the most prepotent of all needs. This means they must be satisfied before any of the higher-level needs can emerge and serve as motivators of behavior. If you are totally lacking in satisfaction of all needs in the hierarchy, your behavior will be motivated by the physiological needs. The other higher-level needs, for all practical purposes, do not exist for you. But when the physiological needs are satisfied, they cease to be motivators of behavior and higher-level needs emerge. Only unsatisfied needs can motivate behavior. Need satisfaction, however, need not be 100 percent. As lower-level needs become relatively satisfied, we are motivated mainly by the next higher level of unsatisfied need. The degree of need satisfaction required depends on the individual.

The safety needs are the next to emerge. These include the need to feel that you will survive and that your physiological needs will continue to be met. A cave dweller made a spear for protection against wild animals and other enemies. Our highly stable political and economic system helps to make most of us feel relatively safe from dangers such as starvation, tyrannical government, and severe economic collapse. The safety needs, for most adult Americans, are not active motivators of behavior. Of course, there are some people whose safety needs are relatively unsatisfied and their lives are dominated by those needs. This may be true in some of our crime-ridden urban areas. But there are other examples of the security needs. Job security, for example, is a major issue in many contracts negotiated by labor unions and employers. Nevertheless, we probably can consider physiological and safety needs as basic survival needs.

The belonging needs are more social in nature. They include social belonging, love, affection, affiliation, and membership needs. The family provides much of this but a business firm also can satisfy them by making the worker feel "needed." Coworkers can also satisfy these needs.

The esteem needs are of two basic types, social-esteem and self-esteem. Social-esteem needs (esteem from others) include prestige, status, and appreciation. They are your needs for relating to other people effectively. Self-esteem needs include competence and self-respect. These needs are very important because success in life leads us to undertake new challenges, whereas repeated failures tend to reduce our willingness to undertake new challenges. Self-esteem and self-actualization needs are our needs for personal growth.

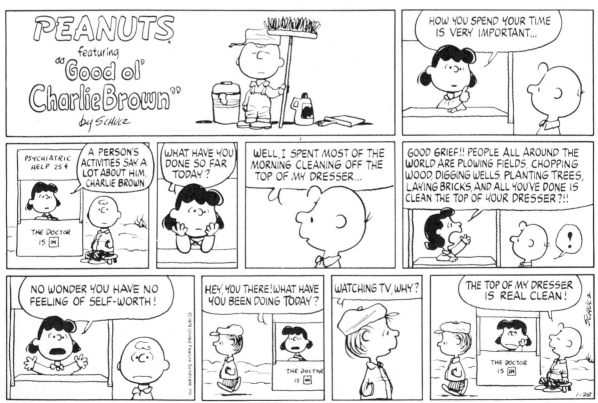

Source: *Peanuts*, © 1979 United Feature Syndicate, Inc.

Self-actualization includes the drive for achievement, creativity, and developing your attributes and capabilities. It is your need to achieve your potential in life, to become what you are capable of becoming. People who are seeking to achieve self-actualization are very concerned about using their time in an effective manner to accomplish tasks that they believe are worthwhile and challenging.

As we mature, we tend to move up in the hierarchy of wants. The behavior of infants, for example, is dominated by the physiological and safety needs. Older children and adolescents are more aware of others and their behavior usually is dominated by social needs. Their primary concern is "fitting in" and "belonging"—being like others with whom they associate instead of "being different." Normally, we tend to be motivated more by ego needs as we mature more fully. At some point in our teenage years, therefore, we become more motivated by self-esteem and self-actualization needs. We want to assert our independence.

THINK ABOUT IT!

Personal and Organizational Objectives and Values

The organizational structure in many firms often serves as a source of conflict between the personal objectives and values of employees and the objectives and values of the organization itself.

Many people today, for example, place a high value on personal freedom, control over their own lives, privacy, equal opportunity and treatment, self-expression, personal involvement, and personal growth. These personal values carry over to their world of work.

But in many large organizations, employees face a bureaucratic structure whose objectives and values are very different. The management hierarchy is based on positional authority, jobs are highly specialized and often boring, policies and procedures spell out required behavior on the job, and the activities and accomplishments of employees are reported in great detail to people higher up in the chain of command. THINK ABOUT IT!

The challenge for business today is to provide jobs for employees that offer rewards beyond those that satisfy only physiological and safety needs. Money, by itself, loses some of its power to motivate as we move up the need hierarchy, which is not to say that money is not a motivator. Money can help in satisfying higher-level needs just as it can help in satisfying physiological and safety needs. For example, many people judge themselves in terms of how much money they earn. For them, money is related to the need for self-esteem. Likewise, money can give social esteem to the person who likes to brag about being a $100,000-a-year executive.

Money, however, basically is an *extrinsic* reward for work, which means that the reward does not come from the work itself. But there are other rewards that are part of the work itself. These are called *intrinsic* rewards. Social esteem can come from job titles and status symbols such as carpeting on the office floor and a key to the executive washroom. Self-esteem comes from competent performance on the job.

In our society the need to achieve one's potential in life (self-actualization) very often involves one's work. Top-level executives and owner-managers, for example, often say that their work is their life. Work can satisfy a wide range of needs for these people. But this view of work is not shared by all people. Some people consider their work to be a sort of necessary evil that must be performed in order to satisfy their basic physiological and safety needs. They tend to look away from the job to satisfy their higher-level needs. As we will see in our next chapter, managers use different approaches to leading their subordinates because managers know that work does not have the same meaning to all people.

Why Do Groups Exist?

In our economy people have become less self-sufficient and more group dependent because of specialization. Groups either enable us to do things that we could not do alone or help us to do them more efficiently.

Human beings are social animals. Our behavior is influenced by our awareness of others, and we tend to behave toward others as we think they expect us to behave. All of us are subject to group influence and pressure. We are pressured to conform to group standards of conduct. Conformity keeps the group together and working toward its goals. *Socialization,* the process by which human beings become social beings, enables a person to become accepted by and integrated into groups. A worker, for example, becomes accepted as a member of a group on the job by learning how to interact with its members.

Groups in the Modern Environment

In a large factory, a boss knows very little about the total personalities of subordinates and vice versa. As long as the job gets done, a boss may not be concerned about the other aspects of a subordinate's life. Life outside of our most intimate, face-to-face groups has, in many cases, become more impersonal.

A person's role in some groups is very formal and governed by rules. This formality is often true of the employer-employee relationship. In a sole proprietorship, the worker and the owner-manager work out pay arrangements, hours of work, and other aspects of the job on a face-to-face basis. In a large corporation, most employees do not even know the president. To the average factory worker, the employer is his or her immediate supervisor. Often the employer is represented by hired managers, and the workers are represented by union negotiators.

The Informal Organization

People on the job work and live together. They develop shared habits, customs, and patterns of behavior and beliefs. This interaction leads to the formation of informal groups. **Informal groups are small, face-to-face groups that spring up naturally as a result of human interaction on the job. They are created by their members to satisfy wants that are not being satisfied on the job by management.**

informal groups

Workers are influenced in their attitudes and behavior by the social groups they create to meet their personal needs. These interpersonal relationships cannot always be controlled by management. Employees interact in ways that are not always prescribed in the employee hand-

TABLE 4-1

Informal and formal dimensions of the business organization

Characteristic	Informal	Formal
1. Nature of the business organization	A social organization	An economic organization
2. Central concern	Human interaction	Profit
3. Members seek to satisfy	Social needs	Economic needs
4. Structure	Informal, determined by voluntary patterns of interaction	Formal, determined by management
5. Communication	Face-to-face, employee grapevine	Chain of command
6. Leaders	Chosen by members	Appointed by management
7. Commitment of members	Emotional	Limited personal involvement
8. Composed of	Small, social groups	Departments
9. Contact among members	Close, personal, face-to-face	Impersonal, often indirect contact through the chain of command
10. Human interaction	Spontaneous and natural	Determined by management

book. A business firm, therefore, is a social as well as an economic organization.

Within every formal organization there is an informal organization. **The informal organization is the entire complex of informal groups that exists within the framework of the formal organization. It exists within the formal organization but is separate from it.** Human interaction in the formal organization is structured by management. Interaction arises naturally in the informal organization as a result of our social nature.

How and with whom a worker chooses to interact can affect that worker's job performance. Some interactions may harm a person's job performance. Others may improve it. An employee may learn good work habits by associating with other more experienced employees. Another employee may learn bad habits by associating with careless workers.

Harry Thompson is a new management trainee at Brigdon Corporation. This is his first job after graduating from City College. As a new employee, Harry was introduced to his immediate boss and several coworkers. He was given information about the company, its objectives, and how he fits into the picture. After touring the plant, meeting a lot of people, and completing numerous personnel forms, Harry returned to his new office. His formal introduction to the job was over.

Suppose that Harry met two old friends who were former students at City College. They graduated one year before him and have been in the management-trainee program at Brigdon since then. Harry probably will ask them questions. Now that he knows all the rules and what he's supposed to do, he asks his friends about "how things really are." If Harry had no old friends at Brigdon, he would try to talk to others who have only recently been hired. They, too, want to "talk it over" with people "on the same level."

Because of his need for information, Harry begins to interact with other people in ways that are not dictated by management. Although he was required to attend the formal orientation sessions, no one told him to seek out the advice of fellow employees. No one told him to let those other employees influence his behavior.

Workers learn customs and develop habits through their job experiences. Doing things "according to the book" often is abandoned in favor of shortcuts they learn on the job. The many informal, interpersonal relationships that exist in a firm lead to the formation of social groups. They are relatively small and their members stick together because they share common values and goals. You become a group member when the group decides that you are a member. A young college graduate assigned to the production department, for example, may find it harder to be accepted than another person closer to the educational level of the group.

informal organization

Group leaders in informal groups are selected from their membership. Thus even though Shannon Arnold may be the foreman appointed by management, Joe Smith is the person to whom the employees under Shannon go to "air their gripes." Joe has the "inside track" with Shannon's superiors. Joe has been around for a long time and knows "what's happening." He understands the workers' problems and knows how to "take care of them."

Groups develop norms, or standards of behavior, and they pressure their members to conform to them. Members who go against those standards are punished. A worker who produces "too much" may be rejected by the group.

Since informal groups are based on interpersonal relationships, any changes that threaten to disrupt them are resisted. When changes in work assignments break up the coffee group, resistance will develop. It may take the form of workers asking why the change was made. It may even lead to a slowdown.

Informal groups, therefore

- are small in size
- are created by their members
- arise naturally and spontaneously
- have leaders
- resist change
- are cohesive (members stick together)
- have close contact among members
- develop norms of behavior
- enjoy emotional commitment of members
- have rapid communication of facts and rumors through the communications "grapevine"
- satisfy needs that are not satisfied by the formal organization

Member Benefits from Informal Groups

A worker usually belongs to several informal groups. Each satisfies different needs. Tom belongs to one group whose members work together in the receiving department. Their physical closeness on the job provides a basis for grouping.

Tom cashes his weekly check in a local tavern where he and several workers from other departments talk over their town's professional football club. They also talk over the "goings on" in their different departments.

Suppose Tom's boss recently hired someone with new ideas on running the department. If Tom and the older employees see this as a threat to their usual ways of doing things, they might form an informal group to "keep the new boss in line."

Sometimes overspecialization of labor places workers in boring jobs. Informal groups help their members relate to the formal organization. Membership in informal groups provides relief from boredom. It enables members to feel human on the job even though they may perform mechanical tasks. Beth Welles works on an auto assembly line. She may not feel that she is a real part of the company, however. Her contacts and experiences in informal groups help her to feel like "somebody."

For some workers, the only needs satisfied by the firm are physiological and safety needs. The paycheck buys groceries and the union contract gives some job security. But the higher-level needs often are unsatisfied. The need to belong is an example.

Beth Welles may know that she is an important part of the lunch group because she is included in their plans. On the other hand, she may feel that the firm would hardly miss her, even if she were to die. Nor does the job itself give her much self-esteem. She is "Beth" only to her immediate boss and close friends. The payroll clerk, the timekeeper, the plant superintendent, and others know her only as badge number 121. She feels unimportant to them. This is not true when she bowls with several coworkers. Thus Beth needs to feel important to herself, and she wants others to look upon her as "somebody."

As individuals mature, they become increasingly conscious of their "selves." They want more independence. A worker who has to punch in, punch out, eat, rest, and wash up at a certain time is, in many respects, being treated like a child. That worker seeks an outlet for developing some degree of independence on the job.

Workers also want to feel that they are doing something worthwhile and that they are important for what they do. Workers who perform similar tasks recognize their particular contributions. An informal group may develop to help maintain a feeling of achievement. All the workers know and respect Jerry as the best person in the plant with an acetylene torch even though Jerry may receive no formal recognition from management. The realities of the informal organization are a vital part of the way a firm works—or doesn't work.

Summary and Look Ahead

An organization is a logical combination of human, financial, and physical resources put together by management so that certain goals can be accomplished. Businesses and their employees seek to accomplish objectives. Company and personal goals, therefore, must be integrated so that employees will strive to accomplish company goals as well as personal goals. Because perfect integration is impossible, firms must suboptimize objectives.

Activities are the connecting link between the objectives and the structure of a firm. Activities are determined by breaking down broad company goals into specific ones for each worker. Departmentation means these activities are grouped and assigned to various departments.

How many subordinates a manager can manage depends on many factors. Upper-level managers, however, usually manage fewer subordinates (a narrow span of management) than do lower-level managers.

Delegation means a superior entrusts part of his or her activities to a subordinate. It involves: (1) assigning responsibility, (2) granting authority, and (3) establishing accountability. Responsibility is the obligation of a subordinate to perform an assigned task. Authority is the right to take the action necessary to accomplish an assigned task. Accountability is the act of holding subordinates liable for performing their assigned tasks and for reporting results to their superiors. There is little delegation in highly centralized organizations because the decision-making power is concentrated at the top.

There are three basic types of organization structures: (1) line, (2) line and staff, and (3) committee. Line authority (the chain of command) is the right to direct subordinates' work, and line functions contribute directly to reaching primary firm goals. Staff functions help the line to perform line functions. Staff people advise and serve line managers. The authority of staff people to issue orders to line personnel is called functional authority.

A firm has a social dimension that is not shown on its organization chart. Maslow's hierarchy of needs is helpful in understanding that workers have needs that must be satisfied on the job. Many of these needs are social needs. If not met by the formal organization itself, these needs lead to the formation of informal groups. The groups are small, face-to-face groups whose members stick together to achieve their goals. Their activities may help or hinder the firm's efforts to accomplish organizational goals. The collection of small informal groups in a firm is the informal organization.

In the next chapter, we look at the organization in terms of its management. We will study the management functions of planning, organizing, staffing, directing, and controlling.

Let's assume you have resisted the urge to start your own business. Let's assume further that you choose to work for a medium- to large-sized firm. This chapter discusses what staff and line positions are. What are *you*, a line person or a staff person?	**LINE OR STAFF CAREER?**

The big difference is that line people make the decisions and control the "mainstream" activities of the firm—producing and selling goods and services. Starting with the first-line supervisor and working up the organization, being "in the line" takes self-confidence and decisiveness—not unlike what it takes to run your own business. It will take a large measure of skills in human relations, too. The higher you get, the more breadth of vision it takes—being able to see the whole picture.

Staff positions are not easy to describe because they are so varied. A personal staff-assistant position often requires helping to deal with important people and important problems, but only with those problems your boss [line] assigns you and without making major decisions of your own. If you are an efficient follower and don't mind "avoiding the limelight," a staff-assistant position may be for you.

If you have attained a special skill—as a lawyer, an accountant, a statistician or creative artist—you may fill a staff-specialist position. This means you do special tasks a line officer hasn't the expertise or the time to do. You might have to write technical reports to help a line manager decide whether to sign an important contract or not. As you progress as a staff specialist, you might head a department of your own, such as the market research department of a firm. This will require more than a specialized skill in that area. It will take some of the same skills in human relations the line person needs.

What are you likely to be best at—line or staff work?

Key Concepts

accountability Subordinates to whom adequate authority has been delegated to fulfill their responsibilities are accountable, or answerable, to their superiors for results. The requirement for subordinates to report results to their superiors.

authority The right to take the action necessary to accomplish an assigned task. Power to make decisions.

centralization The concentration of decision-making power at the top level of an organization. Managers in centralized organizations disperse very little authority throughout the organization.

decentralization The dispersion of decision-making power in an organization. Managers in decentralized organizations disperse considerable authority throughout the organization.

delegation The process of entrusting part of a superior's job (or activities) to a subordinate. Involves the three actions of assigning responsibility, granting authority, and establishing accountability.

departmentation The process of identifying, grouping, and assigning organizational activities to specific departments within the organization. The result is a departmented, or departmentalized, organization.

echelons of management The different layers, or levels, of management in an organization, that is, upper, middle, and lower.

functional authority Authority of the staff to issue orders directly to line managers. This authority is granted only in the staff's area of expertise. An example is a quality control manager who can order the production manager to shut down the plant under certain conditions, such as when a high number of defective products are being produced.

hierarchy of needs A. H. Maslow's ranking of human needs: physiological, safety, belonging, esteem, and self-actualization needs. The lowest level of needs, the physiological needs, are the most prepotent. They are the first to emerge.

hierarchy of organizational objectives A breakdown of broad, overall organizational objectives into divisional, departmental, work-group, and individual worker objectives. The individual worker helps the firm to realize its objectives by helping his or her work group, department, and division to achieve their objectives.

informal groups Face-to-face groups that are created by their members to satisfy needs that are not being satisfied on the job by management. They arise naturally as a result of human interaction on the job.

informal organization The entire complex of informal groups that exists within the framework of the formal organization but is separate from it.

line authority The right to direct subordinates' work. The authority relationship that exists between superiors and subordinates. The chain of command.

line functions Organizational functions that contribute directly to reaching primary firm goals. Production and marketing are line functions in a manufacturing firm.

organization Something that is structured so that human activity can be coordinated to accomplish objectives. The three basic components (people, activities, and physical resources) are related to each other through the organizing process.

organization chart A diagram showing an organization's formal structure at a given point in time. It indicates the tasks that must be performed if the organization is to accomplish its objectives, the chain of command, how the firm is departmented, how the departments relate to each other, the various positions in the organization, and the titles of these positions.

responsibility The obligation of a subordinate to perform an assigned task.

span of management A term that refers to the number of subordinates an individual manager supervises. Also called span of control.

staff Persons who advise, serve, assist, and support line managers in their work of achieving primary company goals. Personal staff perform duties for one line executive to whom he or she is "assistant to." Specialized staff serve the entire firm.

staff functions Organizational functions that help the line to achieve primary firm goals. Quality control and market research are staff functions in a manufacturing firm.

For Review . . .

1. Why is formal structure necessary in a business organization?
2. Why do formal organizations suboptimize personal and organizational objectives?
3. What is meant by the hierarchy of organizational objectives?

4. Why are business organizations departmented?
5. List the six bases upon which an organization can be departmented and give an example of each.
6. How are the concepts of delegation, span of

management, departmentation, and decentralization related?

7. Discuss the relative advantages and disadvantages of (a) the line organization, (b) the line and staff organization, and (c) the committee organization.
8. What does an organization chart indicate? What aspects of organization does it not indicate?
9. Discuss four modifications of the traditional line and staff organization that have been made by some firms.
10. Discuss Maslow's hierarchy of needs.
11. Contrast the formal organization and the informal organization.

. . . For Discussion

1. Are there any organizational objectives that are common to organizations in general (such as charitable, educational, religious, business, or fraternal organizations)? Are there any objectives that are common to all business organizations?
2. For years the federal government and many state legislatures have talked about the need to consolidate many of the activities that are currently spread out over various departments. Why is this? Does this have any implications for business firms? Explain.
3. "Staff positions generally are dead-end jobs in most companies." Do you agree?
4. Do informal groups exist only in large businesses?
5. How might the informal group put pressure on its members to get them to conform to group standards?

Incidents

Last Chance for British Leyland Motor Corporation

"When the Labor government reluctantly agreed to take over nearly bankrupt British Leyland Motor Corp. in 1975, it publicly warned the maker of Jaguar, Morris, Triumph and Rover cars that it would not throw good money after bad. The price of government cash for new-car development and badly overdue plant modernization was to be an end to the constant bickering that has pitted unions against management and against each other. For two years, the warning was mostly ignored, and Leyland continued on the road to collapse.

"[In November, 1977] its prospects for survival suddenly improved. Rejecting the advice of militant [union leaders], Leyland's 100,000 car workers voted 2 to 1 for a package of bargaining reforms that holds at least some hope of ending labor anarchy. The results of the vote came on the first day in office of Michael Edwardes, who was named chairman by the government, getting his term off to an auspicious start. . . .

"Leyland was originally formed by a jerry-built amalgam of smaller companies, and that is now one reason for its troubles. Its crazy-quilt wage bargaining structure forces management to deal with 58 different bargaining units at its 34 plants; executives are involved in some kind of labor negotiation for nearly nine months of every year. Strikes, many prompted by wage differentials from plant to plant, break out frequently, with or without union authorization. . . .

"The government, which now owns 95% of Leyland's stock, has passed the word that it would advance no more cash to Leyland if centralized bargaining were rejected—a move that would have meant the company's demise. The workers apparently believed that London really meant it.

"New Chairman Edwardes, consequently, will have time to try to make sense out of Leyland's disorganized management structure. . . .

"Though he will have to negotiate a company-wide pact, Edwardes is a fervent believer in decentralized management who pledges to use 'ruthless logic' in organizing executive teams to run Leyland as a group of 'profit centers.' He had better hurry. His appointment is for three years . . . and government officials make it clear that they regard those three years as giving Edwardes a 'last chance' to save the company."

Questions

1. Why is there always some degree of conflict between organizational and personal objectives?
2. What advice would you give Mr. Edwardes to help reduce the conflict between the employees and management?
3. Do you think that a decentralized management structure will help Leyland to become profitable? Why or why not?

Source: *Time.*

Lee Iacocca Takes Over at Chrysler

"[In July, 1978], one of Detroit's sharpest marketing men was abruptly ousted after 32 years at Ford, the last eight years as president. . . . Ford had announced a severance agreement with [Lee] Iacocca that granted him a termination payment of $400,000 plus a separation payment of $275,000; he also stood to get $1.1 million in additional payments, on condition he did not go to another auto company. . . .

"[Within a few months, however, Mr. Iacocca was hired by Chrysler to be its new president.] Iacocca insisted on being given a free hand in running Chrysler's day-to-day affairs. . . . [Chrysler's Chairman, John J. Riccardo] announced that he [would] turn over his job as chief executive officer to Iacocca [in 1979] and devote most of his energies to Government relations and Chrysler's finances. . . .

"Riccardo [said] he recruited Iacocca because Chrysler 'needed additional firepower.' While Ford and General Motors [were] both enjoying robust sales and profits, Chrysler [was] in the midst of its worst year since 1975, when it lost $260 million. . . .

"Iacocca [said] that he would like to see his new employer develop a 'sports car,' suggesting that something like the Mustang, which made Iacocca's reputation as a marketing whiz at Ford, may be in Chrysler's future. . . . Whether Iacocca will succeed in turning the company around remains to be seen. But Chrysler is betting a bundle he can do just that."

Questions

1. How important do you think work is to Mr. Iacocca?
2. Why do you think Mr. Iacocca insisted on having a free hand in running Chrysler?

Source: *Time.*

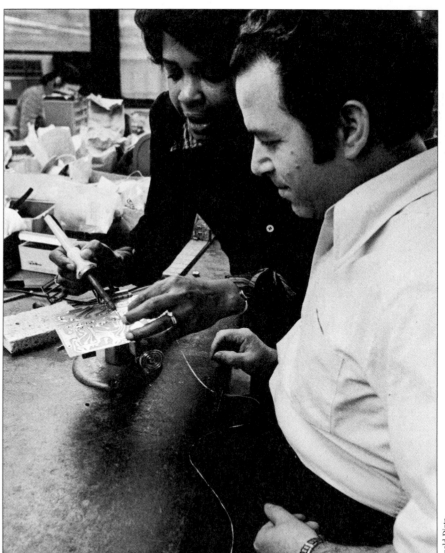

Management

CHAPTER
5

Objectives: After reading this chapter, you should be able to

1. Distinguish between managerial work and nonmanagerial work and relate these types of work to the echelons of management.
2. List and discuss the managerial skills and relate these skills to the echelons of management.
3. Discuss the sources of stress on the job and how managers and workers can deal with stress.
4. List and define the functions of management and tell why they are interdependent.
5. Discuss the concept of management by objectives.
6. Interrelate the systems concept to the practice of management.
7. Contrast Theory X managers and Theory Y managers.
8. Contrast motivational factors and maintenance factors in the motivation-hygiene theory and the theory's relationship to job enrichment.
9. Contrast the "great person" theory of leadership to "traitist theory" and discuss several different types of leadership styles.
10. Illustrate the control process by means of a chart.
11. Identify and discuss the stages in the decision-making process.

Key concepts: Look for these terms as you read the chapter

manager	directing
management	participative management
managerial skills	communication
functions of management	motivation
planning	job enrichment
strategic planning	leadership
operational planning	controlling
management by objectives (MBO)	decision-making process
	routine decision
organizing	nonroutine decision
systems concept	management by exception
staffing	

In the previous chapter we discussed the process of structuring the formal organization. This structure is the framework within which certain activities are performed. Any firm, however, is much more than a structure. It is a "living thing" in which effort is exerted to accomplish results.

Managers perform managerial work and nonmanagers perform nonmanagerial work so that the firm can achieve its objectives. These functions of management are (1) planning, (2) organizing, (3) staffing, (4) directing, and (5) controlling. Let's begin our study of these functions by examining the nature of management.

The Nature of Management

There are two basic types of work in any organization:

- nonmanagerial work (operative tasks)
- managerial work (the functions of management)

Auto assembly-line workers perform operative tasks such as tightening bolts; and football players block, punt, and tackle. But the president of Ford Motor Company or the head coach of the Dallas Cowboys ordinarily do not perform these operative tasks. They spend their time planning company and team strategy and performing the other functions of management.

    A manager is a person who works through other people (subordinates). These subordinates perform operative tasks. A manager "brings together" their efforts to accomplish goals. Of course, nonhuman resources, such as money and materials, also are involved.

    Management can mean the process of managing, a collection of managers, or an area of study. **Our primary definition of management is the process of achieving goals through the efforts of others.** Management is necessary in any organization that seeks to accomplish objectives. Without it, an organization becomes a collection of individuals, each going in his or her own direction with no unifying guidance toward organizational goals. The most important ingredient in a firm's ability to reach its goals is the quality of its managers. To look at it from another angle, poor management is the basic cause of business failures.

manager

management

The Echelons of Management

The concept of the echelons of management was introduced in Chapter 4. Figure 5–1 shows three levels of management that are found in most medium-sized and large firms—top, middle, and lower (operative) management. In very small firms, the owner(s) usually is (are) the only manager. In very large firms, there may be more than three levels of management.

Members of top management work through a greater number of subordinates than middle- and lower-level managers, and they very seldom perform any operative tasks. Members of middle management report to top management. They are accountable for carrying out top management's plans. Their perspective is more short-run than top management's because they are closer to the firm's day-to-day activities. They also perform more operative tasks than top managers. Members of lower management report to middle management. Operating managers are the managers closest of all to the operative tasks in the firm. A foreman on an assembly line, for example, may get some grease on his or her hands and clothing. It is very unlikely that a top-level manager would.

In other words, the higher the level of management, the more time a manager spends performing managerial work. The lower the level of management, the more time a manager spends performing operative tasks. (See Figure 5–2.)

FIGURE 5–1

The management pyramid

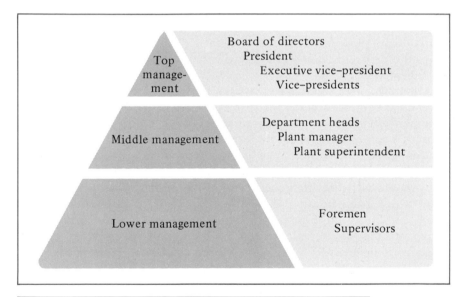

FIGURE 5–2

The relative importance of managerial and nonmanagerial work at various levels of the management hierarchy

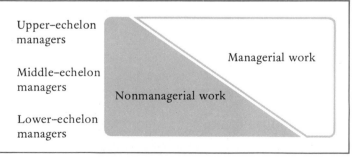

Managerial Skills

All managers, regardless of their level, must have three basic manage-   managerial skills
rial skills:

- **conceptual skills**
- **"people" skills (human relations, communication, motivation, and leadership skills)**
- **technical skills**

Conceptual skills give a manager the ability to see the organization as a whole—to see it as a complex of interacting and interdependent parts. Such skills also allow a manager to see how an organization is related to its environment.

Managers who have these skills can think creatively, analytically, and imaginatively. They can identify and solve problems and come up with new approaches to the management process. They do not look at the organization as a collection of different departments but as a whole. Conceptual skills are crucial for long-range planning and are most important at the upper echelons of management.

People skills include human relations skills, the manager's ability to get along and work with people, including both superiors and subordinates. Managers have to work effectively as group members in order to build a team effort. People skills also include communication, motivation, and leadership skills. They are the most important of the managerial skills and are discussed in more detail later in this chapter.

Effective managers view their subordinates as human assets and strive to create a work environment in which subordinates will put forth their best efforts to reach the firm's goals. Developing this human resource is a crucial task for all managers. People skills, therefore, are equally important at all echelons of management.

Technical skills are the manager's ability to understand and use techniques, methods, equipment, and procedures. It is the ability to understand how "things" operate. These skills are most important at the operative management level. Foremen, for example, must know how to operate the machinery their subordinates use. As a manager moves up the management hierarchy, technical skills become less important relative to the conceptual and people skills.

The higher a manager is in the management hierarchy, the more important it is to have knowledge in many areas. He or she must be a generalist, one who has a broad general knowledge. One of the toughest tasks for some younger managers is to broaden their outlook, to stop looking at their job from the viewpoint of their former job. Fortunately each of the managerial skills can be developed if a person is willing to work hard to learn them. They do not have to be "inborn."

Effective managers are willing to learn. They keep up with develop-

THINK ABOUT IT!

Upper-level Managers Are Very Mobile

> The higher a manager is in the management hierarchy, the more important conceptual and people skills become relative to technical skills. Technical skills are the most difficult to transfer from one industry to another. It is harder for lower-level managers, whose major skill is technical skill, to move from one industry to another than it is for those managers in higher levels. Conceptual and people skills are more transferable. Upper-level managers are very mobile. They can move from one industry to another because all organizations require their conceptual and people skills. THINK ABOUT IT!

ments in their field and in related fields and seek to apply useful knowledge to the management job. Management is partly a science because managers use organized knowledge in carrying out their functions. Production and marketing managers use formulas developed by statisticians to manage inventories, to schedule production, and to plan and control the distribution of their products. They also use knowledge in the fields of sociology and psychology in managing people. They borrow knowledge from other disciplines to improve their managerial skills.

Management also is an art. Through experience, managers develop judgment, insight, intuition, and a general "feel" for the management job. These are subjective skills that are learned through training and experience.

In general, management tends to be more science at the lower echelons and more art at the upper echelons. Staff people, for example, who advise top managers supply them with the "facts" they need to make decisions. In making their decisions, however, top managers often have to temper the objective facts with subjective judgment.

Other Aspects of Managerial Work

Effective managers are goal oriented. They can set goals and put forth the effort needed to accomplish them. They also have a high achievement need and recognize the value of time. Time is one of the scarcest resources of managers, and they know how to manage it productively. They can cram more into an 24-hour day than people who have a lower need for achievement. Hourly workers, such as carpenters and plumbers, receive overtime pay if they work overtime. Managers do not receive overtime pay. Their work hours are not set out as an "eight-hour day." Managerial work also is a stress-creating type of work.

Actually, nonmanagerial and managerial work both involve stress because individuals must subordinate, to some degree, their individuality and personal goals to the organization if it is to be effective. Since managers must work through the efforts of subordinates, they must help them to manage their stress. Line and staff conflict, personality conflicts, the potential for conflict between different departments, and the conflict between labor and management are only a few of the sources of organizational conflict.

Conflict can disrupt the smooth functioning of a firm and contribute to stress among workers and managers. Conflict, however, also can benefit the firm; it often leads to new ways of doing things, and it brings deep-seated problems to the surface where they can be dealt with. The accompanying tension often stimulates the flow of creative new ideas. Management, therefore, should try to control conflict, not eliminate it.

A person who perceives an assigned task to be important but too demanding experiences stress. It is stressful because the person expects that his or her costs and benefits for meeting the challenge are different from those of failing to meet it. It is a person's perception of the task's difficulty that influences the amount of stress that will emerge. People who have a high degree of self-confidence usually will perceive less difficulty in accomplishing a task than people who lack self-confidence.

Stress on the job can come from within a person or from his or her work environment. Internal sources include low self-confidence, poor health, low tolerance for frustration, and a tendency to set unattainable goals for oneself. Examples of external sources are boring and monotonous work, too much responsibility, too little time to do the assigned work, and poor supervision.

Organizations are limited in their ability to control stress because of its highly personal nature. A top manager who is under stress because of family problems, for example, does not want to "hang the laundry out" for all to see. There is, however, growing concern in business to help workers and managers to cope with stress. "Workaholics" can be required to take time off for vacations. Many firms encourage employees to use coffee breaks as "exercise breaks" to help relieve tension on the job.

How a person copes with stress is an individual decision. Some people try to escape it by reducing their achievement drive, drinking excessively, overeating, or taking tranquilizers. Others face it in a more constructive way. Managers who feel under stress because they neglect their children may reorient their value systems and place limits on how much time and effort they are willing to give the company.

In recent years many managers and their companies have become more aware of the importance of coping with stress and strengthening the cardiovascular system. Approaches and techniques range from exercise and recreation to biofeedback and transcendental meditation (TM). Perhaps the major development in stress management has been the trend toward employer-sponsored fitness programs. More than 400 major corporations and perhaps thousands of smaller firms have employee exercise plans. Some firms have their own gyms and some pay all or part of the cost of individual membership in fitness clinics.

The Functions of Management

functions of management

Managerial work consists of performing the functions of management:

- **planning**
- **organizing**
- **staffing**
- **directing**
- **controlling**

Dividing managerial work into functions helps us to understand its nature but, in the real world, managerial work cannot be divided into component parts. These functions are performed at the same time and are interdependent.

Planning

planning

Planning means preparing a firm to cope with the future. It involves setting the firm's objectives over different time periods and deciding on the methods of achieving them.

Setting Objectives

Since a firm is an economic and social organization, its objectives are both economic and social. An economic objective of most firms is to produce and sell products or services that satisfy customer wants at a profit to the firm. Other objectives are:

- to maximize profits
- to achieve a 15 percent rate of return on investment
- to increase market share by 10 percent

Greater awareness of the social responsibility of business has led to growing attention to social objectives. Large corporations especially recognize that cooperation in attaining social objectives is in their long-run interest. Some examples of these social objectives are:

- to provide employment opportunities for the disadvantaged unemployed
- to support the arts
- to improve race relations in the community

Plans can be long-range, intermediate-range, or short-range. These periods, however, are not easily defined in terms of years and months. Long-range planning for Gulf Oil, Xerox Corporation, and United Airlines may cover a period of 10 or more years in the future. Long-range planning for a small apparel store may cover a period of six months to one year. How far ahead a firm plans (its planning horizon) depends on the particular industry a firm is in, its technology, and its products.

Long-range planning makes it easier for a firm to adapt to a changing environment. The purpose is not to show how well the firm can predict the future but to gain insight into the actions the firm has to take in the present to help ensure that it will, in fact, have a future.

There are two basically different types of planning: strategic planning and operational planning.

Strategic planning is concerned with a firm's long-range future and its overall strategy of growth. This is the type of planning for which top-level managers are responsible. **strategic planning**

Operational planning is planning for the day-to-day survival of the firm. Middle and lower-level managers engage mainly in this type of planning. (See Figure 5–3.) **operational planning**

Regardless of the time frame for a particular objective, it generally is accepted that sound objectives should

- be specific
- be measurable and, if possible, quantified
- identify expected results
- be reachable with reasonable effort
- be expressed within a time frame for accomplishing them

The person or department responsible for accomplishing them should have the necessary authority to accomplish them in order to prevent buck passing.

During recent years many managers have been adopting the management by objectives (MBO), or managing by results, approach. The **management by objectives (MBO)**

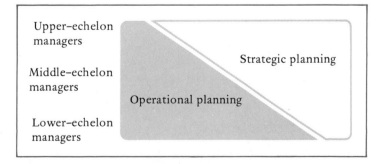

FIGURE 5–3

The relative importance of strategic and operational planning at various levels of the management hierarchy

BUSINESS AND CORPORATE STRATEGIES

> Many large corporations have operations spread throughout many different types of industries. For example, International Telephone and Telegraph (ITT) is in communications, real estate, car rentals, insurance, banking, and book publishing. Such a corporation is called a conglomerate. Planning in these companies requires the chief executive officer to understand the basic difference between business strategies and corporate strategies.
>
> A business strategy usually covers a plan for a single product or group of related products, while a corporate strategy, in today's world of conglomerates, seeks to unify all the business lines of a company and point them toward an overall goal.
>
> Corporate strategies require the chief executive officer to set clearly-defined long-range goals for their total companies and to develop a rational plan for implementing those goals.

Source: *Business Week.*

manager gets together with each subordinate to set his or her objectives. The subordinate participates in goal setting and, if the objectives are accomplished, the subordinate is considered to have performed well. It's the result that counts!

MBO offers the following advantages:

- subordinates know at the beginning of a planning period what is expected of them, thereby reducing their uncertainty about what they are supposed to accomplish
- subordinates often enjoy participating with superiors in determining a method for measuring their performance, which increases their motivation to reach the objectives
- subordinates are given more opportunity to use new approaches to reaching their objectives since MBO does not predetermine the means for reaching objectives
- managers have more confidence in future planning and in predicting results

Managers who use the MBO approach assume that their subordinates (1) have higher-level needs which they desire to satisfy through their work, (2) are creative and have ideas and knowledge to bring to the job, and (3) will work harder to accomplish goals which they help to set.

Supervisor A:

"This MBO is for the birds. Why should I let my subordinates help to set the goals they are supposed to accomplish? This mutual goal setting lets them tell me what they should be trying to accomplish. But my job is to tell them what to accomplish.

"What is worse is that MBO lets workers help decide what acceptable levels of performance are. You can bet that it results in lower employee performance.

"Periodic meetings with each worker to discuss his or her progress toward reaching goals is another requirement of MBO that wastes both my time and my workers' time. Then we're supposed to meet again at the end of the period during which the worker is supposed to have accomplished the mutually agreed-upon goals. The big joke is that the worker and I are supposed to evaluate his or her performance and set new goals for the next period. Thus, not only does a worker help to set goals, a worker also helps evaluate his or her own performance. It's a never-ending cycle of giving away authority to make decisions."

Supervisor B:

"MBO is the best possible way to motivate subordinates. By letting them participate in setting their goals, they know what is expected of them. By letting them participate in evaluating their performance, they know how their performance will be evaluated. In other words, MBO improves boss-worker communication. It is at the heart of participative management. I think it shows workers that their ideas and opinions count.

"MBO helps each worker to better understand how his or her performance is related to the firm's accomplishment of its objectives. It also puts an end to the notion that promotions and pay raises are based on favoritism. Each worker knows what goals he or she is supposed to be working toward and how his or her performance will be evaluated. Supervisors who believe that MBO is no good assume that workers are lazy, unconcerned about accomplishing goals, and indifferent about performance evaluation."

Among the potential problems in implementing the MBO approach are (1) subordinate suspicion that the real purpose of MBO is to get more work out of them, (2) desire to "beat the system" by setting very minimal objectives to make their performance look good, (3) desire to "please management" by setting unrealistically high objectives, and (4) desire to avoid spending time with the boss discussing and writing objectives. Other problems may arise in integrating the various individuals' goals with those of the organization, setting a priority of objectives, and time-scheduling to accommodate them.

Deciding How to Reach Objectives

In planning, managers rely on knowledge of past and present conditions in their environment. They use this to forecast probable future developments and to plan a course of action in accordance with this forecast. Since no one knows for sure what the future holds, managers operate under conditions of uncertainty. The future, however, is not completely uncertain. Some conditions can be more or less taken for granted. We know that our government will not take over private property except under very unusual conditions. We project this knowledge into the future and this reduces the number of planning "unknowns."

Certain internal facts also are under the firm's control. Planners plan in the face of something more than complete uncertainty and something less than complete certainty. They plan under conditions of risk; they have knowledge (or a good guess) about the likelihood of occurrence of some factors, but not all.

Planning and decision making are bound up in a future filled with risk. This is why some managers avoid planning. They argue that it takes them away from "doing" and accomplishing results; they prefer to live only in the present. They do not try to foresee problems; they "cross those bridges when then come to them." This, of course, is very short-sighted.

Usually there is more than one way to reach an objective, but there is no sure way of identifying the "best" way. Most managers will choose the approach they predict will yield the highest return relative to cost. This type of analysis is called *cost-benefit analysis.*

In other words, we set out the various plans that could be used to reach an objective. Underlying each plan is a set of planning premises, or assumptions about the future. Probabilities, or odds, are assigned to each set of premises to indicate our "best guess" as to which ones will become reality. Each plan's expected profit along with its probability of success also are estimated. The plan most likely to be chosen is based on the most realistic planning premises and offers the highest return, given the estimated probability of success in carrying out the plan.

Organizing

We discussed the firm as an organization in Chapter 4. A firm becomes a structured organization through the process of organizing. **Organizing is the management function of relating people, tasks (or activities), and resources to each other so that an organization can accomplish its objectives.** Plans are carried out by the organizing process. Like planning, organizing also is a dynamic process. This means that changes in objectives and plans usually lead to changes in the organization's structure.

The Systems Concept

A firm is something more than the sum of its parts. To understand this, the concept of system is helpful. A system is a complex of interacting parts. The parts are interrelated so that the unified whole is something more than the sum of its parts. The solar system, for example, is a complex of planets that revolve around the sun. From the systems approach, the earth is a part of that system, rather than independent. This way of looking at the earth gives us a different perspective of our planet.

This systems concept also is relevant to businesses. **According to the systems concept, a firm is not the accounting department or the marketing department. It consists of a network of interrelationships among the various departments and their environment.** The marketing research department is a *subsystem* of the firm. However, the firm is a subsystem of its industry, and the industry is a subsystem of the total economic system, and so on. Top management must integrate the various subsystems so that overall system performance can be improved. Top management also must work for acceptance of this view by others in the firm.

The systems view underscores the need for top management to set clearly defined goals and to communicate them to lower-level managers and workers. In judging their effectiveness, credit managers tend to think in terms of reducing bad debts, while sales managers tend to think in terms of annual dollar sales increases. They often view the firm from different perspectives, but they should be striving to accomplish common goals.

The more that company personnel view the firm as a system, the less their actions will conflict and the more efficient the firm will become. The credit manager recognizes that some bad debts are acceptable in order to increase sales. The sales manager recognizes the need to deny credit to customers with poor credit ratings in order to keep bad-debt losses down. This is the essence of the systems view. Another indicator of systems thinking is the responsiveness of a firm to social problems.

(margin notes) organizing

systems concept

When a firm accepts social responsibility, it is viewing itself as a subsystem of the larger socioeconomic system.

Staffing

staffing

An organization is meaningless without people. The quality of its managers and workers probably is a firm's single most important asset. **Staffing includes the recruitment, selection, training, and promotion of personnel to fill both managerial and operating positions in a company.** Because it is so important, we will study it in detail in Chapter 12.

Directing

directing

Assume that we have developed plans, created an organization structure, and staffed it. It now must be stimulated to action through the management function of directing. **Directing means encouraging subordinates to work toward achieving company objectives. It sometimes is called leading, guiding, motivating, or actuating.**

A manager's opinion of subordinates affects how they will be directed. Managers who think subordinates are lazy, irresponsible, and immature rely on rewards and punishments and use formal authority to get things done. Managers who think subordinates are responsible and are striving to achieve goals will likely "let them work." The amount and type of directing that are needed depend largely on the manager's view of his or her subordinates.

The discussion that follows focuses on four basic concepts that relate to the directing function:

- participation
- communication
- motivation
- leadership

"Someday I hope to be as good as he thinks he is."

Source: *Selling Short,* Universal Press Syndicate.

Participation

Managers use whatever personal knowledge they have about their subordinates. They also make assumptions about them in performing the directing function.

participative management

Managers who practice participative management do not rely only on their formal authority to issue orders to subordinates. **Participative management means that the manager encourages and allows his or her subordinates to involve themselves directly in the decision making that will affect them.**

Douglas McGregor has suggested that there are two types of managers, *Theory X managers* and *Theory Y managers.*[1] Theory X managers assume that the average person

- inherently dislikes work
- is, by nature, lazy, irresponsible, and self-centered
- is security oriented and indifferent to the needs of the organization
- wants to avoid responsibility and has little ambition

Because they make these assumptions, Theory X managers believe that the average person must be threatened, coerced, and controlled in order to motivate him or her to work toward company goals.

Theory Y managers make the opposite assumptions about the average person. Theory Y managers assume that the average person is capable of

- developing interest in his or her work
- committing himself or herself to working to reach company goals
- working productively with a minimum of control and threat of punishment

According to McGregor, workers who fit the Theory X manager's set of assumptions do so because of the nature of their work and the supervision they receive. In other words, their jobs and the supervision they receive tend to make the workers dislike their work, become irresponsible, and so on.

Many managers believe that participative management is the key to building *employee morale*, the worker's attitudes about the job and employer. The more that workers view the firm as the source of their need satisfaction, the higher their morale is likely to be.

Some workers, however, *do* fit the Theory X assumptions. A manager who assumes they fit Theory Y assumptions probably will fail to motivate them. Furthermore, good employee morale is no guarantee of high employee productivity. Employees could be very happy on the job and still produce very little. They also could be very unhappy and have low morale and yet be very productive because they are afraid to be fired!

For participative management to work effectively

- there must be adequate time to anticipate problems and make plans because participation requires more time than authoritarian decision making
- subordinates must be assured that their participation is genuine or else they will not see any personal benefit from participating

[1] Douglas McGregor, *The Human Side of Enterprise* (New York: Mc-Graw-Hill Book Company, 1960).

- managers must believe in it and trust their subordinates
- managers must understand that it involves accountability to subordinates as well as superiors because they no longer merely pass
  "orders" down the chain of command

Communication

communication

**Communication is a transfer of information between people that re-
sults in a common understanding between them.** When workers believe
that they are not only "talked down to" but can also talk up the chain,
two-way communication exists. Workers feel more important when
their voice is heard.

Modern managers recognize the advantages of two-way communication. Communication of orders may be initiated at the top. But feedback
(the receiver's response) from people lower in the chain is critical to the
planning and control functions because these people are closer to the
situation than upper-level managers. A production manager who recently installed new machinery on the assembly line wants feedback
from foremen regarding the machinery's performance. Foremen, in
turn, want feedback from assembly-line workers.

Effective communication requires the sender of a message to decide
what information is to be communicated. Then the sender has to put it
in a form, written or oral, that can be interpreted correctly by the receiver. The sender encodes the message and the receiver decodes it. The
communication effort is effective if the result is a common understanding between the sender and the receiver. (See Figure 5–4.)

The channel, for example, could be another person, a telephone, or a
written memo. The channel that is selected may affect the effectiveness
of the communication effort. For example, if the sender wants to convey
a large volume of statistical data to the receiver, a written report probably will be more effective than a phone call.

The dotted lines in Figure 5–4 indicate noise. Anything that interferes
with the communication process is called *noise,* or a barrier to effective
communication. In our earlier example, the foremen may provide feed-

FIGURE 5–4

**The communication
process**

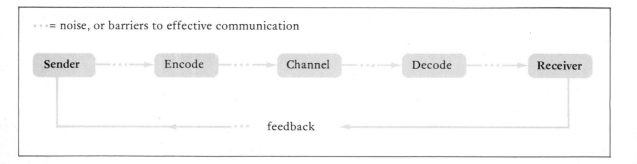

Source: *B.C.*, Field Newspaper Syndicate.

back to the production manager that suggests the new machinery is working well, even if that is not true. The foremen may fear relaying any negative information to the production manager that could be interpreted to mean that he or she made a mistake in buying the new machinery. In such a case, there is no effective two-way communication.

One important communication barrier is semantic confusion. The sender may have trouble putting what he or she wants to convey "into words" that the receiver will understand. This is a big problem when people who are familiar with technical jargon try to communicate with people who are unfamiliar with it. The language barrier often exists between staff specialists and line managers.

Perception, the process through which we assign meaning to objects or events in our environment, is another possible barrier. How you perceive things is influenced by your background and past experiences. Different people can perceive the same object or event in different ways.

Suppose the company president picks up the phone and asks the sales manager for help in getting salespersons to sign pledge cards for a charitable drive. This is the first time the president has ever called the sales manager on the phone. The sales manager, therefore, probably will perceive this call to be much more important than if the president had circulated a memo to all department heads asking for their help in signing up their personnel.

Motivation

Motivation is the result of the drive to satisfy an internal urge. Managers must structure jobs so that they satisfy these urges of individuals if   motivation

**they apply effort. By doing this, managers can motivate their subordi-
nates to work toward company objectives.** As we saw in Chapter 4,
there never can be a perfect integration between organizational and
personal objectives. But the more effectively these objectives are integrated, the more motivated workers are to achieve organizational objectives.

For many years, money has been used as the "carrot" (incentive) to
motivate workers. Money is an effective motivator as long as most
workers are focusing on satisfying their lower-level needs. But for many
workers today, money no longer is the all-powerful motivator.

The Hawthorne Experiments mark the beginning of modern research
into employee motivation and the human-relations movement in management. These experiments were conducted between 1927 and 1932 at
Western Electric's Hawthorne plant near Chicago. The researchers were
studying the effects of the physical work environment on worker productivity. For example, it seemed reasonable to assume that better
lighting would lead to greater employee productivity. The researchers
found, however, that production increased when the lighting level was
raised *or* lowered. The apparent explanation for this surprising result
was the importance the workers felt because they were being studied by
management.

The human-relations movement brought new approaches to motivating and leading employees. Managers have come to understand that
people are people, on and off the job. Workers are not machines. If their
higher-level needs are not satisfied by the formal organization, workers
will create an informal organization to satisfy them.

All managers are responsible for motivating their subordinates, but
managers are limited in what they can do. Foremen are limited by
company policies on wage scales and fringe benefits, and the company's
president may be limited by policies set by the board of directors. Since
the typical employee is said to work at about 30 percent of capacity,
however, motivating them to become more productive is a big challenge
for all managers.

An interesting view of motivation has given managers added insight
into how to motivate employees.[2] Frederick Herzberg's research led him
to conclude that many factors managers often rely on to motivate
workers are not true motivators. He divides job factors that generally
are considered to be motivators into two groups:

- maintenance factors (hygiene factors), such as pay, working conditions, job security, and the nature of supervision
- motivational factors (motivators), such as achievement, recognition, responsibility, advancement, and growth potential

---

[2] Frederick Herzberg, *Work and the Nature of Man* (Cleveland: World Publishing Company, 1966).

Since a manager must work through others to accomplish goals, how those "others" view management is important to a manager's effectiveness. The following are some of the important things a worker expects of management:

Job and Working Conditions

- A job that is safe
- A job that is not monotonous and boring
- A job that enables a worker to use his or her acquired skills
- A job with a future
- A healthful job environment
- Reasonable hours of work
- Adequate physical facilities
- Stable employment

Concern with the Worker as an Individual

- To be treated with dignity
- To feel important and needed
- To be managed by supervisors who can work with people
- The right to be heard
- The right to participate in decision making that will affect him or her

Fair Treatment and Compensation

- To know what is expected in terms of performance
- Objective basis for evaluating performance
- No favoritism
- Equal opportunity
- Fair compensation system
- Fringe benefits
- Pay that reflects his or her contribution to the firm

Opportunity for Advancement

- Opportunity to learn new skills
- Equal opportunity for promotion
- Training and development programs
- Recognition for past accomplishments
- Opportunity to improve his or her standard of living

Maintenance factors occur as part of the work environment. They are job context, or extrinsic, factors that are not part of the work itself. If they are absent or inadequate, they tend to be *dissatisfiers*. Their presence, however, helps to avoid worker dissatisfaction. Thus poor pay and poor working conditions are dissatisfiers but improving them will *not* provide true motivation.

Motivational factors occur as part of the work itself. They are job content, or intrinsic, factors. Motivational factors make work rewarding in and of itself—they are *satisfiers*. Herzberg's motivational factors are similar to the higher-level needs of Maslow's hierarchy.

job enrichment

Herzberg's motivation-hygiene theory has helped in focusing management attention on job content factors in motivating workers. **Job enrichment is the process of redesigning jobs to satisfy higher-level needs and organizational needs by improving worker satisfaction and task efficiency. It gives workers more responsibility, authority, and autonomy in planning and doing their work.**

Some managers believe that job enlargement and job rotation can help in providing more satisfying work for subordinates. *Job enlargement* involves adding new tasks to a job in order to make it less boring and more challenging. It is especially useful for assembly-line jobs that are repetitive and monotonous and do not involve the worker's mental processes. For example, a machine operator's job might be enlarged to include performing maintenance on the machine instead of relying on a maintenance worker to do it.

Job rotation among management trainees has been practiced for many years to give them an overall view of the firm's operations and to prepare them for promotion. This practice has been used at the operative level in recent years. Workers periodically are assigned to new jobs in order to reduce boredom. The new job usually does not require the worker to learn a major new skill; but it does, for example, give assembly-line workers a better understanding of the total production process. They can relate their specialized jobs to the creation of a finished product.

Leadership

leadership

Leadership is a manager's ability to get subordinates to develop their capabilities by inspiring them to achieve. It is a means of motivating them to accomplish goals. A manager should be a good leader and something more. Besides being able to inspire followers to want to achieve, a manager also must perform the other management functions.

Leadership is practiced in different degrees by the people in a firm. The president ultimately is responsible for directing the entire firm. He or she sets the style of leadership in the firm. If the president is a dictator, other managers are likely to be dictators, too.

One of the earliest leadership theories was the "great person" theory. It assumed that certain persons were gifted with leadership talent and that they would arise as great leaders in any situation. Examples of these "born leaders" are Alexander the Great, Napoleon, Abraham Lincoln, Queen Elizabeth I, and Susan B. Anthony.

Another theory is the "traitist" theory. The "traitists" believe that leadership traits don't have to be inborn. They can also be acquired through experience and learning. For years, the "traitists" have been searching for common traits among leaders, but there are striking differences among the lists compiled by various researchers. Some of the more common leadership traits are intelligence, dependability, high tolerance for frustration, persistence, and cooperativeness.

Most of the more recent research on leadership has focused on leadership styles. Figure 5–5, for example, presents a continuum of possible leadership styles. At the left is the boss-centered leader and at the right is the subordinate-centered leader. The general conclusion is that the more subordinate-centered leadership styles are more effective than the more boss-centered styles.

Other commonly used terms to describe leadership styles are

- autocratic, dictatorial, or authoritarian
- democratic, or participative
- laissez-faire, or free rein

Autocratic leaders keep all decision-making authority to themselves, while democratic leaders share it with their subordinates. Laissez-faire leaders try to delegate total responsibility for decision making to their subordinates. They do not want to share their decision-making authority; they want to join the group for decision-making purposes.

FIGURE 5–5

A continuum of leadership behavior

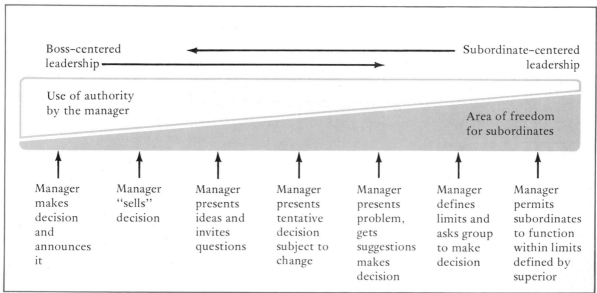

Source: *Harvard Business Review.*

As we suggested earlier, many modern managers regard the more participative styles of leadership as desirable because participative leadership

- permits subordinates to satisfy their higher-level needs (competence, knowledge, self-confidence, feelings of achievement, esteem) through the job
- is an approach to motivating subordinates
- permits managers to receive feedback from operatives at the lowest levels in the firm

In the final analysis, the "best" style of leadership depends on the three elements in the leadership environment:

- the leader
- the followers
- the situation

Participation will not work if the leader cannot inspire subordinates to participate or if the subordinates do not want to participate. Situations that call for quick decisions limit the time available for true participation of subordinates.

Fred Fiedler has developed a *contingency theory of leadership*, which makes it clear that there is no one "best" leadership style.[3] For example, situations that are either very easy or very difficult are handled best by task-oriented leaders. Situations that are only moderately difficult are handled best by subordinate-oriented leaders.

Controlling

controlling

Managers must always monitor operations (evaluate performance) to see if the firm is achieving its goals. This is the management function of controlling. **Controlling involves**

- **setting standards of performance**
- **measuring actual performance and comparing it to performance standards to detect deviations from standards**
- **taking corrective action when significant deviations exist**

As we suggested in our discussion of MBO, planning and controlling are closely related. When spouses prepare a budget, they are planning *and* setting up a control device. Suppose the budget plan is to save $1,000 by the end of the year. If their savings account shows a balance of $200 on July 1, the standard is not being met. Awareness of this should

---

[3] Fred E. Fiedler, *A Theory of Leadership Effectiveness* (New York: McGraw-Hill Book Company, 1967).

A lower-level manager

"I'm a supervisor on a production line. To me, management means attending to detail—making sure that my subordinates do exactly as they are told. The really important work that can't be left up to somebody else to do is what it's all about. I spend a lot of time working right along with my subordinates. I'm not afraid to get my hands dirty!

"As far as management functions go, and I'll admit I never thought of management in those exact terms, most of my time is spent on directing. Controlling would come in second. My job is to get production out of my workers and that means getting them to do a good job and making sure that they do it."

A top-level manager

"I'm president of a large firm that manufactures sporting goods. To me, management means keeping yourself free of detail work so that you can concentrate on thinking about your company's future—where your company will be 10 to 15 years from now. Of course, thinking by itself won't accomplish the job. That's why I've spent several years bringing together the best possible group of executives to carry out my plans for the future.

"Undoubtedly, my most important function is planning."

lead to corrective action. The earlier that they discover the deviation from their saving standard, the quicker they can take corrective action.

Examples of controlling are an office manager's efforts to keep expenditures for typing paper in line with the budget, a plant manager's efforts to keep the number of rejects down to an acceptable minimum, or a marketing manager's efforts to move the firm into production and sale of a new product according to a time schedule.

The elements of control are present in each of the above examples. First there must be a definite idea of what we want to accomplish (a standard). The office manager, for example, cannot exceed the budget for paper. In practice, setting standards is not always simple. How should management evaluate the production department's performance? On the basis of the number of rejects? On the basis of the average time required to produce an average unit of output? On the basis of the average cost of producing an average unit of output? Actually, all are

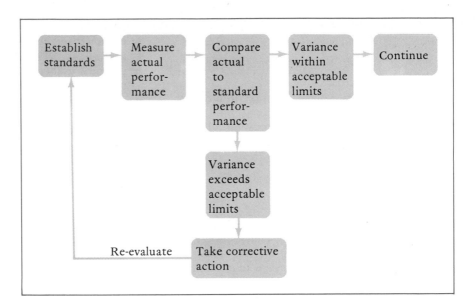

FIGURE 5-6

The control process

important. A 3 percent reduction in rejects along with tripled production costs probably is not desirable. But whether it is or is not depends on the relative importance of avoiding rejects and avoiding cost increases.

Second, a manager measures actual performance and compares it to the established standard. Measurement is not so simple either. There are many problems in measuring employee performance. In some jobs only quantitative results (number of units produced) are important. In other jobs qualitative results (quality of the units produced) are the crucial basis for comparison. Evaluating the performance of higher-level managers is especially complex. We discuss this in Chapter 12.

The final element of control is taking corrective action. It is desirable to detect deviations from standards quickly. The longer that corrective action takes, the more it will cost. (See Figure 5–6.)

The Decision-Making Process

One way to look at managerial work is to think of it as decision making. Everything a firm does is the result of decisions made by managers. Examples are deciding on the firm's goals, what products to make, what equipment to buy, what advertising appeals to use, where to get funds, and where to sell its products.

Like the management functions, decision making is a process—a very complex process. There is no one best way to explain it. We'll look at it in

a logical and straightforward manner. **The stages in the decision-mak-** **decision-making process**
ing process are as follows:

- **recognizing an opportunity or a problem**
- **gathering information**
- **developing alternatives**
- **analyzing alternatives**
- **choosing the best alternative**
- **implementing the decision**
- **evaluating the decision**

The management functions are involved at each stage.

Recognizing an Opportunity or a Problem

A business opportunity must be recognized before it can be exploited. This requires decision making about the nature of the opportunity a firm can undertake. Since a firm's resources are limited, management must decide what types of opportunity can be exploited. The actual exploitation of the opportunity also requires decision making.

Decision making also is needed when management recognizes a problem. Often this is little more than a feeling that "something is not right." Decisions must be made regarding a clear definition of the problem and whether or not anything will be done about it.

Gathering Information

After recognizing the opportunity or problem, the decision maker's next step is gathering information about it. This involves talks with company personnel and outsiders who might provide greater insight. Company records and secondary sources of information such as libraries also might be investigated.

Because of the tremendous capacity of computers to store data, many firms now have *management information systems (MIS)*. These systems are made up of people and machines. People feed in the data needed for decision-making purposes, and these data are processed, summarized, and reported to decision makers who need it. We will have more to say on this in Chapter 14.

Developing Alternatives

After developing a good "feel" for the opportunity or problem and its setting, the decision maker begins to formulate alternative courses of action. The support of others might be sought in brainstorming sessions in which the participants offer ways to deal with the opportunity or problem. Freewheeling creativity is important here, so no evaluation is made of the alternatives offered at this stage. The goal is to stimulate new ways of looking at the opportunity or problem and to develop alternative ways of dealing with it. Creativity is important in developing a list of choices. If there is only one alternative, there is no decision to make!

Analyzing Alternatives

After making a list of alternatives, the decision maker begins to analyze them critically. It's a process of elimination. Alternatives that are unlikely to pay off are eliminated along with those that involve high risk in comparison to expected payoff. Those that remain often are ranked in terms of their expected payoff. The payoff could be stated in terms such as least cost, maximum profit, or maximum customer service.

This process might involve analyzing the projected consequences of each of the remaining alternatives, which is always tough because it involves forecasting the future. Nevertheless, the thought process required here helps to ensure that the decision maker considers the future consequences of present decisions.

Choosing the Best Alternative

In choosing the best alternative, a decision maker establishes a decision criterion and a decision rule. If the goal is to improve delivery service to customers, the decision criterion might be "fastest delivery." The decision rule would be to choose the transportation method that provides the fastest delivery to customers. The decision criterion, however, could have been "lowest cost." Choosing decision criteria requires good judgment concerning the firm's goals and an understanding of the risks involved.

Implementing the Decision

Once the decision has been made (the best alternative or a combination of several of the initial alternatives has been selected), the decision

Source: *Beetle Bailey*, King Features Syndicate.

maker must move toward implementing it. Implementation, of course, also requires decision making in performing the management functions.

Evaluating the Decision

After implementing the decision, the decision maker must evaluate it. Operations must be monitored, or checked, to see whether the decision is being implemented properly. Monitoring also gives the decision maker feedback that helps in assessing whether the "right decision" was made and if corrective actions are needed.

Types of Decisions

There are two basic types of decisions, routine decisions and nonroutine decisions.

A routine decision is a decision that must be faced over and over. The set of circumstances that call for the decision are recurring circumstances. You probably do not consciously decide the route you will take to class each day. Because you face that decision so many times, you probably develop a routine decision for it.

routine decision

Managers also face routine decisions. These often are set up as policies and standard operating procedures. An office manager who sets up a policy of "no smoking in the office" does away with the need to make a decision actively each time an office worker asks if it's all right to smoke in the office.

A nonroutine decision is a nonrecurring decision. The set of circumstances that call for this type of decision does not occur regularly. There are two types of nonroutine decisions, strategic and tactical. Strategic decisions are made by top-level management. Examples are decision making about the types of opportunity that a firm will attempt to exploit (what business the firm will be in) and whether or not the company should buy out a competing firm. Strategic decisions have an important, long-run effect.

nonroutine decision

Tactical decisions have less long-run effect. An example is a decision about where to locate a new warehouse. The dividing line between strategic and tactical decisions, however, often is an arbitrary one.

According to the concept of management by exception (or the exception principle), routine decisions should be pushed as far down in the firm as possible. By granting authority to lower-level managers to make routine decisions, higher-level managers can devote more time to nonroutine decisions.

management by exception

Management by exception is related to the control function. It requires a well-developed observing and reporting system to monitor operations. It also requires setting standards of performance, measuring actual performance, and comparing actual to standard performance. The idea is to allow subordinates to review performance against set standards and bring to the manager's attention only those cases that involve exceptions to normal or acceptable performance. This frees the manager from reviewing performance in situations where performance is in line with standards. He or she can concentrate time and attention on cases of exceptionally good performance and exceptionally poor performance. By studying these cases, he or she can develop ideas for improvement.

There are several potential drawbacks to management by exception. For example, advancing technology may make old standards obsolete. Unless they are re-evaluated from time to time, managers may assume incorrectly that performance is acceptable and operations are going along as planned when, in fact, they are not. If some aspects of operations that are critical to success are not identified in advance, they will go unmeasured by the subordinate. There also is a measurement problem, especially for critical factors such as human behavior. It may be next to impossible for such a system to call attention, for example, to a situation where employee morale is on the decline.

Summary and Look Ahead

Businesses are living things that seek to accomplish objectives. Through the performance of nonmanagerial work (operative tasks) and managerial functions (the functions of management), a firm moves toward the realization of its objectives. The three managerial skills that are required for effective performance of these functions are conceptual, people, and technical skills.

Management is partly an art and a science. Managerial and nonmanagerial work can cause stress on the job. Firms do what they can to help control stress but how a person deals with it basically is a personal decision.

The functions of management—planning, organizing, staffing, directing, and controlling—are performed by managers in the process of achieving goals by bringing together people and other resources. Management is necessary whenever results depend on group effort. There are different echelons (levels) of management in a firm. Its success or failure is traceable to the effectiveness of its managers.

In reality, management cannot be broken down into a series of separate functions. It is a process. This becomes clear when we think of the firm as a system.

We also can view the management task in terms of decision making.

Managers make decisions in performing their functions. There are seven stages in the decision-making process: (1) recognizing an opportunity or a problem, (2) gathering information, (3) developing alternatives, (4) analyzing alternatives, (5) choosing the best alternative, (6) implementing the decision, and (7) evaluating the decision.

Decisions can be routine or nonroutine. Nonroutine decisions can be either strategic or tactical. Truly strategic decisions are made by top management. Management by exception helps to ensure that upper-level managers will have adequate time to devote to strategic decisions.

In the next section, we will study in greater detail the various areas of decision making in the firm. These are called the functional areas—production, marketing, and finance. Do not confuse the functions of management (planning, organizing, and so on) with the functional areas of business. The functions of management are performed in all the functional areas we will study.

MANAGEMENT AS A CAREER

To become a manager is to accept responsibility, to work through others, and to make an organization work. The skills needed include human relations skills, the ability to plan, and the ability to make and stand by your decisions. Managers must also have the self-discipline needed to take orders.

Many of these managerial skills are transferable across a wide range of businesses and in many nonbusiness enterprises. Specific areas include heavy industry, transportation, petroleum exploration, agribusiness, insurance, electronics, the hospitality industry, the health-care industry, local and federal government, and many others. In every case the manager organizes, plans, staffs, directs, and controls.

In nearly every field there are several levels of managers' jobs. It is normal to be promoted through the ranks. However, except in those rare cases where promotion depends mostly on seniority, the promotions get much tougher as you near the top of the organization. It is near the top that the exceptional management skills begin to show. This is where toughness of character, vision and capacity to absorb and interpret complex information are required.

These days it is rare to see a person reach the top of management ranks without a bachelor's degree. Many have more than one degree. In the middle- and lower-management ranks, however, there are many opportunities for people with associate degrees.

Key Concepts

communication A transfer of information between people that results in a common understanding between them.

controlling The management function of setting standards of performance, measuring actual performance and comparing it to performance standards, and taking corrective action, if necessary.

decision-making process Involves recognizing an opportunity or a problem, gathering information, developing and analyzing alternatives, choosing the best alternative(s), implementing the decision, and evaluating the decision.

directing The management function of encouraging subordinates to work toward achieving organizational objectives. Also called leading, guiding, motivating, or actuating.

functions of management Planning, organizing, staffing, directing, and controlling. Together, they constitute managerial work.

job enrichment The process of redesigning jobs to satisfy the worker's higher-level needs and organizational needs by improving worker satisfaction and task efficiency. It gives workers more responsibility, authority, and autonomy in planning and doing their work.

leadership The manager's ability to get subordinates to develop their capabilities by inspiring them to achieve.

management The process of achieving goals by bringing together and coordinating the human, financial, and physical resources of an organization.

management by exception Also called the exception principle. Managers who practice this grant authority to lower-level managers to make routine decisions. This enables upper-level managers to devote more time to nonroutine decisions.

management by objectives (MBO) Also called managing by results. The manager gets together with each subordinate to set his or her objectives. Allows the subordinate to participate in goal setting. The subordinate is considered to have performed well if he or she accomplishes those objectives.

manager A person who works through other people (subordinates). A manager "brings together" their efforts to accomplish goals.

managerial skills Conceptual skills, people skills, and technical skills. All managers need all three skills.

motivation The result of the drive to satisfy an internal urge. Managers must structure jobs so that they satisfy these urges of individuals if they apply effort. By doing this, managers can motivate their subordinates to work toward company objectives.

nonroutine decision A nonrecurring decision. The two types are strategic and tactical.

operational planning Planning for the day-to-day survival of a firm. A major responsibility of middle- and lower-level managers.

organizing The management function of relating people, tasks (or activities), and resources to each other so that a firm can accomplish its objectives.

participative management The manager encourages and allows his or her subordinates to involve themselves directly in the decision making that will affect them.

planning The management function of preparing a firm to cope with the future by relying on knowledge of present and past conditions and forecasting probable future developments. Setting a firm's objectives over different time periods and deciding on the methods of achieving those objectives result in a plan to be followed to reach desired goals.

routine decision A recurring decision, often set up as a policy.

staffing The management function of recruiting, selecting, training, and promoting personnel to fill both managerial and operating positions.

strategic planning Planning for the long-range future. A major responsibility of top-level managers.

systems concept A way of looking at a company. A system is a complex of interacting parts. A socioeconomic system is made up of many smaller subsystems. A given industry is one such subsystem. Firms in that industry are still other subsystems. Each firm has several subsystems, such as a production department and a marketing department. Management effort focuses on integrating the various subsystems of the firm so that overall system performance can be improved.

For Review . . .

1. Why do lower-level managers perform more operative tasks than higher-level managers?
2. Why are the people skills equally important at all echelons of management?
3. Is there any room for judgment in making management decisions? Explain.
4. Should management strive to eliminate all conflict in the firm? Explain.
5. List and describe the five functions of management.
6. Discuss the similarities and differences between operational and strategic planning. Which one is more important? Why?
7. What is meant by management by objectives (MBO)? What are its advantages? What are some of the potential problems in implementing the MBO approach?
8. What is the "systems concept"?
9. Discuss the relationship between Herzberg's motivation-hygiene theory and job enrichment.
10. What is the "best" style of leadership? Explain.
11. List and describe the seven stages in the decision-making process.

. . . For Discussion

1. Why do managers encounter stress on the job?
2. "All managers should practice MBO and be Theory Y managers." Do you agree?
3. It has been said that the president of a company need not be a good manager. All the president need do is possess an ability to select well-qualified subordinates. Do you agree?
4. In general, people in upper management positions need to possess relatively few technical skills, whereas operatives must possess many such skills. Does this mean that people in top management positions can transfer more easily from one type of industry to another than operatives can?
5. Do you think that a company president should direct subordinates in the same way that the boss of a work crew would direct subordinates?

Incidents

A Technique for Improving Two-Way Communication

"No question about it, executives who sit down with employees in no-holds-barred sessions are taking their lumps. But nonetheless, an ever-growing number of them are doing it—so much so that psychologists have given the process a formal, somber-sounding name: deep sensing, defined as the attempt by top managers to find out face to face what is on the minds of the rank and file."

The technique enables top managers to discuss employee gripes and company objectives in direct face to face meetings.

"The setup of sensing meetings varies across the lot. Some involve meals, while others are held in conference rooms. Some companies choose attendees randomly—every sixth name on an alphabetized list of all employees, for example—while others group participants by job category, length of service, or the like. Some use consultants or managers from different divisions to run the meetings, while at others the top manager goes it alone with his people."

Questions

1. Why is two-way communication important in a company?
2. Would a Theory X manager be likely to use this technique? Why or why not?

Broadening Managers

"It looks at first glance like a typical college summer session. The professor lets his voice rise and fall in traditional professorial cadence as he lectures some 65 men and women on the philosophies behind modern-day thought on human equality. The students, sporting jeans and short-shorts, occasionally refer to esoteric concepts chalked on the blackboard as they listen intently and take notes."

The basic purpose of the summer session is to broaden the individuals enrolled in the course.

"But a closer look turns up a surprising number of gray hairs and wrinkles in the class. These are, in fact, not students at all, but middle-to-upper-level executives and their spouses attending Dartmouth College's four-week Dartmouth Institute. They represent some 35 companies as diverse as American Can, Federated Department Stores, and Citibank, all of which have forked over upwards of $5,000 to let these executive couples immerse themselves in existentialism, Shakespeare, and other decidedly nonbusiness subjects. The hope: that the executives would return sufficiently broadened to make more thoughtful decisions."

3. Would this technique lose its morale-building potential if the manager simply listened to employees talk about their problems but he or she did nothing about those problems? Discuss.

Source: *Business Week.*

The goal of DI is to broaden the executives' perspective of their environment in order that they can make more thoughtful decisions. It is assumed that managers who have reached the higher levels of management in their firms already possess management skills.

" 'This is probably the highest order of a management training course,' says Lionel N. Sterling, controller and senior vice-president at American Can Co. 'The dominant management technique of the 1970s is strategic planning, and how can you even contemplate that without understanding the nature of the forces of the world and how we bring our own beliefs and value systems to bear on our decisions?' "

Questions

1. In your opinion, do executives need this type of broadening? Why or why not?
2. Does this program benefit the firms that enroll their executives? Why or why not?

Source: *Business Week.*

ROCKETOY COMPANY 3

After carefully considering his options as to the form of ownership, Terry decided to form a small corporation. Rocketoy's common stockholders are Terry, Joe Phillips, the three Milwaukee investors (Richard Talley, Julia Rabinovitz, and Mike Shultz), and Terry's sister Pam. Terry owns 55 percent of the common stock, Pam owns 5 percent, and the others each own 10 percent.

Terry was elected chairman of the board of directors. In a meeting of the owners, they agreed to fill the top management jobs themselves. Each

department would be headed by that owner who had the most interest and experience in that particular type of work.

This informal arrangement reflected Terry's basic ideas about business. For example, Rocketoy's major organizational objective at the time of incorporation was "to make the highest quality toys possible and to sell them at prices reasonable enough to earn a good return on the owners' investment in the firm." Terry suggested, and the other owners agreed, that this was enough to guide

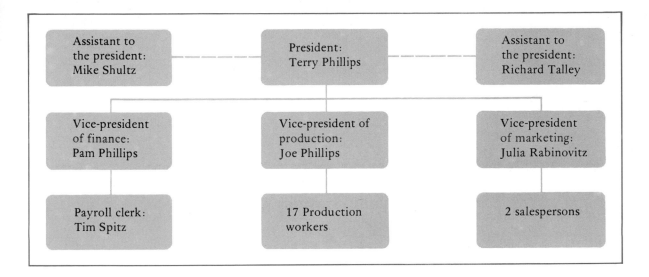

them in running the firm. As Terry said, "We are in business to serve customer wants so that we can make a profit. We don't have to act like a big business. We know each other's abilities and interests and we are all dedicated to making Rocketoy a success. Let's not get bogged down in things like the chain of command and all the other things that take time away from doing. We can informally work out the details of operations as we gain more experience in working with each other. Let's not try to invent problems."

The owners decided on the following positions and titles:

· President: Terry Phillips
· Vice-president of finance: Pam Phillips
· Vice-president of production: Joe Phillips
· Vice-president of marketing: Julia Rabinovitz.

Richard Talley and Mike Shultz were heavily involved in several other business ventures, so they decided not to get actively involved in Rocketoy's management. The other owners agreed that this would be best. But because of their valuable business experience, Terry convinced them to serve as his advisors. Whenever Terry wanted advice, he would be able to turn to Richard and Mike.

Terry, Pam, Joe, and Julia each drew a salary from the business. Because they wanted to keep as much money invested in the business as they could for future growth, they drew relatively modest salaries—Terry $15,000 a year; Pam, Joe, and Julia $12,500 per year. Richard and Mike got $2,000 each per year for their jobs as advisors to Terry.

Rocketoy's work force expanded to a total of 20 workers in addition to the managers. This is shown in the organization chart that Terry prepared for Rocketoy. (See chart.)

Questions

1. Why do you think Terry chose to incorporate his business?
2. Do you agree with Terry that Rocketoy's broad organizational objective is enough to guide its managers? Why or why not?
3. Is Terry a good chief executive? Why or why not?
4. Suppose you could step into Mike Shultz's or Richard Talley's shoes. What advice would you give Terry at this point?

B Y NOW we know what a business firm is. We also know that it must be managed. In this section we discuss what firms do and what types of decisions their managers must make.

Goods and services must be produced and marketed. Thus production and marketing are two basic decision areas of business. Chapter 6 discusses production management. Chapters 7 and 8 introduce the areas of marketing decision making.

Accounting is a necessary tool of management. It helps managers to make better production and marketing decisions. Accounting is examined in Chapter 9.

The third major decision area is finance. A firm's production and marketing activities must be financed. Chapter 10 looks at financial institutions such as banks and securities exchanges, and Chapter 11 discusses financial decisions of the firm.

Because a firm's most important resource is its human resource, we devote two chapters to it. Chapter 12 explores the area of personnel administration. Chapter 13 looks at labor relations.

The role of computers in modern business is examined in Chapter 14. This discussion is accompanied by an introduction to business use of quantitative methods.

After you finish this section, you'll have a good idea of the types of work done by business managers. This may help you to develop a better idea of what types of business careers appeal to you.

Photos: left—Chris Maynard; top right—George W. Gardner, 1973; bottom right—©Magnum Photos.

SECTION THREE

Business Decisions

Producing Goods and Services

CHAPTER 6

Objectives: After reading this chapter, you should be able to

1. Explain the nature of production.
2. Draw a chart illustrating the inputs, processes, and outputs of production.
3. Illustrate the several ways of classifying production processes.
4. Review the management functions and give an example of each as applied to production.
5. Develop a checklist for plant location decisions.
6. Evaluate the dangers of loss of human motivation in a big factory.
7. Explain the process of control as it applies to product quality.
8. Distinguish between value analysis and vendor analysis.

Key concepts: Look for these terms as you read the chapter

production	plant layout
combination	control chart
breaking down	PERT
treatment	CPM
intermittent production	quality control
continuous production	preventive maintenance
automation	obsolescence
labor-intensive	reciprocity
capital-intensive	value analysis
production management	vendor analysis
make-or-buy decision	operations management
plant capacity	

We begin our study of the functional areas of management with a look at production. The traditional management functions of planning, organizing, staffing, directing, and controlling are used as a framework for studying production management. Special emphasis is given to modern planning and control devices.

Production has a special place in American business history. By doing good production work, American firms built our reputation as an industrial leader. In the first part of this century the names Henry Ford, Frederick W. Taylor, and Frank Gilbreth were known throughout the industrial world. They made the terms mass production, assembly line, *and* efficiency expert *familiar by combining new technology with modern organizational techniques and incentives. The result was a fantastic level of output per hour worked. Although the earliest applications of these ideas were in factories, they were in time extended to retailing, services, and other forms of business.*

Industrial production growth continues to be great, as is seen in Table 6–1. Using the year 1967 as typical (the index value for that year equals 100), we can compare the growth of various major industries from 1950 to 1978. Notice that some industries, like rubber products and chemicals, have grown much faster than the average for all products, which has more than tripled in 28 years.

What Is Production?

Production activity creates goods and services. Because of production more wants can be satisfied. Production can also be viewed as a sequence. **It starts with the *input* of resources which are fed into one of several kinds of production *processes*. Finally an *output* of products or services results for use or sale.** Figure 6–1 illustrates this view and makes it easier for us to explain the elements of production management.

production

The Inputs to Production

To produce something, the following set of resources is usually needed as input:

- materials
- capital goods
- the human input

Materials include raw materials such as raw cotton, corn, and crude oil; semimanufactured products such as sheet steel and unfinished lumber; and manufactured parts such as spark plugs, bolts, and tires. Electric power and other energy sources are usually included. Capital goods include the plant investment, which can range from a huge refinery to a barber shop, and equipment such as a lathe or a typewriter.

TABLE 6-1

Industrial production—indexes, by industry, 1950–1978*

Major industry group	1950	1960	1970	1978 (June estimates)
Industrial production	45	66	107	144
Manufacturing	45	65	105	145
Durable manufactures	44	63	101	131
Primary metals	71	74	107	117
Fabricated metal products	57	72	109	142
Machinery	(NA)	56	100	154
Transportation equipment	41	64	90	131
Instruments and related products	26	58	111	171
Clay, glass, and stone products	58	81	106	157
Lumber and products	65	74	106	137
Furniture and fixtures	52	72	99	150
Nondurable manufactures	46	69	111	154
Textile mill products	61	71	106	138
Apparel products	64	82	98	126
Leather and products	92	99	91	76
Paper and products	46	68	113	146
Printing and publishing	49	70	104	129
Chemicals and products	25	53	120	187
Petroleum products	48	77	113	141
Rubber and plastics products	31	54	116	253
Foods	58	78	112	143
Tobacco products	69	90	100	121
Mining	66	83	110	127
Utilities	27	62	128	148

NA: Not available
* 1967 = 100. Based on 1967 Standard Industrial Classification.
Source: Federal Reserve System.

The human input includes

- unskilled labor
- skilled labor
- supervisory skills
- managerial skills

The main distinction between skilled and unskilled labor is ability to perform a special task that cannot be performed by all employees.

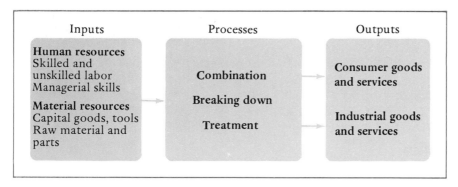

FIGURE 6-1

The production process

Examples of skilled workers include carpenters, pipefitters, and technicians. Supervisors and managers, of course, are responsible for directing the activities of others.

One of the greatest problems facing producers today is the fact that one of the critical inputs, raw materials, is often scarce. As the world's resources are used up, producers are turning to chemical research to find new chemicals for industry—for example, new catalysts. Monsanto Company and Union Carbide, two large chemical producers, have developed new catalysts that enable them to produce acetic acid and plastics from raw materials that are more plentiful than the ones they used in earlier years. This kind of research can reduce the problems created by increasing scarcity of certain raw materials.

Processes

There are several ways of classifying production processes. The first depends on the way that material inputs are dealt with. Thus a process may combine two or more material inputs, break down an input, or treat an input.

Combination means putting parts together. It is the most common process. Cars, pumps, and pencils must go through the process of combination.

Breaking down means removing or at least separating some of the original input, usually a raw material. When a log is cut into two-by-fours or when juice is taken from oranges, the process, which is also very common, is one of breaking down.

Treatment is doing something to an input without adding or subtracting from it. It may involve hardening or softening or cooling or reshaping an input. Smoking a ham or molding a plastic toothbrush handle is a treatment process. The forming of a part out of a basic material is often called *fabrication*.

combination

breaking down

treatment

We can also classify production processes according to a time dimension. They can be intermittent or continuous, and also either for stock or to order.

intermittent production

An intermittent production process starts and stops and starts again, maybe several times. Intermittent production may occur only when stocks fall below a critical level. It may also occur to build up stocks when machines and workers would otherwise be idle. A specialty toolmaker, for example, may nickel-plate certain batches of output and not others. Some products may require special heat treatments. The nickel-plating and heat-treating departments of the firm are used intermittently.

continuous production

A continuous production process, as the name implies, goes on and on. A cola bottling plant repeats the same process countless thousands of times without interruption. The demand for this product is large and easy to predict. **The process, as in the case of most continuous processes, is highly automated. This means that little human supervision is needed. The process of automation is discussed more fully in Chapter 14.**

automation

Most continuous processes produce products *for stock*. This means that output is kept in inventory in anticipation of demand. This could not be done without losing money if the firm did not have good reason to expect a fairly steady demand. The reason is that keeping inventories costs money in several ways. They take up valuable space, they require financing, and they may be damaged or stolen or become obsolete.

The alternative to producing for stock is producing *to order*. This means that the firm waits until there is a specific order in hand before starting to produce. Such production is also called *jobbing*. This kind of production usually uses general-purpose machines and tools—those which can do a variety of jobs. Often production to order is "custom" production in which a specific design or feature is provided for the customer.

labor-intensive

Processes also vary in the amount of human input they need. **Labor-intensive processes depend more on people than on machines.** Some parts of the apparel trade are like this. Labor-intensive processes are most likely to be used when labor is cheap or when there is an artistic element in the work. There are some kinds of jobs, too, in which it is really hard to apply machines because the process varies a lot. Some kinds of farming are still highly labor-intensive as is the making of high-quality jewelry. Today many items of clothing for U.S. markets are made or are partly made by U.S. firms with low-cost labor in less-developed nations.

capital-intensive

The opposite situation exists when machines can do the job better than people. **This calls for capital-intensive processes in which people may have little to do with production. Instead, investment in machin-**

Source: The Picture Cube.

ery is great. The huge petroleum refinery is a classic example of a capital-intensive process. A refinery that may cost hundreds of millions of dollars to build and equip may operate with fewer than 100 employees.

An extreme example of intermittent production to order is a customized stereo-system producer. Such a firm waits for orders, produces a variety of outputs, and tends to be labor intensive. Some parts of the shop may be idle for extended periods and, as a result, the size of its labor force may vary. A similar situation exists in producing heavy machinery, ships, and high-fashion dresses.

A producer of soap powder is at the other extreme. This firm has a heavy investment in special-purpose equipment and operates on a continuous basis. It usually keeps a large inventory of finished products. Other examples of such producers are makers of ballpoint pens, paper towels, and gasoline.

The Outputs of Production

An almost unlimited variety of outputs can result from the production process. Some are very complex products that require both breaking down and combining the inputs. Examples are computers, cargo ships, and scientific equipment. Others are simple products, such as distilled water, which require a simple process.

Services, such as preparation of tax returns, are a kind of product. Services represent an ever-increasing part of total U.S. production and employment. Their production is discussed more thoroughly in a later section of this chapter.

What Is Production Management?

production management **Production management is the application of managerial functions to production.** The inputs, processes, and outputs we have just described require planning, organizing, staffing, directing, and controlling. As we will see near the end of this chapter, this topic is often viewed in a broader way. This broader view, known as *operations management*, is more "systems"- or "process"-oriented than the traditional approach taken here. Meanwhile, we will examine the managerial functions in a production context.

Production Planning

Planning is concerned with the future. It is a mapping out of how things are going to be done. It has short-run and long-run dimensions and requires a forecast of demand.

Planning for production is no exception. It includes planning the product (outputs) and planning for capital, labor, and material needs (inputs). We will emphasize strategic, long-run planning with an emphasis on capital-goods planning and planning for the product itself.

Product Planning

The logical time to start planning for production is when planning the product. This type of planning really involves both production and marketing functions of the firm and is discussed more fully in our chapters on marketing. At this point we will describe just a few features of the product-planning process.

Product planning amounts to answering the following questions:

- What kind of products can be sold at a profit?
- How much can be sold?
- What styles and sizes should be produced?
- What special features should the product have?

The answers to these questions require study in the laboratory to determine the best inputs of raw materials and component parts. In many firms this kind of thinking is done on a continuous basis by a product development department. The basic questions are always "will it sell?" and "can it be produced at a profit?"

The product mix of a firm—that is, the combination of products that it produces—has both market and cost effects. Producing a line of related products has certain advantages from the selling standpoint. Producing several products, whether they are related or not, may affect the unit cost. A local Coca-Cola bottling company could begin to bottle other soft drinks in the Coca-Cola Company's line. This would probably increase its total production volume without adding much cost for plant or equipment. Thus "fixed" costs (such as plant and equipment) would be spread over more units, and the cost per bottle would be reduced.

THINK ABOUT IT!

New Products at Procter and Gamble

In 1978 and 1979, the huge and successful firm of Procter and Gamble ($8.1 billion in sales in fiscal year 1978) had plans to introduce to large-scale distribution an unprecedented number of new products, according to Edward G. Harness, its chairman. The array of new products suggests just how broad Procter and Gamble's product mix is. New products include: Puritan cooking oil, a new disposable diaper, a new cake mix, Wondra hand and body lotion, Rely tampons, a line of disposable drapes and gowns for surgical patients, and new flavors of Pringles' potato chips.

Launching so many new products at the same time is costly, but Procter and Gamble already has good evidence of the new products' acceptability from market testing and other market research. (See Chapter 8 for a discussion of market research.) Heavy costs include capital spending to increase production and research and development spending to keep the new products coming.

Not many firms have product planning activity on the scale of Procter and Gamble, but the nature of the activity and its importance remain the same.

Source: *The Wall Street Journal.*

One question that often arises in planning the product is the decision whether to make a product or a component part or to buy it—the "make-or-buy" decision. If we are talking about a firm that makes only one product, buying it rather than making it would take the firm out of the production business entirely. This could be the right decision if the firm could make more money by buying a product and reselling it than by making it and then selling it.

"make-or-buy" decision

Other factors are involved in the "make-or-buy" question. If it is to be a question at all, there must be a reliable source from which to buy the product or part. There must be a supplier who is willing to meet the buyer's needs in terms of quality, quantity, and delivery schedules. A decision to buy rather than to make often is made for the component parts of an assembled product. The major auto makers, for example, buy many of the component parts of the cars they make. In the construction industry, a contractor often uses one or more subcontractors to produce various parts of the project.

Once a firm reaches a certain size, it might stop buying one or more component parts and begin to make them. This may reduce total costs of production and make the producer more secure about sources of inputs. It may also make the firm less flexible.

Planning the Plant

There are several important questions that relate to planning for the plant itself. These include the decisions of

- where to locate the plant
- how large a plant to build
- how to arrange the plant internally

Plant location can affect overall cost, employee morale, and many other elements of a firm's operation. A manager should weigh carefully any location decision. A checklist such as the one provided in "Guidelines" below could be a great help. The first question is "in what area do we wish to locate?" This refers to a city or county or, perhaps, metropolitan area, but an even broader geographic location decision may be needed first. The factors to consider in selecting an area include input transportation, output transportation, and city and state inducements (such as tax exemptions) and deterrents (such as high real-property taxes). These should be estimated well in advance of making a decision.

GUIDELINES

Things to Consider When Locating a Plant

Area selection

1. Cost of materials and parts transportation
2. Cost of transportation of finished products to customers
3. Location inducements and deterrents by city and state governments
4. Quality and quantity of appropriate labor supply
5. Adequacy of power and water supply
6. Attractiveness as a place to live—climate, schools, safety, etc.

Specific site selection

1. Size
2. Accessibility to highways, railways, or water transport
3. Restrictions on land use, waste disposal, etc.
4. Land costs
5. Availability of leased facilities, such as public warehouses

Input transportation cost depends on the distance of raw material and parts suppliers from the proposed area and the kind of transportation facilities connecting them. Output transportation cost depends on the expected location and density of customers in the proposed area. Sometimes these cost factors make it hard to meet competitors' prices.

Local labor, water and power supplies are sometimes crucial. Southern California, with its large supply of skilled aircraft workers, would have to be a major contender for a new aircraft production plant. Chemical plants, which require large water supplies for processing, cannot ignore sites along the Mississippi River. Especially in times of tight energy supplies, any plant that will use large amounts of energy must consider if there is enough natural gas, petroleum, or coal at the proposed site.

A less tangible factor is the attractiveness of the area as a place to live. Important items here are climate, schools, housing, public parks, police protection, and taxes. A firm trying to decide between two possible locations might make estimates of their comparative profitability, taking into account the expected effects of each location on sales and on the various cost components—especially taxes, transportation, and labor.

Once an area is selected, the next problem is to choose a specific site. The firm makes a survey of available parcels of land that are suitable in terms of size, zoning restrictions, drainage, and access by highway, railway, and water. If several sites are satisfactory, the decision might depend on cost. There is the added possibility of finding a suitable existing plant available for sale or lease which could mean an earlier date for plant opening.

Specific site selection calls for compromise among the items on the checklist. A specific firm's choice may be determined by the emphasis placed on access to a river or on distance from population centers. The site may be selected because it is close to a large university or to a major industrial customer.

Railroads help manufacturers find industrial sites. One major railroad operates a briefing center at which it presents complete descriptions of all available spots to prospective plant builders. This saves firms a lot of legwork and searching costs.

Plant location decisions are becoming more difficult as land in and near major population centers becomes scarce. Also, traffic congestion, crime, pollution control, and plant obsolescence are forcing many plants to leave urban centers. These moves often involve heavy losses in moving or abandoning heavy machinery and equipment.

Once a site is chosen, the next step in planning is to design the building itself. With the help of production experts and architects, the firm must plan plant capacity. **Plant capacity is the limit of the production output of the facility.** A pocket calculator assembly plant, for example, may require 10,000 square feet of space to produce an expected maximum output of 2,000 units a day.   plant capacity

Plant layout describes the relative location of the different parts of the production process in the building or buildings. The planner of a   plant layout

THINK ABOUT IT!

How Profit Expectation Helps Choose a Location

The Dogwood Company is about to choose a location for its new box factory. With help from the accounting, production, and marketing experts, Ned Rink, head of the expansion committee, has come up with cost comparisons. They have narrowed the choice down to the cities of Memphis and St. Louis because they are nearest to the market that is not presently being served. The sales and cost estimates below lead to the conclusion that Memphis is the better choice, assuming that land and plant construction costs are equivalent.

	Memphis		St. Louis	
Estimated annual sales in units		80,000		120,000
Selling price		$5.00		$5.00
Cost of materials	$1.10		$1.20	
Labor	1.20		1.40	
Average transportation to market	1.30		1.10	
Taxes	.60		.80	
Other costs	.20		.20	
Total costs per unit		4.40		4.70
Net profit per unit		.60		.30
Expected total annual profit		$48,000		$36,000

Although volume of sales from St. Louis is greater, unit profit is twice as high in Memphis. It is dollar profit that counts. THINK ABOUT IT!

new calculator assembly plant might plan capacity and layout with the following factors in mind:

- expected output level
- possibility of 24-hour operation
- demand variation by month
- inventory storage needs
- expansion needs
- limits imposed by financing

How much weight is placed on each of these factors might vary according to the type of production process. A calculator assembly plant is a continuous, for-stock, labor-intensive process. It might well be laid out on one floor in a straight line. The parts could be stocked at one end, the several-step assembly process could occur in the center and the inspection, testing, packaging, and shipping could be done at the other end.

Organizing for Production

Some of the departmentation process (referred to earlier in Chapter 4) depends on the type of plant layout. A plant may be arranged according to process or according to product, depending on the number of products being produced and the volume of production. A *process-organized* plant might have a grinding department, buffing department, stamping department, etc. A *product-organized* plant might have a pocket calculator department and a desk calculator department, each of which is arranged on an assembly-line basis. How machines are related to each other often determines the organizational structure, including the number of persons in each department.

Production Organization Structure

Sometimes a firm's organization may have the structural features of both product and process. The organizational chart for the Punch Products Corporation in Figure 6–2 shows such a case in which there are two

FIGURE 6-2

Punch Products Corporation—organization for production

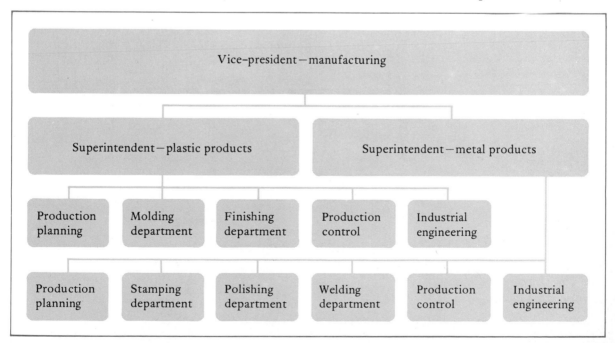

products, each run by a superintendent. Each product group has two or more processes, each of which is in a separate department. This firm is decentralized in that each product organization has production planning, production control, and industrial engineering departments.

The specific organization for production in a firm may be heavily influenced by the nature of the production process as well as by the number and variety of products made. The Switzer Company produces small amounts of 20 different products at different times of the year. This is the reason that production planning, control, and engineering will be centralized. If the 20 products go through many of the same processes, including processes A, B, C, and D, the organization may appear as in Figure 6–3.

Many new restaurant chains provide interesting examples of a trend toward centralization. The Joshua Tree restaurants and others operated by Marriot Corporation in the Northeast have centralized the food preparation function so that most of the outlets do no cooking on the premises. The large, centralized kitchens serve restaurants over 150 miles away and cut operating costs down and keep more uniform food quality standards at the same time.

Other special organization problems are forced on a firm when it grows and acquires competing or unrelated manufacturing firms. Deciding what can be combined, whether to remain decentralized, and other related problems call for careful study.

Production management often faces a tough challenge in keeping human enthusiasm for work, especially when production operations are highly automated. John Bivona's job is to press the green button every time the red light lights up in the boiler room. It is hard for John to see

FIGURE 6-3

Switzer Co.—organization for production

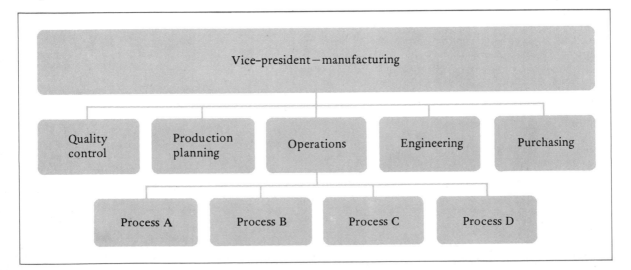

his role in the productive process. This kind of job presents a real challenge to the production manager to make full use of John's ability. Machines can reduce the "humanity" of an organization when they seem to "tell a person what to do." John Bivona's job is less human because of a machine.

A related problem is conflict in the assignment of activities among work groups. Introduction of new technology in the plant may cause work to be distributed in a new way. What the new machines require in the way of work assignment and departmentation may not be accepted by workers or by their unions. In organizing a factory, traditional union definitions of job responsibility—what kind of work a worker can or cannot do in the production process—cannot be ignored by a manager. Recent new regulations by the Occupational Safety and Health Administration (OSHA) which attempt to protect workers have added new limitations to factory design that complicate planning. (See Chapters 12 and 17.)

Staffing and Directing for Production

Staffing and directing together represent the application of the human resource to the production process. Staffing for production is often complicated by the need for highly specialized personnel. More extensive searching processes must be used than in many other kinds of business. The alternative is a long and expensive training program. Another complicating factor is the large role played by unions in manufacturing industries. As we'll see in Chapter 13, labor contracts often restrict or limit personnel managers in the process of hiring, transferring, and promotion, as well as in job assignments and in setting up working conditions.

A production manager must cope with the fact that machines, their timing, their coordination, and their very high costs determine how the production process is carried out. This includes determining the relationship between jobs, the span of management of supervisors, and other factors that must influence the kind of direction a supervisor can give.

The Human Dimension in Production

It is easier to motivate workers to outproduce coworkers than to motivate them to operate at the pace dictated by a machine. How does a manager set a wage rate that all workers think is fair when the principal contributor to productivity is a machine? Also, many production workers fear that automation will put them out of work. This makes it hard to motivate them, especially when their unions oppose automation.

In such situations, harmony is hard to achieve. It may be done by means of cooperation between labor and management. Both sides can agree that greater productivity is good for all. If automation can bring about greater productivity and management can assure the unions and their members that workers will share fairly in this increased productivity, a good working relationship can be built. It takes planning to prepare for the period of change to automation. This planning includes worker retraining and relocation and other guarantees of security for those workers most affected. Wage rates will rise because workers expect to share in the benefits of increased productivity.

Controlling Production

Controlling production involves setting production standards and developing systems for comparing production performance to those standards. There are several different types of production control. They include

- order control
- product quality control
- plant maintenance control
- inventory control
- other production controls

Order Control

When a plant is engaged in continuous, high-volume production of standard products, close control of individual orders is not very important. But in those plants using intermittent production, it is vital to create systems to control the flow of orders. New orders that have never been processed before must be checked to see what operations must be performed. They must be checked for correct sequence and to see that the right tools are on hand. This may require the use of a control chart. **A control chart is a device which shows the standard set of steps to be taken in the performance of a procedure.** It ensures that things will be done as planned. Control charts were first conceived by Henry Gantt in the early 1900s, and today a wide variety of commercial variations of Gantt Charts is available.

control chart

Plants that produce a variety of products on an intermittent basis establish a system of *decision rules* to guide the movement of orders through various manufacturing processes. Suppose there is a question: Which of two orders should be processed first by a given machine? It is not always logical to say that the order with the earliest due date should be processed first. Some firms use a simple "first-come, first-served" rule; others use a "first-come, first-served within priority class" rule for making these decisions. Which rule is best depends on the kind of processing going on in the plant. Regardless, some form of decision rule is necessary in intermittent-process production to guarantee a smooth flow. In recent years, computer simulation techniques have been used to speed up production. These are discussed in Chapter 14.

Important tools used in order to assure a smooth flow of operations include PERT (Program Evaluation and Review Technique) and CPM (Critical Path Method). **PERT is a planning and control tool focusing on the timing of the occurrence of many operations included in a project.** It helps identify and remove bottlenecks. This tool was first applied by the government to speed up completion of vital weapons systems.

PERT

A CPM diagram is illustrated in Figure 6–4. **CPM is much like PERT except that specific estimates rather than variable estimates of elapsed time in operations are used.** Wetherall Utility Buildings plans construction of a standard 20,000-square-foot warehouse by listing the major stages of construction, the time needed for each, and the sequence in which they occur. The letters in parentheses are events. The order of events is indicated by arrows. *Branching* occurs whenever two events can be worked on at the same time. The numbers next to arrow-segments show how many days are needed. A manager can follow a "path"

CPM

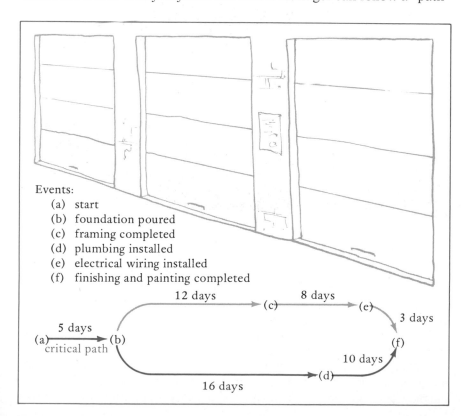

FIGURE 6-4

A CPM diagram

Events:
  (a) start
  (b) foundation poured
  (c) framing completed
  (d) plumbing installed
  (e) electrical wiring installed
  (f) finishing and painting completed

to completion and can tell which chain of events is the longest or "critical" path (ABDF in our example). It is this chain of events that the manager must focus on to cut production time or to avoid delays.

Order control systems must include rapid communication systems, such as special mail service or teletypes or even direct feedback to a central computer. They help management to take action quickly enough to correct flaws in the operation. This is the essence of control.

Product Quality Control

quality control

Clearly, there is a need to control the movement of orders through a production process. There is also a need for quality control. **A quality control system sets up a standard for an input or output and makes comparisons against this standard to prevent nonstandard items from going into or coming out of the production process.** This, however, does not necessarily mean that quality must be kept high. It means that the level of quality must be known and checked so that it can be kept within a certain *range of acceptable quality standards.* Of course, a manufacturer does not always seek to avoid high quality. Lower quality, however, may be acceptable when higher quality control would be too costly. A firm may seek a quality level far below what could be achieved.

The Good Time Corporation makes children's outdoor play products. It produces a backyard slide selling for $49.95. The production manager has specified an inexpensive rust-resistant galvanized nut and bolt for fastening the slide's major parts. These nuts and bolts sell for one cent apiece in large quantities. The manager could have specified chrome-plated nuts and bolts costing eight cents apiece and thus been able to guarantee against rust. But customers paying $49.95 for a backyard slide just don't expect chrome-plated parts, so the added cost is unjustified. This does *not* mean, however, that the production manager would accept even cheaper, lower-quality bolts than the ones selected just to reduce costs by a fraction of a cent. They might cause the slide to fall apart and the firm would lose its reputation as a maker of good, low-priced play equipment.

Production quality control applies to raw materials, parts purchased, the finished product, and to various stages in the production process. Thus certain testing standards and procedures may be used in the purchasing department for all raw materials and parts. Other testing standards and procedures may be used in the production process to guarantee the quality of the finished product.

The Brakewell Bike Company buys tires, tubes, and handle grips from the Mutual Rubber Supply Company in large lots. These components are inspected upon arrival to see if they meet specifications (standards of quality). During the process of manufacture, welded joints of the bicycle frame are inspected and the braking assembly is tested. After an entire bike is assembled, it is lubricated and "test driven" for a quarter of a mile. These tests cost money, but they help build Brakewell's reputation for quality.

It is almost impossible to guarantee 100 percent quality of all inputs and finished products. Ordinarily, this would be too expensive. Most manufacturers, therefore, use sampling in quality control inspection. When a shipment of steel tubing arrives for processing, the purchasing department at Brakewell may require that a sample of 50 twenty-foot sections be examined. Instructions might require that a shipment be accepted if no more than one defective section is found in the sample. This is called *acceptance sampling.* In certain types of production, of course, a 100 percent inspection is necessary because the sale of even one faulty unit could have very serious results.

The basis for classifying a unit as defective depends on what features of the unit are "critical." For steel tubing, perhaps hardness and strength are important. Applying these standards may require mechanical assistance or perhaps it can be done visually. Welds, for example, may be examined visually or by using x-rays, as was done for the Alaskan pipeline. A wide variety of measuring and testing machines exists in industry today. Often, however, a simple visual inspection is sufficient. A balance is needed between the cost of inspection and the cost of failure to meet standards.

Maintenance and Control of Plant and Equipment

In a manufacturing plant—particularly a continuous-process, assembly-line plant—one critical machine breakdown means high costs. During this "downtime" most of the other machinery is idled, and all the workers on the line are being paid even though their machines are idle.

This points up the need for maintenance. **Many firms practice preventive maintenance. This means that they inspect and/or replace certain critical machines and parts on a regular basis to avoid downtime.** Not all firms practice this, however. It may cost more than a firm is willing to pay. The units may be very expensive to replace. Also the cost of interrupting the production process for maintenance work may be too high. Some production managers prefer to "leave well enough alone." They install the highest-quality equipment to start with. This decision is a matter of balancing costs.

preventive maintenance

Control of Inventory Levels

A fourth area of production control is the control of inventory levels. This includes inventories of raw materials, parts, and finished and partly finished products.

There are some good reasons for keeping high levels of inventory. A

Source: Chris Maynard.

firm using assembly-line production is less likely to "run out" of parts and partly finished products. Running out of inventory can mean expensive downtime. This also applies to finished products. Big orders (and possibly big customers) can be lost if deliveries cannot be made as promised. Large stocks protect against this.

There are some equally good reasons for keeping inventories low, however. First, inventories require an investment of funds. A factory that operates with a lower inventory is operating more efficiently—that is, it is producing profits with a smaller investment than a factory with a large inventory. Second, inventories take up scarce space. Third, products in inventory may decrease in value because of deterioration, theft, or damage. **Inventory items also may be subject to obsolescence. This is what happens when something is out of date or not as efficient as newer products.** New inputs or new finished products may be invented or found which would make existing inventories obsolete.

obsolescence

Some firms use mathematical formulas to determine the best inventory levels to maintain. These formulas include such things as order-loss risks, storage costs, interest, expected delivery time, and other factors. They also aid in determining the best quantity of inputs to order and the time interval between orders.

Other Production Controls

As we will see in our discussion of accounting in Chapter 9, there are other important control devices relating to production costs. These include cost systems and various budgeting devices.

Production and Ecology

Many production processes cause problems of ecological balance in the areas where a product is produced and consumed. Extracting coal by strip mining has sometimes caused long-lasting environmental damage. The use of aluminum and glass containers for certain consumer products has contributed to a solid-waste disposal problem. It has brought unsightly litter to our cities and countryside. The manufacturing process itself has poured smoke into our air and poisonous wastes into our waters. Nuclear energy plants, especially since the Three-Mile Island accident, have represented an ecological threat in the minds of many citizens.

For years our factories have made only limited use of waste materials and by-products. They have used these materials only when there was obvious profit in it. There are many recyclable inputs which have little dollar value, but which should be recycled for the sake of our ecological balance. The government is setting new standards, and it is up to production management to do its work within the new limits at a cost that will permit the sale of products at competitive prices.

Materials Management

The variety of materials purchased by a firm—raw materials, partly finished products, finished products, supplies, and capital goods—requires a special managerial effort. These products must be purchased (or made), physically handled, and stored. Capital goods also need to be maintained in working order.

The most highly developed managerial activity in dealing with materials—one that often requires setting up a special department—is purchasing.

The Purchasing Task

The purchasing task can have a critical effect on profits for manufacturers, retailers, and wholesalers. In manufacturing this is especially true when materials and parts are a major part of total manufacturing cost. Many firms establish a separate purchasing department with its own manager. Many large purchasing departments have divisions that specialize in specific types of purchases and divisions for records management and follow-up.

A typical large manufacturing firm must buy fuels, cleaning supplies, lumber, sheet steel, dyes, handtools, nails, electronic calculators, stationery, electrical equipment, paint, food for the company cafeteria, trucks, and many other items. They must prepare for fulfilling these needs by forecasting them and by locating adequate sources of supply. The sources must be adequate in terms of volume, delivery schedule, and quality levels. The purchasing department must be in constant contact with their suppliers' sales offices to keep up with their pricing policies, new product features, and delivery schedules.

Many firms, especially large ones, practice *centralized purchasing* rather than allow individual departments and divisions to make their own purchases. This can result in cost savings from large-volume buying, greater coordination of purchasing and receiving functions, and a more uniform application of standard purchase specifications.

Depending on the nature of the product or service, the purchasing department may provide different types of advice and perform different types of services. When specialized and expensive machinery is needed, the purchasing department must work closely with the production manager whose department will use it.

Often, finance, purchasing, production, and engineering people work together to develop a list of specifications for the equipment and to plan for its financing and procurement. This team approach is helpful in "make-or-buy" decisions, and it helps to ensure that the right machine will be bought. The production manager alone might specify higher quality than is actually needed. If the finance manager were to make the decision alone, perhaps quality would be compromised in order to save money. The team objective is to get the level of quality needed by the using department at the best price. This requires a systems approach to decision making in which the "net" welfare of the firm is the guiding principle.

For less expensive items the purchasing department assumes a larger role. The purchasing department makes its own price and quality decisions for items such as paper clips. Most routine purchases are handled in this way.

Purchasing Policies

Over time, firms usually develop *standard purchasing policies.* For example, some follow a policy of building up inventories when prices are right. The purchasing agent is a "professional purchaser," who generally has a very good idea of when prices are right.

Frank McGee, purchasing agent for the Claxton Art Supplies Manufacturing Company, is in constant contact with several suppliers of quality natural bristle for artists' paintbrushes. He buys only when prices are down because storage costs and product deterioration are not a problem. In March he received notice and samples of a huge shipment available immediately from Korea at a price 20 percent below the typical price. Since he had dealt with this importer before and had been favorably impressed, he ordered a two-year supply of the product.

CAN YOU SETTLE THE ISSUE HERE?

The Purchasing Agent, the Salesperson, and Business Ethics

The purchasing agent is the firm's professional buyer. He or she is a very important person as far as salespeople are concerned. That is why purchasing agents often receive "special favors" from salespersons who want to sell to them. Christmas gifts, free "samples" for the purchasing agent's personal use, and other "favors" are not uncommon.

Is it unethical for purchasing agents to accept "favors" and for salespersons to offer them? CAN YOU SETTLE THE ISSUE HERE?

Some purchasing agents follow a policy of concentrating all their purchases for a specific good or service with one supplier. This is often because that supplier's past performance has been excellent. Other purchasing agents avoid this for fear of "being taken for granted" or "putting all their eggs in one basket." A strike, for example, at a supplier's plant may place the buyer firm in a bad position.

Other purchasing policies involve such matters as taking discounts offered by suppliers. If a supplier offers a *cumulative quantity discount*, all purchases made during a certain period are subject to a discount based on the total volume purchased during that period. This policy builds buyer loyalty but probably reduces the average size of orders. A *noncumulative quantity discount* probably leads to larger orders but may not do much to develop customer loyalty.

Some firms follow a policy of leasing equipment rather than purchasing it whenever possible. Leasing often offers a tax advantage since lease payments are deductible business expenses. It also shifts part of the risk of equipment obsolescence to the lessor and ties up less of the lessee's capital. Just as firms face "make-or-buy" decisions, they also face "buy-or-lease" decisions.

A common purchasing policy involves reciprocity—"you buy from me and I'll buy from you." Reciprocity is widely practiced by industrial marketers and buyers. It makes buyer and seller interdependent and it guarantees the seller a customer but limits the sources of supply. It may also cause buyers to become too lazy in their search for "the best quality at the lowest price."

reciprocity

Value Analysis and Vendor Analysis

The purchasing function is being handled increasingly by professionals. Two tools which are receiving growing attention are value analysis and vendor analysis.

value analysis

Value analysis starts by reviewing existing product specifications as set by user departments. Attention then focuses on identifying and eliminating nonessential cost factors. This review may involve a committee including engineers, cost accountants, production representatives, and others. They review the specifications set by the user department. Wherever a specification is thought to add unnecessary cost, the function of that "spec" is examined to see if it can be eliminated or if a cheaper way of doing it can be found. Such a review requires close contact with potential vendors to verify cost.

The Coca-Cola Company in late 1978 was seriously considering a high-fructose corn sweetener as a partial substitute for sugar in the manufacture of their noncola brand. Such substitution could have been expected to lead to a big cost saving because fructose sweetener was selling at a price 10 to 15 percent lower than sugar. And the change in inputs would have had no significant effect on taste.

Careful investigation of the costs of alternative input components can lead to significant savings. However, a value-analysis decision of this type cannot omit consideration of whether significant loss of quality in the product will occur.

vendor analysis

Vendor analysis is the evaluation of potential suppliers in which the technical, financial, and managerial abilities of vendors are considered and rated in terms of their past performance in these areas. It is a method of substituting facts for feelings in the selection of suppliers.

After a purchasing department has made its analysis of possible suppliers, it is in a position to decide. It makes the decision and sends a purchase order to the supplier. Some purchasing departments, however, invite sellers to submit bids. In some cases, the buyer elects to award the purchase contract to the lowest bidder. This *competitive bidding* requires that the buyer specify in detail what it is that he or she wants to purchase. In other cases, specifications are not so exact, and bids received are subject to further *buyer-seller negotiation* over price and quality. Bids, however, are not used in all cases. The buyer might contact and deal with only one supplier.

A purchasing department is also accountable for following up on purchases already made. Elaborate file systems are used to ensure that deliveries are made on time. This permits quick follow-up on transportation details and expected delivery dates. A final responsibility is for the physical receipt of shipments. This involves checking contents against invoices before giving approval to the accounting department to make payment.

Operations Management—A Broader View

Up to now we have emphasized the use of management techniques for the production of products—production as opposed to marketing or finance, and physical products as opposed to services. This bias is justified on two grounds. First, scientific management was developed in factories, not in retail stores; and second, the next few chapters will be devoted to marketing and finance.

Most of the techniques discussed so far in this chapter can be made to work quite well outside the factory. These methods work in service firms like beauty parlors or repair shops; they also work in distribution firms like wholesalers or truckers.

Operations management is a new, expanded version of the idea of   operations management
production management. It represents a systems approach to all busi-
ness functions with an emphasis on current operations and control
rather than on long-range planning.

An operations management view is likely to conceive of a business, or a part of a business, as a productive system. Such a system normally involves making a series of key decisions within a system, such as are outlined in "Guidelines," on the next page.

This broader view includes such business systems as controlling the billing process for a large medical practice, designing the physical layout of a bank, or locating a new supermarket for a large chain. Let's look briefly at how we might apply operations management techniques to each of these.

Dr. Jenny Wilson opened her office in a suburb of a midwestern city soon after completing her internship. The practice grew very quickly. It was a great success after a few years, but she wasn't doing too well when it came to collecting her fees. A management consultant could have pointed out several specific problems. First, she was not regularly recording and filing fees for house calls. Second, her office assistant was often absent and his replacements made a lot of billing errors. Finally, there was no routine for following up on slow or nonpaying accounts.

The practice of good operations management methods would have resulted in the design of a routine for reporting house-call charges to the office; the hiring of a regular replacement for the office assistant; and the establishment of a past-due bill follow-up procedure and use of a collection agent for extreme cases.

The National Commercial Bank needed to bring its 50-year-old building up to date. An operations management approach to the problem might have started by asking the question, "What has changed between 1930 and 1980 concerning the banking needs of our customers?" Solutions might have included providing a pleasant atmosphere, improved parking, and drive-in facilities. Consultants might also have recom-

GUIDELINES

An Operations Management View of Key Decisions in the Life of a Productive System

BIRTH of the System	What are the goals of the firm? What products or services will be offered?
PRODUCT DESIGN and *PROCESS SELECTION*	What are the form and appearance of the product? Technologically, how should the product be made?
DESIGN of the System	Where should the facility be located? What physical arrangement is best to use? How do you maintain desired quality? How do you determine demand for the product or service?
STAFFING the System	What job is each worker to perform? How will the job be performed, measured; how will the workers be compensated?
STARTUP of the System	How do you get the system into operation? How long will it take to reach desired rate of output?
The System in *STEADY STATE*	How do you run the system? How can you improve the system? How do you deal with day-to-day problems?
REVISION of the system	How do you revise the system in light of external changes?
TERMINATION of the System	How does a system die? What can be done to salvage resources?

Source: Chase and Aquilano, *Production and Operations Management.*

mended closed-circuit TV for greater security (control) and a customer-relations training program for tellers. A systems approach often requires that human inputs be modified along with the plant itself. Good operations management would have recommended such things only after interviewing customers and employees and checking the timing and flow-path of bank customers inside the building as well as their choice of transportation methods to the bank.

Similar analysis and application of operations management techniques could work for the Safeway supermarket chain in choosing a new retail location. Management might have started by checking census data and other sources to find those areas of population growth in the city. They might also check the location of competition, the cost of land, traffic flows, zoning information, and the availability of the right kind of land and/or buildings for lease. The final decision would be made in much the same way as the plant location example earlier in this chapter.

Management of Safeway would consider factors likely to draw customers and factors affecting costs. The greatest motivation, as in the case of all business management, is profit. The methods of estimating profit found in operations management are quite similar to those a large factory might use.

Summary and Look Ahead

Production creates products and services by a variety of processes out of human and material inputs. The management of such a process begins with the planning of the product, the plant, and its location. Production includes special organizational and staffing problems related to the impact of technology. It requires the application of a variety of control devices to assure uniformity of quality of output and efficient production scheduling.

Purchasing has evolved into a science in itself. Centralized purchasing departments develop purchasing policies and procedures to help ensure that the firm gets products and services at required quality at a minimum price.

The mountain of products generated by a giant production system demands an ingenious marketing effort to move them into American markets. Financing a manufacturing plant and its related facilities is also a complex undertaking that requires up-to-date accounting methods. Computers are needed to support production, finance, accounting, and marketing. All of these topics will be examined in the next few chapters. Marketing is the first to be examined. It is such a large subject that we will devote two chapters to it. The first chapter presents an overview of the marketing task and introduces two parts of the marketing mix—product and place, or distribution.

My name is Thomas E. Jones. I am an industrial engineer with the Cummins Engine Company.

My education has led to a B.S. in vocational education from Alcorn State as well as an M.Ed. degree from Southern University. I have had experience as a teacher in vocational education, math, and sciences, which included educational work in Botswana, Africa and with the Job Corps in Indiana. I also had experience as a soil conservationist before coming to Cummins.

My present responsibilities include developing work standards for various production lines and conducting make-or-buy studies to determine whether it is more efficient to manufacture a part in-house or purchase it. I also have developed flow charts for machine operators and machines; conducted machine utilization studies to ensure that machines are being used to their fullest capacity; conducted space studies to determine if there is adequate room for an operator to work with a machine; and developed a training program to familiarize other manufacturing areas with the industrial engineering department's function.

I originally chose to be a foreman to become exposed to the basic functions of the manufacturing environment. I felt this exposure would benefit me greatly in my manufacturing career development. I moved into the industrial engineering area believing it would provide excellent training since I was interested in a manufacturing career.

I chose Cummins because of its outstanding system of promotion and opportunities for cross-functional moves and exposure. I had read that Cummins was one of the top 10 companies to work for and was especially attracted to the fact that Cummins is known for being very "people-oriented."

Key Concepts

automation   A process in which little human supervision is needed.

breaking down   A production process that involves removing or separating some of the original input (raw material), as when logs are cut into boards.

capital-intensive   Production processes depending more heavily on machinery, plant, and equipment than on labor. Capital investment is a major part of production costs.

combination   A production process that involves bringing things together into a new arrangement.

continuous production   Production carried out routinely and without interruption. The opposite of intermittent production (see next page).

control chart   Any of a variety of charts or illustrations guiding the sequence of steps required in production or in the flow of paperwork.

CPM (Critical Path Method)   A planning and control tool used by managers to estimate the time needed to complete various parts of a project, and focusing on the longest or "critical" path.

intermittent production   Production that stops and starts. This happens because the products may require several different kinds of treatments or because stocks must be replenished from time to time.

labor-intensive   A production process involving relatively large amounts of human input. Wages are a major production cost.

make-or-buy decisions   Decisions about the economy of making a product or a component part or buying it.

obsolescence   Growing old, becoming outdated or not as efficient as newer products; applied to technological or fashion products.

operations management   A general term applied to production, financial, and marketing management with an emphasis on the treatment of all three as parts of a system that is subject to improvement by scientific management methods. The focus is on current operations and control.

PERT (Program Evaluation and Review Technique)   A planning and control tool used by managers to estimate how much time it takes to complete various parts of a project so that bottlenecks can be avoided and the project can be done on time.

plant capacity   The limits of the output of a production facility. A major subject of production planning.

plant layout   The internal design of a factory, including the arrangement of the machines used in the manufacturing process.

preventive maintenance   The inspection and/or replacement of certain critical machines and parts on a regular basis to avoid downtime.

production   An activity that results in the creation of goods and services.

production management   The application of the functions of management to a production process. A narrower concept than operations management (see above).

quality control   Means by which the level of quality of inputs and outputs is known and monitored so that it can be kept within a certain range of acceptable quality standards.

reciprocity   A "you buy from me and I'll buy from you" purchasing policy. Two firms agree to supply each other.

treatment   A production process that doesn't add parts to or remove them from something. Examples are cooking meat or painting wood.

value analysis   The reviewing of existing product specifications as set by user departments; the identification of costs and the attempt to cut them where possible.

vendor analysis   An approach to evaluation of potential suppliers that considers the capabilities of vendors and may include a specific vendor rating system. Vendors are rated in terms of their past performance.

For Review . . .

1. Who was Frederick W. Taylor? Check an encyclopedia.
2. Distinguish between production management and operations management.
3. Does continuous production or intermittent production justify larger capital expenditure? Why?
4. Locating a plant near suppliers but far away from customers implies what about the nature of inputs and outputs and their transportation costs?
5. Distinguish between production organization along product lines and along process lines.
6. Does production management have human-relations problems not found in financial or marketing management? Explain.
7. What is reciprocity? Is it a sound basis for purchasing decisions? Why or why not?

8. What are the pros and cons of centralized purchasing?
9. What is the essential idea of value analysis?

... For Discussion

1. Analyze the data in Table 6–1 and explain the great variation in rates of growth of different industries since 1967.
2. Develop a detailed example of the inputs, process(es), and output(s) of a plant in your town. What would happen to the process and output if one input were not available?

3. Draw a simple CPM chart, modifying the example in your text. Identify the critical path. In what sense is it critical?
4. Find a real-life example of buying on a bidding basis and discuss the advantages of this to the buyer.
5. Give an example of the use of operations management in the control of the quality of hamburgers at a McDonald's restaurant. Identify the standard employed.

Incidents

Dutch Pantry Restaurants

More than eighty restaurants operate in the Northeast under the name "Dutch Pantry." These restaurants are serviced by a central commissary in Hummelswharf, Pa. A high proportion of all the food served in these restaurants is prepared centrally at the commissary. This cuts down significantly on the size of the staff and the capital investment in cooking facilities which would be needed if each outlet did all of its own cooking. It also is easier to maintain quality control. This procedure is followed by many restaurant chains, but certainly not by all.

Questions

1. What are the disadvantages of this system over that of individual food preparation in all outlets?
2. How should Dutch Pantry have decided where to locate the commissary originally?
3. How does this system affect: *(a)* the range of decisions made by each outlet's manager; and *(b)* the motivation of the outlet managers and of workers in these outlets?

Source: *The Wall Street Journal.*

Auto Recalls—Product Quality Control the Hard Way

News of a massive new recall of autos, tires, and appliances is hardly news anymore. A specific case announced in 1978 was the voluntary recall by Ford Motor Company of some 1.5 million Pintos and Bobcats. National Highway Traffic Safety Administration (NHTSA) tests of these cars had indicated problems with fuel tank safety in rear-end collisions.

Such recalls are very costly to the manufacturer. In this case, it was estimated that gas tank modifications would cost Ford between $20.00 and $30.00 apiece. Additional costs in terms of damage to the "image" of the product could be great, as could losses from lawsuits.

If Ford had not recalled voluntarily, the firm might have faced a forced recall order issued by the NHTSA. Such an event could have resulted in even higher costs.

Questions

1. How do you think such callbacks will influence future product quality-control practices in auto plants?
2. Could such recalls influence value-analysis systems in purchasing? If so, how?
3. After you have read the next chapter, show how this recall case illustrates the overlap between production management and marketing management.

Source: *The Wall Street Journal.*

ROCKETOY COMPANY 4

Terry Phillips, by now a reasonably experienced corporate executive, began to realize that corporate growth brings with it serious problems. The production facilities of Rocketoy were becoming clearly inadequate. The number and the variety of orders were so large that the firm was two weeks behind schedule on deliveries. Equipment was rapidly "falling apart" despite good maintenance and supervision by Mark Flynn, the assistant production manager. A new plant was essential and Terry called in Uchello and Jaynes, consulting architects, to design it.

Looking ahead at what Rocketoy expected to be the future production level of various products, the seasonal factors, and chances of obsolescence, T. Phillips, J. Phillips, Flynn, and the architects agreed on a one-level, 60,000 square-foot plant with nine "shops" or processing areas as well as office, inspection, packaging, shipping, and receiving areas. The nine processing areas included painting, wood assembly, plastic molding, metal stamping, and five other areas. Each was capable of performing one of the major production processes for one or more of the three types of toys produced—wood, metal, and plastic.

A site was selected near Detroit with excellent access to interstate highways. The site was also close to suppliers of many of Rocketoy's parts and raw materials.

Some differences of opinion arose among Rocketoy's managers. Ms. Rabinovitz and Pam Carter (formerly Pam Phillips) argued that moving the plant to Detroit from Milwaukee would create great morale problems among their loyal production workers who would dislike moving. Finding replacements in Detroit would, at least in the short run, cause lots of problems according to Ms. Rabinovitz and Pam Carter.

Questions

1. Classify some of the production processes at Rocketoy according to the process classifications discussed in the text.
2. Do you agree with the kind of plant arrangement worked out by the architects? Why or why not?
3. Can you think of any alternatives to building a new plant? Explain.
4. What are the criteria for site selection which were not mentioned in the case?
5. How should Rocketoy deal with the problem of assuring quality labor in the new location? What morale problems could arise in addition to those mentioned?

Marketing I

CHAPTER
7

Objectives: After reading this chapter, you should be able to

1. Illustrate the fact that marketing is a matching process.
2. Explain the role of the consumer in the marketing concept.
3. Distinguish among four kinds of utility in a product.
4. Give an example of a marketing mix for a specific product or a service.
5. Show what justifies the existence of middlemen.
6. Describe the principal characteristics of the industrial goods market.
7. Draw up a list of consumer goods and tell which are convenience, shopping, and specialty goods.
8. Identify the bundle of satisfactions offered by a product to its user.
9. Draw a chart illustrating the life cycle of a product.
10. Present arguments for and against a broad product mix.
11. Explain the functions that a package performs.
12. Draw a chart that illustrates how a middleman may bring about economies in distribution.
13. Distinguish between an integrated and a nonintegrated channel of distribution.
14. Provide an illustration of the total cost concept.
15. Describe the ideal distribution task conditions for each of the major modes of transportation.

Key concepts: Look for these terms as you read the chapter

marketing	product life cycle
form utility	planned obsolescence
place utility	product mix
time utility	brand
ownership utility	patent
managerial approach to marketing	trademark
	place (distribution)
marketing concept	channel of distribution
target market	manufacturer's agent
industrial goods	franchised retailer
consumer goods	physical distribution
middlemen	total cost concept
convenience goods	common carrier
shopping goods	contract carrier
specialty goods	private carrier
marketing mix	containerization
product	

This chapter introduces the second important area of decision making for firms—marketing. It builds on concepts developed in earlier chapters on economics and management. It also prepares us for the detailed discussion of marketing activities in the next chapter. We'll see why a "marketing" orientation has been adopted by many firms and how this is reflected in their approach to the customer. We'll also see the difference between utility creation *in production and in marketing and begin a careful look at the marketing mix. At the outset, it will prove helpful to define what is meant by "marketing."*

What Is Marketing?

Marketing is the whole set of activities undertaken to find, influence, and serve customers for products and services. It often means finding out what products and services people already need or want. Sometimes it involves creating or stimulating new wants. These wants, once established, must be satisfied. Marketing activities include such things as marketing research, retailing, sales force management, advertising, and transportation. These activities will be examined in the pages to follow.

marketing

The greater the production ability of a nation or firm, the more important it becomes to improve its marketing ability. The benefits of production technology are wasted in a free economy if the wrong things are produced or if the people don't know about the product. It is vital that every firm design a good marketing program.

In a rich nation like the United States or Canada, there are many choices available to consumers. The more income a family or individual has, the smaller is the proportion of income required for absolute necessities. Wealthy buyers can shift their spending patterns around. As we have seen in Chapter 2, what a buyer has to spend on things other than necessities is called *discretionary income*. Figure 7–1 shows that a family, the Collinses, has 67 percent more after-tax income ($25,000 versus $15,000) than another family, the Browns. However, it also demonstrates that the discretionary part of the Collins's income is 250 percent greater than that of the Browns ($7,000 versus $2,000). Rising income, then, means businesses find it harder to predict what will be bought. This complicates the marketing task and makes it even more important to watch the consumer closely. The consumer's tastes and preferences can change quickly.

In recent years there has been a big increase in the number of *multi-earner families*—families with more than one earner. The rise in job opportunities for women together with the rising number of working wives means a big jump in discretionary income for many families. These multiearner families are reputed to spend more on household help and dining out and less on child-related products and services. They represent a market for luxury products and services.

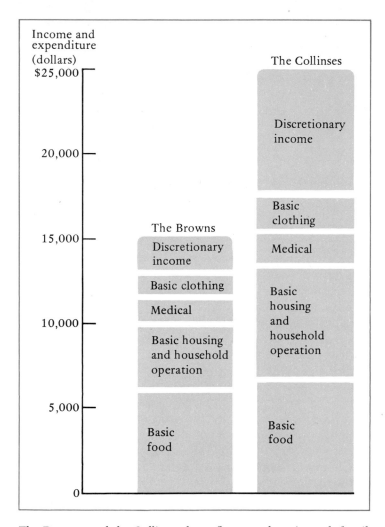

FIGURE 7-1

**Discretionary income
of two families**

The Browns and the Collinses have five members in each family—two adults
and three children between the ages of 5 and 15. The Collins's income after
taxes is $25,000—$10,000 more than that of the Browns. The Collinses spend
$5,000 more than the Browns for necessities—basic food, clothing, housing,
and medical expenses. This leaves them $7,000 to spend as they prefer—
discretionary income. The Browns have only $2,000 in discretionary income.
As income increases, discretionary income increases at a higher rate.

The marketing process must also cope with risks related to technology. A firm never really knows when a competitor will devise a new
product that outdates the firm's present product or that makes its present product unnecessary. Frozen orange concentrate, for example, has
greatly reduced the market for orange-squeezing appliances in the
kitchen.

A full explanation of the function of marketing is helped by expanding on a concept introduced in Chapter 1, the concept of *utility*. The next section explores the relationship between marketing and utility.

Marketing and Utility

The utility of products and services is at the heart of the marketing problem. We can distinguish the following kinds of utility

- form utility
- place utility
- time utility
- ownership utility

We will show how these four aspects of utility relate to the household purchase of sugar.

Form utility is utility resulting from a change in form. It is produced by treatment or breaking-down processes such as those described in Chapter 6. Sugar, for example, becomes more useful after the juice is extracted from the sugar cane or sugar beets and is cooked and refined. The sugar refineries of Louisiana create form utility.

form utility

Form utility, unfortunately, is not enough to satisfy the millions of people who want this sugar for use in their homes. Place utility is needed, too. **Place utility is that aspect of usefulness determined by location.** Refined sugar on a loading dock in Louisiana must be moved to Chicago before its usefulness to a Chicago family can be realized. The train or truck that transports the sugar "up North" creates, in the process, *place utility* for people in Chicago.

place utility

Time utility is somewhat harder to explain. It is that aspect of utility determined by the passage of time as it relates to consumption. It depends on an idea we explored in the early chapters, the principle of *diminishing marginal utility*. Let's take the case of the Jones family in Chicago. They have a pound of sugar in a bowl on the kitchen table. A five-pound bag on the shelf of the Jewel supermarket down the street is not yet fully useful to the Joneses for several reasons. One, as we have seen, is that it needs more place utility. Another is that more time must pass until the present stock of sugar is used up and they "need" more sugar enough to go to the store to buy it. That bag on the Jewel shelf is gaining *time* utility as the bowl of sugar at home is used up.

time utility

Finally, full usefulness of the five-pound bag on the supermarket shelf, as far as the Jones family is concerned, can't be reached until they own it. Because of the concept of private property, this sugar must be *bought*. **Ownership utility is that aspect of the usefulness of a product**

ownership utility

related to the passage of legal title to the final user. When Mr. or Mrs. Jones goes to the store, pays for the sugar, and brings it home to fill the sugar bowl, the *full utility* of the sugar is realized. Marketing activities have been directly involved in the creation of place, time, and ownership utility. How firms do this is the main topic of this chapter and the next.

The Marketing Concept and the Managerial Approach

The broad field of marketing has been analyzed in many ways. Some people study the major institutions (wholesalers, retailers, etc.) involved in the marketing process. Others study the different ways in which various commodities are marketed (marketing of grain, meat, hardware, etc.). Still another method is to divide the total marketing task into its separate functions (buying, selling, risking, etc.).

managerial approach to marketing

Today, the most common way to study the subject is called the managerial approach to marketing. This approach takes the point of view of a firm that must make a variety of marketing decisions, each of which may affect the profit of that firm. We'll use this approach because it is the most popular one today and because it fits the scheme of this book.

marketing concept

The managerial approach makes use of the marketing concept. This is the idea that a firm must coordinate all its activities to satisfy customers and to make a profit in the process. The customer is at the center of the firm's planning. This kind of thinking gives the firm the goal that it needs to operate as a system. If there is a disagreement within a firm, it should be resolved in terms of the marketing concept. To make a profit, you do what best serves the customer. Some believe that marketing management and the marketing concept are also applicable to nonprofit activities such as government programs. One writer has suggested that government programs such as those providing methadone treatment for drug addicts or for getting the general public to use $2 bills would benefit greatly from marketing management application.[1]

The Target Market

target market

If a firm is to adopt the marketing concept, it must define the characteristics of its customers. This set of customers is called the target

---

[1] Charles B. Weinberg, "New Government Programs: The Need for a Marketing Management Approach," *The Collegiate Forum*, Dow Jones and Company, Inc. (Fall, 1977), p. 3.

Source: Chicago Tribune-New York News Syndicate.

"Miss Connally, will you please check with the people in the catalogue department and ascertain if and when the Christmas catalogues were mailed."

market. Aiming at this target guides the firm in designing its marketing program. Often there are certain factors, such as existing investment in production facilities or experience of personnel, that restrict the kind of target at which the firm "aims." In other words, there may be a compromise between the resources already available for marketing and the setting of target markets.

When choosing a target, one thing is usually easy—deciding whether what is produced will be used for its own sake or whether it will be used to make something else or to help provide a service. This is an important distinction.

Industrial goods are products or services that will be used by a firm or an institution to make another product or to provide a service. For example, tractor tires sold to "Caterpillar Tractor" or an examining table sold to a doctor is an industrial good. Manufacturers, hospitals, and lawyers buy products and services for reasons that are different from those of ordinary consumers. These buyers are *industrial buyers*.

industrial goods

Consumer goods are products and services that people buy for their own use—to wear, to eat, to look at, or to live in. We usually call these buyers *ultimate consumers*. Their motives and buying behavior are quite different from those of industrial buyers.

consumer goods

Besides industrial buyers and ultimate consumers, firms must also consider a third kind of customer. These are called middlemen be-

middlemen

cause they usually hold products briefly during the process of bringing them from their producer to their user. Retailers and wholesalers are examples of middlemen. We'll study middlemen later in this chapter when we see how a producer uses them in marketing a product.

Meanwhile, let's clarify the importance of defining the target market by comparing the industrial goods market with the consumer goods market and with other distinctive markets.

The Industrial Market

What are the features of the industrial market? First of all, the target market is generally *smaller* than it is for consumer products. A maker of shoemaking machines has fewer customers than a candymaker or a tuna canner or a TV manufacturer.

Industrial customers are often *more concentrated geographically* than are household or ultimate consumers. Many industries which are the sole users of certain products are centered in one or a few areas. The aircraft industry on the West Coast, the auto industry in Detroit, and the steel industry in the Great Lakes area are only a few examples. A firm selling electronic parts for aircraft is likely to locate in California where many of its customers are.

Industrial buyers are also different from household or ultimate consumers because they have *more formal systems for buying*. This is illustrated in Figure 7–2, which shows the purchase of an air-conditioning system by a large manufacturer.

A firm also has *more clearly defined* and *profit-oriented purchase motives.* Industrial markets can also be especially risky because of the dynamic nature of technology. One change in technology can cause the sudden death of many industrial products (parts, supplies, etc.) that go into the production of one newly obsolete major product. Conversion from the older type of electron tube to solid state parts in TVs and radios hurt many small producers of the older tubes.

Industrial goods include:

- *installations*, such as plants, office buildings, land, and very expensive assets like cranes
- *raw materials*, such as cotton, iron ore, and lumber
- *accessory equipment*, such as typewriters, accounting machines, and small fork lift trucks
- *supplies*, such as maintenance items (brooms and light bulbs); repair items (nuts and bolts to repair equipment); and operating supplies (lubricating oil and typewriter ribbons)

---

1. In early May workers began to complain that it was too hot in the main assembly plant.

2. In mid-May the production manager noted a decrease in productivity and further complaints about the inadequacy of the old air-conditioning system.

3. At a conference between the executive vice-president, the production manager, the comptroller, and the plant engineer on June 1, it was decided to replace the system immediately.

4. The plant engineer prepared a description of the system Sweeny, Inc. needs and a time schedule for installation. These specifications were sent to five local industrial air-conditioning contractors on June 14, with a request for installation bids and proposals.

5. Four proposals are received by July 4. Each is checked by the plant engineer, the purchasing agent, and the production manager. These three confer with the comptroller and the executive vice-president and award the contract to the Acme Company. Their bid was somewhat higher than one of the others, but their reputation for quality is very high and their service and warranty are at least equal to those of all other bidders.

6. On July 10 contracts are prepared by the purchasing agent and signed both by him and by an Acme Company representative. Work is begun the same day.

FIGURE 7-2

Sweeny, Inc. buys an air conditioning system

- *component parts and materials*, such as tires, batteries, and cement
- *business services*, such as uniform rental, security services, and consulting engineers

These products and services have either narrow or broad target markets. The target depends on how widely the products or services are used in industry. Many types of supplies (stationery and fuel), accessory equipment (typewriters), and services (legal assistance) are used by nearly all firms. On the other hand, most types of major equipment or installations, raw materials, and parts have a much narrower market.

The breadth of a market for an industrial product is limited by the product's nature. Who the customers of a given firm are also depends on its location, its experience and good name, its financial strength, and the size and strength of its distribution system.

Governmental and Institutional Markets

Products and services sold to nonprofit institutions, such as federal, state, and local governments, nonprofit hospitals, and schools, are also industrial products. Many of the same products that are sold to businesses are also sold to nonprofit institutions. These are often like industrial firms because they use a formal purchasing system. They often draw up product specifications and request bids from several suppliers.

Marketing to the federal government is a special case because of the complex purchasing system it uses. Many firms sell only to the government. Large defense purchases may involve years of congressional debate and lobbying. All of this makes the federal government a very special kind of target market.

The Consumer Market

Manufacturers that produce goods for ultimate consumers often face a huge, tricky market. The "household" buyer is not as professional or as formal as the industrial firm. However, the high level of income among American consumers leads to the purchase of a fantastic number of different products and services. This affluence also makes possible frequent changes in taste.

These changes, together with the amazing rate of technological progress, cause a rapid "turnover" of consumer products. New products and new brands of products appear daily on retail shelves. Nearly as many soon disappear. The tougher competition for the consumer dollar represents the main challenge in marketing consumer products and services. A number of different marketing strategies are used to meet the challenge, as we will see later in this chapter and in the following chapter.

Classes of Consumer Goods

Although many specific products are hard to classify, it is useful to distinguish three kinds:

- convenience goods
- shopping goods
- specialty goods

This classification depends on frequency of purchase, the product's significance to the buyer, and the buyer's preselection of a specific product brand.

convenience goods   **Convenience goods are items bought frequently, demanded on short notice, and often purchased by habit.** Cigarettes and many foods and drugs are examples. These are usually low-priced products that people don't think much about when buying. They don't make very careful price and quality comparisons.

shopping goods   **Shopping goods are items which are taken seriously enough to require comparison and study.** Most clothing, appliances, and cars fall into this category. Gifts are almost always shopping goods. Stores that sell shopping goods are often grouped together to help customers make price and quality comparisons.

On your next trip to the supermarket, pass by the shelf that displays bath soaps. You'll see many different brands. Some are packaged in fancy foil wrappers. Notice how many different sizes there are. Some soaps are deodorant soaps, some are mild enough for babies, and some have ingredients that promise to give you youthful-looking skin.

But don't we all buy bath soap for the same reason? Isn't the reason we buy soap to wash ourselves? Why are there so many brands of bath soap? CAN YOU EXPLAIN THIS?

CAN YOU EXPLAIN THIS?

Why Are There So Many Brands of Bath Soap?

Specialty goods are those for which strong conviction as to brand, style, or type already exists in the buyer's mind. The buyer will make a great effort to locate and purchase the specific brand. Usually, such products are high in value and aren't purchased frequently. Examples are Leica cameras and Steinway pianos. For some customers, however, a can of soup could be a specialty product. The class depends on the individual consumer's buying behavior. A certain item (a shirt, for example) could be classed in three different ways by three different people. However, there is enough agreement among consumers on most products to make this product-class scheme useful to firms in decision making. Marketers judge the way that most customers will behave toward the product and classify it accordingly.

specialty goods

How a firm classifies a product greatly influences the way it is sold. A manufacturer who considers a product a convenience good will want it to be sold in as many places as possible. If, however, the product is viewed as a shopping good, it is likely to be placed in stores that are near stores selling similar shopping items. A specialty good manufacturer doesn't have to worry as much about the retail location. Since such buyers will go out of their way to locate the product, the firm's distribution channel problem is simplified. These are only a few examples of how the way that consumers classify products may affect the way that they are marketed. Figure 7–3 summarizes the features of the three classes of products.

In summary, consumer goods producers must put themselves in the shoes of the buyer to figure out the probable class in which most buyers will place a given product. This is an application of the marketing concept and makes it more likely that the marketing effort will be truly matched to what consumers want.

To get a better definition of a consumer target market, Batton, Barton, Durstine, and Osborne, a large advertising agency, has developed a "problem tracking" system that shows the process a consumer follows in selecting a product. This "problem tracking" system helps to group

	Convenience	Shopping	Specialty
How far will a buyer travel?	Short distance	Reasonable distance	Long distance
How much does it cost?	Usually low-priced	Usually middle-to-high priced	Usually high-priced
How often purchased?	Frequently	Occasionally	Infrequently
Emphasis on comparison?	No	Yes	No
Purchased habitually?	Often	Never	Not usually
Which advertising media?	Television, newspapers, and general magazines	Television, newspapers, and general magazines	Special-interest magazines and catalogs

FIGURE 7-3

Classes of consumer goods

people with common problems and then suggests specific products and services which can serve such a group or target market. Full-scale marketing, of course, requires other marketing activities to go along with the product or service. The set of activities which marketers use is often called the *marketing mix.*

The Marketing Mix

marketing mix

To apply the marketing concept effectively, a firm must understand the major factors or tools it may use to meet (and to influence) consumers' wants. These factors are called the marketing mix. (See Figure 7–4.) The marketing mix includes four elements, often referred to as the "four p's."[2] They are

- **product**
- **price**
- **promotion**
- **place**

All four elements of the marketing mix are focused on the consumer and are influenced by factors in the environment such as the society, technology, the economy, and the law.

There are many possible combinations of these four major elements. Price, for instance, might play a big role in the mix for selling fresh meat

[2] This concept was developed by E. Jerome McCarthy in many editions of his text, *Basic Marketing: A Managerial Approach* (Richard D. Irwin, Inc.).

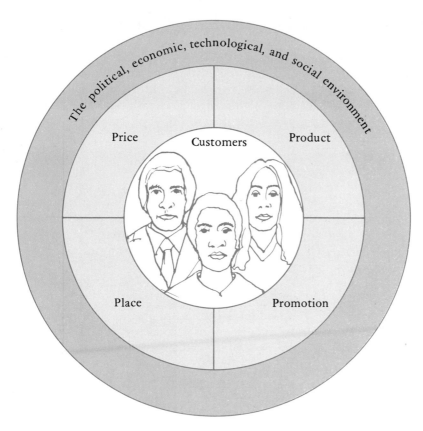

FIGURE 7-4

The marketing mix

but a very small role in selling high-quality perfume. Place might be very important in marketing gasoline but not so important for lumber. Promotion could be vital in toy marketing and yet be of little importance in marketing nails. The product is always important, but it is much more important when marketing a car than it is when marketing laundry detergent or toothpaste. We'll now take a closer look at the product and place elements in the marketing mix. Promotion and price will be treated in Chapter 8.

Product

Decisions about what and how much to produce represent the first step in the product planning process. Good product planning requires coordination with other marketing mix elements and strong customer orientation.

The relationship between a firm and its customers focuses mainly on the product. It should be viewed as a "bundle of satisfactions," which might include a variety of things, such as the guarantee, the

product

brand, the package, and the services that go with it. For example, when a mother buys a sweater for her baby at a department store, she buys warmth and comfort. She is also buying assurance that the product will last and the right to return it if it does not fit. When a man buys a cartridge of razor blades, he is buying comfortable shaves and convenient blade replacement. Buyers of ice cream think of the good taste and possibly the nutrition of what they are buying. This is the product. It is very important for a firm to know what "bundle of satisfactions" customers expect from its product offering.

A retailer's "bundle of satisfactions" or benefits includes those services that might be provided by each of the products sold in the store. It also includes the convenience of the location, the parking facilities, credit, assortment, skill of the salespeople, returned merchandise policy, and all those things that may attract customers. The enjoyment of shopping itself is for many customers a very important part of the "bundle of satisfactions."

The Product Life Cycle

product life cycle

The life history of a product is called the product life cycle. The cycle has four phases: introduction, growth, maturity, and decline.

Figure 7–5 shows a typical life cycle for a product. Notice that the sales volume is very low during the *introduction phase* of the cycle.

FIGURE 7-5

The life cycle of a product

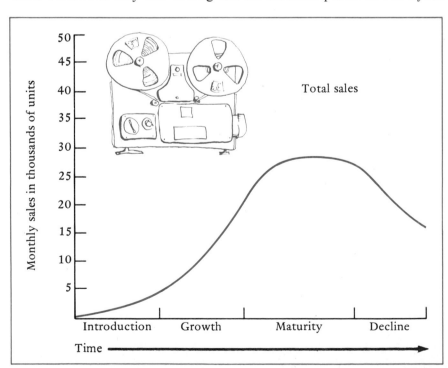

There is a steep increase in sales volume during the *growth phase;* but it begins to level off in the *maturity phase,* the longest part of the cycle. It is hard to tell how long the maturity phase will last and when the *decline phase* begins because we can't predict technological change. Near the end of the maturity phase, firms usually cut back on spending for advertising and other promotional activities. The maturity phase ends when a better product appears or a need disappears and the old product enters the period of decline. The console radio was at one time the chief source of entertainment for millions of Americans. Today it has been replaced by the television and by other home entertainment devices. More recently, CB radios seem to have entered the decline stage.

Within the life cycle of *product classes, individual brands* of products have life cycles, too. The brand's lifetime is shorter than that of the product class. People still drive cars (product class) but they no longer can buy Edsels, De Sotos, and Packards (brands).

Marketers, of course, try to extend the maturity phase of their brands' life cycles as long as the brands are profitable items. Arm and Hammer baking soda entered a period of decline when homemakers decreased their use of the product for baking. The brand's life cycle was extended, however, by advertising new uses—as a deodorant for kitty litter boxes, refrigerators, and kitchen sink drains. There are limits to product and brand life cycle extension, however. Eventually, it is a good idea to introduce completely new products and brands to replace dying ones.

When a product is no longer purchased, it is *obsolete.* Obsolescence is usually the result of a change in consumer tastes or in technology. A firm spends money on research and development (R&D) to improve its product so that it won't become obsolete. Sometimes R&D leads to an entirely new product, which takes the place of the old product, making it obsolete. For example, buggy whips, wringer washing machines, and automobile running-boards are now obsolete.

When a firm intends to replace its products, it is called planned **obsolescence.** Business has been criticized for this practice on the grounds that it is wasteful and somewhat deceptive. Many people feel that they are not getting a full lifetime out of the appliances and other durable products they buy. When obsolescence occurs because of new technical features, it is *technological obsolescence.* (See Figure 7–6.) Where the appearance or style is changed, it is *fashion obsolescence.* Promotional activities help to create this type of obsolescence by making customers dissatisfied with the "old" product.

planned obsolescence

One of the most critical and delicate marketing tasks occurs when a firm introduces a new product. Only one out of perhaps twenty new products is successful. Most firms try to avoid such expensive failures by using marketing research. This reduces, but doesn't by any means prevent, the chance of loss.

Many firms hire consultants to test out new product ideas so that they

FIGURE 7-6   Almost yearly since they were first used, business machines have suffered some technological obsolescence. These two units, produced many years apart by the same firm, suggest how great the obsolescence can be.
Source: Burroughs Corporation.

will increase their chance of success. Consulting firms like Booz, Allen and Hamilton, Inc. have helped to introduce aerosol shaving cream, latex paint, the Wearever corn popper, a dog shampoo, and over 250 other consumer and industrial products.

The success of a new product depends on its ability to perform a service customers will buy at a price that more than covers the firm's cost of making and selling it. It also depends on good introductory promotion and strong distribution. Chevrolet's huge dealership organization was extremely helpful in introducing the subcompact Citation. The competitive advantages of Chevrolet did not stop the firm from doing a lot of consumer research before introducing the Citation. Chevrolet wanted to ensure a long life cycle by getting the product just right.

Services also require innovation to succeed. Recently, Japan Air Lines introduced "Sky Sleeper Service" on many trans-Pacific flights. For an additional charge, passengers from New York to Tokyo may have the use of one of the five beds installed in the airline's Boeing 747s. This is a significant improvement in long-distance air travel for many customers.

The Product Mix

product mix   **A manufacturer's or a retailer's product mix is the combination of products it produces or sells.** General Mills produces hundreds, while

Coca-Cola produces a much smaller number. The size of the product mix affects marketing policy.

First of all, there is safety in numbers. A firm with a broad product mix has a kind of insurance against the dangers of obsolescence. Also, economies of scale often make the difference between success and failure. A firm with many products can spread its overhead cost over the entire product mix. This means savings in production costs if the products are manufactured in the same factory. It also cuts unit distribution cost. A firm can save on distribution costs by using the same salespeople or transportation system for all the products in its mix. Thus General Mills' salespersons can represent many products when they call on customers, and can ship in larger, more economical quantities.

At the retail level and, to some extent, at the wholesale level, firms with many products (a broad product mix) have an advantage in the form of product exposure. When a shopper goes into a department store to buy luggage, he or she will see many other products. The shopper may buy some of these other products as well. This couldn't happen in a single-product store.

There are advantages sometimes to having a single product, or a "narrow" product mix. A firm with a narrow product mix can be more easily promoted as a specialist than a firm that produces many kinds of products. On the other hand, it is usually the multiproduct firm that has the competitive advantage. The users of each of its products may hear about and become interested in the other products made by the same firm. This is most likely if the products all bear the same brand, such as Heinz.

Packaging

All the elements that constitute the broad concept of "product" must be considered in developing the product mix. Among these is the *package*. In recent years, packaging has become a more important part of product policy. Packaging does several things:

- protects the product
- divides the product into convenient units, for example, a six-pack of Pepsi
- becomes part of the product, like a razor blade dispenser or spray can of deodorant
- helps with promotion by making the product easy to spot on the shelf and easy to remember from an advertisement

Brands and Labels

A brand is "a name, term, symbol, or design or a combination of them, which is intended to identify the goods or services of one seller or   brand

"About this '101 Tips for Consumers' I bought—there are only 97 tips in it."

Source: *Pepper and Salt*, Cartoon Features Syndicate.

group of sellers and to differentiate from those of competitors."[3]
Brands usually include both a *name* and a *symbol*. The key to successful branding is making a lasting impression in customers' minds. A good brand name such as *Charmin* or *Seven-Up* is distinctive and easy to remember. A manufacturer's advertising program achieves utmost success when the brand name, like Scotch Tape, becomes a household word, but it then runs the danger of losing its exclusive use of a name on the grounds that it has become "the" name used by Americans. Such is the case with the words aspirin and elevator. At one time these were brand names.

The advertising agency of Benton and Bowles selected the name *Light 'n Luscious* as the brand name for a new diet dessert because they felt that a name should reflect the position of a product in the market. In this case, the brand name was intended to tell the customer that the product provides fewer calories and yet delivers the taste that dessert lovers expect.

Brands also play a role in the marketing strategy of wholesalers and retailers. Brands developed by such middlemen are called *distributor's brands* or *private brands*. Sears' Kenmore appliances and Craftsman tools are examples. They are produced by other firms for Sears. Large grocery chains do the same thing. They generally make a larger profit

---

[3] Committee on Definitions, Ralph S. Alexander, chairperson, "Marketing Definitions: A Glossary of Marketing Terms," (Chicago: American Marketing Association, 1960), p. 8.

per unit on private brands. The K-Mart Company, which for years has concentrated on nationally advertised brands, has recently started a policy of adding its own private-label products with an economy appeal.

Many major retailers of grocery and related products have begun to sell unbranded products, sometimes called *generics*. These products, such as paper towels, dog food, green beans, and laundry detergents, are priced even below private brands and may have some features that make them less attractive than manufacturer's-brand or private-brand items. String beans or peas may not be uniform in size in generic packages, although the nutrition is equal to that of branded items.

Legal protection is available for products and brands. This is especially important for small firms, who can't spend so much on advertising. **A patent protects an invention, a chemical formula, or a new way of**   patent **doing something from imitation. It makes it very hard for a competitor to copy this new product or new idea for a period of 17 years.** The United States Patent Office supervises this activity. It accepts applications for patents and, if an idea is "patentable," it is registered and protected. The Polaroid Land Camera is a good example. **The patent**   trademark **office also protects a name printed a certain way or a symbol which, when registered, is called a trademark.** Once the trademark is accepted by the patent office, it is protected for a period of 20 years and it can be extended for a like period indefinitely. Miller's Lite beer and the Ford Fiesta are examples of trademarks. They are also, of course, brands.

One of consumerism's goals is the informative labeling of products. Such labeling helps a buyer to make a more informed choice among products, particularly when self-service is involved. The label describes in simple terms the content, nutrition, durability, precautions, or other special features of a product. It might also indicate the grade or standard of quality of the item as established by industrywide agreement or by law.

Informative labeling can lead to better purchase decisions *only* if the labels are read. How many people today even understand the long-standing meat and milk quality standards? Some consumers want a massive consumer education program to teach buyers the benefits of using label information.

Much of a firm's product policy is governed by its decision to *segment* or not to segment the market. As will be explained in Chapter 8, it is often wise to design special marketing mixes for each segment. The product is usually at the center of a segmentation strategy.

Place

Both time and space separate a manufacturer from its customers. These "gaps" occur as a result of differences between the production rate and the consumption rate and because the final users of products are more

place or distribution

widely scattered than the producers. **There is also a wide range of functions which must be performed in the process of bringing products to their final users whether these be households or industrial users. These functions make up the place or distribution element in the marketing mix.** The products flow through the *channel of distribution.*

What Is a Channel of Distribution?

channel of distribution

A channel of distribution is the firm, or usually the set of firms, directly involved in selling a product. Channels also make up for the difference between one manufacturer's product mix and the product mix a consumer wants. Since these two mixes rarely match, other firms are often needed to complete the marketing process. For example, General Foods and General Mills each produce many consumer products. But a grocery shopper wants their products *and* the products of other firms such as Procter and Gamble, Campbell, Heinz, Armour, Borden, and so on. Wholesalers bring these products together and make them available to retailers, such as grocery stores. This enables the grocery shopper to buy, in one place, a broad assortment of products. These firms, except for the producer, are usually called *middlemen.* The type and number of such middlemen describe the distribution channel. (See Figure 7–7.)

If a manufacturer of a consumer product were completely consumer-oriented and cost were no object, the firm would probably send out salespeople to call directly on every household. The cost of such careful attention, however, is almost always too great. The final decision about how to get products to customers requires a compromise between cost control and providing the best service and convenience.

The final development of a channel depends on

- the number of customers
- the functions which the channel is expected to perform
- the costs of alternative channels
- the importance of controlling the marketing process

Thus a maker of lathes selling to a handful of industrial firms may sell directly to customers. A maker of toothbrushes selling to millions of customers, by contrast, will need a long (several levels of middlemen) channel. A firm making several different appliances with high unit profit margins, like Singer, can operate its own retail stores because the overhead cost is spread over several products. A manufacturer of blankets could never afford to do so.

A gasoline manufacturer who wants to treat customers with great care may operate its own service stations. However, the mood of many gasoline producers is changing on this subject because of the attractiveness of self-service and of keeping gas prices down in the face of rising crude oil costs. A Gulf Oil Corporation spokesman has said that

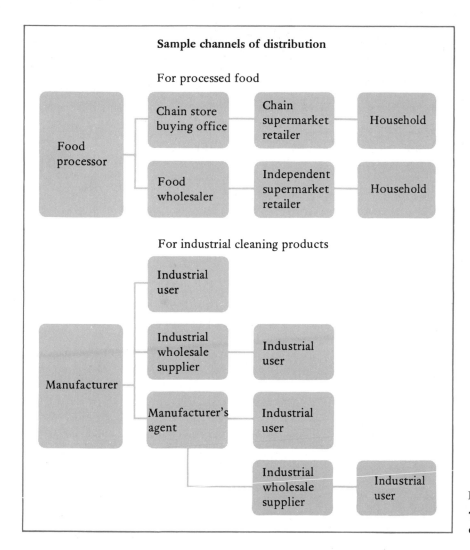

FIGURE 7-7

Typical channels of distribution

brand loyalty for gasoline is fading as prices rise and self-service be-comes generally accepted.

The Principal Middlemen

There are three basic types of middlemen:

- merchant middlemen
- agent middlemen
- facilitating middlemen

Merchant middlemen actually take title to the products that they sell, while *agent middlemen* do not. *Facilitating middlemen,* like transportation firms, participate in the transportation and storage of the product, without actually buying and selling it.

Examples of merchant middlemen include *wholesalers* and *retailers.* These firms regularly buy stocks of products and resell them. Retailers are involved in selling a wide variety of consumer products. Food, for example, is sold mostly through food and grocery retailers known as supermarkets, some of which are parts of large chains (Kroger, Safeway, A&P) and some of which are independent. Independent supermarkets usually buy from independent wholesalers, while chain stores receive products from their own firm's central distribution points, which perform the wholesaling function.

The top part of Figure 7–7 shows a typical channel of distribution used by a processor of a food product. This firm sells to a central buying office of a large food chain which, in turn, distributes to its retail stores. These, of course, sell to households. Other important retailer types include department stores, drug stores, variety stores, discount houses, and vending machine operators. The latter are expanding the range of products they can handle. A businessman in Pennsylvania, for example, operates 20 vending machines which sell live night crawlers and other baits to fishermen.

Agent middlemen include manufacturer's agents, brokers, and selling agents. These firms are involved in selling a wide variety of products, including consumer products and industrial products. **A manufacturer's agent is paid a commission to represent manufacturers of several noncompetitive lines in a limited geographic territory. Without taking possession of products, such an agent aggressively seeks to establish these products in this territory.**

A manufacturer's agent may help a producer of industrial cleaning products to introduce the line in California. Since the agent gets paid a commission only for the actual sales made, this can be a more efficient way of distributing in a new territory, rather than dealing directly or exclusively through wholesale industrial suppliers. The bottom part of Figure 7–7 shows the "set" of channels that a manufacturer of industrial cleaners might use. In some cases, this firm sells directly to large industrial users, using its own sales force. In other cases, the producer sells to industrial suppliers (wholesalers) who sell to industrial users (usually the smaller customers). Another method is to use the manufacturer's agent to reach either users or wholesale industrial suppliers. It is common for a national manufacturer to use different channels of distribution in different parts of the country.

The more direct (shorter) a channel is, the more control a manufacturer has over distribution, because there are fewer middlemen to coordinate. Control is improved by means of franchising. **A franchised retailer is tied closely by contract to a manufacturer and its operations**

manufacturer's agent

franchised retailer

are strictly supervised. Examples of franchised outlets include McDonald's and other fast-food firms, as well as auto dealers and many gas stations. Franchising is discussed in detail in Chapter 15.

Facilitating middlemen are not pictured in Figure 7–7, although they may be involved in each case. These are railroads, warehouse companies, insurers, and other firms who facilitate or help in distribution but are not directly engaged in buying or selling.

Are Middlemen Necessary?

At some time you might have heard a friend say that she got a great bargain from a store because it bought "direct from the factory," or "eliminated the middleman." Your friend assumed that the price was reduced by the profit that would have gone to the middleman. Such a claim would lead you to believe that middlemen are unnecessary and expensive and should be abolished. Let's examine this claim.

The Glammer Company is a hardware wholesaler. Glammer buys saws, nails, electrical fixtures, adhesives, and camping equipment from five different manufacturers. Glammer buys a rail carload of each product each month. It sells most of these five products to 50 retail hardware stores in central Iowa. The retailers make small purchases of some of the five products every week or two from Glammer. The hardware retailers also buy from three to six other wholesalers in order to keep a complete inventory.

Why don't the retailers buy all the items they carry direct from the manufacturers? The answer is clear—they save money by buying through the wholesaler. The Glammer Company simplifies the number of purchases and sales and reduces unit shopping costs and record keeping. It provides quicker delivery to the retailers than they could get by dealing directly with the manufacturers. Figure 7–8 illustrates this principle. Each connecting line represents a transaction. Clearly, shipping in carload lots is much cheaper than the many small shipments which would be needed for direct sales from manufacturers to retailers.

There are great economic advantages in a system of distribution that uses a wholesaler. This middleman

- buys in large quantities and sells in small quantities
- makes it possible for the retailer to simplify its buying process by carrying a broad line of items
- often takes credit risks which manufacturers might not accept
- guarantees delivery on short notice so that retailers need not keep large stocks

In most cases, wholesalers and their margins (the difference between the costs of products to them and what they sell them for) are justified.

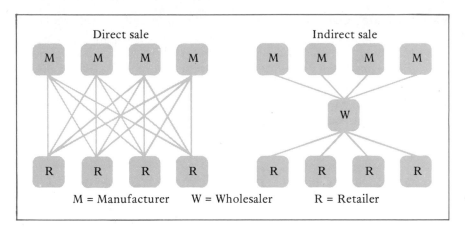

In the absence of the wholesaler, each retailer would find it necessary to deal with all four manufacturers. Each manufacturer would also have to deal with all four retailers. With the introduction of the wholesaler, each retailer and each manufacturer need deal with only one intermediary—the wholesaler. Thus the wholesaler reduces the number of transactions (represented by the connecting lines) and makes it possible to increase the average size of transactions. This increase brings about economies of scale and thereby justifies the existence and the profit margin of the middleman.

If the wholesaler did not exist, all of these activities could not be conducted without raising prices.

If your friend got a real bargain from the retailer who "eliminated the middleman," she probably made the purchase under very special circumstances. Maybe the retailer is practicing *leader pricing* with this one product. Practicing leader pricing means setting a price low on a widely bought item to attract buyers to a store who, it is hoped, will buy other products also. The retailer could also be part of a chain operation with a very high volume of sales. In any case, the functions usually performed by the wholesaler have to be performed by someone. This costs money.

Physical Distribution

physical distribution

The growth in volume and variety of products sold, together with new transport technology, have turned the attention of manufacturers toward the problem of physical distribution, or *logistics*. **Physical distribution is concerned with the physical movement of raw materials and semimanufactured products into and through the plant, and the movement of finished products out of the plant to the ultimate consumer or industrial user.**

The Total Cost Concept

At one time physical distribution management was mainly concerned with minimizing the cost of transportation. This is a narrow view since the transportation cost may be less than half of the total cost of physical distribution. **Modern firms apply the total cost concept, which considers all costs related to a particular means of physical distribution.** In addition to transportation, there are storage costs and "out-of-stock" costs. Concentrating only on transportation rates is shortsighted.

total cost concept

Some firms have developed distribution systems that depend on electronic computers to schedule the flow of products from manufacturer to consumer or industrial user. They select the best location for intermediate storage points and the best means of transportation. These computer-based systems take into account the costs of transporting and storing as well as the cost of "running out" of merchandise. Such accurate cost systems are common where the channel is under the control of a retailer or manufacturer. The objective of modern physical distribution management is to achieve a *balance* between costs and service. The firm usually establishes a desired level of customer service and then seeks to minimize the cost of providing that level of service.

The Modes of Transportation

Firms have a choice among railroads, motor trucks, air freight, and, in some cases, ships and barges or pipelines to move their products. Decisions like this are in the hands of the *traffic manager*. This important decision maker keeps track of the in-and-out flow of materials, delivery dates, and storage space with the goal of coordinating all aspects of physical distribution and thereby ensuring customer satisfaction at the lowest cost. Recent history, as can be seen in Figure 7–9, has seen some dramatic shifts in the relative importance of the various modes of transportation.

There is a legal relationship between a firm that wants to move freight (the shipper) and the transportation firm (the carrier) that will handle the actual transport. Carriers (railroads, truckers, shipping companies, etc.) can be

- common carriers
- contract carriers
- private carriers

A common carrier offers its services to the general public at uniform, published rates. These carriers' rates and services are supervised by public agencies. Railroad rates, for example, are regulated by the Interstate Commerce Commission (ICC).

common carrier

contract carrier

When a firm needs to move freight that can't be moved by a common carrier, it may call on a contract carrier. A contract carrier is a firm, such as a trucking company, that negotiates long- or short-term contracts with shippers to handle their freight. It is a private contract between the shipper and the carrier. The shipper may want *customized service* and may want a guarantee of availability without investing in its own truck or barge fleet.

private carrier

If a manufacturer or middleman owns and operates its own transportation, it is called a private carrier. This kind of operation is justified when a large, predictable volume exists and common or contract carriers are not as economical or can't do exactly what the shipper needs. Many oil companies, for example, own fleets of ships to transport their oil.

Each of the major modes of transportation has its good and bad points. The railroad's major advantages are its cost advantages for "long hauls" and for bulky items where water transportation is not available. The railroad also provides reliable service, since varying weather conditions do not often affect it. Economies of scale are evident in railroading

FIGURE 7-9

Percent distribution of ton-miles of domestic intercity freight traffic, by type of transportation: 1929–1978

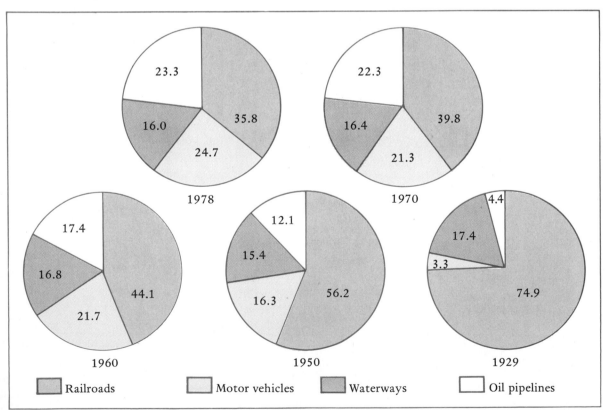

Source: *Yearbook of Railroad Facts.*

since one diesel engine can pull one or many loaded cars. This enables the railroad to spread the cost of the motive power over a large number of shipments.

The major limitations, however, also relate to *economies of scale*. Less-than-carload lots (l.c.l.) are not well-suited to rail movement. Modern railroads use mechanized loading and unloading equipment that is designed to handle single, large units. Small shipments require very costly manual handling. Furthermore, the more cars that can be moved with one engine, the lower the cost to move each car. Therefore, the small shipper may find its shipment waiting on the siding while a large train is being made up.

The major advantage of motor truck transport is flexibility. Trucks can go anywhere there is a road. Thus by truck the shipper can reach many more potential customers than by other modes.

As in the case of the rails, there are many different types of trucks, some of which are highly specialized. Since the required investment is rather small, many shippers own and operate their own trucks. Door-to-door service is possible with trucks, and service is speedy.

Water transport is important in both domestic and foreign commerce. The major advantage is low cost. Low-value, bulky products move at very low rates by barge. As bulk goes up and value goes down, the advantage of water transport increases. On the other hand, as delivery time becomes more important, barges become less attractive. Accessibility to waterways and ports is, of course, necessary.

Pipelines are the most "invisible" of the modes, although they move many millions of tons of goods over many miles. Thousands of miles of pipelines move crude and refined petroleum, chemicals, and natural gas. Pipelines are almost completely unaffected by weather and, once they are installed, the cost of operation is very low. Very little labor is involved in operating them.

In the not too distant past, airplanes were considered basically "people carriers." At best, they could move only very high-value, low-bulk cargo. The arrival of the jet age and jumbo jets, the increased number of airports, and sophisticated materials-handling techniques have changed many of these ideas. Air transport is speedy, safe, and can help the shipper in reducing other elements of total distribution costs. Many airlines appeal to the shipper on the basis that if it is willing to spend a little more money on transportation, its other distribution costs can be reduced. One major problem is the great rise in fuel costs which has led some airlines to discontinue service to smaller cities.

Our discussion of physical distribution would be incomplete without some discussion of containerization. **Containerization is the practice of using standard large containers, preloaded by the seller, to move freight.**

containerization

Modern containers move many types of freight. They are loaded at the shipper's plant, sealed, and moved to the receiver's plant. Instead of many individual items being individually handled, the entire container is mechanically handled. They move with great efficiency from truck to train (piggyback), from train to ship (fishyback), and from truck to plane (birdyback). This is called *intermodal transportation.* The savings in distribution cost can be great because of reduced theft and damage as well as lower transportation rates on intermodal movements.

Summary and Look Ahead

Marketing is a very large part of the economic activity in the United States. Its role is becoming central to business planning as firms adopt the marketing concept. The reason for this is that business profit and the national rate of economic growth depend on the growth of consumption. Businesses must learn more about their customers and concentrate on satisfying them if they are to succeed.

It is convenient to think of the set of customers that a firm wants to appeal to as its target market. This target might consist of customers in the industrial market and/or customers in the consumer market. Industrial goods can be classed as installations, raw materials, accessory equipment, component parts and materials, and supplies. Consumer goods can be classed as convenience goods, shopping goods, and specialty goods.

The kind of product and the target market help to define the "marketing mix" or combination of product, place, promotion, and price that a firm will use. Product policy is the focal point of the marketing mix of many firms, who keep a close eye on the product life cycle and try to keep products alive and profitable. Research and development helps to keep old products alive and to replace them with new products. Packaging and branding are also vital parts of the product element in the marketing mix.

Place or distribution is of equal importance because each product must reach its target customer at a reasonable cost and with some of the services that those target customers demand. Middlemen, such as retailers and wholesalers, help to form channels of distribution. Facilitating middlemen such as railroads and warehousing companies cooperate in the distribution process.

In Chapter 8 we go on to complete our examination of the marketing mix. Special attention will be given to the methods of promotion and pricing techniques. We will also look at the strategies of product differentiation and market segmentation and discover the role of marketing research in the planning of the marketing mix. The subject of consumerism is also discussed in more detail.

My name is Shirl Mendonca. I am a marketing trainee with Philip Morris, USA.

I received an associate of arts degree from the College of the Sequoias in Visalia, California and went on to Columbia University for a BA in economics. I later got my MBA from Fordham. While at Columbia I decided to pursue a marketing career. I took a part-time job with Philip Morris while still going to school. When I completed my BA degree, I accepted a full-time position with Philip Morris as a merchandising analyst.

A merchandising analyst gathers, develops, and interprets data relating to the merchandising programs for our customers and data on our market share in the cigarette industry. This position is a part of the National Accounts Department, which services major retail classes of trade (that is, supermarkets, convenience stores, drug stores, etc.).

The position also required administrative responsibilities for the departmental budget, sales force brochure content and development, interdepartmental communications, and project presentations.

Within a year there was an opportunity to enter the marketing trainee program. This is a two-year program at Philip Morris for entry into most marketing management positions. In the course of this program, I spend approximately three months in each of several different departments of the tobacco marketing division. These departments include Brand Management, National Accounts, Sales, Media, Marketing Research, etc.

In each of these areas I am learning what resources are available and how the departments interact with the key marketing function. Most importantly, I am learning how departments make decisions in very large corporations.

I chose Philip Morris because of my interest in consumer product marketing. I was challenged by the New York City business environment and, specifically, by the dynamic reputation of Philip Morris as one of the best consumer product marketing firms. Finally, Philip Morris has a very broad training program and is very interested in the welfare of its employees.

Key Concepts

brand A name, term, symbol, or design, or a combination of them used to identify the goods or services of one seller or a group of sellers and to differentiate from those of competitors.

channel of distribution The set of firms directly involved in selling a product.

common carrier A carrier that offers its services to the general public at uniform rates to all, for example, railroads.

consumer goods Products and services used by consumers for their own satisfaction, not for producing other products or services.

containerization The method of shipping products in standard container units. It simplifies handling at points of transfer, loading, and unloading.

contract carrier A carrier that makes temporary contracts with individual shippers to move their freight.

convenience goods Items bought frequently, demanded on short notice, and often habitually purchased, like cigarettes or gasoline.

form utility The increase in value of products because form has been changed or separate parts have been combined, which increases the usefulness of the products.

franchised retailer A retail firm operating under a licensing agreement with a franchise grantor. Examples include car dealerships and fast-food restaurants.

industrial goods Products sold to business firms, such as installations, accessory equipment, component parts and materials, supplies, and raw materials to make another product or to provide a service. Industrial services are sometimes included.

managerial approach to marketing An approach to marketing that focuses upon marketing decisions and how they are made.

manufacturer's agent An agent middleman representing a manufacturer or manufacturers in a specific region for a given commission.

marketing A set of activities undertaken to find,

influence, and serve customers for products and services. Includes product design, place, promotion, and pricing activities.

marketing concept The guiding philosophy that says a firm must be consumer-oriented and that the entire firm must recognize this fact in order to make a profit.

marketing mix A certain combination of the elements of price, product, promotion, and place (or distribution) manipulated by a firm in order to achieve its marketing objectives.

middlemen Firms that participate in buying and selling products as part of a channel of distribution. Middlemen that take title are merchant middlemen. Those that do not are agent middlemen.

ownership utility The actual transfer of title to a product creates the utility of ownership.

patent Legal protection of a process, invention, or formula by the federal government. Protects against imitation for a period of 17 years in the United States.

physical distribution The physical movement and storage of products. This has provided the main opportunity to apply technology to reduce costs of marketing. Also called logistics.

place (distribution) An element in the marketing mix concerned with the movement of products through a channel from producer to consumer or industrial user.

place utility The increase in the value of a product by changing its location.

planned obsolescence Intentionally scheduled replacement of a previous product or model by the same firm that produced the previous product or model.

private carrier A transportation system owned by a manufacturer or middleman for the exclusive use in moving its own products.

product An element in the marketing mix consisting of the entire "bundle of satisfactions" made available for sale. It includes the package, brand, and physical characteristics.

product life cycle   The evolution of a product through periods of introduction, growth, maturity, and decline/obsolescence.

product mix   All products offered for sale by a firm.

shopping goods   Consumer products whose purchase is taken seriously enough to require comparison and study.

specialty goods   Items for which strong conviction as to brand, style, or type already exists in the buyer's mind and for which he or she will make a great effort to locate and purchase a specific brand.

target market   The set of customers, present and potential, to which a firm directs its attention when it designs its marketing mix and the policies associated with it.

time utility   The increase in value resulting from the passage of time.

total cost concept   A way of viewing or planning transportation and storage so as to minimize total costs.

trademark   A legally protected name, symbol, or combination of name and symbol registered with the U.S. Patent Office.

For Review . . .

1. Why is the marketing task more complex in an economy where there are high levels of discretionary income than in one where the people live at the subsistence level?
2. If a product possesses only form utility, is it useful to a customer? Why or why not?
3. Why is there a demand for industrial products?
4. When you purchase a new toaster, what "bundle of satisfactions" are you buying? How about a tube of toothpaste?
5. How long does a product "live"? Why does a fashion product "live" a shorter time than a hardware item like a wrench? Explain the concept of "life cycle" as applied to these two types of products.
6. Has packaging become more important or less important in selling consumer products in recent years? Discuss.
7. Why does the distribution channel for an industrial product differ from a convenience consumer product channel? How does it differ?
8. How is it that "middlemen" exist even though they must cover their cost of operation and make a profit? Are their functions necessary? Why or why not?

9. Draw a chart illustrating four different channels of distribution that a manufacturer of toys might use. Could these be shortened?
10. What are the main advantages of rail transportation over water transportation?

. . . For Discussion

1. Do you think that high mass consumption is desirable? Why or why not?
2. How is the marketing concept related to the economic problem we discussed in Section One?
3. If a firm adopts and implements the marketing concept, all of its actions are oriented to the satisfaction of its target market. Is that desirable? Discuss.
4. Name six brand names that you think have good "memory value." Name six that you think are poor. What makes the difference?
5. Discuss the application of the total cost concept to the distribution of expensive flowers from farms in California to florists in the New York City area.

Incidents

Private Delivery Services versus the Postal Service

Place or distribution is a critical element in the marketing of some of the advertising media we will examine in the following chapter—newspapers and magazines. For years the United States Postal Service has been the major means of distribution for many such "products." With the recent rises in postal rates, however, national newspapers and magazines have been switching in part to private delivery services. Major users of private delivery services have been such national publications as *The Wall Street Journal* and *Reader's Digest*.

Firms in the private delivery business, such as Inland Carriers, Inc. of Southern California, have made their success on good quality service coupled with somewhat lower labor costs than those of the United States Postal Service. As the use of such services broadens, unit costs of delivery will be reduced and the price advantage of these firms will be improved.

Questions

1. What kind of utility is created by the delivery?
2. In what way might private delivery of a newspaper provide a greater "bundle of satisfactions" than delivery by the Postal Service?
3. Why is it that some magazines are distributed by methods other than mail or private delivery? Discuss.

Source: *The Wall Street Journal.*

Used Clothing in Major Department Stores?

Macys' and Abraham & Straus, major New York department stores, opened "antique" clothing departments in 1978 featuring used clothing—cleaned and repaired, of course. Styles from the thirties, forties, and fifties are featured. This idea represents a major departure in policy for big department stores and raises some interesting questions about product mix, product life cycles, and market segmentation.

Questions

1. Do you foresee any problems for the departments selling brand-new clothing because of the used clothing department? Discuss.
2. How does the concept of product life cycle fit into this incident?
3. Is the market segment appealed to by these "antique" clothes the same as that appealed to at the time these clothes were first made? Discuss.

Marketing II

CHAPTER
8

Objectives: After reading this chapter, you should be able to

1. Describe how an advertising agency serves a large seller of consumer products.
2. Compare the advantages of the various media.
3. Act out with another student an example of personal selling as it should be done.
4. Show the difference between the cost and the demand approaches to pricing in a small dress shop.
5. Describe two possible strategies for introducing a new product.
6. Compare the strategies of differentiation and market segmentation.
7. Name and explain two different approaches to market research.
8. Describe a case of conspicuous consumption.
9. Find an example in the newspaper of consumerist activity and discuss its effect on the marketing mix of a firm.

Key concepts: Look for these terms as you read the chapter

promotion	trade position discount
advertising	functional discount
advertising agency	market penetration pricing
advertising media	
AIDA process	skimming pricing
personal selling	inventory turnover rate
publicity	price lining
public relations	product differentiation
sales promotion	market segmentation
price	marketing research
oligopoly	secondary research
price leadership	primary research
monopolistic competition	conspicuous consumption
markup	
pricing model	

We continue with the marketing mix. This will include a careful examination of promotion with special attention to advertising institutions, messages, and media as well as a brief description of sales management and personal selling. The price element of the marketing mix is examined also. This leads to a review of the role of markets and the introduction of a group of pricing strategies. The chapter closes with a look at marketing research and a further discussion of consumerism.

Promotion

Promotion is probably the most dynamic, aggressive, and persuasive element of the marketing mix. It includes all communication by a firm with its customers or potential customers for the purpose of expanding sales, directly or indirectly. Promotion is communication that

promotion

- gains attention
- informs
- teaches
- reminds
- persuades
- reassures

Because of the dynamic nature of competition, promotion must be viewed as a *process*. It is the process of sending messages through a variety of media. A cartoon commercial message, for example, is sent to families through the medium of television. The choice of a medium can influence the way that the message is received. For example, it would probably be a mistake to promote burial insurance during a TV situation comedy program. The principal methods of promotion are advertising and personal selling. Of somewhat less importance are the methods of sales promotion, publicity, and public relations. Let's discuss these methods and how they relate to one another.

Advertising

Modern Americans are familiar with the process of advertising. They are being subjected to it during a large part of every day of their lives, much of it through TV. **Advertising includes all nonpersonal promotional activity for which a fee is paid.** The special feature of advertising is its ability to reach large numbers of people at the same time and at a moderate cost per contact. It is done through the principal advertising media of television, consumer magazines, newspapers, business publications, radio, direct mail, and billboards. It is carried on by such institutions as advertising departments of firms or advertising agencies. The

advertising

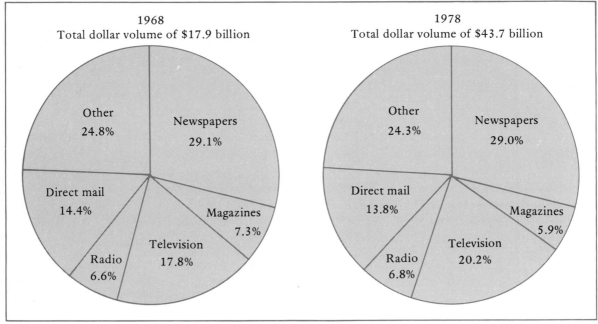

1968
Total dollar volume of $17.9 billion

Other
24.8%

Newspapers
29.1%

Direct mail
14.4%

Magazines
7.3%

Radio
6.6%

Television
17.8%

1978
Total dollar volume of $43.7 billion

Other
24.3%

Newspapers
29.0%

Direct mail
13.8%

Magazines
5.9%

Radio
6.8%

Television
20.2%

Source: McCann-Erickson, Inc.

FIGURE 8-1

Share of total advertising volume by media: 1968 and 1978

volume of advertising in each of the major media is shown in Figure 8–1. The use of TV continues to grow at the expense of direct mail and magazines.

Individual firms spend most of their advertising budgets on *brand,* or *selective, advertising.* This means that the purpose is to promote the particular brand of product sold by that firm. Sometimes firms also engage in *institutional advertising,* which promotes the good name of the firm as a whole. When a group of firms advertise a general class of product without mentioning brands, this is called *primary demand advertising.* You have probably seen ads urging you to drink more milk or eat more beef.

Advertising Institutions

The principal institutions involved in making advertising decisions are

- the advertising departments of firms
- advertising agencies
- the media—newspapers, television stations, magazines, and so on
- research organizations employed to evaluate the effectiveness of advertising

Let's examine the functions of each.

Most large- and medium-sized firms have a separate department to oversee advertising activities. If a firm has adopted the marketing concept, its advertising department is under the authority of the top marketing executive. This provides for coordination of advertising with other promotional activities and with the rest of the marketing mix. Advertising departments serve as communicators between the firm and the advertising agency.

The principal creative centers for advertising for most medium-sized and large firms are their advertising agencies. An advertising agency specializes in performing advertising functions for other firms. It serves its clients by planning advertising campaigns, by buying time and space in the broadcast (radio and TV) and print (newspapers and magazines) media, and by checking that ads appear as agreed. Sometimes ad agencies perform additional marketing functions, such as marketing research and public relations. Agencies are normally paid a 15 percent commission based on the dollar amount of advertising placed in the media. They also charge additional fees if they perform marketing research or other special services for their clients.

advertising agency

The advertising media carry the message designed by firms and their agencies to many receivers (customers or potential customers). The most important media are newspapers, television, direct mail, and magazines, in that order. Since 1968, the largest gain in the share of total advertising volume has been made by TV. The other major media have lost share except for radio. Direct mail and magazines were the big losers.

advertising media

An advertiser selects media (often with an agency's help) with a number of factors in mind. The marketing executive must first ask "Which medium will reach the people I want to reach?" If a firm is selling turkey breeding equipment, it might select *Turkey World*, a business paper read mostly by turkey breeders. If it is selling silverware, it might choose a magazine for brides. If it is selling toothpaste, the choice might be a general audience television program or a general audience magazine like *Reader's Digest*.

Another important factor in media choice is the medium's ability to deliver a message effectively. Some messages need visual communication and some need the added dimension of color. Foods are an example of products that benefit from color in communication. Selling an electric organ requires a sound-oriented medium. Some messages need color, sound, and motion. This is only available in color television, the medium with the greatest set of "communicating tools."

There are other special considerations in media selection. For example, print media are more permanent. They can communicate several times or be taken to the store as a shopping aid. Some media (radio, television, and daily newspaper) provide frequent communication and relatively short "lag" time before the ad will appear. Finally, there is the cost per contact with a customer or prospect. This will vary greatly, but the one-dimensional media, such as radio and newspapers, are usually inexpensive per contact. TV costs more. An ad appearing on a national telecast of a Super Bowl or other major sports event can cost hundreds of thousands of dollars! Even this could be relatively cheap per contact because of the huge audiences who tune in to such events. Ninety-five million people saw the 1978 Super Bowl.

S. C. Johnson and Sons, Inc., a manufacturer of a variety of household products, entered the shampoo market in 1978. The firm undertook a large advertising campaign for Agree shampoo in 25 women's magazines, Sunday newspaper supplements, and network TV. It supplemented these traditional media with a huge mailing of samples of the product. For this kind of product, sending samples is a common occurrence. It is usually classified as a kind of sales promotion.

How an Advertisement Works

AIDA process

Much of what advertising can do can be shown by careful examination of a particular advertisement. **A promotional process can be thought of in terms of how it works on a particular receiver or prospective customer, leading him or her through the stages of attention, interest, desire, and action—the AIDA process.**

Headlines are usually attention-getters and interest-builders. Sometimes they go a long way toward building desire, too. Copy, in many ads, is the desire-builder or convincer because it gives facts and anticipates objections by the reader. The signature is usually the familiar company trademark or brand name. It says who is sending the message. Sometimes it is accompanied by a coupon or an action-inducing offer.

THINK ABOUT IT!

Advertising and the Professions

There is growing controversy concerning the role that advertising should play in the professions. Even the mass advertising media are being used by some professionals despite years of tradition to the contrary.

Their use of mass media is the result of a U.S. Supreme Court ruling last year (1977) that struck down an Arizona bar regulation barring advertising by lawyers.

Should what, up to now, has been only a small-scale adoption of traditional marketing techniques, become widespread in the professions, it will be interesting to see what kind of marketing mix they will employ. What advantages will this new form of competition bring to lawyers, dentists, and physicians? What advantages will it bring to their clients? THINK ABOUT IT!

Source: *Business Week.*

The color ads shown in this chapter display a variety of appeals or themes used to "reach" customers. The advertiser uses an appeal, such as sex or prestige, that fits the product and the customer the firm wishes to influence.

The arrangement of parts in a print ad—illustration, headline, and copy—is called the *layout*. Ideally, the layout makes it easy to "carry the reader through" the phases of attention, interest, desire, and action. A similar AIDA "game plan" can also be used in personal selling.

Advertising Complaints and Regulation

Because advertising is such an obvious part of the lives of Americans, it is not surprising that it is subject to much criticism and government regulation. Complaints come from consumer groups, conservationists, sociologists, and economists about the effects and some of the methods of advertising.

Some complaints relate to *truth in advertising*. Some exaggeration about the quality of products has always been permitted, but there are limits to the degree of exaggeration that is permitted. The Federal Trade Commission has, in recent years, imposed stiffer penalties for false and misleading advertising. Its ground rules provide that all statements of fact be supported by evidence. In some cases, the FTC has required the guilty firm to run corrective advertising. The makers of Listerine mouthwash were required, for example, in their advertising to correct the impression which they had created in earlier advertising that Listerine is effective in controlling colds or sore throats. The Food and Drug Administration and the Federal Communications Commission also have increased their efforts to control advertising abuses. Most states have passed laws to control deceptive advertising. These laws are called "Printer's Ink" statutes and their level of enforcement varies greatly from state to state.

Other questions about advertising that are worth discussing are:

- Are we being brainwashed?
- Is much of competitive advertising wasteful?
- Does advertising lead to monopoly and high prices?
- What effect is advertising having on the values of our people?

While some of these questions have merit, it is hard to imagine how the great productivity and wealth of our economy could have happened without the stimulating effect of modern advertising.

Personal Selling and Sales Management

In some situations there is no substitute for one-to-one human persuasion. All of us experience it nearly every day. There is a lot that one person can do to convince another of a point of view. This could mean one's willingness to try a new brand of beer or to change an attitude toward a politician. However, persuasive talent cannot serve a business effectively unless it is properly managed.

personal selling

Personal selling includes any direct human communication for the purpose of increasing, directly or indirectly, a firm's sales. The special quality of personal selling is its individuality—the one-to-one relationship between the seller and the buyer—and the fact that the seller may give very special attention to the buyer's needs. The tone of personal selling can vary widely. It can be like that of a sideshow barker or of a skilled computer salesperson. The style is different, but the goal is quite similar—to sell. Both hope to guide the receiver through the AIDA process. See Figure 8–2 for a typical example of how a salesperson might follow this process. Advertising and personal selling are complementary; they work well together.

FIGURE 8-2

A typical personal selling sequence

Salesperson (S)	Prospect (P)
Enters situation with thorough knowledge of product, incomplete knowledge of prospect's needs. Is confident.	Enters situation with a poorly formed idea of need, very little information about salesperson or product. Some distrust and hostility toward salesperson.
1. Attracts attention of P by setting up appointment and, perhaps, by indicating some awareness of the needs of P.	2. Greets S, attitude improved by the pleasant, interested manner of S.
3. Begins to show how product can solve a problem that P has.	4. Becomes more deeply interested, but brings up certain objections regarding price and quality.
5. Answers P's objections by describing credit plan and explaining how the service department of S's firm can overcome the problems in (4) by P. Asks for the order.	6. Finds another reason to object to signing order, but the objection is mild.
7. Answers last objection and closes with "If you'll just give me your O.K. on this, we can make delivery on the first of the month."	8. Agrees to buy on a trial basis.
9. Thanks P, checks over details of order. Later, checks on P's satisfaction.	10. May experience some post-sale doubt, but reassures self of wise decision.

"How did you know I sell door-to-door?"

Source: *Marketing Molehills,* American Marketing Association.

Salespeople operate in many different ways, but most of them

- do some "prospecting" and/or "qualifying." This involves developing lists of prospective customers and screening them for likelihood of purchase and profitability as customers
- get to know their products and services in every way possible, including strong points and weak points
- formulate sales strategies that best suit their product and their customer as well as their own personal talents
- learn to answer objections raised by customers
- learn to be persistent, positive, and confident enough to close the sale
- follow up to ensure customer satisfaction

There are special problems in managing a sales force that are not usually as serious in the management of other personnel. To be successful, salespeople must be confident in themselves and in their product. Their morale must be kept high. Sales managers are often handicapped in trying to maintain high morale because they usually lack continuous personal contact with sales personnel.

The sales manager's responsibilities include

- building an effective sales force
- directing the sales force
- monitoring the sales effort

To build a sales force, the sales manager must develop recruiting sources and techniques, devise methods of selecting from the recruits, and maintain an effective sales training program for those selected. Directing the salespeople includes developing workable pay plans, which might include salaries, commissions and/or bonuses, and programs for appealing to higher-order motivations such as those discussed in Chapter 4. The third task, that of monitoring sales effort, is a special form of control. The sales manager must, therefore, set up standards, such as sales quotas and sales expense budgets for sales territories, products, and individual salespeople. He or she must also make regular comparisons of actual sales results to such standards and make the necessary corrections. Corrective action may range from redefining sales territories to additional sales training to dismissal of ineffective sales employees.

Other Promotional Methods

publicity

Publicity is a communication through the news media as a legitimate part of the news. It is usually an inexpensive means of promotion, because its only cost is preparing the news story or press release. But only items considered "newsworthy" by the press are used and, very often, carefully prepared items are never printed or broadcast. Often, news stories (like the announcement of the new models of Ford Motor Company) may be cut down by newspapers for lack of space. Thus publicity is a promotional method over which the firm has little control. Also it is limited to reporting facts.

public relations

Public relations and sales promotion are harder to define. **Public relations includes any personal communication with the public or with government (lobbying) that seeks to create goodwill for the firm. Its effect on sales is usually indirect and long-run.**

sales promotion

Sales promotion includes special events directed at increasing sales. Special sales, coupon offers, contests, games, entertainment features, and trading stamps are examples. Some would include specialty advertising devices such as matches, calendars, and ballpoint pens. Others might add "PMs" or "spiffs," which are cash payments to retailers and their employees to promote a manufacturer's products. The use of sales promotion methods varies greatly by industry. Trading stamps have declined somewhat in popularity. However, A&P has returned to using stamps, including the Gold Bond and S&H varieties, in some parts of the Midwest and East in recent years.

Price

In a competitive world dominated by advertising, price still plays a part. **The price element in the marketing mix includes the dollar cost to customers as well as the conditions of sale.** Most firms still concentrate much of their effort on the problem of setting price. How this process fits into the firm's planning is a different story for almost every firm. The role of price in the mix is not as great as it once was. The importance of careful pricing, however, cannot be ignored.

price

Market Conditions and Pricing

The key concepts of price, market, supply, and demand were introduced in Chapter 2. These explanations were limited to a rather narrow range of market conditions (perfect competition). These conditions include: a large number of buyers and sellers, a homogeneous product, easy entry into the market, and market information in the hands of buyers and sellers. A homogeneous product in a market means that the buyers do not perceive any difference between the products of the competing firms. Easy market entry occurs when no large capital investment is needed for new sellers to enter the industry. The necessary market information includes facts about the numbers of competitors and supply and demand conditions.

As consumers we know that all these conditions rarely exist. The more common kinds of market conditions are oligopoly and monopolistic competition. **An oligopoly means there are only a few sellers of the same or slightly different products.** The market for automatic washing machines, for example, might be classified as oligopolistic. There are few sellers and price competition is rare.

oligopoly

In oligopoly one of the stronger competitors may sometimes raise price, and it is likely that others will follow suit. This is called price leadership.

price leadership

Monopolistic competition occurs in a market with many sellers, each of whom sells a somewhat differentiated product. This is most common in the retail and service markets. Location and quality of service are the differentiating factors. New competitors can easily enter the market. This prevents the typical competitor from making large profits.

monopolistic competition

Monopsony, a situation in which there is one large buyer in the market, often occurs also. Large manufacturers, for example, are often the only buyers of a wide range of component parts. This gives them market power over several or many small suppliers of these parts.

There is such a great array of markets and products in the developed Western nations that labels such as *oligopoly* and *monopolistic competition* are not adequate. They help us understand some of the price behavior, but they are not enough to guide price decisions. Such theoretical market concepts don't account for the use of the marketing mix elements other than price. Price is *only one* of the competitive tools.

Setting Basic Price

Under the guidelines of pricing objectives, firms must set basic prices. There are two different approaches to setting basic price that must be understood. These are the cost approach and the demand approach. (See Figure 8–3.)

The Cost Approach

markup

The cost approach to setting basic price involves "building" unit selling prices on the basis of cost. This approach is simple when the cost of one unit is easy to identify. **A markup is an addition to cost to reach a selling price.** It is usually expressed as a percentage. Mr. Schultz, who operates a men's clothing store, uses a percentage markup applied to his unit costs for an item or group of items. Thus he might buy 100 suits at $40 apiece and apply a 50 percent markup on cost, resulting in prices of $60 per item for his customers (150 percent of $40). Schultz might use this same percentage markup on all items in his store. If so, his basic price policy is a very simple one with a cost basis. He probably has allowed demand factors to influence his markups only in an indirect way.

Mr. Schultz probably knows from past experience about how much his customers are willing to pay. But he does not look at consumer price attitudes very closely because cost-plus pricing is so easy for him. He also knows that, over the years, the policy has allowed him enough gross margin (the difference between total dollar sales and costs of goods sold) to pay his rent, his clerk's salary, and other costs of operation, and to leave him a fair profit. These calculations will be covered more completely in the next chapter when we discuss the income statement in accounting.

Manufacturers may also use a cost approach to pricing. However, it is not always easy for them to identify costs attached to a given unit of output. Cost accounting systems have been developed to aid in this task.

Manufacturers who sell to governments often use cost-based pricing because government buyers frequently specify such pricing, sometimes called *cost-plus*. In some cases the federal government is the *only* cus-

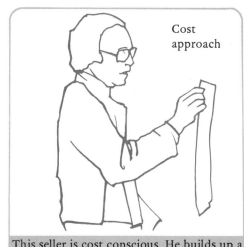

Cost approach

This seller is cost conscious. He builds up a price for what he is selling. He adds all the costs—manufacturing, transporting, dealer margins, etc., and a profit.

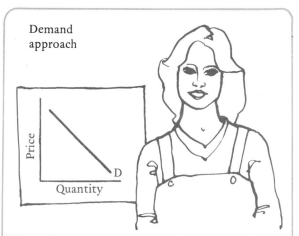

Demand approach

This seller wants to sell! She examines the market and estimates the quantity demanded for the product at various prices—with an eye on her competitors.

FIGURE 8-3

Two approaches to price

tomer of a firm. The government often requires cost-plus pricing which allows the contractor to cover cost and to make a certain profit.

The Demand Approach

In its most extreme form, the demand approach to pricing neglects the cost side. It is more in tune with the marketing concept than the extreme cost approach because it considers possible customer reaction. More precisely, it estimates the amounts which are likely to be sold at different prices (the slope of the demand curve). The most extreme form of demand-approach pricing would set prices very low to sell the greatest number of units.

The Sayles Company, for example, is owned by a former salesperson whose past experience (remote from production costs) leads him to accept the demand approach, giving only some thought to costs. Mr. Sayles realizes that costs, in the long run, must be covered if he is to stay in business. He is, however, more likely to accept lower prices than a cost-oriented firm would, because he is accustomed to thinking in terms of sales growth. He knows that customers and competition must be considered in order to build sales.

Combined Approaches

Many firms set prices by making both cost and demand estimates. These are translated into profit estimates at various unit price and sales levels.

This may also involve the use of *marginal analysis*, which estimates the "best" price and level of production from a profit standpoint.

Pricing models might be developed in firms that have trained economists and computers at their disposal. **A pricing model is an equation or set of equations that represents all the important things in a pricing situation to help decide on the "best" price.** Past experience in pricing and knowledge of the market conditions help to determine the equation that best predicts pricing results. This process is known as *model building*. No matter how carefully it is done, it still requires judgment about what other human beings will do and what their tastes and needs will be.

pricing model

Discounts

Specific prices actually charged by a manufacturing firm often vary from the basic price. Such variations generally result from an established discount policy. Discounts from "list" prices are granted for a number of reasons. For instance, it is common for a firm to offer small discounts for prompt payment of bills. These are called *cash discounts*. Another typical discount is the *trade position discount*. A wholesaler who normally sells to retailers, for example, may make a special sale to another wholesaler at a discount from the regular price to retailers. **Any discount granted because of a difference of position in the distribution channel is called a trade position discount.**

trade position discount

functional discount

Sometimes a functional discount is granted to a customer in return for services rendered. A retail grocer, for example, may receive a discount or allowance from a detergent manufacturer if the grocer features the manufacturer's brand in local newspaper ads. Some would argue

". . . Second tire at half-price when you buy the first tire at double-price. . . . !!"

Source: *Pepper and Salt*, Cartoon Features Syndicate.

How Ads Work

Examples of different advertisements appear on the following pages. Consider the format of each advertisement. What different appeals does each use to attract its particular audience? Are they effective?

We prepare peas for Leslie.

At Gerber, we think Leslie is a very special person. So we prepare peas in a very special way. Although the common garden pea is uncommonly rich in vitamin A, important B vitamins and C, some of these riches last for only a few hours after the pea is picked. In that short time, we begin to capture the nutrients so essential to Leslie's good health. Peas are just one example of the Gerber commitment to produce wholesome baby food. And there are probably easier, less costly ways to prepare them. But we didn't skimp on the other 30 million babies we've helped feed since we began. And we aren't about to start with Leslie.

STRAINED PEAS

Gerber
Babies are our business...
and have been for over 50 years.
Gerber Products Company, Fremont, MI 49412

We know a lot about food because we care a lot about babies.

(1) The illustration draws your attention and helps to get the message across by reinforcing the headline.

(2) The headline can be used as an attention getter, a "teaser," and/or to help get the message across. This one accomplishes all three tasks.

(3) The copy explains by giving facts. It expands on the message given in the headline and illustration. It explains the nutrition available in Gerber peas.

(4) The signature is usually the advertiser's brand name, trademark, and/or slogan. It identifies the advertiser. Gerber's trademark is familiar to many customers.

It's obvious that in this ad beautiful, clear skin is the principal selling point. The lovely young woman tells the whole story. She makes it perfectly clear that Johnson's Baby Oil is not only for babies.

The layout (mostly the illustration of an ad) is vital to its effect. In the ad above, nearly perfect symmetry is used to attract the eye of the reader while displaying the beauty of the products. On the right, with the help of the striking colors of the product and the graceful lines of the models, the reader's eyes are led from the headline to the copy and signature below. The layout is both beautiful and functional. Shape is often crucial to overall ad success.

Securities Processing.
In 1970, Wells Fargo began clearing securities directly on both coasts.
For the first time, it was possible to trade at both ends of the continent through one bank, and stretch the trading day by six hours.
A lot of things have changed since 1970.
But none of the above.

Pioneering. Wells Fargo Bank.

This is an unusual advertisement for securities clearing service by Wells Fargo Bank. The copy is all in headline-sized letters and the "old west" illustration focuses on the institution's name and its long history and experience.

that this practice is not really a discount but rather a simple purchase of a service.

Still another common discount is the *quantity discount* which involves reduced unit prices as the size of the order increases. A firm's discount policy makes its pricing more flexible in special competitive situations. However, it is often also the cause of serious legal problems concerning price discrimination laws.

Pricing New Products

Some special considerations arise in pricing a new product. There are two opposite approaches: market penetration pricing and skimming pricing.

WHAT DO YOU THINK?

Consumer Credit—Curse or Blessing?

If the typical American household were denied credit, its standard of living would likely be lowered. Ours is a credit economy. Consumers can enjoy products during the time they are paying for them. This runs the gamut from houses to cars to clothing to practically anything. But some people believe that some of us go overboard with credit. In some cases this leads to personal bankruptcy. Money and credit managers for the nation are concerned that consumers are overburdened with debt, especially with the higher mortgage notes people are having to meet these days.

At any rate, two amendments to the Truth-in-Lending law are important. The Fair Credit Billing Act gives people who buy products on credit certain rights in their efforts to get their monthly bills corrected. If you have an error on your statement and you notify the store in writing, the store must respond within 30 days. It has 90 days to correct the error or to explain why the statement is correct. During that period you do not have to pay the disputed amount nor do you pay finance charges on it. The store cannot report your account as delinquent to a credit bureau during that time either.

The other amendment, the Equal Credit Opportunity Act, makes it illegal for lenders to deny credit to a person on the basis of sex.

Is consumer credit a curse or a blessing to the consumer? What about sellers? What about our economy? WHAT DO YOU THINK?

market penetration
pricing

To feature low price when introducing a new product is called market penetration pricing. The firm's goal is to build a large initial market share and to build brand loyalty before competitors can enter the market. The initial low price discourages some competitors who foresee smaller profit at such a low price.

skimming pricing

Some firms, however, prefer to charge a high initial price and put greater stress on other marketing mix elements. The goal is to get the greatest early revenue from sales to recover product development costs before competitors enter the market. This is called skimming pricing. It is often used by small firms, by firms with large development costs, and by firms that are not well protected by patents and good reputations. This policy amounts to "getting it while the getting's good." When a small manufacturer of plastic toys introduces a novel, low cost product, the manufacturer is likely to practice "skimming." The firm may charge $1.95 at retail on an easily imitated item that costs $.23 to make. This enables it to maximize immediate return on its investment. A drug manufacturer is likely to do the same with a new antibiotic. Sometimes such pricing brings about legal problems for the firm that practices it.

Retail Pricing

Most prices charged in retail stores are determined by a markup mechanism. Ms. Jill Gladney runs a jewelry store. She knows that, on the average, her costs of doing business—including salaries, rent, and desired profit—have amounted to about 50 percent of sales revenue. She also knows that the cost of goods she buys for resale accounts for the other 50 percent. She might plan prices so that, considering special "sales" to sell slow-moving items, she would realize a 50 percent gross margin (difference between gross sales and cost of goods). Thus her average initial prices might need to be more than double the cost of goods. A shipment of rings costing her $100 apiece might be marked up to $250 and finally sold at $200, just enough to provide a gross margin of 50 percent of sales.

Jill Gladney's initial markup could be expressed two ways: it represents $150/$250 or 60 percent of the originally established sales price and $150/$100 or 150 percent of the original cost price. It should always be made clear whether a percentage markup is expressed in terms of cost or in terms of expected selling price. Of course, Ms. Gladney may assign different markups to different classes of items in her inventory, depending on competitors' practices and her experience in the turnover rate of various items.

inventory turnover rate

The inventory turnover rate in a particular period of time is determined by dividing cost of goods sold by the average inventory value. Thus if the inventory is worth $200 on January 1 and $300 on December

31 and if the cost of goods sold in that year amounted to $2500, the average inventory is $250 and the turnover rate is 10.

If Ms. Gladney uses different markups on different items, she will try to average them out to provide her desired *gross margin*. Sometimes retailers use very low markups on certain items to attract customers. This is known as a *leader item*. The goal is to increase sales of items carrying higher margins. Such practices may be illegal if it is shown that the item is sold below cost. Some firms use illegal "bait and switch" schemes. This means advertising one inexpensive item that is really not available and then convincing people to buy a more expensive substitute when they arrive.

An apparel retailer may make ten purchases of men's sport coats in a season. Marking up each of these by the same percentage might result in ten different prices for sport coats. **Partly to simplify choices for cus-** **tomers and partly to simplify the job of the salespeople, the retailer** **may use price lining—grouping the products at three or four sales price** **levels.** Thus Bill's Men's Wear might make ten purchases of coats in a cost range from $21.50 to $48.50 per unit and present them to customers in the $39.95, $49.95, and $89.95 price range. This makes it easier for the salesperson to get the customer to "trade up." He comes into the store expecting to buy the $39.95 sport coat he saw in the newspaper ad and finally buys the $49.95 or $89.95 coat, after comparing quality and listening to the salesperson's advice.

price lining

The prices selected by Bill's Men's Wear are "odd" amounts and they were close to the next "$10 break." Partly out of tradition and partly because of a slight psychological effect, retailers tend to set prices at $49.95 rather than $50. A price starting with forty "sounds" like more of a bargain than one starting with fifty. Prestige stores, such as Neiman-Marcus, however, often use "even prices" to bolster their status.

Special promotions such as "one-cent sales" and "two-for-one sales" are also a part of the art of pricing. They require careful estimation and experience in order to result in overall profits for the retailer.

Product Differentiation and Market Segmentation

A firm must understand the consumer in order to practice either of two important marketing strategies. **Product differentiation is a process of** **convincing customers that one brand is different from (and better than)** **the competition's. It can be done by stressing distinctive product fea-** **tures or the product's guarantee, its service, or its availability.** It can also be done by an advertising campaign that emphasizes product features or creates the impression of special product advantages. (The government, of course, regulates advertising to prevent false claims.)

product differentiation

market segmentation

A strategy of product differentiation may treat customers as one general target group to be aimed at with one common marketing mix. **A strategy of market segmentation, however, calls for making a special marketing mix for a special segment of the market or several different mixes for several different segments.** The idea is that there is really more than one set of needs to be satisfied within the general market for a product. If a firm believes it will improve its market position, it might make a different version of the product to satisfy the special needs of each group or market segment.

Consider the case of a producer of wristwatches. Such a firm might design one marketing mix to satisfy the "jewelry" watch market and another to satisfy the "time-telling" watch market. There might be important differences in product design, perhaps gold cases with gems for one and waterproof steel cases for the other. Advertising themes for one would emphasize romance or prestige, while the other might emphasize accuracy, durability, and price. They might even use two different sets of retail stores. The expensive ones might be sold in jewelry stores and the cheaper ones in drug and variety stores. Deciding which of these means of segmentation to use requires a study of the market and the cost of segmenting.

Other bases for segmenting markets for certain products might be

- age of customers
- sex of customers
- income level
- personality traits
- educational level
- lifestyles

THINK ABOUT IT!

Why an Uncola?

Most of us are very familiar with the advertising campaign by Seven-Up to establish itself as the "Uncola." Why an "Uncola?" Why an "un-anything?" Some analysts see this as a special kind of market segmentation.

It could be assumed that the main market for soft drinks is already captured by the "big two" cola brands and that a cola drink is the standard drink of mainstream America. If this is so, doesn't it make sense that there is, particularly among younger people, a large number of people who see themselves as different from the mainstream? Isn't it possible that Seven-Up customers are a segment of the soft drink market who share a common lifestyle—off beat and definitely out of the mainstream? THINK ABOUT IT!

In some extreme cases it might be profitable to set up many segments based on combinations of such factors. An extreme segmentation would provide "custom" design for each buyer. In this case each individual customer is a segment. Profitable segmentation requires good consumer knowledge on the part of the seller. Revlon, Inc. broke tradition when it introduced the perfume brand "Charlie." This masculine name appealed to a large segment of "liberated, freewheeling" women and sales reached $10 million in the first year. Homelite, a manufacturer of chain saws, recently discovered that a fourth of its customers are women. This fact undoubtedly influences the definition of the market segments it wants to reach.

Knowing the Consumer

Intelligent decisions about marketing strategies—whether they relate to product, price, promotion, or channel of distribution—require a clear understanding of those who are or might become customers. This kind of decision calls for marketing research. **Marketing research means**   marketing research **applying the scientific method of problem solving to marketing problems. It usually involves getting information from the people who make up the market.**

Two general approaches to the study of the market are the demographic approach and the behavioral approach. The former collects facts about people, families, or firms who are thought likely to become customers. It concentrates on counting and tabulating. The behavioral approach uses ideas from psychology about human behavior and attitudes. It seeks to understand why buyers feel and behave the way they do.

The demographic features of a market of ultimate consumers are such things as the age, sex, race, and income of its members. Often, a firm makes assumptions about the relationship between these characteristics and the likelihood of a person buying a product. These assumptions may be based on past knowledge about customers. For example, we might assume that only persons over age 60 are interested in a certain health tonic. We might also assume that only persons with incomes of $50,000 or more will be interested in a trip around the world.

Assume that a firm decided which characteristics are related to consumption of its product. Now it seeks information about the number of prospects in the area to be served. It may find this information in U.S. Census publications or other government or private sources. **Looking**   secondary research **things up in already-available materials is called secondary research.** On a local basis, a census tract map, accompanied by important facts about people in each tract, can be very valuable to a marketer. (See Figure 8–4.) In each of the numbered sections of the map is a tract. The Bureau of the Census reports income, age, and other important market data for each tract in metropolitan areas. Just think what a manager planning to locate a shopping center could do with this kind of information!

primary research

The firm might also do some primary research. Primary research is getting new facts for a specific purpose. For example, the Swiss Clock Company may include in each package of its product a "registration" card. They request the buyer to fill in facts about herself or himself and mail it in to the company. These cards tell the firm about the people who buy their clocks.

Instead of finding out who the customers are, what they buy, when

FIGURE 8-4

Census tracts in the Akron, Ohio standard metropolitan statistical area

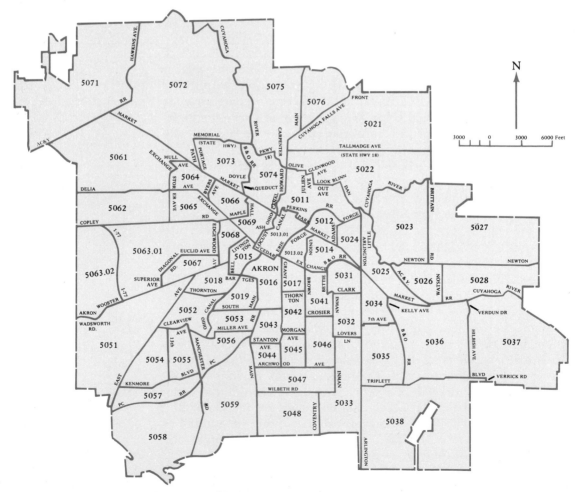

Source: Bureau of the Census.

they buy, etc., the behavioral approach asks the question "why do they buy?" This approach assumes that what people buy often depends on complex motives that can only be understood by psychological probing. Experts in human motivation test a sample of people to find out the basis for their product choice. The researcher might try to find, for example, what a particular brand name "means" to certain people. These researchers often use techniques borrowed from psychologists to discover motives and/or attitudes that customers might ordinarily try to hide.

The firm of McCollum, Spielman and Company, specialists in advertising research, has developed a new way of testing consumer awareness and recall of TV ads. The new system tests three groups of 100 to 120 people in three parts of the country at the same time. A videotaped interviewer asks the people questions about commercials after they have seen them, along with entertainment programs. These tests help tell how much repeating a commercial improves the chance that a viewer will remember it. It is a specialized and advanced type of marketing research.

Regardless of the approach, marketing research must be undertaken on a continuous basis. You need only look at the changes in products for sale in the last few years to see how dynamic the market is. How long ago was it that we had never heard of home smoke detectors, food processors, and household computers? Consumer tastes and values change so fast that a firm must keep its eyes open to the future. This requires marketing research.

Patterns of Consumption

In the last thirty years in the United States, we have witnessed wide swings in attitudes toward discretionary spending (spending beyond basic needs). **Some people have spent more for conspicuous consumption. This means spending in a visible way so that your neighbors will be aware of your wealth and "good taste."** This kind of "show-off" buying frequently happens when people have extra buying power for the first time. They're trying to tell others that they have made it. How often is a new car or a color TV bought to "keep up with the Joneses"? Much of this kind of buying was an indirect result of the G.I. Bill. This education program for veterans of World War II, Korea, and Vietnam helped to bring millions of young people from poor families into jobs with higher economic and social status.

A large number of our younger adults in the late 1960s reacted strongly to conspicuous consumption. Many rejected the middle-class consumption pattern. Of course, this rejection was not limited to the

conspicuous
consumption

kinds of products purchased. It included the entire lifestyle, the politics, the religion, and most of the values of their parents. This rejection caused many people of all ages to question the values of the majority, including the value of high-level consumption. These doubts are still alive.

Even stronger doubts about high-level consumption and the accompanying waste were caused by the oil crisis that began in the early seventies. It made people wonder about the good sense of "gas-guzzling" cars and other wasteful practices we have accepted because of wealth. If oil is running out, what about our other scarce resources? Does our "throwaway" mentality make sense? Will Americans really have to reduce their scale of living? Some believe that businesses may have to engage in *demarketing*—marketing activities aimed at making adjustments to shorter supplies of certain materials or energy. Electric and gas utilities, for example, used to persuade us to use more. In recent years, we have been told to adjust our thermostats to save energy.

Consumerism

As we have seen earlier, *consumerism* is a movement to strengthen the power of users in relation to the power of suppliers. This movement is still strong and centers around the idea of certain basic consumer rights:

- the right to choose
- the right to be informed
- the right to be heard
- the right to safety

This specific list (see Figure 8–5) was endorsed by the President of the United States as early as 1962.

Throughout the 1960s and 1970s, the consumer movement grew and began to include an ever-larger list of objectives. Leadership in the movement has been provided primarily by Ralph Nader, who first became well known when he wrote a book critical of General Motors and the Corvair in 1966. By pointing out the defects in the Corvair, Nader succeeded in gathering support throughout the country. With a broad base of support in the Congress and good press coverage, the consumer movement got several important laws passed. The new laws gave consumers more protection in the areas of packaging, product safety, and information on consumer financing plans. Much of the "grass roots" support came from young people. Many young lawyers on the local and national level worked to draw up and pass consumer laws and to put public pressure on businesses to become more consumer-conscious.

The right to choose from an adequate number of products and brands

The right to be informed of all the important facts about the product or service (price, durability, health and safety hazards, etc.)

The right to be heard by producers and government when treated unfairly or when a question or complaint arises

The right to safety in the use of all products and services

FIGURE 8-5

The basic rights of consumers

The young people who comprised "Nader's Raiders" were often involved in other related movements, such as the ecology movement and the movement to end the Vietnam war. With the end of the Vietnam war, the appearance of an energy crisis, and the economic recession of the early seventies, there was some weakening, or at least a shift in emphasis, in the consumerism movement. Certainly auto emissions control has taken a back seat to better mileage. More emphasis has also been given to protection of consumers from inflation, especially in the area of health care.

In any case, the consumerism movement is still alive and well. It still has some very important meaning to marketers of products and services. Reaction to the movement by firms has varied a lot. Some view it as a threat to the free enterprise system. Others view it as an annoyance. Still others see it as a warning that the marketing concept is not being satisfied.

Those who view it as a real threat are fighting it in the courts and the Congress. These who view it as an annoyance figure they can overcome it with a good public relations campaign. Those that take the marketing concept seriously and recognize consumerism as a symptom of the failure of their application of that concept are likely to review the quality of the marketing research or the marketing mix they are now using.

The Gillette Company, for example, has appointed a vice-president for product integrity. This officer is directly responsible for the safety and quality of Gillette's more than 800 products. He has power to re-

**TWO POINTS
OF VIEW**

**Consumer
Protection**

The Firm:

This consumer movement is going to ruin us! We just get our
new model on the market and bang! The self-appointed
guardians of the people are starting a campaign against us.
They're writing to the Federal Trade Commission and the
State Products Safety Board and they're even giving TV interviews saying that the ZINGER is a death trap and that it has a
faulty braking system.

We market researched that car and know we've built in the
features that customers said they wanted—super styling,
bucket seats, stereo system—the works. It's got all the latest
accessories, too. I call that real consumer responsiveness! We
have been pioneers in applying the marketing concept.

The Consumer Advocate:

The marketplace does not provide consumers with guarantees
to protect them from unscrupulous manufacturers like the
ZINGER Company. The average consumer doesn't know
enough about technical products like cars to know if he or
she is getting gypped. All it takes is a high-pressure ad campaign and a lot of superficial gadgets to convince him or her
to buy.

Consumers need protection. They need product safety
codes with heavy penalties for those firms who don't follow
them. At present, only the consumer movement—people like
Ralph Nader—are around to prevent consumers from making
dumb mistakes. Without us they are almost helpless against
the marketing skills of the giant corporations. Corporations
don't care who gets hurt as long as they make their profit.

move them from the market any time they fail to meet standards he sets.
He can also modify advertising claims or prevent new product introduction. This executive caused the recall of more than $1 million of
antiperspirants because there was a question about the quality of one of
the ingredients.

Many firms have taken similar steps that do much more than "pay lip
service" to consumerism. This, they believe, does not hurt the long-run
profit of their firms. Rather, they wonder about the survival of firms that
do not react positively to public complaints and thereby bring on op-
pressive government controls. We will discuss consumerism again in
Chapter 17.

Marketing of Services

Sales of services have been growing at a rapid rate in recent years. (See Table 8–1.) A service is like a product in that it provides a benefit, but it is unlike a product in that it is not a concrete, physical object. More than 40 percent of what consumers spend is for services. Services represent a big part of what firms buy, too. A service may be quite personal, such as the service provided by a physician or beautician. It can be impersonal as well. Banks, insurance agents, and people who do repair work provide impersonal services in the sense that the human tie between the producer and consumer is not close. In any case, it is usually hard to separate the service from the person who provides it. It almost always requires that the producer be a specialist. Fran Tarkenton and Roger Staubach provide the service of entertainment on the football field. They are highly paid because they are specialists. The same is true of a heart surgeon or an actress. Insurance agents are specialists, too, as are plumbers and electricians.

Since we have defined the product part of a marketing mix in terms of the "bundle of satisfactions" it provides, it follows that marketing of services is not very different from marketing of products. There are a few differences, though. Perhaps the biggest difference is the simple fact that most service producers have not paid as much attention to market-

TABLE 8-1

Selected service industries—receipts, by kind of business, 1970–1977 (in millions of dollars)

Kind of business	1970	1974	1977 (2nd qtr.)
Business services	31,082	42,364	15,443
Advertising	NA	11,574	4,069
Advertising agencies	NA	9,448	3,437
Automobile services	10,040	15,187	5,548
Automobile repair shops	NA	9,455	3,371
Motion pictures, amusement and recreation services	10,256	14,161	4,798
Personal services[1]	12,746	13,785	4,385
Laundries, laundry services, cleaning and dyeing plants	NA	4,886	1,525
Beauty shops	NA	2,974	981
Barber shops	NA	927	257
Hotels, motels, tourist courts, trailer parks, camps	7,417	10,236	3,879
Hotels, motels, tourist courts	NA	9,314	3,485
Miscellaneous repair services	4,602	8,465	3,354

NA: not available.
[1] Includes items not shown separately.
Source: Bureau of the Census.

ing as they should. Only recently have bankers, for example, realized the importance of the marketing concept. They have begun to think in terms of attracting and pleasing customers and of differentiating their services.

Medical services are limited in the use of promotion by ethical codes. However, there is often a need for developing the marketing mix by improving the human dimension of the service (product) and by improving access to doctors' offices and hospitals (distribution). Pricing, in the competitive sense, has been discouraged by ethical codes in medicine, law, and other professions. However, for some specialists, high fees are viewed as a positive marketing factor. The whole question of lack of price competition in the professions is hotly debated these days and may be changing.

For most services all four parts of the marketing mix—product, place, promotion, and price—should be developed. Success in marketing services, even more than in marketing tangible products, depends upon knowing the buyer well and serving his or her needs. This is especially true for personal services where success means treating each client as an individual market segment.

For many services the distribution part of marketing is a little different. Usually the producer and distributor are the same. In most cases there is no "channel" of distribution as we normally think of it. Yet, the location of the bank branch or the watch repair shop or even the doctor's office must be considered carefully. A successful TV repair shop often provides home pickup and delivery. A marketer of rented apartments in a distant suburb might offer private commuter bus service to tenants. This is just another way of distributing.

The marketing of services has a long way to go, however. The sooner service producers realize that the marketing concept applies to their "product," the better off the consumer will be.

Summary and Look Ahead

Promotion is primarily composed of advertising and personal selling activities that complement one another. Advertising reaches large numbers of people, while personal selling is more aggressive and tailored to the individual customer. Both seek to convince the potential customer that a product or service is worth buying. They use a wide variety of appeals to do so.

Price is capable of administration. Firms emphasize a cost approach, a demand approach, or a combination approach in setting basic price. They may offer a variety of discounts and try to control prices at the retail level. There are special pricing problems related to new products and to retail stores.

Marketing strategies such as product differentiation and market segmentation have great influence on the selection of specific elements in the marketing mix. For the mix to really fit the target market, a firm must know that target by means of marketing research. Complete marketing research involves the use of primary and secondary research. Such research, if used to diagnose customer needs and wants, can go a long way toward making firms more responsive to the consumer movement, if firms take their job of satisfying the consumer seriously. As services become a larger part of what is produced, wider and more intelligent applications of marketing are being made to such services.

In the following chapter we turn to the subject of accounting. We will explore the methods of financial and managerial accounting and prepare for later introductions to the world of finance.

My name is Jim Bunch. I am a marketing representative with the Armstrong Cork Company. I received my bachelor's degree in business with a marketing major from the University of Southern Mississippi.

Armstrong flooring products are distributed through wholesale distributors. My primary responsibility is to work with one of these wholesalers in marketing Armstrong flooring products. I work closely with the wholesaler to aid in maximizing sales to retailers and profits. I make sales presentations to the wholesaler on new pattern and flooring introductions, proposals for local implementation of national promotional programs, incentive plans for motivating the wholesaler's sales force, and suggestions on inventory control. All of these things help the wholesaling firm to differentiate itself.

I also have an assigned territory for which my objective is to increase sales of Armstrong flooring products to mass merchandisers and installed-floors accounts targeting the residential remodel/replacement market. My activities here include making sales presentations on new products to major accounts, developing and promoting local retail advertising programs, training retail salespeople, and developing and implementing new merchandising and display methods.

Why the Armstrong Cork Company? Because of my retail experience, I decided to major in marketing with the hope of using this experience and my degree to work for a large department store chain as a management trainee. I enjoy dealing with people and felt I would have an advantage with prior retail management experience. One of my marketing professors, however, recommended I interview with the Armstrong Cork Company, which I learned was known for its residential flooring products. After being in the clothing business, selling floors didn't sound too exciting, but I decided to look into the company and what opportunities it might offer.

During the interview and subsequent trip to Lancaster, Pennsylvania, I discovered that Armstrong was a leader in the resilient flooring industry and that joining the company offered me an opportunity to be exposed to all the phases of marketing a product, from market research and product concept to the manufacturing of that product and the distribution network all the way to Mrs. Consumer. I would get experience in all the latest advertising, merchandising, and promotional techniques available. There was a tremendous opportunity for advancement, and I was most impressed with the professionalism and caliber of the people I met.

I was fortunate to receive an offer from Armstrong and plan to make it a career. However, I feel my experience thus far with Armstrong has provided me with the skills that are universal and that would allow me to compete successfully in the marketing of almost any product in any industry.

Key Concepts

advertising   All nonpersonal promotional activity for which a fee is paid by an identified sponsor. It is complementary to personal selling.

advertising agency   A firm that produces and places advertisements in media and may arrange total programs of advertising for its clients.

advertising media   Any means by which advertising can be carried: radio, television, print, etc.

AIDA process   Short for attention, interest, desire, and action—the process of selling sought by advertising and personal selling.

conspicuous consumption   Spending in a visible way so that neighbors will be aware of the wealth and "good taste" of the spender.

functional discount   A discount given to a channel member (middleman) for performance of a specific marketing function. An example is an advertising allowance.

inventory turnover rate   The cost of goods sold divided by the average inventory. A high turnover rate indicates efficiency in the use of resources.

marketing research   The systematic gathering, recording, and analyzing of data concerning the marketing of products and services.

market penetration pricing   A pricing strategy for introducing a new product. Setting a price low to secure a market share for the product.

market segmentation   Designing a special marketing mix for a special segment of the market or several mixes for several different segments.

markup An addition to cost by a middleman. A middleman adds a markup to the cost of an item in order to compute selling price. It can be expressed in money terms or as a percentage.

monopolistic competition A market condition existing when many sellers compete for customers by offering differentiated products.

oligopoly A market condition existing when a few firms sell highly similar products and dominate a market.

personal selling Direct contact of salesperson with a prospective buyer and a face-to-face sales effort.

price An element in the marketing mix which includes monetary cost and the terms of sale.

price leadership A situation common in oligopoly markets in which one firm sets a price and others follow suit in the interest of price stability and avoidance of price competition.

price lining Setting retail prices at standard preset levels, such as $6.95, $8.00, etc., for items bought at a variety of wholesale prices to simplify consumer decisions and pricing administration.

pricing model A mathematical formula to help firms set the best basic price.

primary research Obtaining original information for a specific research objective. In marketing, it often requires use of questionnaires directed toward the target market.

product differentiation Making products or services appear different from those of the competitors, thereby attracting buyers or commanding higher prices.

promotion An element in the marketing mix which includes all communication a firm has with its present or potential customers for the purpose of expanding sales, either directly or indirectly.

publicity Information about a company or its product that is considered "news" by the media and is reported by them with no charge to the company.

public relations Communication with the public or with the government that seeks to create goodwill for the firm as a whole.

sales promotion Any of a variety of devices to increase sales, including trading stamps, contests, and special attractions.

secondary research Research into materials previously developed by someone other than the present researcher. The present researcher benefits from work done earlier for another purpose. Libraries are a frequent source for this kind of research.

skimming pricing A pricing strategy for introducing a new product. Setting a high initial price in order to get maximum quick return on product development costs, often in anticipation of entry of competition into the market within a short period.

trade position discount A discount given to middlemen in proportion to their position in the channel of distribution. A wholesaler usually gets a larger one than a retailer.

For Review . . .

1. What are the various functions of promotion?
2. Name the important advertising media in the order of their volume in the United States.
3. What is the AIDA process? How does it apply to personal selling?
4. What are the broad responsibilities of a sales manager?
5. Describe perfect competition. How common is it in the United States today?

6. Compare the two approaches to setting basic price.
7. What is the difference between cash discounts and trade position discounts?
8. Contrast the policies of "skimming" and "penetration" pricing.
9. What is product differentiation? Give an example.

10. Contrast the demographic and behavioral approaches to marketing research.

... For Discussion

1. Write a brief piece of copy for a television commercial announcing a new chain of sandwich shops called "Margy's" to be introduced in your city next month.
2. Write a paragraph giving advice to a salesperson for a hardware wholesaler going out on his or her route for the first time.

3. Is price as important a part of the marketing mix today as it was 50 years ago?
4. Why is marketing research necessary?
5. Two divergent views of the proper relationship between buyer and seller are "let the buyer beware" and "let the seller beware." Which is the "proper" view? Why?
6. Why is a consumerism movement under way in the United States when consumer power is a basic characteristic of capitalism?

Incidents

Perrier Water

After a long period of paying very little attention to sales in the United States, the French bottlers of Perrier mineral water launched a very successful marketing effort aimed at Americans. Sales jumped from $1 million in 1976 to over $30 million in 1978. While this is only 1 percent of the United States soft drink market, it is still a fantastic marketing success.

The product is a naturally bubbly spring water popular in Europe for a long time. In America it has been sold on the basis of its natural carbonation and its "snob appeal" because of its French origin.

Principal users have been upper- to upper-middle-income adults.

Questions

1. Do market leaders such as Coke and Pepsi have anything to worry about? Explain.
2. How would you imagine that Perrier's distribution channel differs from those of the leading colas? Its promotional effort? Discuss.
3. Discuss the pricing strategy that you would recommend for this product.

KSTP Switches to ABC

Even relationships between TV stations and the big networks can be upset by changes in consumer behavior. The owners of a Minneapolis station demonstrated the power of the listener-consumer by responding to the fact that their network program ratings were falling.

"They let everyone know it—forcefully—at the start of the season when they informed NBC that on Mar. 1 KSTP-TV will drop its programs and begin carrying the shows of the leader, ABC-TV. The decision severs a 30-year relationship between the network and the station. Moreover, it momentarily throws the market into confusion, because the KSTP-TV switch affects the programming of two

other stations. It could even have national ramifications, as leading stations in other markets consider their futures with NBC or CBS."

Questions:

1. What factors do you think KSTP management took into consideration in reaching this decision?
2. Why do you think it is important for a local TV station to carry highly rated network programs?
3. If you were a local firm considering advertising on KSTP, how would their switch affect your decision and why?

Source: *Business Week.*

ROCKETOY COMPANY 5

Before Rocketoy's new plant in Detroit was half completed, sales reports reaching Terry's desk showed that sales of two of Rocketoy's most successful nonseasonal plastic products were down 20 percent from the previous year. Terry called in the vice-president of marketing, Julia Rabinovitz, for an explanation. Julia gave several possible causes of the sales decline.

First, she had been told by several of Rocketoy's salespersons that some of the customers were placing trial orders with a toy manufacturer in West Germany. This manufacturer produced two high-quality toys that were very similar to Rocketoy's. The major difference was price. The imported toys sold at retail in the United States for 75 percent of the retail price of Rocketoy's two toys. Julia suggested that retail toy buyers were growing more price conscious.

Julia also suggested that recent cost increases for plastic had led to a reduction in the thickness of the plastic used to make several Rocketoy products, including the two "problem" products. She thought that this hurt Rocketoy's reputation for making quality toys. In fact, Rocketoy had received 150 letters from retail customers complaining about the "shoddy" toys. Three customers said they were reporting the problem to the Consumer Product Safety Commission in Washington, D.C. They claimed that their children had received cuts on their hands. Jagged pieces of plastic became exposed when the toys broke under normal play activities. Julia and Terry worried about this problem. They knew that three competitors had had to remove several of their toys from the market as a result of safety problems. Julia suggested, however, that this was a production problem beyond her control.

Julia's third explanation of declining sales was the declining birth rate in the United States. The two "problem" toys appealed to children between the ages of two and four years. Julia said that since the number of potential users of these toys was declining, it could only be expected that sales of these toys would decline as well.

Julia also suggested that many parents were complaining about the tremendous volume of advertising aimed at children. Rocketoy had once concentrated its advertising on Saturday morning children's television shows. Many parents had complained that the constant bombardment of television commercials was bad for their children. Several parents had written to Rocketoy and had accused the company of taking advantage of children. Julia knew that several government agencies were investigating these types of complaints from parents. As a result, Rocketoy had decided to reduce its advertising several months ago.

Finally, Julia said that more and more toys were being sold through discount stores. Rocketoy had always refused to sell through discount stores because many toy store owners said they would stop buying Rocketoy products if Rocketoy sold to "price-cutting" discount stores. Julia said that this had become a big problem for Rocketoy and something had to be done about it.

Questions

1. Should Rocketoy reconsider its plans for the new plant? Why or why not?
2. What action, if any, should Rocketoy take regarding the new competition from West Germany?
3. Who are Rocketoy's target market: children, or their parents? Discuss. Are there any other targets?
4. With respect to the marketing mix, Rocketoy has problems with product, place, price, and promotion. Discuss the nature of these problems and how you would deal with each of them for each element in the marketing mix.

Accounting

Objectives: After reading this chapter, you should be able to

1. Distinguish between financial and managerial accounting processes.
2. Identify the three principal tasks of accounting.
3. Describe what a CPA does.
4. Prepare a chart showing the major information flows of accounting.
5. Explain the relationship between transactions and accounts.
6. Complete both of the principal accounting equations.
7. Draw up a simple example of the two principal financial statements.
8. Explain the purpose of the two principal financial statements.
9. Demonstrate how an investor might use the statements of a firm he or she may wish to invest in.
10. Explain and use at least one of the "key" ratios.
11. Show how a budget may be used in internal control.

Key concepts: Look for these terms as you read the chapter

accounting	current asset
financial accounting	fixed asset
managerial accounting	depreciation
Certified Public Accountant (CPA)	current liability
	accrued expense
account	income statement
assets	gross profit
equity	key ratio
liability	tangible net worth
owner's equity	current ratio
revenue	budget
expense	sales forecast
transaction	responsibility accounting
basic accounting equations	product cost accounting
balance sheet	

If you were asked to describe or evaluate a firm, how would you do it? A lot would depend on why the request was made and who made it. If the request came from a new employee, you might want to describe the wage and promotion policies and the working conditions of the firm. If it came from a new customer, you might want to describe the quality of your product and your delivery price, and credit policies. But what if you were the executive vice-president of a firm and the president asked you to evaluate the sales growth of the firm over the last five years? Or what if the president asked you to make a report on the firm's financial position to a bank that may lend the firm a million dollars?

The last two requests could not be met completely by the use of words. These two requests are common, however, and they both require the use of accounting.

What Is Accounting?

Accounting has been defined in many ways. We will define it as a process of recording, gathering, manipulating, auditing, and interpreting information that describes the assets and operation of a firm and aids in decision making.

accounting

This process is guided by certain widely accepted principles and rules. These principles are especially important when a manager must reach people outside of the firm. They play a smaller role when accounting is for internal use. We call the internal processes *managerial accounting* and the external process *financial accounting*. Both financial and managerial accounting are useful to managers.

Financial accounting helps the manager to "keep score" for the firm. It watches the flow of resources and lets those who have an interest in them know where they stand.

financial accounting

Managerial accounting calls attention to problems and the need for action. It also aids in planning and decision making. It is aimed more at *control* and less at *valuation* than financial accounting. It is also less traditional.

managerial accounting

Like any tool, accounting must be designed to do its various jobs (scorekeeping, calling attention, and helping in decision making) quickly and at a fair cost. The accounting system must provide clear and efficient estimates of financial facts. What it produces must be, above all, *relevant*. Accounting is relevant when it is useful to managers, creditors, investors, or government agencies in doing their jobs. Accounting is a much broader activity than simple bookkeeping. Bookkeeping is simply the mechanics of accounting—the recording of financial data.

What Is an Accountant?

An accountant is much more than a person who keeps the books. Accountants know basic procedures for recording transactions quickly, accurately, and with maximum security. They know enough about the law to build a system of accounts that reflects those laws, especially tax laws. They know where to find specialized information about laws and the answers to other tough questions, especially as they relate to the firm they serve. For example, an accountant for a forest products company would keep a library relating to land valuation and the use of natural resources. He or she must also be aware of the history and policies of the firm.

Certified Public Accountant (CPA)

Certified Public Accountants (CPAs) are accountants who have fulfilled the legal requirements of their states for knowledge in accounting theory, practice, auditing, and law and who are licensed to sign legally required financial reports. Often their knowledge must be broader because they deal with the accounting processes of many different firms. Their duty to report the financial positions of firms extends to the general public as well as to the firm that hires them. Much of the independent CPA's work is classified as auditing (checking the accuracy of records). Some accountants serve government directly and develop a much more specialized skill in reporting and checking the spending of public funds. Careers in accounting, then, are usually classified as in private, public, or governmental accounting.

In the last two decades the process of increasing specialization in the accounting profession has been made evident by the introduction of the following financial certification programs:

- CDP or Certificate in Data Processing
- CFA or Chartered Financial Analyst
- CBA or Chartered Bank Auditor
- CMA or Certificate in Management Accounting
- CIA or Certified Internal Auditor

Accounting to Whom and for What?

Accounting traces a sequence of information flows. Figure 9–1 indicates something about who is "accounted to." Employees at the operating level use accounting to "account to" managers (A) who must use accounting to "account to" owners (B). The firm's managers must also "account to" creditors and future creditors (C) and to government agencies (D).

The flow of information is quite varied—and some of the bits of information reaching managers do not go any further, but are retained for internal purposes (E). Much of the same information is contained in flows B, C, D, and E, although it takes different forms and emphasizes different kinds of facts, depending on who is to read it. Firms have many uses of their own for this information, as we will see when we discuss managerial accounting.

What are "accounted for" are the firm's resources, expressed in dol-

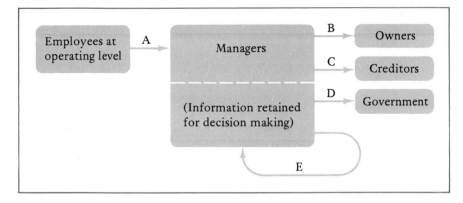

FIGURE 9-1

The flow of accounting information

lars and cents (usually cost) terms. In some cases units other than money are accounted for, but the units are usually money. Non-monetary units, such as products made in a factory or coupons received by a retailer are related to managerial accounting. First, we will consider financial accounting.

Financial Accounting

Financial accounting is an old and traditional practice designed to "keep tabs" on a firm's assets and to protect its owners' property rights. It also has many built-in safeguards for outsiders who want to know about the firm's financial condition. Financial accounting is a scorekeeping process.

Financial accounting is a general system because it includes the entire firm (or entity). Managerial accounting, on the other hand, usually focuses on one activity within the firm. We will discuss this in a later section of this chapter.

Transactions and Accounts

A basic idea in accounting is that of an account. This is a register of financial value. The set of accounts kept by a firm represents all those separate classes of values, both positive and negative, and the changes in value that occur. There are four principal kinds of accounts:

account

- asset accounts
- equity accounts
- revenue accounts
- expense accounts

WHAT DO YOU THINK?

Auditors' Responsibility for Uncovering Fraud

Auditors are responsible for checking to see if a client has followed accepted accounting principles in reporting its results of operations. Recent discovery of fraud in the financial reporting of major firms has led to some serious questioning by the Congress, by regulatory agencies, and even by the accounting profession itself of the adequacy of present auditing practices. The possibility of suing auditing firms for not uncovering fraud has also been raised.

A large CPA firm, Peat, Marwick, Mitchell & Co., has pointed out that traditional auditing practices are not enough to detect management fraud in world-wide businesses tied together by computer. New tools quite different from ordinary auditing are needed. Some believe lawyers should accompany CPAs; others recommend that auditors should automatically "blow the whistle" to government when suspicions arise instead of bringing discoveries to the firm's management. Should auditors be responsible for uncovering fraud? WHAT DO YOU THINK?

assets
    Assets are things with a positive dollar value that are owned by a firm. Their value is registered in asset accounts. Usually a firm keeps a large number of asset accounts. Examples are Land, Cash, and Accounts Receivable (money owed to the firm by customers).

equity
    An equity account is a register of claims or rights of different groups to a firm's assets. These include the claims of outsiders and the claims of owners.

liability
    The claims of outsiders are called a firm's liabilities. An example of such an account is Notes Payable, which shows what a firm owes in the form of promises or orders to pay.

owner's equity
    The claims of insiders, or owners, are kept in owner's equity or capital accounts. Examples of these are Retained Earnings and Common Stock Outstanding.

revenue
    A revenue account is a register of gross earnings or inflows of value to a firm during a given time period. The most important revenue account is Sales. It includes the total selling price of all goods or services sold during a given time period.

expense
    Expense accounts are measures of the using up of resources in the normal course of business in a given time period. A typical example is Wages Paid.

transaction
    The term *transaction* is used to describe any change in an asset or an equity. If we buy raw material for cash, we must reduce the Cash account balance and increase the Raw Material account balance.

Source: *Cathy,* Universal Press Syndicate.

For a better idea about how the basic types of accounts are related, we will study some basic accounting equations that underlie the financial statements.

Important Accounting Equations

An equation represents the fact that two expressions are equal. One expression is placed on the left side of the equality sign, and the other expression is placed on the right. For example, $3x + 4 = 16$. **Basic accounting equations are equations that explain the basic system of relationships in financial accounting.**

basic accounting equations

The first basic accounting equation represents the fact that the sum of the assets equals the sum of the equities (claims on assets) and that these equities include liabilities and capital (or owner's equity). This basic accounting equation, then, is

$$\text{Assets} = \text{Liabilities} + \text{Capital}$$

or

$$\text{Assets} = \text{Equities}$$

If one side of the equation (assets) is increased or reduced, then the other side must be increased or reduced by exactly the same amount, just as in algebra. Some transactions, of course, affect only two individual assets or only two equity accounts. They do not affect the totals on either side of the equation, as in our earlier example concerning the cash purchase of raw materials.

A second equation reflects current operations. It is as follows:

$$\text{Revenues} - \text{Expenses} = \text{Net Profit}$$

Current revenue minus the expenses incurred in gaining that revenue equals *net profit.* Net profit measures the success of the firm's current

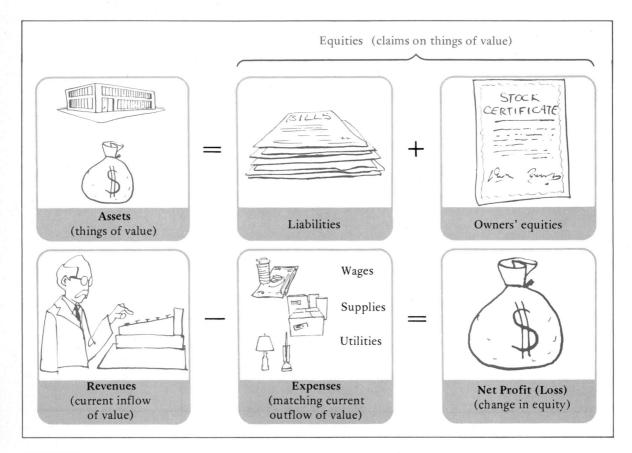

Equities (claims on things of value)

Assets
(things of value)   **=**   Liabilities   **+**   Owners' equities

Revenues
(current inflow
of value)   **−**   **Expenses**
(matching current
outflow of value)   Wages
Supplies
Utilities   **=**   **Net Profit (Loss)**
(change in equity)

FIGURE 9-2

**Two basic equations that
sum up financial
accounting**

operations during the period. When expenses exceed revenues, there is
a net loss for the period. Net profit is also an index of the change in the
owner's equity that occurs during the period. The capital account, Retained Earnings, is increased by profitable operations and reduced by
payments to owners. Net profit is added to or net loss is deducted from
retained earnings. The basic equations are summarized in Figure 9–2.

Financial Statements

You have probably seen financial statements in a newspaper or in a
firm's annual report. Two of them, the balance sheet and the income
statement, have been widely used for more than a century. These statements are useful for managers, investors, and creditors. They are central
to financial accounting.

The Balance Sheet

A business is a living, functioning entity. **A balance sheet (also known as a statement of financial position) presents a picture of a firm at one point in time.** Family albums filled with snapshots of children as they grow represent a record of that growth for their parents. A file of x rays kept by a doctor records the progress a fractured bone makes in healing. Likewise, a set of balance sheets drawn at the end of each year, over a period of years, depicts the rate of growth and nature of the growth of that firm.

Figure 9–3 is a balance sheet for Gloria's Dress Shop as of December 31, 19*3. This is a more detailed way of expressing the first basic accounting equation: Assets = Equities. The firm's assets are divided into three major classes: current assets, fixed assets, and other assets.

Current Assets

A current asset is one that the firm normally expects to hold no longer than a year. Examples are cash (currency and checking account), accounts receivable, merchandise inventories, and prepaid expenses. Accounts receivable are amounts owed to the firm from its normal operations. In this case, they are amounts owed by customers for dresses purchased from the firm recently. As of December 31, 19*3, 43 different customers owed the firm the total sum of $18,000 "on account."

Merchandise inventory consists of all goods purchased for resale but not yet sold. Most retailers must take an inventory of stock at the end of

balance sheet

current asset

FIGURE 9-3

Gloria's Dress Shop, Inc. Balance Sheet (December 31, 19*3)

Current assets:			Current liabilities:		
Cash	$ 6,000		Accounts payable	$10,000	
Accounts receivable	18,000		Accrued expenses payable	1,000	
Merchandise inventories	10,000		Estimated tax liability	7,000	
Prepaid expenses	2,000		Total current liabilities		$18,000
Total current assets		$36,000			
Fixed assets:			Other liabilities:		
Land		4,000	Bonds payable		10,000
Building	$ 8,000		Stockholders equity:		
Less depreciation	4,000	4,000	Common stock	$25,000	
			Retained earnings	1,000	26,000
Other assets:					
Goodwill		10,000			
Total assets		$54,000	Total equities		$54,000

the year to determine the value of their goods for balance sheet purposes. At the end of the year, Gloria's counted $10,000 worth of goods for sale.

Prepaid expenses might include prepaid insurance premiums which have not yet been used by the firm. Gloria's purchased a fire insurance policy on July 1, 19*3, and the premiums were paid one year in advance. Thus, the firm now owns something of value—that is, a prepaid insurance policy, only half of which has been "used."

Two current assets not shown in Figure 9–3 are *marketable securities* and *notes receivable*. The former are stocks and bonds of other firms and government bonds held by a firm as short-term investments. The latter represent short-term loans to customers or others.

Fixed Assets

fixed asset

A fixed asset is a tangible resource that is expected to remain useful for more than a year. Such an asset is valued at its cost to the firm. When a firm buys a building, it is listed among the firm's fixed asset accounts at a value equal to its purchase price.

depreciation

As an asset loses value, it suffers depreciation. This loss of value is charged off as an expense and the stated value of the fixed asset is reduced on the balance sheet. In Figure 9–3 $4,000 has been deducted from the value of the building because of depreciation. This means that this fixed asset is "half used up."

There are many acceptable methods of figuring depreciation in traditional accounting. The simplest is called *straight line depreciation*. It provides for charging equal parts of the original cost of an asset in each year of its expected life. Thus Gloria's firm is using straight line depreciation on the building which was purchased four years before the date of the balance sheet. This building, the only *depreciable* asset Gloria has, will be fully depreciated four years after the date of this balance sheet.

One other general class of asset is included in Figure 9–3. It is an intangible asset known as *goodwill*, which results from years of good business reputation. According to accepted accounting principles, goodwill is assigned a dollar value only when it is bought by the firm. In other words, when the corporation bought the assets of the previous sole proprietorship, it was estimated that the corporation paid $10,000 more than the tangible net worth of the proprietorship (the difference between the value of tangible assets and the liabilities).

Current Liabilities

Under the liabilities section of Figure 9–3, the current liabilities total $18,000. This figure includes the $10,000 due to suppliers, $1,000 of accrued expenses, and $7,000 in estimated taxes owed. **These are current**

current liability

liabilities because they will be paid off within a year.

Accrued expenses illustrate a major accounting principle—accrual. accrued expense
Expenses are charged against revenue in the period in which the firm
benefits from them. An accrued expense is used up but not paid for yet.
Gloria's accrued expenses are the result of some work performed by
several salesclerks during the Christmas season who had not yet been
paid as of the end of the year.

Long-term Liability and Owner's Equity

Gloria's owes bondholders $10,000. This is a long-term liability because
it won't be paid off within a year. Stockholders' equity is listed at $26,000
including the original "stated value" of the stock when it was issued and
$1,000 in retained earnings (earnings of previous years which have been
put back into the firm). Together these add up to what the owner's
claims on assets are—*owner's equity*. If the firm were still a proprietorship, the owner's equity would simply be listed on the balance sheet as
"Gloria Smith, Capital." The owner's equity, then, is the claim of the
owner against the firm's resources.

In any case, the sum of the equities is always equal to the sum of the
assets. The basic accounting equation always holds. The $54,000 in cur-
rent, fixed, and other assets have claims upon them (equities) in the
amounts of $18,000 (current liabilities), $10,000 (bondholders), and
$26,000 (stockholders or owners).

The Income Statement

The balance sheet, or statement of financial position, shows a "cross
section" of a firm's resources and equities at one point in time. **The** income statement
income statement, on the other hand, shows what actually happened
over a period of time to explain some of the differences between
successive balance sheets. It summarizes the revenue and expense
accounts, just as the balance sheet summarizes the asset and equity
accounts. Figure 9–4 illustrates Gloria's income statement for the period
ending December 31, 19*4, one year after the statement in Figure 9–3.

Revenues

Gloria's sold $267,000 worth of dresses this year. The selling price of the
dresses is used in this valuation rather than the original cost. Sales are
net because any discounts or returns and allowances granted to customers have been subtracted from the gross sales.

From net sales is deducted the actual cost of goods sold. The cost of
goods sold is calculated as follows. First, a physical inventory of goods in
stock at the end of the year is taken. The cost of these goods is then
subtracted from the sum of the cost values of (a) the inventory a year

Net Sales	$267,000	(100.0%)
Less cost of goods sold	152,000	(56.9%)
Gross profit	$115,000	(43.1%)
Less expenses:		
Wages and salaries paid	$68,200 (25.5%)	
General and administrative expenses	38,000 (14.2%)	
Interest expenses	1,500 (0.6%)	107,700 (40.4%)
Net profit before taxes		$ 7,300 (2.7%)
Taxes (paid and accrued)		2,000 (0.7%)
Net profit after taxes		$ 5,300 (2.0%)
Less dividends		4,000 (1.5%)
Added to retained earnings		$ 1,300 (0.5%)

FIGURE 9-4

Gloria's Dress Shop, Inc. Income Statement (year ending December 31, 19*4)

earlier and (b) purchases made during the year. Gloria's had $10,000 in inventory at the beginning of the year, bought $180,000 more during the year, and had $38,000 remaining when the closing inventory was taken ($10,000 + $180,000 − $38,000 = $152,000).

Expenses

gross profit

The difference between net sales and cost of goods sold is gross profit. Figure 9–4 shows a few expense accounts, including wages and salaries, general and administrative expenses, and interest expenses. Wages and salaries include Gloria's salary, wages of a bookkeeper and a janitor, and wages and commissions paid to salespersons. General and Administrative Expense includes depreciation, office expenses, utilities, and insurance. Interest Expense includes interest paid to the Second National Bank for a loan made and repaid during the year. Net Profit Before Taxes, then, is $7,300 from which taxes paid or accrued are deducted in the amount of $2,000. Notice the taxes that apply to this year's operations—whether paid or not—are rightfully deducted from this year's revenue. This is another example of the principle of accrual. Figure 9–5, the new balance sheet, shows an estimated tax liability in the amount of $1,000. This means that, of the tax bill for the previous year, only half had been paid by the close of the year.

Returning to Figure 9–4, the final deduction ($4,000) is made for dividends paid to stockholders, leaving $1,300 of the net profit for the year in the business as retained earnings. Thus we have traced the summarized revenue and expense transactions during the year.

Current assets:			Current liabilities:		
Cash	$17,000		Accounts payable	$10,700	
Accounts receivable	22,000		Accrued expenses payable	1,000	
Merchandise inventories	38,000		Estimated tax liability	1,000	
Total current assets		$77,000	Total current liabilities		$12,700
Fixed assets:			Other liabilities:		
Land		4,000	Bonds payable		10,000
Building	$ 8,000				
Less depreciation	5,000	3,000			
Other assets:			Stockholders' equity:		
Goodwill		10,000	Common stock	$69,000	
			Retained earnings	2,300	71,300
Total assets		$94,000	Total equities		$94,000

FIGURE 9-5

The usefulness of the income statement, especially for internal purposes, is increased when it includes a "percentage of net sales" column
as does Figure 9–4. This feature makes the income statement easier to
compare to those of earlier years, to those of other firms, and to industry
averages.

**Gloria's Dress Shop, Inc.
Balance Sheet
(December 31, 19*4)**

Financial Accounting—Users and Uses

Before we begin a discussion of key ratios, we will describe two specific
cases tying in accounting processes and their use.

How Dr. Franklin Used Accounting

William Franklin is a retired doctor who has invested a large part of his
savings in the common stock of the Marshall Corporation, a producer of
steel tubing. He owns 2,000 shares, which represent about three percent
of Marshall's outstanding stock. Dr. Franklin is interested in getting a
reasonable return on his investment in the form of common stock dividends.

This investor does not know any of the corporation's officers or managers personally, and he lives in a town in which none of the firm's
plants is located. He needs information, so he must rely on the firm's
financial statements to judge the quality of his investment.

Let's review how these statements came to be. Dr. Franklin could not
have made a wise decision about his investment if someone (probably
Marshall's treasurer or comptroller) had not set up an information col-

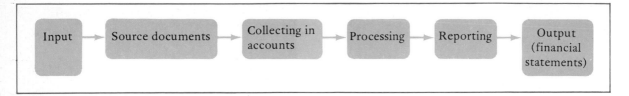

FIGURE 9-6

How the Marshall Corporation generated its financial statements

lecting, processing, and reporting system (see Figure 9–6) that did the following things:

- retained facts about financially significant events on a variety of source documents
- classified these into accounts
- summarized accounts in financial statements
- distributed statements to stockholders

First, the firm's operations were scanned to identify financially significant events (those having a bearing on the firm's profit), and these were entered on some kind of source document. For example, when the office manager bought an order of stationery, he or she signed a purchase order describing the items to be purchased and the amount to be spent. The purchase order, or perhaps a copy of the invoice (list of items shipped) made out by the stationery store, is a source document for the purchase event.

The second step involved recording the dollar amount and the nature of the event in some form of register (account) set up in advance by the comptroller. This is the classifying function. The basic facts found in the purchase order were entered on a punched card, together with a code number indicating the kind of expense. The card (along with many others) was fed into the firm's computer and stored for later use.

At the end of the quarter, Marshall's accounting department took all the stored bits of data, such as the stationery purchase record, and processed them. The department also added up all company expenditures by type and constructed Marshall's quarterly financial statements.

The reporting function has also been fulfilled. The statements, first printed by the firm's computer, were checked by the accounting staff and published for distribution to stockholders. This is how Dr. Franklin got the financial statement he needed to evaluate his investment. He can calculate earnings per share (total profit divided by the number of outstanding shares of common stock) and other financial ratios from these statements. He can, of course, get similar earnings-per-share and dividend data about other firms from his stockbroker.

Checking a Prospective Customer

Suppose Hydraspace Company wishes to sign a long-term contract with the Marshall Company that will make Hydraspace the supplier of an

Source: *Pepper and Salt*, Cartoon Features Syndicate.

"I can explain my excessive and unexplainable deductions. When I made out the return, I was at the lowest point in my biorhythm chart."

important part for Marshall's major product. It's important for Hydraspace to know about Marshall's financial condition so that it can be sure that Marshall can pay on time. Hydraspace will use a number of sources of information for this purpose. They will depend a lot on Marshall's past financial statements, especially those statements that indicate Marshall's ability to pay its current bills.

Marshall's accounting system should be able to provide a summary of its past payment behavior if the firm wishes to give this information to Hydraspace. In practice, this kind of information is accumulated by independent credit reporting services, such as Dun and Bradstreet, and sold to their customers.

Once the contract is negotiated and the first shipment of parts has been made, Hydraspace becomes a trade creditor of Marshall. For further insight about how a creditor might interpret financial statements, we now turn to the subject of ratio analysis.

Important Financial Ratios

The numbers on the financial statements take on more meaning when they are related to each other. For instance, the net profit of a firm is

WHAT DO YOU THINK?

Valuation of Inventories— FIFO or LIFO?

The method traditionally used by most firms to value inventories of raw materials or component parts or goods purchased for resale is known as FIFO (first in-first out). This means, for example, that if a new shipment of 1,000 units of steel plate costing $20.00 per unit is received by a fabricator who already has 500 units in stock costing $15.00 per unit, the fabricator will charge out all of the $15.00 units to the production cost of finished products before charging any of the $20.00 units.

LIFO works the opposite way, so that the fabricator would charge the more recently purchased units to production costs first. In these times of rapid inflation there has been a shift from FIFO to LIFO among American firms. This has the effect of increasing costs of production and reducing profit (and income tax) as reported by the firm. There has not been a real loss in such a case, but rather an indefinite postponement of profit-reporting and of the accompanying income tax.

Compare below the two alternative income statements such as might be reported by the steel fabricator we discussed above:

		LIFO		FIFO
Sales (40 finished units)		$1,000.00		$1,000.00
Cost of goods sold:				
Steel plate	$800.00		$600.00	
Other costs	100.00	900.00	100.00	700.00
Profit before taxes		$100.00		$300.00
Income taxes (assume 50% rate)		50.00		150.00
Net income after tax		$ 50.00		$ 150.00

LIFO makes the tax bill lower in times of inflation. If prices of materials were stable, there would be little effect on profits if a firm switched from FIFO to LIFO or the other way around. Which system is better in the long run? WHAT DO YOU THINK?

more meaningful when it is mathematically related to that firm's sales or to the stockholder's equity. Such relationships are usually expressed as financial ratios or "key" ratios.

key ratio

A key ratio is a value obtained by dividing one value on a financial statement by another value. A particular firm's financial condition can

be judged by comparing several important key ratios of items from its financial statements to typical key ratios of similar types of firms. Dun and Bradstreet publishes typical key ratios for a variety of types of firms. Such typical ratios are presented in Figure 9–7.

Let's look at several of these ratios and see how Gloria's Dress Shop compares with other women's ready-to-wear stores as reported by Dun and Bradstreet. First, let's look at a ratio that measures overall performance, net profit to tangible net worth.

Tangible net worth is equal to stockholder's equity minus goodwill (goodwill is an intangible asset). It is a conservative measure of owner's equity. From Figure 9–5 we see that Gloria's tangible net worth equals $61,300. From Figure 9–4 we see that net profit after taxes is $5,300. The ratio, then, is $\frac{5,300}{61,300} = 0.0865$, or 8.65 percent. Now, turn to the typical ratio of net profit to tangible net worth in women's ready-to-wear stores as found in Figure 9–7. The last item in the table pertains to women's ready-to-wear stores. The circled figure in the third column represents the median or typical net profit/tangible net worth ratio for such stores in that year as reported by Dun and Bradstreet. Gloria's ratio is higher than average (8.65% versus 6.82%). This suggests that Gloria's is "healthier" overall than the average store of its type.

tangible net worth

Gloria's will compute this ratio and others each year to measure its financial strength. Banks or investors will compute such ratios to see whether they should lend money to Gloria's when the firm requests it. Let's look at some other ratios which measure specific things about a firm.

A short-term key credit ratio which is widely used is the current ratio. It is computed by dividing current assets by current liabilities. The result indicates how easily current debt could be paid off with current assets. On December 31, 19*4 (Figure 9–5) Gloria's current ratio was $\frac{77,000}{12,000} = 6.06$. This is excellent and it means that Gloria's is quite solvent; it can easily pay off the current debt. Compare this ratio to the typical one in the first column (circled) of Figure 9–7. The average women's ready-to-wear store had a current ratio of only 2.63.

current ratio

The sales-to-inventory ratio can be used to point out problems related to product design, performance by the sales force, and buying policies. Gloria's sales-to-inventory ratio is computed from Figures 9–3, 9–4, and 9–5:

$$\frac{\$267,000 \text{ (sales)}}{\frac{1}{2}(\$10,000 + \$38,000) \text{ (average inventory)}} = \frac{267}{24} = 11.1$$

This is better than the average ratio of 6.1 shown in column 8 of Figure 9–7.

FIGURE 9-7

Typical key ratios

Line of Business (and number of concerns reporting)	Current assets to current debt	Net profits on net sales	Net profits on tangible net worth	Net profits on net working capital	Net sales to tangible net worth	Net sales to net working capital	Collection period	Net sales to inventory	Fixed assets to tangible net worth	Current debt to tangible net worth	Total debt to tangible net worth	Inventory to net working capital	Current debt to inventory	Funded debts to net working capital
	Times	Per cent	Per cent	Per cent	Times	Times	Days	Times	Per cent	Per cent	Per cent	Per cent	Per cent	Per cent
5722 Household Appliance Stores (88)	3.90 / **2.49** / 1.71	8.00 / **3.66** / 1.24	20.68 / **11.21** / 2.73	31.73 / **16.67** / 6.90	6.63 / **4.01** / 1.97	8.44 / **5.05** / 3.22	14 / **30** / 47	7.0 / **4.9** / 3.3	7.3 / **15.8** / 55.6	33.0 / **71.2** / 146.7	54.2 / **111.9** / 287.0	46.8 / **100.0** / 137.6	56.0 / **73.0** / 103.5	8.8 / **47.1** / 95.8
5944 Jewelry Stores (99)	5.18 / **3.37** / 2.29	9.74 / **4.60** / 1.59	15.46 / **8.52** / 3.81	22.05 / **9.83** / 4.18	3.08 / **1.95** / 1.19	3.15 / **2.22** / 1.56	— / — / —	3.6 / **2.4** / 1.8	4.5 / **10.0** / 29.2	24.6 / **41.3** / 100.0	44.7 / **75.9** / 184.3	71.1 / **91.8** / 121.4	27.2 / **47.4** / 71.5	15.5 / **38.0** / 60.2
5211 Lumber & Other Bldg. Materials Dealers (156)	4.70 / **2.76** / 1.89	5.42 / **3.24** / 1.43	17.45 / **11.43** / 4.47	21.77 / **14.23** / 5.75	6.29 / **3.85** / 2.47	7.32 / **4.43** / 2.96	34 / **44** / 64	9.0 / **5.8** / 4.2	9.0 / **22.2** / 42.8	20.4 / **47.4** / 100.9	58.2 / **102.7** / 168.9	53.9 / **76.7** / 99.5	45.0 / **75.7** / 105.9	13.8 / **36.0** / 79.2
5399 Misc. General Mdse. Stores (99)	10.37 / **3.84** / 1.95	4.50 / **2.33** / 0.95	15.26 / **6.15** / 1.04	21.82 / **13.14** / 4.74	5.75 / **3.62** / 1.75	7.73 / **4.30** / 2.54	— / — / —	7.1 / **4.0** / 2.7	9.3 / **20.5** / 54.2	15.6 / **58.0** / 118.9	61.3 / **100.0** / 156.7	62.9 / **88.4** / 145.7	20.7 / **38.7** / 73.0	11.7 / **23.5** / 64.2
5511 Motor Vehicle Dealers (92)	1.90 / **1.53** / 1.33	2.43 / **1.46** / 0.60	19.73 / **13.82** / 4.08	28.46 / **16.55** / 7.17	14.29 / **10.28** / 5.86	18.06 / **12.88** / 8.73	— / — / —	9.4 / **6.7** / 5.7	10.2 / **21.7** / 64.7	90.0 / **140.0** / 242.0	135.1 / **200.0** / 324.1	135.4 / **185.8** / 258.3	75.2 / **88.9** / 111.8	21.4 / **29.6** / 77.6
5231 Paint, Glass & Wallpaper Stores (35)	4.81 / **3.06** / 1.86	6.27 / **3.48** / 2.06	25.08 / **12.79** / 6.58	33.15 / **23.60** / 14.95	5.44 / **4.14** / 2.29	8.34 / **5.04** / 3.79	— / — / —	9.7 / **7.7** / 4.4	18.3 / **35.2** / 65.8	20.0 / **37.1** / 80.3	34.2 / **94.3** / 238.1	55.4 / **80.0** / 103.5	35.0 / **63.9** / 110.9	20.3 / **54.4** / 78.6
5732 Radio & Television Stores (63)	3.50 / **2.20** / 1.35	7.12 / **3.26** / 0.87	28.96 / **13.20** / 2.53	49.35 / **21.39** / 8.63	9.98 / **3.64** / 1.16	10.31 / **6.38** / 3.09	— / — / —	6.8 / **5.0** / 2.9	8.3 / **19.8** / 42.2	21.8 / **68.2** / 180.5	35.5 / **102.5** / 211.7	85.9 / **128.8** / 194.6	41.3 / **64.2** / 110.3	18.8 / **39.0** / 97.0
5261 & 5191 Ret. & Wholesale Nurs. Lawn, Gdn. & Farm Sup. (79)	3.19 / **1.83** / 1.27	6.12 / **3.16** / 1.10	17.25 / **10.11** / 2.01	52.45 / **22.22** / 7.15	5.75 / **3.87** / 2.49	13.94 / **7.90** / 4.27	— / — / —	13.7 / **9.5** / 4.6	18.0 / **35.3** / 75.6	28.6 / **60.4** / 125.9	47.8 / **82.0** / 161.2	49.8 / **92.6** / 177.5	67.3 / **114.5** / 173.3	8.6 / **37.2** / 114.6
5661 Shoe Stores (102)	8.04 / **4.05** / 2.34	8.60 / **3.54** / 0.53	18.30 / **8.90** / 0.75	32.91 / **11.56** / 4.09	4.32 / **2.50** / 1.69	5.62 / **3.34** / 1.93	— / — / —	4.9 / **3.7** / 2.5	3.8 / **12.6** / 30.5	12.8 / **29.8** / 78.0	23.9 / **46.9** / 154.9	75.4 / **95.4** / 127.4	19.1 / **35.1** / 57.5	8.1 / **24.6** / 52.4
5331 Variety Stores (60)	10.54 / **3.51** / 2.57	5.42 / **2.10** / 0.65	15.25 / **6.99** / 1.52	21.36 / **10.00** / 2.35	4.44 / **2.99** / 1.14	5.11 / **4.09** / 2.64	— / — / —	5.0 / **4.3** / 3.2	8.9 / **16.8** / 34.8	9.3 / **31.4** / 56.4	33.1 / **52.6** / 121.0	65.9 / **97.8** / 131.1	13.8 / **35.8** / 50.0	11.3 / **30.2** / 60.3
5621 Women's Ready-to-Wear Stores (181)	5.35 / **2.63** / 1.92	6.17 / **2.13** / 0.33	16.17 / **6.82** / 0.38	22.92 / **10.16** / 1.51	5.95 / **3.83** / 2.28	6.93 / **4.54** / 2.81	— / — / —	7.8 / **6.1** / 4.0	8.1 / **20.8** / 46.9	24.2 / **59.1** / 117.7	49.3 / **103.7** / 270.1	55.0 / **72.8** / 115.2	40.0 / **74.6** / 109.0	9.1 / **28.3** / 63.7

— Not computed. Necessary information as to the division between cash sales was available in too few cases to obtain an average collection period usable as a broad guide.

Source: Dun & Bradstreet, Inc.

FIGURE 9-7 (continued)

How the ratios are figured

Although terms like "median" and "quartile" are everyday working language to statisticians, their precise meaning may be vague to some businessmen.

In the various ratio tables, three figures appear under each ratio heading. The center figure in bold type is the **median;** the figures immediately above and below the median are, respectively, the **upper** and **lower quartiles.** To understand their use, the reader should also know how they are calculated.

First, year-end financial statements from concerns in the survey (almost exclusively corporations with a tangible net worth over $100,000) are analyzed by Dun & Bradstreet statisticians. Then each of 14 ratios is calculated individually for every concern in the sample.

These individual ratio figures, entered on data-processing cards, are segregated by line of business, and then arranged in order of size—the best ratio at the top, the weakest at the bottom. The figure that falls in the middle of this series becomes the **median** for that ratio in that line of business. The figure halfway between the median and the top of the series is the **upper quartile;** the number halfway between the median and the bottom of the series is the **lower quartile.**

In a statistical sense, each median then is the **typical ratio figure** for all concerns studied in a given line. The upper and lower quartile figures typify the experience of firms in the top and bottom halves of the sample, respectively.

Current assets to current debt   Current assets are divided by total Current Debt. Current Assets are the sum of cash, notes and accounts receivable (less reserves for bad debt), advances on merchandise, merchandise inventories, and Listed, Federal, State and Municipal securities not in excess of market value. Current Debt is the total of all liabilities falling due within one year. This is one test of solvency.

Net profits on net sales   Obtained by dividing net earnings of the business, after taxes, by net sales (the dollar volume less returns, allowances, and cash discounts). This important yardstick in measuring profitability should be related to the ratio which follows.

Net profits on tangible net worth   Tangible Net Worth is the equity of stockholders in the business, as obtained by subtracting total liabilities from total assets, and then deducting intangibles. The ratio is obtained by dividing Net Profits after taxes by Tangible Net Worth. Tendency is to look increasingly to this ratio as a final criterion of profitability. Generally, a relationship of at least 10 percent is regarded as a desirable objective for providing dividends plus funds for future growth.

Net profits on net working capital   Net Working Capital represents the excess of Current Assets over Current Debt. This margin represents the cushion available to the business for carrying inventories and receivables, and for financing day-to-day operations. The ratio is obtained by dividing Net Profits, after taxes, by Net Working Capital.

Net sales to tangible net worth   Net Sales are divided by Tangible Net Worth. This gives a measure of relative turnover of invested capital.

Net sales to net working capital   Net Sales are divided by Net Working Capital. This provides a guide as to the extent the company is turning its working capital and the margin of operating funds.

Collection period   Annual net sales are divided by 365 days to obtain average daily credit sales and then the average daily credit sales are divided into notes and accounts receivable, including any discounted. This ratio is helpful in analyzing the collectibility of receivables. Many feel the collection period should not exceed the net maturity indicated by selling terms by more than 10 to 15 days. When comparing the collection period of one concern with that of another, allowances should be made for possible variations in selling terms.

FIGURE 9–7 (continued)

How the ratios are figured

Net sales to inventory   Obtained by dividing annual Net Sales by Merchandise Inventory as carried on the balance sheet. This quotient does not yield an actual physical turnover. It provides a yardstick for comparing stock-to-sales ratios of one concern with another or with those for the industry.

Fixed assets to tangible net worth   Fixed Assets are divided by Tangible Net Worth. Fixed Assets represent depreciated book values of building, leasehold improvements, machinery, furniture, fixtures, tools, and other physical equipment, plus land, if any, and valued at cost or appraised market value. Ordinarily, this relationship should not exceed 100 percent for a manufacturer, and 75 percent for a wholesaler or retailer.

Current debt to tangible net worth   Derived by dividing Current Debt by Tangible Net Worth. Ordinarily, a business begins to pile up trouble when this relationship exceeds 80 percent.

Total debt to tangible net worth   Obtained by dividing total current plus long term debts by Tangible Net Worth. When this relationship exceeds 100 percent, the equity of creditors in the assets of the business exceeds that of owners.

Inventory to net working capital   Merchandise Inventory is divided by Net Working Capital. This is an additional measure of inventory balance. Ordinarily, the relationship should not exceed 80 percent.

Current debt to inventory   Dividing the Current Debt by Inventory yields yet another indication of the extent to which the business relies on funds from disposal of unsold inventories to meet its debts.

Funded debts to net working capital   Funded Debts are all long term obligations, as represented by mortgages, bonds, debentures, term loans, serial notes, and other types of liabilities maturing more than one year from statement date. This ratio is obtained by dividing Funded Debt by Net Working Capital. Analysts tend to compare Funded Debts with Net Working Capital in determining whether or not long term debts are in proper proportion. Ordinarily, this relationship should not exceed 100 percent.

Source: Dun & Bradstreet, Inc.

Dun and Bradstreet has been a pioneer in the development and analysis of key ratios. For many years it has published "industry average" ratios for many kinds of firms. This provides benchmarks by which the financial status of similar firms may be evaluated.

An overview of modern accounting must also include discussion of some of the internal management tools. Although financial accounting helps, a good manager needs some managerial accounting tools, too.

Managerial Accounting

Managerial accounting provides information for a manager's own use. It helps management to plan, to measure and control performance, to set prices, and to analyze situations. The biggest difference between managerial and financial accounting is the lack of traditional rules and principles in managerial accounting. Management is free to make up its own systems.

Because managerial accounting practices are less rigid, different systems will be found in every firm. The idea is to keep any kind of record or summary of costs and revenues that managers need for planning or control purposes. They might want to evaluate other managers or to judge the success of new products or a new piece of equipment.

Such special accounting is needed because regular financial accounts aren't enough to measure the performance of departments or products or managers within the firm as a whole. They focus, rather, on overall firm profit.

If the Norton Sales Company wishes to evaluate the performance of its salesforce, it must maintain adequate records of the salesforce's activities. Suppose those records show that the average travel expenditure per salesperson has been 11.2 cents per month per square mile of sales territory. After analysis, the sales manager decides to adopt this average amount as a standard. Any salesperson whose expenses exceed the average would be checked out. This shows how accounting can be used to control selling costs.

Managerial accounting can be used to set minimum order sizes, to decide whether to shut down a production line, to help a manager allocate funds for growth among territories, or to set standards for the entertainment of customers. Such managerial accounting activities fall under one of two headings: budgeting or cost accounting.

Budgeting and Cost Accounting

By tradition, financial accounting is not expected to provide predictions of a firm's condition. Predicting is a risky business, but it must be done. Managers use special managerial accounting tools to help them make predictions. One such device is the budget.

A budget is a formal dollar-and-cents statement of expected per- **budget**
formance. It is a means of (1) requiring managers to plan carefully for the future; (2) causing managers to examine present and past performance critically; and (3) helping to coordinate the plans made by different parts of the firm. A budget may be very specialized, or it may be general. It may be a short-term (one year or less) or a long-term budget.

The sales forecast is the starting point for a general (master) budget. **sales forecast**
It predicts what sales will be over a certain period of time. This fore-cast depends on what effect the marketing manager thinks the planned changes in the marketing mix will have on sales. Sometimes the sales

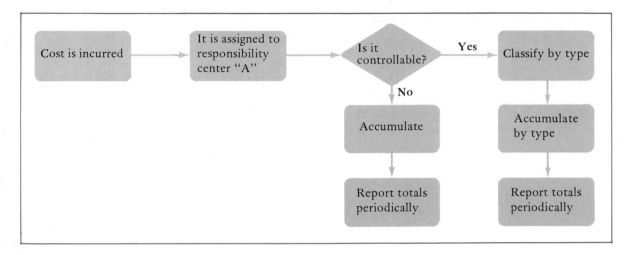

FIGURE 9-8

The responsibility accounting process

responsibility accounting

product cost accounting

forecast is tied to a projection of Gross National Product or to industry sales forecasts. Larger firms, employing a staff of economists and computer facilities, often construct models to predict sales. Whether it be made by such a method or by a simple assumption of a 5 percent increase over the current year, the sales forecast is a keystone for planning.

Cost accounting includes responsibility accounting and product cost accounting. **Responsibility accounting involves setting up responsibility centers in a firm. These are used to classify cost information so as to evaluate the performance of various parts of the firm and their managers.** The costs of operating the shipping department, for example, may be collected in a shipping department responsibility center. Figure 9–8 shows how responsibility accounting works.

Product cost accounting systems also use cost centers to allocate all costs to the various products made by a firm. This gives a firm a better idea about which products are profitable and which are not. Some firms use *standard* product cost accounting systems. Standard costs assigned in such a system are those that should have been incurred, not those actually incurred. Differences between actual and standard costs are called *variances* and are charged to *variance accounts*.

Manual versus Computer-based Accounting Systems

For many years accounting activities were restricted in what they could do because they were manual. They started with a handwritten record of a transaction that was later copied by hand into a summary book of some kind for monthly or weekly tallying purposes.

One of the biggest questions in petroleum accounting circles today is how to evaluate oil reserves held by the larger firms that explore for and produce petroleum. The two methods used by the industry traditionally have been the "successful efforts" method and the "full cost" method. The first method takes the cost of the unsuccessful efforts ("dry holes") and charges these off immediately. The second method lumps in all developmental costs (regardless of success of effort) and assigns this value to oil reserves, to be written off over the life of the reserves.

Robert Mims reported that

In addition to new data on reserve quantities, annual exploration and development costs, and estimates of future cash flow, the SEC also wants oil and gas companies to start calculating the current dollar value of future revenues from these proved reserves. These supplementary disclosures will have to accompany financial data filed with the commission for fiscal years ending after Dec. 25, 1978.

But if the SEC takes the next step and develops what it calls "reserve recognition accounting" (RRA), within perhaps three years something like this current value of reserves will appear on the asset side of petroleum company balance sheets.

This proposal for gas and oil accounting, if finally adopted, would be a "revolutionary" step in financial accounting practice, a discipline not noted for radical change in methods. If you were an accountant for the oil and gas industry, how would you react to RRA? If you were a member of the SEC, how would you set the guidelines for evaluating oil reserves?

Source: *Business Week.*

Such simplified manual systems still exist in small businesses, but they are gradually being replaced by machine-based systems. Some of these systems depend on modern cash register equipment, and some depend on punched cards and computers. Although every accounting system is a data processing system, we now restrict the use of the term *data processing* to machine-based systems.

A data processing system must do the following:

- select relevant data describing the business transaction and prepare a document containing such a description
- classify and store these input items in appropriate places and summarize them for future use

- convert such information into proper form for use by decision makers
- prepare reports, such as financial statements

A computer-based accounting system requires still another step to convert the source document to a form that can be handled by the system. In the typical case the original document is converted to machine-readable form and stored either in card form, in the computer's own memory, as punched cards, or on magnetic tape. In Chapter 14 we will see how such computer storage makes it easier to classify, summarize, and report.

Summary and Look Ahead

Accounting's task is threefold: (1) to "keep score" of the use of financial resources; (2) to draw attention to problems; and (3) to assist in decision making. Financial accounting does the first task and managerial accounting does the second and third.

Accounting principles guide managers in making and interpreting financial statements. Two principal financial statements represent the focus of the financial accounting process: (1) the balance sheet, and (2) the income statement. Key financial ratios are applied to values reported on the financial statements to help make comparisons of the performance of a single firm over time, or to make comparisons among firms in the same year.

Managerial accounting is internally oriented. Planning for financial (and other) resources can be greatly assisted by a variety of budgeting techniques. Cost accounting is another broad component of managerial accounting. It usually takes the form of responsibility accounting or product cost accounting. In either case, costs must be identified and assigned so as to improve internal managerial control of operations.

A basis has now been established for the subject to be analyzed in our next two chapters, "Financial Institutions" and "Financial Decisions and Insurance." With a basic knowledge of the financial institutions and the basic language of financial statements, it will be possible for us to examine the kinds of decisions made by financial managers and how they are made.

My name is David L. Morgan, III. Presently, I am a senior staff auditor with Arthur Young (AY) and Company, an international public accounting firm.

I received my bachelor of science degree with a major in accounting from the University of New Orleans in 1974. One year later, while working at AY, I passed a comprehensive three-day uniform examination and received my license as a Certified Public Accountant (CPA) in the state of Louisiana.

My first year at AY was spent becoming acquainted with public accounting and the process of auditing. An audit involves using specified standards and procedures to render an independent examination of a company's accounting and financial records. It usually is performed to express an opinion on the company's financial statements.

After the first year, my responsibilities, experience, and direct client contacts were increased. I became more involved in each audit and began to develop a better knowledge of accounting principles and auditing standards. This experience has helped me to attain my present level as Senior Staff Auditor with AY.

At AY, the audit senior has the primary responsibility for the day-to-day conduct of the audit. This includes a wide variety of duties, such as planning the audit approach, supervising assistants, and coordinating the engagement with the client and the AY manager and partner.

My first association with an engagement usually begins with the audit manager discussing the timing of the current year's audit with me and the assistants with whom I will be working. If it is a first-year audit, the manager and I will discuss the nature of the new client's business, locations, and any special requirements. For continuing engagements in which the AY manager and senior have an understanding of the client from prior years' audits, initial planning consists of reviewing last year's workpapers, correspondence files for any items that may have been communicated between AY and the client during the year, and discussions with the manager.

At AY we often go to the client's office for interim field work, usually several months before the end of the client's fiscal year. At an interim point in the year, we develop our approaches to reviewing the client's system of internal controls, coordinate with the client the accounting information we will need for the

ARTHUR YOUNG

audit, and begin our testing. This approach is documented in a written audit plan.

Year-end field work consists of the completion of all our testing, which was begun at the interim point, and the development of the most important and interesting part of my job, the audit report and financial statements. While the financial statements are the primary responsibility of the client, the AY senior, manager, and partner work with the client to ensure proper financial statement presentation in accordance with generally accepted accounting principles and various technical, Securities and Exchange Commission (SEC), and other guidelines.

Another interesting part of my job is writing what AY refers to as a Management Letter. During the course of our work we try to identify areas where our client can make changes to help improve controls and efficiency of operations. At the end of the audit, we formalize the comments in an annual Management Letter which we discuss with the client. It always is rewarding to see our comments implemented and actually helping the client's business.

Public accounting is the most challenging commitment I have ever undertaken. A career in public accounting offers exposure to a variety of clients and industries, interesting work, an opportunity to develop both technically and professionally, and unusual growth potential—from first-year assistant, to senior, to manager, and finally to partner and a share of the partnership profits and responsibilities. The income potential for a CPA in public accounting also is unusually high. Public accounting, however, requires considerable overtime, travel, and continuing education.

The experience gained in public accounting with a large international firm such as Arthur Young and Company is valuable even for those whose career paths do not, for one reason or another, lead to partnership in the firm. It offers potential opportunities to develop in private practice or to join a local CPA firm, or it may lead to a rewarding career outside public accounting in industry.

All of the "Big Eight" accounting firms are quite similar in their impressive roster of clients and their educational and training programs. The friendly and relaxed people and atmosphere of Arthur Young played an important role in my decision to choose a career with AY.

Key Concepts

account   A register of financial value. There are four basic kinds of accounts: asset accounts, equity accounts, revenue accounts, and expense accounts. Account balances are changed by transactions.

accounting   The recording, gathering, manipulating, auditing, and interpreting of information that describes the assets and operation of a firm. The two main types of accounting are financial and managerial.

accrued expense   A liability created by incurring an expense in one period but not paying for it until the next.

assets   A firm's resources such as land, cash, and accounts receivable.

balance sheet   A statement or list of the assets and equities of a firm at one point in time. Also called a statement of financial position.

basic accounting equations   Two equations that explain the basic system of financial accounting:
(1) Assets = Equities *or* Assets = Liabilities + Capital
(2) Revenues − Expenses = Net Profit

budget   A financial forecast showing expected income and expenditures for a given period of time.

Certified Public Accountant (CPA)   An accountant who has fulfilled the legal requirements of his or her state for knowledge in accounting theory, practice, auditing and law and who is licensed to sign legally required financial reports.

current assets   Cash or property that can be quickly converted to cash. Examples are accounts receivable, inventories, short-term notes receivable.

current liability   Debts that must be paid in less than one year.

current ratio   Measure of liquidity. Current assets divided by current liabilities.

depreciation   A deduction in the balance sheet to indicate a decline in value of a fixed asset over time.

equity   Claims on resources or assets. The two major types of equity are owner's equity and liabilities.

expense   The using up of resources. Expenses are deducted from the revenues in the pursuit of which they were incurred. The result is net profit or loss.

financial accounting   The accounting process directed toward the flow of resources, communicating with people outside the firm.

fixed asset   An asset which, when originally acquired, is expected to have a lifetime of more than one year.

gross profit   Sales minus cost of goods sold. The amount of profit before operating expenses are deducted to compute net operating profit.

income statement   A financial statement showing revenues, expenses, and profits of a firm during a given period of time.

key ratio   A financial ratio computed from items on the financial statements of a firm and used to evaluate the credit risk or financial strength of a firm. Typical ratios are published by Dun and Bradstreet.

liability   The claim of a nonowner against a firm.

managerial accounting   The accounting process when internally directed to facilitate the firm's management.

owner's equity   The claim of owners against resources of the firm. Often referred to as *capital*. In a corporation it is called *shareholder's equity*.

product cost accounting   Systems for allocating costs to products produced by a firm.

responsibility accounting   A method of classifying cost information and thereby evaluating the performance of the components of the firm (responsibility centers) and their managers.

revenue   Inward flow of value to a firm, mostly from sales.

sales forecast   An estimate of the sales that will be

made in a future period of time, thus making budget construction easier.

tangible net worth   A conservative measure of owner's equity that excludes goodwill from assets.

transaction   Any financially significant event. A transaction causes a change in the balance of a firm's accounts (usually two at a time).

For Review . . .

1. What kinds of information are communicated by means of accounting? Give two examples.
2. To whom is the accounting process directed? What are its three principal tasks?
3. Must all accountants be CPAs? Discuss.
4. What are the basic accounting equations? Show how a change in one side must result in a change in the other.
5. What are the major classes of accounts on a balance sheet?
6. What is meant by the principle of accrual? Explain by giving an example involving rental expense.
7. Construct a simple budget of your own weekly expenses.
8. In what way could an accounting system help to control salespeople's entertainment expenses? Explain.

9. What is product cost accounting? What is a variance? How are these two concepts related?
10. What must a good data processing system do?

. . . For Discussion

1. What do we mean when we say that financial accounting is relevant?
2. Is it possible for a transaction to occur without affecting the balance of any account?
3. What is the functional relationship between a balance sheet and an income statement?
4. What kind of business is Dun and Bradstreet in? Ask any manager what his or her relationship with this firm is, if any.
5. What is the relationship between managerial accounting and the management function of controlling as discussed in Chapter 5?

Incidents

Self-Regulation for Accountants?

The Securities and Exchange Commission (SEC) has responded somewhat favorably to the accounting profession's recent efforts to regulate itself. It does have some reservations, however. The most important comments in a recent SEC 1,300-page report on accounting self-regulation pertain to the proposals for "peer review" by the American Institute of Certified Public Accountants. This private professional group's proposal dictates that a CPA firm with SEC-registered corporations as clients would have to be examined periodically by

outside auditors. The SEC has expressed doubt concerning the validity of the system and wants it to be a more open, public process than the AICPA originally proposed.

Questions

1. How does the responsibility of a CPA differ from that of an accountant working for a manufacturer?
2. If CPA's have special obligations to the public,

why then does the SEC not give full approval to the proposed system?

3. What interest does the general public have in the assurance that financial statements of large

corporations are prepared honestly and in accordance with generally accepted accounting principles?

Source: *The Wall Street Journal.*

Inflation and Financial Statements

The Federal Accounting Standards Board (FASB) has proposed ways for large corporations to tackle the problem of inflation in accounting.

"The board admits that it does not have all the answers to inflation accounting. As a result, it will permit a company to experiment with one of two alternatives. A corporation may present key operating, asset, and market data using current costs to determine whether corporate performance has kept pace with the ravages of inflation. Or a company may disclose essentially the same information in constant dollars by adjusting its numbers with the official consumer price index to show whether its purchasing power has been maintained."

Questions

1. Assuming you are a potential investor in IBM or General Motors, how would you view the new FASB proposal?
2. What are the arguments which large firms might advance against inflation accounting requirements?
3. What kind of educational program for investors might be necessary when and if such reporting becomes widely applied to accounting practice?

Source: *Business Week.*

Financial Institutions

CHAPTER 10

Objectives: After reading this chapter, you should be able to

1. List and discuss the major financial institutions in our business system.
2. Develop an example showing how the commercial banking system creates money.
3. Demonstrate how the Federal Reserve System controls the money supply in the United States.
4. Tell the difference between promissory notes and drafts.
5. Give examples of several types of preferred stocks and several types of bonds.
6. Compare the services offered by investment banks with those offered by brokerage houses.
7. Tell the difference between listed and unlisted securities.
8. Compare the workings of the over-the-counter market with the workings of the securities exchanges.
9. Translate a quote for a stock or bond as reported in *The Wall Street Journal* into dollar-and-cents terms.
10. Compare speculating with investing.
11. Discuss the role of the Securities and Exchange Commission in the securities market.
12. Compare the workings of commodity exchanges with the workings of securities exchanges.

Key concepts: Look for these terms as you read the chapter

money	reserve requirement
commercial bank	margin requirement
savings bank	promissory note
savings and loan association	trade draft
trust company	trade acceptance
credit union	public market
life insurance company	bond
factoring company	investment bank
commercial finance company	brokerage house
sales finance company	securities exchanges
consumer finance company	over-the-counter market (OTC)
commercial paper house	margin trading
demand deposit	short selling
time deposit	mutual fund
prime rate of interest	prospectus
Federal Reserve System	commodity exchanges

All firms need money to begin a business and to remain in it. Money is the lifeblood of a firm—it enables a firm to buy buildings, equipment, inventories, and to pay its employees. Money flows into a firm as sales revenues and flows out as the expenses of doing business and as a return to the owners.

But where does a firm get money? Some of it comes from the owner's (or owners') original investment in the firm. Some of it comes from profits that are reinvested in the firm. Often, however, that is not enough. Most firms need the services of financial institutions to provide them with the money they need.

Types of Financial Institutions

Without money, business as we know it could not exist. Money is anything that people generally will accept in payment of debts. Paper currency and coins issued by a recognized government are legal tender in that nation. If you owe a debt that is stated in money terms, your creditor must accept your payment in legal tender.

But that is not all there is to money. Most American workers, for example, are paid with checks. Many workers deposit their checks in their checking accounts and pay their bills with checks. This is possible because of our modern banking system. **Money, therefore, means paper**   money **currency, coins, and checking account balances.**

There are many different types of financial institutions. Their customers include consumers, businesses, and nonbusiness organizations. As the nature of these customers' needs change and as the laws that regulate financial institutions change, new types of financial institutions appear and old ones may disappear. The same, of course, is true of the types of services they offer. The following discussion focuses on the major types of financial institutions in our business system:

- commercial banks
- savings banks
- savings and loan associations
- trust companies
- credit unions
- life insurance companies
- factoring companies
- commercial finance companies
- sales finance companies
- consumer finance companies
- commercial paper houses

Commercial Banks

The heart of our banking system is the commercial bank. **A commercial**   commercial bank **bank is a privately owned, profit-seeking firm that serves individuals,** nonbusiness organizations, and businesses. Commercial banks offer checking accounts and savings accounts, make loans, and offer many other services to their customers. They are the main source of short-term loans for business firms.

Table 10–1 lists several types of services offered by many commercial banks. Commercial banks chartered by the federal government are national banks. Those chartered by state governments are state banks. Both types are closely regulated.

Perhaps you have read about "banking panics" or "runs on banks" that occurred in the history of banking in the United States. The last series of major panics occurred during the Great Depression. Depositors lost faith in the economy and wanted to withdraw their funds from banks. A typical bank could not possibly pay off all its depositors if they wanted to withdraw on the same day, because it kept only a small percentage of its customers' deposits in cash. Thus many banks failed. They simply could not call in all their outstanding loans that fast.

Congress created the Federal Deposit Insurance Corporation (FDIC) in 1933. All national banks must carry deposit insurance and most state banks voluntarily do so. Each insured bank pays a fee (based on its total deposits) for this insurance. The FDIC uses these funds to pay off depositors (up to $40,000 per account) who have accounts in banks that fail. The FDIC has authority to examine all insured banks.

Nationally chartered banks are audited by the comptroller of the currency and state banks are audited by state banking authorities. Day-to-day operations of banks are regulated with respect to the maximum interest rate they can pay on deposits and the types of investments they can make. Their lending policies are also subject to review.

TABLE 10-1

Some important services provided by commercial banks to business firms

1. Checking accounts
2. Safe deposit boxes
3. Storage of idle cash in certificates of deposit
4. Short-term loans (1–6 months)
5. Long-term loans
6. Loans to a firm's customers
7. Exchange of U.S. dollars for foreign currencies
8. Exchange of foreign currencies for U.S. dollars
9. Advice to business people on financial matters
10. Registration of corporations' stocks
11. Transferring ownership of corporations' stocks
12. Safeguarding property entrusted to them

Savings Banks

Savings banks are not as numerous as commercial banks. **A savings bank serves small savers by accepting their deposits and paying them interest on their savings. Savings banks invest the funds mainly in real estate mortgages and government securities.**

savings bank

There are two types of savings banks. Stock companies are owned by stockholders who earn dividends from net profit. Mutual companies are owned by the depositors. Most savings banks arc mutual companies. Stock savings banks, for the most part, have developed into commercial banks.

Mutual savings banks in the New England states and New York offer "negotiable order of withdrawal" (NOW) accounts. These accounts enable depositors to write checks on their interest-bearing savings accounts to pay their bills.

Savings and Loan Associations

Another financial institution is the savings and loan association (S&LA). **A savings and loan association accepts deposits from the general public. It lends funds mainly for mortgages on homes and other real estate.**

savings and loan association

An S&LA can be a mutual company (owned by depositors) or a stock company (owned by stockholders). S&LAs also help businesses to finance the purchase of real estate. The Federal Savings and Loan Insur-

THINK ABOUT IT!

The Need for Saving

As we saw in Chapter 1, an economy must produce more than it currently consumes in order to add to its capital equipment. Its people must be willing and able to postpone some consumption to produce saving that can be used to add to the economy's capital equipment (new investment).

Not only is the U.S. rate of personal saving the lowest of all the major industrial countries, but the U.S. rate has fallen from the level of a decade ago, while the rates in many other industrial nations have risen, and so has the percent of their gross national products that go into capital investment. In Japan, for example, the rate of saving increased from 20% in 1970 to 24.3% in 1977, and in Canada it has more than doubled in the same period.

Look at Figure 10–1. THINK ABOUT IT!

Source: *Business Week.*

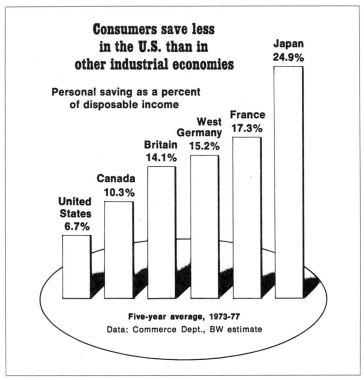

**Consumers save less
in the U.S. than in
other industrial economies**

Personal saving as a percent
of disposable income

Japan
24.9%

France
17.3%

West
Germany 15.2%

Britain
14.1%

Canada
10.3%

United
States
6.7%

Five-year average, 1973-77
Data: Commerce Dept., BW estimate

FIGURE 10-1

Personal saving as a percent of disposable income, selected countries, 1973–1977 average

Source: *Business Week.*

ance Corporation (FSLIC) insures each account in member S&LAs up to $40,000.

Trust Companies

trust company

Another financial institution that serves individuals and businesses is the trust company. **A trust company safeguards property—funds and estates—entrusted to it. It also may serve as trustee, transfer agent, and registrar for corporations and provide other services.**

A corporation selling bonds to many investors appoints a trustee, usually a trust company, to protect the bondholders' interests. A trust company can also serve as a transfer agent and registrar for corporations. A transfer agent records changes in ownership of a corporation's stock. A registrar certifies to the investing public that stock issues are correctly stated and in compliance with the corporate charter. Other services include preparing and issuing dividend checks to stockholders and serving as trustee for employee profit-sharing funds. Commercial banks in many states also provide trust services.

Credit Unions

Credit unions are important to business because they lend money to consumers to buy durable goods like cars and furniture. **A credit union is a cooperative savings association formed by the employees of a company or nonbusiness organization.** Members (owners) can add to their savings accounts (share accounts) by authorizing deductions from their paychecks or by making direct deposits. Members also can borrow from the credit union. The cost of borrowing usually is lower than that from other lenders because the credit union is owned and operated by its members. The National Credit Union Administration (NCUA) insures each account in member credit unions up to $40,000.

credit union

Some state-chartered credit unions are authorized to offer 30-year residential mortgage loans. Until recently, federally chartered credit unions were limited to 10-year maturities on such loans. Now, they also are authorized to make 30-year residential mortgage loans.

Life Insurance Companies

An important source of funds for individuals, nonbusiness organizations, and businesses is the life insurance company. **A life insurance company is a mutual or stock company that shares risk with its policyholders for payment of a premium.** Some of the money it collects as premiums is loaned to borrowers. We discuss life insurance in greater detail in our next chapter.

life insurance company

Factoring Companies

An important source of short-term funds for many firms is the factoring company. **A factoring company (or factor) buys accounts receivable (amounts due from credit customers) from a firm. It pays less than the face value of the accounts but collects the face value of the accounts. The difference, minus the cost of doing business, is the factor's profit.**

factoring company

A firm that sells its accounts receivable to a factor "without recourse" shifts the risk of credit loss to the factor. If an account turns out to be uncollectible, the factor suffers the loss. However, a factor is a specialist in credit and collection activities. Using a factor may enable a firm to expand its sales. The firm does not have to tie up as much of its own money in accounts receivable financing when it uses a factor. In effect, the firm trades accounts receivable for cash. The factor notifies the firm's customers to make their payments to the factor. This also often reduces the firm's collection costs.

Commercial Finance Companies

commercial finance company

A commercial finance company is similar to a factor. **A commercial finance company makes loans to firms with accounts receivable, inventories, or equipment used as security for the loans. Unlike a factoring company, it does not collect the accounts or share the credit risk.** Ordinarily the client's customers do not know that their accounts have been pledged as security for a loan. They continue to make payments to the client. This is called a nonnotification plan.

Commercial finance companies borrow from commercial banks to increase their lending ability. Sometimes clients use commercial finance companies rather than commercial banks if their credit positions are too weak to satisfy a bank.

Sales Finance Companies

sales finance company

A major source of credit for many firms and their customers is the sales finance company. **A sales finance company specializes in financing installment purchases made by individuals and firms.**

When you buy a durable good from a retailer who is on an installment plan with a sales finance company, the loan is made directly to you. The item bought serves as security for the loan. Sales finance companies enable many firms to sell on credit, even though the firms could not afford to finance credit sales on their own.

General Motors Acceptance Corporation (GMAC) and General Electric Credit Corporation are sales finance companies. These are "captive" companies because they exist to finance installment contracts resulting from sales made by their parent companies.

Sales finance companies also finance installment sales to business firms. Many commercial banks also have installment loan departments.

Consumer Finance Companies

consumer finance company

An important source of credit for many consumers is the consumer finance company. **A consumer finance company makes personal loans to consumers. Often these loans are made on a "signature basis," and the borrower pledges no security (collateral) for the loan. For larger loans, collateral may be required, such as a car or furniture.**

These companies do not make loans to businesses. But they do provide the financing that turns many "would-be" customers into "paying" customers.

PLASTIC MONEY

Already 590 million of them fatten Americans' wallets and purses, and the easy, pay-later access to goods and services that credit cards offer extends to such exotica as Nevada divorces, surgical work and, in some areas, bail money. . . . Americans spend $16 billion a year on cards, and the total is expected to soar to about $50 billion in the late 1980s.

Still, there is much room for expansion. Of the 50 payments of various kinds that the average U.S. family makes each month, cards are used for only two or three. To increase that share, card issuers are coming out with many new services:

Split billing. In the high-spending travel-and-entertainment card field, Diner's Club [has introduced] the "Double-Card." A subscriber gets two cards: one for personal use, another for business expenses. . . .

Rebates. Visa, which with nearly 60 million holders has overtaken the long-time leader in the field of multipurpose cards, Master Charge (50 million), is testing in several Midwest states an Executive charge card aimed at big-spending businessmen. Among its attractions: cardholders get a 1% rebate on all charges.

Direct debiting. Though Visa and Master Charge cards have traditionally been issued only by commercial banks, other lending institutions are preparing to jump into the field. A mutual savings bank in Washington State has issued a card that directly debits a customer's savings account for the amount he charges. Some 60 banks are now issuing Visa cards that debit directly against a cardholder's checking account.

Most of the new action by card firms is in a long-somnolent field: traveler's checks. American Express has about 65% of the world market, despite recently heating competition. . . . Diner's Club is offering checks through an arrangement with Thomas Cook & Sons; they are free, while American Express charges $1 per $100 in checks. [In late 1978, Master Charge and Visa were] also considering a traveler's check venture.

The lure of the card business and the reason that the newcomers are prepared to sell checks without a fee, lies in the "float"—all that money from checks that have been bought but not yet cashed. The check issuer has free use of the funds. . . . American Express studies indicate that people already keep approximately $1 billion in cash stashed away for rainy days. If consumers could be persuaded to convert that cash to traveler's checks, it would substantially increase the float. American Express's float totals about $2 billion at any moment; the company invests this money mainly in long-term tax-exempt securities, and pockets the income.

Source: *Time.*

Commercial Paper Houses

Large corporations often borrow money by issuing *commercial paper.* Commercial paper is an unsecured promise to pay back a set amount of money at a stated date in the future, usually within 60 to 180 days. It is a type of promissory note, which we will discuss later in this chapter. Promissory notes are one of the most widely used credit instruments for getting short-term funds. The good faith of the issuing corporation is the backing for commercial paper. The interest rate on this paper usually is lower than that on loans from commercial banks.

commercial paper house   **A commercial paper house is a financial institution that buys commercial paper directly from issuing corporations and resells it to buyers such as pension funds, trust departments in commercial banks, and other corporations with extra temporary cash on hand.** In some cases a commercial paper house acts as a middleman who charges a commission for bringing the issuing company and a buyer together.

The Commercial Banking System

Of all the financial institutions we have discussed, the commercial bank is the most important to businesses. Let's discuss commercial banking in greater detail.

Commercial Bank Deposits

For many years there has been a careful distinction between two types of deposits in commercial banks: (1) demand deposits and (2) time deposits.

demand deposit   **A demand deposit is a checking account.** Customers who deposit coins, currency, or other checks in their checking accounts can write checks against the balances in their accounts. Their banks must honor these checks immediately. That is why checking accounts are called demand deposits. Demand deposits are the most important type of money in our economic system. They account for about 80 percent of the total money supply.

time deposit   **A time deposit is one that is to remain with the bank for a period of time. Interest is paid to depositors during the time their money is on deposit in the bank.** The bank, of course, uses this money to make loans to its customers. The bank pays interest to its depositors and it charges interest to its borrowers.

There are two basic types of time deposits: (1) regular passbook accounts and (2) certificates of deposit (CDs). Passbook accounts are intended mainly for small individual savers and nonprofit organizations. Depositors put their savings in these accounts and, for all practical purposes, there is no required amount of time that they must be left on deposit. Although a bank can require 30-days notice before withdrawals can be made, this is seldom done.

The certificate of deposit (CD) is a deposit that is made for a certain period of time. The time period can range from 30 days for large amounts of money (usually $100,000 or more) to several years for smaller amounts ($1,000). CDs are available to all savers. The interest rate paid on a CD is higher than that paid on a regular passbook account. But a saver must give up 90 days of interest if a CD is cashed in before its maturity date.

TABLE 10-2

The twenty largest banks in the United States

Bank	Assets[1] 12/31/78 $ Mil.	Deposits[2]		
		Total 12/31/78 $ Mil.	Time/ Demand %	Foreign %
1. BankAmerica (San Francisco)	94903	75828	75/25	46
2. Citicorp (New York)	87191	61115	85/15	68
3. Chase Manhattan (New York)	61172	48546	68/32	56
4. Manufacturers Hanover (New York)	40606	32409	56/44	38
5. Morgan (J.P.) (New York)	38536	28603	70/30	50
6. Chemical New York	32770	24906	69/31	40
7. Continental Illinois (Chicago)	31059	21160	77/23	43
8. Western Bancorp. (Los Angeles)	25957	21162	61/39	10
9. Bankers Trust New York	25863	18755	60/40	39
10. First Chicago	24066	17466	82/18	44
11. Security Pacific (Los Angeles)	21633	16968	69/31	22
12. Wells Fargo (San Francisco)	18611	14819	73/27	11
13. Marine Midland Banks (Buffalo)	14289	11315	69/31	33
14. Charter New York	13975	11104	58/42	35
15. Crocker National (San Francisco)	13925	11212	69/31	13
16. Mellon National (Pittsburgh)	11685	8477	67/33	26
17. First National Boston	11557	7816	74/26	53
18. Northwest Bancorp. (Minneapolis)	10906	8462	67/33	5
19. First Bank System (Minneapolis)	10436	7969	64/36	2
20. First International Bancshares (Dallas)	10025	7610	66/34	29

[1]Total assets as of Dec. 31, 1978

[2]Total deposits as of Dec. 31, 1978. Time (including savings) deposits and demand deposits together will total 100%. Foreign deposits subtracted from 100% will equal total domestic deposits.

Source: *Business Week.*

S&LAs, savings banks, and commercial banks offer regular passbook accounts and CDs. By law, S&LAs and savings banks are allowed to pay one-fourth of 1 percent per annum higher interest than commercial banks. Share accounts in credit unions are similar to passbook savings accounts. Federally chartered credit unions also can offer share certificates, which are similar to CDs, with maturities of 90 days or longer.

In June of 1978 a new type of CD appeared, money market CDs. These CDs in commercial banks pay a rate of interest that is equal to the average rate of interest on six-month U.S. Treasury bills. The interest rate on money market CDs changes from week to week. S&LAs and savings banks originally could pay one-fourth of 1 percent higher interest than the U.S. Treasury bill rate. But in March of 1979 government regulators removed the one-fourth percentage point extra interest for an average interest rate on Treasury bills of 9 percent or more. The regulations also prohibit compounding of interest on the certificates. Money market certificates are six-month CDs and the minimum deposit is $10,000. Federally chartered credit unions also can offer money market CDs.

Another new development occurred in 1978. For the first time commercial banks were authorized to offer automatic transfer accounts. These allow depositors to move money automatically from time deposits to demand deposits. Suppose you have a savings account and a checking account in the same bank. You tell the bank how much you want to keep in your checking account and you write checks against your account. When a check that would cause your balance to drop below the minimum reaches the bank, the bank will transfer money automatically from your savings account to cover the difference. Different banks have different fees for this service.

During recent years there have been many changes in the regulations that apply to financial institutions and the distinction between demand deposits and time deposits is becoming less clear. For example, telephone and preauthorized transfer accounts enable people who have savings accounts in commercial banks, S&LAs, and savings banks to use these time deposits for transaction purposes. Some S&LAs offer point-of-sale (POS) terminal service which enables savers to make withdrawals and deposits from savings accounts by using remote computer terminals in retail stores. Telephone transfers also enable savers at savings banks, S&LAs, and commercial banks to shift their deposits from time to demand deposits. Federally chartered credit unions also can offer credit union share drafts which enable savers to withdraw funds via third-party payments. We can expect further changes in the services that financial institutions can offer in the years ahead.

REGULATION OF FINANCIAL INSTITUTIONS

By deciding that existing laws do not sanction such experiments as the automatic transfer of funds between checking and savings accounts, a federal appeals court may be forcing Congress to redesign the nation's archaic banking legislation. Because it is impossible to isolate any one area, all the festering issues of banking regulation—interstate branching, interest-rate ceilings, electronic funds transfer, Federal Reserve membership, and a host of others—must be taken up by Congress at one time. To speed Congress along, the court stayed implementation of its ruling until January 1.

The court decision that was rendered in April, 1979 has far-reaching implications for financial institutions.

Until that Apr. 20 decision, the year 1979 was shaping up as a sleepy one for banking legislation on Capitol Hill. But then the U.S. Court of Appeals for the District of Columbia stunned the nation's financial industry by ruling that automatic transfer service (ATS) is illegal. The court also ruled that the thrift industry's off-premises check-cashing units and the credit unions' checklike share drafts are illegal as well.

As we noted earlier in this chapter, the age-old distinction between time deposits and demand deposits has become less clear during recent years.

Specifically, the court was taking dead aim at the 46-year old law that prohibits financial institutions from paying interest on demand deposits—something that banks, thrifts, and credit unions had gotten around recently with the blessing of regulators. But, actually, the court sent a pointed message to Congress demanding to know why the nation's banking laws have failed to keep pace with developments in the financial markets.

Among other changes, many people expected that Congress would authorize the offering of negotiable order of withdrawal accounts to consumers across the country.

By extending nationwide the negotiable order of withdrawal (NOW) accounts that are allowed in New England and New York, Congress could defuse pressures from legislators who want to end the ban on interest-paying accounts.

Source: *Business Week.*

Commercial Bank Loans

As we will see in the next chapter, commercial banks are the major source of short-term loans for businesses. Although they make long-term loans to some firms, commercial banks prefer to specialize in providing short-term funds.

prime rate of interest

Borrowers pay interest on their loans. Large firms with excellent credit records pay the prime rate of interest. **The prime rate of interest is the lowest rate charged to borrowers. This rate changes from time to time because of changes in the demand for and supply of loanable funds.**

A secured loan is backed by collateral such as accounts receivable or a life insurance policy. If the borrower cannot repay the loan, the bank sells the collateral. An unsecured loan is backed only by the borrower's promise to repay it. Only the most creditworthy borrowers can get unsecured loans.

Deposit Expansion

Suppose you saved $100 in 50-cent pieces, took them to a commercial bank, and opened a checking account. Some portion of your $100 is likely to stay in your account. Your bank can earn interest by lending some of it to borrowers.

Banks subject to federal regulation must keep some portion of their demand deposits in vault cash or as deposits with a Federal Reserve Bank. These are legal reserves. Let's assume that the reserve requirement is 10 percent. Your bank, then, must keep $10 of your $100 deposit in legal reserves. It has $90 to lend.

Now suppose Tom Powers borrows that $90 from your bank. Tom has $90 added to his checking account. Assume that Tom writes a check for $90 payable to the Acme Store. Acme's bank ends up with a $90 deposit. But Acme's bank only has to keep 10 percent of $90 ($9.00) in legal reserves. Acme's bank, therefore, can lend out $81.00.

This is the process of *deposit expansion*. It can continue as shown in Table 10–3. The commercial banking system does create money in the form of demand deposits. Of course, the process of deposit expansion is much more complex in practice. General economic conditions, for example, influence the willingness of bankers to make loans and the willingness of borrowers to borrow.

But as you can see from Table 10–3, your original deposit of $100 in coins could result in an increase of $1,000 in new deposits for all banks in the commercial banking system. Remember, we are assuming a reserve requirement of 10 percent. Thus your original deposit of $100 in coins could expand by 10 times (the reciprocal of the reserve require-

Bank	New deposit	New loan	Legal reserve
Your bank	$100.00	$90.00	$10.00
Bank 2	90.00'	81.00	9.00
Bank 3	81.00	72.90	8.10
Bank 4	72.90	65.61	7.29
Bank 5	65.61	59.05	6.56
Bank 6	59.05	53.14	5.91
Bank 7	53.14	47.83	5.31
Bank 8	47.83	43.05	4.78
Bank 9	43.05	38.74	4.31
Total for first nine banks	$612.58	$551.32	$61.26
Total for entire banking system	$1,000.00	$900.00	$100.00

TABLE 10-3

How the commercial banking system creates money

Note: Assume a reserve requirement of 10 percent.

ment, $\frac{100}{10}$) or to $1,000. If the reserve requirement were 20 percent, your original deposit could expand by only 5 times ($\frac{100}{20}$) or to $500. Our example in Table 10–3 assumes that no borrower takes part of his or her loan in cash and that the banks want to lend as much as they legally can. Otherwise, the increase would be less than $1,000.

The Federal Reserve System

To understand how commercial banking works, we must discuss the Federal Reserve System. **The Federal Reserve System (the Fed) was created by the Federal Reserve Act of 1913. The Fed is the central bank of the United States. Its main purpose is to control the nation's money supply.**

Federal Reserve System

The Board of Governors

The board of governors of the Federal Reserve System is composed of seven members who are appointed by the President of the United States with the advice and consent of the Senate. Each member is appointed to a 14-year term. The board of governors provides general direction to the 12 Federal Reserve Banks. It can audit their books, and it coordinates their operations in the public interest.

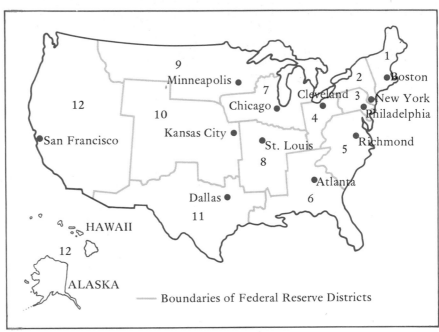

FIGURE 10-2

Federal Reserve Districts

Source: *The Federal Reserve Board.*

Federal Reserve Banks

The United States is divided into 12 districts, each of which has a Federal Reserve Bank (FRB). (See Figure 10–2.) Each FRB is owned by member commercial banks in its district. How many shares a member bank has in the FRB in its district depends on the member bank's size. But the nine directors of the board of directors of an FRB are not elected like board members in a business corporation. If this were permitted, the large commercial banks in a given FRB district would control the election of its board of directors.

Of the nine directors of an FRB, a maximum of three can be bankers, three must be businesspersons, and three are appointed by the board of governors of the Fed to represent the general public. Member commercial banks in each FRB district elect the directors who represent banking and business. These member banks are divided into three classes—large, medium, and small banks. Each group elects one director to represent banking and one member to represent business.

The Federal Open Market Committee (FOMC)

The Federal Open Market Committee (FOMC) is composed of 12 members (the 7 members of the board of governors and 5 FRB representatives). The FOMC sets the Fed's open-market policy. It directs the FRBs either to buy or to sell government securities.

The Federal Advisory Council

Another important part of the Fed is the Federal Advisory Council. The Federal Advisory Council is composed of 12 members, one from each Federal Reserve Bank. The council's task is to advise the board of governors and to make recommendations to it.

Member Banks

Of the roughly 14,000 commercial banks in the United States, only about 5,700 are members of the Federal Reserve System. But all national banks must be members. State-chartered banks can join if they meet the Fed's requirements. Actually, all of our major commercial banks are members of the Federal Reserve System.

Operations of the Fed

The following activities of the Fed are important to member banks, businesses, investors, and consumers:

- controlling the money supply
- lending to member banks
- setting the reserve requirement
- setting the margin requirement
- setting interest ceilings
- using other credit controls
- clearing checks
- protecting consumers

Controlling the Money Supply

The major tool the Fed uses to control the money supply is its open market operations. If the FOMC wants to increase the money supply, it directs FRBs to buy government securities. The FRB pays for these securities by crediting the reserve accounts of the member banks that sell the securities. This increases member bank reserves at the FRB and, therefore, increases member banks' lending ability.

If the FOMC wants to decrease the money supply, it directs FRBs to sell government securities. Purchases by member banks reduce their reserve accounts at their FRBs. This reduces member banks' lending ability.

Lending to Member Banks

A member bank that wants to borrow at its FRB may present commercial paper to the FRB. The FRB will discount this paper—give the member bank less than the face value of the commercial paper. The *discount rate*, in effect, is the FRB's interest rate on member bank borrowing.

Each FRB sets its own discount rate subject to approval by the board of governors. Raising the discount rate makes member banks less willing to borrow, tends to raise the interest rate member banks charge their borrowers, and reduces the money supply. Lowering the discount rate has the opposite effects. It encourages member banks to borrow, tends to lower the interest rate member banks charge their borrowers, and increases the money supply.

Setting the Reserve Requirement

reserve requirement

The board of governors sets the reserve requirement. **The reserve requirement is the percentage of its deposits that member banks have to keep in vault cash or as deposits with their FRBs.** Lowering the reserve requirement increases the money supply. Raising it decreases the money supply.

Setting the Margin Requirement

TABLE 10-4

Federal Reserve System actions to stimulate or slow down the level of business activity

The margin requirement is the percentage that buyers of corporation securities must pay in cash when they buy securities. The remainder of the purchase price is borrowed from the broker. Raising the margin

To *stimulate* business activity	To *slow down* business activity
1. Buy government securities: This increases the money supply because these purchases by FRBs increase member-bank reserves and their ability to make loans to businesses and consumers.	1. Sell government securities: This decreases the money supply because these sales by FRBs decrease member-bank reserves and their ability to make loans to businesses and consumers.
2. Lower the discount rate: This increases the money supply by increasing the willingness of member banks to borrow at their FRBs, thereby making possible more loans to businesses and consumers.	2. Raise the discount rate: This decreases the money supply by decreasing the willingness of member banks to borrow at their FRBs, thereby making possible fewer loans to businesses and consumers.
3. Lower the reserve requirement: This increases the money supply by requiring member banks to keep less cash in their vaults or on deposit with their FRBs.	3. Raise the reserve requirement: This decreases the money supply by requiring member banks to keep more cash in their vaults or on deposit with their FRBs.

The Fed's effectiveness in controlling the money supply depends heavily on the proportion of all commercial bank deposits that are held by members of the system and, therefore, are subject to Fed policies and regulations. In 1978 roughly 73 percent of all deposits in our commercial banking system were held in member banks of the Federal Reserve System, down from 81 percent in 1970.

Over the past few years the number of commercial banks that are members of the system has declined. Although all national banks must belong, some newly organized state-chartered banks are choosing not to join and some are leaving the system. A major reason for this is the reserve requirement. Member banks must keep set percentages of their demand and time deposits on reserve in noninterest bearing accounts at their Federal Reserve Banks. Because of the declining number of member banks, the Federal Reserve Board has asked Congress to pass two bills. One would allow the Federal Reserve Banks to pay interest on member banks' reserve accounts at the Federal Reserve Banks. The other would allow the Federal Reserve Board to set reserve requirements for all commercial banks—members and nonmembers. The intent is to reduce the competitive disadvantage of member banks in competing with non-member banks. THINK ABOUT IT!

requirement discourages investors from buying securities. Lowering it has the opposite effect.

margin requirement

Setting Interest Ceilings

By raising the maximum rate of interest that commercial banks can pay on savings accounts, the Fed seeks to increase the willingness of people to save. This brings in deposits to member banks and increases their ability to lend. Lowering the maximum rate, of course, has the opposite effect.

Using Other Credit Controls

The Fed can also use consumer credit controls and real estate credit controls to regulate the volume of credit. It sometimes uses "moral suasion" when it tries to influence bankers to do what it believes is in the economy's best interest. The Credit Control Act of 1969 allows the Fed, at the request of the President of the United States, to impose a broad range of credit controls, including regulation of minimum down payments and maximum maturities on consumer loans.

Clearing Checks

The Fed also helps in clearing bank checks. Suppose Aaron draws a check on his account in bank A and mails it to Bob who deposits it in bank B. If both banks are in the same city, the clearing process is handled through the local bank clearing house association.

If Aaron's bank were in Miami, Florida, and Bob's bank were in Montgomery, Alabama, the check would be cleared by the Atlanta Federal Reserve Bank since both cities are in the Atlanta District.

If Aaron's bank were in Miami and Bob's bank were in Los Angeles, Aaron's check would have to be sent to the bank in Miami for collection. The transit process here is handled by the two Federal Reserve Banks— one in Atlanta and the other in San Francisco.

Protecting Consumers

Although our discussion has centered mainly on the Fed and business activity, the Fed does function in the interests of all of us. The Fed's efforts to control inflation are an example. We will cite one other example.

The Consumer Credit Protection Act of 1968 ("Truth in Lending" Act) is administered by the board of governors of the Fed. The law requires banks, finance companies, and sellers who sell on an installment basis to disclose the annual interest rate borrowers actually pay. The law applies to consumer transactions, not business or commercial transactions.

Thus a store that charges 1.5 percent interest per month must disclose the annual percentage rate (APR) as 18 percent. A finance company that lends you money must disclose the interest rate on an annual basis.

Credit Instruments

As we'll see in the next chapter, trade credit is the major source of short-term financing for businesses. Instead of borrowing money from banks to finance their purchases, buyers get credit directly from their suppliers. Buyers can do this under three types of trade credit arrangements:

- open-book account
- promissory notes
- drafts

Open-book Account

With an open-book account (often referred to as *trade credit*), the seller of merchandise bills the buyer when the ordered merchandise is shipped to the buyer. No credit instruments are involved because the seller simply includes the bill along with the shipment of merchandise to the buyer. The bill, or invoice, includes the payment terms. Usually the bill is due within 30 days but a cash discount may be offered for early payment. For example, a 2 percent cash discount off the invoice amount may be offered for paying within 10 days of the invoice date. More than 80 percent of all purchases of merchandise are financed through open-book accounts.

An open-book account, however, requires that the seller know the buyer's ability to pay and his or her record for making prompt payment. If the seller is not confident about the buyer's creditworthiness, the seller can use promissory notes and drafts to offer credit to the buyer. These involve much more formal arrangements than open-book accounts.

Promissory Notes

A promissory note is a written promise by a customer (borrower or "maker") to pay a certain sum of money (principal and interest) to a supplier (payee) at a specified future date. Although promissory notes are used in some industries in place of open-book accounts, they are used most often in credit sales to customers who have poor credit ratings or who are slow in making their payments on open-book accounts.

promissory note

FIGURE 10-3

A promissory note

| No._____ | _____ 19__ | $_____ |

_____ after date the undersigned (jointly and severally if more than one) promise(s) to pay to the order of _____

_____ Dollars

payable at _____

Each and every party to this instrument, either as maker, endorser, surety or otherwise, hereby waives demand, notice, protest and all other demands and notices and assents to any extension of the time of payment or any other indulgence, to any substitution, exchange or release of collateral and/or to the release of any other party.

Address Only

Signed By

C 83

Source: The First National Bank of Boston.

The seller feels more secure in selling to such a buyer when the seller has a note signed by the buyer.

If a promissory note is negotiable, the supplier can sell it to another party. Suppose Supplier sells merchandise to Buyer. Supplier takes Buyer's promissory note for $1,000 to be paid in 180 days at 10 percent interest per year. If Supplier wanted to get the money sooner, Supplier could sell the note to the bank. Supplier gets $1,000 (the face value of the note) minus a fee for this service. Supplier might get less, however, if the bank wants to earn more than 10 percent per year on a loan. Buyer pays $1,000 plus interest to the bank on the due date. If Supplier sells the note with recourse, the bank can collect from Supplier if Buyer fails to make good on the note.

Usually, however, banks prefer to discount notes. Suppose Buyer B signed a note for the $1,000 loan with the bank. The bank discounts the note by deducting its interest in advance. Buyer B gets $950, not $1,000. Buyer B pays 10 percent interest on a note of $1,000 but only gets $950 in money. The effective rate of interest earned by the bank is roughly 10.5 percent.

Drafts

There is a big difference between a promissory note and a draft. A promissory note is a *promise to pay* that is made by the maker, the person who promises to make the payment. A draft is an *order to pay* that is made by the drawer, the person who is to receive the payment.

When Supplier (drawer) ships merchandise to Buyer, Supplier sends two documents. One is the bill of lading. This is a written document from the carrier (transportation company) acknowledging receipt of the merchandise for delivery and setting out the terms of the shipping contract. The other document is a trade draft. **A trade draft is prepared by the supplier and it orders the buyer to pay a certain amount of money for the merchandise.**

trade draft

There are two types of drafts: (1) sight drafts and (2) time drafts. If Supplier sells to Buyer with a sight draft, Buyer must pay the sight draft as soon as Supplier presents it for payment. A time draft specifies a certain future date on which the draft must be paid.

trade acceptance

A trade draft becomes a trade acceptance when the buyer signs it (accepts it). The buyer must sign it in order to get the merchandise from the carrier. The trade acceptance is returned to the supplier. If it is a sight draft, Supplier (drawer) has the bank present it for immediate payment by Buyer (drawee). If it is a time draft, Supplier can hold it until the date specified on the trade acceptance and then send it to Supplier's bank, which will present it to Buyer for payment. If Supplier

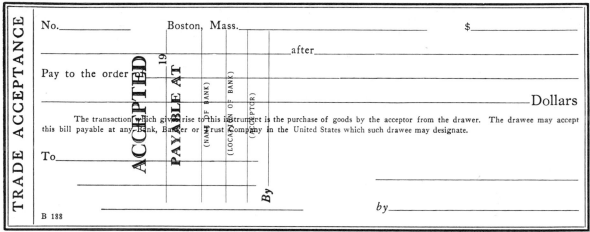

Source: The First National Bank of Boston.

FIGURE 10-4

A trade acceptance

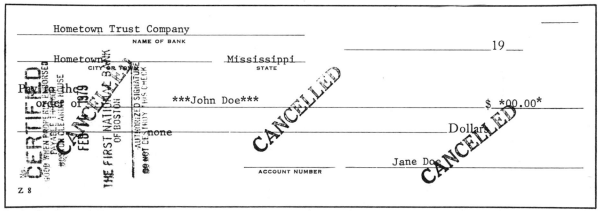

Source: The First National Bank of Boston.

FIGURE 10-5

A certified check

wants the money earlier, it can discount the trade acceptance at Supplier's bank.

Suppose Supplier does not want to use a trade draft but is unwilling to accept a check drawn on Buyer's account. Seller can require Buyer to pay with certified checks or cashier's checks. A certified check is a check stamped by a bank as certified. The bank immediately deducts the amount of the check from Buyer's account. This ensures that the check will not "bounce." The bank charges a small fee for this service.

A cashier's check is a check written by a bank's cashier. The check is drawn on the bank itself (not on Buyer's account) and the payee is

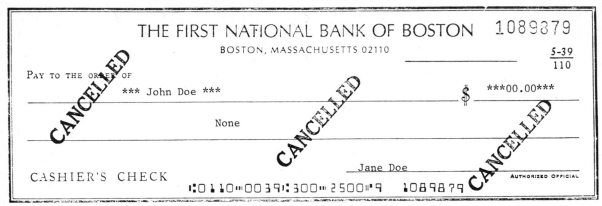

Source: The First National Bank of Boston.

FIGURE 10-6

A cashier's check

specified on the check. The bank collects the amount of the check from Buyer plus a small fee, or it charges Buyer's account.

The Public Market

Up to this point, our discussion of financial institutions has focused mainly on sources of short-term funds for businesses. The only major exception is life insurance companies, which are an important source of long-term funds for some firms.

With very few exceptions, most large- and medium-sized corporations use the public market as a source of long-term funds. **The public market is made up of millions of people who buy stocks and bonds and the business and nonbusiness organizations that also invest in corporate securities. Also included in the public market are the various securities "middlemen" who bring buyers and sellers of securities together.**

public market

Stocks and Bonds

The two major vehicles by which a firm gains access to the public market are stocks and bonds. As we saw in Chapter 3, only corporations issue stock. While a firm need not be a corporation to issue bonds, it usually must be a well-financed and sound firm if it is to attract any buyers of its bonds. You may want to review the discussion of common stock and preferred stock in Chapter 3. (See Table 10–5.)

Stocks

Three different concepts of value associated with common stock are

- book value—the difference between the dollar values of what a company owns (its assets) and what it owes (its debts, or liabilities) divided by the number of shares of common stock.
- market value—the price the shares of stock are selling for on the market. This changes daily in response to supply and demand.
- par value—the value the corporation that originally issued the stock certificate may have printed on it. This is called par value stock. If no value is placed on the stock certificate, it is called no-par stock.

In most cases, the book value, market value, and par value of a corporation's stock are three different amounts of money.

Three other terms are also important:

- stock split
- cash dividend
- stock dividend

A stock split gives stockholders a greater number of shares but does not change the individual's proportionate ownership in the corporation. Sue Adams, for example, owns 100 shares of IBM common, which is

TABLE 10-5

Types and characteristics of preferred stock

Type	Characteristics
1. Cumulative preferred	1. Dividends not paid in one year or more cumulate and must be paid before common stockholders receive dividends.
2. Noncumulative preferred	2. Dividends not paid in one year or more need not be paid in future years but, in a given year, must be paid before common stockholders receive any dividends.
3. Fully participating preferred	3. Once the dividend stated on the stock certificate is paid and the common stockholders receive the same sum, preferred shareholders share in any remaining dividends.
4. Nonparticipating preferred	4. Shareholders are entitled only to the dividend stated on the stock certificate.
5. Convertible preferred	5. Preferred shareholders can convert their preferred stock to common stock at their option.
6. Redeemable preferred	6. Preferred stock issued with a call price at which price the issuing corporation can legally require the holder to sell his or her shares back to the corporation.

Source: *Agatha Crumm*, King Features Syndicate.

selling at $400 per share. The market value of her shares is $40,000. If the directors vote for a 4-for-1 stock split, Sue will have 400 shares valued at $100 per share. The total market value of her shares right after the split is still $40,000. The purpose of the split is to reduce the selling price per share. This may make the stock attractive to more buyers, increase the demand for it, and raise its selling price.

A cash dividend is a payment of cash to stockholders. It rewards them for their investment in the corporation.

If a corporation wants to keep its cash, it might declare a stock dividend. This is a payment to stockholders in additional shares of stock rather than payment of cash. A 20 percent stock dividend means that each stockholder gets two new shares for each ten he or she already owns. A stock dividend is a way to reward stockholders when a firm wants to reinvest its earnings in the business. It conserves cash. Like a stock split, a stock dividend does not increase the stockholder's share of ownership in a corporation.

Bonds

Although all corporations issue common stock, not all issue bonds. Stockholders provide equity (ownership) capital, while bondholders are lenders. Stock certificates indicate ownership, while bond certificates indicate indebtedness.

All levels of government issue bonds as do many nonbusinesses. **A bond is a written promise to pay. It indicates that the borrower will pay the lender, at some stated future date, a sum of money (the principal) and a stated rate of interest.** Bondholders have a claim on a corporation's assets and earnings which comes before that of common and preferred stockholders.

Most bond issues are sold to many individuals. The agreement under which they are issued (the indenture) names a trustee to represent the

bond

Types	Characteristics
1. Secured bonds	1. Backed by security pledged by the issuing corporation. This can be sold by the trustee and the proceeds used to pay off the bondholders if the corporation fails to pay principal and/or interest.
(a) Real estate mortgage bonds	(a) Secured by real property.
(b) Chattel mortgage bonds	(b) Secured by movable property.
(c) Collateral trust bonds	(c) Secured by stocks and bonds in other corporations which are owned by the issuing corporation.
2. Unsecured bonds (debentures)	2. Not secured or backed by specific assets but by the general credit and strength of the issuing corporation.
3. Registered bonds	3. Owner's name is registered with the issuing corporation and is printed on the certificate. Interest is mailed to him or her by the corporation or its trustee.
4. Coupon bonds	4. Owner's name is not registered and does not appear on the certificate. Owner must clip coupons from the bond and present them to the corporation's bank.
5. Convertible bonds	5. Can be converted to common stock at the bondholder's option.
6. Serial bonds	6. The issuing corporation issues a large block of bonds which mature at different dates.
7. Sinking fund bonds	7. The issuing corporation makes annual deposits with the trustee so that those deposits, along with earned interest, will be available to redeem the bonds upon maturity.
8. Redeemable or callable bonds	8. Can be called in or redeemed prior to maturity.

TABLE 10-6

Types and characteristics of bonds

bondholders' interests. This trustee is usually a large bank or trust company. Table 10–6 describes several important types of bonds.

Investment Banks and Brokerage Houses

Two very important financial institutions are investment banks and brokerage houses. They are crucial to the purchase and sale of stocks and bonds.

Investment Banks

An investment bank (or underwriting house) does not accept deposits from the general public. It helps corporations to sell new issues of stocks and bonds.

investment bank

    Suppose the Jaron Corporation decides to expand its plant and wants to sell $10,000,000 worth of bonds. It might contact an investment bank to help with the sale. If its study of Jaron's financial condition is favorable, the bank would offer to buy Jaron's bonds. If Jaron accepts, the cash is made available to it. The investment bank then sells the bonds. The bank earns a profit by charging a commission for its services or by selling the securities at a price higher than it paid for them.

If the risk of selling a large issue of stocks and bonds is too great for one investment bank, several may combine in a syndicate to underwrite the issue. Each bank agrees to take a portion of the securities offered for sale.

Brokerage Houses

brokerage house

A brokerage house is a firm that buys and sells securities that previously have been issued by businesses and governments. It buys and sells securities on behalf of its investor-clients.

Large brokerage houses perform many functions for corporations and investors:

- They engage in investment banking when they help corporations to sell new securities issues.
- They perform a brokerage function when they buy and sell previously issued securities on behalf of their investor-clients.
- They perform a credit function when they finance purchases made on credit by securities buyers (margin purchases).
- They perform a research function when they compile information about firms.
- They perform an advisory function when they use the information gathered through research to advise their corporate clients on issuing new securities and when they advise their investor-clients on buying and selling securities.

Securities Exchanges

securities exchanges

Securities exchanges are set up by brokerage houses to reduce the cost and increase the efficiency of financial investment. Buyers and sellers of securities can deal with each other through members of the exchanges. Members of an exchange own "seats" on that exchange. Only members can trade on an exchange.

Most large brokerage firms hold seats on most of the 17 exchanges in the United States. Of course, there are securities exchanges in other countries also.

A corporation does not receive any money from the sale of its securities on stock exchanges. If Joe Smith buys 100 shares of Chrysler Corporation common on an exchange, the money goes to the party who sold the shares, not to Chrysler.

Listed Securities

Securities traded on organized stock exchanges such as the New York Stock Exchange (NYSE) and the American Stock Exchange (AMEX) are called listed securities.

The NYSE is made up of roughly 1,400 individual members who hold seats on the exchange. Owning a seat enables a brokerage firm to buy and sell on the NYSE floor. The securities of most major corporations are listed here. Only those that have been traded for some time on other exchanges and are widely held can be listed on the NYSE. A fee must be paid before a security can be listed.

Buying a Listed Security

Suppose you want to buy a listed security. If you have never "dabbled" in the market, your first step is to go to a branch office of a brokerage house and open an account. A corporation has only a certain number of outstanding shares (issued by the corporation and owned by investors). If you want to buy some of those shares, you must deal with people who own them. The brokerage house brings you (the buyer) and someone else (the seller) together.

When you go to the brokerage house, you will be introduced to an account executive. This person is often called a stockbroker because he or she works for a brokerage house. If you are serious about becoming an investor, take the time to become familiar with your account executive. Be truthful about your investment goals and your financial situation. Because all of your dealings with the brokerage house will be handled by and through your account executive, you must know and understand each other.

After talking with your account executive, Ms. Perkins, you decide to buy some Westinghouse common stock. You ask her what the selling price is. Ms. Perkins uses an electronic device on her desk to tell her the last price at which the stock sold. Now you must make a decision. If you tell Ms. Perkins to buy "at market," she will buy the number of shares you want at the lowest price offered. If that price is $80 per share, you would pay $8,000, plus commission, if you buy 100 shares.

But suppose you want to pay no more than $70 per share. You can place a "limit order" with Ms. Perkins. Your order would not be filled unless she could find someone willing to sell for $70 or less per share.

If you place an "at market" order, Ms. Perkins contacts her firm's New York office. That office contacts its representative on the New York Stock Exchange floor who goes to the "post" where Westinghouse stock is traded. That floor person buys the shares at the offering price. No delay is involved because someone is always willing to sell if a buyer is willing to pay the seller's asking price.

Within minutes, Ms. Perkins will get an electronic message direct from the exchange floor telling her that the transaction is complete. Meanwhile, the seller's account executive sends his or her client's stock certificate to Westinghouse's transfer agent, who cancels it and issues a new certificate in your name. This may be held by your account executive for safekeeping or sent to you.

The Over-the-Counter Market

over-the-counter market (OTC)

Most securities are unlisted. Unlisted securities are not listed on any of the organized securities exchanges. They are traded in the over-the-counter (OTC) market. **The over-the-counter market is a complex of dealers who are in constant touch with one another. Stocks and bonds of locally owned corporations are generally traded on the OTC market. All new issues of stocks and bonds, most government bonds, and the stocks of most banks, mutual funds, and insurance companies are traded here.**

Security dealers in the OTC market often buy securities in their own name. They expect to sell them at a higher price to their clients. These dealers also buy shares at the request of their clients. Dealers receive a commission for this. Dealers selling to one another charge a wholesale price and sell to their customers at a retail price.

The National Association of Securities Dealers, Inc. (NASD) is the self-regulatory organization for the OTC securities market. In 1971 it created a computerized communications system that collects, stores, and reports price quotations to brokers and dealers. This system is called NASDAQ—NASD Automated Quotations. Brokers and dealers are connected together by this system, which enables them to get up-to-the-second price quotations. Thus a broker can get a price quote on a security that is quoted by NASDAQ merely by pushing a button. This makes possible more efficient trading of securities in the OTC market.

Stock and Bond Prices

Stocks and bonds traded on the exchanges and the OTC market are listed and reported in the financial section of many daily newspapers. *The Wall Street Journal* gives more detailed coverage.

Stock Prices

Figure 10–7 is reproduced from *The Wall Street Journal*. The corporation's name is shown along with the number of shares sold (expressed in

FIGURE 10-7

Stock and bond prices reported in *The Wall Street Journal*

38 THE WALL STREET JOURNAL, Monday, March 19, 1979

Friday's Volume
36,643,550 Shares; 296,200 Warrants

TRADING BY MARKETS

	Shares	Warrants
New York Exchange	31,770,000	296,200
American Exchange	....	....
Midwest Exchange	1,921,800	....
Pacific Exchange	1,244,900	....
Nat'l Assoc. of Securities Dealers	790,450	....
Philadelphia Exchange	528,200	....
Boston Exchange	262,700	....
Cincinnati Exchange	116,800	....
Instinet System	8,700	....

NYSE – Composite

Volume since Jan. 1:	1979	1978	1977
Total shares	1,620,540,427	1,250,271,550	1,352,063,102
Total warrants	7,565,749	3,948,800	6,607,800

New York Stock Exchange

Volume since Jan. 1:	1979	1978	1977
Total shares	1,425,585,867	1,091,856,980	1,153,703,312
Total warrants	7,262,900	3,952,100	6,584,800

MOST ACTIVE STOCKS

	Open	High	Low	Close	Chg.	Volume
Texaco Inc	26	26½	25¾	26¼	+ ¼	593,100
Texas Intl	11	12½	11	12½	+ ⅛	454,800
Gulf Oil	26	26¾	25⅞	26¾	+ ⅝	352,500
Occident Pet	20⅜	21	20¼	20⅞	+ ⅝	352,000
Exxon	53⅜	54⅛	53¼	54	+ ¾	349,000
Hughes Tool	44½	47⅝	44½	47⅛	+2⅞	339,200
Searle GD	14⅝	15⅛	14⅝	14⅞	+ ⅜	301,300
Amer Hess	29⅞	31	29⅞	30⅞	+1	280,800
LouLd Exp	26¾	27¼	26½	26⅝	.....	251,800
StdOil Ind	59⅞	60⅞	59⅝	60½	+1⅜	235,700
Halliburtn	64¾	68⅞	64¾	67¾	+2⅞	230,800
Cont Oil	32¾	33⅛	32⅝	32⅞	+ ¾	224,600
Norton Sim	16	16	15⅝	15⅞	– ⅜	222,200
Gen Tire	25½	25½	24¾	25¼	– ¼	219,000
Scott Paper	18⅝	18¾	18½	18⅝	.....	215,300

52 Weeks High	52 Weeks Low	Stocks	Div.	Yld %	P-E Ratio	Sales 100s	High	Low	Close	Net Chg.
		– A–A–A –								
39½	29⅛	ACF	2.10	6.3	7	44	33¼	33	33⅛	– ¼
23⅝	15½	AMF	1.24	7.6	7	240	16⅜	16⅛	16⅜	+ ⅛
32⅞	16⅛	AM Intl	.28	1.4	7	383	20¼	19⅝	19¾	– ⅛
14¾	8⅞	APL	1	10.	..	44	10	9⅞	9⅞	– ⅛
31⅜	19	ASA	1	3.9	..	128	25⅜	25¼	25⅜	.....
14⅞	8½	ATO	.48	4.1	5	115	11⅝	11¼	11⅝	+ ¼
40	29	AbbtLb	1	3.2	13	486	31⅝	30¾	31½	+ ½
23¾	13⅛	AcmeC	1.20	6.7	5	4	17⅞	17⅞	17⅞	.....
6¼	3⅜	AdmDg	.04	1.1	5	17	3¾	3⅝	3⅝	– ⅛
13	10¾	AdaEx	1.28e	12.	..	49	11¼	11	11⅛	+ ¼
8½	3⅞	AdmMl	.20e	4.4	6	11	4⅝	4½	4½	.....
45¾	34⅜	AetnaLf	2.70	6.1	5	x1120	44⅜	43⅝	44	+ ⅜
26¾	17⅝	Ahmans	1	4.6	4	5	21⅝	21⅝	21⅝	– ⅛
4	2	Aileen		..	..	30	2½	2⅜	2½	+ ⅛
31⅞	23⅛	AirPrd	.60	2.2	9	295	27⅛	27	27	+ ⅛
26¾	15¼	AirbFrt	1	4.9	10	18	20⅜	20⅛	20¼	.....
15¼	11¼	Akzona	.80	6.5	7	27	12⅜	12⅛	12⅜	.....
9½	7¾	AlaP dpf	.87	10.	..	22	8⅜	8⅛	8⅜	+ ⅛
113	97½	AlaP pf	11	11.	..	z1350	100½	100	100½	+ ½
102	84½	AlaP pf	9.44	11.	..	z150	85½	85½	85½	.....
87¼	76	AlaP pf	8.16	11.	..	z280	77¼	77	77	+ ⅜
87	73	AlaP pf	8.28	11.	..	z150	75	75	75	– ½
18	14⅛	Alagsco	1.40	9.3	7	3	15	15	15	.....
22¼	13½	AlaskIn	.66	3.5	13	388	19½	18⅞	19⅛	+ ⅜

CORPORATION BONDS
Volume, $12,120,000

Bonds	Cur Yld	Vol	High	Low	Close	Net Chg
APL 10¾97	13	20	85	85	85	– ½
ATO 4⅜s87	cv	2	67	67	67	– ½
AbbtL 7⅝96	8.1	5	93⅝	93⅝	93⅝	+ ⅛
AlaBnc 9½84	9.5	5	99⅞	99⅞	99⅞	– ⅞
AlaP 3⅛s84	4.3	14	72¾	72¾	72¾	+1⅞
AlaP 9s2000	11.	12	84½	83⅛	83⅛	–1⅜
AlaP 8½s01	10.	3	82⅞	81	82⅞	+ ⅜
AlaP 7⅞s02	10.	10	75⅞	75½	75⅞	+2⅞
AlaP 7¾s02	10.	6	75¼	75¼	75¼	.....
AlaP 8⅞s03	11.	7	84	84	84	.....
AlaP 8¼s03	11.	7	78¼	78	78¼	+ ¼
AlaP 9¾s04	11.	5	92⅝	92⅝	92⅝	– ¾
AlaP 10⅞05	11.	16	99½	99¼	99¼	–2⅝
AlaP 10½05	11.	54	97½	96¼	96¼	+ ¼
AlaP 8¾07	10.	11	83⅜	82	83⅜	+1⅛
AlaP 9½08	11.	10	89¾	87⅞	87⅞	.....
AlaP 9⅝08	11.	5	89⅜	89⅜	89⅜	– ⅝
Alaska 6s96	cv	37	83	82	83	+2½
AlldC 5.2s91	5.9	5	87⅞	87⅞	87⅞	+ ⅜
AlldSt 4½92	cv	5	98½	98½	98½	–1½
Alcoa 5¼s91	cv	30	105	103	105	+2¼
AluCa 9½95	9.9	14	96¼	96¼	96¼	.....
AMAX 8s86	8.7	4	91½	91½	91½	.....
Amerce 5s92	cv	5	75¼	75¼	75¼	– ¼
AForP 5s30	9.2	1	54⅝	54⅝	54⅝	....
AAirl 4¼s92	cv	4	55	55	55	– ¼
AAirl 11s88	11.	8	103½	102½	102½	.....
AAirl 10⅞88	11.	2	102	102	102	....
ABrnd 8⅛85	8.7	10	93¼	93¼	93¼	.....
ACan 6s97	7.9	10	75⅝	75⅝	75⅝	+1¼
AExC 8½s85	8.9	11	96	96	96	....
AHosp 5¾99	cv	10	100¾	100	100¾	– ¼
AInvt 8¾s89	10.	2	87½	87½	87½	+ ⅛
AMF 4¼s81	cv	3	92¼	92¼	92¼	.....
AmMot 6s88	cv	131	86	80	86	+1½
ASug 5.3s93	8.5	1	62¼	62¼	62¼	.....
ATT 3¼s84	4.2	62	77	76⅞	77	.....
ATT 4⅜s85	5.5	91	79⅛	79	79	– ⅛
ATT 2⅝s86	3.8	46	69¼	69¼	69¼	.....
ATT 3⅞s90	6.0	30	64⅝	64¼	64⅝	+ ⅛
ATT 8¾00	9.3	127	94¾	94⅜	94½	+ ⅛
ATT 7s01	8.8	27	79⅝	79⅜	79⅝	+ ⅛
ATT 6½s79	6.7	7	97⅝	97 5-16	97⅝	+ ⅛
ATT 7⅛s03	8.9	141	80	79¾	80	+ ¼
ATT 8.80s05	9.3	58	94¾	94¼	94¼	– ⅜
ATT 7¾s82	8.1	15	95½	95½	95½	+ ½
ATT 8⅝s07	9.3	16	93¼	92⅝	92¾	.....
Amfac 5¼94	cv	8	67¾	67⅜	67¾	+ ⅛
Ampx 5½94	cv	5	63¾	63¾	63¾	– ⅛
Anhr 6s92	7.4	10	81¼	81¼	81¼	.....
AppP 7¼s79	7.3	10	98 11-16	98 11-16	98 11-16	+9-16
Arco 8.70s81	9.0	10	97¼	97	97	– ¼
ArizP 9½s82	9.6	3	98¾	98⅝	98¾	+ ⅜
ArizP 9.8s80	9.8	5	99¾	99¾	99¾	.....
AshO 4¾93	cv	10	122¾	122½	122½	– ¼
AshO 8.2s02	9.2	10	89	89	89	+1
AsCp 9¼90	9.7	15	95½	95½	95½	+ ⅜
AsCp 8⅝81	8.8	12	97¾	97½	97¾	+ ⅞
AsCp 8.2s87	9.1	5	90¼	90¼	90¼	.....
AsInv 5⅛79	5.2	3	97 21-32	97 21-32	97 21-32	–11-32
Atchsn 4s95	6.6	1	60¼	60¼	60¼	+ ⅛
AtlCEl 9¼83	9.4	2	98¼	98¼	98¼	+ ¼
ARich 8⅝00	9.3	6	93	93	93	.....
AvcoC 5½93	cv	63	63⅝	63½	63½	– ⅜
AvcoC 7½93	10.	15	73½	73¼	73¼	– ⅜
AvcoC 9⅝01	cv	5	129	129	129	.....
AvcoF 7⅞89	9.0	9	88½	87½	87½	–2⅜
AvcoF 11s90	10.	15	105	105	105	+1
BPNA 9s80	9.1	13	98¾	98¾	98¾	+ ¾
Bally 6s98	cv	265	115¼	112	114½	+3
BalGE 10s82	9.9	5	101¼	101¼	101¼	....
BalGE 9⅜08	9.8	20	95½	95½	95½	+ ⅛
BkCal 6½96	cv	1	78½	78½	78½	–1½
BkNY 6¼94	cv	8	89¾	89¾	89¾	+ ¼
Banka 8⅞05	9.5	20	93⅞	93½	93½	– ¾
Banka 8¾01	9.6	29	92¾	91½	91½	–1⅛
BaxL 4⅜s91	cv	153	106	104¾	106	+ ½

Source: *The Wall Street Journal.*

High Low 50½ 35	Ajax Co. 1.25	P-E ratio 20	Sales 15	High Low 45¼ 43	Close 45	Net change +½
The highest and lowest price paid for one share during the current year.	Company name and $1.25 per share dividends annually.	The current market price per share of stock divided by the past 12 months' earnings per share. This is the price/earnings ratio.	Total shares traded on this date in round lots.	The highest and lowest prices paid per share for this day.	Price per share at the closing of the market for this day.	The increase or decrease between the closing price per share today and the closing price per share on the previous day.

FIGURE 10-8

Reading the financial section of *The Wall Street Journal*

round lots of 100 shares). Prices are quoted in dollars and fractions of a dollar ranging from ⅛ to ⅞. A quote of 50⅝ means that the price per share is $50.63. Figure 10–8 explains the meaning of the various columns.

Bond Prices and Bond Yield

Bond prices also change from day to day. These changes provide information for firms about the cost of borrowing funds.

Prices of domestic corporation bonds, U.S. government bonds, and foreign bonds are reported separately. Bond prices are expressed in terms of 100 even though most have a face value of $1,000. Thus, a quote of 85 means that the bond's price is 85 percent of par or $850.

A corporation bond selling at 155¼ would cost a buyer $1,552.50 ($1,000 par value times 1.5525) plus commission. U.S. government bonds, however, are quoted in $\frac{1}{32}$ points. A $1,000 par bond quoted at 101$\frac{8}{32}$ would cost $1,012.50 ($1,000 times 1.0125) plus commission. In the financial pages, the selling price would be shown as 101.8 rather than 101$\frac{8}{32}$. The interest rate on bonds is also quoted as a percentage of par. Thus, "6½s" pay 6.5 percent of par value per year.

The market value (selling price) of a bond at any given time depends on (1) its stated interest rate; (2) the "going rate" of interest in the market; and (3) its redemption or maturity date.

If a bond carries a higher stated interest rate than the "going rate" on similar quality bonds, it will probably sell at a premium above its face value—its selling price will be above its redemption price. If a bond carries a lower stated interest rate than the "going rate" on similar quality bonds, it will probably sell at a discount—its selling price will be below its redemption price. How much the premium or discount is depends largely on how far off in the future the maturity date is. The maturity date is indicated after the interest rate. (See Figure 10–7.)

Suppose you bought a $1,000 par value bond in 1977 for $650. Its stated interest rate is 6 percent and its maturity or redemption date is 1997. You paid $650 for the bond and its interest rate is 6 percent per year of par value. You get $60 per year in interest. Based on your actual investment of $650, your yield is 9.2 percent. If you hold it to maturity, you get $1,000 for a bond that originally cost you only $650. This "extra" $350, of course, increases your true, or effective, yield.

Stock and Bond Averages

To give investors an overall idea of the behavior of security prices, several types of stock and bond averages are reported. The Dow-Jones Averages and the Standard & Poor's Index are two such averages for stocks. The Dow-Jones Averages include: (1) the average of 30 industrial stocks; (2) the average of 20 transportation stocks; (3) the average of 15 public utility stocks; and (4) a composite average of the preceding 65 stocks. Standard & Poor's Index covers 500 leading stocks.

Common stocks on the NYSE are averaged so that an investor can tell in dollars and cents how much an average share changed in price on a given day. The Dow-Jones Bond Averages and several others provide information about the behavior of the bond market.

Speculating and Investing

Speculating

Some people think that buying stocks and bonds is a way to get rich quick. They buy on the basis of hot tips. This is called speculative trading. Speculative trading means buying or selling securities in the hope of profiting from near-term future changes in their selling prices.

Sometimes amateur speculators do "strike it rich," but the losers far outnumber the winners. Speculating is most popular during a *bull market,* when stock prices as a whole are rising and there is a great deal of optimism among speculators. Speculating is less popular in a *bear market,* when stock prices as a whole are falling and there is a great deal of pessimism among speculators.

Margin Trading

A speculator has to pay cash for securities bought only when the margin requirement is 100 percent. Otherwise, the speculator buys partly on credit.

margin trading

Margin trading enables speculators to buy more shares for a given amount of money because they are buying partly on credit. Brokers put up the shares they sell on margin as collateral for the loans they make from banks to finance their clients' margin purchases. As long as the price of a stock bought on margin rises, there is no problem. The banker's collateral increases in value. But if its price falls, the banker wants more cash from the broker or wants to sell the shares.

In the 1920s many speculators were buying on 10 percent margin. When stock prices began falling, bankers started selling, in large volume, the stocks they held as collateral. This helped to bring on the eventual collapse of the stock market.

Short Selling

Speculators may also make a profit from selling stocks when prices are falling. Martha Todd, an established client of Broker B, believes that the selling price of GM common stock will fall in the next few weeks. It is now selling at 65. Martha does not own any GM stock but "borrows" several shares from her broker. Many investors do not take possession of the stock certificates they own. They let their brokers keep them for them. Thus brokers can "lend" some of this stock to their other clients.

short selling

Martha tells her broker to sell 500 of these borrowed shares at 65. If the price subsequently falls, Martha buys the shares to "cover" her earlier sale. She buys in, say, at 55. She thus makes a $10 profit on each of the 500 shares (less commission). But if the price went up instead of down, Martha would have incurred a loss. This practice is called short selling. **Short selling means selling a security that you do not own by borrowing it from your broker. At some time in the future, you must buy the security to "cover" the short sale.**

Investing

Unlike a speculator, an investor invests in securities for the longer haul. Before even considering investing, much less speculating, you should have a cushion of cash reserves and adequate insurance. You should be able to choose when you want to sell your shares and not be forced to sell them because you need cash for an emergency.

Your approach to buying and selling securities should be logical. Your investment goals should guide your buying and selling decisions. The kinds of goals may vary among investors but each investor should have definite goals.

An important goal for investors is to protect their invested dollars. You could do this by putting your money in a safe deposit box. But this earns nothing and, because of inflation, the buying power of those dollars declines. You would be wiser to put your money in an insured savings account. You might also buy U.S. government bonds. All those are highly liquid investments. They can be quickly converted into cash. Furthermore, they are very safe investments. In fact, they involve almost no risk at all. But to increase your earning potential, you will have to make riskier investments.

How Much Risk?

Of course, different investment strategies involve different degrees of risk. Investing in preferred stocks of established and profitable corporations is less risky, for example, than investing in common stocks of new ventures. But in terms of return, the new venture might prove to be the better investment. In other words, risk and return tend to be inversely related.

There is no one answer to the question of how much risk you should assume in your investment program. You have to consider your financial situation, age, investment goals, patience, self-discipline, etc. To put it simply, if your goal is to get rich quick, you will have to take a lot more risk than someone else whose goal is to get rich more slowly.

Balancing Objectives

The typical investor wants a safe investment that will return regular earnings and has a lot of potential for future growth. But it's hard to satisfy all three objectives.

Investing in securities involves keeping up with developments in the economy and in the industries and firms in which you invest. If you don't have the time or "know-how" to do this, you might invest in a mutual fund. **The owners of a mutual fund pool their investment dollars and buy securities in other businesses. Buying one share in a mutual fund makes you part owner of all the securities owned by the fund.** You spread your risk over a broad range of securities. Mutual funds are professionally managed. Before they were created, only people with large sums to invest could afford to hire professional managers to oversee their portfolios (the stocks and bonds that they own).

mutual fund

Securities Regulation

Both the issuance of new securities and trading in previously issued securities are regulated by state and federal laws. At the state level, blue-sky laws apply mainly to the sale of new securities. Their purpose is to prevent corporations from issuing securities that have nothing of value to offer the buyer. Issuing corporations must back up securities with something more than just "the blue sky." These laws also generally require the licensing of stockbrokers and the registration of securities before they can be sold.

At the federal level, the Securities Act of 1933 protects the public against interstate sales of fraudulent securities. It is a "truth in securities" law. Issuers of new securities are required to file a detailed registration statement with the Securities and Exchange Commission (SEC) before the securities are offered for sale to the public. This registration statement must disclose all information about the company that might affect the value of its securities, such as earnings, financial condition, and officers' salaries. In addition, every prospective buyer of the securi-

prospectus
ties must be given a prospectus. **A prospectus is a summary of the registration statement that is filed with the SEC. It includes information about the firm, its operations, its management, the purpose of the proposed issue, and any other things that would be helpful to a potential buyer of those securities.**

The Securities and Exchange Commission was established by the Securities Exchange Act of 1934. The SEC is a five-member commission appointed by the President with the consent of the Senate. It has a staff of about 1,500. The Securities Exchange Act requires *all* corporations whose securities are listed on national securities exchanges to file registration statements with the SEC and to file annual reports with the SEC to update their registration statements.

The Securities Exchange Act was amended in 1938 by the Maloney Act, which created a private trade organization, the National Association of Securities Dealers (NASD), to regulate the over-the-counter market. The SEC, however, retains final authority to regulate securities dealers in the over-the-counter market.

The Investment Company Act of 1940 brought the operations of mutual funds under the SEC's jurisdiction. The Securities Investor Protection Act of 1970 established the Securities Investor Protection Insurance Corporation to provide insurance protection to investors who buy securities but leave them with their brokerage houses for safekeeping. It also provides insurance protection to investors who leave cash with their brokerage houses.

The SEC licenses brokerage houses and establishes codes of conduct for them. A person who owns more than 10 percent of a firm's stock must register as an "insider" with the SEC. Such a person must file a report with the SEC if he or she does any trading in that stock. Insiders are not allowed to sell their firm's stock "short." The purpose is to prevent insider manipulation of the stock's selling price.

In recent years the SEC's regulatory power over exchanges has been broadened and the self-regulating authority of the exchanges has been narrowed. The SEC has revised the commission system used by brokerage houses. Fixed brokerage commissions have been replaced by negotiated commissions on both large and small transactions.

The NYSE is also challenging trading in listed stocks off the exchanges. Today many smaller investors as well as big institutional investors want to deal off the exchanges.

The securities exchanges are working on a plan for a single nationwide stock market. In line with this, price and volume data for securities traded on all major exchanges are reported by composite stock tickers.

Despite its broad regulatory powers, however, the SEC does not pass on the relative merits of a given security. The SEC does not guarantee an investor a profit from the purchase and sale of securities.

AN EXPERIMENTAL STOCK EXCHANGE

In 1975 Congress ordered the nation's stock exchanges to work toward a national securities market—a system in which all securities dealers can compete for the public's orders. Accordingly, the Securities and Exchange Commission has authorized several types of experimental exchanges in recent years. One is the fully computerized Cincinnati Stock Exchange (CSE).

> The CSE eliminates the familiar trading floor with its frenzied brokers and specialists confronting each other to buy and sell shares. Instead, there is only the silent glow of cathode-ray tubes quoting the stock prices normally quoted by specialists.
>
> The biggest difference between the CSE and the other exchanges is that the role of the specialist is taken over by the computer, which can even store limit orders—those above or below the prevailing market price—and execute them according to price and time of receipt.

Source: *Business Week.*

Commodity Exchanges

There are also organized markets for commodities (corn, sugar, pork products, copper, silver, wheat, etc.) in the United States and other countries. **Commodity exchanges provide a market for commodities much as securities exchanges provide a market for stocks and bonds. They are voluntary trade associations whose members must follow specified trading rules.** They are regulated by the Commodity Futures

commodity exchanges

Trading Commission (CFTC). The Chicago Board of Trade is the world's largest commodity exchange.

Most commodity exchanges deal only in cash trading. Cash trading involves the actual buying and selling of commodities for delivery. A sales contract may call for immediate delivery or delivery at a specified date in the future. The contract is fulfilled upon delivery.

The larger commodity exchanges also have futures markets. In futures markets, traders buy and sell contracts to receive or deliver a certain quantity and grade of a commodity at a specified future date. Prices are set on the exchange floor by traders. Most futures trading does not result in the physical exchange of goods.

Suppose you expect the price of wheat to go down. You sell a futures contract for wheat you don't actually have. You sell at $3 per bushel. The price goes down to $2.90 and you then buy to "cover" your sale. You make 10 cents per bushel in profit (less commission). But if the price had gone up instead of down, you would have incurred a loss.

Suppose instead that you expect the price to go up. You buy a futures contract in June at $3 per bushel for delivery in October. In July, October futures are selling at $3.25 per bushel. You sell in July at $3.25. Your purchase and sales contracts cancel each other. But you make 25 cents per bushel in profit (less commission). If, however, the price had gone down instead of up, you would have incurred a loss.

Although many people have made fortunes on the commodities exchanges, it is no place for amateurs.

Summary and Look Ahead

The commercial bank is at the heart of our banking system. It is the most important source of short-term funds for business firms. Our commercial banking system creates money in the form of demand deposits. The Federal Reserve System (the Fed) is the central bank of the United States. Its main job is to control the nation's money supply.

In addition to commercial banks, there are many other financial institutions—savings banks, savings and loan associations, trust companies, credit unions, life insurance companies, factoring companies, commercial finance companies, sales finance companies, consumer finance companies, and commercial paper houses.

Important credit instruments used in everyday business are promissory notes and drafts. The need for cash is declining in proportion to the number of transactions. Electronic banking may someday even make ours a "checkless" society.

The public market is made up of the millions of people who invest in corporate securities and the "middlemen" who bring them together for buying and selling. A corporation that issues new stock may use the services of an investment bank to help sell the securities. Brokerage houses buy and sell previously issued securities for their clients.

A speculator looks mainly for short-term profits from buying and selling securities—in some cases (short selling) by selling something he or she does not own. An investor takes a longer view. Speculating is very popular during bull markets and much less popular in bear markets.

Commodities like grain and copper are traded on commodity exchanges such as the Chicago Board of Trade. The cash market involves the actual buying and selling of commodities, whereas most futures trading does not result in the physical exchange of goods.

Just as banks and the commodity exchanges are regulated, so are the securities exchanges, brokerage houses, and stockbrokers. The Securities and Exchange Commission (SEC) has broad regulatory power, but it does not assure any investor of making a profit from trading in securities.

In the next chapter, we will see how businesses use these financial institutions. Our topic there is financial management.

My name is Ginger G. Cooper. I am an assistant banking officer and manager of a branch office of The Citizens and Southern National Bank in Atlanta, Georgia. We have 125 such offices throughout the state.

My interest in a business career began as a result of selling advertisements in our high school yearbook. After graduation I attended college for one year before deciding to join the business world as a staff member of a small bank in my hometown. The excitement and challenge of serving our customers' banking needs and being a part of the financial community inspired me to return to college so that I might have the best possible background to pursue a management-level position in the field of banking. I graduated from Auburn University with a degree in business administration and joined the C & S Bank because I was impressed with its reputation and its position as Georgia's largest banking institution.

After several years' experience in the field of branch banking, I became manager of a retail banking office on the outskirts of downtown. It is my responsibility to see that this branch operates in a smooth and professional manner and meets our goals for production and quality of service. Customer service is

of primary importance to us at C & S, and we work very hard to handle the needs of our customers and the community as we develop new business in our market area.

As a retail branch, our office offers a full range of banking services to the individual. Six staff members work with me in fulfilling our business goals, and I am responsible for the hiring and career development of these people.

We find branch banking provides a great deal of variety, excitement, and satisfaction as we meet the public. I am very satisfied with my career choice and am proud to be a viable part of my community as a representative of The Citizens and Southern National Bank.

Key Concepts

bond A certificate of indebtedness. A written promise to pay made by the borrower (government, business firm, other organization) to its bondholders.

brokerage house A firm that buys and sells securities that previously have been issued by businesses and governments. It buys and sells on behalf of its investor-clients.

commercial bank A privately owned, profit-seeking firm that serves individuals, businesses, and other organizations. Major services are accepting demand deposits and making short-term loans. It also provides many other services such as accepting time deposits, exchanging foreign currency for U.S. currency, and giving financial advice.

commercial finance company A company that helps firms finance their accounts receivable. It may buy a firm's accounts receivable at a discount or lend money on accounts receivable that are pledged as security for a loan. Also makes loans secured by inventory or equipment.

commercial paper house A company that buys commercial paper directly from issuing corporations and resells it to buyers or acts as a middleman who, for a commission, brings the issuing corporation and a buyer together. Com-

mercial paper is a promissory note written by a business firm to obtain short-term working capital from a lender.

commodity exchanges Voluntary trade associations whose members engage in trading commodities. Provide a market for commodities such as copper, pork, cotton, etc.

consumer finance company A company that makes personal loans to individuals, often on a signature basis which involves no collateral. This type of company does not make loans to businesses.

credit union A cooperative savings association that is owned by its depositors who work for the same employer or are members of the same nonbusiness organization. Also makes loans to members.

demand deposit Checking accounts of individuals, businesses, and other organizations.

factoring company Also called a factor. A company that buys accounts receivable from a firm. It pays less than the face value of the accounts (it buys them at a discount) but collects the face value of the accounts from its client's customers. The difference, minus the factor's cost of doing business, is the factor's profit.

Federal Reserve System (the "Fed") A banking

system created by the Federal Reserve Act of 1913 to regulate the nation's money supply. Its 12 Federal Reserve Banks are privately owned, but their operations are controlled by the board of governors of the Federal Reserve System.

investment bank A firm that helps corporations to sell new issues of stocks and bonds. Does not accept deposits from the general public. Also called an underwriting house.

life insurance company A mutual or stock company that shares risk with its policyholders for payment of a premium. A source of long-term funds for some business firms.

margin requirement The percentage that buyers of securities must put up in cash when they buy them. It is set by the board of governors of the Federal Reserve System.

margin trading A person who buys securities partly on credit financed by his or her stockbroker engages in margin trading.

money Anything that people will generally accept in payment of debts. In the United States, coins, paper currency, and checking account balances are considered money.

mutual fund An investment company. The owners of a mutual fund pool their investment dollars and buy securities in other businesses and government securities.

over-the-counter market (OTC) A complex of securities dealers who buy and sell securities for investors without using a securities exchange.

prime rate of interest The lowest rate of interest charged by commercial banks to their most creditworthy borrowers.

promissory note A written promise to pay a certain sum of money (principal and interest) made by a borrower (maker) to a lender (payee) at a certain time in the future.

prospectus A summary of the registration statement that is filed with the Securities and Exchange Commission when a company proposes to issue new securities. It includes information about the firm and the purpose of the proposed issue. It must be made available to prospective buyers before they buy the issuing corporation's securities.

public market Individual and institutional investors who buy stocks and bonds. Also includes the various securities middlemen who bring buyers and sellers of securities together.

reserve requirement The percentage of deposits that member banks of the Federal Reserve System must keep in vault cash or as deposits with their Federal Reserve Banks. It is set by the board of governors of the Federal Reserve System.

sales finance company A firm that specializes in financing installment purchases made by individuals and firms.

savings and loan association An association of depositors who deposit their savings in savings accounts. Accepts deposits from the general public and makes mortgage loans mainly on homes and other real estate.

savings bank A bank that serves small savers by accepting their deposits and paying them interest on their savings.

securities exchanges Places where buyers and sellers of securities deal with each other through members of the exchanges. The exchanges are set up by brokerage houses to reduce the cost and increase the efficiency of financial investment.

short selling The selling of a security that a person does not own by borrowing it from his or her broker. At some time in the future, the person must buy the security to "cover" the short sale.

time deposit A deposit that is made for a period of time. Savings accounts and certificates of deposit are examples. Interest is usually paid on a time deposit.

trade acceptance A draft (order to pay) from a seller that has been signed (accepted) by a buyer.

trade draft A draft (order to pay) prepared by the seller of merchandise that orders the buyer to pay a certain amount of money for the merchandise.

trust company A company that safeguards funds and estates entrusted to it. Also may serve as trustee, transfer agent, and registrar for corporations.

For Review . . .

1. Contrast: *(a)* a factoring company and a commercial finance company and *(b)* a sales finance company and a consumer finance company.
2. Explain how the commercial banking system creates money.
3. Suppose the Fed wants to stimulate business activity. What should it do regarding: *(a)* the purchase or sale of government securities; *(b)* the discount rate; and *(c)* the reserve requirement?
4. What is the major difference between a promissory note and a draft?
5. Explain why business firms sometimes use cashier's checks.
6. List and define three different concepts of "value" for common stock.
7. What is the purpose of *(a)* a stock split; *(b)* a stock dividend; and *(c)* a cash dividend?
8. What is a brokerage house?
9. What is the purpose of a stock exchange?
10. How do listed securities differ from unlisted securities?
11. What is a stockbroker?
12. Is speculation more likely to exist during a bear market or a bull market? Explain.
13. What is a mutual fund? Explain how it works.
14. Does the Securities and Exchange Commission guarantee the value of a corporation's stocks and bonds to investors? Explain.
15. What is the purpose of a commodity exchange?

. . . For Discussion

1. Federal Reserve Banks often are referred to as "banker's banks." Why?
2. Why might a bond's market value (selling price) be above its face value (redemption price)?
3. Why might a small retailer sell its accounts receivable to a factoring company?
4. How do commercial paper houses help to increase the efficiency of short-term financing by large firms?
5. Why do speculators engage in margin trading and short selling?

Incidents

A Big Cash Buildup

In the spring of 1978 the biggest corporations in the United States had about $80 billion of cash on hand. Business people lacked confidence in the economic outlook and were not anxious to make long-run investments in new plant and equipment.

"Some cash-rich companies have peculiar problems that hamper their ability to spend. The business investments of giant International Business Machines Corp., which has about $5 billion in cash, are restricted by antitrust considerations. That company has so far confined its investments largely to government securities. Westinghouse Electric Corp. is hanging on to much of its $671 million in anticipation of settling $2 billion worth of uranium contract disputes."

Questions

1. Explain how a commercial paper house helps corporate borrowers to secure short-term financing and helps lenders to find an attractive rate of interest on the extra cash they have on hand.
2. What actions would you recommend to the Federal Reserve Board in order to help increase the confidence of business people in the economy's future?

Source: *Business Week.*

Big Boom in Gambling Stocks

"[During the spring and summer of 1978, a gambling stock boom got underway on the New York Stock Exchange and the American Stock Exchange.] The prime mover was Resorts International, which set off the gambling stock boom by opening the first . . . casino in Atlantic City, N.J., in May 1978. . . .

"Resorts' Class A stock rose $13 in four days on the American Exchange, closing at a high of $123.50. That was a 560% increase since Jan. 1. Not bad for a company that [had] never paid a cash dividend. . . . Some others, with their rises from April through August [1978]: Caesars World, 583%; Playboy, 351%; Bally, 283%; Del Webb, 281%; and Harrah's, 213%.

". . . [T]he speculation turned even wilder (in August, 1978) after a bullish report by Merrill Lynch cited the gambling industry's 'potential to be one of the high growth segments of the economy during the next five years.'

"Finally the exchanges moved, lifting the initial margin requirements for gambling issues from 50% to 75%—meaning that buyers would have to put up at least $750 for every $1,000 stock purchase. The Big Board said it was acting 'to insure the protection of public investors and the maintenance of a fair and orderly market.'"

Questions

1. Do you think the people who participated in this bull market were basically speculators or investors? Explain.
2. In what ways do speculators and investors differ?
3. Why do you think the NYSE and the AMEX raised the margin requirement on gambling stocks?

Source: *Time.*

Financial Decisions and Insurance

CHAPTER 11

Objectives: After reading this chapter, you should be able to

1. Identify the three principal duties of a financial manager.
2. Demonstrate a case in which a manager balances the twin objectives of liquidity and profit in the use of working capital.
3. Draw a chart showing the normal flows of working capital in a manufacturing firm.
4. Explain the relationship between technology and fixed capital needs.
5. Illustrate the use of two major sources of short-term credit—trade credit and commercial bank loans.
6. Contrast the advantages of issuing bonds with the advantages of issuing preferred stock for getting long-term funds.
7. List four kinds of risks that can be reduced by good management techniques.
8. Distinguish between pure and speculative risk.
9. Show how the law of large numbers is used to figure insurance premiums.
10. Demonstrate the principle of coinsurance.
11. Contrast the procedures of voluntary and involuntary bankruptcy.

Key concepts: Look for these terms as you read the chapter

working (short-term) capital	pure risks
liquidity	speculative risks
opportunity costs	law of large numbers
long-term capital	insurable risks
capital budget	insurable interest
lease	property and casualty
debt financing	insurance
equity financing	principle of indemnity
maturity	life insurance
trade credit	merger
line of credit	amalgamation
revolving credit	holding company
secured loans	recapitalization
floor planning	reorganization
sinking fund	bankruptcy
self-insurance	

In the two previous chapters we studied the communications devices of accounting and the financial institutions available to financial managers. In this chapter we'll see how a manager uses the services of commercial banks, stockbrokers, and insurance companies in managing the firm's financial affairs. Accounting systems provide the basis for most of these financial decisions.

The Financial Manager and Financial Planning

Financial decisions are made by the financial manager (who may be called the comptroller or the vice-president for finance). This executive projects the firm's long- and short-term financial needs and meets them with the help of banks and others. He or she is the chief guardian of the owners' equity. The financial manager's job is to get the best return on the owners' investment without taking unnecessary risks.

Company presidents may include noneconomic or social objectives in their decision making, but financial managers must think of dollars and profit. Financial managers specialize in funds and their allocation. They help to provide the president of a firm with a purely economic, profit-maximizing point of view.

A financial manager's responsibilities are

- to identify and satisfy the firm's short term (working) capital and long-term capital needs in the face of uncertainty
- to evaluate and select from alternative sources of funds
- to manage risk while maximizing the firm's return on assets

Uses of Funds

As we have seen, there are two basic financial needs, each with its special characteristics. These needs are for working capital and long-term capital. We need to understand these uses of funds more completely, starting with the uses of working capital.

Working Capital

Working capital is a term applied to a firm's investment in short-term assets, the current assets we discussed in Chapter 9. It includes those assets that flow regularly in the day-to-day operations of a firm—cash, accounts receivable, and inventories (see Figure 11–1, where flows are identified by the numbers in parentheses). The complete flow pattern of

working capital

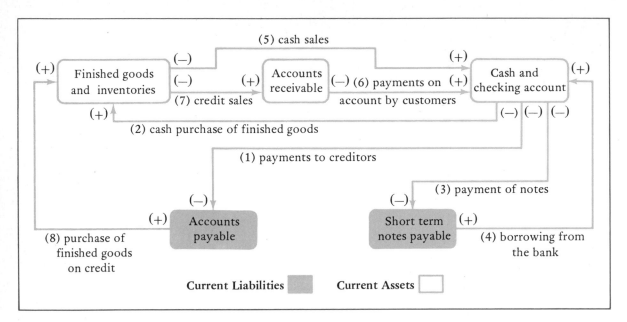

FIGURE 11-1

Flows of working capital. Notice that decreases in liabilities (–) are accompanied by decreases in assets (–) and increases in liabilities (+) are accompanied by increases in assets (+).

working capital includes two current liabilities: accounts payable and short-term notes payable (usually payable to a commercial bank).

Cash and checking accounts are reduced by

(1) payments to creditors

(2) cash purchase of finished goods

(3) payments of notes to bank

and increased by

(4) borrowing from the bank

(5) cash sales

(6) payments on account by customers

Accounts receivable are increased by

(7) credit sales

and decreased by

(6) payments on account by customers

Finished goods inventory is increased by

(2) cash purchase of finished goods

(8) purchase of finished goods on credit (if this were a manufacturing firm, finished goods inventory would also increase from internal processing of materials)

and decreased by

(5) cash sales

(7) credit sales

Accounts payable are decreased by

   (1) payments to creditors

and increased by

   (8) purchase of finished goods on credit

Short-term notes payable are increased by

   (4) borrowing from the bank

and decreased by

   (3) payment of notes to bank

This is a simplified version of the working capital flow because there are other inventories besides finished goods, especially when manufacturing processes are involved.

To compute net working capital we deduct the balance of current liabilities from the gross working capital (total current assets). Working capital must be handled carefully by the financial manager so as not to interrupt or slow the regular operations of the business. **The firm needs to have enough cash coming in to meet bills, wages, and other current payments. This ability to make payments that are due is the test of a firm's liquidity.** If the Mangham Feed Store has a payroll of $800 due next Monday as well as a repair bill of $500 due on the same day, the manager must examine Mangham's liquidity. If the firm has only $200 in its checking account and expects no significant cash inflow before Monday, some borrowing may be in order, maybe from the bank. If Mangham borrows $1,500 from the bank, the firm increases its gross working capital, but its net working capital stays the same because it has created a new current debt, a note payable to the bank. The firm could have found some temporary cash in other ways, as we will see.

The financial manager seeks to balance liquidity with profit. The goal is to minimize idle cash balances by keeping "near cash" on hand. This means earning assets or investments that pay interest to the firm, but that are also easy to "cash in" when needed. Examples are certificates of deposit (CDs) in banks or short-term government securities such as Treasury bills. Tying up cash in long-term investments such as bonds of another firm does not meet the goal of balancing liquidity with profit because these bonds might not be convertible into cash quickly or might involve some loss owing to changes in their market value.

Credit sales represent another use of short-term funds. A firm that sells "on credit" uses its funds to finance its customers' operations. The credit manager and the sales manager often disagree on credit policies. The sales manager sees this as a means of increasing sales. The credit manager sees it as a waste of working capital and maybe as a source of losses if credit customers fail to pay debts.

liquidity

IS CONSUMER DEBT TOO LARGE?

Although many economists and social observers seem to think that consumer credit is out of hand, the facts in the graph below suggest that consumer credit managers are, in the long run, setting credit policy and making credit decisions that are warranted. A sensible measure of the safety of consumer debt burden is the ratio of consumer debt repayments to after-tax income. The graph indicates that this ratio has remained nearly constant at 20 percent from 1963 to 1978. In other words, the average American consumer since 1963 has had to pay one fifth of his or her income to meet current debts—mostly home mortgage payments and installment purchases. This constant percentage also suggests that the American people themselves are practicing some restraint in credit buying.

Debt-burden barometer
(consumer debt repayments as a percentage of after-tax income)

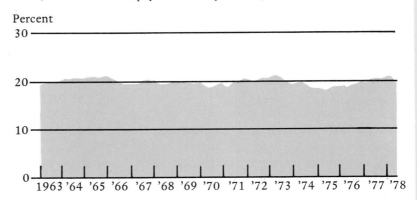

Source: *The Wall Street Journal.*

The financial manager seeks to achieve a balance. The firm wants profits to increase if more working capital must be tied up in accounts receivable. If the increase in receivables results from purchases by proven paying customers, profits will increase. The Mangham Feed Store may be wise to avoid selling on credit to a young farmer whose farm is poorly managed. Even if the debt will be repaid, it might take a long time to collect—tying up valuable working capital. The financial manager uses Dun and Bradstreet or other credit reporting services to judge possible credit customers. An example of a credit report is presented in Figure 11–2. It provides many financial facts about the customer to help measure the risk of selling to Arnold Metal Products.

© *Dun & Bradstreet, Inc.*

| BE SURE NAME, BUSINESS AND ADDRESS MATCH YOUR FILE | ANSWERING INQUIRY | This report has been prepared for: SUBSCRIBER: 008-001042 |

THIS REPORT MAY NOT BE REPRODUCED IN WHOLE OR IN PART IN ANY MANNER WHATEVER.

FULL REVISION

FULL REVISION

D-U-N-S NO. 04-426-3226   APR 21 197-   SUMMARY
ARNOLD METAL PRODUCTS CO.   RATING   DD1
                           METAL STAMPINGS
53 S MAIN ST   STARTED   1957
DAWSON MICH 49666   SIC NOS   PAYMENTS DISC-PPT
    TEL 215 999-0000   34 69   SALES $177,250
                                                     WORTH $ 42,961
                                                     EMPLOYS   10
    SAMUEL B. ARNOLD, PARTNER   HISTORY   CLEAR
                                                     CONDITION STRONG
                                                     TREND   UP

PAYMENTS   (Amounts may be rounded to nearest figure in prescribed ranges)
AS OF   PAYING   HIGH   NOW   PAST   SELLING   LAST SALE
         RECORD   CREDIT   OWES   DUE   TERMS   WITHIN
01/7-   Disc   3000   1500   -0-   1 10 30   2-3 Mos
02/7-   Disc-Ppt   2500   1000   -0-   1 10 30   4-5 Mos
03/7-   Disc-Ppt   2000   500   -0-   2 20 30   6-12 Mos
03/7-   Disc   800   400   -0-   1 10 30   1 Mo

FINANCE   On Apr 21 197- S. B. Arnold, President, submitted the following statement dated
         Dec 31 197-
         Cash $ 4,870   Accts Pay $ 6,121
         Accts Rec   15,472   Notes Pay (Curr)   2,400
         Mdse   14,619   Accruals   3,583
                      -----------   -----------
             Current   34,961   Current   12,104
         Fixt & Equip (4,183) 22,840   Notes Pay (Def)   5,000
         CSV of Life Ins 2,264   NET WORTH   42,961
                      -----------   -----------
             Total Assets 60,065   Total   60,065
         Annual sales $177,250; gross profit $47,821; net income $8,204.
         Fire insurance mdse $15,000; fixt $20,000. Annual rent $5,000.
         Signed Apr 21 197- ARNOLD METAL PRODUCTS CO by Samuel B. Arnold, President.
                           --0--
             New equipment purchased last Sep was financed by bank loan. Monthly payments
         on loan are $200.
             Arnold reported sales for the three months ended Mar 31 were up 10% compared
         with the same period last year. Increase was attributed by management to addi-
         tional capacity provided by new equipment.
             Profit is being made and retained resulting in an increase in net worth. Cur-
         rent debt is light in relation to worth. Inventory turnover is rapid.

BANKING   Balances average high four figures. Loans granted to low five figures, secured
02/7-   by equipment, now owing high four figures. Relations satisfactory.

HISTORY SAMUEL B. ARNOLD, PARTNER   GEORGE T. ARNOLD, PARTNER
             Style registered Feb 1, 1965 by partners.
             S. ARNOLD, born 1918, married, 1939 graduate of Lehigh University, 1939-50 em-
         ployed by Industrial Machine Corporation, Detroit, and 1950-56 production manager
         with Aerial Motors Inc, Detroit. Started this business in 1957.
             G. ARNOLD, born 1940, single, son of Samuel. Graduated in 1963, Dawson Insti-
         tute of Technology. Served U.S. Air Force 1963-64. Admitted to partnership Feb 1965.

OPERATION   Manufactures perforated metal stampings for industrial concerns. Sells on net
         30 day terms. Has twelve accounts. Territory greater Detroit area. EMPLOYEES: Ten
         including partners.
         LOCATION: Rents 5,000 square feet in one story cinder block building in normal con-
         dition. Located in central business section of main street. Premises neat.

         04-21 (980   /1   )5842/02   1 051
         First National Bank, 80 S. Main St., Dawson, Mich.

THIS REPORT, FURNISHED PURSUANT TO CONTRACT FOR THE EXCLUSIVE USE OF THE SUBSCRIBER AS ONE FACTOR TO CONSIDER IN CONNECTION WITH CREDIT, INSURANCE, MARKETING OR OTHER BUSINESS DECISIONS, CONTAINS INFORMATION COMPILED FROM SOURCES WHICH DUN & BRADSTREET, INC. DOES NOT CONTROL AND WHOSE INFORMATION, UNLESS OTHERWISE INDICATED IN THE REPORT, HAS NOT BEEN VERIFIED. IN FURNISHING THIS REPORT, DUN & BRADSTREET, INC. IN NO WAY ASSUMES ANY PART OF THE USER'S BUSINESS RISK, DOES NOT GUARANTEE THE ACCURACY, COMPLETENESS, OR TIMELINESS OF THE INFORMATION PROVIDED, AND SHALL NOT BE LIABLE FOR ANY LOSS OR INJURY WHATEVER RESULTING FROM CONTINGENCIES BEYOND ITS CONTROL OR FROM NEGLIGENCE.
9 R2-3 (741212)

FIGURE 11-2

A credit report

Source: *Dun & Bradstreet, Inc.*

Another current asset shown in Figure 11–1 is the inventory of finished goods. Raw materials are changed into finished goods through the production process. Between these two stages, they are called goods in process. The financial manager seeks to reduce excess inventories at all three stages. There may be a conflict with the production manager, who wants to keep large inventories of inputs so as to keep the production line running smoothly.

Suppose that the sales manager of the Wonder Mattress Corp. forecasts a 10 percent increase in sales during the next year. The production manager bases estimates of raw materials needs on this sales forecast. Now, suppose further that the purchasing agent can receive a 12 percent discount if the order of raw materials is increased by 20 percent rather than by 10 percent. Should the financial manager approve this use of funds to earn the additional discount?

This depends on whether the Wonder Mattress Corp. could use the additional funds tied up in raw materials more profitably elsewhere. If the raw material is perishable or if storing it would be costly, the larger order would probably not be approved. On the other hand, if the price of raw materials is expected to rise, the manager would probably approve the larger order. The value of a systems approach to decision making is clear here. Better decisions are made when finance, marketing, and production are viewed in terms of their overall goal of helping to increase the firm's profit.

Still another use of working capital involves the current asset "prepaid expenses." You can buy a three-year fire insurance policy on your home, for example. Paying the three-year premium in one lump sum means that you are prepaying your insurance coverage. The same is true for a firm.

A financial manager carefully evaluates the option to pay insurance premiums in advance. The choice depends on the other uses that could be made of those funds. Prepaying expenses is wise when the savings exceed the opportunity costs. **Opportunity costs are costs of losing the option to use the funds in another way.** Let's assume that for the Sanford Ice Cream Company the savings from paying a lump sum for three years of fire insurance coverage, rather than paying on a year-to-year basis, amounts to $100. Assume further that Sanford's comptroller could have earned $150 of interest on the prepaid part of the expense during the last two years of the policy life. Clearly, the comptroller would not prepay in this case. The current (and expected) interest rate is a major factor in making all such financial decisions because it helps to determine what unused dollars can earn.

A manager should have an overview of the flow of working capital such as we saw in Figure 11–1. He or she must understand this flow and the timing of it from one use to another. If the firm has a good sales forecast and a good collection policy, it can achieve the goal of providing enough working capital but not too much.

opportunity costs

Long-term Capital

long-term capital

Long-term capital is the firm's investment in fixed assets. Such capital is committed for at least one year (usually much longer), and it requires a different perspective. The amounts are larger and the risk is greater. A big mistake could cause the firm to fail.

Long-term capital is invested in land, buildings, heavy machinery, and other fixed assets that, to a large extent, determine the direction in which the firm is going. When RCA went into the computer business, it directed a large part of its long-term capital into assets that could not be sold without loss. RCA management assumed that such an investment would be profitable. This decision proved to be wrong, and RCA later sold its computer holdings at a loss of millions of dollars. Ford had a similar experience with the Edsel. Auto makers in the 1970s had to decide how much production capacity to convert to subcompact cars. General Motors, for example, invested $2.7 billion to develop the Chevrolet Citation, the Buick Skylark, the Oldsmobile Omega, and the Pontiac Phoenix.

Financial managers must take a long-run view of the firm's operations. They use some of the accounting devices referred to in Chapter 9. **One is the capital budget. This projects the expected need for fixed assets for a period of five to ten years.** This long planning period means that budget makers must use every scrap of information about the long-range plans and expectations of the firm. They must take the environment into account, too. This includes technological events outside the firm and changes in consumer needs and tastes that might require changes in plant machinery and equipment.

capital budget

Technology is especially hard to predict. It is difficult to say when a competitor might come up with a product or a process that makes your own obsolete. For firms that sell a standard product such planning may depend only on a forecast of sales. The Parker Nail Co. (see Figure 11–3) prepared its sales forecast primarily from government projections for the home construction industry in its market area and from knowledge of competitive behavior and costs.

Some steel producers have plants that are nearly obsolete because of recent developments in production technology. Yet these firms must

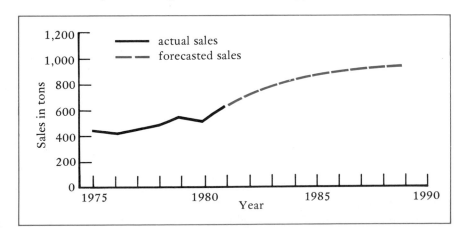

FIGURE 11-3

A sales forecast for the Parker Nail Co.

compete with foreign steel producers whose plants, in many cases, are newer and use the latest equipment and techniques. The capital budgeting problem in this case is to find sources of funds to enable the firm to update plant and equipment.

Consider the great technological change that has occurred in the airline industry. The propeller-driven airplane has been replaced by jets. An airline must face the possibility that even recently bought planes will soon become obsolete. If they do, a decision must be made whether or not to replace them and, if so, with what. Some airlines did not place orders for the Boeing 747 for some time after it was introduced. Fuel costs have since caused some airlines to reduce or stop their use. Meanwhile, the airplane manufacturers are spending large sums to develop more fuel-efficient planes. The demand for individual high-technology products is not easy to predict.

Each capital investment decision depends on the expected payoff. Such decisions call for expert planning in the use of long-term capital. In some cases firms will avoid the risk of long-term asset purchase by resorting to leasing.

The Alternative of Leasing

lease

One way of avoiding the need for long-term financing for land, buildings, or equipment is to lease them. **A lease is an agreement to grant use of an asset for a period of time in return for stated regular payments.** Leasing such assets has several advantages over borrowing funds for their purchase:

- It reduces the outstanding debt of the firm.
- Leased equipment may be replaced with more modern equipment without the losses that result from replacement of owned equipment.
- It is often a tax advantage to lease because the entire lease payment is tax deductible.
- A lease is usually a known, predictable cost factor, and, in a sense, is an aid in financial planning.

The decision to lease, however, is not always so obvious. There are advantages to outright ownership. Often the cash payments on a lease are considerably higher than the equivalent financed purchase payments. Also there are often restrictions on the way a firm might use or modify leased assets. Such restrictions don't apply to owned equipment.

A bank or a manufacturer often leases computer equipment instead of buying it. Such leasing can be viewed as a "source of long-term funds" rather than as an alternative to borrowing. In other words, what might have required a large part of a firm's long-term borrowing capacity is not needed, and other long-term projects can be considered.

Evaluating and Selecting Sources of Funds

Once a financial manager determines the needs for short- and long-term funds, the question is "who will provide them?" For some firms there is little choice. For most, however, there is some choice of sources of funds. The basic choice is between debt financing and equity financing.

Debt financing is the use of borrowed funds. This could mean a major corporation issuing bonds or it could mean a barber shop borrowing $1,000 for 60 days from a local bank.

debt financing

Equity financing means the provision of funds by the owners themselves. This could involve issuing stock or using retained profits. U.S. nonfinancial corporations since 1970 have used somewhat more equity financing than debt financing. Debt to equity ratios, however, have been on the rise.

equity financing

Criteria for Evaluation of Sources

There are several important features of financing that help a firm decide between the use of debt and equity. These are shown in Figure 11–4. **Maturity is the factor of time of repayment. When a debt matures, it must be paid.** If funds are internal, they need not be repaid at all. If they are borrowed, the date of maturity (due date) may vary.

maturity

Equity and debt financing also differ in the way they affect the claims on assets and earnings. To issue bonds means that the new bondholders will get the designated interest payment before stockholders get any dividends. They have a prior claim on income. Bondholders also come first in the event that the firm goes out of business. They are paid off out of the proceeds of the sale of the firm's assets before stockholders receive anything.

Still another factor in the choice of debt or equity capital relates to control of the corporation. If a firm issues more common stock and this stock is bought by newcomers to the firm, the original common stockholders may lose control over the election of the firm's board of directors. They might lose some influence over policy decisions. A bond sale would not run such a risk for the controlling shareholders.

Of course, the main reason businesses borrow in the first place is that they feel they can earn a higher return on borrowed dollars than the cost or interest they must pay to their lenders. To improve earnings by borrowing is called *leverage*.

Financial markets also play a role when a firm seeks new sources of capital. Sometimes there is a lot of money available to lend and sometimes there is not. The final selection is often a compromise between what management would like most and what suppliers of capital are willing to give.

FIGURE 11-4

Comparing debt and equity financing

A large firm that pays its bills on time and has a high current ratio is in the best position for selecting from among financing sources. Small firms may overcome the advantage of larger firms by building a good credit record and practicing good money management.

Sources of Short-term Funds

Funds sources differ depending upon the length of time for which the funds are needed. When the need is for the short term, usually one year or less, it is generally in order to supply current asset needs such as cash, accounts receivable, and inventories. However, some of these current asset needs represent a predictable minimum amount—what the firm *knows* it will always need. (See Figure 11–5.) This means that much of this part of current asset needs can be supplied from the same long-term sources that serve fixed asset needs. These sources will be discussed in the next section.

The variable current asset needs are partly of a seasonal nature and partly just plain unpredictable. All of these variable short-term needs and some of the "fixed" current assets needs can be met from three principal sources:

- trade credit (open book account)
- commercial bank loans
- secured loans made by a variety of lenders

Trade Credit

Trade credit or "open book account" differs from other types of short-term credit because no financial institution is directly involved. It is simply credit extended by sellers to buyers. To the seller trade credit means accounts receivable. To the buyer it means accounts payable. When one firm (manufacturer, wholesaler, retailer) buys materials or

trade credit

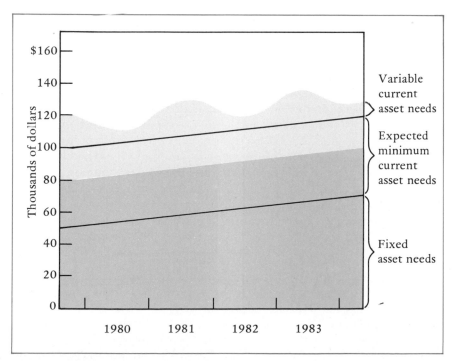

FIGURE 11-5

Asset needs and their financing by source

merchandise from another, the transaction is handled in open book accounts. There are no complex credit papers. The buyer records a new account payable. The seller makes an entry showing a new account receivable. Nearly 90 percent of sales are handled that way.

In effect, the seller "lends" the buyer money for the time between receipt of the goods and payment for them. Without this type of credit, many firms could not survive. The same type of credit exists between the consumer and the retailer. When you "charge" the purchase of a TV on your account, the seller is really lending you money for a while. Instead of calling this an open book account, most people call it a charge account.

Most trade credit involves cash discounts for early payments. Invoice terms of "2/10, net/30" mean that the buyer can deduct 2 percent of the invoice price if paid within 10 days; otherwise it is due in 30 days. In other words, the buyer is "giving up" the use of the seller's money for 20 days in exchange for a 2 percent discount. This is equal to an annual rate of 36 percent. (There are eighteen 20-day periods in a year and $18 \times 2\% = 36\%$.) Thus many firms will often borrow from their banks at rates as high as twelve percent per annum in order to take advantage of cash discounts.

Commercial Banks

The commercial bank, as we saw in Chapter 10, accepts time and demand deposits and lends a part of these funds to businesses for their short-term commercial needs. Commercial banks are the most popular credit source among smaller business borrowers.

Depending on the current balance between the demand and supply of commercial credit, bankers will adjust standards for lending. When money is short, bankers are likely to become more careful about those to whom they lend money. In any case, a bank will always check a new borrower's past credit record and ability to manage. The banker will screen loan applications also on a basis of the current ratio of the firm as well as on the basis of some of the other key credit ratios. The bank loan officer may obtain a credit report such as the one presented in Figure 11–2.

A banker expects that the loan will be repaid normally out of seasonal declines of inventories and accounts receivable held by the borrower. The bank and borrower must agree on four principal terms of a commercial loan:

- the general nature of the arrangement
- the interest rate
- the quantity and type of security (if any)
- the repayment date

Firms that have a continuing need for funds from the bank often use a line of credit or revolving loans. **When a line of credit is set, the bank stands ready to lend up to this amount to the borrower with some restrictions.**

line of credit

    A revolving credit agreement, on the other hand, is a very formal and specific agreement that guarantees funds for a period of time with strict rules limiting the borrower.

revolving credit

THINK ABOUT IT!

Borrowing to Save Money

When this business manager bought supplies from Acme Paper Co., they sent a bill for $1,000 with terms of 2/10, net/30. He had the choice of paying $980 by June 10 or the full amount by July 1.

    Since he had no spare cash, he went to the Friendly National Bank and talked to the vice-president. She offered him a loan of $980 for 20 days at an annual interest rate of 10 percent. Total interest cost was only $5.44 ($\frac{20}{360} \times 10\% \times \$980 = \$5.44$). He saved $14.56 as follows by borrowing from the bank to pay the bill early:

Bill saving	$20.00
− Bank interest	5.44
Net Saving	$14.56

An important new source of short-term credit is the commercial paper house referred to in the previous chapter. This middleman finds buyers for the notes of issuing companies. Buyers could be insurance companies or pension funds, for example.

Secured Loans

secured loans

Many commercial loans to smaller firms and to firms with lower credit ratings are "secured" loans. Here, the lender is protected by a pledge of the borrower's assets. Secured loans also may be arranged by firms that have reasonably good credit records and wish to borrow unusually large sums or want favorable interest rates. Items pledged as security for loans may include accounts receivable, inventories, equipment, or stocks.

floor planning

A special kind of secured financing is called floor planning. An auto dealer who gets a shipment of new cars signs a note to a bank or other financing agency for the amount due. Title passes to the lender, who pays the bill. A trust receipt serves as a substitute for the actual asset. The bank holds the trust receipt for the cars until they are sold and the loans are paid.

Commercial banks are also the major institutions involved in the use of the other credit instruments described in Chapter 10—promissory notes, drafts, acceptances, and certified checks.

Other lending institutions that are used by firms for short-term financing include factors, commercial finance companies, and sales finance companies.

Sources of Long-term Funds

The sources available to corporations for long-term funds are much more numerous than the sources available to partnerships and sole proprietors. But in all cases, there is some choice between internal (equity) and external (debt) financing.

Sources for Corporations

Corporate long-term capital is available in the public market by means of stock issues and bond issues. As we have seen, there are several types of stock and several types of bonds. Issuing preferred stock is a source of growth funds for corporations with stable earnings. Common stock is more likely to be issued when good growth is expected but earnings are considered to be unpredictable. The "new" common stockholder, or shareholder, joins the "old" common stockholder on an equal footing. Depending on the relative size of "old" and "new" common stockholdings, the "old" shareholders may risk loss of or reduction in their control over the firm's affairs.

A corporation that needs additional debt financing for the long run may issue bonds. Firms have an implied right to borrow as long as it is done for the company's benefit.

A major decision in a bond issue is selecting a method to pay off bondholders. The most attractive way for a strong, growing firm is by debt replacement—relying on the ability of the firm to exchange maturing bonds for new bonds or for stock. **In other cases, firms set up a sinking fund to retire maturing bonds. This means putting aside money each year from profits to pay them off.** This is more likely to be done in a firm that is not expanding or that might find this investor protection feature the only way to attract bond investors. Also, using a sinking fund will bring the interest rate on the bonds down.

A profitable firm has the option of using profits to pay dividends or to "plow back" into operations. Plowing it back permits fixed asset growth without the use of money markets. It is a form of equity financing.

Common shareholders may or may not favor such financing, depending on their investment goals. Investors who view their shares as "growth stock" expect it to appreciate over the long run. They don't demand immediate dividends. Others invest for immediate income. They prefer to receive regular (and large) dividend checks rather than have profits stay in the business.

Conflict often exists among shareholders concerning the "dividend versus retained earnings" policy. Managers and shareholders may conflict on this point, too, unless managers are also shareholders. The availability of large amounts of capital is usually more attractive to managers than it is to shareholders. Retained earnings (a form of equity financing) has no maturity date and does not dilute managerial control as common

TWO POINTS OF VIEW

Stockholders Often Disagree

Stockholder A

"Right, we will have to build a new production plant in the southern region in the next couple of years. But the important thing is to finance it by issuing a new block of common stock. We've already got a pretty heavy load of bonds outstanding, and retained earnings just have not been large enough. Besides, if we put all of our earnings into expansion, we won't be able to pay a decent dividend."

Stockholder B

"You're all wrong, buddy. Plant expansion should be financed by issuing $5 million worth of debenture bonds. That way, the chances are that common stockholders like you and me will be able to gain greater returns in the long run. The profits from the new plant will far exceed the cost of servicing the debt. This multiplies our earning power. It gives us leverage. Besides, to issue additional stock will dilute our control of the corporation. Let's use somebody else's money to grow. So what if current dividends will be smaller than usual. I can wait."

stock does. Like common stock, retained earnings place no prior claim on income or assets. Financial managers are attracted to retained earnings as a source because they are not subject to the evaluation of the marketplace in their use of such funds.

Another outside source that has been available for long-term funds in recent years is insurance companies. Such companies have huge reserves to invest. They make these funds available, especially to large corporations, for long-term expansion at rates similar to or somewhat lower than those paid to bondholders.

Sources for Noncorporate Firms

Sole proprietorships depend on the personal funding of the owner-manager for equity financing. Partnerships have the same limitation except that there are two or more partners who may contribute fixed capital.

All forms of ownership may generate new funds internally if the firm succeeds. The amount available, in part, depends on the amount of retained earnings. In addition, the amount charged for depreciation of assets is "available" for current or long-term financing because, although depreciation reduces net profit, this value has not actually left the firm in the short run. Depreciation is not the same as a current expenditure.

Equity capital is available for an indefinite period of time and has a subordinate (after creditors) claim on the firm's earnings and assets. It can lead to dilution of control of the present owners if a new partner is added.

Risk Management

Owning and using resources lead to risks of many kinds. Risk is the possibility of loss. To protect these resources and to deal with these risks is the third major task of a financial manager.

Kinds of Risks

There are risks in everything and the degree of risk may vary greatly. In lending money, we risk loss. In buying things, we risk the possibility of defective merchandise. In running a factory, we risk liability for accidents to employees or visitors. In owning buildings and cars, we run risks of fire, vandalism, and theft. We risk that secret processes or designs will be discovered, and we risk the death of corporate officers. All of these threaten the firm's resources and must be dealt with if the firm is to survive and prosper.

Self-insurance and Risk Avoidance

There are three basic approaches to dealing with risk. They can be used in combination. One is to assume risk yourself. The second is to avoid or reduce it. The third approach is to shift the risk to others. (See Figure 11–6.)

Many firms practice self-insurance of certain types. This means assuming your own risk and preparing for loss. If, for example, a large chain of shoe stores sets aside regularly a certain amount to cover the possibility of fire in one of its outlets, it is practicing self-insurance. The idea is that, with a very large operation, some fire damage is bound to happen. Instead of paying insurance firms, the self-insurer pays itself.

Such a practice, of course, makes a firm very conscious of ways to avoid fires so as not to have to spend its reserved funds. It will install

self-insurance

FIGURE 11-6

How a business manages risk

1. **Risk assumption:** Self-insurance against fire, theft, etc.

2. **Risk avoidance and/or reduction:** Sound business management enables the firm to avoid unnecessary risk (i.e., credit policies that grant credit only to persons with good credit records) and/or reduce risk (i.e., safety training to teach employees safe work habits).

3. **Shifting risk:** Shifting the risk to another party such as an insurance company.

sprinklers, inspect heating systems, prevent unnecessary smoking in the stores, and take other steps to minimize risk. There are many other types of operational precautions a firm can take to reduce or avoid risks in different phases of its business.

Mechanized cash control systems help to protect against theft, as do basic cash audit procedures and regulations for writing checks and making cash purchases. Related procedures provide for systematic purchasing (sometimes on a sealed-bid basis) to avoid losses because of favoritism in buying or commercial bribery. Usually, more than one signature is required for approval of purchases over a certain amount. Careful inspection of both quantity and quality of goods received also plays an important part in resource control.

Firms that deal in new ideas and processes must maintain secrecy. This includes careful personnel screening and constant development of employee loyalty. Also included are normal security precautions such as checking visitors to plants. Careful patent protection is another means of protecting this kind of resource from being copied by competitors.

There is always a danger that changes in market conditions will hurt a firm. A retailer may find some goods hard to move. To avoid losses, he or she may use one of several legal devices which allow the return of merchandise to the producer or wholesaler. When a wholesaler wishes a neighborhood hardware store to stock a new line of expensive barbecue grills, the wholesaler may offer them *on consignment*. This means the retailer takes no risk that the grills won't sell. The retailer pays only for those sold at retail.

To protect against sudden rises in the cost of needed supplies, a firm might also have a policy of stocking up large quantities when the market is down. Such protective measures complement the role of insurance, which is our next topic.

Shifting Risk and the Use of Insurance

Insurance companies assume the risks of their policyholders for a price. A firm pays a premium for a policy that pays if it sustains certain types of losses. The policy specifies the types of risk that are covered, the amount of coverage, and the premium.

The insurance company is a professional risk taker, but it takes only certain types of risks. Insurance is available only for pure risks. **Pure risks are those which offer only a chance of loss. There is no chance of gain.** Examples are risk of fire and risk of death.

pure risks

Speculative risks are "gambles" in which there is possible gain as well as loss. Placing a bet at the race track is one obvious example. Going into business is another, because the quality of a new product or

speculative risks

the quality of management may lead to profit or loss. Insurance is not available for such speculative risks.

The federal and state governments are also in the insurance business. State governments operate unemployment and worker's compensation insurance programs. The federal government operates the social security program and other programs, such as savings account insurance on accounts in banks and mortgage insurance to lenders under VA and FHA programs.

Firms deal with insurance companies for the same reasons that individuals do. Most homeowners, for example, carry fire insurance rather than bear the entire burden of the risk themselves. The same is true of firms. Insurance companies combine the risks of many policyholders—firms or individuals—into a group.

THEN AND NOW

Trend Toward Risk Managers

The traditional role of the insurance manager in a firm has been that of buying the right insurance. As lawsuits and jury awards for damages rise and insurance rates go up, more and more firms are de-emphasizing insurance and emphasizing risk management. In other words, buying insurance is the "last step." If risk can be eliminated or greatly reduced or if self-insurance is feasible, "bought" insurance may not be necessary. This is in keeping with a systems concept of management.

The Risk Insurance Management Society membership doubled in a recent five-year period. More and more firms are looking for good risk managers to replace the more traditional insurance buyer. These risk managers are earning roughly $30,000 per year and half of them report directly to a vice-president.

Source: *The Wall Street Journal.*

The Law of Large Numbers

Insurance firms study the past to see how many people die each year at age 50 or age 60 or at any age. They develop mortality tables from these facts. Mortality tables are used to predict the number of policyholders who will die in a given year. **This prediction depends on the law of large numbers. In other words, if the insurance firm has a large number of policyholders, it can pretty well predict from the mortality tables how many of them will die in a year.**

law of large numbers

The same principle applies to other insured risks such as risks of fire or theft. Past experience and the law of large numbers give insurance firms a fair idea of how much they will have to pay out in claims. They set their premiums at a level that will allow them to cover expected claims as well as to cover operating costs and profit.

The loss-predicting experts (actuaries) of the Eagle Fire and Windstorm Insurance Co. know from historical records that in a year, on the average, 100 buildings of the 5,000 they insure against fire losses actually suffer fire losses. They also know that in the recent past, the average loss per building has been $20,000. Ignoring the effect of the rising cost of building repairs for the moment, the actuaries can set an average premium of something over $400 per year per insured structure. It must be somewhat higher than $400 to cover the expected $2 million payout ($20,000 × 100) plus its costs of operation and a profit margin. The predicted loss could, of course, be underestimated, in which case premiums would have to rise the following year. Recent high rates of inflation in building costs have of themselves forced rates up significantly every year for the last several years, regardless of the changes in the frequency of fire losses.

Of course, an insurer attempts to avoid writing insurance for a group if the peril (danger) insured against would damage all members in the group at the same time. For example, a fire insurance firm would not concentrate all its coverage in one section of a city. A major fire there could affect too many policyholders and could ruin the insurance firm.

The risk from the insurance firm's point of view relates to how accurately it can predict total losses within a group of policyholders. If the probable range of losses is great, the risk is great.

What Is Insurable and Who Can Be Insured Against Its Loss?

insurable risks

Insurance firms judge what kinds of dangers or perils they can insure against. These are what they consider to be insurable risks. An insurance company desires a reasonable amount of evidence dealing with the size and frequency of past losses. For the law of large numbers to work, a large number of objects must be insured. For a risk to be insurable, it must be measurable in dollars, too. Losses must also generally be unintentional to be insurable. A proprietor who is known to have burned his or her own store down may not recover for the loss.

insurable interest

People or firms have an insurable interest when they can show that they would suffer a loss from the thing insured against. If the McElroy Store leases a building at their main place of business, they can buy insurance protecting them against losses sustained by a fire in the building, even though they don't own it. They could suffer a great financial loss from such a fire. A corporation, because it has an insurable interest in the life of its president, can buy an insurance policy on his or her life. We will discuss life insurance after describing another major class of insurance—property and casualty insurance.

Property and Casualty Insurance

Under the general heading of property and casualty insurance we traditionally include perils of fire, windstorm, flood, theft, burglary, accident, loss of health, and liability due to negligence. We will use fire insurance as a principal example of how property and casualty coverage works.

property and casualty insurance

Firms and households insure buildings and houses against fire. Suppose a company's warehouse originally cost $50,000 and its current cost to rebuild is $75,000. It has a $100,000 fire policy and the building is totally destroyed by fire. **Under the principle of indemnity, the insured cannot collect more than the actual cash value of the loss, that is, $75,000.**

principle of indemnity

Total destruction by fire is rare. Thus most business property is underinsured. Insurance companies use a coinsurance clause to induce firms to carry adequate coverage, usually 80 percent of the market value of the property. The policy with an 80 percent coinsurance clause works like this: Suppose Samantha Butte owns a motion picture theater that would cost $100,000 to rebuild. If she buys only a $50,000 fire insurance policy and suffers a $30,000 loss from fire, the insurer would pay only $18,750 of the loss. This is computed as follows. The insured gets paid a fraction of the loss equal to the amount of the policy divided by 80 percent of the cost to replace. In this case it was $50,000/80,000$ or $\frac{5}{8}$. Five-eighths of $30,000 = $18,750.

Fire insurance protects against damage by fire or lightning. Most firms buy added coverage (allied lines) against perils such as windstorm, riot, water, smudge, etc.

There are several different forms of auto insurance. Comprehensive auto insurance covers loss due to windstorm, fire, hail, theft, etc. Collision insurance covers damage from collision with another vehicle or a stationary object. Bodily injury liability insurance protects the insured against claims resulting from death or injury of another person due to the insured's negligent operation of a car. A medical payments feature pays hospital and doctor bills for persons injured in the insured's car. Property damage liability insurance pays for damage done by the insured to other cars, houses, or property. Uninsured motorist protection covers the policyholder for his or her bodily injury caused by an uninsured negligent driver.

Burglary policies provide coverage in cases of forced entry. Theft insurance protects against larceny regardless of how the property is stolen. Fidelity bonds give the employer protection against employee theft of company funds.

Accident policies pay the insured for certain medical expenses due to accidents. Health policies pay expenses related to loss of health, whether due to an accident or sickness. Many firms provide group health insurance for their employees. Under a sick-leave plan, part of the worker's salary is paid when he or she cannot work due to sickness or accident. In the case of total disability, an income protection plan pays a certain percentage of the employee's salary while he or she is disabled. Major medical expense insurance provides coverage for long-term hospital stays and doctor bills. Many employees add to this coverage hospital money plans that pay a certain amount for each day the insured is in the hospital.

Public liability insurance protects firms and individuals from claims made by people who use the insured's facilities or products. Product liability insurance rates have skyrocketed in recent years.

THINK ABOUT IT!

Product Liability and Industry Self-Insurance

The option that businesses have of insuring themselves rather than relying on insurance companies is not a very practical one for most individual firms. The pressure of high rates, however, can lead to some inventive variations on the principle of self-insurance.

> Alarmed by skyrocketing premiums and even cancellations of product liability insurance, a chemical industry group has launched an experiment in coverage that could point the way for other "high-risk" industries. The Chemical Specialties Manufacturers Assn. in September formed a self-insurance program based in Bermuda that began writing policies at a fast clip almost from day one, including several for companies that have signed on as CSMA members just to get coverage.

> Such initiative on the part of an industry group might point the way to major changes in the structure of insurance for business. It certainly demonstrates the adaptiveness of business when it is faced with a financial problem. THINK ABOUT IT!

Source: *Business Week.*

Most states require employers to provide for medical expenses and weekly benefits to workers injured on the job. The employer pays the premiums.

Other important types of coverage include title, credit, and marine insurance and surety bonds. Title insurance protects the property owner against loss due to defects in title to real property. Credit insurance protects creditors against losses on uncollectible accounts receivable. Ocean marine insurance covers the ship and its cargo against theft, sinking, collision, etc. Inland marine insurance covers mainly land transportation modes. Surety bonds protect the insured against loss from nonperformance of a contractual obligation. A contractor might have to furnish a surety bond that a building will be completed by a certain date.

Life Insurance

Life insurance provides a degree of financial security to the insured's family or firm. The insurer pays a cash benefit to a surviving person or firm upon the death of the person insured. Life insurance has grown rapidly in the last twenty years. (See Figure 11–7.)

life insurance

Three major classes of life insurance policies are:

- term policies
- ordinary life policies
- limited payment policies

Term life insurance policies are issued for definite time spans such as 5–10–15 years. If the insured dies, the policy's face value is paid to his or her beneficiary. If the insured outlives the term of the policy, the insured receives nothing. Term insurance is pure protection.

FIGURE 11-7

Assets of American life insurance companies

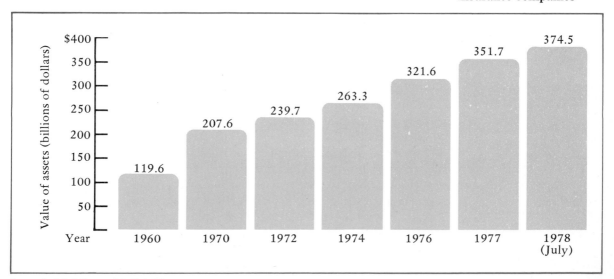

Source: *Statistical Abstract of the United States.*

Under ordinary life insurance, the insured pays premiums until death, at which time the beneficiary receives the policy's face value. If the insured person cancels the policy during his or her life, that person is paid the cash surrender value of the policy, which increases during the life of the policy. Thus a savings element is provided in addition to protection. The insured can also borrow money against the current cash value of the policy.

Under limited payment life insurance, premiums are paid for a stated number of years, usually in the 20–30 year range. At the end of the period, no further premiums are due. The policy is "paid up" but remains in force (that is, will pay the face value whenever the insured dies).

Many employers provide group life insurance plans for their employees. The premiums are lower than those on individually purchased policies. All told, the life insurance companies of the United States represent a huge part of the assets of the nation (see Figure 11–7) and, as such, can have much influence over the financial climate of the country.

Extraordinary Financing Arrangements

Sometimes, special conditions lead a firm to make extraordinary financing arrangements. These arrangements include devices for external expansion as well as the processes of recapitalization and reorganization.

External expansion can be achieved through

- merger
- amalgamation
- creation of a holding company

merger

In a merger one firm (the absorbing firm) keeps its identity and another firm is absorbed and loses its identity.

amalgamation

In an amalgamation both firms lose their identity. A new corporation is formed and shareholders of both former firms receive stock in the new corporation in exchange for their old shares.

holding company

A holding company owns the stock of one or more other corporations and controls them. When the holding company is itself an operating firm, it is known as an operating holding company. Control can be exercised without majority ownership by means of proxies. (See Figure 11–8.)

Mergers represent the most important form of combination of firms. Over the years they have been the subject of close scrutiny by govern-

Merger

Bigger Bottle Co. acquires Tiny Cork Co.

Only Bigger Bottle remains

Tiny Cork shareholders get some Bigger Bottle stock instead

Amalgamation

Bigger Bottle Co. and Tiny Cork Co. amalgamate to form Bottles and Corks, Inc.

All shareholders get new stock and the old corporations disappear

Holding company

Containershares, Inc. buys stock of Bigger Bottle and Tiny Cork

Original firms continue to operate

ment agencies including the Federal Trade Commission, the Department of Justice, and the Securities and Exchange Commission. These agencies are discussed more fully in Chapter 17. The volume of mergers continues to be quite great, however. It is reported that there were 455 corporate name changes in the first half of 1978, more than double the number in the same period a year earlier. The name changes include mergers as well as cases of the "spinning off" of divisions to independent ownership.

Mergers are so common that there are now many merger brokers operating in the United States. The very large mergers are usually arranged through investment bankers, but merger brokers usually handle smaller mergers. Even large firms may use a broker to find a suitable merger partner because this could keep the proposed buyer's name secret and thereby keep the share purchase price down. Small companies seeking either to buy another firm or to sell out to another firm may go through a merger broker because they may not have the ability to search around for appropriate "partners in merger."

Mergers occur for many reasons, such as to achieve economies of scale in production or distribution, to fill out product lines, or to com-

FIGURE 11-8

Methods of expanding a firm

"In 1976, Alfred and his company were swallowed up by a conglomerate, and we haven't seen him since."

recapitalization

bine technological skill with financial capacity. Tax reasons may also enter into merger plans.

Recapitalization occurs when a firm changes its capital structure to meet changing conditions. It does not raise more capital. It may involve replacing a high-yield preferred stock with a lower-yield preferred stock or floating a new bond issue to replace a maturing one. Sometimes a stock split is used to attract investors. Recapitalization often requires that the corporation amend its charter or receive permission of the Securities and Exchange Commission.

Suppose that the management of the Parkway Bolt Co., a fast-growing corporation, feels that its heavy dependence on 11 percent bonds to raise long-term capital has been too much of a drain on earnings (high interest cost). It might prefer to recapitalize by issuing a new block of common stock and by using the proceeds to retire half of the outstanding bonds. This would free profits for "plowing back" into the capital needs of a growing firm. Of course, the original common shareholders (and perhaps the SEC) would have to approve this proposal.

Reorganization is an involuntary process. It occurs when a firm is in very serious financial trouble and the court steps in to protect creditors. Sometimes creditors force an out-of-court reorganization.

Firms go into debt (both long- and short-term) with the hope that they will be able to pay the interest and principal out of earnings. If this doesn't work out over the period of indebtedness, the firm is in trouble. A firm that cannot meet its maturing financial obligations is insolvent. **If, in addition, its liabilities are greater than its assets, the firm is bankrupt. Such a firm is said to be in bankruptcy.**

Under voluntary bankruptcy, a person or firm files a petition in federal court claiming inability to pay debts because the debts exceed available assets. This petition asserts willingness to make all assets available to creditors under court supervision.

Under involuntary bankruptcy, a person's or firm's creditors seek to have a debtor declared bankrupt by proving that the debtor committed one or more acts of bankruptcy as defined in the law. Once a defendant is declared bankrupt by the court, the procedure is the same as it is in voluntary bankruptcy.

(margin terms) reorganization

(margin terms) bankruptcy

Summary and Look Ahead

The financial manager's job is complex and requires a variety of talents. One must be aware of present and future needs for working capital and fixed capital. Capital budgeting helps in performing this task. The financial executive must also evaluate and select sources of funds. He or she thinks in terms of maturity, claims against assets and income, and control of the firm when deciding how to get funds. For short-term funds, trade credit and commercial banks are the major sources. Stocks, bonds, and retained earnings are the sources of most long-term funds.

To protect the firm's resources, a financial manager must think of ways to avoid, reduce, or shift risk. Insurance companies play a major role in risk shifting for firms as well as for individuals.

In addition to the ordinary long-term financing sources (retained earnings and stock and bond issues), extraordinary means for long-term financing are sometimes needed. These include external expansion devices—recapitalization and reorganization.

In the next chapter we will begin to explore how the human resource is dealt with by studying personnel. We will also see how a firm maximizes its use of people by understanding human motivation and social groups.

My name is Kim Flippen. I am a management intern with the Prudential Insurance Company of America.

I took an A.B. degree at Mount Holyoke College. During my junior and senior years I thought heavily about my future, and a career for me in business was a strong possibility. In my senior year I developed a research project on management in the small company. This exposure, as well as the emphasis on expanding opportunities for women in business, led to my decision to go to work directly and to postpone graduate study.

I examined companies which offered management training programs, trying to determine their commitment to employee development. I wanted to be sure that, in the capacity in which I worked, my abilities would be enhanced. While I expected to perform well regardless of the position, I wanted to be certain that a good match would be made between my abilities and the company.

In the short time I have been with Prudential, I have been given the opportunity to prove myself in numerous ways. The company encourages a "take-charge" attitude, where a person assumes full responsibility for a project, to create, innovate, and implement. This is the attitude that attracted me to Prudential and which keeps me interested. Each person is valued for what he or she can contribute and is viewed with an eye to the potential he or she represents.

Prudential offers several professional training programs in various areas of the company for high-potential college graduates. It was one of these programs, the Management Internship, which attracted me. Organized into rotational assignments of six-to-nine-months duration, the internship imparts the necessary technical, supervisory, and managerial skills that contribute to effective management. The ultimate aim of the program is to create a pool from which future executives may be tapped.

Within an assignment, the intern may work on a single, one-time project, or several projects which require the full attention of a staff member. The diversity of Prudential enables the intern to pursue interests in insurance marketing, insurance services, public relations, investments, and computer operations just to name a few. Regardless of the area, the aim of the assignment is the same: to challenge the abilities of the intern; to cultivate the intern's strengths while minimizing weaknesses; to encourage the intern to fulfill his or her potential.

My current assignment is in the Community Affairs Division of the Public Affairs Department. An important function of Community Affairs, along with several other divisions, is the implementation of programs arising from the company's corporate social responsibility. The division's activities at the corporate headquarters in Newark address the needs of that city and the surrounding areas. My activities included a seminar on rape prevention, the development of an English as a second language course for employees who speak little or no English, and a week-long career education seminar for high school seniors.

In every assignment I was expected to take command of the project, devise my own research and methodology, and follow up on its implementation. I appreciate the independence, and I believe my performance has benefited from it.

Key Concepts

amalgamation A method of combining corporate firms by which both original firms lose their identity and all old stock is exchanged for stock of the new, combined firm.

bankruptcy A condition of insolvency (inability to meet current debt) combined with liabilities greater than assets.

capital budget A projection of expected needs for fixed assets over a five-to ten year period.

debt financing Obtaining funds by going into debt (for example, issuing bonds).

equity financing Financing by selling additional shares of stock or obtaining additional funds from a proprietor or partner.

floor planning A method by which sellers of consumer durables finance these products so that they do not have to pay for them until they have sold them.

holding company A corporation owning all the common stock of one or more other firms so that the operation of those firms is coordinated and controlled.

insurable interest A financial involvement or dependency on a person or thing, the loss of which may be insured against.

insurable risk That risk against which an insurance firm will write a policy.

law of large numbers The fact that the likelihood of a peril within a large group of policyholders may be estimated fairly closely.

lease An agreement to grant use of an asset for a period of time in return for a periodic payment.

life insurance Insurance that protects a person or firm from a degree of financial loss in the event of death of the insured. It is also available in a variety of forms that permit policyholders to save as well as to insure.

line of credit A set amount of credit made available to a person or firm by a lending institution.

liquidity The quickness and ease with which an asset can be turned into cash.

long-term (fixed) capital Assets committed for more than one year or funds used for the purchase of such assets.

maturity The date on which a debt obligation becomes due.

merger A combination of formerly independent business firms under the name of one of the firms.

opportunity cost The cost of losing the option to use funds in another way.

principle of indemnity The principle that the insured may not collect more than the amount of the loss sustained.

property and casualty insurance   A general category of insurance other than life insurance. Includes fire, theft, liability, and many other kinds.

pure risk   An opportunity for financial loss without opportunity for financial gain.

recapitalization   A change in capital structure to reflect changing conditions internal or external to the firm.

reorganization   An involuntary process by which a court steps in to protect creditors from loss due to poor financial conditions in a firm.

revolving credit   Commercial bank credit under a formal agreement. It guarantees the borrower funds for a period of time under strict rules.

secured loans   Commercial bank loans in which assets of the borrowers are pledged as security.

self-insurance   The practice of preparing for losses by saving systematically instead of buying an insurance policy.

sinking fund   A fund set aside over the lifetime of bonds for their retirement.

speculative risk   A risk in which there is a chance for gain as well as a chance for loss.

trade credit   Credit extended a firm by its suppliers.

working capital   Current assets used in business operations or funds employed for the acquisition of current assets.

For Review . . .

1. Briefly explain why it is important to distinguish short-term financing from long-term financing.
2. What specific uses are made of working capital?
3. What are some examples of fixed capital needs? Give an example of a firm with great fixed capital requirements and another with very small fixed capital requirements.
4. What factors may affect the supply of credit to a small manufacturer?
5. How do debt and equity financing differ in terms of their maturity? Their claims on income?
6. Going back to Chapter 10, describe the principal types of stocks, common and preferred, that are used by corporations.
7. Describe two of the operational precautions that a firm might apply in order to protect its resources.

8. What is the law of large numbers? How does it relate to the size of insurance premiums?
9. Describe two types of property insurance.
10. How does a firm become bankrupt?

. . . For Discussion

1. Where do preferred stocks fit into the debt versus equity financing decision?
2. What capital need is served by "open book account" or trade credit? Compare this source to the commercial bank.
3. Why can some firms use self-insurance while some others cannot?
4. Explain how probability mathematics enters into premium setting in the insurance industry.
5. Why are merger brokers becoming more widely used? Discuss their function.

Incidents

The Lee National Corporation

The Lee National Corporation proposed a merger with a privately held company owned by certain of its current officers and directors and another private investor. A minority group of shareholders asked for an injunction in the New York State courts to block the merger, claiming that the officers and directors involved in the merger would "unlawfully . . . enrich themselves" by the merger. Proponents responded that an independent appraiser had determined that the proposed share payment price in the budget was fair and that the merger was needed to get fresh capital into the company.

Questions

1. If you were a minority shareholder, what position would you take, assuming the share price

was equal to the most recent market price of the stock?
2. What role do you think government should play in such a case?
3. What are alternative methods of "getting fresh capital into the company"?

Source: *The Wall Street Journal.*

Product Liability Laws—Shifting Responsibility

A shift in court decisions concerning product liability is contributing to inflation in the prices of manufactured consumer products. *Business Week* reports on the impact of this trend as follows:

"The costs of product liability are becoming a horrendous problem for U.S. industry. Last year alone manufacturers and retailers paid an estimated $2.75 billion for product liability insurance, compared with an estimated $1.13 billion in 1975—and with rising deductibles they are self-insuring still more, though nobody knows by how much. Some even speculate that the U.S. is on the way to be-

coming a 'no-fault' economy, in which producers and sellers will be held responsible for all product injuries."

Questions

1. How does such a shift in product liability laws affect the introduction of new products?
2. How does this shift affect investments in product design and testing?

Source: *Business Week.*

ROCKETOY COMPANY 6

After 15 years of growth as a corporation and a successful move from Milwaukee to Detroit, the Rocketoy Company is financially sound. Its credit rating is good, and an analysis of its financial statements by a large national CPA firm indicates that it is a very good prospect for continued success if growth funds can be acquired. Presently there is common stockholders' equity worth $4,000,000. All of it is held by the original stockholders except for Richard Talley, who sold his holdings to Terry Phillips. Terry now owns 65 percent of the outstanding stock. Bonds are outstanding in the amount of $1,000,000. Half of this amount is maturing (will become due) within a year.

Including the retirement of maturing bonds and capital expansion needs as found in the capital

budget, Rocketoy needs $6,000,000 in long-term capital funds in the following two-year period. Pam Carter, the vice-president of finance, still holds 5 percent of the outstanding stock at the time. She proposes issuing $2,000,000 in 11 percent bonds maturing in 20 years and selling 40,000 shares of stock at $100 per share. This would double the number of shares outstanding. Her brother, the president, is concerned about this proposal because he does not have personal funds sufficient to maintain majority ownership under such a plan. But he does see the advantages of the plan, too. Joe Phillips, Mike Shultz, and Julia Rabinovitz could easily purchase 10,000 additional shares each. Investment bankers have advised that up to $4,000,000 in 11 percent bonds could be sold at par.

Questions

1. Assuming the expansion needs are genuine and you are Terry Phillips, would you oppose Pam's plan? Why or why not?
2. What are the advantages of Pam's plan?
3. What are the advantages of selling $4,000,000 in bonds?
4. What compromises could you suggest?
5. What information about the toy market would you want before reaching a decision?

Personnel

CHAPTER 12

Objectives: After reading this chapter, you should be able to

1. Compare a firm's human asset with its nonhuman assets.
2. Explain the meaning of human resource management.
3. Explain the significance of the systems concept to personnel management.
4. List and discuss the major federal laws that outlaw discrimination in employment.
5. List and discuss the tasks of the personnel department.
6. Discuss the nature of affirmative action recruiting.
7. Differentiate among the three types of interviews used in the selection process.
8. Compare job-skill training, management development, and organization development.
9. Compare the merit rating system with the management by objectives approach to appraising employee performance.
10. Discuss the equity theory of compensation.
11. Discuss the significance of the Occupational Safety and Health Act to employee safety and health programs.

Key concepts: Look for these terms as you read the chapter

human resource	management development
personnel administration	organization development (OD)
personnel management	performance appraisal system
personnel department	
management inventory	merit rating system
job analysis	seniority
job description	wage and salary administration
job specification	
recruiting	piece rate
affirmative action plan	incentive pay
job application form	wage
preliminary employment interview	salary
	promotion
selection tests	Occupational Safety and Health Act (OSHA)
in-depth interview	
background investigation	resignation
final selection interview	exit interview
bona fide occupational qualification (BFOQ)	dismissal
	discharge
employee orientation	
job-skill training	

Any firm's success, in the final analysis, depends most on the quality of people who work for it—its personnel, or human resource. This resource includes workers and managers at all levels in the firm, from top to bottom.

Top management, of course, is responsible for staffing the firm with good personnel. Staffing is a vital function of management. Its importance, unfortunately, is sometimes underestimated. Personnel administration is concerned with setting broad company policy regarding the firm's management of its human resource.

Top management delegates to the firm's personnel manager the task of implementing its human resource policies at the firm's "operations" level. Usually this involves setting up a personnel department. This staff department is accountable for building and keeping a good work force.

In this chapter we will discuss the firm's approach to human resource management. In practice, all managers participate in managing this vital resource. But most of the specialized activities of human resource management are delegated to the personnel manager. Our main focus, therefore, is on the nature of personnel management activities.

The Human Resource

A firm's most important resource (or asset) is its human resource—the personnel who staff the firm. This includes workers and managers— maintenance workers, salespersons, assembly-line workers, typists, and managers at all levels. A firm's human resource makes its nonhuman resources productive because, without good personnel, the best-equipped and well-financed firm will not function well.

human resource

Only during recent years, however, has management come to recognize the crucial importance of the human resource. If you look at a firm's balance sheet, you will find listed current assets such as cash, accounts receivable, and inventories. You also will find fixed assets such as machinery, equipment, and buildings. But there is usually no specific accounting for the human asset—an asset without which the firm would fold up. There are practical problems in human-asset accounting but the significance of the human resource is being recognized and steps are being taken to further its development.

Personnel Administration

personnel administration

The broadest possible view of a firm's human resource is that of personnel administration. **Personnel administration is top management's effort to develop an overall effective workforce that includes managers and workers at all levels in the firm. It is human resource management on a grand scale.**

Top management sets the tone for the firm's approach to its human resource management. All managers, however, participate in managing this resource. Production managers, for example, help to train and to motivate plant superintendents who, in turn, help to train and to motivate supervisors. Supervisors, in turn, help to train and to motivate their subordinates.

Personnel Management and the Personnel Department

personnel management

Top management's policies regarding human resource management are carried out through the practice of good personnel management. **Personnel management consists of recruiting, selecting, training, developing, compensating, motivating employees to good performance, and terminating employees. It is concerned with building and preserving the firm's human resource.**

personnel department

As we said earlier, managing personnel is part of every manager's job. But as firms grow, they create a specific staff department to help their managers manage people. Top management delegates to the firm's personnel manager the task of carrying out its human resource policies at the firm's "operations" level. He or she does this by managing the personnel department. **A personnel department is a staff department that is created to advise and help line managers to manage their personnel. It is headed by a personnel manager.**

Personnel work can be divided as follows:

- determining human resource needs
- searching for and recruiting applicants to fill those needs
- selecting applicants for employment
- training and developing personnel
- appraising employee performance
- compensating employees
- promoting employees
- providing personnel services
- performing other personnel activities
- terminating employees

The role a personnel department plays in a firm depends on the authority granted to it by top management. As a staff department, it advises and helps line managers to recruit, select, train, and motivate workers. Final decisions about personnel matters, therefore, are made by the line managers. In some firms, however, the personnel manager has functional authority over specified personnel activities. He or she, for example, actually may make hiring and promotion decisions.

The systems view of management is important in modern personnel management. Production managers, for example, can turn to personnel managers for assistance in determining how the introduction of automation will affect the firm's staffing. Will some workers have to be discharged? Can they be shifted to other types of jobs within the firm? Will their skills have to be upgraded?

Personnel activities also help in relating the firm to its environment, such as when a new plant location is evaluated for suitable workers in its labor force. Other examples are the personnel department's encouragement of employee support of charitable fund-raising drives and blood-donor programs for the local community.

Personnel departments also are stepping up their use of computers. Payroll processing and employee record keeping are two activities that are computerized in many firms. Some firms also are using a *personnel management information system (PMIS)* to help in developing the human resource.

For example, a firm could enter into its PMIS detailed data about the kinds and combinations of skills that exist among its current employees. When new jobs open up, the personnel department can check the PMIS to see if current employees have the needed skills. This might save the firm a lot of time and money recruiting new employees and improve the morale and productivity of current employees. Great care, of course, is needed to ensure that the PMIS is not used to violate an employee's right to privacy. In general, workers must be told why the firm needs information, and they must be given the chance to refuse to give that information.

Personnel Management Tasks

Determining Human Resource Needs

The best place for a new firm to start in determining human resource needs is to state the company objectives. This statement helps in preparing an organization chart, which provides a skeleton of the firm's need for managers and workers.

In the case of established firms, some workers and managers already staff the firm. But these firms continually must study their need for personnel. Some of the present employees may be approaching retirement or leaving to take jobs with other employers. They must be replaced.

Forecasting Human Resource Needs

There are two basic ways to determine a firm's human resource needs. One approach involves no advance planning. The need is recognized as urgent only when a present employee leaves or a new job opening must be filled.

The other approach is to anticipate needs before they become urgent. This involves forecasting the number and types of positions that will be opening up and making a time schedule of when they probably will open up. Ideally the firm should take its sales forecast and "back into" production scheduling and financial forecasting. This helps it to get a better fix on the exact number and types of jobs to be filled.

management inventory

A firm's management inventory is an example of a technique that can be used in determining the reserve of managerial talent on hand for promotion to higher positions and in making projections regarding future need for managers. **The management inventory is a list of present managerial positions along with the names and personal data (age, experience, length of service, etc.) of the persons holding them.**

One indicator of good human resource planning is stability of employment. Drastic ups and downs in a firm's employment levels and periods of excessive overtime pay followed by periods of layoffs and shortened work weeks are evidence of poor human resource planning. Many state unemployment insurance programs penalize employers who have a poor record for providing stable employment. The "experience rating" of these employers results in their paying higher unemployment taxes. Furthermore, laying off and rehiring workers is costly.

It is wise to avoid having to hire or lay off a large number of workers on short notice. Well-managed firms try to plan ahead. For example, the forecast of personnel needs may indicate reduced future need for employees. If this is known far enough in advance, attrition (people retiring and people quitting for other reasons) can bring the workforce down to an efficient level. This is better than laying off a lot of workers on short notice.

Specifying Human Resource Needs

job analysis

Job analysis helps a firm to specify its human resource needs. **Job analysis involves defining the jobs that must be done if the firm is to reach**

its objectives. Each job is studied to determine what work it involves
and what qualifications are needed by the persons who will fill it.

From the job analysis, the job description (or position guide) is pre-
pared. **A job description outlines the nature of a given job—how the job**   job description
relates to other jobs; the specific duties involved; and the tools, ma-
chinery, and supplies needed are stated in writing. (See Figure 12–1.)

FIGURE 12-1

Hanes
Corporation   EXEMPT POSITION DESCRIPTION

Date: May 2, 1979   Position: Employee Benefits
                                                   Supervisor
Incumbent   Cathy Cook   Reports to: Ted Williams
Written By: Cathy Cook   Department: Personnel
Approved By: *Ted Williams*   Division: Bali
                     5/2/79   Location: Winston-Salem, N.C.

POSITION OBJECTIVE
     The incumbent has primary responsibility for the
administration of group insurance, retirement and retirement savings
plans, workmen's and unemployment compensation programs, the
affirmative action plan and employee communications. In addition,
the incumbent assists in the planning, development, administration
and communication of employee benefits plans to all domestic and
foreign locations.

DIMENSIONS
     Cost of Employee Benefits Programs: $360,000
     Employees Affected: 400 Employees (Domestic)
                            1800 Employees (Foreign)

NATURE AND SCOPE
     This is one of three positions reporting to the Director of
Personnel, Bali Company; the other two are Managers of Personnel
(Domestic and Foreign).
     The responsibilities of the incumbent include:

1.   Maintain administrative procedures for all group insurance
     programs, retirement plans, retirement savings plans,
     employee stock option plan, workmen's and unemployment
     compensation programs, etc. Prepare or revise, maintain and
     distribute materials necessary for proper plan administration
     (i.e., claim forms, enrollment cards, administration manuals,
     booklets, etc,).

2.   File insurance claims for Winston-Salem, New York and Sales
     employees.

3.   Administer Retirement Savings Plan, Stock Purchase Plan,
     Retirement Plan etc. for all employees.

4.   Training of personnel at all domestic locations to administer
     benefits programs.

5.   Conduct benefits surveys as needed, summarize results and
     make recommendations based on findings.

```
Exempt Position Description
Employee Benefits Supervisor
Page 2
```

6.   Prepare a yearly analysis of existing benefits' costs for the company.

7.   Conduct cost and/or feasibility studies of benefits' costs and other programs as requested by the Director of Personnel.

8.   Participate in benefits planning committee activities.

9.   Develop and maintain audit checklists to insure that administrative requirements are satisfied.

10.   Respond to employee questions.

11.   Assist in the development and coordination of various personnel/benefits policies, employee handbooks, service awards programs, handicapped provisions, etc.

12.   Prepare timely reports as assigned (affirmative action reports, labor turnover reports, absenteeism reports, premium statements, birthdays, Employment Security Commission Report of New Hires, OSHA Safety Reports, etc.)

13.   Prepare annual Affirmative Action Plan (numerical and written plan for Bali Company), assist in establishing goals and advise Directors where an affirmative action goal is open, notify recruiting sources of affirmative action policy, maintain current log of all personnel (Winston-Salem) by job group, post all employments, terminations, transfers, promotions. Coordinate other employment statistics for New York, Gastonia and Winston-Salem.

14.   Assist in various special assignment projects.

15.   Act as liason with employees, insurance carriers, corporate benefits department, medical community, and management on matters involving Bali's benefit programs.

16.   Advise employees of benefit changes through oral and written presentations in all locations.

17.   Coordinate responsibilities of a part-time Personnel Clerk.

18.   Serve as editor of Bali Division newsletter coordinating all reporting from domestic and foreign locations.

FIGURE 12-1 (continued)

Source: Hanes Corporation.

job specification

From the job description, the job specification is prepared. **A job specification states the personal qualifications needed by the person who is to fill each job—education, skills, experience, etc.**

Management inventories, job descriptions, and job specifications help make a firm's human resource needs more concrete. They give the personnel manager a clearer idea of what types of employees are needed and permit more effective evaluation of people who apply for jobs. They help in matching specific workers with specific jobs.

Firms that do not prepare job descriptions and job specifications have to take the opposite approach to matching jobs and people. They hire people and build the job to fit the qualifications of the people who are hired.

Searching for and Recruiting Applicants

A firm that waits for recruits to come to it has to be satisfied with whatever shows up. This is a poor approach. **Recruiting is the task of attracting potential employees to the firm. It should be a continuous process for most medium- and large-sized firms.** "Beating the bushes" to find recruits when the firm is in desperate need for new employees should be avoided because the recruiter will have to be less selective in choosing. Recruiting for the long range is beneficial because

recruiting

- it forces a firm to take stock of its present workforce and to plan for future human resource needs
- it helps to eliminate the chance that new employees will be selected from among a small number of applicants
- it may give a firm an edge over competitors, because it will be able to hire people who are not available to "panic" recruiters

The nature of the search task depends on the jobs being filled and the general conditions in the job market. The more skills needed, the more complex is the search process. The supply and the demand for people possessing certain skills also affects the search. Recruiting practices also have been affected in many ways by antidiscrimination legislation.

Antidiscrimination Legislation

Federal, state, and local laws that seek to remove discrimination in employment have their most direct impact on a firm's personnel department. Personnel departments in many firms, for example, have a manager in charge of affirmative action plans and related programs. **An affirmative action plan is a detailed statement by a firm describing how it will go about actively recruiting and upgrading members of minority groups and women.** Table 12–1 discusses several major federal laws that pertain to employment discrimination.

affirmative action plan

Personnel managers must be keenly aware of these laws because the costs of violations can be very high. The U.S. Supreme Court has ruled that firms that defend themselves successfully against charges of un-

TABLE 12-1

Major antidiscrimination laws

The Equal Pay Act (1963)	Outlaws any pay differentials based on sex. The Wage and Hour Division of the U.S. Department of Labor says that "men and women performing equal work in the same establishment under similar conditions must receive the same pay if their jobs require *equal skill, equal effort,* and *equal responsibility."* Jobs must be "substantially" the same, but not necessarily identical, for the law to apply.
The Civil Rights Act (1964)	This act (especially Title VII) and its 1972 amendment (the Equal Employment Opportunity Act) outlaws job discrimination based on race, color, religion, sex, or national origin. Requires employer to post notices saying that the employer is an equal opportunity employer and does not discriminate. Enforced by the Equal Employment Opportunity Commission (EEOC), which can file suits against employers and unions who continue to discriminate after the EEOC has tried to gain compliance through conferences and persuasion.
Executive Order 11246 (1965)	Requires federal government contractors and subcontractors with more than $50,000 in government contracts to take "affirmative action" to end discrimination. The Office of Federal Contract Compliance Programs (OFCCP) in the U.S. Department of Labor enforces the order.
The Age Discrimination in Employment Act (1967)	Prohibits employers to engage in job discrimination against people between ages 40 and 65. A 1978 amendment extends the age to 70. Enforced by the U.S. Department of Labor.
The Rehabilitation Act (1973)	This act (Section 504) bans employment discrimination against the handicapped, who are otherwise qualified, by government contractors or any employers receiving any kind of federal assistance.

lawful bias in hiring or promotion decisions must prove that the claim of discrimination was "frivolous, unreasonable, or groundless" in order to force the losing side to pay the legal fees.

In addition to the EEOC and the U.S. Department of Labor, the U.S. Civil Service Commission and the Civil Rights Division of the Department of Justice are active in enforcing equal employment opportunity. The Civil Service Commission reviews the policies of all federal agencies and consults with state and local governments to establish and improve merit rating systems. The Civil Rights Division can bring suits against private employers or labor unions that engage in a "pattern or practice of discrimination."

Some states and cities also have fair employment practices (FEP) acts that outlaw discrimination on the basis of race, religion, sex, national origin, and age. Some of these laws also protect the handicapped from employment discrimination.

In the U.S. Supreme Court's decision in the *Regents of the University of California* v. *Bakke* case in 1978, the Court said that rigid quotas based solely on race are forbidden but that race might legitimately be an element in judging students for admission to universities. That case does not apply specifically to affirmative action employment and promotion programs. But another case does deal with the issue of affirmative action programs in business.

Kaiser Aluminum and Chemical Company and the United Steelworkers of America agreed in national labor contracts in 1974 and in 1977 that the firm would set up affirmative action programs in training for skilled crafts. The firm would fill 50 percent of the training positions with white males and 50 percent with blacks, other minorities, and women.

Brian Weber, a white male worker at a Kaiser plant in Louisiana, sued the company and the union in 1974 when two black workers with less seniority than Weber were chosen for a craft training program. Weber claimed *reverse discrimination* and two lower federal courts ruled that Kaiser's program was illegal because it fostered racial bias against Weber. Kaiser appealed the case to the U.S. Supreme Court, which agreed to hear the case.

The Kaiser program accepted trainees at the firm's 15 plants in the United States on the basis of seniority within their racial group. If Kaiser had accepted trainees on overall seniority at the plant, only whites could have made it.

The U.S. Supreme Court had to decide whether employers with no proven history of racial bias illegally discriminate against whites when giving preference to minority workers. A trial jury and the Fifth U.S. Circuit Court of Appeals both held that a firm may install affirmative action programs only if it first admits bias or if the government has found that the firm has discriminated against minorities in the past.

In June, 1979 the U.S. Supreme Court ruled that Brian Weber had not been a victim of reverse racial discrimination. In a 5-to-2 decision, the Court said that the plan negotiated between Kaiser and the United Steelworkers of America was a temporary measure that was not designed to maintain racial balance, "but simply to eliminate racial imbalance."

The Court noted that preferential selection of craft trainees at the plant would end as soon as the percentage of black skilled craft workers in the plant approximates the percentage of blacks in the local labor force.

Source: *The Times-Picayune.*

Affirmative Action Recruiting

The underlying philosophy of affirmative action recruiting programs is that it is not enough for employers to have no intent to discriminate in hiring and promotions. If their personnel practices result in an adverse effect on minorities and women, then affirmative action must be undertaken to eliminate that adverse effect.

In addition to traditional sources of recruits that are discussed below, employers under affirmative action plans turn to community action agencies, colleges with large enrollments of women and minorities, employment agencies that specialize in placing women and minorities, and ads in magazines that appeal mainly to women and minorities. Past discriminatory practices often have resulted in women being placed in "deadend" clerical jobs. Affirmative action employers, therefore, search within their own firms to identify those women who want to advance up the job ladder and are able and willing to prepare for promotion.

The EEOC can require employers to maintain an "Applicant Flow Record." This indicates, for each job applicant, "name, race, national origin, sex, referral source, date of application, and position applied for," as well as specific company records for members of minority groups and females who are not hired. Also required is information regarding who made the decision not to hire and the reasons for not hiring.

Mechanics of Recruiting

Sources of recruits include unemployed workers, present and past employees, their friends and relatives, and workers who are taking their first jobs. Employees who have jobs with other employers but are dissatisfied also often are receptive to job offers.

The extent of the search depends largely on company policy. A firm with a policy of not promoting from within will conduct an extensive external search. But excluding present employees in the early search may have a bad effect on their morale. The personnel department must remember that building and maintaining employee morale are basic tasks. The systems view is essential here because the various personnel activities are interrelated. The advantages of external search must be balanced against those of internal search.

Among the many methods of recruitment are word-of-mouth, advertisements, government and private employment agencies, vocational, technical, and college recruiting. Word-of-mouth recruiting, however, can be illegal if the "word" finds its way only to white male Anglo-Saxons.

As a college student, you know that many firms recruit on college

FRENZIED
RECRUITING

Three-day work weeks. Sign-up bonuses as high as $7,000. A key to the company hot tub. Free orthodontia for all the children.

These are just a few of the goodies handed out by electronics companies in California's "Silicon Valley," some 40 miles south of San Francisco. It is the scene of a frenzied recruiting drive for anybody with a scientific skill—and many with no skills at all.

Some 500 companies are locked in a desperate recruiting battle for a severely limited number of workers.... In personnel offices, linear engineers and microsystems programmers are spoken of in awed whispers, as if they were deities....

This activity is part of the explosive growth of the microelectronics industry, which since 1963 has transformed Santa Clara County, whose heart is Silicon Valley, from a bucolic orchard to a crazy quilt of low-slung buildings and endless seams of freeway.... Partly because of a post- Viet Nam decline in trained electronics workers coming out of the military, the valley's personnel officers are searching to fill an estimated 5,000 openings.

Helicopters hover above local picnic grounds, trailing long banners promoting the attractions of working at different firms. The Sunday editions of the San Jose *Mercury-News* bulge with up to 50 pages of help wanted ads. Television commercials promise job applicants VIP treatment if they deign to drop in for an interview.

... Additional perks often include payments for the selling costs on the recruit's old home, free lodging while house hunting, conferences with tax specialists (in hopes of setting up tax shelters) and membership in a country club.

Source: *Time.*

campuses. You should pay close attention to the Appendix, in which we discuss how to prepare student data sheets, résumés, letters of inquiry, and how to approach an employment interview.

Recruiting Managers

There are two basic sources of management recruits: (1) promotion from within the present managerial and nonmanagerial ranks and/or (2) going outside the firm. Promoting from within boosts employee morale because it demonstrates that a manager can move up the management hierarchy in his or her present firm. Recruiting outsiders, however, may bring needed "new blood" into the firm.

"The Public Employment Service found VW an American workforce."

Marvin McFadden
General Director of Personnel
Volkswagen Manufacturing Corporation
of America

"When Volkswagen decided to build Rabbits in New Stanton, Pennsylvania, we designated the Pennsylvania Bureau of Employment Security's Job Service to do the bulk of our staffing.

"By the time we reach full production, this state government agency will have reviewed 60,000 applications to find us 3500 of the best assembly, maintenance, office and front-line supervisory personnel in the area.

"And even before Volkswagen decided on New Stanton, we used the Employment Service's labor market statistics to help us decide among plant sites."

Analyzing a labor market. Staffing a whole plant. Filling one key vacancy. The Public Employment Service can serve decision makers many ways.

If you'd like to know more, send for our free report, "Working for a Working America". Mail this coupon to: Bill Heartwell, Executive Vice-President, Interstate Conference of Employment Security Agencies, Inc. 444 North Capitol Street, N.W., Washington, D.C. 20001.

YES, send me a copy of "Working for a Working America".

NAME _____

TITLE _____

COMPANY/ORGANIZATION _____
_____

ADDRESS _____

CITY _____

STATE _____ ZIP _____

Source: Interstate Conference of Employment Security Agencies.

Selecting Applicants for Employment

If the personnel department succeeds in getting applicants, its next task is to select the best ones. A personnel department that sets out to find the best person for the job will undertake more intensive recruiting and selection processes than if it were content merely to screen out the worst applicants.

Building the organizational structure and staffing it are two interrelated management tasks that involve matching jobs and people. Some firms design jobs first and recruit and select people who fit into those jobs. They emphasize fitting applicants to particular jobs. Some other firms hire employees and build the organization around them. They adjust jobs to fit the people who are available to fill them. This approach may be taken when a firm feels that it has employment "quotas" to fill or when exceptionally qualified people are available to fill existing vacancies. Of course, some firms take both approaches.

The Job Application Form

The job application form (application blank or biographical inventory) is prepared by an employer and filled in by a job applicant. The applicant provides job-related information that helps the reviewer to determine if the applicant has the needed education, experience, training, etc., for the job. The care with which an applicant fills out this form can tell a lot about him or her. It usually is the basis for the potential employer's first impression about the applicant as a person. (See Figure 12–2.)

job application form

Antidiscrimination laws make it illegal to require an applicant to supply data regarding religious preference, color, race, sex, or nationality. Many firms that formerly required applicants to attach photos to the job application form have dropped the practice. This helps to ensure the applicant that his or her race will not be considered in the employee selection process. A job application form that asks for "wife's name" but does not ask for "husband's name" makes it rather obvious that the firm assumes that all applicants will be men.

The Preliminary Employment Interview

The preliminary employment interview is the first time that the employer and the applicant meet face-to-face. The employer usually is represented by an interviewer who informs the applicant of job openings and the applicant has an opportunity to ask questions and to discuss skills, job interests, and so on.

preliminary employment interview

Great care also is needed to avoid discrimination in conducting these interviews. For example, questions such as "Do you plan to have children?" or "What does your husband think of your going to work?" should be avoided. Otherwise, the firm may be subject to lawsuits or to government action. Job interviews are discussed more fully in the Appendix.

Selection Tests

Selection tests are used to measure an applicant's potential to perform the job for which he or she is being considered. These tests include

selection tests

FIGURE 12-2

A job application form

APPLICATION FOR EMPLOYMENT AS FIELD REPRESENTATIVE

ALLYN AND BACON, INC. — 470 ATLANTIC AVENUE — BOSTON, MASS. 02210

Return to: _____ (   ) ELHI   (   ) COLLEGE

PLEASE FURNISH COMPLETE ANSWERS TO ALL THE QUESTIONS. WRITE NEATLY IN INK (OR USE TYPEWRITER)

DATE _____ Social Security No. _____

NAME _____ U.S. Citizen: Yes _____ No _____
    Last   First   Middle

HOME ADDRESS _____ Tel. No. _____
        Street   City   State   Zip Code

Is any additional information relative to a change of name, use of an assumed name or nickname necessary to enable a check on your work record? Yes ___ No ___
If "Yes", please identify name or names used and the period of time in which they were used on page three.

Present condition of health _____ Are you willing to have a physical examination by our doctor? _____

Number of days ill during last two years and types of illness _____

Have you ever applied for a position with Allyn and Bacon before? _____ When? _____ Where? _____

Have you any friends or relatives with Allyn and Bacon? _____ Who? _____ Relationship _____

Draft Classification _____ If deferred, state basis _____

U.S. Military Service _____ / _____ / _____ / _____
            Branch   Date Entered – Discharged   Nature of Discharge   Rank

Member of Reserves? _____ Active? _____ Inactive? _____ Date Active Reserve Duty Completed? _____

List all military, business and social organizations to which you belong (Note A) EXCEPT organizations of a religious or racial character or that indicate national

origin of its members: _____

In order to have a complete overview of your qualifications, please complete the following sections in conjunction with your employment history.

Education	Name of School	Where Located	FROM Mo. Yr.	TO Mo. Yr.	Course of Study	Graduate?	Degree
Prep or High							
College							
Other Education							

What was your standing and average in H.S.? _____ In College? _____

What was your college major? _____ Extra curricular activities? _____

To what undergraduate clubs or organizations did you belong? (See Note A above) _____

_____

Are you studying now? _____ What and where? _____

What further courses do you expect to take? _____ Where? _____

Referred to Allyn and Bacon, Inc. by _____

Toward what type position do you want to work? _____

When can you start work? _____ Minimum income requirement: _____

Source: _Allyn and Bacon._

intelligence tests, aptitude tests, performance tests, interest tests, and personality tests. Of course, not all firms will use all of the selection tests we will discuss. The size of the firm and the type of job, for example, influence the types of selection tests that will be used.

Intelligence tests measure general verbal ability and specific abilities such as reasoning. Aptitude tests measure ability, such as mechanical aptitude or clerical aptitude. Performance tests measure skill in a given type of work, such as typing. Interest tests (inventories), such as the Kuder Preference Record, are designed to predict whether a person will like to perform a particular task. Personality tests (inventories), such as the California Psychological Inventory, measure some aspect (or aspects) of a person's total personality. They are designed to predict whether a person will be able to accept a lot of stress on the job, work well with other people, and so on.

These tests help to determine if applicants match up to job requirements, but they are far from perfect. While it may be easy to measure a typist's ability to type by giving a performance test, not all jobs require such specific skills. Testing is more successful in spotting an applicant's shortcomings than in picking guaranteed successes. It is hard, for example, to test for job motivation, which plays a big part in a person's success or failure on the job. Selection tests should supplement (not substitute for) judgment and other information that is available on an applicant.

The use of selection tests is controversial. Some people believe that the tests are biased. Intelligence tests, for example, have been attacked because of their alleged white, middle-class cultural bias. It is unlikely that a person with a disadvantaged background who is applying for a job would be familiar with such words as *hors d'oeuvre* or *cutlery*. To that person, these things are "little sandwiches" or "knives, forks, and spoons." Unless the test is meant to measure his or her knowledge of such things, using those words may introduce cultural bias.

Critics argue that selection tests should measure a person's ability to do the job or measure the person's ability to be trained to do it. Other people argue that a job involves more than the ability to do a given task. For example, a recruit's ability to get along with others is important on the job and should be considered. To stay within the law, selection tests should be carefully designed to measure ability to do the specific job for which an applicant is being considered. The U.S. Supreme Court has ruled that tests can be used for employment decisions only if the tests are proven to predict job performance and are related to the job itself.

Proving that selection tests can predict job performance is, in itself, a major task. For several years the EEOC and the other government agencies charged with the job of eliminating discrimination in employment have insisted that employers validate the tests they use—prove that the tests can predict the applicant's ability to do the job for which he or she is applying. Because this is time-consuming, costly, and extremely tough to do, some firms have stopped using these tests, especially firms that do not have trained psychologists in their personnel departments. Many of them began placing more reliance on personal interviews and reference checks. The potential for bias here, however, probably is even greater than it is for tests.

The newer "bottom-line" concept in employee screening has been adopted by the EEOC, the Department of Justice, the Department of Labor, and the U.S. Civil Service Commission. Under this approach, employers may not have to go the "validation route" in proving that their screening processes are nondiscriminatory. If the number of minorities and women that actually are hired suggests that discrimination does not exist in the firm, there is no problem in using the tests.

The In-depth Interview

An applicant who passes the selection tests may be scheduled for an in-depth interview, especially if he or she is applying for a higher-level job. **An in-depth interview is one conducted by trained specialists from the personnel department to shed light on the applicant's motivation, ability to work with others, ability to communicate, etc.**

in-depth interview

Effective interviewing requires a lot of skill on the interviewer's part. But many interviewers simply lack interviewing skills. This is one of the main reasons that the interviewing process is under criticism. Many interviews probably are less valid as predictors of job success than some of the psychological tests that the U.S. Supreme Court has ruled illegal because of their potential for perpetuating illegal discrimination.

The Background Investigation

After in-depth interviewing, an applicant's references are checked. **In a background investigation, the applicant's past employers (if any), neighbors, former teachers, etc. are questioned about their knowledge of the applicant's job performance, character, and background.**

background investigation

There is a lot of controversy here, also. An employer has the right to look into an applicant's suitability for a job, but it is easy to go overboard and invade the applicant's privacy. Reference letters often are used by employers to obtain information about job applicants. While it's relatively easy for the applicant to find a few friends who will say "good things" about him or her, former employers and supervisors have tended to be more critical in their assessments. Since reference letters now are open for review by the person about whom they are written, former employers tend to say only complimentary things in writing. A growing number of employers are refusing to provide reference letters other than those that state the person's period and status of employment. Some employers, therefore, now are making personal telephone calls to former employers of job applicants.

LIE DETECTORS

> Whatever their problems or stated objectives, U.S. businesses have found a surprising range of applications for lie detectors. Not only are they looking for thieves, junkies, liars, alcoholics, and psychotics among their workers; increasingly the machines are being used to screen out applicants with health problems without resort to more expensive physical exams.

Source: *Business Week.*

The Final Selection Interview

If the results of the background investigation are satisfactory, the applicant may be called in for a final selection interview. As is true of the in-depth interview, a final selection interview is more likely when the applicant is applying for a higher-level job. **In the final selection interview, all company personnel who have interviewed the prospect are present, along with the manager under whom the applicant will work. The manager is the person who makes the decision whether or not to hire the applicant.** Any hiring decision, however, is contingent on passing the company's physical (and perhaps, psychological) exam.

final selection interview

In recent years there has been some controversy regarding physical and psychological exams. As long as they pertain to job-related requirements, there is no problem. But when a firm sets standards that are not job-related, trouble arises. Weight and height requirements often have been used to discriminate against women. There also is no excuse for denying physically or mentally handicapped persons a job if the handicap cannot hurt job performance.

The concept of the bona fide occupational qualification (BFOQ) is important in preparing job specifications and in the employee selection process. A BFOQ is an occupational qualification based on sex, age, religion, or national origin that is justified and legal as a basis for discrimination in selecting job applicants. The EEOC allows employers to set BFOQs if they can be justified. For example, a dress designer who wants to hire a female fashion model can use sex as a BFOQ to screen out male applicants. Airlines can use age as a BFOQ to screen out applicants for pilot positions if the applicants are over a certain age, provided the employer can prove that age is related to job performance (safety).

bona fide occupational qualification (BFOQ)

BFOQs always must be related to the job being filled. Thus an employer cannot refuse to hire a female applicant simply because the employer thinks the job is too physically demanding. Male applicants for jobs as flight attendants or women applicants for sales jobs that require travel with men cannot be rejected because of their sex. Race has never been upheld as the basis for a BFOQ.

Selecting Managers

Applicants for management positions are screened in somewhat the same way as other employees. Unlike most workers, who normally are being selected for specific jobs, managers are selected for careers. Job requirements and criteria for success are much harder to define for managers. Furthermore, whereas operative jobs generally require manual skills and other skills that may be easy to test, managerial skills are harder to test. This is why many firms rely very heavily on interviews in selecting managers.

In recent years the use of assessment centers has become popular in selecting managers. Graduating college seniors who are applying for a management trainee position may be given the standard personality, interest, and intelligence tests, but they are supplemented by giving the candidates a series of typical management problems to solve as a group. For example, a group may be set up as a "company" to manufacture and market a product. The members are observed by experienced managers who get together to make an overall evaluation of each candidate's performance. Their judgments are passed on to the persons who are making the selection decision.

Training and Developing Employees

Up to the point of hiring, the main goal of personnel activities is to accept or reject the applicant. After the employer tells the applicant that he or she is hired, the "point of hire" has been passed. The employer then can ask for personal information that it may have been illegal to request earlier. For example, medical insurance inquiry cards legally can require age and sex data. The only time such information could be requested legally of an applicant is when the prospective employer needs the information to comply with EEOC Applicant Flow Record requirements. Of course, it still is illegal to engage in discriminatory practices after the person is hired. (See Figure 12–3.)

Employee Orientation

employee orientation

Employee orientation (induction or indoctrination) involves introducing the new employee to the job and to the firm. It is the first, and probably most critical, phase of the employee's training. An applicant gets some orientation to the firm and the job during the selection process, but it only touches the surface. For an employee, the orientation

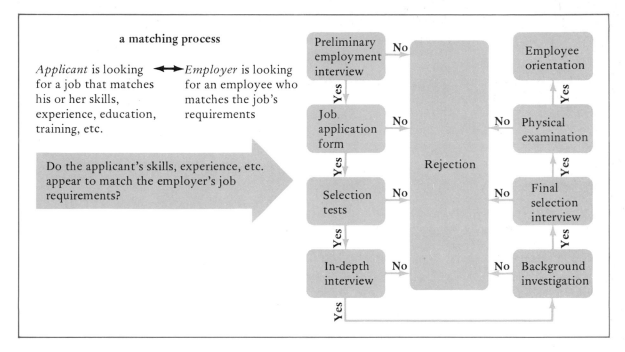

a matching process

Applicant is looking ←→ *Employer* is looking for a job that matches his or her skills, experience, education, training, etc.

for an employee who matches the job's requirements

Do the applicant's skills, experience, etc. appear to match the employer's job requirements?

Preliminary employment interview — No → Rejection

Yes

Job application form — No → Rejection

Yes

Selection tests — No → Rejection

Yes

In-depth interview — No → Rejection

Yes

Background investigation — No → Rejection

Yes

Final selection interview — No → Rejection

Yes

Physical examination — No → Rejection

Yes

Employee orientation

FIGURE 12-3

The sequence of steps an applicant may go through in the employee selection process

should be much more formal and complete. Serious-minded employees want to know what is expected of them on the job. If the orientation is skimpy or mishandled, they will experience a lot of stress at the outset and they may leave the firm, and a potentially fine resource is lost.

A good orientation program helps to relieve the new employee's feelings of insecurity in a new environment. He or she is told about the firm's history, its products, and its operation. Company policies and rules are explained as are company-sponsored employee services. Often these are spelled out in a personnel manual, or employee handbook. To acquaint the new employee with the firm, a tour of the plant often is made, coworkers are introduced, and the new employee's questions are answered.

The personnel department coordinates the orientation program, but the new employee's supervisor plays the major role. Effective supervisors know that the time they devote to orientation can save them "headaches" later in disciplining and answering questions from new employees who received a poor introduction to the job.

Employee Training

Job-skill training teaches employees specific job skills. It can be done on the job or away from the job.

job-skill training

On-the-job training (OJT) can be used to teach new employees their jobs or to teach new skills to experienced employees. OJT is best suited to teaching simple jobs. The trainee works under the guidance of an experienced worker who advises and shows the trainee how to do the job.

Away-from-the-job training is used when a higher level of skill is required and when OJT is too dangerous, or causes too much interruption of the workflow in the plant. The trainee may go to a company-sponsored training program either at the plant or in the company's training school. He or she is trained on the same machines that are used in the plant, but the training is done in a classroom. This often is called *vestibule training*.

Training is an ongoing process because new employees must be trained and those with longer service must be retrained. The rapid pace of technological change means that employee skills become obsolete much faster. Thus the techniques of in-company training also are changing. Computers, closed-circuit TV, programed text materials, video-cassettes, and other technical aids are being used. The millions of dollars that firms spend every year training their employees pay off in improved morale and productivity.

Management Development

management development

Management development refers to efforts to prepare people for managerial positions and to improve the managerial skills of present managers. Among the techniques of management development that are used, especially in larger firms, are

- lecture
- case method
- simulation
- laboratory training

The lecture method is good for presenting facts but not for developing managerial skills. For example, it is a good way of informing managers of the meaning of new laws that regulate business activity. In the case method, participants are given a problem situation which they must analyze and solve as if the case situation were real. Its major drawback is that it often fails to develop the emotional involvement of the participants. Examples of simulation are management games and role-playing. Simulation techniques force trainees to act out real business behavior that is supposed to give them practice in decision making. In a management game, for example, several teams compete against each other. Each team is a separate "company." Role-playing emphasizes the human aspects of management. A trainee might play the role of a supervisor who is disciplining a subordinate or evaluating the performance of a subordinate.

One of the newer management-development techniques is T-group training (also called sensitivity training, laboratory training, or encounter groups). Small discussion groups become involved with real (not simulated) problems that exist within the training group itself. The purpose is to help trainees learn about their individual weaknesses, how groups work, and how to behave more effectively in interpersonal relations.

Organization Development (OD)

Management development is concerned mainly with the manager as an individual. In recent years a lot of attention has been focused on the organization as a whole. **Organization development (OD) is a re-education process that is used to change the culture, values, and behavior of the entire organization in order to improve its effectiveness in reaching its objectives and in solving problems.** By improving the organization, it is assumed that the employees' value to it increases. OD uses knowledge in the fields of psychology and sociology to improve organizations. OD programs are based on the systems view of management and can lead to organizational changes, such as redesigned jobs and participative work groups.

organization development (OD)

Appraising Employee Performance

The personnel department also helps to develop a formal performance appraisal system to enable supervisors to rate their subordinates' job performance. A good performance appraisal system provides a basis for measuring an employee's contribution to the firm. It reduces employee suspicion that promotions and pay raises are based on favoritism rather than performance. Since there are several types of performance appraisal systems, it is important for supervisors and subordinates to understand the system that is used by the firm.

performance appraisal system

Traditional performance appraisal systems require a manager to appraise a subordinate's work habits and personal traits. In the merit rating system, each employee's job performance is appraised every six months or every year. Initiative, ability to work with others, dependability, etc., are appraised. There is, of course, a lot of room for error in rating these personal traits and work habits objectively.

merit rating system

Because of these problems, some firms rely mainly on an employee's seniority as a basis for granting pay raises and promotions. **Seniority refers to an employee's length of service. The longer that service, the more seniority an employee has.** It is a lot easier to be objective in measuring seniority than in measuring initiative or ability to work with others. This is why labor unions favor the seniority system. By and large,

seniority

TWO POINTS OF VIEW

Employee Evaluation

Supervisor A:

"As a supervisor, I have to evaluate my subordinates every six months. The people over in the personnel department keep tabs on these evaluations for use when promotions open up and for granting pay raises. Honestly, I think it's a lot of bull. If I rate any of my subordinates low, it's a bad reflection on me. After all, my job is to inspire them to good performance. For example, if I check the box that says 'poor attitude toward job,' in effect I'm admitting that I'm failing as a manager.

"On the other hand, if I give 'top grades' to my subordinates, I look good to them and to my boss. It sort of reminds me of school and the lousy grading system. You can bet that all of my subordinates always get good marks."

Supervisor B:

"As a supervisor, I want to evaluate my subordinates every six months. I have an obligation to my subordinates to rate their performances realistically and objectively. They want to know where they stand and how well they are progressing on the job. I also have an obligation to my superiors to make the best use of my subordinates.

"As a manager, I must work through others. The more that I can help them develop into good employees, the more valuable they are to me, to the company, and to themselves."

"Since you like to state things in football terms, McDonnell, it's fourth and long yardage for your career."

Source: *Selling Short,* Universal Press Syndicate.

however, this approach dodges the issue of appraising employee performance.

As we saw in Chapter 5, the management by objectives (MBO) approach can be used in rating employee performance. It does away with some of the subjective elements in a merit rating system. But it requires mutual trust and respect between boss and subordinate, ability to communicate effectively with each other, and faith in each other's abilities.

Compensating Employees

wage and salary administration

Wage and salary administration is the process of developing and implementing a sound and fair method of compensating employees. It involves setting pay ranges for all jobs in the firm and setting a specific amount of pay for each employee.

Compensation is important to employees because pay is the main factor that determines the standard of living for most American families.

It is the major source of buying power. Although pay is important in an economic sense, it also is important in a psychological sense. Many workers, for example, measure their importance to their employers in terms of their pay.

To an employer, employee pay is a cost of doing business. Although wage and salary administrators want to hold this cost down, they know that low pay usually leads to low employee morale. Low pay does not always mean more profit to the firm. We must consider labor productivity. It is better to pay a worker $10 per hour for producing 100 units of output than it is to pay a worker $5 per hour for producing 30 units. An employer is wise to view pay as an incentive to greater effort, not as a cost that should be reduced.

A firm's compensation system also can be important to the firm's various publics. Take the case of a large firm that builds a plant in a small town. If the local labor supply cannot meet the new plant's needs, the firm may have to pay "above-average" wages to attract some employees away from other employers or cause some to move to the area. An employment boom might occur in the town.

Determining the Basis for Payment

A worker's pay can be based on

- output produced
- time spent on the job
- a combination of output produced and time spent on the job

Some workers are paid a piece rate. Each worker is paid a certain rate for each acceptable unit of output produced. A worker who sews together a pair of overalls could be paid a piece rate. This method, of course, can be used only when each worker's labor can be identified with specific units of output.

piece rate

To encourage greater worker productivity, some firms offer incentive pay. For those units produced by a worker above the normal output per day (the quota), the piece rate is increased. Suppose the quota is 100 pairs of overalls per day. A worker gets $.35 for each pair sewed together. Meeting quota means a daily payment of $35. If a bonus (incentive payment) of $.05 were paid for each pair produced above quota, a worker who produced 120 pairs would receive $43 for that day's work (100 pairs × 35 cents + 20 pairs × 40 cents, or $35 + $8 = $43).

incentive pay

A worker paid on the basis of time spent on the job gets paid by the hour, week, or month. **A worker paid on an hourly rated basis receives a wage.** Thus a worker who gets $6 per hour and works 40 hours a week gets $240 in wages for that week. Hourly workers can get overtime pay by working extra hours.

wage

A worker paid a fixed amount on a weekly, biweekly, or monthly

salary

basis receives a salary. Salaried workers usually work for a fixed amount of pay per year. Most white-collar jobs are salaried jobs. Salaried workers usually do not get overtime pay.

A salesperson might be paid a base salary plus a commission for sales made. This is a combination of time spent on the job and output produced. If a salesperson gets a bonus for selling more than the quota, the pay plan provides incentive.

Features of Wage and Salary Administration

There are four main features of wage and salary administration:

- wage and salary surveys
- job evaluation
- performance rating
- incentive plans

Wage and salary surveys are conducted to determine the general pay level in the firm's community and industry. In setting its pay rates, the firm can pay above, at, or below the prevailing pay level in the industry or community. If top management wants to recruit the best talent available, the firm may be willing to pay "above-market" rates. If there are large numbers of unemployed people who have the skills the firm needs, the pay level may be set at or below the prevailing level. Of course, other factors, such as minimum wage laws and the presence or absence of a union must be considered. After determining the general pay level, the focus shifts to determining what other firms are paying for comparable jobs.

Job evaluation is a method for determining the relationship between pay rates for particular job classifications. For example, how much pay should typists, receptionists, accountants, and salespersons receive? Important factors here are the prestige and status attached to different jobs, the desirability of the work, and the amount of skill, experience, or education needed to perform a given job.

Instead of setting one pay rate for each job, a series of rates (steps, or pay ranges) are set for each job. New employees usually start at the base rate for the job, and the worker advances to higher rates as he or she gains experience, proficiency, and seniority. This is called performance rating. Some firms set pay ranges on a strictly judgment basis; others develop detailed rating systems, or point systems. Under "the relative desirability of the type of work," for example, the firm might set point values for such things as danger and exposure to pollution. Regardless of approach, the goal is to come up with a pay range that is fair for each job in the company.

Finally, wage and salary administrators must decide how much each

"*About my raise, boss . . . I had in mind something a little more inflationary.*"

Source: *Dunagin's People*, Field Newspaper Syndicate.

individual worker should receive. Firms with incentive plans pay the base rate only for a "normal amount of production," as determined, for example, through a time study. Employees who produce more than the normal amount get an extra incentive bonus.

The Equity Theory of Compensation

Equity theory is important in wage and salary administration. Equity, in this case, is the *perceived* fairness of what a worker does compared to what he or she receives from the employer. The worker exchanges his or her inputs (such as skills) for outputs (tangible and intangible rewards from the employer) and compares the inputs and outputs to those of other workers doing the same job.

The worker is concerned with the fairness of the pay as he or she perceives it. This perception is based on a comparison the worker makes between his or her input and output with the inputs and outputs of other people doing the same job. Inequity results when there is an imbalance between the inputs and outputs as a result of the comparison process. Pay inequity has been a major issue in the women's movement. Many women argue that they do the same work as men (equivalent inputs) but receive lower pay (unequal outputs).

Workers who feel that their inputs are greater than their outputs might try to get a pay raise, reduce their inputs, quit the job for a more equitable job, or learn to live with dissatisfaction. On the other hand, workers who feel their inputs are less than their outputs may put forth more effort on the job or re-evaluate their inputs to "prove" to themselves that they actually are not being overpaid.

Compensating Managers

An owner-manager's compensation is tied to the firm's profit. But with professional managers, this is not always the case. Many of the same factors that determine a worker's pay affect how much a manager will receive. But there are no union wage scales to serve as guidelines.

Fringe benefits (employee benefits in addition to salary) are very important to managers in high income-tax brackets. Deferred income plans enable them to receive part of their compensation after retirement. Income deferral shelters some earnings from the high tax rates they pay in their working years. A firm tries to "lock in" good executives by offering many benefits that hinge on their staying with the firm. Liberal retirement benefits are an example.

Promoting Employees

promotion

A promotion means moving up to a higher position in the firm, usually one that involves more pay and more challenge. It is a way of compensating an employee for good performance in the previous job.

Firms set up promotion programs to decide which employees are promotable. The personnel department can help by developing "career ladders" that will encourage promising employees to take the risks involved in being promoted.

You probably have heard jokes about the employee who got a promotion but no raise in pay. To many people a promotion means more than a pay raise. It is a clear form of recognition for good performance, and it moves the employee up the firm's job ladder. In most cases a promotion is much more visible to others than is a salary increase.

As we saw earlier some approaches to evaluating employee performance are more objective than others. But employees do want to be rated. The important thing is that the system used is fair, is understood by employees, and is consistently and objectively used. Performance in the present job should be the basic factor in determining an employee's promotability to a higher job.

Providing Personnel Services

Employee benefits, or fringe benefits, are compensation other than wages or salaries—company-paid tuition for employees who attend college, cafeterias, credit unions, group life and medical insurance, paid vacations, and retirement programs. Fringes account for about 35 percent of the typical worker's compensation and their cost is growing about twice as fast as wages and salaries.

A recent innovation in fringes is flexible benefit plans, or "cafeteria plans." The employer offers a basic core of benefits to all employees and each individual employee is allowed to "buy" additional benefits to suit his or her own needs. Employees "buy" these benefits with their benefit credits, based on, for example, salary or length of service. Thus a single male employee fifty years of age might choose to pass up maternity coverage for additional pension contributions.

Employee benefits help to build employee morale, which can help in reducing absenteeism and labor turnover. *Absenteeism* occurs when workers fail to report to work, and *labor turnover* occurs when they quit their jobs. Both lower employee productivity. To employers, this means rising costs and less ability to compete, especially with foreign firms. To

WELL PAY

Sick pay is one of those necessary and sensible corporate institutions that are often abused. If an employee is hung over or simply does not feel like working because it is a lovely day, he can call in with a feigned case of the blahs. That escape hatch from the workaday world is being mildly threatened by a new-fangled idea aimed at throwing dedicated malingerers into a dilemma: well pay.

Now being tried in several small and medium-size companies on the West Coast, well pay rewards people for doing what they are supposed to do: to work regularly and on time. Some results have been impressive. Reports James Parsons, 59, president of Parsons Pine Products of Ashland, Ore., maker of nearly 80% of the nation's wooden mousetrap bases: "Our absenteeism has dropped 30%, and our tardiness is almost zero." Parsons' incentive: an extra day's pay at the end of every month to workers who are punctual. Reichhold Chemicals' fiberglass manufacturing division in Irwindale, Calif., offers half an hour's pay for each week a worker completes a full shift without illness or absence. The bonuses are called "sweet pay" (for Stay at Work, Earn Extra Pay).

Source: *Time.*

workers, it means little hope for good raises. To society, it means more inflation. When overall wage increases outstrip productivity gains in the economy, the result is higher prices for the products and services people buy.

Employee Safety and Health

Employee safety and health programs are two personnel services that help to reduce absenteeism and labor turnover. The personnel department creates and implements the company-wide safety and health program. This program helps to reduce lost time due to accidents and illness. It raises productivity and boosts morale by making jobs safer and more healthful.

A good safety and health program helps to reduce job accidents by eliminating the cause of accidents and the injuries that often result from them. Accidents are caused by unsafe working conditions and/or careless and unsafe activities of employees. Once the causes of accidents are known, measures can be taken to reduce or eliminate them. Likewise, by studying employee activities, steps can be taken to eliminate poor work habits.

Occupational Safety and Health Act (OSHA)

In 1970, the Occupational Safety and Health Act (OSHA) was passed to help ensure that every working man and woman in the nation has a safe and healthful work environment. The law set up the Occupational Safety and Health Administration to enforce it.

JOB HEALTH

The 10 industrial hygienists employed by labor unions may seem utterly unequal to the task of monitoring—much less solving—the on-job health problems of 20 million unionized workers. But the unions' employment of such professionals is a clear sign that organized labor is increasingly asserting itself on occupational health issues rather than leaving them to the shifting priorities of the Occupational Safety & Health Administration. While companies now spend much time fighting OSHA regulations, they may soon face more formidable challenges from unions on the health front.

Source: *Business Week.*

OSHA covers office workers as well as factory workers. Some provisions of the law relate mainly to housekeeping requirements, such as keeping work areas uncluttered, while others set out requirements for equipment safety, the construction of buildings, etc. Originally, the Occupational Safety and Health Administration was expected to seek voluntary compliance with its regulations, and it was assumed that a few fines and other penalties would be enough to secure compliance. But from the start, this agency has been the source of a lot of controversy. Unclear regulations, the high cost of complying, and uncertainty about the agency's authority to make uninvited inspections caused a lot of complaints. In more recent years, therefore, the agency has toned down some of its activities and requirements. For example, the U.S. Supreme Court has ruled that OSHA searches that are conducted without a warrant or the employer's consent are unconstitutional. OSHA, however, does *not* have to provide evidence of a probable violation in order to get a warrant.

Performing Other Personnel Activities

The personnel department also plays a major role in formulating employee discipline policy and in explaining it to workers. Actually, discipline is used only when other approaches to correct employee performance problems have failed. Although most workers abide by the rules, some workers do break them. Disciplinary action is administered by the worker's supervisor. For first offenses, it usually means an oral reprimand in private. The more serious the offense and the greater the number of prior offenses, the stiffer the penalty. After oral warnings, there are written warnings, disciplinary layoffs, and discharge from the company.

In past years only unionized firms had to be concerned about challenges to their discipline policies. But in recent years challenges have come from other sources. An employee can only be disciplined for what he or she has done, not because of who he or she is. Otherwise, the discipline will violate antidiscrimination laws. It's also illegal to discipline an employee who, for example, gives information that helps convict the employer of a charge of polluting the environment. The employee does have the right of free speech.

Personnel departments also provide many other types of services. During periods when business is slack, management must decide what to do with employees whose services are no longer needed. One department may have to cut its work force while another may need more workers. The personnel department might help the two department managers to shift workers between departments, help in a retraining effort if that is needed, or help to develop a plan for sharing the available work among employees—shorter work weeks for all workers or layoffs in order of seniority.

Employers who have to cut back their permanent work forces often try to minimize the problems of workers who are being discharged. If a

FLEX TIME

"Flex time," or flexible working hours, as opposed to fixed working hours, is making entry into the labor force easier for many workers, especially women workers. The concept of part-time work has been in existence for a long time. But flex time is a more recent innovation. For example, it enables working mothers to fulfill their other responsibilities without having to give up an opportunity for a full-time job.

The concept of flex time is built around a core of working hours, for example, 10 a.m. to 2 p.m. All employees are required to work between those hours. Each individual employee, however, is given the opportunity to select other hours of work to make up a full work week. Although it presents scheduling problems, flex time also makes it possible for some employees to work full-time instead of having to settle for part-time work.

plant closing is being considered, the personnel department might help these workers find jobs with other firms. It also might handle the job of paying them severance pay.

Terminating Employees

Eventually every employee will leave the company's service. This may come about by death, retirement, voluntary resignation, dismissal, or discharge.

Retirement

Many firms have retirement plans as one of their fringe benefits. Employees whose service has been good over their working years get compensation from the firm during their nonworking, or retirement, years. It is a type of deferred compensation.

Some employees are ready for retirement much earlier than others. But most retirement plans are based on the employee's age. This requirement forces some workers who perhaps should retire earlier to stay on the job. It forces others to leave perhaps before they would like to and even though they are still good workers. The Age Discrimination in Employment Act has been extended to cover workers up to age 70. In most cases, forced retirement at age 65 no longer is legal if the employee wants to stay on the job and is mentally and physically able to do so.

Some workers, however, want early retirement and their employers grant it. They also help the employee to adjust to this new lifestyle by providing various types of counseling services.

The Employee Retirement Income Security Act of 1974 (the "Pension Reform" act) protects the pension rights of workers if the employer goes out of business or if the worker quits or is dismissed after a certain period of employment. The term *vesting* means that the worker's right to his or her accumulated pension benefits is guaranteed to the worker. The law does not require an employer to set up a pension plan but it does set up regulations for company or union plans. A Pension Benefit Guarantee Corporation was created to pay workers whose pension plans fail because of employer bankruptcy or union corruption.

The law benefits retired workers who receive pension benefits. It also provides portability to workers who change jobs. Thus workers who leave a firm before retirement are eligible to receive whatever benefits they earned when they reach retirement age. Furthermore, if the worker takes a job with another employer, the worker's pension credits can be transferred from the old pension fund to the new one, if the new employer agrees to this.

Voluntary Resignation

Resignation occurs when an employee voluntarily leaves the employer's service. There are many reasons for employee resignation. Some employees want to leave to take a job with another employer. In fact, a lot of firms try to hire away good employees from other firms. Some employees quit in order to dramatize a point of difference with higher-ups.

resignation

Because of the poor effect on morale, a wise employer does not want to hold on to an employee who can improve his or her position at another firm. **But it is a good practice to conduct an exit interview with an employee who is quitting the firm. The purpose of an exit interview is to determine the reasons why an employee is leaving.** Perhaps the work environment could be changed to discourage others from leaving.

exit interview

Dismissal

Dismissal is an involuntary temporary or permanent separation of the employee. Some workers are laid off temporarily when business is slack. Of course, a layoff can become permanent if laid-off workers are not called back.

dismissal

Union contracts usually specify that a laid-off worker's right to be recalled, based on his or her seniority, will not continue beyond a certain period of time, usually one or two years. This means that a layoff which lasts longer than that period of time results in the loss of the worker's claim to other employee benefits that are based on seniority. In other words, if he or she is rehired, he or she comes back as a new employee.

Discharge

discharge

Discharge is a permanent involuntary separation due to a permanent layoff or outright firing of an employee. It sometimes is called "industrial capital punishment." A firm might permanently lay off workers in a plant when it is closed down. An employee might be discharged because of an inability to do the job or serious violations of work rules.

Summary and Look Ahead

A firm's most important resource is its human resource, its personnel. Top management is responsible for putting together and keeping intact a productive work force that includes managers and workers. This is the task of personnel administration.

Top management delegates to the personnel manager the task of carrying out its human resource philosophy at the firm's operations level. Usually, this means setting up a personnel department headed by a personnel manager. This is a staff position created to advise and assist line managers in managing their personnel.

The personnel department's main activities are (1) determining human resource needs; (2) searching for and recruiting applicants to fill those needs; (3) selecting applicants for employment; (4) training and developing personnel; (5) appraising employee performance; (6) compensating employees; (7) promoting employees; (8) providing personnel services; (9) performing other personnel activities; and (10) terminating employees. (See Table 12–2.) All of these activities are interrelated and are vital aspects of human resource management. It is crucial that all of these activities are conducted with awareness of antidiscrimination laws.

In the next chapter, we look at labor relations. The viewpoint for personnel management is the employer-individual employee relationship. In labor relations, the viewpoint is the employer-union relationship. The focus is on the employees as a group, as members of one or more labor unions. Labor relations activities often are referred to as "industrial relations." But even when line managers handle negotiations with labor unions, the personnel department is responsible for providing advisory services through their labor-relations specialists.

TABLE 12-2

**The personnel
department's activities,
objectives, and procedures**

Activities	Objectives	Procedures
1. Determining human resource needs	To specify the firm's need for applicants	(a) Study company objectives (b) Study organization chart (c) Forecast human resource needs (d) Develop management inventory (e) Perform job analysis (f) Prepare job description (g) Prepare job specification
2. Searching for and recruiting applicants	To attract applicants to the firm	(a) Specify sources of recruits (b) Recruiting
3. Selecting applicants for employment	To select the most desirable applicants	(a) Prepare job application form (b) Conduct preliminary interview (c) Administer selection tests (d) Conduct in-depth interview (e) Conduct background investigation (f) Conduct final selection interview (g) Schedule physical examination
4. Training and developing employees	To build and maintain a productive work force	(a) Handle job orientation (b) Perform job-skill training (c) Aid in management development
5. Appraising employee performance	To rate employee performance objectively	Develop performance appraisal system
6. Compensating employees	To develop a fair and equitable system for paying employees	Wage and salary administration
7. Promoting employees	To reward productive employees in order to utilize the human resource more effectively	Developing promotion policies
8. Providing personnel services	To build and enhance employee morale	(a) Provide fringe benefits (b) Employee safety and health
9. Performing other personnel activities	To advise and assist line managers in coping with special personnel problems	(a) Formulate employee discipline policy (b) Retrain employees (c) Share work among employees (d) Counsel employees
10. Terminating employees	To facilitate the exit of employees from the employer's service	(a) Retirement (b) Resignation (c) Dismissal (d) Discharge

**Hanes
Corporation**

My name is Cathy Cook. I am an employee benefits supervisor in the Personnel Department of the Bali Company Division of Hanes Corporation. I graduated from Surry Community College in Dobson, North Carolina with an Associate Degree in Applied Science.

As employee benefits supervisor, I am primarily responsible for the administration of employee group insurance, the retirement and retirement savings plans, workmen's compensation, and unemployment compensation. I assist in the planning, development, administration, and communication of employee benefits to all domestic and foreign locations. In addition to administering the benefits program, I am responsible for preparing the company's affirmative action plans, tracking turnover and absenteeism, preparing orientation programs, and writing employee handbooks and other employee communications. I have begun training in the field of salary administration. I also serve as editor of the Bali Division newsletter.

I began work as benefits coordinator in the personnel area after seven years of secretarial experience. After one year of experience in this job, I was promoted to supervisor. I selected the personnel area because of the many areas of learning involved and the opportunity to work more closely with employees.

Key Concepts

affirmative action plan A detailed statement by a firm describing how the firm will implement a program of actively recruiting and upgrading members of minority groups and women.

background investigation Checking up on a job applicant's references to help in assessing his or her suitability to the job.

bona fide occupational qualification (BFOQ) An occupational qualification based on sex, age, religion, or national origin. Allowed by the EEOC if the qualification is job related and can be justified.

discharge A permanent involuntary separation due to permanent layoff or firing of an employee.

dismissal A temporary or permanent involuntary separation of an employee.

employee orientation The process of introducing a new employee to the job and to the firm. Also called induction or indoctrination.

exit interview An interview conducted with an employee who is leaving the firm. Its purpose is to find out the reasons for leaving.

final selection interview The last in a series of interviews of a prospective new employee. It comes after the in-depth interview.

human resource The personnel who staff a firm, including both workers and managers.

incentive pay Payments made to a worker who exceeds his or her quota under a piece-rate system. In general, the purpose is to encourage and reward increased employee productivity.

in-depth interview The interview given to an applicant who passes the selection tests. It is conducted by trained specialists from the personnel department to shed light on the applicant's motivation, ability to work with others, ability to communicate, etc.

job analysis Defining the jobs that must be done if a firm is to reach its goals.

job application form A form prepared by an employer to be completed by a job applicant. The applicant gives a written summary of his or her education, experience, skills, etc. Also called an application blank or a biographical inventory.

job description A listing and description of the nature and requirements of a job. Prepared from the job analysis.

job-skill training Training an employee how to do a job. It can be done on the job or away from the job. Its main purpose is to teach specific job skills.

job specification A statement of the personal qualifications (education, skill, experience, etc.) needed by the person who is to fill each job. Prepared from the job analysis.

management development Training present and potential managers to improve their managerial abilities. It focuses mainly on developing the manager's conceptual and human relations skills.

management inventory A list of present managerial positions in a firm and the names and personal data of the persons who hold those positions.

merit rating system An approach to evaluating employee performance. Performance is appraised periodically by each worker's supervisor. Performance criteria include personal traits and work habits.

Occupational Safety and Health Act (OSHA) A 1970 federal law that set up the Occupational Safety and Health Administration "to assure so far as possible every working man or woman in the nation safe and healthful working conditions."

organization development (OD) A re-education process that is used to change an organization so that it will be more effective in reaching its objectives. It is based heavily on concepts from sociology and psychology.

performance appraisal system A system used by management to measure and evaluate employee performance on the job.

personnel administration Top management's efforts to develop good company personnel, including both managers and workers. It is the broadest possible view of the firm's human resource and sets the tone for the firm's approach to managing that resource.

personnel department A staff department headed by a personnel manager which advises and assists line managers in managing their personnel. Performs personnel tasks such as recruiting and training.

personnel management The task of implementing top management's policies regarding human resource management. Includes activities such as recruiting, selecting, training, developing, compensating, motivating, and terminating employees. It is the job of the personnel manager who heads the personnel department. More generally, it refers to the duty of all managers to manage their personnel.

piece rate A method of paying workers. Each worker is paid a certain rate for each acceptable unit of output produced.

preliminary employment interview A job applicant's first interview with a prospective employer.

promotion Moving up to a higher position on a firm's job ladder. Usually involves more pay and more challenge.

recruiting The task of attracting potential employees to a firm.

resignation An employee's announcement that he or she is voluntarily leaving an employer's service.

salary Fixed compensation to an employee who is regularly paid on a weekly, biweekly, or monthly basis.

selection tests Tests given to job applicants whose preliminary employment interview and job application forms were satisfactory. Their purpose is to select the best applicants and to reject the others. They include aptitude tests, intelligence tests, performance tests, personality tests, and interest tests.

seniority An employee's length of service. The longer that service, the greater the seniority. It can be computed on the basis of length of service with the firm, length of service in a particu-lar job or department, or length of membership in a labor union.

wage Compensation to a worker who is paid by the hour.

wage and salary administration The process of developing and implementing a sound and fair method of compensating employees.

For Review . . .

1. Does "personnel administration" mean the same thing as "personnel department"? Explain.
2. Why might a firm create a personnel department?
3. Give an example that illustrates how a personnel management information system (PMIS) could benefit a firm.
4. List the ten phases of personnel work and tell how antidiscrimination laws can affect performance of those personnel activities.
5. What purpose does a management inventory serve?
6. Explain how the use of assessment centers can help in selecting managers.
7. What should be covered in an employee orientation program?
8. List and discuss four techniques of management development.
9. Why is it important to have a good performance appraisal system?
10. List and discuss the four main features of wage and salary administration.
11. What is the equity theory of compensation?

. . . For Discussion

1. When a firm buys a new typewriter, it expects that its value will diminish with the passage of time. The typewriter becomes "used up." Is the same true of a new management trainee who recently began working for the firm?
2. Applicants for managerial positions usually are given more "subjective" tests than are applicants for nonmanagerial jobs. Why is this? Are there any potential dangers?
3. Should a firm retrain employees whose skills have become obsolete if it can hire persons already possessing the needed skills?
4. Do you think that it is fair for a firm to have a policy of not promoting from within?
5. Do you think that it is proper for a retailing firm to require job applicants to submit to a polygraph (lie-detector) test as a condition of employment? Is it fair to require all salespeople to take a polygraph test every six months in order to keep their jobs?

Incidents

The Climate Survey

"Last year more than 100,000 employees—ranging from production workers to senior managers—minced no words in telling their bosses exactly what they thought of them, the company they work for, and their fellow workers. But instead of being fired, they were encouraged to sound off. Their companies were using a management tool called climate surveys, which not only get employee opinions out in the open but force managers to face up to—and correct—often unpleasant situations."

The climate survey is a technique for improving two-way communication in an organization.

"Giving employees a say, of course, is nothing new. Attitude surveys—which sample employee opinions companywide on such general topics as pay, benefits, and the like—have existed for decades. But climate surveys zero in on individual departments or work units of about 15 or fewer employees, and ask such questions as 'Does your boss make assignments clear?' and 'Do you get recognition for a job well done?' What is more, they offer a no-holds, two-way feedback process—an interpersonal exchange between managers and subordinates—in which unwarranted employee gripes can be explained away and legitimate ones handled."

Questions

1. Can a climate survey provide the manager with information that can be used to improve his or her managerial skills? Explain.
2. Why is two-way feedback so important between managers and subordinates?
3. How might a personnel department assist managers in using this technique?

Source: *Business Week.*

Eastern Airlines' "Save-Your-Job" Program

When Frank Borman took over as chairman of Eastern Airlines in early 1976, the company was in deep financial difficulties. In order to help turn the company around, Mr. Borman started up two new programs. First, he persuaded Eastern's 36,000 employees to accept a wage freeze in return for a profit-sharing program for five years.

In mid-1977 Mr. Borman also persuaded Eastern's employees to accept a 3.5 percent wage deferral in order to help reach a profit target of 2 cents on every revenue dollar Eastern collected. The program was a kind of "Save-Your-Job" program that was named the "Variable Earnings Program." Under the program, Eastern returns all of the 3.5 percent contribution if the profit targets are met. Eastern keeps the difference from the contributions if profits fall below the target. If, however, earned profit exceeds the target, the employees can collect up to 3.5 percent more than their normal pay.

In early December of 1978, Eastern's employees received more than $60 million in deferred earnings and profit-sharing bonuses. This included all the employees' deferred wages for the first eleven months of 1978 and the first installment on the profit-sharing program.

Questions

1. How would you describe Mr. Borman's concept of the human resource?
2. Do you think the Save-Your-Job Program helped Mr. Borman to turn the company around? Why or why not?
3. If you had been an Eastern employee when the new program was announced, would you have agreed to participate? Why or why not?

Source: *The Times-Picayune.*

Labor Relations

CHAPTER 13

Objectives: After reading this chapter, you should be able to

1. Explain how the Industrial Revolution changed the "world of work" for workers and led to efforts among workers to form unions.
2. Describe the general nature of labor-management relations prior to the 1930s.
3. Give examples of how the legal environment prior to the 1930s was hostile to unionization.
4. List the major federal labor laws and discuss the major provisions of each.
5. Discuss the National Labor Relations Board's role in certifying a union as the exclusive bargaining agent for a firm's employees.
6. Show how a local union, a national union, and a labor federation are related to each other.
7. Distinguish between craft and industrial unions.
8. Give examples of political, social, and economic objectives of unions.
9. List several important reasons why workers join unions.
10. Cite specific issues that might lead to labor-management conflict.
11. Explain how employees and employers collectively bargain through union and management representatives.
12. List and discuss labor and management's "weapons" in dealing with conflict.
13. Appraise the future prospects for the union movement in the United States.

Key concepts: Look for these terms as you read the chapter

labor union	closed shop
collective bargaining	union shop
collective bargaining agreement	right-to-work laws
blacklists	agency shop
unfair lists	open shop
injunction	guaranteed annual wage
Norris-LaGuardia Act	supplemental unemployment benefits (SUB)
Wagner Act	
National Labor Relations Board (NLRB)	bargainable issues
Fair Labor Standards Act	escalator clause
Taft-Hartley Act	conciliation
Landrum-Griffin Act	mediation
craft unions	voluntary arbitration
industrial unions	compulsory arbitration
local union	grievance procedures
national union	strike
union federation	picketing
lobbying	boycott
	lockout

The relationship between employer and employees is crucial in a firm. When the relationship is between the employer and the employees as individuals, it is called employee relations or personnel relations. In many firms, however, the employees belong to labor unions. The relationship between the employer and the employees' union(s) is called labor relations. In this relationship, a third party, the union, comes between the employer and the employees. No longer does the employer deal with an employee solely as an individual.

In labor relations, management representatives bargain with union representatives over wages and working conditions for unionized employees. In some firms the personnel manager does the bargaining for the employer. But as unions have become more powerful, labor relations specialists are increasingly found in unionized firms.

We begin this chapter with a brief look at the history of the union movement in the United States and the major federal laws that deal with unions. We will also look at why workers join unions, the nature of labor-management relations, and the future of unions in the United States.

Why Unions Began

Individualism is a basic characteristic of capitalism. Labor unions, however, are based on the idea of collective action. **A labor union is an organization of employees formed for the purpose of dealing collectively with their employers in order to further the interests of those employees.**

labor union

The dealing that occurs between the employer and the union is called collective bargaining. **Collective bargaining is the process of negotiating a labor agreement between union representatives and employer representatives and also involves the ongoing process of administering an existing labor agreement.**

collective bargaining

The contract negotiated between employer and union representatives is called the collective bargaining agreement. It sets forth the terms and conditions under which union members will offer their labor services to an employer.

collective bargaining agreement

To explain the apparent conflict between capitalism's emphasis on individualism and unionism's emphasis on collective action, let's briefly study the history of unionism in the United States.

The Work Environment

Before the Industrial Revolution, many workers were skilled artisans. Production was organized around the domestic system. Shoemakers, for example, worked in small shops located in their homes. They bought materials needed for making shoes, made the shoes, and sold them. They were more like independent business owners than workers. They worked for themselves.

The Industrial Revolution changed this. The domestic system was largely replaced by production in factories. Many formerly independent artisans became employees who worked for firms owned by others. Workers lost control over buying, producing, and selling activities. These became activities of organized businesses. The only thing over which workers could have any control was in offering their services to employers. Thus workers began to organize in order to control that supply collectively.

Furthermore, many skilled artisans became machine operators in big factories. Mechanization (substituting machines for human labor) was also seen as a threat by many workers. To deal with this threat to their security, workers began to organize unions. The "fear" of being replaced by machines still is a fact of life for many workers in our highly mechanized and automated production system.

Wages paid to employees are a cost of doing business for the employer. Workers feared that employer efforts to reduce this cost would lead to job scarcity, low wages, and poor working conditions. Labor responded to these concerns by organizing unions for collective action.

Thus the Industrial Revolution brought rapid changes in the "world of work." But the human problems of this revolution, especially for workers, were not quickly solved. Although organization was a way for workers to deal with their changed world, workers were going to have an uphill battle to have their right to form labor unions recognized.

The Legal Environment

There were many political and legal barriers to collective bargaining. Employers viewed their employees' efforts to unionize as an attempt to deprive the employers of their private property. Courts held that unions were criminal or civil conspiracies against trade and property. The employment contract was between the individual worker and the employer, not between the employer and employees as a group. The balance of bargaining power, therefore, was in favor of the employer.

The employer-employee relationship also became much less direct as firms grew in size. Managers who were themselves employees dealt with other employees. Communication among owners, managers, and workers became more formalized through the chain of command. Since the courts tended to side with employers, big business had the upper hand. Because of mounting public concern, however, laws were passed to place the worker on a more even footing with the employer.

Labor Legislation

Early in the book, we discussed the economic philosophy of laissez faire. This philosophy was at the heart of our economic system from its beginnings up to the Great Depression of the 1930s. Most Americans rejected government interference in business affairs.

There were, however, some efforts among workers to form unions prior to the 1930s. But for the most part these efforts lacked widespread public acceptance and support. In many cases efforts to organize workers were violent. For example, the Haymarket Riot in Chicago in 1886 resulted in the death of 7 police officers and 4 workers and injury to 66 people who were protesting the use of police to break up employee efforts to strike. The result of this and other violent acts was to weaken the labor movement. The rights of private property and freedom of individual contract were used to justify antiunion moves by employers.

For many years, employers battled with workers sympathetic to unions. For example, employers circulated blacklists among themselves. **Blacklists contained the names of workers who were known to be in favor of unions.** These blacklisted workers were refused employment.

Labor unions circulated their lists also—"unfair lists." **Unfair lists contained the names of employers whom unions considered unfair to workers because these employers would not hire union members.** Furthermore, violent strikes and riots were much in evidence during the nineteenth and early twentieth centuries.

But during the early 1930s, things began to change. As much as 25 percent of the American labor force was out of work during the Great Depression. Laissez-faire economics began to lose public support and government turned its attention to getting workers back to work. It began to play a bigger role in the economy. Laws were passed to guarantee workers the right to form and join unions.

Following is a brief summary of the major federal labor laws. Individual states take various positions on labor law in intrastate commerce (commerce within a given state).

The Norris-LaGuardia Act of 1932

Congress passed the Sherman Antitrust Act in 1890. This act prohibits "every contract ... or conspiracy in restraint of trade or commerce

blacklists

unfair lists

among the several states, or with foreign nations. . . ." The Sherman Act was the first of several acts passed by Congress to prevent monopolies.

But it was not clear whether the Sherman Act applied to labor unions. The courts, however, generally held that it did. This is why unions were considered conspiracies against trade and property by the courts.

To clear up the confusion, Congress passed the Clayton Antitrust Act in 1914. This act said that unions were not subject to the Sherman Act. The Clayton Act prohibited the use of the injunction in labor disputes unless the employer could prove that irreparable injury to property or property rights was threatened. **An injunction is issued by a court. A mandatory injunction requires performance of a specific act. A prohibitory injunction orders the defendant to refrain from certain acts.** Employers typically sought and were granted injunctions to prevent their workers from forming unions or engaging in strike activity.

injunction

The Clayton Act, however, was narrowly interpreted by the courts and actually led to increased use of the injunction in labor disputes. The loopholes were closed by the Norris-LaGuardia Act of 1932. **The Norris-LaGuardia Act prohibits employers from using the injunction unless they can meet the strong requirements set out in the act. It also outlaws the yellow-dog contract.** (This contract required an employee to agree, as a condition of employment, not to join a union.)

Norris-LaGuardia Act

The Wagner Act of 1935

Three years after passage of the Norris-LaGuardia Act, the Wagner Act (the National Labor Relations Act, NLRA) was passed. This prolabor law showed that Congress wanted to equalize the bargaining power of labor and management. **The Wagner Act, often called labor's "Magna Charta," strengthened the right of workers to form unions without fear of employer reprisal. It lists several employer practices that are unfair to labor.** (See Table 13-1.)

Wagner Act

The Wagner Act created the National Labor Relations Board (NLRB) to administer the act. The NLRB investigates cases of alleged unfair labor practices committed by employers and issues orders to prevent them. The NLRB's duties were increased by later laws, as we will see.

National Labor Relations Board (NLRB)

The Fair Labor Standards Act of 1938

The Fair Labor Standards Act of 1938 defined the normal working week, required time-and-a-half pay for all hours over forty worked by an employee during a week, and established a federal minimum wage. It set the stage for later congressional action relating to discrimination on the basis of age, sex, race, color, and national origin.

Fair Labor Standards Act

Norris-LaGuardia Act (1932)
1. Greatly limits the use of the injunction by employers engaged in a labor dispute
2. Outlaws the yellow-dog contract

National Labor Relations Act (NLRA), or Wagner Act (1935)
1. Makes it illegal for employers to
   a. interfere with the rights given workers under the act
   b. interfere in the organization or operation of a union
   c. discriminate against workers who file charges or testify under the act
   d. discriminate in hiring and firing because of union affiliation
   e. refuse to bargain collectively with unions
2. Created the National Labor Relations Board (NLRB)

Fair Labor Standards Act (1938)
1. Defines the normal work week (40 hours)
2. Requires time-and-a-half pay for overtime
3. Established a federal minimum wage

Labor-Management Relations Act, or Taft-Hartley Act (1947)
1. Makes it illegal for unions to
   a. coerce workers to join unions
   b. coerce employers to discriminate against workers who do not join unions
   c. refuse to bargain collectively with employers
   d. set excessive or discriminatory union dues
   e. force an employer to pay for services which were not performed or offered to be performed
2. Outlaws the closed shop
3. Permits states to pass right-to-work laws
4. Provides for injunctive processes in national emergency strikes and in certain types of illegal strikes

Labor-Management Reporting and Disclosure Act, or Landrum-Griffin Act (1959)
1. Requires unions and employers to file reports with the Secretary of Labor
2. Set up rules for election of union officers
3. Guarantees each union member the right to
   a. attend and vote in union meetings and elections
   b. vote on proposals to increase union dues
   c. testify and bring suit against the union for violations of the act and for discriminatory treatment
   d. receive a hearing before the union can take disciplinary action against him or her

The Taft-Hartley Act of 1947

TABLE 13-1

Major federal labor laws

Between 1935 and 1947, employers tried to curb legislative and judicial actions, which they claimed had placed them at a disadvantage in collective bargaining. They thought that the NLRB showed a prolabor bias in its actions. Furthermore, the Wagner Act listed only unfair practices of management, not of unions.

Because of growing public awareness of the effects of inflation, which were often blamed on union-won wage hikes, and the wide publicity given to some union excesses, Congress passed the Labor-Management

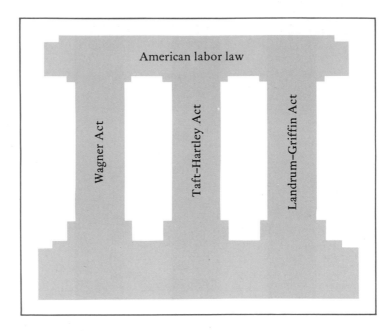

FIGURE 13-1

The pillars of American labor law

Taft-Hartley Act

Relations Act, or Taft-Hartley Act, in 1947. **The Taft-Hartley Act is a "promanagement" act that lists several practices that are unfair for unions to commit.** These and other provisions are also listed in Table 13-1.

The Landrum-Griffin Act of 1959

The Labor-Management Reporting and Disclosure Act is also known as the Landrum-Griffin Act. **The Landrum-Griffin Act is a labor reform amendment to the Taft-Hartley Act. Its purpose is to ensure democratic operation of unions and to give employers added protection from unscrupulous union practices and leaders.** (See Table 13-1.)

Landrum-Griffin Act

Passage of this law was aided by the McClellan Senate committee's investigation of labor racketeering. In their investigation, committee members had uncovered cases in which some union leaders were engaged in blackmail, arson, and other practices such as embezzling union funds for personal use and accepting bribes and payoffs from employers for union protection.

The Organizing Drive

Prior to the Wagner Act, unions had a hard time organizing workers. Threats, coercion, and intimidation by both unions and employers were

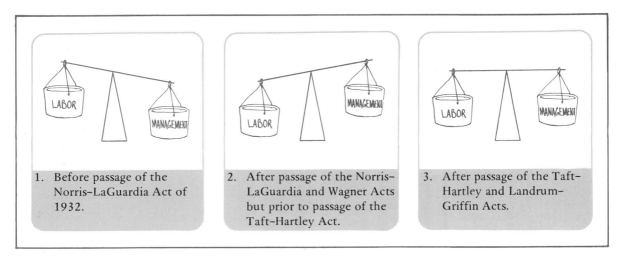

1. Before passage of the Norris–LaGuardia Act of 1932.

2. After passage of the Norris–LaGuardia and Wagner Acts but prior to passage of the Taft–Hartley Act.

3. After passage of the Taft–Hartley and Landrum–Griffin Acts.

FIGURE 13-2

How some observers view the balance of labor-management bargaining power

used to force workers either to join or not join a union. The Wagner Act made the NLRB responsible for preventing unfair practices committed by *employers.* The Taft-Hartley Act made it responsible for preventing unfair practices committed by *unions.* The NLRB also holds elections to determine whether or not a firm's employees want a union and, if so, which one.

A union might try to organize a firm's workers when it is trying to break into new geographical areas, when some workers in a firm are members and it wants to cover other workers, or when it is attempting to outdo a rival union. Thus, in some cases, a union might try to organize workers for purposes other than helping a group of employees to help themselves.

Different industries vary in the degree to which they are unionized. Industries in which a few firms dominate are easier to organize because the workers are more concentrated than in industries where many firms exist. Thus the auto industry is more unionized than the retailing industry. Furthermore, industrywide bargaining is more likely where there are few firms.

It is not as profitable for unions to organize highly automated industries that employ only a few workers as it is to organize industries that employ many workers. To make organization a paying proposition, a union must expect the dues from new members to more than offset the costs of organizing them. This is generally the case, except when a union is trying to break into an area or industry where unions are weak. Thus the organizing effort in the South and in highly unorganized industries, such as many of our growing service industries, is progressing.

Management often becomes aware of union organizing effort through the grapevine. These "rumblings" may set off a countereffort by management to slow the drive. Management must know, however, what it can legally do. A do-nothing approach is rare today. Employers can exercise the right of free speech to present their side of the story to the workers.

Suppose that a union is trying to organize employees of the Vinson Company. The union has won over several employees and is enlisting their help in winning over other Vinson employees. If the union secures signed authorization cards from at least 30 percent of these employees, it can ask the NLRB to hold a representation election to see if a majority of employees want the union. If the union wins, it is certified as the employees' exclusive bargaining agent.

A problem may arise regarding the right of different types of workers to join or not join the union. For example, supervisors cannot be included in a bargaining unit along with nonmanagement workers. Supervisors do not have bargaining rights under the Taft-Hartley Act. They can form their own union but management does not have to bargain with it. The NLRB has final authority in determining the appropriateness of the bargaining unit it certifies. Professional and nonprofessional employees may not, however, be included in the same bargaining unit unless a majority of the professional employees wish to be included.

Union Organization

Like business firms, unions also have organized structures. In fact, some workers are as far removed from the top officials in their national organizations as they are removed from the top managers of the firms for which they work.

craft unions

The two basic types of union are craft and industrial unions. **Craft unions are organized by crafts or trades—plumbers, barbers, airline pilots, etc. Craft unions restrict membership to workers with specific skills.** In many cases members of craft unions work for several different employers during the course of a year. For example, many construction workers are hired by their employers at union hiring halls. When the particular job for which they are hired is finished, these workers return to the hall to be hired by another employer.

Craft unions have a lot of power over the supply of skilled workers. This is because they have apprenticeship programs. For example, a person who wants to become a member of a plumber's union will have to go through a training program. He or she starts out as an apprentice. After the training, the person is qualified as a "journeyman" plumber.

industrial unions

Industrial unions are organized according to industries—steel, auto, clothing, etc. Industrial unions include semiskilled and unskilled workers. Prior to 1955 the American Federation of Labor (AFL) housed craft unions. The Congress of Industrial Organizations (CIO) contained industrial unions. In 1955 the two merged into the AFL-CIO.

Industrial union members typically work for a particular employer for a much longer period of time than the craft union member. But an industrial union does have a lot of "say" regarding pay and personnel practices within unionized firms.

The local union is the basic union organization. A local of a craft union is made up of artisans in a local area. A local of an industrial union is made up of workers in a given industry in a local area.

    local union

Many local unions are affiliated with a national union. **A national union is the organization set up to bring all the locals together for bargaining purposes.** There are close to 200 national unions in the United States. Some, however, are called international unions. These are unions that have members in other countries. For example, the United Automobile Workers is an international union. It is made up of local unions in the United States and Canada.

    national union

A union federation can exist at the national or the local level. **A union federation represents the unions that comprise it in presenting labor's views on political and social issues, and it helps to resolve conflicts among its affiliated unions.**

    union federation

The AFL–CIO is a national federation. It is made up of many, but not all, national unions. For example, the International Brotherhood of Electrical Workers is affiliated with the AFL–CIO, whereas the International Brotherhood of Teamsters is not.

There also are union federations at the local level. Local unions in a city, for example, come together in a federation to represent labor's views on political and social issues. The federation also may help to settle disputes among its member unions.

Union Objectives

The long struggle by unions to have their right to exist recognized has resulted in their general acceptance today—at least in acceptance of the idea that workers have a right to form unions. Union objectives are

- political
- social
- economic

Political Objectives

During the nineteenth century union objectives were basically political, since unions were fighting for recognition of their right to exist. This involved them in the political process. Once this right was recognized, unions shifted their emphasis to that of advancing the economic interests of their members. But unions do have political goals.

Unions as the Representatives of Labor

Unlike union movements in most Western-European nations, the union movement in the United States is a minority movement. Only about 24 percent of our nonfarm workers are unionized. (See Table 13–2.) Furthermore, there has been a decline in the percentage of our nonfarm labor force that is unionized over recent years. (See Figure 13–3.) Nevertheless, politicians speak of the "labor vote." There are two dimensions here: (1) the organized (unionized) and (2) the unorganized (nonunionized). The ability of labor leaders, however, to deliver the labor vote is questionable. Most Americans probably vote on issues other than the candidates' pro- or antilabor views.

But organized labor does try to speak for the labor force. We have no separate labor party in the United States. Our political system, therefore, provides no formal mechanism for the expression of labor's views. Union leaders attempt, with varying degrees of success, to make up for this lack.

Unions and Lobbying

lobbying

Unions and business both engage in lobbying. **Lobbying is efforts by a group of persons who have the same special interest. These persons,**

TABLE 13-2

Characteristics of national and international union membership

	1960	1968	1976
Total union membership (thousands)	18,117	20,258	21,006
Percentage in AFL–CIO	83.2	77.0	78.7
Percentage in independent or unaffiliated unions	16.8	23.0	21.3
Percentage males	81.8	80.6	80.0
Percentage females	18.2	19.4	20.0
Percentage white-collar	12.2	15.7	18.4
Percentage blue-collar	87.8	84.3	81.6
Percentage of total labor force in unions	23.6	23.0	20.1
Percentage of nonagricultural workers in unions	31.4	27.9	24.5

Source: *Statistical Abstract of the United States.*

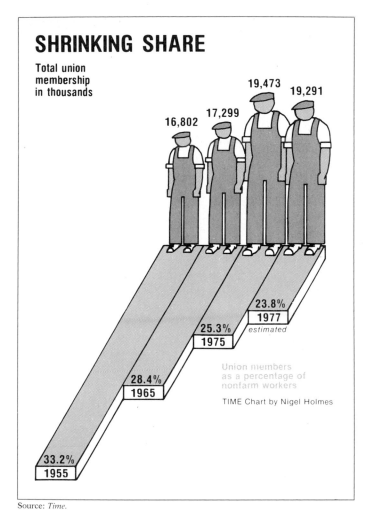

SHRINKING SHARE

Total union membership in thousands

16,802

17,299

19,473

19,291

23.8%
1977
estimated

25.3%
1975

Union members as a percentage of nonfarm workers

TIME Chart by Nigel Holmes

28.4%
1965

33.2%
1955

Source: *Time.*

FIGURE 13-3

Union members as a percentage of nonfarm workers

called lobbyists, seek to influence the passage of laws or to influence their administration or enforcement.

The labor lobby is powerful and well organized. The AFL–CIO's Committee on Political Education (COPE) lobbies for passage of pro-labor laws and helps prolabor candidates get elected. It attempts, with varying degrees of success, to speak as the representative of labor, both in and out of unions. Among recent legislative goals of unions are

- restricting imports of foreign-made products
- restricting American firms from setting up plants in low-wage countries overseas
- raising the federal minimum wage

• amending the Taft-Hartley Act to make it easier to organize workers
• passing national health legislation
• passing consumer protection legislation
• passing various types of social welfare programs
• passing full-employment legislation.

THE MINIMUM WAGE

The Fair Labor Standards Act of 1938 set a federal minimum wage of 25 cents per hour and it was scheduled to rise to 40 cents by 1945. Over the years, the minimum has been raised several times. Effective dates of increases in the federal minimum wage are as follows:

February 1967	$1.40
February 1968	1.60
May 1974	2.00
January 1975	2.10
January 1976	2.30
January 1978	2.65
January 1979	2.90
January 1980	3.10
January 1981	3.35

Unions generally are among the strongest supporters of increases in the minimum wage. Organized labor, for example, fought hard in 1977 to win Congressional approval of the increases scheduled for 1978, 1979, 1980, and 1981. Opponents alleged that a higher minimum wage would: 1) reduce the number of jobs available for young people; 2) lead to more inflation; and 3) cause many marginal workers to be laid off. Some opponents in 1977 favored a lower minimum wage for teenage workers than for adult workers. Congress rejected this proposal, as it had done in 1971 and 1974.

Business, of course, also engages in lobbying. As we said in Chapter 3, the concept of countervailing power includes unions, business, and government. Perhaps the best known of the business lobbies is the National Association of Manufacturers.

Social Objectives

Union leaders typically view their job to be serving their members' interests. But in order to recruit new members and improve their public "image," union leaders are showing greater interest in the problems of workers in general, as suggested in the above list of legislative goals of unions.

Unions that excluded minorities and women in the past have opened the door to them. They have set up programs to do away with discriminatory practices and to upgrade the skills of the disadvantaged unemployed.

Economic Objectives

Union leaders are elected by union members. Thus those leaders seek to satisfy their members' economic needs. Higher wages, job security, and good working conditions often are called "bread and butter" issues. They are central issues in the collective bargaining process.

Improved Standard of Living

Unions seek to improve their members' standard of living. In the past this meant getting higher wages. The pay envelope, however, is no longer the only concern of union members. Many want more leisure time. They want to work fewer hours but make more pay per hour. The entire package of fringe benefits is part of the improved standard of living that unions seek. Working conditions, pensions, paid vacations, and so on are important bargaining issues. Inflation in recent years has led union members to demand that labor contracts protect their standard of living. We will discuss this later in the chapter.

As we have seen, the 40-hour work week was established by the Fair Labor Standards Act in 1938. In the past rank-and-file workers generally preferred to get higher wages and more benefits instead of more time off. But, in more recent years, preference for time off has been growing. During periods of slack business activity in the 1970s, for example, interest revived in spreading the available work and improving the security of people who had jobs by reducing work hours. In 1978 the All Unions Committee to Shorten the Work Week was set up. Shortening the work week by extending vacations, providing more sick leave and holidays, and allowing for a variety of so-called go-to-hell days are a goal of the committee.

Security Objectives

The growing security consciousness of American workers is reflected in union goals. The seniority provision in most contracts spells out the worker's rights when layoffs, transfers, and promotions occur. Employees are ranked in terms of length of service. Those with longer service get better treatment.

Much conflict exists regarding seniority. Women and minority groups for example, typically have less seniority and are the first to be laid off and the last to move up to higher jobs. These workers tend to oppose the tradition of seniority.

Union security is another issue. The three major forms of union security are

- the closed shop
- the union shop
- the agency shop

closed shop

The strongest type of union security is the closed shop. **In a closed shop an employer can hire only union members.** The Taft-Hartley Act outlaws the closed shop. Some states, however, do allow it. This, of course, is permissible only if the employer is not engaged in interstate commerce.

union shop

The Taft-Hartley Act permits the union shop. **In a union shop an employer may hire nonunion workers even if the employer's present employees are unionized. New workers, however, must join the union within 30 days of being hired or else be fired.** Roughly 90 percent of all unionized blue-collar workers work under a union shop agreement.

right-to-work laws

The Taft-Hartley Act permits individual states to pass right-to-work laws. **Right-to-work laws outlaw the union shop.** (See Figure 13–4.) They weaken union bargaining strength and make organizing efforts more difficult. A firm's unionized and nonunionized employees are paid the same wage for the same work. Union members believe that non-union employees take advantage of union-won benefits without paying union dues. Unions have been lobbying for years to repeal that section of the Taft-Hartley Act which allows states to pass right-to-work laws.

agency shop

Some states permit an agency shop. **In an agency shop all employees for whom the union bargains must pay dues but need not join.** This is a compromise between the union shop and the open shop.

open shop

In an open shop an employer may hire either union and/or nonunion labor. Employees need not join or pay dues to a union in an open shop.

guaranteed annual wage

Another security issue is job security, especially in highly automated industries. The guaranteed annual wage reflects the worker's concern about job security. **The guaranteed annual wage is a provision in a labor contract that maintains the workers' income level during a year.** Most labor contracts that provide for this guarantee the worker a minimum amount of work during the contract period. This lends stability to the worker's employment. Some contracts provide for early retirement, lengthy vacations, and sabbatical leaves for employees.

The security of unions themselves is also in question. Our most organized industries—steel, auto, transportation, etc.—are almost totally unionized and are rapidly automating. Prospects for new members are not

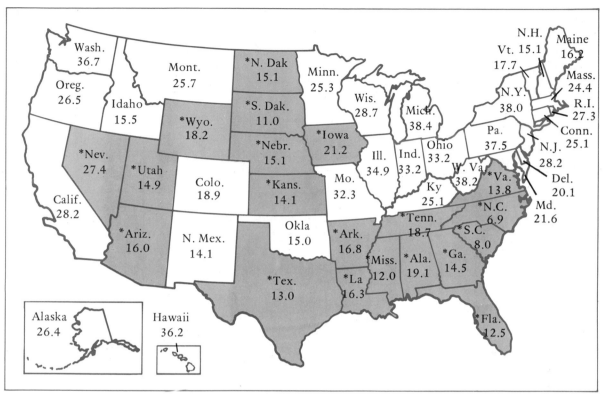

Source: *Statistical Abstract of the United States.*

FIGURE 13-4

The percentage of the nonagricultural labor force that is unionized in each state (shaded states have right-to-work laws)

attractive. Furthermore, the stronghold of unions—blue-collar labor—is diminishing as a percentage of our labor force. Thus unions have sought new areas for growth, such as government workers and white-collar workers.

Working Conditions

Suppose that a long strike has been settled. Nevertheless, some locals of the national union remain on strike. The national contract covers major issues such as wage rates and fringe benefits. But specific provisions on rest periods, sanitary facilities, washup periods, and so on vary from plant to plant. These disputes over working conditions are worked out by the local union and the specific plant.

Although the average working conditions in business today are much better than those during the "sweat-shop" days of the Industrial Revolution, dirty and dangerous jobs still exist. Brown lung, black lung, lead poisoning, and asbestosis are some examples of dangerous industrial diseases. As we saw in the previous chapter, the Occupational Safety

**TWO POINTS
OF VIEW**

The Right to Work

Labor:

"Sure, a worker in a union plant in a state without a right-to-work law does have to belong to the union. The majority rules, and the majority of the workers who voted did vote to organize our union. Under the law, two persons doing the same job must be paid the same wage and receive the same fringe benefits. It would be unfair for a person who doesn't pay union dues to enjoy the same benefits won by a union that is supported by members' dues. Freeloaders should have to pay their fair share.

"To say that unions are unnecessary is plain hogwash. Do away with the union and see how employee-oriented most employers are. Business firms exist to make a profit. The less they pay to their workers, the more they keep as profit. The claim that union leaders have no incentive to do a good job is a lot of XXX! No law requires any firm's employees to form a union. If they weren't benefiting from the union, the members could have it decertified as their exclusive bargaining agent.

"Finally, consider one important point. The majority of the states that have right-to-work laws are in the South and the Southwest. If these laws were so good for business, why aren't these states more industrialized? Surely, business managers are smart enough to locate their plants where labor cost is low and labor productivity is high."

Management:

"A worker should not be forced to join a union in order to hold a job in my company. Granted, employees do have a right to form a union. But an employee should have a right not to join. Yet the NLRB certified a union as exclusive bargaining agent for my production workers, even though not all of them voted to unionize. Now all of them have to pay dues or else be fired. They don't have freedom of choice in a state without a right-to-work law.

"Unions have done a lot for the worker in the past, but they are not needed today. Social security, workers' compensation laws, minimum wage laws, job safety laws, and enlightened management take away the need for unions.

"When you think about it, a customer who isn't satisfied with our product can stop buying it. But if one of our unionized workers isn't satisfied with the union, he or she must still pay dues, because there is no right-to-work law in our state. What reason do union leaders have to do a good job?

> "Finally, when bargaining time rolls around for one of our suppliers and its union, we often build up our inventory of that supplier's product. This is done in case there is a strike at that plant. A strike would cut off our supply source. The end result, of course, is higher prices to consumers to make up for the cost of carrying extra inventory."

and Health Act was passed, with major support from unions, to help improve the situation.

Why Do Workers Join Unions?

Let's assume that workers are not required to join unions in order to get or keep their jobs. Why, then, would they join?

First, there is strength in numbers. An individual worker's demands may receive little attention from management. Those same demands, when expressed by an organization of workers, are likely to receive a lot more attention. The individual worker's threat to strike, for example, would cause little interruption of the workflow in a plant. A collective strike, however, could easily cripple the workflow.

Second, union members are represented in collective bargaining by professional negotiators. The employer is also represented by professional negotiators. The outcome is likely to be better for each worker than if each negotiated by himself or herself.

A third reason is the feeling of power that workers get from union membership. Although the employer-employee negotiations are handled by professionals, the workers at least have a chance to vote for union officers and also have veto power over any "settlement" that is reached regarding wages, fringe benefits, and working conditions.

Finally, many workers believe that union membership is necessary to keep employers interested in and concerned with the well-being of their workers as human beings. We will discuss this in greater detail later in the chapter.

Sources of Labor-Management Conflict

In the United States labor and management bargain within a framework of certain shared, basic common beliefs. Negotiations in some other countries take on an air of class warfare—the "working class" is pitted against the "capitalists." In the United States today the vast majority of unions accept the capitalist system. It is within that framework that labor and management bargain.

There are, of course, some basic differences in outlook between labor and management. We will look at several sources of conflict and discuss each from a "labor viewpoint" and a "management viewpoint."

The Loyalty Issue

Some employers think that the presence of a union reduces employee loyalty to the firm. When the collective bargaining process results in a pay raise, for example, the employees may think that the union "won" the raise—it was not "granted" by management. Union people, of course, question whether the raise would have been granted in the absence of the union.

The Jobs Issue

Some workers think that a firm's major goal should be to provide jobs for workers. Recent problems with unemployment have made many workers very concerned with the prospect of being laid off. They want job security.

Our federal government also looks to private firms as the major source of jobs for people. It is committed to a policy of full employment. When jobs in private industry cannot absorb all those people who are willing and able to work, many people want government to step in as the "employer of last resort." In other words, many workers believe they have a right to a job.

In some countries (Japan, for example) a worker enters into a sort of long-term unwritten contract with his or her employer. In return for good service, the worker is more or less guaranteed lifetime employment. Some American workers would like to have a similar guarantee.

If employers cannot or will not provide this guarantee, some union people believe government should provide it. In 1975 the Full Employment and Balanced Growth Bill (the Humphrey-Hawkins full employment bill) was introduced in Congress and unions lobbied for its passage. That bill would have committed the federal government to use its full resources to reduce unemployment to 3 percent within four years after it was passed. The bill, however, was not passed. In 1978 a watered-down version was passed. It expresses the federal government's desire to reduce unemployment to 4 percent by 1983, but the act does not authorize any government spending to attain that goal. Whereas the original bill did not mention inflation, the version that passed in 1978 also sets a goal of reducing inflation to 3 percent by 1983.

In the United States, some labor contracts provide for supplemental unemployment benefits. **Supplemental unemployment benefits (SUB) are payments made by employers to the workers they have laid off.** The concept developed in 1955 in the auto industry. The idea is to deal with the problem of short-term joblessness among auto workers during yearly model changeovers. The employer pays a certain amount of money into a fund for each hour an employee works. The accumulated funds are used to make payments to workers who are laid off. The problem is that the SUB concept is not designed to deal with longer-term unemployment.

This leads to demands by some workers and their unions for shorter work weeks and extended vacations. The purpose is to spread the available work around to more workers. But workers want more pay per hour to keep their same take-home pay. Some managers argue that pushed up wages lead to higher costs, which are passed on to consumers in the form of higher prices.

supplemental
unemployment benefits
(SUB)

TABLE 13-3

**The twenty largest
unions in the
United States**

Union	Number of members (in thousands)
Teamsters	1,889
Automobile workers	1,358
Steelworkers	1,300
Electrical (IBEW)	924
Machinists	917
Carpenters	820
State, County, and Municipal (AFSCME)	750
Retail clerks	699
Laborers	627
Service employees	575
Meat cutters	510
Clothing and textile workers	502
Communications workers	483
Teachers (AFT)	446
Hotel and restaurant	432
Operating engineers	420
Ladies' garment workers	365
Musicians	330
Paperworkers	300
Mine workers	277

Source: *Statistical Abstract of the United States.*

Finally, another aspect of the jobs issue is the fear of union people and other workers that new machines and automation are cutting out jobs. In the publishing industry, for example, linotype operators and compositors are being replaced by fewer workers who operate computerized typesetting machines. This was a major issue in the 1978 strike against New York City's newspapers.

Automation has made some jobs obsolete but unions often try to protect the members' whose jobs are taken over by machines. Some employers, in order to maintain labor peace, are willing to keep these people on the payroll even if their services are not needed. The Taft-Hartley Act makes it illegal for unions to force an employer to pay for services which are not performed *or offered to be performed.* (See Table 13–1.) The term *featherbedding* often is interpreted to mean paying workers for work they do not do. Actually, this is featherbedding only if the workers also do not offer to perform the work. In practice, however, workers sometimes are paid for doing work that could be done faster and more efficiently by a machine. The result, of course, is higher costs for the firm and higher costs to consumers for its products.

The "Right to Manage" Issue

bargainable issues

An employer must bargain with a union that is certified by the NLRB. The employer does not have to grant the union everything it wants, but both parties must bargain in good faith on bargainable issues. **Bargainable issues are aspects of the work or job environment that are subject to collective bargaining between union and management representatives.** Examples include vacations, holidays, rest periods, wages, seniority regulations, transfers, promotions, layoffs, and size of work crews.

The scope of these bargainable issues has been broadened over the years. A nonunion worker's wage and fringe benefits are set by the employer, except to the extent that the worker can bargain for himself or herself. Those of a union member are set through the collective bargaining process. The union bargains for the employee. The employer's right to move a plant to another location may be subject to collective bargaining. Because the area of managerial discretion is narrowed when a union is present, nonunion companies usually try to provide good working conditions to discourage employee interest in unions.

Some unionized companies favor including a statement of management rights in their contracts with unions. In some cases these are very specific. An example is a statement that management retains the right to institute technological changes. Other firms believe that a specific listing of management rights can become too restrictive. The union could contend that anything that is omitted from the list is outside the exclusive

Some Americans still feel uneasy about labor unions. Much of this is probably because a lot of the publicity unions get is bad. Strikes are discussed in terms of lost production time, unions often are blamed for inflation, and cases of union corruption get a lot of news coverage.

Some people, even some union members, think that unions are too powerful and "un-American." They want tighter government control of unions. Many of them want to deny food stamps and unemployment benefits to workers who are on strike.

Emotions run high when we talk about unions. But unions have played a major role in improving our society. Few people would want a return to the conditions of labor during the Industrial Revolution. Unions help make democracy work. Labor has a voice in the political process without dividing society into warring classes. Unions have helped create our large middle-income group of consumers without which many firms would have a lot fewer customers. Do unions benefit society? WHAT DO YOU THINK?

domain of management. These companies tend to include only a very general statement of management rights in their contracts.

When employees are unionized, all personnel decisions come under close scrutiny by the union. Personnel policies on pay, job transfers, promotions, discipline, fringe benefits, etc., are written into the collective bargaining agreement. Unionization also often results in more centralization of decision-making authority over personnel matters. Decisions on discipline, job transfers, etc., may be removed from lower-level managers in order to exercise more control over these aspects of the collective bargaining agreement.

The NLRB also has ruled that an employer must give a union statistical data on minority and women employees in order to protect workers from discrimination. The same is true regarding job applicants so that the union can monitor collective bargaining agreements that contain provisions against discrimination.

The Seniority Issue

Unions often are critical of wage and salary plans that are not based on seniority. Labor argues that any other system is subjective and/or interferes with the collective bargaining process. Union work rules, for example, may impose obstacles to using the MBO approach to appraising employee performance. We discussed the seniority issue in Chapter 12. But management resists basing all pay and promotion decisions on seniority alone, on the grounds that it ignores employee productivity.

The Productivity Issue

The productivity issue has become very important in recent years, as we saw in Chapter 6. Productivity means the ability to produce. In measuring productivity, we compare output in relation to input. The output is products and services and the inputs are labor and capital. If we can get more output from the same input or a lesser input, productivity has increased.

Output per worker-hour is one measure of how efficient we are in producing products and services. Whereas ten years ago American labor's productivity was increasing by about 3 percent per year, it now is closer to 2 percent. This is a major problem when American firms must compete with foreign firms whose labor productivity is increasing at a higher rate. In Japan, for example, it has been averaging about 7 percent over the last ten years. (See Figure 13–5.)

Management often blames declining productivity on restrictive union work rules, a decline of the work ethic, taxes and inflation that reduce their incentive to invest in new machines, and government regulations, such as OSHA and the Environmental Protection Act, which require firms to invest in financially nonproductive areas.

Unions, however, argue that management too often is unwilling to

FIGURE 13-5

Annual rates of increase in labor productivity for selected countries, 1967–1977

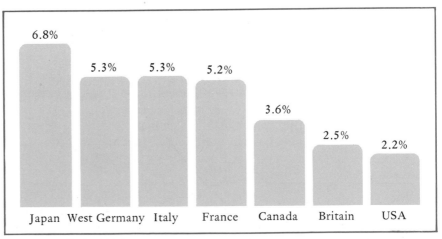

Source: Bureau of Labor Statistics.

invest in training programs to upgrade labor skills. Other criticisms include poor product engineering, which places American-made products at a disadvantage in world markets, poor communication between workers and managers, too much red tape in big firms, a dehumanized work environment, and lack of effective cooperation with unions in trying to improve the standard of living of workers.

When increases in productivity do occur, management and labor often disagree over how much of the increase in output is due to labor and how much is due to capital. If a worker doubles his or her output per worker-hour, the worker wants to be paid more. But management argues that at least part of the increase in the worker's productivity is due to the fact that the worker works with a new and better machine. At any rate, if all of the increase in output is paid to the worker in higher wages, management would have little or no incentive to invest money in new plant and equipment. The result, according to management, is rising costs, less profit, and eventually, a business failure because of inability to compete.

The Inflation Issue

A growing number of labor contracts include cost-of-living escalator provisions. **An escalator clause means that, during the period of time covered by a labor contract, wage hikes will be granted on the basis of changes in the cost of living. These hikes are called cost-of-living adjustments.** Some are tied to increases in the consumer price index. This helps to ensure that the worker's standard of living will not deteriorate because of increases in the cost of living. The worker is sheltered from inflation. This helps to avoid demands for big "catch-up wage hikes" when a current contract expires and a new one is being negotiated. In some cases unions want to bargain for shorter pacts and to reopen negotiations when their contracts do not protect their members adequately from inflation.

In general, management acceptance of the escalator clause is growing, but most employers would prefer to have an upper limit on the cost-of-living benefits they might have to pay during a contract period. In fact, bargaining over the formula to use for making cost-of-living adjustments can be tough.

Table 13–4 shows the average income before and after income taxes for people in various occupations between 1967 and 1978. Notice the percentage change in income after taxes and the effects of inflation. Steelworkers, autoworkers, and petrochemical workers whose union contracts include escalator clauses fared well relative to people in non-union jobs. Social security recipients pay no income taxes on their benefits, which increased more than threefold over the period.

escalator clause

TABLE 13-4

The real story of earnings

THE REAL STORY OF EARNINGS

Occupation	Average income 1967	1978	After tax income 1967	1978	% change in income after taxes and effects of inflation
Social Security recipient					+ 59 %
Steelworker	7,548	20,923	6,580	16,932	+ 32
Autoworker	7,647	19,971	6,670	16,114	+ 24
Petrochemical worker	8,273	21,085	7,163	17,072	+ 22
Truck driver	7,134	16,805	6,203	13,779	+ 14
U.S. Army major	11,616	26,074	10,171	21,856	+ 10
Plumber	11,149	22,360†	9,515	18,045†	+ 4.5
Policeman (municipal)	6,482	13,190	5,665	11,164	+ 0.9
Fed. civil servant* (Grade 7)	6,734	13,014	6,182	11,824	− 2.1
Computer programmer	9,984	19,604	8,429	15,798	− 4.1
Engineer (journeyman)	12,420	23,976	10,585	19,141	− 7.5
Corporate lawyer (middle level)	17,208	33,552	14,353	25,636	− 8.6
Accountant*	7,000	12,800	6,105	10,884	− 8.8
U.S. Senator	30,000	57,000	24,047	42,168	− 10.3
Librarian	7,305	11,894†	6,359	10,262†	− 11.1
Welfare recipient (per family)	1,894	3,089	1,894	3,089	− 16.5
University professor	17,158	30,353	14,311	23,077	− 17.5

After tax income computed by the Tax Foundation, Inc. (assuming 3 dependents)   *Starting salaries   †1977

Source: *Time*.

The Nature of Collective Bargaining

Collective bargaining sessions between union and management are conducted by professional negotiators. In preparing to bargain on a new contract, the union sets up a negotiating team long before the current contract will expire. This team develops a list of demands that will satisfy the union membership while also having a fairly good chance of finally being accepted by management. It also is common for the union members to vote a strike authorization that will go into effect if the current contract expires and a new one has not been negotiated.

Employers also prepare in advance. The management negotiating team tries to anticipate the union's demands and prepares for them. For example, if management expects the union to bargain for a large wage hike, management negotiators will enter the bargaining sessions armed with forecasts concerning the impact of the higher wages on the firm's ability to compete against other firms in the industry.

During the early bargaining sessions, the union side presents its demands first and the management side proposes changes in the old contract that it would like to include in the new contract. Any issues brought up for discussion can be objected to by either labor or management. But as we have seen, the law requires both to bargain in good faith on bargainable issues. Suppose management believes that one of the union's demands infringes on the employer's area of managerial discretion and it refuses to bargain on this point. The union might file a complaint with the NLRB which will decide if the issue is bargainable.

By now, both sides have their demands on the table and it may look as if there is little chance of coming to an agreement. The union "wants all" and management is unwilling to give up anything. The bargaining process then focuses on the concessions stage. Each team is authorized to make concessions in order to narrow the gap between labor's demands and management's offers.

The closer the bargainers get to the expiration date of the current contract, the harder they work to hammer out a new contract. Around-the-clock bargaining sessions may be held to come up with a contract. The union negotiators, however, are not authorized to accept the contract they eventually work out with management. They can recommend it to the membership but rank-and-file union members must vote on it before it can be binding. If they ratify (accept) it, a formal and binding contract is prepared and signed by labor and management.

But suppose the two bargaining teams get deadlocked in their negotiations. They can call in a neutral third party to help in breaking the deadlock.

In conciliation the neutral third party's task is to prevent negotiations from breaking down. If negotiations break off, the conciliator tries to get the two parties back to the bargaining table. The conciliator, however, has no authority over either party.

conciliation

Mediation goes a step further. **In mediation, the neutral third party's task is to suggest a possible compromise.** The mediator tries to persuade the parties to settle the dispute. Like the conciliator, the mediator has no authority over either party.

mediation

Some states have mediation services but most mediators are provided by the Federal Mediation and Conciliation Service. This agency was set up by the Taft-Hartley Act.

Arbitration is another process that may be used in settling labor-management conflict. Very few labor contracts, however, provide for arbitration as an approach to negotiating a labor contract. **In voluntary arbitration a neutral third party hears both sides of the dispute and settles the issue. The two parties decide voluntarily to submit the dispute to arbitration and both parties usually are bound by the settlement.**

voluntary arbitration

compulsory arbitration

Compulsory arbitration is compelled by federal or state law. The arbitrator's settlement is binding. Compulsory arbitration is used only when essential public services are involved. An increasing number of states are turning to this method of settling strikes by government workers.

The President can use an injunction to stop strikes if they "imperil the national health or safety." President Carter used an injunction to force striking coal miners back to the mines in 1978. That strike was held to be a national emergency strike. If the miners had refused to obey the back-to-work order and violence had broken out, the President could have called out federal troops to help prevent any further violence. The President also could have sought Congressional action to authorize seizure of the mines. The miners, however, did obey the back-to-work order.

Grievance Machinery

Although most employers used to believe that unions were all bad, this is not the case today. A firm may benefit from the presence of a union. Unions can help in managing employee discontent by bringing problems to the surface where they can be dealt with through collective bargaining. In all firms, whether they are unionized or not, there is the problem of integrating individual goals with those of the firm. Workers may express their individual discontent through work slowdowns or quitting. A union, however, provides a mechanism for channeling this discontent to management while, at the same time, keeping the workforce intact. Thus employer-employee communication improves when the union serves as a feedback mechanism. Supervisors who want to initiate changes in work procedures often will discuss it with union representatives before they "announce" the changes. This gives the supervisor the chance to "sell" the proposed changes to the union representative who, in turn, may help "sell" them to the union members.

The collective bargaining agreement enables management and labor to coexist. The rights of each are stated. But no such contract eliminates the chance that problems will happen. No contract could cover every situation in which trouble might occur. Also, problems sometimes arise over the interpretation of the contract.

A grievance is something that causes a worker to complain. Not all complaints, however, are grievances—only those complaints that relate to alleged violations of the labor contract or the law are grievances. To deal with grievances, labor contracts include grievance procedures. **Grievance procedures spell out the sequence of steps a grieved employee should follow in seeking to correct the cause of the grievance.** These procedures are set up to reduce the chance that employee gripes will cause a breakdown in labor-management relations.

grievance procedures

Suppose Homer Anderson's supervisor tells him to do a task that Homer does not think is part of his job. He might take the matter up with his union steward (a union representative in the plant) who would then take it to Homer's boss. If the issue is not settled at this stage, it goes to a higher union official who takes it to a higher manager. As we said earlier, contract arbitration is very rare. But grievance arbitration is common in collective bargaining.

Weapons of Labor and Management

Most grievances are settled through grievance procedures. Sometimes, however, issues divide labor and management so much that they resort to certain weapons. This is likely to happen when employee discontent is widespread, the parties are unable to agree on a new contract, or there is a dispute over contract terms.

Labor's Weapons

Labor's main weapons are

- the strike
- the picket
- the boycott

(See Table 13–5.)

A strike is a temporary withdrawal of all or some employees from the employer's service. The presumption is that they will return when their demands are met or a compromise is worked out. The strike is the union's ultimate weapon. It ordinarily will not be used, however, unless the union has the financial resources to ride it out.

strike

Picketing means that persons (pickets) form a picket line and walk around a plant or office building with placards (signs) informing other workers and the general public that the employer is held unfair to

picketing

Strikes	
1. Primary strike	The employer's workers withdraw from their jobs for their direct and immediate benefit.
2. Secondary strike	B Company's union strikes to force B to bring pressure on C Company because the union has a gripe with C.
3. Sympathy strike	A strike called by one union primarily for the benefit of another union.
4. National general strike	All the workers in the nation strike.
5. General strike	All or most of the workers in a particular industry go out.
6. Sitdown strike	The workers cease working but do not leave their place of employment.
7. Slowdown strike	The workers "slow down" rather than cease working altogether. This type of strike is most effective in mass production industries.
8. Partial strike	Only part of the work force strikes, but those who go out are strategically selected to place the employer in a difficult position.
9. Wildcat strike	Some union members go out even though the union did not declare a strike.
Pickets	
1. Primary picket	The employer's workers walk around the building or place of employment with placards informing other workers and the public that the company is held unfair to labor.
2. Secondary picket	Several employees of X Company (with whom the union has a gripe) picket Y Company, a customer of X Company, in order to induce Y to cease buying from X Company.
Boycotts	
1. Primary boycott	The workers refuse to do business with (buy from) their employer.
2. Secondary boycott	The boycotters cause third parties to the labor dispute to refrain from dealing with the employer of the boycotters.

TABLE 13-5

Types of strikes, pickets, and boycotts

labor. Strikes usually are accompanied by picketing, but picketing may take place without a strike.

In general, picketing is protected under the right of free speech as long as it does not include any fraud, violence, and/or intimidation. An effective picket may keep other employees who belong to different unions from entering a plant. If a picket line around a plant is honored by truck drivers, the picketed firm finds itself without deliveries.

boycott

In a boycott a union tries to get people to refuse to deal with the boycotted firm. There are primary and secondary boycotts. Suppose that the employees of Company Y are involved in a dispute. They might send circulars to Y's customers and suppliers asking them not to do business with Y. This is a secondary boycott.

Secondary strikes are generally legal. Secondary pickets enjoy some protection as an exercise of free speech. The legality of a secondary boycott depends on its purpose, the means used to carry it out (degree of coercion, etc.), and the remoteness of the third party to whom pressure is applied. The Taft-Hartley Act allows the NLRB to secure a federal court injunction against unions that engage in illegal strike, picket, and/or boycott activity. These tools of labor power are also used by nonunionized labor and minority groups—especially the boycott and the picket.

Management's Weapons

Management's main weapons are

- the lockout
- the layoff
- the injunction
- the employer's association

For many years management used the lockout to counter labor's threat to strike or to organize. **In a lockout employees are denied access to the plant until they accept the employer's terms of employment.** This weapon is now used mainly as a defensive weapon once a strike is called.

lockout

Today the layoff is more effective. A general strike against steel makers that lasts long enough to deplete their inventories leads to layoffs in steel-using industries. Although autoworkers who are laid off claim they are "behind" the steelworkers, a lengthy steel strike brings hardship to the autoworkers. This may lead to indirect pressure on the steelworkers to reach an agreement.

The Norris-LaGuardia Act greatly limited the use of the labor injunction. But employers who can prove that unions are engaging in unlawful practices can seek injunctive relief in the courts.

Employers' associations are important in industries with many small firms and one large union that represents all workers. Member firms in an industry might contribute to a strike insurance fund. The fund could be used to help members who are struck. They are similar in purpose to strike insurance funds built up by unions.

Firms or industries with labor problems often publicize their side in newspapers and other media to gain public support. Unions also do this. The strength of public opinion sometimes leads to new laws.

The Future of Unionism

As we have seen, the percentage of our labor force that is unionized has declined over recent years. The future of the union movement in the

United States will depend largely on the success with which unions can organize people in geographic areas, industries, and occupations that traditionally have not been unionized.

During recent years there has been some movement of people and industry from the older industrialized Northeastern states to the Sunbelt states of the South and Southwest. Some of the Sunbelt states are highly nonunionized and unions will have to step up their organizing efforts to increase membership in these states.

In Chapter 1 we said that our economy is undergoing a basic change from an industrial economy to a postindustrial economy in which the service industries are growing more rapidly than manufacturing industries. Workers in the service industries traditionally have not been highly unionized. Many work part-time and the typical firm is small. This makes it harder and more costly for unions to organize these workers than it is to organize full-time workers in large factories. Unions will have to intensify their organizational efforts in the service industries.

White-collar workers now account for about half of our labor force. In the past some union leaders assumed that these workers were hard to unionize because of their tendency to identify more closely with their employers than with unions and blue-collar workers. But during recent years many white-collar workers have been experiencing many of the same problems blue-collar workers have faced. Mechanization and automation in factories gave rise to fears about job scarcity and stimulated unionization. More recently the effects of automation are being felt in white-collar occupations. Some clerical workers, for example, are facing loss of jobs and rapidly changing job requirements as employers use computers to automate office operations. Unions will have to appeal to these and other white-collar workers, including professionals such as teachers, nurses, and interns in hospitals.

The service industries also employ a large number of women and minorities. For years the working woman worked to supplement her family's income. Some worked only part-time and many remained in the labor force for only a few years. As a result, many women felt that any union-won benefits they might enjoy would not make up for the union dues they would have to pay or the income they would lose during strikes. Women, like minorities, also tend to have reservations about the seniority system and the "male hardhat" image that some unions project.

Career-oriented women, however, view work differently from their earlier counterparts. Along with the sexual revolution there are now new ideas about marriage and family. For many women work has replaced the family as their primary concern in life. As a result, the percentage of our labor force accounted for by women is increasing and unions will have to make even stronger efforts to appeal to them.

Federal labor laws exclude federal, state, and local governments in defining the term "employer," and the Wagner Act does not recognize the right of government workers to strike. In 1962 President Kennedy issued an Executive Order that, for the first time in our history, supported the unionization of federal government workers. In 1966 Congress passed legislation that enabled postal workers to unionize.

Although unions for federal government workers are similar to unions for workers in private industry, there are some differences. The U.S. Civil Service Commission, for example, still has a great deal of control over personnel policies and regulations. Most government jobs are white-collar jobs and, therefore, most unionized federal government workers are white-collar workers. This is the segment of white-collar workers that unions have been most successful in organizing.

Since the number of government jobs is increasing so rapidly, particularly at the state and local level, greater effort to organize government workers has been made and will continue to be made. The financial problems of local and state governments will probably continue and, perhaps, get worse. Part of the problem is the rising demands of newly unionized public employees in the face of limited city and state revenues. Meanwhile, it appears that taxpayers are growing more reluctant to vote for tax increases. For example, many blue-collar union workers supported the passage of California's Proposition 13 in 1978. In addition to cutting property taxes, it also eliminated some jobs in state government. Some of these jobs were held by unionized white-collar government employees.

In recent years there has been talk of unionizing the armed forces of the United States. Opponents cite the possibility of striking soldiers refusing orders to fight while proponents claim that an all-volunteer force needs a union to protect military personnel as employees of the United States government against efforts to reduce defense costs. Although unionization of the armed forces is a relatively new idea in the United States, the armed forces of Belgium, Denmark, Norway, West Germany, Sweden, and the Netherlands are unionized.

Summary and Look Ahead

A labor union is an organization of employees formed for the purpose of collective bargaining with the employer. Union and employer representatives negotiate a collective bargaining agreement, which is a contract that sets forth the terms and conditions under which union members will offer their labor services to an employer.

The earliest attempts of workers to form unions were frustrated by court rulings which held that unions were criminal or civil conspiracies against trade and property. Gradually, public sympathy shifted in favor of unions, and laws were passed to guarantee the worker the right to join a union. The Norris-LaGuardia Act, the Wagner Act, and the Fair Labor Standards Act were passed during the 1930s. These "prolabor" laws shifted the balance of power in favor of labor and led to a reaction in the form of "promanagement" laws during the 1940s and 1950s—the Taft-Hartley Act and the Landrum-Griffin Act.

The National Labor Relations Board (NLRB) holds elections and certifies unions as bargaining agents. Once a union is certified, union and management must bargain in good faith on bargainable issues. Examples of these issues include vacations, seniority regulations, and wages.

The two basic types of unions are craft and industrial unions. Craft unions are organized by crafts or trades, such as plumbing and carpentry, and they restrict membership to workers with specific skills. Industrial unions are organized according to industries, such as auto and steel, and they include semiskilled and unskilled workers. The union organizational structure includes local unions, national unions, and union federations.

Unions have political, social, and economic objectives. Both businesses and unions engage in lobbying to promote and protect their special political interests. In recent years unions also have shown greater interest in the problems of workers in general. As part of their social objectives, unions are helping to do away with discriminatory practices. Their economic objectives include an improved standard of living for their members, greater union security, and improved working conditions.

The three major forms of union security are: (1) the closed shop; (2) the union shop; and (3) the agency shop. In a closed shop an employer can hire only union members. The Taft-Hartley Act outlaws the closed shop if the employer is engaged in interstate commerce. In a union shop an employer can hire nonunion workers but they must join the union within 30 days of being hired. Some states have right-to-work laws which outlaw the union shop. This is permitted under the Taft-Hartley Act and unions have been fighting for repeal of this provision in the Act. In an agency shop all employees for whom the union bargains must pay dues but need not join. In an open shop employees need not join or pay dues to a union.

Many factors can lead to labor-management conflict. These include seniority rights, working conditions, the scope of bargainable issues, labor productivity, and management's right to manage.

Collective bargaining sessions between union and management are conducted by professional negotiators. Each side starts by presenting its demands and this is followed by a series of concessions. If they become deadlocked in their negotiations, the bargaining representatives can resort to conciliation, mediation, and arbitration. Grievance procedures also spell out the sequence of steps a grieved employee should follow in seeking to correct the cause of the grievance.

When labor-management conflict results in a standoff, labor uses its weapons—the strike, the picket, and the boycott. Among management's weapons are the lockout, the layoff, the injunction, and the employer's association.

The union movement has always been a minority movement in the United States. In recent years unions have sought to increase their membership by growing in new directions, such as organizing government employees and white-collar workers. This is necessary because of the declining percentage of the labor force that is in blue-collar jobs.

In the next chapter, we will study computers and quantitative analysis in business. Few developments can rival the impact that computers have had on business.

My name is James A. Wilkinson. Presently, I am manager of labor relations policy at United States Steel.

I received the bachelor's degree in economics and business at Georgetown University, Washington, D. C., in 1967 and the doctor of jurisprudence degree from Duquesne University, Pittsburgh, Pennsylvania, in 1978. I joined U. S. Steel in 1974 as a staff assistant in the company's labor relations department, and two years later was made assistant manager of labor relations policy. In 1978 I became manager of labor relations policy.

Prior to joining U. S. Steel, I served as an environmental and energy coordinator, Office of Management and Budget, Executive Office of the President, in Washington, D. C. I also served as a deputy executive secretary, Cost of Living Council, as well as an adjunct lecturer in management at Marymount College, Arlington, Virginia.

Labor relations involves contract negotiation and administration, both of which require dealing with people. What makes a career in labor relations so interesting is that the daily problems one encounters are never quite the same since either the issues are a little different or the people involved have changed. I chose labor relations as a career because the intellectual challenge associated with the collective bargaining process involves getting people to agree with positions they were not originally prepared to accept and because normally the process results in the peaceful resolution of legitimate disputes.

As the manager of labor relations policy my duties fall into four broad areas. Primarily, I am responsible for the develop-

United States Steel Corporation

ment and implementation of corporate-wide policy to assure the consistent administration of over 60 collective bargaining agreements with over 30 national and international unions. I handle both steel and coal arbitration cases involving those agreements. I serve as liaison with other departments of U. S. Steel, including law, personnel, accounting, benefits administration, and public affairs, in matters which have labor relations policy implications. I also serve as the focal point for inquiries from government agencies and other private sector companies on labor relations matters.

I also have been actively involved in the Personnel Policy Committee of the Pittsburgh United Way and have participated in the contract negotiations of the Pittsburgh Symphony Orchestra.

Key Concepts

agency shop   A type of union security. All employees for whom the union bargains must pay dues but need not join.

bargainable issues   Aspects of the work or job environment that are subject to collective bargaining between union representatives and management representatives. Examples are wages and fringe benefits.

blacklists   Lists circulated among employers containing the names of workers who were known to be in favor of unions. Blacklisted workers were denied employment. The use of blacklists is now illegal.

boycott   In labor relations a boycott is a union's attempt to get people to refuse to deal with the boycotted firm. Also used by other groups to get people to unite against another person, business, nonbusiness organization, or country and to agree not to buy from, sell to, or associate with that person, organization, or country.

closed shop   A type of union security. Only members of the union can be hired by an employer. Outlawed in interstate commerce by the Taft-Hartley Act.

collective bargaining   The process of negotiating a labor contract between union representatives

and employer representatives and the on-going process of administering an existing labor contract. The parties bargain in good faith on bargainable issues.

collective bargaining agreement   The contract negotiated between employer and union representatives which sets forth the terms and conditions under which union members will offer their labor services to an employer.

compulsory arbitration   A method of settling a dispute between labor and management. A neutral third party decides how the dispute is to be settled and it is binding on both parties. Used only when essential public services are involved. Compelled by federal or state law.

conciliation   A method of settling a dispute between labor and management. A neutral third party tries to prevent negotiations from breaking down. If negotiations break off, the third party (conciliator) tries to get the disputants back to the bargaining table.

craft unions   Unions organized by crafts or trades—plumbers, carpenters, machinists, etc. Membership is restricted to workers with specific skills.

escalator clause   A provision in a collective bargaining agreement that wage hikes will be granted on the basis of changes in the cost of living. These hikes are called cost-of-living adjustments.

Fair Labor Standards Act A 1938 law that defines the normal working week, requires time-and-a-half pay for all hours over forty worked by an employee during a week, and establishes a federal minimum wage.

grievance procedure The sequence of steps an aggrieved employee should follow in seeking to correct the cause of a grievance. A grievance is a complaint about an alleged violation of a collective bargaining agreement or the law as it applies to a worker. Included in most collective bargaining agreements.

guaranteed annual wage A provision in a collective bargaining agreement that maintains the worker's income at some agreed-on level during a year.

industrial unions Unions organized according to industries—steel, auto, clothing, etc. Include semiskilled and unskilled workers.

injunction An order issued by a court. A mandatory injunction requires performance of a specific act. A prohibitory injunction orders the defendant to refrain from certain acts. In labor relations, an injunction granted to an employer orders employees to return to work or not to strike.

labor union An organization of employees formed for the purpose of dealing collectively with their employers in order to further the interests of those employees.

Landrum-Griffin Act A 1959 law that requires unions and employers to file financial reports with the Secretary of Labor and that contains provisions to ensure democratic operation of unions. A labor-reform amendment to the Taft-Hartley Act.

lobbying Efforts to influence the passage, administration, or enforcement of laws.

local union The basic union organization. A local of a craft union is made up of artisans in a local area. A local of an industrial union is made up of workers in a given industry in a local area.

lockout An employer's tool in labor disputes. Employees are locked out or denied access to their place of employment until they accept the employer's terms of employment.

mediation A method of settling a labor-management dispute. A neutral party suggests a possible compromise of the dispute.

National Labor Relations Board (NLRB) Created by the Wagner Act, the board investigates cases of alleged unfair labor practices committed by employers and unions and issues orders to prevent them. It is responsible for holding elections to determine whether or not a firm's employees want a union and, if so, which one.

national union The organization set up to bring all the local unions of a particular craft or industry together for bargaining purposes.

Norris-LaGuardia Act A 1932 law that prohibits employers from using the injunction in labor disputes unless employers can meet the strong requirements set out in the act. Also outlaws the yellow-dog contract.

open shop An employer may hire either union and/or nonunion workers. Employees need not join or pay dues to a union.

picketing a means of communicating with others. Persons (pickets) form a picket line and walk around a plant or office building with signs informing other workers and the general public that the employer is held unfair to labor.

right-to-work laws State laws permitted under the Taft-Hartley Act that outlaw the union-shop type of union security.

strike A temporary withdrawal of all or some employees from an employer's service.

supplemental unemployment benefits (SUB) Payments to laid-off workers made by their employers.

Taft-Hartley Act A 1947 law that outlaws the closed shop, permits states to pass right-to-work laws, provides for injunctive processes in national emergency strikes and in illegal strikes, requires unions to bargain in good faith with employers, and makes it illegal for unions to discriminate against workers who do not join unions if they are not required to do so as a condition of continued employment.

unfair lists Lists circulated among workers containing the names of employers whom unions considered unfair to workers because these employers refused to hire union members.

union federation Represents the unions that comprise it in presenting labor's views on political and social issues; it also helps to resolve conflicts among its affiliated unions. Exists at national and local levels.

union shop A type of union security. An employer whose employees are unionized may hire non-union workers, but they must join the union within 30 days of being hired or else be fired.

voluntary arbitration A method of settling a dispute between labor and management. A neutral third party decides how the dispute is to be settled. The two parties decide voluntarily to arbitrate the dispute. The parties are usually bound by the agreement.

Wagner Act The National Labor Relations Act (NLRA) of 1935. Referred to as labor's "Magna Charta," it spells out employer practices that are unfair to labor. The act created the National Labor Relations Board (NLRB).

For Review . . .

1. Discuss the Industrial Revolution from the viewpoint of the typical worker during that period.
2. Prior to the 1930s, how did employers resist their employees' efforts to form unions?
3. List the major federal labor laws and discuss their main provisions.
4. Why is the Wagner Act referred to as labor's "Magna Charta"?
5. Why is the Taft-Hartley Act considered by many to be "promanagement"?
6. Discuss the role of the National Labor Relations Board (NLRB) in labor-management relations.
7. Is the scope of "managerial discretion" narrowed when a firm's workers form a union? Explain.
8. Distinguish between a craft union and an industrial union.
9. List and discuss two major economic objectives of modern unions.
10. In light of the declining proportion of our labor force that is engaged in blue-collar jobs, what are unions doing to increase their membership?
11. List and discuss four issues that might lead to labor-management conflict.
12. List and discuss the "weapons" of labor and management.

. . . For Discussion

1. Does a union have a responsibility to persons or groups other than the members of that union?
2. Do the employees of a firm whose management is "employee-oriented" have a need for a union?
3. How would you explain the fact that most American workers do not belong to a union?
4. Suppose that you are in charge of selecting a location for a new plant to be built next year by your firm. Would the absence or presence of state right-to-work laws influence your decision making?
5. What should businesses, government, and unions do to increase the productivity of American workers?

Incidents

General Motors and the United Auto Workers

The United Auto Workers (UAW) and General Motors (GM) held heated discussions for several weeks during 1978 over GM's alleged antiunion "southern strategy."

The UAW had accused GM of opening new plants in the South in order to avoid the unionization of its workers. GM, however, said that the construction of new plants in the South was based on sound business practices, not a desire to avoid the UAW. The UAW contended that GM refused to hire unionized GM workers from other plants who wanted to transfer to GM's new plants in the South. Many of GM's workers in its northern plants originally were from the South. But an hourly worker at GM who wanted to transfer to a new plant had to show up in person, on his or her own time, at the new plant to make a regular job application.

Under a new hiring policy agreed to by the UAW and GM in 1978, a GM worker has only to inform GM that he or she wants to transfer and the worker will receive preferential treatment as job applicants are reviewed.

Give-backs and Collective Bargaining

"What the boss once gave away, the boss now wants back.

"That is the message unions are hearing as employers in numerous fields adopt a harsher negotiating stance over fringe benefits and work rules that hamper production.

"Upset that companies are seeking to erase costly benefits or working practices from contracts, union leaders have coined a new phrase: give-backs. Corporate executives say a more apt description is buy-backs, because they are offering higher wages in exchange for the concessions.

"By whatever name, the result is hard-nosed bargaining and a scattering of strikes in such diverse fields as railroading, coal mining, construction, steelmaking, railway-car building and publishing. Instead of getting hung up on the size of

Questions

1. Do you think that the existence of right-to-work laws in the southern states had any bearing on GM's decision to build new plants in the South? Explain.
2. Why did GM agree to the new hiring policy?
3. Is it fair for GM to grant preferential treatment to job applicants from its other plants when they apply for jobs in the new plants? Why or why not?

Source: *Associated Press.*

wage increases, bargainers in these and other industries are haggling over such issues as crew sizes, coffee breaks and production quotas.

"'There is definitely a demand by almost all employers to get productivity increases,' says W. J. Usery, Jr., former Secretary of Labor and now a private mediator and consultant. 'With inflation as it is, they must increase output if they are to continue to increase wages.'"

Questions

1. Why are employers trying to win these "give-backs" or "buy-backs" from unions?
2. In your opinion, are fringe benefits as important to workers as wages? Why or why not?

Source: *U.S. News and World Report.*

ROCKETOY COMPANY 7

Rocketoy's workforce had expanded to a total of 300 workers. In spite of its size, Rocketoy's management was able to preserve the good employer-employee relationship that had existed ever since the company was founded. Furthermore, Rocketoy had a profit-sharing plan that enabled its employees to share in the firm's profit. According to Terry the plan gives each worker a real stake in the company. He believed this was crucial in getting them to put forth their best efforts.

Joe Phillips was still vice-president of produc-

tion. Terry had noticed "people problems" between Joe and ten young production workers who had recently been hired. Terry asked these ten workers to come to his office to discuss the situation. He wanted to take steps to solve the problem between the workers and "Uncle Joe."

The ten workers showed up in Terry's office and it became apparent that the "people problems" between Joe and his workers were a lot more serious than Terry had thought. They accused Joe of treating his subordinates like children.

Charlotte Ethridge was the most outspoken. She accused Joe of playing the "father role." Charlotte cited an example. Two months ago, a promotion opened up. The former supervisor of the loading dock retired and the obvious choice for the job was Pauline Williams. She had the most seniority in the entire production department and she wanted the job. Pauline was a good worker and had never had any trouble with Joe or anyone else at the plant.

But Joe passed over Pauline and gave the promotion to Gordon Hooker. Gordon had less seniority than Pauline but Joe believed he would be a better choice for the job because the loading dock supervisor sometimes has to "be tough" to keep things moving.

After the meeting, Terry thought the situation over. He knew Joe was not ready to retire. Terry also felt that he owed him a lot. Without his help, Rocketoy might never have gotten started.

But Terry did understand the source of the workers' complaints. He recalled Joe's discussing with him the reasons he promoted Gordon Hooker over Pauline Williams. "Terry, I know I'm out of step with some of the newer thinking. If Pauline were a man, I'd have given her the promotion. She really deserved it. But—she is a 28-year-old woman. Can you imagine the problems I'd have with her as supervisor on the loading dock?"

At first Terry decided to let Joe run his department as he saw fit. But during the next three months Charlotte "stirred up" several of the pro-

duction workers. At first it was mainly Charlotte and the other nine workers who had visited Terry's office. But it soon spread. Complaints about Joe began multiplying rapidly.

Before long, union organizers tried to unionize Rocketoy's production workers. The Pauline Williams "incident" was a big issue. Rocketoy's workers were the only ones among the big toy manufacturers who were not unionized.

Questions

1. Discuss the meaning of a "good employer-employee relationship."
2. Do you think that a profit-sharing plan for employees helps to make employees feel that they have an ownership interest in the company for which they work? Explain.
3. Do you think that Terry should have called the ten workers in for a talk? Explain.
4. Could Terry have done anything to prevent the problem as outlined by Charlotte Ethridge? Discuss.
5. Once the problem involving Pauline Williams was out in the open, what should Terry have done about it? Explain.
6. How successful do you think that the union organizers were in unionizing Rocketoy's production workers? Discuss.
7. If you were Terry, what would you have done to try to keep Rocketoy a nonunion company? Explain.

The Computer and Other Business Tools

CHAPTER 14

Objectives: After reading this chapter, you should be able to

1. Describe one important way that a computer enters your life.
2. Illustrate the complementary relationship between people and computers in doing a job.
3. Explain what makes a system automated.
4. Compare manual, mechanical, and electronic data processing systems.
5. Draw a diagram of a computer system.
6. Recognize common input-output devices for computers.
7. Explain the function of a language such as COBOL.
8. Explain the impact of minicomputers on business.
9. Contrast several ways that people react to computers.
10. Discuss some of the jobs available that are related to computer operation.
11. Compute an arithmetic mean and median.
12. Prepare a breakeven chart.

Key concepts: Look for these terms as you read the chapter

computer	COBOL
computer program	documentation
data processing	quantitative tools
punched card	statistics
hardware	arithmetic mean
central processing unit (CPU)	median
	mode
outside data storage systems	frequency distribution
input-output (I-O) devices	histogram
on-line system	sample
time sharing	breakeven analysis
controllers	operations research (OR)
software	model building
FORTRAN	linear programing

In this chapter we'll first discuss what a computer is and what it can do. We will examine the major components of a computer and the programing and other things needed to make it work. We'll also study some of the practical problems met in using computers. Finally, we will turn to statistics and mathematical techniques used by business firms. Topics include breakeven analysis and linear programing.

What Is a Computer?

A computer or, more exactly, a computer system is an electronic ma-   computer
chine capable of storing huge amounts of data and performing mathe-
matical calculations very quickly. It is also called an electronic data
processing system. Computers are an important part of many thousands
of business firms.

What a Computer Does

Computers play a big role in your everyday life. Stop and think about it!
They do some of the little everyday things like figuring your bank balance or the size of your family's bill at Sears. A computer might even
prepare your quarter or semester grade report. Computers do thousands of repetitive operations like these. They perform very efficiently
for a big institution like a corporation or a university. They store a huge
mass of information and make thousands of routine calculations. They
allow big companies to communicate with many customers.

Suppose you use your VISA card to buy gas at a service station. The
attendant uses it to print your account number before you sign
the charge slip. This slip ends up being processed by a computer. The
amount of your purchase is added to your VISA bill. Because of the
great speed and accuracy of computers, thousands of transactions, like
your purchase of gasoline, can be quickly and accurately processed.

But a computer can do a lot more than routine data processing. Think
of its role in our space program! Without computers, moon landings
would have been impossible. In fact, much of the progress in science
and technology has depended on computers. Computers touch your life
in at least these two ways—as a go-between for large institutions and the
people they deal with and as an instrument that speeds up technological
and economic progress.

Businesses use computers to

- prepare payrolls
- analyze past-due accounts receivable
- prepare and mail out bills
- keep social security and tax records
- keep track of inventories
- simplify reordering of goods

There are many other jobs, too, that require speed, flexibility, and accuracy in data processing. In Chapter 9 we examined the flow of data required for performing such functions. Computers make accounting systems work quicker and more accurately.

YOU BE THE JUDGE!

The Computer's Personal Touch

Have you ever received a personal letter from a computer? What about that big sweepstakes letter you got from your favorite magazine publisher? Wasn't the letter informing you of the contest addressed to you personally? Didn't the salutation of the letter say "Dear (your name)?" Wasn't your name mentioned at several places in the letter? How nice of such a big company to take the time to be so friendly and personal! Think of what it had to pay for typing all those personal letters!

Of course, you know the letters were not from a computer. They were from the publisher. But the publisher had help from a computer-controlled typing or printing system. Hundreds of thousands of letters come out looking like personal letters because of the computer. Such "personal communication" should flatter you. But is it really personal communication or just another piece of "junk" that is typical of the computer's ability to impersonalize company–customer relations? YOU BE THE JUDGE!

Smaller computers are now finding their place in brand-new functions. Many income tax preparation firms are using them to figure out and print tax returns. Garages are using specialized computers to find out what is wrong with your car. In fact, small special-purpose computers called *microprocessors* are being built into cars and appliances to improve their performance in many ways, such as to produce better engine performance. High-technology firms like Texas Instruments are pouring hundreds of millions of dollars into research for new ways to apply these electronic marvels.

It is obvious from what we have seen in our earlier chapters about production, marketing, finance, and accounting that much of the success or failure of a firm depends upon its ability to *accumulate, process, organize,* and *retrieve* information. The accounting department needs to collect data concerning transactions and periodically produce financial statements. The production department needs to keep records of inventories and costs of production and to estimate production schedules. Financial managers need to measure cash flows and construct capital budgets. All of these and many additional jobs in all but the smallest firms require the speed and accuracy and data-handling capacity of the computer. A successful firm needs to be able to gather, store, combine, and use this mass of data at a reasonable cost, a cost which is lower than the benefit it brings. If a computer is well designed and well used, it can do this.

Some firms, such as Xerox corporation (see the advertisement reproduced on page 480), have developed whole new combinations of technology (computers, duplicators, printers, telecopier transceivers, electronic typewriters) called *information management* systems. These are said to increase productivity without really threatening the work ethic, an important component of the Protestant ethic. They represent a technological response to what some are calling "the information explosion."

Computers can't predict the future, but they can help to make the future manageable, given complete and accurate data and a good understanding of the causes of success. Informed decisions are almost always better than those which are uninformed.

Master or Servant?

Some people fear that computers are "taking over" civilization. The truth is that, although the computer can perform millions of simple computations in a very short period of time or solve amazing problems, it is still only a servant. Some say it is not even a servant, but only a tool in the hands of people.

Whether we call it a servant or a tool, it still is a great multiplier of human power. It does some jobs that people could never do. It can work tough math problems at fantastic speeds without a mistake.

At the same time, there are some tasks the computer will never do and that only people can perform. People can set values of things and create things. A computer cannot judge a beauty contest or write real poetry. The relationship between people and computers is complementary—they can work very well together.

INFORMATION MANAGEMENT. DOES IT THREATEN THE WORK ETHIC?

The American work ethic has always assumed that if you worked hard, your efforts would be rewarded.

We wouldn't argue with that. But we would like to amend it a little.

The way we see it, working hard isn't nearly as important as working well.

Information Management isn't a way of sidestepping hard work. It's a way of making it more productive.

For example, there's no virtue in having to spend hours typing, retyping and re-retyping documents. So we make electronic typing systems that let you type, revise and retrieve information in a lot less time. Which gives you a lot more time to create and perfect it.

To make information easier to work with, we make a full range of copiers, duplicators and computer printers. Ones that not only reproduce, but can reduce, collate or even print in color.

To make information more accessible, we have Telecopier transceivers and communicating typewriters that transmit information crosstown or cross-country in minutes.

We even offer computer services that let you manage information without having to manage a computer.

So you see, Xerox information management systems are actually the epitome of the work ethic.

They work harder. So you can work better.

XEROX

XEROX® and Telecopier® are trademarks of XEROX CORPORATION.

Source: Xerox Corporation.

Basic Computer-Related Ideas

Before discussing how businesses use computers, let's discuss two important ideas related to the use of computers. These are automation and data processing.

Computers and Automation

In earlier sections of the book we used the term automation. An activity or process is automated when it is possible to set its controls in advance so that it can work a long time without human attention.

Some automated processes are fairly simple and don't require computers. An example is a household heating and air-conditioning system. The thermostat permits the system to operate without much human interference.

A petroleum refinery is a more complex system. There are many points in the refining process at which information must be fed continuously into a computer. The information relates to things such as the rate of flow, temperature, and so on. The refinery's central computer has been programed so that it uses this information to control the refining process.

Programing, as we will see in greater detail later in this chapter, is the process of telling a computer what to do. **A computer program is a detailed set of instructions in a special computer language.**

computer program

The computer automatically makes certain computations and relays instructions to machinery in the factory. It does this in accordance with the program fed into it at an earlier time. Thus valves are opened and closed and temperatures are raised and lowered automatically.

Computers and Data Processing

As we saw in Chapter 9, all businesses need to accumulate, store, manipulate, interpret, and report data. This is called data processing. It includes financial and nonfinancial data. Governments and other non-business institutions need to process data too. These data processing needs vary a lot because of the great differences in the type and the size of data flows among these institutions. In all cases, however, there is a need to keep accurate tallies of all those numbers that are important to these institutions—counting hospital admissions or adding cash collected by a grocery store or figuring the net profit of Gulf Oil Corporation.

data processing

The size of the data flow (need) and the financial resources of the institution (ability to pay) determine the scale and complexity of its data processing system. Not all firms need, nor can they afford, computers.

On a very small scale, such as would be found in a small rural gasoline service station, no machines at all may be involved. Keller's Service Station in Bush, Texas, uses only a pencil and a loose-leaf notebook to record sales and expenses.

A more complex data processing system (a mechanical system) may

punched card

require converting the original document to a more easily handled form such as a standard punched card (IBM card). These cards have space for 80 characters across and 12 positions in each of the 80 "columns." Numbers and letters are punched on a card by a keypunch machine. This machine works like a typewriter. But in addition to printing, it makes small holes in the card. The vertical position of a hole in a column indicates a number. Two vertical holes in a column indicate a letter. Notice the top of the card in Figure 14–1. A keypunch usually prints the letters or numbers across the top of the card while it punches.

Data on punched cards can be processed in many ways. A sorting machine reads the holes in one column of a deck of cards and sends each card to a special pocket in the machine. Each pocket represents a certain number or letter punched on the card. All cards sent to a particular pocket have the same hole punched in a particular column.

A collating machine organizes or collates separate decks of cards into one combined deck. Accounting machines also do data processing jobs. A worker in a furniture store's billing department can take a deck of punched cards that represent customer credit purchases and print bills for those customers with an accounting machine. This is a mechanical data processing system. This kind of system is rapidly becoming obsolete, although some of its parts (keypunches, sorters, etc.) are still widely used to support modern computer systems.

Computers are also known as electronic data processing (EDP) systems. They are generally much more complex and powerful than mechanical data processing systems. EDP systems are used by nearly all large companies today and by growing numbers of middle-sized firms.

FIGURE 14-1

Punched card

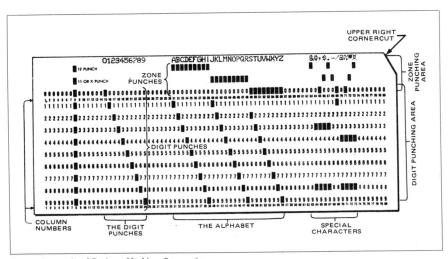

Source: International Business Machines Corporation.

EDP systems differ from mechanical systems in many ways. One of the main differences is that EDP systems allow instructions to be fed into the system rather than wired in on the control boards as found in mechanical systems.

Computer Hardware

Any discussion of computers usually falls under two headings: the *hardware* and the *software*. **The hardware consists of the machinery and electronic components.** Let's examine the various parts of the hardware and what they can do.

hardware

The tasks performed by the hardware, in logical order, are

- input
- storage and/or manipulation
- output

The tasks of inputting, storing, manipulating, and outputting are performed by four kinds of parts or components: (1) input devices; (2) central processing units; (3) outside data storage systems; and (4) output devices. (See Figure 14–2.)

The heart of any computer is its central processing unit (CPU). The CPU includes an internal memory for storing data, an arithmetic unit for performing calculations, a logic unit for comparing values and helping to "make decisions," and a control unit that actually operates

central processing unit (CPU)

FIGURE 14-2

Hardware components of a computer system

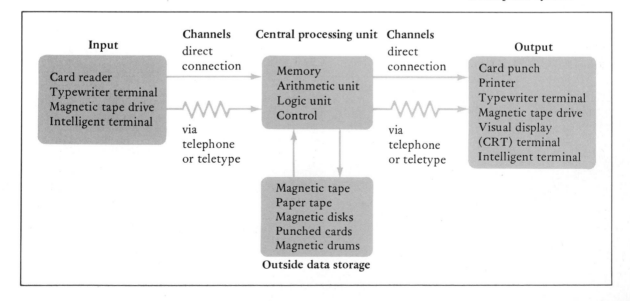

the computer and sends instructions for controlling all of the other components.

A computer's internal memory can be added to by means of outside data storage systems. There are separate systems for storing information, such as magnetic disks, magnetic tape, decks of punched cards, and punched paper tape. (See Figure 14–3.) Information can be recorded on any of these devices and fed back into the computer itself at any time. Outside memory devices are usually used for information that is not needed constantly in the operation of the computer system. More frequently used data or programs are stored in the internal memory, which provides much faster access.

outside data storage systems

FIGURE 14-3

Some of the devices used to store, enter, and retrieve data from computer systems

Magnetic disk

Magnetic tape

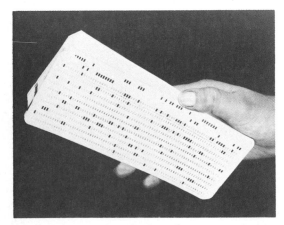

Punched cards

Paper tape

Source: International Business Machines Corporation.

The input and output (I-O) devices are the hardware used in getting information in and out of the computer. These pieces of hardware are, as a group, also called *peripheral* equipment. Information may be put into a computer by means of a card reader, a typewriter terminal, or a magnetic tape unit. Typewriters and magnetic tape input units also serve as output devices. Automatic card punching units, visual display units similar to a TV screen (CRTs), and a variety of high-speed line printers also can serve as output devices. Some line printers can print out hundreds of lines of information per minute. In some cases smaller computers, sometimes called "intelligent terminals," serve as input and output units for the larger computers and do simple processing by themselves. All input and output devices operate at much lower speeds than that of the central processing unit.

input and output (I-O) devices

A few years ago many marketing researchers used computers primarily to tally the findings of surveys. In fact, mechanical tabulating systems were often enough.

Market research experts of today are predicting radical new computer hardware applications to their profession. Among these are a CRT display device and computerized questionnaires for carrying out telephone surveys; optical scanners for tabulating sales data at supermarkets and other retail outlets; self-administered questionnaires completed by shoppers at consoles set up in shopping malls; and large computer-accessible data tapes containing demographics and product usage for studies of market segments. Computers even help to make large numbers of automated phone calls for marketing and marketing research purposes.

Many of these new systems have already undergone field testing. What will the computer mean for the future of marketing research?

THEN AND NOW

Computer Hardware and Tomorrow's Market Research

One important modern idea involves the use of remote input-output devices. The input or output unit may be far away from the central processing unit. When the operating needs of a business require that information be fed into or retrieved from the CPU by someone located at some distance, it is possible to do so by means of telephone lines. **A computer system that employees use constantly to get operating facts, such as parts availability or accounts receivable balances, is called an on-line system.** When data are collected for a period of time before being processed, this is called *batch processing*.

on-line system

time sharing

The use of remote I-O devices (peripherals) also facilitates an on-line process known as time sharing. This involves connecting several devices to the same computer so that several different firms or different users in the same firm can use it at the same time. The computer's high-speed calculation makes this possible. A computer can "handle" several jobs at the same time because the CPU operates much faster than any of the input or output devices. Several departments of a firm can use the same system at the same time. The inventory clerk in a warehouse can be typing in data on a newly arrived shipment of bolts while the payroll department is feeding in a magnetic tape containing information needed to print this week's paychecks. There is no noticeable interruption of either input. **Devices known as controllers regulate the "traffic" of peripheral hardware into the CPU.**

controllers

Time sharing also makes it possible for many small firms to use computers at a moderate cost. They pay only for the time during which they are connected to the central computer. A small business, for example, may make a time-sharing contract with a local bank that has excess computer capacity. The small business's only investment is the cost of the teletype or other I-O device.

"We think you'll fit right in here, Farbish . . . you're hired!"

Source: *Pepper and Salt*, Cartoon Features Syndicate.

The Bay Trucking Company operates a fleet of 20 trucks in California. It must maintain an accurate file of scheduled truck usage, including full information on dates, times of shipment, cargo sizes and types, and so on. The central office needs to be able to tell a prospective customer if and when a particular shipment can be made. By means of a teletype or visual display unit an employee can "call up" the computer at the Whitten National Bank of California eighty miles away and get an immediate report on what will be available in the next two weeks. This information is stored in a special part of the memory of the bank's computer.

The bank computer's CPU "handles the traffic" of Bay Trucking's computer needs as well as the needs of many other firms. The fee that Bay Trucking pays the bank is less than the cost of setting up its own small computer, and it may help the bank afford its large system. Of course, when the time-sharing arrangement was originally made, Bay Trucking needed the help of programers and others involved in the bank's computer system to learn how to use the computer correctly.

Computer Software

Computer software consists of things which complement the hardware, such as computer languages, internal systems, and programing. Software is just as important as hardware. In fact, experts predict that data processing expenditures of the future will include larger and larger proportions spent for software. Hardware can do nothing until it receives instructions.

software

A set of instructions is called a *program*. Writing such instructions is called *programing*. These instructions can reach the computer's control unit only if they are in a language that the computer understands. The kind of language a computer understands varies even among models of the same computer manufacturer. New software developments, however, make it possible to write instructions for the computer in a language that is nearly like human language. Some of these languages are FORTRAN, BASIC, COBOL, RPG, and PL/1.

FORTRAN is short for "formula translator." It is the most widely used language and has the widest variety of applications. It can do simple tasks as well as complex mathematical computations. BASIC and PL/1 are simpler languages somewhat like FORTRAN, but they are easier to learn. They have, however, fewer applications.

FORTRAN

COBOL is a specialized business language that is extremely close to English and is used for accounting and other business data processing. RPG stands for "report program generator."

COBOL

A business student can make good use of all of these languages. They are rather simple to learn. With the proper educational tools you can

```
10   READ X
20   IF X = −99.99 THEN 50
30   LET T = T + X
40   GO TO 10
50   PRINT "THE SUM IS"; T
60   DATA 30, 25, 63, 91, 11, −99.99
70   END
```

FIGURE 14-4

A BASIC program for finding a sum

learn BASIC or PL/1 in a few days and FORTRAN or COBOL in a few weeks.

The BASIC program in Figure 14–4 tells a computer to do a series of steps in the order of the program line number at the left of each line. Line 10 says to read the first number in the first DATA line. This is the number 30 in this case. Line 20, in effect, tells the program when to stop adding. It does this by picking a "dummy" number, −99.99, which is placed at the end of the DATA list. Line 20 says: "When you come to the dummy number (−99.99), skip to line 50." Line 30 is the actual adding process. It tells the computer to set up a counter, T, and to add the next value of X in the DATA line to this counter. Line 40 says to start the cycle at line 10 again. The computer continues the cycle of lines 10 to 40 until it reaches the dummy number, −99.99. Next, line 50 says to print the words "THE SUM IS" and the final value of T, which is 220. Line 70 tells the computer to stop the program.

This may seem like an awful lot of trouble for a simple addition. It is. But if there were hundreds of numbers and much more complex mathematics than addition, it would be worth the trouble.

Documentation

documentation

An important part of software is known as documentation. This means an explanation, often in diagram form, of what a program does and of the logical steps required to be performed by the program.

In recent years there has been a big change in the way that computer experts believe that programs should be documented. This change stems from an important new idea in software called *structured programing*. This new programing is said to be much more efficient than traditional programing, and it involves a new documentation system which includes *HIPO diagrams* and *structure charts*. It is the wave of the future, but it has not yet affected the way that the majority of business program development is done. The more traditional form of documentation is known as a *block diagram*. It is illustrated in Figure 14–5.

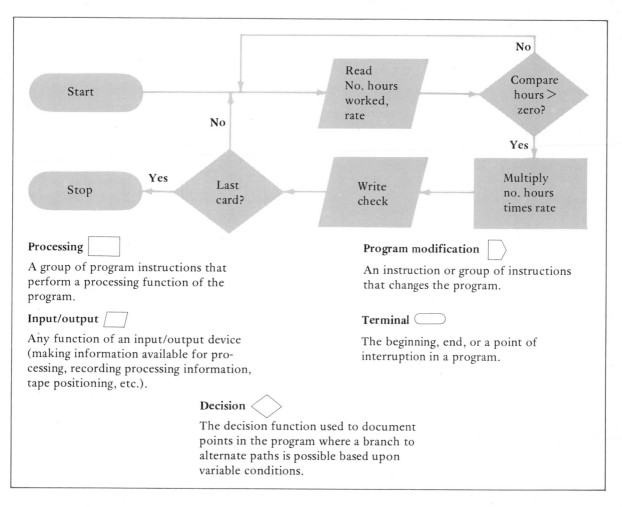

Processing ☐

A group of program instructions that perform a processing function of the program.

Input/output ▱

Any function of an input/output device (making information available for processing, recording processing information, tape positioning, etc.).

Decision ◇

The decision function used to document points in the program where a branch to alternate paths is possible based upon variable conditions.

Program modification ⬠

An instruction or group of instructions that changes the program.

Terminal ⬭

The beginning, end, or a point of interruption in a program.

One form of documentation is known as a block diagram or flowchart. This describes a program that reads hours worked and hourly rate from a record, skips records of workers who have not worked during the week, computes total wages earned for the week, and writes the paycheck. Standard flowchart symbols are also explained. Gradually, new forms of documentation under the general heading "structured programing" are beginning to replace traditional flowcharts.

FIGURE 14-5

How Are Computer Systems Selected and Installed in a Firm?

A sad fact about the typical use of computers in businesses is the lack of sufficient planning before installing the systems. This is caused by a variety of things. Consider this typical sequence of events leading up to the installation of a computer system at the Ajax Bolt Company.

Selecting a System

Ajax is a middle-sized manufacturer with an outdated, partially manual system of processing data. The information systems in the production, marketing, and finance departments are all somewhat different. The system at Ajax's newly acquired subsidiary is completely different. There is a serious need for a modern computer-based information system.

The subject came up once before at a board of directors meeting. The need began to be realized, though, when Ajax's president, Sam Black, visited a competitor's plant. He saw the fancy computer room over there, with all the blinking lights and spinning reels of tape. Sam also noticed the lower volume of paper work and learned that the competitor's profits had improved since the system was installed.

The next time the computer firm's sales representative visited Ajax, Sam listened closely to the strong sales pitch. The salesperson presented what seemed to be a very good application of the computer company's

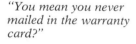

"You mean you never mailed in the warranty card?"

Source: *Pepper and Salt,* Cartoon Features Syndicate.

hardware and software to Ajax's needs. Being a smart businessman, Sam arranged for three computer firms to make presentations to his staff. After study and comparison of the proposals (which were all similar), Ajax picked a medium-priced computer made by the firm with the best service reputation of the three.

Ajax's need for a computer system was clear. But Sam Black did not take the best approach. Ideally, Ajax should have started by hiring an independent systems consultant or a permanent systems analyst. This person would have talked to all department heads to develop a complete set of concepts of the firm's needs. Next, with the analyst's help, Ajax would have examined the computers made by several manufacturers, including a variety of components that best fitted Ajax's needs. Finally, the necessary programing, testing, and installation would have been done.

Under this plan, Ajax would have had a better understanding of its needs. This understanding would not have been limited by the ready-made systems of a given manufacturer and by such a firm's "outsider's

---

GUIDELINES

Selecting a Computer System

Hardware evaluation:

- What are the costs involved? The rent, lease, or purchase price as well as the costs of operation and maintenance must be considered.
- Can it perform to your satisfaction? This includes adequate work volume capacity and speed.
- Is it compatible with the system already in operation?
- Is it expandable to meet your growth expectations?
- Can your staff be trained to run it?

Software evaluation:

- Do packaged programs fit your needs and staff expertise?
- Are programs documented adequately?
- Are the operating system, compilers, etc. reliable?

Vendor evaluation:

- What are the maintenance capabilities of the vendor?
- Does the local office of the vendor provide programing and systems support?
- What support will the vendor provide during conversion?
- What is the record of the vendor as to past performance, consistency during negotiations, etc.?

Source: *Louisiana Business Survey.*

view" of Ajax's problems and operations. In other words, it's wise to define your true computer needs first. Guidelines such as those presented on the previous page can help a lot.

Other Options

Firms that are thinking about a new computer, of course, have other options open to them besides the choice from among hardware manufacturers. First of all, they now have the choice of leasing from manufacturers or of leasing from computer leasing firms. The latter are independent "middlemen" who can often provide combinations of various manufacturers' hardware components which might more closely meet the needs of the user than can the products of one manufacturer. Often, a user can save money by using the services of a middleman.

Another option that is available is the leasing of a line connected into an existing large system with time-sharing capabilities. Such an arrangement can be made with a large user such as a bank or with a leasing firm. This option, of course, is not feasible for a firm that needs a large, complex data processing capacity. Another option for the small firm is to let a computer service firm take over its data processing needs entirely.

Minicomputers

In recent years the revolution in tiny computer circuits has led to the development of a whole new set of business "minicomputers." The minicomputer, which costs only one-fortieth as much as a large computer, can do much more than one-fortieth the work. The low cost of models made by many vendors has made the computer available to hundreds of thousands of smaller firms. Although many of the managers of these smaller firms might still be skeptical about having their own system, the financial reasons for not doing so are rapidly disappearing. These small systems have been marketed with broad accounting packages and specialized programs tailored for many industries. They can do payroll, general ledger, billing, inventory and sales analysis; and clerks, secretaries and floor salespersons can learn to use them with minimal training.

In the larger firm, minicomputers may have an equally large impact. Larger firms, in recent years, have felt the pressure of mounting data processing loads and a shortage of trained computer operating staff. This problem has caused them to centralize data processing in larger, more powerful computers. It seems, however, that centralization, in turn, has often led to conflict between those actually using the systems and those controlling them at data centers. The falling costs of mini-

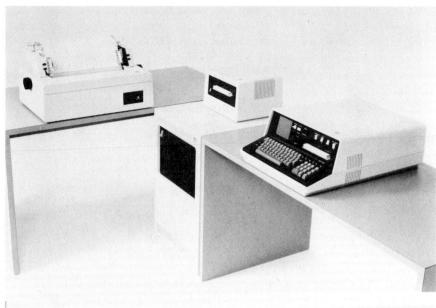

IBM 5110 Computing System

Source: International Business Machines Corporation.

computers has started to reverse the trend toward centralization of data processing. Firms that wish to implement decentralized management philosophies, then, can avoid the frustration created by large centralized computers.

Minicomputers can also be linked to large computer systems so that maximum flexibility can be achieved. The mini can serve both as a form of intelligent terminal and as an independent data processor.

How People React to Computers

Human reactions to the computer range from worship to outright fear. Most people who know computers reject these extremes. Rather, they learn that the computer is a marvelous tool. They find that people and computers can bring their different abilities together and that this combined power can be used very effectively.

Fear of the computer takes different forms. Some fear that people will become so dependent on complex control systems that a small human error could produce chaos. The Three Mile Island near-disaster and the SALT negotiations are reminders of the basis for such fears. Some people fear the computer because they feel it can bring about mass unemployment. Others fear it because it brings change in the firm—new ways of doing things. Still others fear the computer for another reason. They know that the government and many private agencies have stored huge quantities of personal data about private citizens and feel that this is a violation of their right to privacy. This is a special problem because of the prevalence of electronic spying.

Closely related is the fear of loss through "computer crime." Clever thieves have, in many cases, discovered ways to abuse computer systems, often in bank accounts or in payroll systems, for their personal gain. This is a growing problem which computer system designers are working on. Naturally, not much is publicized about techniques being used to combat such theft. Space-age thieves are too clever.

One measure which is being tested specifically to avoid the theft of private information is coding, not unlike the coding used in military and CIA communications. Such codes are being developed by specialized computer consulting firms for use by all kinds of businesses. All messages on SWIFT, a computer network linking 500 international banks, are being sent in coded form. Bank customers who use automatic tellers to transact business are being issued "secret passwords" to help protect against electronic thievery.

Sometimes people (even managers) feel that a computer will solve all their problems like magic. This can cause as many problems for a firm as

TWO POINTS OF VIEW

Converting to a Computer System

Gregory Snare has been head bookkeeper for 30 years at Wing Fanbelts, Inc. He feels that the company does not need a computer system. He is quoted as saying, "We can't expect to keep our customers or employees happy if they feel they are dealing with a computer. They want the feeling that human beings are taking care of their accounts and their payrolls. Besides, half of my clerical staff would quit. They feel it would only be a matter of weeks before they would be fired!"

Dave Delaney, the company's new vice-president, disagrees strongly. "We have grown 300% in the last five years. The volume of business demands computerization of our accounting. Bills are often late and we've had several payroll errors recently. If we convert to a computer system, all of these problems will disappear. The people in Snare's department have no reason to fear for their jobs. We'll retrain them to work with the computer. The XYZ Computer Company will do all of the training and installation. Our business will grow much faster and we'll have a more modern image!"

Who has the more realistic point of view? Could there be still another viewpoint?

fear of the computer. The truth is that managers must plan very carefully. They must get accurate data and a "debugged" program (one in which all the problems have been worked out) before they can count on using a computer's output. Someone invented the phrase GIGO (garbage in–garbage out) to describe how much the computer depends on reliable human input. A chimpanzee is unlikely to be able to count his toes even with a computer's help!

While computers have grown to be a vital part of business activity, a parallel growth has occurred in the use of mathematics and statistical tools. The fact that these two things have grown at the same time is not a coincidence. **Many of the mathematical and statistical tools depend on computers for their practical application. We refer to this whole set of mathematical and statistical applications to business as quantitative tools.**

quantitative tools

Some Quantitative Tools for Management Decisions

The use of quantitative tools by managers is increasing. Whereas managers in the past often relied only on their own judgment, modern managers strengthen their judgment by collecting and organizing data to support it. We will examine some basic statistical concepts and some examples of quantitative tools used today.

Statistics for Business

Managers have dealt with numerical data in their decision making for many years. These numerical data and methods of summarizing them are called statistics. Data may represent internal facts, such as number of units sold, or external facts, such as the population of the states in which a firm does business.

statistics

It is often helpful to summarize numerical data by using special kinds of averages. For example, we may wish to refer to average family income in the United States or to the average number of years of school completed. An average is a summary figure that describes the facts we are studying. There are three principal types of averages:

- the arithmetic mean
- the median
- the mode

The arithmetic mean is an average computed by first adding numbers, finding the total, and then dividing that total by the number

arithmetic mean

TABLE 14-1

Ages of employees in the receiving department

Employee	Age
Harold	30
Janet	28
Gordon	38
Clyde	27
Susan	27
Richard	34
Thomas	26
Total	210

of numbers that were added together. Look at Table 14–1. It is a list, or array, of the ages of seven employees in the receiving department of a factory. It also shows that the sum of their ages is 210 years. We can compute the arithmetic mean of their ages, their average age, by simply dividing 210 years by 7. The answer, of course, is 30 years. This is the most common form of average.

median

    Another measure of an average is called a median. It means the middle number when numbers are listed in rank—from smallest to largest or vice versa. To find the median of the ages of the employees in Table 14–1, we first rank ages in an array, starting with the youngest. The list becomes 26, 27, 27, 28, 30, 34, 38. The middle number is 28 years (Janet's age). There are three people older than Janet and three who are younger.

    To find a median of an even number of numbers, we still rank the numbers and then take an arithmetic mean of the two "middle" numbers only. If we added Paul, aged 29, to our list the median would be 28.5, which is the arithmetic mean of the two middle numbers, 28 and 29.

mode

    A third average is called a mode. It is the most common or frequent number in a list. In our example, only two people are the same age. Clyde and Susan are both 27, so this is the mode. Their age, 27, is the modal age.

    These types of "averages" are different ways of making a summary measurement of a characteristic of a group. Which one is best depends on the use to which the measurement is put and how the raw data are distributed.

    Suppose we collected statistics on family incomes in your home county and organized them into five groups. The statistics might appear in grouped form as shown in Table 14–2. This is called a frequency distribution.

frequency distribution

    A frequency distribution is a table that shows how many members of a larger group fall within various classes or subgroups. In this case it shows how family incomes are distributed among five income intervals or ranges. There are, for example, 420 families who received less than

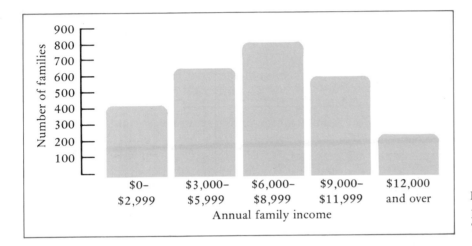

Annual family income	Number of families
$ 0– 2,999.99	420
3,000– 5,999.99	652
6,000– 8,999.99	809
9,000–11,999.99	602
12,000 and over	248
Total	2,731

TABLE 14-2

Frequency distribution of family incomes

FIGURE 14-6

Histogram of data in Table 14–2

$3,000, and 652 who received at least $3,000 but less than $6,000. Of course, the same information could have been provided by giving a whole list or array of all families and their income. The frequency distribution gives a clear summary of what family incomes are in the county without the extreme detail of such a list. It also tells us more than a single average of incomes could tell. It shows something about how incomes are dispersed or scattered around the average income. Figure 14–6 shows the same information in the form of a histogram. **The histogram, or bar chart, portrays a frequency distribution in vertical or horizontal columns whose length, measured on an accompanying scale, indicates the number or percent in each class.** The average, frequency distribution, and histogram are examples of descriptive statistics. Managers use them in preparing reports that describe their business operations or marketing data.

histogram

Sampling

Another widely used tool is the *statistics of sampling*. **A sample is a part of a larger group called a universe or population. It is intended to take**

sample

the place of the larger group and to convey some information about that larger group. Political analysts, for example, base their projections of winners in elections by studying a relatively small number of voters (the sample). The time, costs, and effort involved in interviewing every voter (the universe) would be too great. By interviewing a sample of voters, a pollster can make a good estimate of the election results.

Businesses also use sampling. Suppose a manufacturer of light bulbs wishes to guarantee that its bulbs will last a certain number of hours. The company might find, based on a study of a sample, that the average bulb life is two hundred hours. It would be unrealistic to base the guarantee on a study of all the light bulbs it produces. Its entire inventory would have to be "burned out." So it tests a sample of these bulbs.

A TV program sponsor uses a rating to decide whether to keep a particular program. A TV rating firm such as A. C. Nielsen cannot check all viewers in the country. Think of the cost! Nielsen contacts a sample drawn from all viewers and then estimates the national audience from the sample.

Some samples are selected in such a way that certain things can be estimated about the larger group with a given degree of confidence. Other samples are not drawn according to strict mathematical rules but still try to approximate the characteristics of the larger groups. They don't provide a measurable degree of confidence in their accuracy, but they are cheaper to get and are more often used than the other (random) kind because of the lower cost.

Breakeven Analysis

breakeven analysis

A useful management tool in both production planning and pricing of products is breakeven analysis. Breakeven analysis demonstrates the profitability of various levels of production. The breakeven point shows at which level total costs are exactly equal to total sales revenue. As you can see in Figure 14–7, the number of units produced is measured on the horizontal scale and dollar costs and revenues are measured on the vertical scale. The sales revenue line starts at the zero point (lower left corner). Since the product sells for $100, this line moves up $1,000 each time it moves to the right by 10 units. If we make and sell 20 units, we get $2,000 in revenue.

Costs are of two kinds: fixed and variable. *Fixed costs* occur whether we produce zero or 20 or 1,000 units. These costs are often called *overhead costs*. They include depreciation on plant, insurance, and other costs that do not vary with the level of production. In this case fixed costs are $1,000.

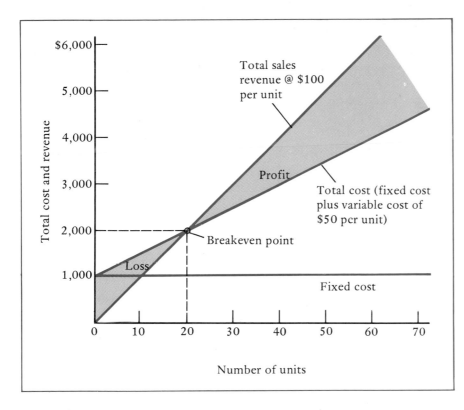

FIGURE 14-7

A breakeven chart

Variable costs depend on the number of units produced and sold. These might include raw materials, labor, and other costs that go into each unit produced. For each unit we produce and sell, it costs us $50 more—in addition to fixed costs. The effect of variable cost is represented by another line sloping up from the $1,000 mark on the left vertical axis. This line, since it starts from the $1,000 fixed-cost level, also measures total cost at various levels of production. If 20 units are made, the total cost is $2,000, consisting of $1,000 in fixed costs and $1,000 (20 × $50) in variable costs. If 25 are made, the total cost is $2,250.

At the level of 20 units of production, the cost and revenue lines cross. This is the *breakeven point*, the production level beyond which the firm begins to make a profit. For each additional unit made and sold the firm realizes an increase of $50 in profits. This is so because unit revenue minus unit variable cost ($100 − $50) equals $50.

A breakeven chart can help a plant manager decide several things. It can help a manager decide whether to install expensive new machines that would change the production cost structure. It can help to set prices or help to decide whether to buy or to lease a plant. A retailer could also use a breakeven chart to make similar decisions.

Operations Research

In recent years many new mathematical tools have been developed. Many were originally developed to analyze and solve military problems. The army's problems in assigning personnel are a lot like the problems found in business. Assigning aircraft is similar to a business assigning salespeople or distributing inventory among warehouse locations.

operations research

Determining how many units of a product to keep in its warehouse is a tough problem for a company selling hundreds of products around the world. Mathematical means are available to help with such a problem. Others are suited for scheduling operations and for making other common decisions. **The various quantitative techniques used for scheduling or allocating things are called operations research (OR). They include linear programing, waiting-line theory, and game theory.** Sometimes the term *management science* is used to describe the same thing.

Computers enable managers to apply these techniques. Otherwise, the mathematical calculations might take years to perform. Several examples of the use of operations research in business follow.

Model Building

Sometimes the best way to understand and solve a problem is to create a simplified model of it. An organization chart, as we saw in Chapter 4, is a model of organizational relationships. It is a very simple model. It does not show all the formal and informal relationships that exist.

model building

An architect builds a model of a bridge to evaluate certain structural ideas. It is subjected to tests of strength. If the results are favorable, the architect feels more confident in the design. The same is true in business. Managers, however, cannot usually build that kind of model themselves. They may, however, call on a specialist to build a mathematical model or simulation of a problem situation. **Such model building represents the way in which several important factors (variables) work together to explain how other factors such as profits or sales vary.**

The equation $S = bY + cV - dR$ could be a simple model explaining variation in sales of Blanche's restaurant. (See Figure 14–8.) S stands for total annual sales of the firm. Y stands for total projected income of Macon, Georgia, where Blanche's is located. V means number of expected visitors to Macon, and R is the number of rainy days expected in the year. The letters b, c, and d are called *coefficients*. They are values to be multiplied times the values of Y, V, and R, respectively. It would then be possible to forecast sales with some degree of assurance, if we could plug in good estimates of Y, V, and R. The coefficients must be estimated

$$\begin{bmatrix} \text{Expected} \\ \text{sales of} \\ \text{Blanche's} \\ \text{Restaurant} \end{bmatrix} = b \begin{bmatrix} \text{Next} \\ \text{year's in-} \\ \text{come of} \\ \text{Macon,} \\ \text{Georgia} \end{bmatrix} + c \begin{bmatrix} \text{Predicted} \\ \text{number} \\ \text{of visi-} \\ \text{tors to} \\ \text{the city} \end{bmatrix} - d \begin{bmatrix} \text{Predicted} \\ \text{number} \\ \text{of rainy} \\ \text{days} \end{bmatrix}$$

$$\mathbf{S} = b\,\mathbf{Y} + c\,\mathbf{V} - d\,\mathbf{R}$$

FIGURE 14-8

a simple model

from past testing of this model. A model can help in other things besides forecasting. Making a model can help the manager of Blanche's understand better the operations of the firm and the market.

A model is tested by seeing how it fits the real facts (variables) in the past. If it seems to work, it can be used to predict what might happen if the firm takes a certain action. A marketing manager who wants to introduce a new product might introduce it as a new variable in the model to see what it does to the other variables, including profit levels. There are, of course, no guarantees of accuracy.

By using model building, the decision maker can see what will happen if a particular course of action is chosen. The likely outcome of a particular decision can be predicted by plugging it into a model of the problem situation, without the "real" decision being made. Without a model, the outcome could be determined only by actually making the decision.

Linear Programing

Managers must make informed decisions about how resources will be allocated. **Linear programing is a mathematical tool used to allocate resources in the "best way" so that a desired objective is maximized or minimized.** This desired objective may be the greatest profit, the least cost, or another "best" result for the firm.

linear programing

Linear programing is widely used in problems such as determining the best (optimum) inventory level or plant location. A manager who must select a location for a new plant would find this technique helpful. It could allow him or her to minimize the total cost of getting raw materials into the plant, getting finished products to warehouses, and moving them to customers. Actually, these are only a few of the many variables that influence plant location decisions. A linear programing technique considers all variables in order to arrive at a "best" location. It can be applied in a situation when there are limited resources (time and money) and a value (profit or cost) that is to be maximized or minimized. The limitations are called *constraints*. For an example, see Figure 14-9.

The Purple Advertising Agency has $1,000 to spend and 10 working days to complete the job for the Wrought-Iron Hinge Company's ad campaign. They want to produce the largest amount of sales possible. Past experience shows that the average newspaper ad produces $3,000 in sales and the average radio ad, $4,000.

It costs $33.33 each to run newspaper ads and $100 each to run radio ads. It takes a day to prepare a newspaper ad and half a day for a radio ad. Purple can only work on one ad at a time. The question is how many newspaper ads to run and how many radio ads. The problem must be solved in terms of producing maximum sales.

In mathematical terms, the agency must maximize the expression $S = 4,000R + 3,000N$, where R equals the number of radio ads and N equals the number of newspaper ads. S equals expected sales.

The constraints or limits to the values of N and R in the solution are in the form of linear inequalities:

$$33.33N + 100R \leq 1,000$$
$$N + .5R \leq 10$$

The upper inequality says that the $1,000 must be spent at the rate of $33.33 per newspaper ad and $100 per radio ad. The lower inequality says the 10 days must be used at a rate of one day per newspaper ad and half a day per radio ad.

Solving these as you would a set of simultaneous equations gives values of $N = 6$ and $R = 8$. This combination will give maximum sales revenue in the amount of $50,000.

FIGURE 14-9

Linear programing and the advertising budget

Summary and Look Ahead

How the special talents of computers fit in with unique human talents is gradually being learned as people and computers work together solving business problems. Computer hardware and software together comprise a computer system that can serve a firm in many ways.

Computers are used in information storage and retrieval and in data manipulation and organization. Computers, together with people who know how to use mathematical tools, can greatly improve management ability. These helpful tools include statistics, breakeven analysis, and several types of operations research. They fit in well with the use of modern computers.

In the next chapter, we focus on the special problems related to running a small business. We will look at the risks and the opportunities, the advantages and the pitfalls of running your own business.

My name is Leo M. Johnson. I am a senior inspection technician at Magnetic Peripherals, Inc., a subsidiary of Control Data Corporation, one of the nation's largest computer technology firms. I received my associate degree in electronics technology from Eastern Oklahoma State College in Wilburton, Oklahoma.

Soon after graduation, I was hired by my present employer as an electrical-mechanical tester technician. Within two years I had moved up to positions as systems test technician and then as quality assurance technician.

In my present position as senior inspection technician I am responsible for test development of flexible disk-drive printed wire assemblies at the Magnetic Peripherals division of Control Data. I have also been assigned to training technicians and product correlation work at an affiliated production site in Tampa, Florida.

I came to work for Control Data because I was convinced that here I had an opportunity to pursue a career in the growing field of electronic technology. My impressions are still very positive about career growth opportunities and financial rewards.

CONTROL DATA CORPORATION

Key Concepts

arithmetic mean A kind of "average" computed by adding a group of values and dividing the total by the number of values.

breakeven analysis A technique for estimating the relationships among volume of operation, costs, and sales revenue. Costs are divided into fixed and variable parts. When sales revenues equal total costs, the firm breaks even.

central processing unit (CPU) The device which performs the actual calculations and logic in a computer system. It includes an internal memory, an arithmetic unit, a logic unit, and a control unit.

COBOL A specialized language that is extremely close to English and is used for business data processing.

computer An electronic data processing system that stores great amounts of data and manipulates data quickly and accurately.

computer program A detailed set of instructions to a computer in a special computer language.

controller A device to regulate the flow of multiple sources of data (terminals, etc.) into the CPU.

data processing The accumulation, storage, sorting, interpretation, and reporting of facts, mostly in numerical form.

documentation Explanation or illustration of a computer program.

FORTRAN Short for "Formula Translator." FORTRAN is a science-oriented computer language.

frequency distribution A means of describing a large group of values. Intervals or ranges of values are established first. Then the number of values falling within each interval is computed and listed next to the interval.

hardware The electronic and mechanical components of a data processing system.

histogram A graphic representation of a frequency distribution, using bars or columns to indicate frequency.

input-ouput device Any piece of equipment that

allows information to be fed into a computer or permits the computer to make information available to its user (for example, a typewriter). Also called peripheral equipment.

linear programing   A quantitative technique used to allocate resources in the best way so that some desired objective is maximized or minimized. Desired objectives might be greatest profit or least cost.

median   The middle value of a group of values ranked in order of magnitude.

mode   The most frequent value in an array.

model building   A model is a simplified version of a set of relationships. By simulating the real-world operations of the firm through model building, the decision maker can see what will happen if he or she chooses a particular course of action.

on-line system   A computer system that permits direct and continuous access by employees to stored information.

operations research (OR)   Various complex quantitative techniques used by managers to assist them in decision making.

outside data storage systems   Means of storing data other than in the CPU itself. Magnetic tape and disks are examples.

punched card   A paper card that is used in computers to store and transmit information by means of specially arranged holes made in the card.

quantitative tools   Methods of using mathematics and statistics to help solve business problems and understand facts.

sample   A part of a larger group that represents the larger group.

software   The programs, languages, and routines used in electronic data processing. Software complements hardware.

statistics   Data; also the science of manipulating, interpreting, and summarizing data.

time sharing   A method whereby a number of users may utilize the facilities of a single computer at one time.

For Review . . .

1. Name the three major hardware components of a computer. How are they interrelated?
2. What is a computer language? Name two common ones.
3. What kinds of business processes make good use of the rapid repetitive capabilities of a computer?
4. What is a computer program?
5. Explain what is meant by documentation. Draw a simple block diagram.
6. Contrast the alternatives of computer leasing and time sharing.
7. Fixed costs are $100 and variable costs are $1 per unit. How many units must be sold at $2 to break even?
8. Name two input devices and two output devices.
9. What can supplement the memory component of a CPU?
10. Why do managers develop models?

. . . For Discussion

1. Besides the trips to the moon, what startling modern accomplishments do you think never could have happened without computers?
2. Review the experiences you had yesterday and try to determine which of these were in some way influenced by the existence of computers.
3. Do you think that computers will someday dominate us? Why or why not?
4. Can you "invent" a business problem that linear programing could solve? What are you maximizing or minimizing?
5. What happens to the breakeven point when the sales price goes up?

Incidents

Giant Foods, Inc.

In many of its supermarkets in the Washington, D.C. suburbs, Giant Foods, Inc. has installed computerized checkouts that read the universal product codes on groceries and print a detailed receipt quicker than any clerk could do with a typical cash register. Every item is spelled out by name. The stores report savings in labor cost and greater accuracy in bills. Also, a continuous check is provided on food stocks, which makes reordering a lot simpler.

Questions

1. What are the advantages that you can identify from the shopper's point of view?
2. What are the shopper's disadvantages, if any? Do they vary by type of retail customer?
3. Do any costs rise in this system? What are they?
4. Which characteristics of the computer are demonstrated here?

Source: *The Wall Street Journal.*

Computer Comes to the Ranch

Wallace and Maurice Harrell are modern day cattlemen with many of the tools of the space age at their command. In recent years they began to keep track of customers, pasture, and herds on a Datapoint computer. The computer has taken record-keeping functions away from cowboys and helps to plot feedlot expenses and the cattle's weight gains. In addition, the computer can be programed to provide sixty pieces of data on each animal on the ranch. It can guide the owners in their dealings in futures contracts and other pricing decisions.

Questions

1. What additional uses can you think of for the computer on a large modern farm or ranch?
2. Would problems of adaptation of personnel be likely to come up when a computer is first installed in such an environment? Discuss.

Source: *The Wall Street Journal.*

YOU CAN LOSE your perspective by thinking of business firms only as national corporations. Firms come in all sizes and dimensions. For many firms there is a need to "think small" or a need to "think international."

We will adjust our sight in Chapter 15 to take a look at businesses that are quite small and that have many problems peculiar to small business.

In Chapter 16 we will look at businesses that have an international perspective. There we examine the special challenges and opportunities involved in conducting business across national borders.

SECTION FOUR

Special Types of Business

Small Business

CHAPTER 15

Objectives: After reading this chapter, you should be able to

1. Explain, in your own words, the meaning of a "small business firm."
2. List and discuss three ways by which a person might become a small business owner.
3. Give two or more reasons why small firms can compete effectively with larger competitors.
4. Compare the benefits and burdens of entrepreneurship.
5. List and discuss the first steps in starting your own business.
6. List and discuss the benefits of franchising to the two parties to a franchising agreement.
7. Explain, in your own words, why the Small Business Administration was created.
8. Identify and describe the major types of programs sponsored by the Small Business Administration to aid small business.
9. Identify the challenges to survival faced by small firms.

Key concepts: Look for these terms as you read the chapter

Better Business Bureau (BBB)	SBA direct loans
Chamber of Commerce of the United States	SBA participating loans
	SBA guaranteed loans
economic development council	Small Business Investment Company (SBIC)
franchiser	Service Corps of Retired Executives (SCORE)
franchisee	Active Corps of Executives (ACE)
franchising agreement	
Small Business Administration (SBA)	Small Business Institute (SBI)

Although our discussions on production, marketing, finance, personnel, and accounting in earlier chapters apply to all firms regardless of size, there are several aspects of small business that merit separate treatment. If you have ever considered going into business for yourself or if you already have done so, you will be especially interested in this chapter.

Most people who go into business for themselves start out in small businesses. A small business is a firm that is small in relation to its competitors. "Smallness" relates to such things as number of employees, dollar sales volume, and funds invested in the firm.

We also discuss how and why a person might start a small business. Then we look at the pros and cons of going into business for yourself. After that, we take a close look at franchising. Franchising is a way of doing business that has enabled many people to go into business for themselves.

The Small Business Administration plays an important role in helping entrepreneurs to start and to keep their firms going. We will examine the nature of this assistance.

In the end, however, a small business owner's success (or lack of it) is the result of good (or poor) management. As you will see, it's still possible to make "big money" by going into business for yourself. On the other hand, it's just as possible to lose everything you have invested.

What Is a Small Business?

In Chapter 3 we saw that there are roughly 11 million sole proprietorships, 1 million partnerships, and 2 million corporations in the United States. Many of these firms are small businesses. But "small" is a relative

THINK ABOUT IT!

What Is a Small Business?

For business loan purposes, the Small Business Administration defines a small business as one that is independently owned and operated, not dominant in its field, and that meets employment or sales standards developed by the agency. For most industries these standards are as follows:

- *Manufacturing.* Small, if average employment in the preceding four calendar quarters did not exceed 250, including employees of any affiliates; large, if average employment was more than 1,500. If employment exceeded 250 but not 1,500, SBA bases its determination on a specific size standard for the particular industry.
- *Wholesaling.* Small, if yearly sales are not over $5 to $15 million, depending on the industry.
- *Retailing and Service.* Small, if annual sales or receipts are not over $1 to $5 million, depending on the industry.

In some instances, the SBA uses other standards. As an entrepreneur, you should ask the nearest SBA field office which standard applies to your type of business.

Source: U.S. Small Business Administration.

term. For example, you might consider American Motors to be a "small" company in comparison to General Motors. But, compared to many other business firms, American Motors is very large.

The Small Business Administration (SBA) uses different "measuring sticks" to define what is meant by "small." For manufacturing firms the SBA usually defines a firm with 250 workers or fewer as small. Aircraft manufacturing firms are an exception. They are considered small if they have 1,500 workers or fewer. In the service industries firms are defined as small in accordance with their annual dollar sales. The dollar cutoff point varies by type of service industry.

There is no single definition of small business that is entirely satisfactory. Let's say, then, that a small business is one that can be started with a relatively modest investment of funds by the owner or owners. Of course, what is "relatively modest" is just that—it is relative to the industry in which the firm exists. Some industries, however, are made up almost entirely of small firms. Examples are barber shops, beauty parlors, and sandwich shops. The concept of relative size in its industry has little real meaning in these cases.

THINK ABOUT IT!

Big Businesses and Small Businesses Complement Each Other

Many big firms depend on thousands of small businesses to supply them with parts, services, supplies, and finished products for resale. For example, giant retailers like J.C. Penney and Sears have contracts with thousands of firms to supply them with products for resale. Giant manufacturers like Ford and Chrysler buy component parts for their cars from many suppliers. In many cases these supplying firms are small firms. The big firms are customers of small firms and small firms are the suppliers for big firms.

But small firms also often are customers of big firms that supply them. For example, retailers buy products that are produced by large manufacturers and resell them to household consumers. This relationship provides small retailers products to resell, and it gives large manufacturers access to the millions of consumers who shop in small retail stores. Both large and small firms benefit from these complementary roles. THINK ABOUT IT!

In addition to being small in size, a small business also usually is

- localized in its operations. Its owner(s), employees, and customers often live in the same town in which the firm is located. This,

FIGURE 15-1

You read about this one on Wall Street Journal's front page

WORLD-FAMOUS CHRISTMAS CAKE

ORIGINAL
DeLuxe TRADE MARK
"that famous Corsicana, Texas
Fruit Cake," since **1896**

BAKED TO ORDER

Shipped to your business friends and their families. Never sold in stores.

Here's the distinguished Christmas Cake we've baked in the little town of Corsicana, Texas for 82 years. Not only does the DeLuxe excel all gifts in its price range (shipped to executives in 158 different lands last year), it's unconditionally guaranteed *the best fruit cake you or friends ever tasted, or your money refunded!*

Crammed with prime-harvest fruits and crisp Texas pecans, DeLuxe is custom-baked and shipped fresh and moist from our kitchens. We guarantee delivery any place in the world. Please call or mail your order now. (Refer to box #.) Enclose check, or use Mastercharge or VISA with number, expiration date, signature. Include gift list; tell us how to sign gift cards. (Bakery's remarkable history comes in every tin.) SEE GIFT PRICES ABOVE COUPON.

ORDER YOUR GIFT CAKES TODAY

1-24	25-99	100+
2 lb. @ $ 6.95	2 lb. @ $ 6.75	2 lb. @ $ 6.55
3 lb. @ $ 9.85	3 lb. @ $ 9.55	3 lb. @ $ 9.25
5 lb. @ $15.95	5 lb. @ $15.45	5 lb. @ $14.95

Discounts apply to assorted sizes. Prices include holiday packaging and postpaid delivery. (Prices effective through Dec. 31, 1978)

COLLIN STREET BAKERY
Box   , Corsicana, Texas 75110, U.S.A.
Phone: 214-874-6511   Cable: Fruitcakes

Please ship:_____ 2 lb.; _____ 3 lb.; _____ 5 lb.
☐ Ship to me.   ☐ Ship to attached list, showing addresses, sizes, wanted dates.
☐ Payment enclosed. Or charge to my
☐ Master Charge ☐ Visa

Card No. _____
Expires: _____
Signature _____
Name _____
Address _____
City _____
State _____ Zip _____

Source: Collin Street Bakery.

of course, is not always the case. For example, the Collin Street
Bakery ad in Figure 15–1 appeared in *The Wall Street Journal.*
This bakery ships cakes to customers all over the world.

• a sole proprietorship, a partnership, or a family-owned corporation. There very seldom is any separation of ownership and management. The owners usually run the business directly.

Becoming a Small Business Owner

A person becomes a small business owner in one of three ways:

• by taking over the family's business
• by buying out an existing firm
• by starting a new firm

Each way has its own set of problems and opportunities.

Taking Over the Family Business

Not too long ago, it was common for a father to train his son to take over
the family's business someday. Usually these firms were very small and
employed only family members. The oldest son was expected to keep
the business going after the father stepped down. This meant the father
made the choice of occupation for his son. A grocer's son would become
a grocer. A barber's son would become a barber.

During the twentieth century, this method of becoming one's own
boss lost much of its appeal. Apprenticeship under the father generally
has been replaced by formalized education.

Nevertheless, every year many firms are taken over by relatives of the
former owners. In many cases the person taking over a firm is the
spouse or one of the children. But this often is not planned in advance
and makes it very hard for the person taking over, especially when the
former owner is not there to help the new owner.

Buying Out an Existing Firm

Many people go into business by buying out an existing firm. In many
cases an agreement can be reached whereby the seller helps the new
owner to learn the business from the ground up. It is good practice to
have a written contract outlining the duties of the former owner after
the new owner takes over.

Sometimes, buying out an existing firm means buying it from a surviving spouse. This presents a different problem, since the owner is not there to help the new owner to get oriented to the firm. In many of these cases the surviving spouse has neither the desire nor the ability to continue the firm. This fact points out the need for a plan to continue the firm after the owner's death. However, many small business owners do not ever prepare such a plan.

A person might go into business with the intention of selling out after the firm becomes a going concern. Some companies are formed to buy out small firms that have good growth potential. Often, these firms give financial and managerial help to promising new firms and offer to buy them out. In some cases they "go public." This means that they become corporations and sell shares of stock to the public. Some investors want to buy stock in new ventures.

Starting a New Firm

In the previous examples the business owner takes over an existing business. It has an established customer base and is a going concern. A person who starts a new firm, however, must build a going concern.

A new firm is not troubled with many of the problems that accompany the takeover of a firm that has been in business for some time. There are no dissatisfied customers, no fixed plant or store location and layout, and no bad debts for a new firm. The owner has the opportunity to build the firm from the ground up.

Many young people today are turned off by the thought of working for somebody else. They want personal and direct involvement that can be best achieved when they are their own bosses. Going into business may reflect a search for identity.

In a typical college town there are small firms that were started by college students who recognized profit opportunities. Examples are small clothing stores that cater to young adults, swimming pool maintenance firms, and home or apartment maintenance services.

Some colleges now offer courses in entrepreneurship or in starting a new business firm. While some students don't have the money to start a business right after graduation, many want to do it after they gain the necessary funds and experience.

Opportunities in Small Business

There are countless opportunities for small firms to serve ultimate consumers and industrial users. Opportunity exists in manufacturing, agriculture, retailing, wholesaling, and even in the extractive industries. Each year thousands of new firms are opened to exploit opportunity in those fields. Many start out as small firms.

The big question is: "How does a would-be entrepreneur learn how to spot opportunity?" It is partly a matter of being sensitive to the environment. The highly successful Baskin-Robbins 31 Ice Cream Stores had its beginning back in 1945. Mr. Baskin and Mr. Robbins recognized an opportunity to sell hand-packed, quality ice cream in attractive stores. The trend at that time was toward sales of prepackaged ice cream through supermarkets. But they believed that customers would go out of their way to buy delicious ice cream that was sold in attractive specialty stores, even if it meant paying more for it.

REALIZING THE AMERICAN DREAM

Kaleidoscope, Inc. is a high-quality mail-order catalog business that was started by Susan Edmondson in Atlanta. At the time she started her firm, Ms. Edmondson was working as a counselor to adolescents for $30 a day. But she wanted to go into business for herself.

Ms. Edmondson recognized market opportunity—the growing trend among women to buy from catalogs. Kaleidoscope's catalog features designer ready-to-wear and accessories, limited-edition art, furniture, decorative home accessories, unusual toys, gourmet items, and gifts for men. It also offers tours to foreign countries.

Ms. Edmondson's initial investment in her business was $5,000. Within five years of starting, her sales reached $20 million. As she puts it, "I guess I've realized the American dream."

Source: *The Times-Picayune.*

One of your authors recalls a success story of a former student. This was just before the widespread popularity of prewashed denim jeans. As a part-time sales clerk in a "jeans shop," the student recognized a growing preference for prewashed jeans among young people. He wanted to try "something on his own" so he bought 100 pairs of jeans from his employer. He had them washed by a commercial laundry so that they "looked old." He gave ten pairs free to college students to wear. They were asked to take orders from people who wanted the "new look" in jeans. The cost of the jeans that were given away, the laundering costs for 100 pairs, and the commissions he paid to his "salesforce" amounted to $845. His "take" on the whole deal was $1,500, leaving a profit of $655.

He now owns a very successful clothing store that caters to young men and women.

We could discuss many such success stories. What they teach is that opportunity always exists but hardly ever "knocks at your door." In a competitive economy you can be sure that it never knocks twice! Opportunity does not come to you. You must discover it!

Some people say that opportunity has all but dried up for small businesses. They argue that only large corporations can afford to hire the talent needed to spot trends and to capitalize on them. But bigger does not necessarily mean better as far as business is concerned. A large discount chain store can't give its customers the personal attention a small clothing store can give. A big manufacturer with many products can't give any one of them the attention a small firm can give to its one or two products. A small firm is usually more adaptable than a large firm. It often can react to change a lot faster.

Should You Go Into Business for Yourself?

Let's assume for a minute that you want to become your own boss. You have a rich uncle who will lend you the money to get started. If that's not enough to tempt you, you also can assume that you have a product or service that will definitely lead to a good profit if you can succeed as a manager. Should you go into business for yourself?

Given these assumptions (and they may be very unrealistic), you still must evaluate a third vital input—you, the entrepreneur. Before you make your decision, you must consider your goals in life. Then you must determine whether you have what it takes to reach those goals.

The Basic Requirements

Ask yourself the following questions to see whether you have the basic requirements for starting your own business:

1. Are you afraid of risk?
2. Are you unable to put off enjoying the "good life" today because you are afraid you won't be here tomorrow?
3. Are you overly security-conscious?
4. Do you have trouble getting along with people?
5. Do you lose interest in things that don't work out as quickly or as well as you thought they would?
6. Are you a thinker and not a "doer"?
7. Are you a "doer" and not a thinker?

8. Are you easily frustrated?
9. Do you have trouble coping in situations that require quick judgments?
10. Do you "cave in" under stress?
11. Does your family make unreasonable demands on your time?
12. Are you emotionally unstable?
13. Are you unable to learn from your mistakes?
14. Are you "too good" to do manual labor?

If you answered "yes" to several of these questions, you probably are not ready to start your own business. In any case, this sort of thinking is very important in deciding whether you measure up to the job of being your own boss. If you do measure up, then you can begin to weigh the benefits and the burdens of starting your own firm.

The Benefits of Entrepreneurship

Perhaps the best thing about being your own boss is the sense of independence you feel. You get a great deal of personal satisfaction from being directly involved in guiding your firm's growth. It is also possible to make a sizable personal fortune. You not only draw a salary but you also own the firm, the value of which may increase manyfold over the years.

Owning your business also is good for your ego. The entrepreneur fulfills the "American dream." You are respected by others because you are not a "cog in a wheel." You are "the wheel!" For many people, achieving their true potential means the same thing as becoming their own boss. Clearly, it gives you personal, economic, and social benefits.

The Burdens of Entrepreneurship

Being in business for yourself, however, requires your full attention. You usually will not leave the office or shop at 5 P.M. Nor do you leave job problems at the office or shop. They follow you home as business problems and business homework. This means you have less time for your family.

A person with very limited abilities may be able to hold a job in a large company by doing just enough to get by. Maybe others will cover up for his or her shortcomings. There is, however, no one to "carry you" when you are in business for yourself. Incompetence is the major cause of business failures. (See Table 15–1.)

While you may not have to report to a boss, you often have to bend over backwards for your customers. You have to contend with creditors,

Underlying causes	% Manu-facturers	% Whole-salers	% Retailers	% Con-struction	% Commercial services	% All
Neglect	1.2	0.4	1.0	0.8	0.8	0.9
Fraud	0.9	0.7	0.4	0.2	0.6	0.4
Lack of experience in the line	7.8	11.5	14.4	7.6	10.2	11.3
Lack of managerial experience	11.5	12.0	15.8	16.1	14.3	14.6
Unbalanced experience[2]	23.5	22.5	22.2	21.5	24.1	22.6
Incompetence	51.8	48.5	40.8	47.7	41.7	44.6
Disaster	0.4	0.4	0.5	0.4	0.3	0.5
Reason unknown	2.9	4.0	4.9	5.7	8.0	5.1
Total %	100.0	100.0	100.0	100.0	100.0	100.0
Number of failures	1,122	887	3,406	1,463	1,041	7,919
Average liabilities per failure	$1,088,344	$690,788	$141,679	$287,232	$344,559	$390,872

[1]Classification failures based on opinion of informed creditors and information in Dun & Bradstreet reports.

[2]Experience not well rounded in sales, finance, purchasing, and production on the part of the individual in case of a proprietorship, or of two or more partners or officers constituting a management unit.

Source: Dun & Bradstreet, Inc.

TABLE 15-1

Causes of 7,919 business failures in 1977[1]

employees, suppliers, government, and others. In short, you are never completely independent.

When you work for somebody else, you may be paid a salary based on a normal work week of 40 hours. If you work 50 hours, your pay will be greater (if you get paid on the basis of the number of hours worked). If you are a manager, your salary is based on a normal work week, even if it is usually more than 40 hours. As your own boss, however, you might work for many months and not be able to take a penny out of the business. Your profits may have to be reinvested to meet short-term demands for cash or for long-term growth. Thus you may not be able to draw a salary during the period it takes to get the firm to become a truly going concern. Many small business owners fail to anticipate this when they start out. It is a major cause of new business failures.

Starting a Small Business—The Preliminaries

It's a sad fact that many people who want to start their own firms do not do so because they just don't know how to do it. Some people think that there is so much red tape involved that you need a team of lawyers to start a firm. At the other extreme, some people open shop without even checking to see if they need permits or licenses. Both views are wrong.

Starting a business always requires careful planning of preliminary details. A firm does not come into being by itself. It takes planning. A good pamphlet to get is the Small Business Administration's *Checklist for Going Into Business* (Small Marketers Aid No. 71). In the following discussion, we will outline some of the steps in getting started. It is very general because the laws of different cities and states differ on how to start a business.

Financing

Perhaps the most important step in starting a new business is estimating the amount of money needed to get started. Underestimating can result in failure to get the business off the ground. Start off with a ballpark

**RECOGNIZING
A BUSINESS
OPPORTUNITY**

The ideal lawn mower would be one that makes no noise, consumes no gasoline, emits no noxious fumes, does not rust when left out in the rain—and besides all that, is self-starting and fertilizes grass while cutting it. Anette van Dorp, . . . an enterprising agriculture student in Bonn, West Germany, concluded . . . that such a machine already exists—only it is called a sheep. So she persuaded her mother Doris, the wife of a prosperous architect, to lend her $15,700, and . . . set up . . . Rent-a-Sheep Co. It buys sheep from farmers and rents them to businesses and home owners who want their grass cut cheap.

Customers must take a minimum of five sheep for the whole summer and graze them on at least 1¼ acres of lawn that is free of chemicals. The fee: $7.80 per sheep per season. That barely covers insurance on the animals. But Anette and her partners, Mother Doris . . . and Brother Tom . . . expect to make a sizable profit in the fall by taking back the sheep—by then nicely fattened—and selling them to butchers and breeders.

Rent-a-sheep requests have been pouring in from all over Germany, and Doris is thinking of expanding the business by selling partnerships to individuals. For them, the sheepfold could be a tax shelter: Germany levies no taxes on individuals' capital gains from the sale of assets (other than real estate) held for six months, which is just about as long as [Rent-a-Sheep Co.] plans to own its sheep.

Source: *Time.*

estimate and refine it as you learn more about the business you are considering. At the least, you should know, for example, whether $200,000 or $20,000 is needed.

This ballpark figure will help you determine if the venture is feasible for you. It also will influence your thinking about the form of ownership. Can you go it alone as a proprietor or should you consider taking in a partner or partners? What about incorporating? If you decide on a partnership, for example, you should set the minimum percentage of ownership in the firm that you are willing to settle for. You should keep that in mind when looking for a partner or partners.

In most cases it is not wise to put all your personal assets into the business. Financial reserves, such as a personal savings account, are needed to help you over the hump in getting your firm off to a good start. It's easy to become too optimistic about the chances of early success. Don't count on quick profits to help finance operations in the beginning. The firm may be in operation for one or more years before it shows a profit. And even then you may be taking out little or no salary from the business. This is another reason why you need some personal financial reserves. Beginning entrepreneurs tend to *over*estimate sales revenues and *under*estimate costs.

Let's assume, however, that you have added up the funds you can afford to put into the business and have decided to be the sole owner of the firm. Those funds, along with any money you can borrow from friends and relatives, may be all you have for starting operations. If you are to get any additional funds, they must come from other sources, such as

- commercial banks
- mortgage loans
- government agencies, such as the Small Business Administration

Commercial banks may be willing to lend you money if you can show that your proposed venture is sound. Be prepared to show the banker projected income statements and document your need for additional start-up funds. Don't rely only on your friendship with the banker. There is an old joke about bankers not lending money to people unless they can prove that they don't need it! This joke has a lot of truth to it. Unless you have a good personal credit history, it isn't easy to borrow.

You also may be able to take out a mortgage loan on your house. But remember, as a proprietor or as a general partner, you may lose your personal and real property if your business fails.

Some other possible sources of financing are various local, state, and federal government agencies. One of these, the Small Business Administration, is discussed later in this chapter.

As we saw in Chapter 11, money will flow into and out of your business as you carry on your business activities. Cash inflow comes mainly from selling your product or service. Cash outflows are necessary to pay for supplies, salaries, telephone, etc. Some of these expenses are start-up expenses that have to be paid only one time. For example, you do not have to pay a deposit to the telephone and electric company every month. But other expenses, such as wages and supplies, are recurring sources of cash outflows.

The main element in estimating cash inflows and cash outflows is timing. You must meet your bills as they come due. It's important for you to plan your cash flows carefully. It's a good idea to seek help from an experienced accountant. He or she, for example, can help you learn to use leverage to maximum advantage. Your accountant can show you that buying the equipment you need on time allows you to pay off the purchase price with cash inflow from your operations. Skillful use of trade credit also can help. If you are in a retail business, you may be able to buy merchandise from a wholesaler on credit and pay off the wholesaler with money you receive from sales of that merchandise to your customers. Your accountant also will point out the pros and cons of leasing equipment rather than buying it. A brief review of Chapter 11 would be helpful.

Licenses and Permits

Before you start operations, you must have the required licenses and permits. Which ones you will need depends on state and local laws.

In many cities or counties you will need a certificate of occupancy from the city or county department of safety and permits. This certifies that your type of business is permitted in your location under local zoning codes. For example, you could not open a pet shop in a location zoned exclusively for single-family residences. Nor could you set up a steel foundry in a location zoned light commercial.

In some states, cities, and counties you must get an occupational license to engage in any business activity or profession. These licenses are usually available from state and local departments of revenue. The cost depends on anticipated annual gross receipts and the type of business activity.

If your business deals with food, you probably will need a local food permit. These are usually issued by city or county health departments.

If you plan to sell beer, liquor, wines, soft drinks, or tobacco, you probably will need a state beverage or tobacco permit. Requirements here vary a lot among the states.

Suppose you wanted to go into business for yourself by selling lamps door to door. You might find yourself in trouble if you don't have a local vendor's permit.

The best advice on licenses and permits is to check with the local chamber of commerce, the local sheriff's office, or the state and local departments of revenue. Because of recent financial squeezes in many local governments, you'll need a greater number of licenses and permits than you might expect!

Taxes

You also will have to pay various types of taxes. Three common types are

- sales taxes
- self-employment tax
- employer taxes

Most states collect retail sales taxes. In these states, you must register with the state's department of revenue in order to comply with the law. This permits you to collect the tax for the state.

Many cities levy their own sales taxes. Again, you must register with the city revenue or finance department, tax collector, school board, etc.

If you are self-employed and earn at least $400 per year, you must pay a self-employment tax. Check with the local Internal Revenue Service (IRS) office.

If you hire employees, you must withhold federal (and perhaps state and city) income taxes as well as social security taxes from your employees' wages. You must also pay your own share of their social security taxes. You'll pay taxes for unemployment insurance. You'll have to get a federal tax number from the IRS. The IRS has two publications that will help you. Its *Mr. Businessman's Kit* contains tax forms that you will have to file. Its *Tax Guide for Small Business* tells how to fill them out.

Sales taxes collected and taxes withheld from employees' salaries and wages should be kept separate from the firm's other funds. The business owner is personally responsible for these funds and has to turn them over to the proper tax officials at set intervals of time.

Insurance

Before you start operations, you should have business insurance. Your selection of an insurance agent is an important step. The agent can give advice on the types of coverage you'll need in your line of business. But be sure to shop around for the best combination of price and coverage.

If you hire employees, you must carry workers' compensation insurance. This covers employees who are injured or killed on the job. The premium is based on your estimated payroll.

Information Sources

In starting your new firm, you may need more information on many aspects of your business. Of course, if you are in a large city, you will have access to more sources than if you are in a rural area or a small town. The following discussion covers some of the basic sources.

Better Business Bureau (BBB)

Many cities have a Better Business Bureau (BBB). A BBB is a non-profit organization of business firms that join together to help protect consumers and businesses from unfair business practices. Businesses "police" themselves through the workings of the BBB. Suppose you have doubts about buying from a particular supplier. You can call the local BBB to ask if any complaints have been filed against that supplier. If you have trouble with a supplier, you can file a complaint against that firm. It's a good idea to join the BBB.

Chamber of Commerce of the United States

Many cities also have a Chamber of Commerce. **The Chamber of Commerce of the United States is a national organization of local chambers of commerce in cities and states throughout the United States. Its purpose is to improve and protect our free enterprise system.** A local chamber of commerce is a useful source of data on business conditions in that area. Active involvement in the local chamber can put you in contact with potential customers and suppliers.

economic development council

Some cities have an economic development council. **An economic development council is an organization of business firms and local government officials. It seeks to further the economic development of the area in which it is located.** It is a good source of data on the local economy. In many areas local governments cooperate with local action groups to aid small businesses. A check of local libraries may help you to find other information you might need in starting your business.

Outside Assistance

Starting your own business takes a lot of planning. Running your business also takes a lot of know-how. Unlike most larger firms, however, you will not have a staff of experts in your firm to help solve tax problems, insurance problems, legal problems, and financial problems. In fact, lack of expertise in these areas is one of the major reasons why some entrepreneurs fail.

Remember, you are not out "to do it all without any outside help." Often, whether you can get that outside help will be the main factor in your success as an entrepreneur. At the minimum, you should know an

"I'm horrified," says California Attorney Max Goodman. "It just sounds cheap," huffs another prominent member of the Los Angeles County Bar Association. Still another calls it a "crime."

What has aroused these and other members of the bar association is a small retail emporium known as The Law Store, which has been open for business since the spring [of 1978] in Los Angeles' Sherman Oaks, next to Mogo's Mongolian Barbecue and a subpoena's throw from Super Cow's Soft Frozen Yogurt. The Law Store customers pay $9.95 to pick up a store telephone and consult with one of eight part-time attorneys in the West Los Angeles offices of Group Legal Services, Inc., owner of the store. For an additional $10, attorneys will write routine letters or make simple phone calls for customers. Sold also are a variety of "packages," telephone advice and preparation of forms used for simple wills ($30), changes of name ($75) and uncontested divorces ($125). These and step-parent adoptions ($75) are the hottest sales items.

"What people need," says one of The Law Store's founders, Attorney Stuart Baron, 40, "is accessibility, an attorney to talk to, the ability to pick up the phone and call somebody." Indeed, according to a recent American Bar Foundation study, 36% of Americans have never used an attorney. In 1973, with that untapped market in mind, Baron and his partner, Attorney Blair Melvin, 44, founded Group Legal Services. Today the firm offers round-the-clock legal consultations by phone to 20,000 California families for annual fees ranging from $35 to $60. For Baron and Melvin, The Law Store seemed a logical next step, and two additional stores will be opened soon.

Source: *Time.*

accountant, a banker, an insurance agent, and a lawyer to whom you can turn for advice.

Franchising

During the 1960s franchising became a very popular way of going into business for many people. Familiar examples are Holiday Inn, Pizza Hut, Wendy's, Midas Muffler, and Baskin-Robbins outlets.

There are two parties in franchising. Each has certain duties or obligations and each receives certain benefits. **The franchiser is the firm that licenses other firms to sell its products or services.** Wendy's International, Inc., is a franchiser.

franchiser

franchisee

The party that is licensed by the franchiser is called the franchisee. **A franchisee has an exclusive right to sell the franchiser's product or service in his or her specified territory. Each franchisee is an independent business owner.** Wendy's International, Inc., licenses independent franchisees to make and sell Wendy's hamburgers. Each franchisee pays an initial fee and yearly payments to Wendy's International, Inc., for the right to use the Wendy's trade name and to receive financial and managerial assistance from the franchiser.

FIGURE 15-2

A franchising agreement

WENDY'S INTERNATIONAL, INC.
DEVELOPMENT AGREEMENT

<u>INDEX</u>

WDEV001

Source: Wendy's International, Inc.

The franchiser and the franchisees are related to each other through the franchising agreement. **A franchising agreement is a contract between a franchiser and its franchisees that spells out the rights and obligations of each party.** (See Figure 15–2.)

franchising agreement

Many fast-food franchisers are owned by parent firms in the food and beverage industries. For example, PepsiCo owns Pizza Hut, Royal Crown Cola Company owns Arby's Inc., Pillsbury owns Burger King, Heublein owns Kentucky Fried Chicken, and General Foods owns Burger Chef.

Franchising and the Franchisee

Among the potential benefits of franchising to franchisees are:

- franchisee recognition
- management training and assistance
- economies in buying
- financial assistance
- promotional assistance

Franchisee Recognition

A person who wants to go into business in the fast-growing service industries (such as the fast-foods industry) will run into many obstacles. Perhaps the most important one is becoming known. A new Joe's Hamburger Joint just doesn't have the instant recognition that Joe Jones would get as a Wendy's franchisee.

A franchiser enjoys widespread consumer recognition because the units are all basically alike. A Midas Muffler shop in Atlanta, Georgia is very similar in appearance and operation to one in Los Angeles, California. The franchiser usually provides the franchisee with a blueprint for constructing a building that will be just like all other franchised outlets.

Source: *Funky Winkerbean* Field Newspaper Syndicate.

The franchiser also insists on standardized operation of all outlets. These are spelled out in the franchiser's operations manual and are backed up with standardized forms and control procedures so that all outlets look and operate alike. This is important in a society where people are highly mobile. A newcomer to a town feels a lot safer about buying a Wendy's hamburger than he or she might feel about eating one at Joe's Hamburger Joint. A traveler is more relaxed about staying at a Holiday Inn than he or she might be about staying at The Three Oaks Motel.

Management Training and Assistance

A major reason why many small firms fail is the owner's lack of management skills. Many franchisers operate training schools for their franchisees. They learn business skills like record keeping, buying, selling, and how to build good customer relations.

Ongoing training is also important. Many franchisers send representatives to give their franchisees advice and assistance. Franchisees with special problems can turn to the franchiser for help. Thus franchisees are not left entirely on their own in managing their businesses.

Economies in Buying

A franchiser either makes or buys ingredients, supplies, parts, and so on in large volume. These are resold to franchisees at lower prices than they would pay if each of them made or bought them on their own. In the past some franchisers required franchisees to buy their supplies from them. Even if a franchisee could get a better deal from another supplier, he or she had to buy from the franchiser to keep the franchise. This is no longer legal. A franchisee who can get a better price without sacrificing quality can buy from any supplier.

Financial Assistance

A franchisee can get financial assistance from the franchiser to go into business. Usually, a franchisee puts up a certain percentage of the cost of land, building, equipment, and initial promotion. The rest is financed by the franchiser, who is paid back out of revenues earned by the franchisee. The franchising agreement spells out the amount of financing the franchiser will provide and the terms of repayment. The franchiser also provides working capital by selling to franchisees on account.

In some cases the two parties agree on a joint venture arrangement. The franchisee does not pay back the money put up by the franchiser. Instead, the franchiser becomes a part owner of the franchisee's business.

Finally, franchisees may find local banks more willing to grant loans than if they were completely on their own. Bankers know that a reputable franchiser will license only dependable franchisees and will help them to be successful.

Promotional Assistance

Franchisers usually supply their franchisees with various types of promotional aids. These include in-store displays, advertising mats for use in local newspaper advertising, radio scripts, publicity releases, and many others. Franchisers also help them to develop their promotional programs.

Franchising and the Franchiser

Among the potential benefits of franchising to franchisers are:

- franchiser recognition
- promotional assistance
- franchisee payments
- franchisee motivation
- franchisee attention to detail

Franchiser Recognition

A franchisee benefits from being able to use the franchiser's name and products at his or her location. The franchiser benefits by expanding the area over which the trade name is known. A franchiser can achieve national and, perhaps, international recognition much faster by franchising than by any other form of expansion. This increases the value of the franchise to both parties.

Promotional Assistance

A local franchisee pays a lower rate for newspaper advertising than a national franchiser. By sharing the cost of advertising, the franchiser and the franchisee both benefit. This is called cooperative advertising. Also, by using local radio and TV advertising in franchise areas rather than blanket network coverage, the franchiser may avoid wasted coverage—advertising in areas that don't have a franchisee. There are benefits from "localizing" promotion to suit customer tastes in a given area or to tie in with local events. Furthermore, a franchisee can promote the business as being locally owned. This may give the franchisee a competitive advantage over chain store operations in some areas.

Franchisee Payments

The franchising agreement sets out the amount and type of payments that the franchisee will make to the franchiser. Sometimes the franchisee pays a royalty based on monthly or annual sales. In some cases the fee is fixed at a certain amount and is payable monthly or annually. Often the fee is determined on the basis of the market size in the franchisee's territory. In still other cases a combination of these methods is used. Less frequently, the franchiser gets only a one-time payment from the franchisee. Also, keep in mind that franchisees increase the funds available to a franchiser for expansion purposes through their payments of fees.

Franchisee Motivation

Some large chain stores have trouble recruiting and developing well-motivated store managers. These hired managers are not independent business owners. Franchisees are their own bosses. Their profits belong to them. A franchisee is, therefore, more likely to accept long hours and hard work than a hired manager.

Franchisee Attention to Detail

The headquarters of a chain store operation must keep payroll, tax, and other records on all of its units. It must be concerned with local laws regarding sales taxes, licenses, permits, and so on. In a franchise operation, keeping records and complying with local laws are the job of local, independent franchisees.

Franchising and You

Do you have a future in franchising? The answer depends on your willingness to work, your ability to find a good franchise opportunity, and your ability to buy into the operation. Many independent business owners have been very successful as franchisees. Remember, however, that a franchisee is not totally independent. He or she must work within the limits of the franchising agreement. This is intended to help ensure the franchise's success.

There are, however, some possible drawbacks. Franchising has become a get-rich-quick scheme for some "fast" operators. These fast-talking promoters will try to develop a franchise operation around practically anything. If you are thinking of becoming a franchisee, check into the franchiser's reputation for honesty and record of past performance.

Also, carefully read and take time to understand any proposed franchising agreement. Some make promises that the franchiser cannot fulfill. Don't be in a rush to "sign up before someone else does." Look for clauses that might permit the franchiser to buy you out at his or her

David Darren has been a franchisee of a large franchiser in the fast-foods field for the past three years. David's business has been very successful. He has had a good working relationship with Rachel Petersen, the district representative of the franchiser. David always consulted Rachel on important business matters and followed her advice on running his business.

Last week David had lunch with his nephew, Sam. Sam is a college student majoring in business. He wants to go into business for himself after he finishes school.

When David told Sam about the terrific opportunities in franchising, Sam reacted rather negatively. "But, Dave, you're not your own boss. You're pretty much the same as a store manager—just like the person who manages an A&P or a Kroger. The only differences are that franchisers make you think you're boss and make you risk your own money. You really work for them—you're an employee, not an independent businessman." David was somewhat upset by Sam's assessment. CAN YOU SETTLE THE ISSUE HERE?

discretion. If necessary, consult a lawyer to help you to understand the proposed agreement.

Look out for oversaturation (too many firms) in that particular type of operation in your area. This is why location is so important. Show-business people and gimmicky promotions are poor substitutes for facts about market potential in a given location. Some of the best-promoted franchises have failed because they were poorly conceived.

Fortunately, the "franchising fever" of the 1960s has died down. But, as in any type of investment, franchising has its risks and rewards. On the balance, however, it still offers a lot of promise to would-be entrepreneurs. But don't be sold on the rewards without considering the risks. Be careful! Ask for the names and addresses of current franchisees. Talk to them. They can give you more objective insight. But don't be all-trusting here, either. They might be looking for someone to sell out to!

Recent legislation provides protection for the novice franchisee. Under Federal Trade Commission (FTC) regulations that went into effect on July 21, 1979, franchisers are required to make detailed information available to people who are interested in becoming franchisees. Franchisers have to give prospective franchisees a disclosure statement at least 10 days before a franchising agreement is signed or any money changes hands. The new rule also forbids franchisers from making claims about actual or potential sales or profits which cannot be backed up.

The Small Business Administration (SBA)

Small Business
Administration (SBA)

The Small Business Administration (SBA) is an independent agency of the U.S. government. It was created in 1953 to promote and protect the interests of small business firms.

Throughout our history the small business owner has been admired and respected. The entrepreneurial spirit is most closely associated with the small business owner's dedication to thrift and hard work. The owner realizes the dream that anybody can become his or her own boss if he or she can get enough money to start a firm and keep it going through hard work and know-how.

During this century, however, several basic changes took place in our economy. Many Americans lost sight of the dream of going into their own businesses. For many, "making a living" meant working for somebody else. Growing fear of risk among Americans led many of them to turn away from playing the role of entrepreneur. The high failure rate was enough to scare off many would-be entrepreneurs.

Big business interests were promoted in Congress by well-financed and well-organized lobbies. A large corporation could lobby for favorable laws. So could its trade association. A small firm could not afford to do this. Nor were they well organized into trade associations.

Because of those and many other reasons, the SBA was created. It gave substance to our national policy that small business should be encouraged and helped. It was intended to help ensure that competition would not lead to survival of only large firms.

SBA Financial Assistance

Commercial banks are the major source of credit for small firms. A small business owner with a good record of repayment and successful management can set up a line of credit with a local banker. A banker, however, is not anxious to lend money to a new firm, especially when the owner lacks business experience and the venture is very risky.

The money needed to get started is called seed capital. If a person needs more money than he or she has in savings plus what a bank will lend, the SBA can help. As a general rule, though, the SBA will lend money to an entrepreneur only after he or she has been turned down by

If you are the owner of an established firm you should

1. prepare a balance sheet
2. prepare an income statement
3. prepare a statement showing your personal net worth
4. list any collateral you can offer as security for the proposed loan, along with each item's estimated market value
5. prepare a statement that outlines how you will use the loan
6. take all the above to your banker and apply for a bank loan
7. if you are turned down for a bank loan, ask the bank to consider making an SBA participating loan or an SBA guaranteed loan
8. if you are turned down on a participating or a guaranteed loan, you should go to another bank and apply again
9. if you are turned down at the second bank, go to the nearest SBA office with your statements and apply for an SBA direct loan

If you are setting up a new firm you should

1. prepare a detailed statement of the type of business you want to establish
2. prepare a detailed statement of your prior personal and managerial experience
3. prepare an estimate of how much money you can invest in the business and how much you will need from other sources
4. prepare a statement showing your personal net worth
5. prepare an estimate of your proposed firm's income and expenses for the first year of operation
6. list any collateral you can offer as security for the proposed loan, along with each item's estimated market value
7. take the above to your banker and apply for a bank loan
8. if you are turned down for a bank loan, ask the bank to consider making an SBA participating loan or an SBA guaranteed loan
9. if you are turned down on a participating or a guaranteed loan, you should go to another bank and apply again
10. if you are turned down at the second bank, go to the nearest SBA office with your statements and apply for an SBA direct loan

Source: U.S. Small Business Administration.

private lenders because of the high risk of the proposed venture. This risk may relate to the nature of the proposed business activity and/or the person's lack of business experience.

Three basic types of SBA loans are

- direct loans
- participating loans
- guaranteed loans

All are term loans which means they must be paid back within a certain number of years. The proceeds can be used for almost any purpose, ranging from ordinary working capital needs to building a plant or store.

SBA direct loans   **SBA direct loans are made entirely with the SBA's own funds.** Usually these are made only for high-risk businesses.

In other cases the SBA might participate with banks in making loans. **SBA participating loans**   **SBA participating loans supplement loans made from banks.** In these cases the proposed business activity and the entrepreneur's talents are considered sound enough to merit getting some seed capital from private lenders.

SBA guaranteed loans   **In SBA guaranteed loans the money comes from a bank, but the SBA guarantees 90 percent of the loan.** This helps many entrepreneurs to get loans who might otherwise be turned down.

The SBA prefers participating loans and guaranteed loans. These enable private lenders to get in on the lending and reduces criticism of government interference in business affairs. It also enables the SBA to get more mileage out of the funds it has to lend.

Small Business Investment Companies (SBICs)

Congress passed the Small Business Investment Act of 1958 to make it easier for small firms to get long-term capital to finance their growth. **Small Business Investment Company (SBIC)**   **This act authorized the SBA to license Small Business Investment Companies (SBICs). An SBIC is a privately owned and privately operated company that is licensed by the SBA to supply straight loans and/or equity-type investments to small firms for expansion and modernization.** Often an SBIC also will provide management assistance to small firms.

An SBIC finances small firms in two ways: (1) by straight loans and (2) by equity-type investments. In a straight loan the SBIC will take collateral that banks will not accept. This, of course, makes it easier for the small firm to get a loan. The borrower and the SBIC negotiate the interest rate, subject to the laws in the state where the agreement is reached. An SBIC's transactions with small firms are private arrangements, but they must operate within SBA regulations.

An SBIC generally prefers, however, to participate in the growth of the small firms it finances. There are several ways to do this. First, the

Some people believe that business failures represent a tremendous waste of resources. Buildings and stores become vacant, bank loans are not paid off, employees are laid off, tax collections go down, and the entrepreneurial spirit dies. Some of these people believe that government should control the entry of entrepreneurs into business. For example, before a person could open a clothing store, he or she would have to apply for and receive permission from the local government. This permission would be granted only if there is a demonstrated need for this proposed business firm in the community. This, they say, would at least increase the chances of success and reduce the social and personal costs due to business failures.

On the other hand, some people believe that government control of entry into business would destroy the free enterprise system. These people are especially upset with the notion that a business failure is a disgrace. Sure, nobody goes into business to fail. But a failure, according to them, is not totally bad. Entrepreneurs can and do learn from their failures. A business failure is not necessarily a personal failure. J. C. Penney and F. W. Woolworth, among others, failed in their first business undertakings. But they learned from their mistakes.

small firm can issue warrants to the SBIC in return for a loan. These warrants enable the SBIC to buy common stock in the firm, usually at a favorable price, during a specified period of time. Second, the small firm could give a debenture (a certificate indicating indebtedness) to the SBIC in return for a loan. The SBIC could either accept repayment of the loan, or it could convert the debenture into common stock in the small firm. Finally, the SBIC could receive common stock in the firm in return for advancing it funds for expansion.

In effect, SBICs give the small business owner access to equity capital without the need to make a public stock offering. SBICs range from the very small to the very large. Stock in some of them is publicly traded. Because of their key role in financing small business, Congress has authorized tax incentives to encourage investment in SBICs.

SBA Management Assistance

The SBA also gives management help to small firms through its Office of Management Assistance. SBA loan approvals often require applicants to take positive steps to improve their management skills. Since poor management is the main reason why small firms fail, the SBA wants to develop the managerial talent of small business owners. Financial assistance has no lasting benefit to an owner who lacks basic management skills.

The SBA cosponsors management training courses with public and private educational institutions to instruct small business owners in the functions of management. It also sponsors management conferences and problem clinics. Management conferences usually run for one day to help owner-managers keep up with the latest developments in business. For example, a tax conference might examine the impact of changes in tax laws on management decision making. A problem clinic brings together small groups of business owners who face a common problem. They work under the guidance of a moderator to consider solutions to the problem. The SBA also provides more specific help to small business owners who have special problems and aids those who want to go into business for themselves. The SBA field offices have professionals on their staffs to counsel small business owners.

Service Corps of Retired Executives (SCORE)

The SBA's Service Corps of Retired Executives (SCORE) is a group of retired executives who volunteer their services to small firms that need management counseling. There is no charge to the firms except to pay the executives for out-of-pocket expenses they incur during their consultations.

Active Corps of Executives (ACE)

The SBA's Active Corps of Executives (ACE) is a group of active executives from all major industries, trade associations, educational institutions, and many of the professions, who volunteer their services to small firms that need management counseling. Like SCORE, there is no charge except for out-of-pocket expenses.

In a typical case a SCORE or ACE volunteer is assigned to a firm that has requested help from the SBA. The volunteer visits the firm to analyze its problems and to make suggestions for solving them.

Small Business Institute (SBI)

The SBA also sponsors the Small Business Institute (SBI). In the SBI program small business owners with problems are counseled free of charge by faculty members and senior and graduate students from collegiate business schools. The SBA contracts with the schools to provide this service. If you have the opportunity, enroll in such a course. You'll learn a lot about small business management.

SBA Publications

The SBA publishes a wide variety of booklets written by specialists in all areas of business. It also publishes an entire series of *Management Aids* that discuss general management problems. The SBA's *Technical Aids* deal with specific problems related to plant operation. *Marketing Aids* discuss management problems in retailing and wholesaling. Any

Starting and Managing a Small Business of Your Own
Starting and Managing a Service Station
Starting and Managing a Small Bookkeeping Service
Starting and Managing a Small Building Business
Starting and Managing a Small Restaurant
Starting and Managing a Carwash
Starting and Managing a Swap Shop or Consignment Sale Shop
Starting and Managing a Retail Flower Shop
Starting and Managing a Pet Shop
Starting and Managing a Small Retail Music Store
Starting and Managing a Small Retail Jewelry Store
Starting and Managing an Employment Agency
Starting and Managing a Small Drive-In Restaurant

SBA field office can provide you with a list of free management-assistance publications and a list of booklets for sale.

Government Contracts and Minority-owned Small Business

The SBA helps small firms get government contracts. Its earliest effort focused on military supply contracts. In more recent years the SBA also has succeeded in getting other government agencies to seek bids from small firms.

The SBA and the Office of Minority Business Enterprise (OMBE) in the Department of Commerce operate special programs to aid minority-owned small firms. Between 1968 and 1977, for example, the federal government awarded $2.2 billion dollars in government contracts to 3,700 minority-owned firms, and it allocated $1.3 billion for direct loans or consultant services for minority-owned firms. President Carter in 1977 ordered all federal agencies to double their purchasing from minority-owned firms during 1978 and 1979.

The Senate Small Business Committee, in a study of the SBA's minority business program, found that a major problem of minority business is survival outside the "set-aside program." Minority "set asides" are government contracts that are awarded to minority-owned firms without competitive bidding. Federal agencies remove contracts from competitive bidding and give them to the SBA to be awarded to minority-owned firms. The SBA and the OMBE are working to see that a greater number of minority-owned firms can survive under normal competitive conditions.

Survival and Growth of the Small Firm

Each year thousands of new and old firms go out of business because they cannot meet the competition. Most of these failures are small businesses.

Small firms often are at a disadvantage in competing with larger firms. Larger firms use banks mainly as a source of short-term funds because they can borrow for the longer term from other lenders, such as insurance companies. They also can issue more stocks and bonds. Small firms, for the most part, depend mainly on their local bankers for borrowed funds.

A small firm's loan may take as long as ten years to repay. This, by itself, makes the small firm's loan risky. Their loan applications also are checked more closely to see if they can meet monthly loan payments, and they usually pay higher interest rates than larger firms. Whereas a larger firm can shop around for a low interest rate, a small firm usually has to deal with a local banker. This is why the small business owner's relationship with his or her banker is so important.

Lack of funds is a major problem of many small firms. Too many firms are started on a shoestring, and the owner often realizes too late that he or she needs more funds.

Some small firms have trouble because of the manner in which they handle their funds. A firm that starts off with too much money tied up in fixed assets, such as plant and equipment, runs into a shortage of working capital to finance accounts receivable, pay off trade creditors, and maintain adequate inventories.

Small firms also find it hard to estimate and control expenses. They often lack the advanced cost control methods and accounting procedures of larger firms. Also, small firms ordinarily don't have dependable data concerning the market potential for their products and services.

Sometimes the owner pays himself or herself too much salary. Living too high on the firm's profits robs it of funds needed for growth. This is why self-discipline is so vital to small business success.

To survive, an entrepreneur must be constantly alert to new opportunities and careful about spending. The keys to survival are

- creativity
- determination
- careful planning
- willingness to work

Many small firms, however, are started by people whose primary motivation is to escape from the "rat race." Many of these entrepreneurs really don't want their own firms to go through "growth pains." To

FIGURE 15-3

Business failures

Business Failures include those businesses that ceased operations following assignment or bankruptcy; ceased with loss to creditors after such actions as execution, foreclosure or attachment; voluntarily withdrew leaving unpaid obligations; were involved in court actions such as receivership, reorganization or arrangement; or voluntarily compromised with creditors.

Total Listed Concerns represent the total number of business enterprises listed in the Dun & Bradstreet Reference Book. This Book includes manufacturers, wholesalers, retailers, building contractors and certain types of commercial services including public utilities, water carriers, motor carriers and airlines. This count by no means covers all the business enterprises of the country. Specific types of business not listed are: financial enterprises including banks, mortgage, loan and investment companies; insurance and real estate companies; railroads; terminals; amusements; and many small one-man services. Neither the professions nor farmers are included.

Failures vs. Total Turnover: Failures do not represent total business discontinuances. As defined in Dun & Bradstreet's statistics, failures include concerns involved in court proceedings or voluntary actions involving loss to creditors. An entrepreneur may discontinue operations for a variety of reasons, such as loss of capital, inadequate profits, ill health, retirement, etc., but if his creditors are paid in full, he is not tallied as a failure by the D&B definition. Failures comprise only a small percentage of total discontinuances, although they represent the most severe impact upon the economy and pinpoint the most vunerable industries and locations in a specific time period. Every year, several hundred thousand firms are started, almost an equal number discontinued, and even more transfer ownership or control. Each business day, more than 5,000 changes are made in listings in the Dun & Bradstreet Reference Book; new names are added and discontinued businesses deleted, name styles are altered, and credit and financial ratings are revised up or down. This is all evidence of the dynamic change and turnover constantly taking place in the business population.

Source: Dun & Bradstreet, Inc.

SITUATIONS THAT TEND TO FAVOR SMALL FIRMS

1. When a product does not lend itself to large-scale mass production, such as custom-tailored clothing and custom-made kitchen cabinets.
2. When customer convenience is more important than price and selection, such as in the case of small convenience food stores that offer late-night shopping and fast checkout to hurried shoppers.
3. When demand and/or supply fluctuates with seasons of the year, such as fresh produce that is harvested locally and sold at roadside markets by truck farmers.
4. When potential sales in a market are not large enough to attract a large firm, such as small communities that have many small retail shops rather than a major department store.
5. When large firms compete with each other for the big market segment and ignore one or more smaller segments, such as health food retailing, which escapes competition from big chain supermarkets.
6. When the product or service being offered requires a lot of personal attention to the customer by the seller, such as hair styling and funeral direction.

many, running their own firms amounts to little more than something they have to do to prove that they can do it.

Although there is nothing wrong with wanting to remain small, small business owners should consider the benefits of a planned strategy of growth.

A firm that offers only one service or product is in deep trouble if demand falls off sharply. Growth may enable a firm to achieve the benefits of specialization and economies of scale. By expanding production and sales, fixed costs may be spread out over a greater volume of output. Putting on two shifts of workers, for example, may enable the plant to operate more efficiently.

A small firm that is growing may provide greater motivation to employees. Aggressive and growth-oriented employees don't want to work for a firm that is not growing. Of course, there is the chance for greater profits from growth. Because business opportunity is dynamic, a firm also should strive to be dynamic.

Many small firms are started by people who want to sell out to someone else eventually, maybe to a larger, growth-oriented corporation. An aggressive strategy of growth may make this possible at an earlier date.

Relatively few small, new firms are successful enough to make profit in their early years to match their owners' expectations. This, of course, often proves to be a big disappointment to these entrepreneurs.

Some entrepreneurs react by lowering their expectations. Often, this takes away their motivation to excel. Some others, however, react by trying harder to "make it." There are still others who "throw in the towel" and admit failure. What accounts for these different reactions? CAN YOU EXPLAIN THIS?

A firm that doesn't grow also may find it harder to borrow money. The greater the competition among borrowers for loanable funds, the greater the disadvantage of being a "standstill" operator. But the wisdom of any approach to growth depends mainly on the owner's skill and vision. A small firm can grow in many ways. It can expand its present business. A small gift shop in a downtown location, for example, might expand by opening a branch in a suburban shopping center.

Some small firms don't grow simply because they lack direction. Maybe the owner spends too much time running the firm and not enough time thinking about growth. Many small firms have been launched into aggressive growth strategies, including new lines of business, by bringing in some "new blood."

Merger is another way to grow. By joining together, two small firms might enjoy economic benefits and be able to exploit opportunity that neither could by itself.

Seeking new customers is always a way to grow. Two often overlooked sources for small firms are government contracts and export sales.

Of course, there are other avenues to growth. The approach that is best for a firm depends on its resource strengths and weaknesses and on its environment.

Summary and Look Ahead

The entrepreneurial spirit is alive and well in modern America. Many Americans, including a growing number of young people, want to start their own firms. The opportunities are there for those who can spot opportunity and exploit it.

But it takes work, know-how, and a determination to succeed in the face of chilling statistics on failures of new, small firms. Lack of funds and management know-how are the most often cited causes of failure.

There are possible benefits and definite headaches involved in going into business for yourself. The best approach is to be realistic in assessing them. Don't let the dream of becoming your own boss turn into a nightmare.

We presented a summary of the first steps in starting a firm. Local requirements may differ, so you must study them carefully.

Franchising is still a growth industry. It provides good opportunities for those who want to start their own business, but it does not guarantee success.

The SBA helps small business in many ways. It gives financial and managerial help, lobbies for small business interests, helps small firms to get government contracts, and is committed to helping minority business enterprise. The SBA can help you to get started and to stay in business.

Small firms must face the challenges of survival and growth. Recognizing the challenges to survival is an important first step in developing the ability to survive. The same is true about growth.

In our next chapter we will look at international business. Here, too, there are challenges and opportunities for small, medium-sized, and large firms.

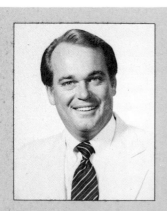

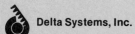

Delta Systems, Inc.

My name is Charles Nelson. I received the bachelor of business administration degree from the University of Mississippi in 1974 and my master of business administration in 1977 from the University of Southern Mississippi.

I had several employment opportunities with a number of firms after receiving my bachelor's degree, but I had a strong desire to be my own boss. I then decided to work on my master's degree in business administration. I wanted to broaden my knowledge of business to prepare as fully as possible for the challenges I knew I would face in setting up a new firm. My strong need for independence and a basic conviction that my dream of being my own boss could become reality with a lot of hard work and dedication are among the major reasons why I decided to strike out on my own. I also got a good deal of encouragement from my family and friends. But I also was aware of the fact that it takes much more than desire to succeed in your own business. I knew that starting my firm and realizing my dream would be the biggest challenge I had ever faced. But I was willing to take the risk.

In 1977 four members of my family and I incorporated a new business, Delta Systems, Inc., in Houston, Texas. Ownership is divided as follows: $24\frac{1}{2}$ percent, $24\frac{1}{2}$ percent, $24\frac{1}{2}$ percent, $16\frac{1}{2}$ percent, and 10 percent. Thus no one stockholder alone can exercise control over Delta's management. We chose the Subchapter S form in setting up the corporation under the incorporation laws of the state of Texas.

Delta manufactures a new type of mineral-fiber pipe insulation, which is used to insulate pipes that carry hot oil and superheated steam. Our major customers are petrochemical firms and electric power plants. I spent five years developing the machinery and the process that are used in manufacturing the insulation.

A considerable amount of research also was necessary to define precisely the types of customers who could use the product and how they could be reached. In other words, I started with an idea for a new type of pipe insulation and then proceeded to determine if it could be marketed profitably. After a lot of careful research, I decided that our product filled a need in the industrial market. Because of a lack of funds to get started, I approached several members of my family with a proposal to incorporate. They were excited about the firm's potential based on the research data that I presented to them and we set up Delta Systems.

As is true of any new firm starting out, there were problems. One of the biggest problems in the beginning was starting the business with a very limited amount of money. It took a considerable effort to gather statistical data and interview prospective buyers of Delta's product to demonstrate to the other incorporators that we really had a marketable product—one that was needed and could be sold at a profit. Another major problem in getting started was production scheduling. Since the product was new on the market, we could not turn to past sales data as a basis for projecting sales. And since production scheduling depends on sales forecasting, I knew we had to do as accurate a job as possible of sales forecasting. I also quickly learned how important a good cost accounting system is in running a manufacturing firm. Experience has proven to be one of the greatest teachers. Many of the problems that I faced early in the business would be of much lesser consequence now that I have had some experience in the business.

During the first few months after going into business, I performed practically every job in the firm. This included designing the machine that manufactures the pipe insulation, opening bank accounts, designing catalogs, soliciting orders, working on the production line, training a growing number of employees, record keeping, answering customer inquiries, and even sweeping the floor. As the company has grown, I find myself spending more time managing other people. I also am learning that I must be willing and able to delegate to others because there simply are not enough hours in a day to do everything myself. Incidentally, my typical working day starts at 6 a.m. and often runs until midnight.

I would encourage any young man or woman who wants to go into business for himself or herself and has a want-satisfying product or service to market to try it. There is no greater personal satisfaction than watching your firm grow into a going concern. But do not underestimate the time and effort you must dedicate to making your dream a reality. Success will not come overnight.

Key Concepts

Active Corps of Executives (ACE) An advisory service of the Small Business Administration. Members are currently employed executives who volunteer their services to small firms.

Better Business Bureau (BBB) The Council of Better Business Bureaus, Inc. is made up of local BBBs in many cities. A BBB is a nonprofit organization of business firms that join together to help protect consumers and businesses from unfair business practices.

Chamber of Commerce of the United States A national organization whose main purpose is to improve and protect our free enterprise system. Many cities have local chambers that belong to the national organization.

economic development council An organization of business firms and government officials that promotes the economic development of an area.

franchisee A person or firm that is licensed by a franchiser to sell its products or services in a specific territory under a franchising agreement.

franchiser A person or firm that licenses franchisees to sell its products or services in specified territories under a franchising agreement.

franchising agreement The contract between a franchiser and his or her franchisees.

SBA direct loans Loans made to entrepreneurs entirely with SBA funds.

SBA guaranteed loans Loans made to entrepreneurs by commercial banks and guaranteed up to 90 percent by the SBA.

SBA participating loans Loans made to entrepreneurs with SBA funds and with funds secured from private sources.

Service Corps of Retired Executives (SCORE) An advisory service of the SBA. Members are retired executives who volunteer their services to small firms.

Small Business Administration (SBA) An independent agency of the U.S. government created in 1953 to promote and protect the interests of small business firms.

Small Business Institute (SBI)   An SBA program that provides counseling of small business owners by faculty members and senior and graduate students from collegiate business schools.

Small Business Investment Company (SBIC)   A privately owned and privately operated company that is licensed by the SBA to provide long-term financing and management assistance to small firms.

For Review . . .

1. Why is it so difficult to define "small business"?
2. Discuss the three ways a person might become a small business owner.
3. Discuss the basic requirements for becoming a successful entrepreneur.
4. Discuss the benefits and burdens of entrepreneurship.
5. List and discuss the preliminaries of starting a small business.
6. Why is it important for an entrepreneur to consult an accountant, a banker, an insurance agent, and a lawyer?
7. Explain how a franchising agreement works.
8. Explain how the two parties to a franchising agreement benefit from franchising.
9. What is the SBA?

. . . For Discussion

1. Why would a person who wants to go into business choose to become a franchisee?
2. Suppose you are a banker. A person comes to you and asks for a loan to help him or her get a new business started. What information would you want before acting on the loan request?
3. Why is the failure rate so high among small businesses?
4. How can small, independently owned grocery stores compete against giant chains such as Safeway and Kroger?

Incidents

Taking on IBM

"Even in the rarefied scientific atmosphere at IBM, Gene M. Amdahl was always something special. Chief designer of the early IBM 704 and a key man behind the revolutionary 360, Amdahl directed IBM's advanced computing-systems project and wound up as an elite IBM Fellow, free to pursue whatever research he wished. But Amdahl, a soft-spoken physicist who was raised on a South Dakota farm, soon became unhappy. He wanted to design a machine that would outperform IBM's big 370/165 computer, but the company wasn't interested. So Amdahl quit IBM to go into business for himself.

"That was [in 1970]. [By 1976], after a few false starts, near-bankruptcy and $47 million in development costs, Amdahl . . . succeeded where such

giants as RCA and General Electric have failed. His tiny Amdahl Corp., with headquarters in Sunnyvale, Calif., is successfully challenging IBM on its strongest ground—the top-of-the-line computers that cost more than $5 million. . . .

"Though plenty of scientists have left IBM to set up their own computer companies, few have succeeded—and for a time, it seemed as if Gene Amdahl wouldn't either. On the strength of his reputation, he raised an initial $20 million from Fujitsu, Ltd., a large Japanese electronics firm, West Germany's Nixdorf Computer AG and American venture capitalist Edgar F. Heizer Jr. But in 1973, on the eve of Amdahl's first public stock offering and just after it had completed the first working model of the computer that was to compete with the IBM 165, IBM unveiled its 370/168, a giant machine with an enhanced memory that Amdahl couldn't match. Amdahl abruptly canceled the stock offering and cut operations drastically.

". . . But the company's backers hung on. A new management team was brought in, leaving Amdahl himself free to concentrate on design as the firm scrambled to come up with a more competitive computer. [In 1975], Amdahl stunned the computer world with a machine that could process 50 percent more data than a 168 in the same amount of time, while costing 10 to 15 percent less. . . ."

Entrepreneurial Studies

In recent years there has been a growing demand from college students for courses in entrepreneurship.

"Typically, an entrepreneurial studies program includes lectures from the instructor and from managers of small businesses on such topics as patent law, small-business bookkeeping, new-venture evaluation, risk-taking guidelines, the development of suppliers and customers, and the negotiation of new acquisitions. Class assignments often include case studies of successful and unsuccessful small-business ventures, as well as discussions of regulations that relate to new businesses.

Questions

1. How would you explain the high failure rate of scientists who left IBM to go into business for themselves?
2. How would you explain the willingness of the West German and Japanese firms and the American venture capitalist to provide financial backing to help Mr. Amdahl go into business?
3. What reasons do you think Mr. Amdahl had for going into business for himself?

Source: *Newsweek.*

Students prepare a detailed business plan for a proposed venture and 'sell' it to a panel of venture capitalists and entrepreneurs."

Questions

1. How would you explain the popularity of entrepreneurial studies programs?
2. Suppose you already have decided to go to work for a large corporation instead of going into business for yourself. Would taking courses in entrepreneurship benefit you? Would it benefit your potential employers? Explain.

Source: *Business Week.*

International Business

Objectives: After reading this chapter, you should be able to

1. Explain the principle of absolute advantage and the principle of comparative advantage.
2. Differentiate between natural, tariff, and nontariff barriers to international trade and give examples of each.
3. List and discuss the arguments used to justify tariffs and present counterarguments to those justifications.
4. Give examples of how the United States government aids American firms in conducting international business.
5. Distinguish between a country's balance of trade and its balance of payments.
6. Discuss the effects of fluctuating foreign exchange rates on international trade.
7. Give reasons why firms import and export products.
8. Compare exporting and foreign operations as strategies for entering foreign markets.
9. List and discuss several important environmental factors that affect multinational business.

Key concepts: Look for these terms as you read the chapter

absolute advantage	devaluation
comparative advantage	foreign exchange rate
international trade	combination export manager
state trading company	
trade barriers	Webb-Pomerene associations
tariffs	piggyback exporting
import quota	multinational company (MNC)
embargoes	
exchange control	cartel
tax control	regional trading bloc
dumping	expropriation
General Agreement on Tariffs and Trade (GATT)	contract manufacturing
	foreign licensing
balance of trade	joint venture
balance of payments	

Up to now we have discussed business mainly in terms of American firms operating in America. In this chapter we look at international business. Business activity is becoming more international in character. By and large, the days of political and economic noninvolvement with other nations are gone. American-made products are exported to almost every nation in the world. Marlboro cigarettes and Pepsi-Cola are even found in Russia. Some of our large corporations sell more abroad than they sell in the home market. Many of them also have set up manufacturing and marketing operations overseas.

But foreign firms also export products to us. Familiar examples are Japanese cameras, Colombian coffee, West German cars, and French perfumes. A less familiar example is Russian tractors. Foreign firms also have manufacturing plants in the United States and invest heavily in American business. Volkswagen has a plant in Pennsylvania and West German chemical plants operate in South Carolina. Arabs own office buildings, farmland, and hotels in the United States. The firms that make Pepsodent toothpaste, Calgon bath oil, and Foster Grant sunglasses are controlled by foreign firms.

International business creates new types of business opportunity, stimulates international contact, and leads to new business practices and new business challenges. Ours is truly an exciting age of international business. Let's begin with a discussion of the reasons why nations trade with each other.

Why Nations Trade

As we saw in Chapter 1, within rather broad limits greater specialization makes possible greater output. But specialization requires exchange, or trade. The greater the market, the greater the opportunity to exchange and specialize. These processes do not have to be limited to the people within a country. Broadening the scope of the market makes greater exchange and specialization possible. This is one reason why nations buy from and sell to each other. Let's examine some basic principles of trade that explain why nations specialize in certain kinds of products.

The Principle of Absolute Advantage

A country enjoys an absolute advantage in producing a product when   absolute advantage
either (1) it is the only country that can provide it, or (2) it can produce it at lower cost than any other country. If a product can be produced only in Switzerland, any other countries that want it must trade with Switzerland. If a product can be produced at a lower cost in France than in any other country, other countries must either trade with France to get it or pay the higher cost of producing it themselves.

If all nations followed this principle, each would specialize in producing the product or products in which it enjoys an absolute advantage. Each would import all others that it wished to have. Let's assume that Japan and the United States are the only countries in the world. If Japan can produce steel more cheaply than the United States, Japan has an absolute advantage in steel production. We would import steel from Japan. Suppose the United States has an absolute advantage in producing grain. According to the theory, we should specialize in producing grain and import Japanese steel. The Japanese should specialize in producing steel and import our grain. Both countries would be better off.

The Principle of Comparative Advantage

Suppose the president of a large firm can type faster than his or her secretary. The president, therefore, enjoys an absolute advantage over

THINK ABOUT IT!

The Principle of Comparative Advantage

Assume that skilled labor is the only factor of production in the United States and Japan. A Japanese worker can make 16 radios or 4 TVs per day. An American worker can make 4 radios or 2 TVs per day. Thus the Japanese worker is four times as efficient in making radios and two times as efficient in making TVs as the American worker.

	Radio	TV	Radio—TV ratio of advantage
Japanese worker	16	4	4:1
American worker	4	2	2:1

Without trade the Japanese have to give up 4 radios to get 1 more TV. The Americans have to give up 1 TV to get 2 more radios.

Trade can take place and be profitable for both Japanese and American consumers at any ratio of exchange between 4:1 and 2:1. The ratio of exchange is determined largely by the relative bargaining strength of the trading partners. Suppose, therefore, that Japan specializes in radios and the United States specializes in TVs. They settle on a radio-TV ratio of 3:1. Thus the Japanese give up 3 radios to get a TV. The Americans give up 1 TV to get 3 radios. This is the principle of comparative advantage. THINK ABOUT IT!

the secretary in typing ability. But should the president spend time typing? Although he or she is a better typist than the secretary, the president is, more important, a much better decision maker than the secretary. The president is wiser to attend to the duties of president rather than type. The choice here should not be based only on absolute advantage.

The same is true of countries. Suppose a country can produce everything its people consume more efficiently than all other countries. It can still benefit from trade. Trade would enable that country to specialize in producing those products in which it is the most productive. Decisions made to cope with the economic problem are made on the basis of the best use of our resources. While the company president may be making good use of limited time by typing, he or she is not making the best use of that time. Comparative advantage rather than absolute advantage should guide decision making here. **Comparative advantage means that a country should specialize in producing those products in which it has the greatest comparative advantage or the least comparative disadvantage in relation to other countries.**

comparative advantage

The products a given country will produce depend on many factors, such as presence of natural resources, cost of labor and capital, and nearness to markets. International trade enables each nation to use its scarce resources more economically. Its people can enjoy a higher standard of living. Since our exports account for only about 5 or 6 percent of our GNP, some Americans believe that trade is not important to the United States. They point to countries whose exports account for half or more of their GNP and say that they are the ones who benefit from trade. The fact is that some of our industries depend on exports for sales. Also, many of them need imports such as tin, nickel, natural rubber, asbestos, and chromium. To restrict trade would hurt us.

TABLE 16-1

Selected major exported and imported commodities of the United States, 1977

Exports	Millions of $	Imports	Millions of $
Motor vehicles and parts	11,797	Petroleum and products	41,526
Chemicals	10,812	Machinery	17,663
Electrical machinery	10,285	Automobiles and parts	15,842
Grains and cereal preparations	8,755	Iron and steel	5,804
Construction machinery	4,406	Chemicals	4,970
Soybeans	4,393	Nonferrous metals	3,938
Mineral fuels, lubricants, etc.	4,184	Coffee	3,861
Coal and related products	2,730	Metal ores	2,234
Textiles	1,959	Textiles	1,772

Source: *Survey of Current Business.*

Suppliers	Millions of $	Customers	Millions of $
Canada	29,356	Canada	25,749
Japan	18,663	Japan	10,522
West Germany	7,215	West Germany	5,982
United Kingdom	5,068	United Kingdom	5,380
Mexico	4,685	Mexico	4,806
Venezuela	4,072	France	3,503
Indonesia	3,491	Venezuela	3,171
Italy	3,038	Italy	2,788
France	3,031	Brazil	2,482
Brazil	2,246	Australia, incl. New Guinea	2,376

Source: *Survey of Current Business.*

TABLE 16-2

Major trading partners of the United States, 1977

Our exports create jobs for people who produce them and get them to overseas markets. This includes manufacturers, transportation firms, banks, and insurance firms. The same is true of our imports. Some people complain that importing a car "robs" American auto workers of jobs. But it also creates jobs for people involved in the job of importing the car and places American dollars in the hands of citizens in the selling country which they can use to import other American products.

State Trading

international trade

International trade involves the exchange of products between one country and other countries. Our main concern is the international operations of business firms. But some foreign trading does not directly involve privately owned business firms. Government agencies carry out this type of trading.

For example, our foreign aid program is administered by the U.S. government. Although American firms produce the products sent overseas, the amount of aid and the opportunity it represents for American firms is determined by government. An American maker of farm machinery, therefore, might sell some tractors to the U.S. government. The firm's role in this international flow of resources is very limited. Government plays the big role.

Essentially the same thing occurs when the U.S. government negotiates sales for American firms to overseas buyers. The U.S. Department of Defense actively promotes sales of American weapons to some foreign countries.

The volume of trade with the communist nations has increased in recent years. Since the Soviets view foreign trade as an instrument of foreign policy, politics play a large role in their trade with the noncommunist world. Trade with those countries is handled through the USSR's state trading companies.

A state trading company is a government-owned operation that handles trade with foreign countries and/or firms. An American firm selling to the People's Republic of China sells to one of seven state trading companies. These companies do the actual buying for the Chinese. The American firm does not deal directly with the people who will finally use the product.

state trading company

Barriers to International Trade

International trade among people in free economies is carried out mainly by private business firms in those countries. But trade barriers can affect the willingness and ability of firms to sell in foreign markets. **Trade barriers are obstacles that restrict trade among countries. They can be divided into three groups:**

trade barriers

- **natural barriers**
- **tariff barriers**
- **nontariff barriers**

Natural Barriers

Even if a product can be produced more cheaply in country X than in country Y, the cost of shipping it to Y might wipe out the production cost advantage. Distance, therefore, is a major natural barrier to international trade. Technology has helped us to reduce many of the natural barriers. Because of the jet airplane, distance between countries is measured in hours of flying time. This especially has helped to increase international trading of products that spoil rapidly. The big problems are the "created" barriers, tariff and nontariff barriers.

Tariff Barriers

Tariffs are duties or taxes that a government puts on products imported into or exported from a country. Governments rarely impose

tariffs

tariffs on exports because they generally favor exporting products to other countries. Tariffs serve two main purposes:

- to generate tax revenue—revenue tariff
- to discourage imports—protective tariff

A revenue tariff raises money for the government that imposes it. Since the purpose is not to reduce imports of the product on which the tariff is imposed, revenue tariffs usually are rather low. They were important during our early history when we had very little domestic industry. By taxing products coming in from abroad, our government raised revenue. Today, the United States has few revenue tariffs but many of the less developed nations use them to raise money for their governments. Of course, the final effect is that their people pay more for

TABLE 16-3

Arguments for tariffs

Argument	Reasoning
1. The infant industry argument	1. Tariffs are needed to protect new domestic industries from established foreign competitors. Once imposed, they are hard to remove. The industry that "grows up" under such a tariff tends to need it in adulthood.
2. The home industry argument	2. American markets should be reserved for American industries by building "tariff walls" around domestic industries regardless of their maturity levels. American consumers pay higher prices, and these tariffs are easily matched by other nations. The principle of comparative advantage is completely overlooked.
3. The cheap wage argument	3. Keep "cheap foreign labor" from taking American jobs. When labor is a large cost of producing a product, firms in low-wage countries can sell it in America at lower prices than American manufacturers. In periods of high domestic unemployment, this argument influences policy. Keeping such products out of the United States denies potential foreign buyers the American dollars with which to buy our products.
4. The defense preparedness argument	4. Certain skills, natural resources, and industries are vital to defense preparedness. They should be protected during peacetime in case of war. Our government grants subsidies to American shipbuilders. These equalize the cost of constructing ships in the United States and other, lower-wage countries. The United States would need domestic shipbuilding capacity in the event of war, when we might not be able to rely on foreign firms to build them. Many skills, resources, and industries far removed from defense preparedness are similarly protected because producers lobby for protection from foreign competition.

the products they import since the foreign sellers add the tariff to their selling prices.

A protective tariff discourages imports. It is set high enough to discourage imports of the product on which the tariff is imposed. They usually are levied on products from abroad that are priced lower than comparable products produced in the domestic market. Our government, for example, imposes a protective tariff on some textile imports in order to protect the American textile industry. Table 16–3 summarizes the major arguments used to justify tariffs.

There are three ways of setting tariffs: (1) ad valorem; (2) specific duty; and (3) combination ad valorem and specific duty.

An ad valorem tariff is one levied as a percentage of the imported product's value. It is used mainly for manufactured products. A specific duty is one levied on an imported product based on its weight and volume. It is used mainly for raw materials and bulk commodities. The duty is figured on the basis of pounds, gallons, tons, and so on. In a combination ad valorem and specific duty, both types of tariffs are imposed on an imported product.

Nontariff Barriers

There are many nontariff barriers to trade. They include

- import quotas
- embargoes
- exchange control
- tax control
- government procurement policies
- government standards
- customs procedures
- subsidies and countervailing duties

Import Quotas

Most quotas apply to imports although some countries also impose quotas on exports. **An import quota places a limit on the amount of a product that can enter a country.** It may be an absolute limit, in which case all imports stop when the quota is filled. In some cases, a quota is combined with a tariff so that a limited amount can enter the country duty free. Additional imports carry a tariff.

import quota

In 1977 the U.S. placed a quota on Japanese-made color TV imports and Taiwan began to step up its exports of color TVs to the U.S. The U.S. was considering imposing a quota on Taiwan-made color TVs as it had done on Taiwan-made textiles and footwear.

Embargoes

embargoes

Embargoes prohibit the import and/or export of certain products into or out of a country. This may be done for health purposes (the embargo on the import of certain kinds of animals), for military purposes (the embargo on the export of military equipment to certain countries), or for moral purposes (the embargo on the import of heroin). Embargoes also are used for political purposes; for example, the United Nations Security Council has placed an embargo on arms shipments to South Africa. Domestic industries that face stiff competition from imports sometimes lobby for embargoes for economic reasons.

Exchange Control

An American firm that opens a branch plant overseas wants the branch's profits to go to its American owners. If the branch is in West Germany and West Germans buy products produced in that plant, they pay for the products with marks. But the American owners want dollars. If West Germany is short on dollars, it might stop the branch from sending the profit to America. This is done by limiting the amount of marks that can be converted to dollars. It is called exchange control.

exchange control

Exchange control means government control over access to its country's currency by foreigners.

YOU BE THE JUDGE!

Should the United States Restrict Trade with Countries Because of Their Alleged Restrictions of Human Rights?

Some people believe the United States should not trade with countries that do not live up to our standards of human rights. They say that economic pressure is a peaceful way to get them to change their ways. Other people, however, argue that the United States should not interfere in the internal affairs of other countries, especially when human rights in the United States may not be the ideal to use as a model.

Should the United States restrict trade with countries that some people allege are restricting human rights? YOU BE THE JUDGE!

Tax Control

tax control

Foreign-based firms are reluctant to invest in countries that practice tax control. **A country's government practices tax control when it uses its authority to tax to control foreign investments in that country.** Underdeveloped countries, for example, need revenues but have no tax base at home. Taxing foreign-owned firms is an easy out. In extreme cases tax control can lead to virtual control of these firms by a country's government.

Government Procurement Policies

Most nations give some preference to domestic firms in government purchase contracts. The Buy American Act, for example, gives American firms a 6 percent price preference over foreign firms in bidding for federal government contracts. As long as the bid prices of American firms are not more than 106 percent of the bid prices of foreign suppliers, American firms will be awarded the government contracts. Many states have similar laws that give preference to domestic firms when awarding state government contracts.

Government Standards

Government regulations concerning safety and health and other product standards also can serve as nontariff barriers. Sometimes these regulations are used to keep foreign products out of the market.

Customs Procedures

All imports into the United States are subject to customs duties but exports are free of duty. Customshouse brokers are licensed by the U.S. Treasury Department to help importers complete the documentation that is necessary to clear imports through customs.

Each nation has its own customs procedures. Consider, for example, the issue of customs valuation codes. Each nation chooses its own method for placing a value on imported products for customs purposes. Some countries have objective criteria. Others leave it up to the discretion of customs officials and this can discourage exporters from selling in those countries.

Subsidies and Countervailing Duties

Some governments subsidize some of their domestic industries. Japan, for example, subsidizes its computer industry. These subsidies take different forms—extended coverage of operating losses, tax incentives, credit guarantees, and so on.

Some countries also use export subsidies that result in a price for a

A JAPANESE STATE MONOPOLY

U.S. officials in Tokyo have accused the Japan Tobacco & Salt Public Corp., one of the nation's most profitable state monopolies, of discrimination in marketing U.S. cigarettes in Japan. U.S. tobacco companies complain that the government retails foreign-made cigarettes, half of which are American, at as much as 60% above the price of domestic brands. As a result, foreign brands hold only 2% of the market.

Source: *Business Week.*

product in a foreign market that is lower than the product's domestic price. An importing country that finds its domestic industry being harmed by subsidized foreign competition can impose a countervailing duty on the product to offset the amount of the foreign government's subsidy.

dumping

Dumping means shipping substantial quantities of a product to a foreign country at prices that are below either the home-market price of the same product or the full cost (including profit) of producing it.

TABLE 16-4

Some examples of governmental assistance to international business

Under the United States Antidumping Act, firms that complain that foreign competitors are dumping must show that prices are lower in the

Institution	Purpose
1. Foreign Trade Zones	1. The Foreign Trade Zones Act of 1934 permits the creation of foreign trade zones in the United States. These are areas into which goods can be imported without being subject to customs duties or quotas. Often, the imported materials are manufactured into finished products that are re-exported or enter into domestic commerce. If re-exported, they are not subject to any tariffs. If they enter into domestic commerce, they are subject to regular tariffs.
2. The Export-Import Bank (Eximbank)	2. This agency was created in 1934 by the U.S. government to reduce domestic unemployment. It makes loans to exporters who cannot secure financing through private sources. It also makes loans to foreign countries who use the funds to buy American-made goods.
3. The Foreign Credit Insurance Association (FCIA)	3. Eximbank and the private American insurance industry created the FCIA in 1961. A firm can buy insurance from FCIA to cover political risk (such as expropriation and loss due to war). Comprehensive coverage can be bought to cover business risks (such as credit default). The exporter can also buy insurance coverage on credit sales to foreign customers. FCIA places American exporters on a more equal footing with exporters whose governments provide financial assistance to them.
4. The International Bank for Reconstruction and Development (World Bank)	4. The World Bank began operations in 1946 to advance the economic development of member nations by making loans to them. These loans are made either directly by the World Bank using its own funds, or indirectly by the World Bank's borrowing from member countries.

importing country and that the domestic producers in the importing country are being directly harmed by the alleged dumping. Only then will the U.S. Treasury Department investigate the situation.

In recent years dumping has been a special problem, especially involving Japanese-made steel. Trigger prices were published in 1978 for most steel products. These trigger prices are the prices below which the Treasury Department will start a dumping investigation on its own. If the investigation shows that the foreign firm did engage in dumping, countervailing dumping duties will be assessed on the dumped products in order to wipe out the price advantage.

TABLE 16-4 (continued)

Institution	Purpose
5. The International Monetary Fund (IMF)	5. The IMF began operations in 1947 to promote trade among member countries by eliminating trade barriers and promoting financial cooperation among them. It enables members to cope better with balance of payments problems. Thus, if firms in Peru wish to buy from American firms but Peru lacks enough American dollars, Peru can borrow American dollars from the IMF. It pays the loan back in gold or the currency it receives through its dealing with other countries.
6. The General Agreement on Tariffs and Trade (GATT)	6. GATT was negotiated in 1947 by member nations to improve trade relations through reductions and elimination of tariffs. GATT has resulted in tariff reductions on thousands of products.
7. The International Development Association (IDA)	7. The IDA began operations in 1960 and is affiliated with the World Bank. It makes loans to private businesses and to member countries of the World Bank. In addition to the IDA, there are similar organizations that make loans to governments and firms in certain country groupings. The Inter-American Development Association, for example, is for countries belonging to the Organization of American States.
8. The International Finance Corporation (IFC)	8. The IFC began operations in 1956 and is also affiliated with the World Bank. It makes loans to private businesses when they cannot obtain loans from more conventional sources.
9. Domestic International Sales Corporation (DISC)	9. In December 1971 Congress authorized American firms to form tax-shelter subsidiaries (DISCs) to handle their export sales. The purpose is to spur exports and encourage American firms to enter the export market. A firm can defer some of its taxes on export earnings by establishing a DISC.

Removing Trade Barriers

General Agreement on
Tariffs and Trade
(GATT)

Governments can help to promote trade by reducing or removing trade barriers. Agreements also have been entered into between countries to relax trade barriers. Bilateral agreements are made between two countries. Multilateral agreements are made between three or more countries. **One of the most important multilateral agreements is the General Agreement on Tariffs and Trade (GATT). It is a treaty that is administered by a permanent secretariat through which member countries act jointly to reduce trade barriers.** In operation since January 1, 1948, it provides a framework for multilateral tariff reduction negotiations. Over the years GATT has resulted in tariff reductions on thousands of products and has worked to eliminate nontariff barriers to international trade.

The Bureau of International Commerce (BIC) in the U.S. Department of Commerce organizes trade missions, operates permanent trade centers in many foreign countries, and sponsors national and regional export expansion councils. The U.S. Department of State provides information and promotion services to American firms interested in overseas business. Its Agency for International Development (AID) encourages American firms to invest in underdeveloped countries. Table 16–4 discusses several ways our government aids international business.

Many agencies and groups promote international business. Many state and municipal government programs seek to boost exports. State industrial development commissions, governors, and mayors often go overseas to lure foreign firms to their areas.

Private efforts are also important. The Chamber of Commerce of the United States provides information and advice to firms interested in selling overseas. The National Foreign Trade Council is a group of firms engaged in international business. It provides information and advice to its members. Members of world trade clubs in many American cities share their knowledge and experiences in overseas business. When banks, insurance firms, transportation firms, ad agencies, accounting firms, and marketing research firms help and promote international business, they bring new business to themselves.

The Balance of Trade and the Balance of Payments

In order to understand the importance of international trade to the United States, we should understand the concepts of the balance of trade and the balance of payments. An understanding of the role of gold in international trade also is important.

The Balance of Trade

An export from one nation is an import to another nation. International trade is a two-way street. Some governments, however, see it as a means of gaining an economic "edge" over other countries. National pride and mutual distrust cause many nations to view trade as desirable only if their exports are greater than their imports.

A nation's balance of trade is the difference between the money values of its exports and its imports. If it exports more than it imports, its balance of trade is favorable. If it imports more than it exports, its balance of trade is unfavorable.

balance of trade

Long ago nations relied on gold for settling trade imbalances. A country that imported more than it exported (an unfavorable balance of trade) paid for its excess imports by shipping gold to the creditor nations. Because a nation's gold supply was considered a measure of its strength, a government would restrict imports and grant tax breaks to firms that exported products. This enabled it to hold its gold.

The United States had enjoyed a favorable balance of trade for many decades prior to 1971. In that year, the value of our imports first exceeded the value of our exports. Except for 1970, 1973, and 1975, our balance of trade was unfavorable during the 1970s. (See Figure 16–1.)

FIGURE 16-1

The U.S. balance of trade, selected years (in billions of dollars)

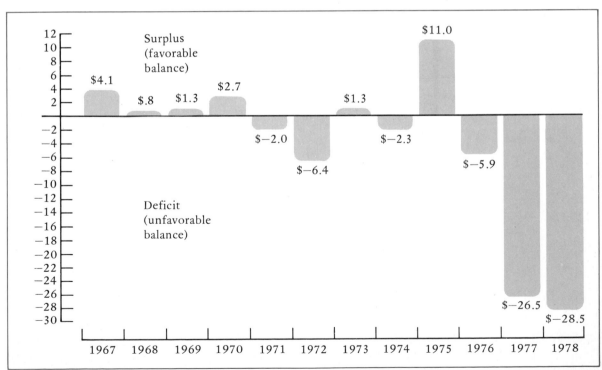

Source: *Survey of Current Business.*

Our huge oil imports largely accounted for this. For example, the United States imported oil worth nearly $50 billion in 1979. To understand how all this affects international business, let's discuss the balance of payments.

The Balance of Payments

balance of payments

A nation with a favorable balance of trade can have an unfavorable balance of payments. **A country's balance of payments is the difference between its receipts of foreign money and the outflows of its own money due to imports, exports, investments, government grants and aid, and military and tourist spending abroad.** For the United States to have a favorable balance of payments for a given year, the following would have to be true. Our exports, foreign tourist spending in America, foreign investments in America, and earnings from overseas investments must be greater than our imports, American tourist spending overseas, our foreign aid grants, our military spending abroad, the investments made by American firms abroad, and earnings of foreigners from their investments in America.

In almost every year since 1950, America's balance of payments has been unfavorable. Although our balance of trade was favorable during the 1950s and 1960s, spending by American firms and tourists abroad, foreign aid, and military spending abroad more than offset the effect of a favorable balance of trade. Our unfavorable balance of payments position was made even worse by our unfavorable balance of trade during most years in the 1970s.

The Role of Gold

Between the latter part of the nineteenth century and the beginning of World War I, the world's major trading nations were on the international gold standard. Each valued its currency in terms of gold and offered to convert its currency into gold when requested to do so by a foreign holder of its currency.

The economic problems caused by World War I ended the international gold standard and the nations went on a gold exchange standard. All countries revalued their currencies in terms of gold. But instead of just counting gold, they also included sterling and U.S. dollars as part of their gold holdings. Thus many nations' currencies were backed by gold, sterling, and U.S. dollars. The U.S. dollar became a reserve currency.

The gold exchange standard fell apart during the Great Depression of the 1930s. The United States devalued the dollar in 1933 by raising the price of gold from $20.67 to $35 per ounce. **Devaluation means reducing the value of a currency in relation to gold or in relation to some other**

devaluation

standard. This made American products cheaper for foreigners to buy which, in turn, led many other countries to devalue their currencies. Because of these competitive devaluations, the major trading nations set up the International Monetary Fund (IMF) in 1944. The value of each nation's currency was fixed (pegged) in relation to each of the other currencies. Exchange rates between currencies were stabilized.

By the end of World War II, many countries were using the U.S. dollar as a reserve currency because they had faith in the dollar's stability. But as U.S. balance of payments deficits became chronic during the 1960s, some foreigners began to question our ability to convert their dollars into gold. In 1971 we had a $6.3 billion deficit in our balance of trade and many nations lost faith in the dollar. They wanted gold. These "runs on the dollar" got so severe that, in 1971, the United States stopped paying gold in exchange for dollars held by foreigners.

THE EUROPEAN CURRENCY UNIT

Beginning January 2, [1979], the governments of West Germany, France, the Benelux nations and Denmark [started] taking steps to ensure that their currencies move up or down, more or less, in unison. In addition, the members created a new form of money, the European Currency Unit, or ecu. For now, at least, the ecu will not be paper money used by the man in the [street] to pay his bills, but simply a bookkeeping device for Europe's central banks to settle debts with each other.

The idea of a currency union has been around since the European Community started in 1957. What advanced it . . . was the . . . decline of the U.S. dollar, which has unsettled Europe's money and hurt E.C. economies. Every time the dollar dropped against the strong German mark, it also dropped—less so—against most of Europe's other, not-so-strong currencies. This caused annoying changes in the exchange rates between countries. Export trade was slowed because businessmen had to calculate and recalculate prices, and multinational companies postponed transborder E.C. investments because they could not forecast investment returns easily in their own currency.

It was decided . . . that each currency would be assigned a set value against all the others and would be allowed to fluctuate only 2¼% above or below this point.

Under the system, if any member country's currency rises or falls out of this narrow band, its government will be obliged to adjust the price and pull it back in. A country can do this by buying or selling its own currency on international markets.

Source: *Time.*

In late 1971 a new agreement was reached under which member nations of the IMF would maintain "par values" of their currencies. Each was valued in relation to the others (rate of exchange) but its value was allowed to float (fluctuate) by up to 2.25 percent from its par. As part of the deal, the United States agreed to devalue the dollar in 1972 from $35 per ounce of gold to $38 per ounce. But the resulting exchange rates could not be maintained and the United States again devalued the dollar in 1973 from $38 to $42.22 per ounce of gold. Before the 1972 devaluation, the American dollar was worth $\frac{1}{35}$ of an ounce of gold. The 1973 devaluation meant that the dollar was worth $\frac{1}{42}$ of an ounce of gold.

Member nations of the IMF also stopped holding their exchange rates within the agreed upon margins against the U.S. dollar. The result was further declines in the value of the dollar in relation to other currencies.

FIGURE 16-2

The price of gold, 1970-February 1979

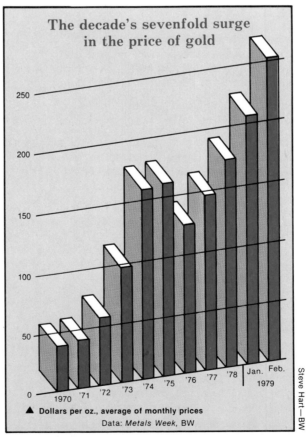

Source: *Business Week.*

Condition	Result
1. U.S. balance of trade and balance of payments are unfavorable (deficit).	1. The supply of U.S. dollars overseas increases and this usually leads to a decline in the exchange rate of the dollar.
2. Demand for the U.S. dollar is strong and the Federal Reserve does not want the exchange rate of the dollar to rise.	2. The Federal Reserve will sell dollars to U.S. banks in exchange for foreign currencies. This reduces the supply of foreign currency available for business transactions and increases the supply of U.S. dollars. This puts downward pressure on the exchange rate of the U.S. dollar.
3. The exchange rate of the U.S. dollar declines.	3. American importers pay more dollars for the products they import. This fuels inflation in the United States and tends to reduce importing by Americans.
4. The exchange rate of the U.S. dollar declines.	4. Foreign buyers need less of their currency to pay for products imported from America. This tends to increase American exports.

TABLE 16-5

Fluctuating foreign exchange rates

This led President Carter to take bold steps in late 1978 to stabilize the value of the dollar.

Since 1933 gold had been held by the U.S. government only for use in redeeming dollars owned by foreigners. American citizens could not legally hold monetary gold. On January 1, 1975, however, it became legal for American citizens to own gold, and they have paid widely fluctuating prices for it. (See Figure 16–2.) This is the price paid for it by private citizens. Trading in gold among private citizens is something separate and apart from the price that a government puts on its currency in relation to gold. As Americans become concerned about inflation and the value of the dollar, some of them invest in gold. The price of gold, therefore, tends to go up on the world market. In the fall of 1979, the price exceeded $400 per ounce of gold.

The Payment Problem

Because buyer and seller are in different countries, international transactions sometimes present a payment problem. Methods of payment vary widely. While cash payment appeals to the seller, the buyer may look at it as seller suspicion of the buyer's creditworthiness. It also ties up the buyer's working capital if payment must accompany an order.

With open account, the exporter ships the merchandise to the buyer and the exporter's commercial invoice indicates the buyer's liability to pay. This is risky unless the exporter is sure of the buyer's willingness and ability to pay.

The most common method of payment is with drafts, or bills of exchange. Drafts provide documentary evidence of financial obligation. A draft drawn on and accepted by an importer is a trade acceptance. A draft drawn on and accepted by a bank is a bank acceptance. A commercial letter of credit is issued by the importer's bank showing that the bank accepts the draft drawn on it by the exporter. Of course, the importer must apply for and be granted this credit to be issued a letter of credit.

There also are other methods of payment. An exporter who ships materials from the United States to be used in a construction project for the U.S. government may be paid directly by the U.S. government. In some cases exporters accept bonds issued by the importer's government when that government is short on foreign exchange. In still other cases barter transactions are made. Importer and exporter agree to swap products for products and there is no currency involved. In the late spring of 1979, for example, some American grain producers were attempting to negotiate barter transactions with several Arab nations. The Americans wanted to barter bushels of grain for barrels of oil.

Because of the growing importance of international business, many foreign banks have banking connections in the United States. Some foreign banks operate branch offices and agencies in the United States. A branch office's main job is to keep in contact with banking developments in the United States and to promote goodwill. Agencies usually do not accept deposits from Americans, but they operate foreign exchange and perform other services for firms in their home countries and in other countries. In some cases foreign banks have set up full-scale banks in America.

American banks also do the same. Big American banks have foreign branches in many countries. They also operate foreign departments in their banks in the United States to finance imports and exports. American banks also enter into correspondent relationships with foreign banks. Correspondent banks are far more numerous than foreign branch banks. An overseas correspondent bank of an American bank handles its transactions in that country. Of course, the foreign bank's American correspondent handles that bank's international dealings in the United States.

This international banking facilitates international business by converting foreign currencies into U.S. dollars and vice versa. These banks buy foreign exchange from some customers and sell it to others. This is the foreign exchange market. But since exchange rates between currencies can fluctuate from day to day, there is some risk in dealing in different currencies.

Source: *Dunagin's People*, Field Newspaper Syndicate.

"Our problems began when we went on the paper standard."

For example, an American exporter that sells products to a German firm probably will receive payment in marks. The American firm must convert these marks to dollars. How many dollars those marks will buy can change from day to day, depending on the foreign exchange rate. **The foreign exchange rate is the ratio of one currency to another. It tells how much a unit of one currency is worth in terms of a unit of another.** Thus the mark may be worth 40 cents when the exporter made the deal and only 38 cents when payment is received. Suppose the deal involved 1,000 marks. They were worth $400 when the sale was negotiated but only $380 when the American exporter received payment.

foreign exchange rate

Exporting and Importing

We've used the terms *exports* and *imports* in our discussion of trade. Imports are things that enter into a country from other countries. Exports are things that go from one country to other countries.

Why Firms Export Products

Exporting is a special kind of selling. Exported products cross over national borders. But these borders are political borders. They are not related to the nature of business activity. Some mass production industries have to produce in large volumes to get the cost-per-unit down to a low level. If the home market is too small to absorb this output, these firms look overseas for additional customers. For example, almost every American household has a refrigerator. The typical family buys a new one only when the old one wears out. Without exports, sales of refrigerators would be limited to new households and a replacement market.

Closely related is the product life cycle concept. Whereas the refrigerator is in the maturity stage in the United States, it is in the growth stage in many other countries. This means that the profit potential is greater in those countries.

Often, selling costs abroad are lower than selling costs in the home market. The American market is highly competitive. Many firms produce similar products and compete directly with one another. If there is less competition in a foreign country, the exporter might enjoy lower marketing costs there.

The demand for many products is seasonal. Many American firms shift their off-season production into foreign markets where the product is in season. This may lower production cost as a result of better production scheduling.

Finally, a firm might find it more profitable to expand its market coverage to foreign countries than to develop new products for sale at home. Its skills may be put to best use by producing and selling its traditional product rather than by taking on the risks of developing new products.

Why Firms Import Products

Importing is buying. American firms import bananas and coffee because they are not available in the United States. Sometimes domestic sources must be supplemented by foreign sources. Thus American imports of crude petroleum are growing as our domestic supply is shrinking. (See Figure 16–3.) Imagine how our economy and lifestyles would be affected if these products could not be imported.

Prices of foreign products often are lower than like products in the United States. As we saw in Chapter 13, the productivity of labor has been increasing at a higher rate in some foreign countries than in the United States. This has been a challenging problem for many of our

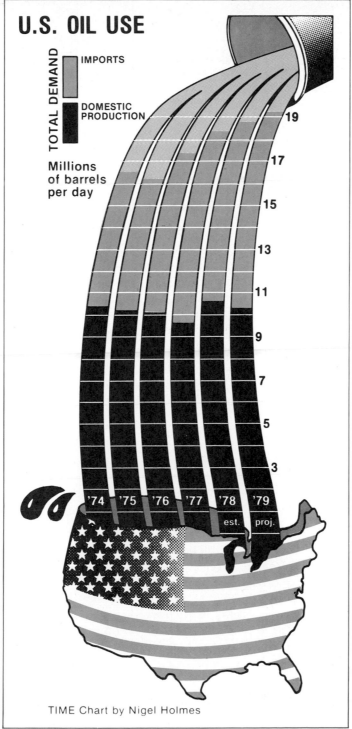

FIGURE 16-3

U.S. oil consumption, domestic production and imports

Source: *Time.*

industries—such as the textile, steel, and shoe industries—as they try to survive the competition from lower-priced foreign products.

Importing products from foreign producers may lead to reciprocal exporting of products to them. This is true for nations and for individual firms.

Imported products also may have prestige value. Some Americans, for example, are willing to pay extra for imported wines, perfumes, cars, and cameras. At one time American-made products, as a rule, were superior to foreign-made products. In recent years this has changed. "Made in Japan" no longer means "low quality" to Americans.

Types of Exporting

A firm's involvement in exporting products can range from a minimal commitment all the way to considering exports as necessary for the firm's survival and growth.

Unintentional Exporting

Many firms' products are exported without their knowledge. For example, a supplier of a part used by Ford Motor Company in making farm tractors might be unaware that the part ends up on a tractor used by a farmer overseas.

Many firms have resident buyers in foreign countries. These buyers buy products in those countries and send them to their employers. Thus an American firm might be selling to a resident buyer for an Italian firm without knowing it.

Unsolicited Exporting

Sometimes, a firm might get an unsolicited order from an overseas buyer. Unlike the examples above, the firm is aware that the customer is overseas. Often, however, the firm may not be interested in selling overseas. Many firms, especially small ones, have a mistaken notion that selling overseas involves too much "red tape." Various U.S. government agencies and programs, as we have seen, help these firms to do business overseas. The U.S. Department of Commerce helps small firms to get involved in exporting. The Small Business Administration's publication *Export Marketing for Smaller Firms* is also helpful.

Intentional Exporting

Intentional exporting means that the exporter is committed to selling abroad. But there are degrees of commitment. At one extreme are firms

Company	Main export products	1977 exports (millions of dollars)
General Electric	Gas turbines, aircraft engines, power generating equipment, appliances, motors	$2,100
Caterpillar Tractor	Earth-moving & materials-handling equipment	1,900
Boeing	Commercial aircraft	1,470
McDonnell Douglas	Commercial & military aircraft	1,130
Lockheed	Commercial & military aircraft, aerospace items	1,030
Du Pont	Synthetic fibers, plastics, agricultural chemicals, health care products	1,000
Dow Chemical	Plastic intermediates, caustic soda, magnesium	900
United Technologies	Jet engines, aircraft equipment, telephone & power cables, helicopters, elevators	890
Eastman Kodak	Photographic film, papers, chemicals & equipment	850
Sperry Rand	Computers, farm machinery, hydraulic equipment	850
Westinghouse Electric	Nuclear power plants, electrical generators & equipment, defense equipment	800
Weyerhaeuser	Logs, pulp, liner board, lumber	710
International Harvester	Trucks, farm & construction equipment, gas turbines	660
Union Carbide	Chemicals, agricultural products, plastics, metals, batteries	640
Textron	Helicopters, staplers & staples, pens, machine tools	540
Chrysler	Cars & trucks	530*
Monsanto	Chemicals, plastics, fibers	530
Northrop	Military aircraft	500
Rockwell International	Automotive, aerospace, electronic products	470
Grumman	Military & executive aircraft	430

* Excluding shipments under the U.S.-Canada automotive free trade pact.
Source: *Business Week.*

TABLE 16-6

The 20 biggest U.S. industrial exporters

who consider their export business to be secondary to their domestic sales. Such a firm might accept orders from overseas buyers but not seek them. It might have a small department that accepts orders from foreign buyers. At the other extreme, a firm might have a large, well-staffed, and well-financed division that seeks export sales.

At intentional exporter must decide how to handle its export business. In direct exporting the firm handles the export task itself. In indirect exporting outside specialists handle the export task for the firm.

Which approach is best depends on such factors as the company's size, its export volume, the number of foreign countries involved, the investment required to support the operation, the profit potential, the risk present, and the desires of the overseas buyers. If the firm exports many products, it may go direct with some and indirect with the others.

Some firms are afraid to get involved in exporting because they don't know how to do it. **The combination export manager can help. This middleman represents several exporters and handles all the work involved in moving their products overseas.**

combination export manager

Many firms, especially small and medium-sized ones, cooperate with each other in their exporting. **Webb-Pomerene associations are made up of American firms that compete in the United States but work together in expanding their sales overseas.** Their actions are not subject to our antitrust laws if they do not reduce competition in the United States and as long as the members do not engage in unfair methods of competition. These associations help American firms to compete with foreign firms that are not subject to American antitrust laws.

Webb-Pomerene associations

Another type of cooperation is piggyback exporting. **In piggyback exporting, one firm (the carrier) uses its overseas distribution network to sell noncompetitive products of one or more other firms (riders).** For example, Sony (the carrier) distributes Whirlpool, Schick, and Regal Ware (riders) in Japan.

piggyback exporting

Foreign Manufacturing Operations

Exporting means selling products that are produced in one country to customers in another country. The products themselves are transported from the exporting country to the importing country. When American firms export products to overseas buyers, the sale helps our balance of trade and payments.

In recent decades there has been a tremendous growth of a different type of international business—foreign manufacturing operations. Since the end of World War II, American-based firms have invested heavily in building plants in foreign countries. This has played a big part in rebuilding the economies of the Western European nations and Japan after the war. Although the American firm may not export products to build and operate the overseas plant, it does export other resources, such as technology to build it, managerial skills to run it, and perhaps money to finance its construction.

Foreign manufacturing operations represent a much greater commitment to international business than exporting. Sales of overseas

GLOBAL CARS

> Henry Ford sold his Model A in Europe in 1903. General Motors Corp. traces its European connection to the creation of the GM Export Co. in 1911. But until recently Detroit has regarded the products of its affiliates overseas as almost as "foreign" as those turned out by non-U.S. companies. No longer. By the early 1980s, worry European competitors, Detroit will use its muscle to blitz overseas markets on two fronts: through its subsidiaries in Europe and via direct exports from the U.S. of a bevy of "internationally sized" models.

Source: *Business Week.*

subsidiaries in which American firms hold majority ownership add up to four or five times the dollar volume of our exports.

Suppose an American-based firm sets up a plant in a foreign country to produce products for sale in that country and, perhaps, for export to other countries. The sales of that overseas plant do not show up as exports from the United States. But a large proportion of our exports are accounted for by sales of American firms to their overseas subsidiaries.

The Multinational Company

A multinational company (MNC) is a firm that is based in one country (the parent country) and has production and marketing activities spread in one or more foreign (host) countries. The greater the number of these host countries, the more "multinational" the company is. Such a firm truly becomes a global enterprise.

multinational company (MNC)

We tend to think of firms such as IBM, Procter and Gamble, Coca-Cola, and General Electric Company as American firms. But they are global firms that look at the world as their base of operations. Many such firms sell more overseas than they sell in the United States.

Of course, the United States is not the parent country for all multinational firms. For example, Switzerland's Nestlé does more than 90 percent of its business outside of Switzerland. Royal Dutch Shell and Unilever Corporation do more than 80 percent of their business in host countries. (See Table 16–7.)

The multinational company has become more visible and controversial since the end of World War II. Some people believe it is not subject to enough social control. These people question the allegiance of a firm headquartered in one country but having operations in scores of other

Company	Country	Net sales (1977) Millions of U.S. dollars	Net profits (1977)
1. Royal Dutch/Shell Group	Netherlands-Britain	$43,647.3	$ 2,572.8
2. British Petroleum	Britain	23,035.0	688.0
3. National Iranian Oil	Iran	22,399.9	19,410.2
4. Unilever	Britain-Netherlands	17,470.0	499.8
5. Philips	Netherlands	13,790.2	280.4
6. Fiat	Italy	13,143.5	72.4
7. Veba	Germany	13,064.6	73.5
8. Daimler-Benz	Germany	12,337.1	233.7
9. Volkswagen	Germany	11,520.5	199.9
10. Cie. Française des Pétroles	France	11,372.0	48.1
11. Hoechst	Germany	11,113.1	103.5
12. Siemens*	Germany	10,915.8	281.6
13. B-A-T Industries	Britain	10,857.9	367.1
14. ENI	Italy	10,532.7	− 138.8
15. Renault	France	10,476.1	4.3
16. Nippon Steel**	Japan	10,459.3	71.3
17. Toyota Motor***†	Japan	10,288.1	525.1
18. Bayer	Germany	10,204.0	150.7
19. Nestlé	Switzerland	10,111.8	417.7
20. Nissan Motor**	Japan	10,100.7	362.8

TABLE 16-7

The twenty giants of industry outside the United States

*Fiscal year ended Sept. 30, 1977   **Fiscal year ended Mar. 31, 1978
***Fiscal year ended June 30, 1977

†All Toyota Motor Co. sales are to Toyota Motor Sales Co., which markets Toyota products worldwide. Toyota Motor Sales earned $113.2 million on $11.9 billion in sales in the fiscal year ended Mar. 31, 1978

Source: *Business Week.*

countries. Some people think they are too powerful, both economically and politically.

Why Foreign Manufacturing Operations?

Several factors help to explain the growth in foreign manufacturing operations. One is the growth in buying power in some countries. This helps to create enough demand for some products so that it is more profitable for their producers to set up manufacturing operations there instead of exporting the finished products from the United States.

Another factor is the growing spirit of nationalism in many countries, especially in the underdeveloped countries that export raw materials.

Nations that produce raw materials have been at a trading disadvantage with the industrialized nations for a long time. They argue that foreign-based firms come in and "take" their natural resources and export them to the industrialized nations where they are manufactured into products. These countries argue that the foreigners get the high-paying manufacturing jobs, their governments get taxes from the firms, and the workers spend their money at home. They also believe that they are in a poor bargaining position against the big firms. This is why some less developed nations have formed cartels. **A cartel is a group of business firms or nations that agrees to operate as a monopoly. Thus they regulate prices and production.** Although cartels are illegal in the United States, they are legal in some other countries.

cartel

Instead of exporting their raw materials to the more developed countries, less developed nations want the using firms to set up manufacturing plants in their countries to use the raw materials there. This creates local jobs, gives the government some control over the MNC's operations, and increases the tax base.

Consider another example of nationalism. In order to encourage local production, some governments erect barriers against importing selected products that MNCs wish to sell there. These barriers practically force these MNCs to set up local manufacturing and marketing operations instead.

Still another factor is the lower cost of producing in some countries. This can be due to factors such as lower labor costs, lower interest rates on borrowed money, lower taxes, government subsidies, and better availability of raw materials.

Finally, the formation of regional trading blocs in some areas of the world may favor foreign operations for some firms. **A regional trading bloc is a group of countries that agrees to eliminate barriers to trade among member nations.** In 1958, for example, Belgium, France, Italy, Luxembourg, the Netherlands, and West Germany formed the European Economic Community (EEC), or the European Common Market. Since then, Denmark, Ireland, and the United Kingdom have joined. Negotiations were completed in 1978 for Greece to join in 1981. Spain and Portugal also have asked to join.

regional trading bloc

There are no tariffs on exports and imports among member countries. For example, there is no tariff on French imports in West Germany. But all members apply a common external tariff on products entering from nonmember countries. Thus an American exporter is at a disadvantage in competing with a French firm to export products to other Common Market countries. Many American firms have set up subsidiaries in member countries to get behind this tariff wall.

There are, of course, several risks in engaging in foreign operations. Each nation has its own system of government, laws, and money.

expropriation

Sometimes, foreign-owned firms receive discriminatory treatment by host-country governments.

Perhaps the biggest political risk of setting up a plant overseas is the risk of expropriation. **Expropriation means that the government of a country takes over ownership of a foreign-owned firm located in its country.** The firm that is taken over may then be sold to private citizens of the expropriating country. In some cases the owner is paid part or all of the market value of that property. Confiscation, however, means that the government does not compensate the owner. When the expropriating government keeps ownership and runs the expropriated firm, it is called nationalization.

A firm that engages in foreign operations also must consider the attitude of its home-country government. The U.S. government's attitude toward American firms that invest abroad depends largely on the situation and the time. It involves foreign policy and the national interest. Political differences with some nations may cause our government to discourage American firms from investing in them. The U.S. balance of payments problem sometimes leads our government to restrict

FIGURE 16-4

U.S. direct investment abroad, 1977 (direct investment position: $148.8 billion)

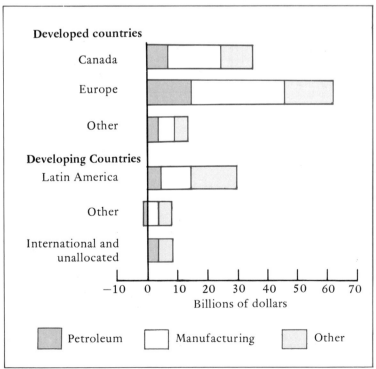

Source: *Survey of Current Business.*

foreign investment by American firms. On balance, however, our government encourages and helps American firms to do business overseas.

Foreign Operations in the United States

As we have seen, American-based MNCs have been engaged heavily in foreign operations since the end of World War II. In recent years there has been a tremendous increase in foreign investment in the United States. Some of it has been oil money from the Arab nations. But a lot of this investment is due to the decline of the U.S. dollar relative to many other currencies. This enables foreigners to invest here at very attractive prices. Of course, our highly stable political system also helps to attract foreign investment.

Foreign investment in the United States takes many forms. Some

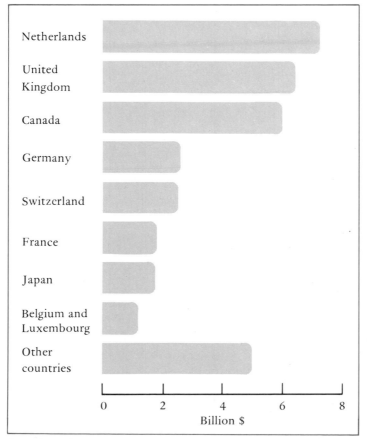

FIGURE 16-5

Foreign direct investment in the United States, 1977 (direct investment position: $34.1 billion)

Source: *Survey of Current Business.*

foreign-based MNCs are building plants here from the ground up while others are buying controlling interest in some existing American firms. Other examples are foreigners buying U.S. government securities, securities of U.S. corporations, and real estate (hotels, office buildings, farm land) for investment purposes.

A GERMAN BANK TRIES TO BUY THE WORLD TRADE CENTER

> To would-be climbers, tightrope walkers, King Kong and New York tourists, it is the World Trade Center, at 1,350 ft. the second tallest building in the world, behind only Chicago's Sears Tower (1,454 ft.). . . . The Deutsche Bank of Frankfurt, which in terms of assets (about $50 billion) ranks fourth in the world . . . has approached the W.T.C.'s owner, the Port Authority of New York and New Jersey, about buying the colossus for resale to as yet unspecified German clients.
>
> Whatever happens to it, the Germans' approach is another evidence of the craving of foreign capital for a haven in the safe, solid U.S. Deutsche Bank viewed the W.T.C. as a sound investment in prime U.S. urban real estate. . .

Source: *Time*.

Other Types of Foreign Operations

As we have seen, firms can enter a foreign market by exporting to it or by setting up their own manufacturing and marketing subsidiaries overseas. Other entry strategies include contract manufacturing and foreign licensing.

Contract Manufacturing

contract manufacturing

In contract manufacturing the firm that wants to do business in a foreign country enters into a contract with a firm there to produce the product. This arrangement is popular with big consumer products firms such as Procter and Gamble. P&G might contract out the production work to a foreign firm but P&G takes on the marketing task.

Foreign Licensing

foreign licensing

The main difference between contract manufacturing and foreign licensing is that a licensor-licensee relationship usually extends over a longer period of time. **In a foreign licensing arrangement, licensees are licensed to manufacture and market products in their countries. The licensor gets an agreed-upon percentage of the licensee's sales revenues.** PepsiCo sells its concentrate to the Soviets who bottle the product under license for sale in the Soviet Union.

Some firms engage in foreign assembly through a licensee. The parent firm exports parts to the licensee who assembles the finished product. This is popular because tariffs on unassembled products are lower than those on assembled products.

Ownership of Foreign Operations

An overseas operation can be a wholly owned subsidiary of the parent firm or a joint venture. There are no local part-owners when the parent owns the subsidiary outright. Outright ownership gives the parent firm maximum control and makes it easier to coordinate subsidiary operations with those of the parent.

In international business, a joint venture means a partnership of two   joint venture
or more firms that are based in different countries. They share ownership and control of the venture's operations and property rights. The partners can be two foreign firms that are doing business in a host country, a foreign firm and a government agency, or a foreign firm and a locally owned firm.

The majority of foreign subsidiaries of American-based MNCs are wholly owned. But there is a strong worldwide trend toward requiring joint ventures. For example, since 1973 Mexico has limited to 49 percent the proportion of a new investment that can be foreign-owned.

The Multinational Business Environment

Decision making in the multinational firm is complex since it must cope with a variety of foreign environments. In some cases it has to adapt to the environment in a country. In other cases it is best to be innovative or to do things differently. Deciding when to adapt and when to innovate is often tough.

For example, consider leadership styles. If an American-based firm is operating a plant in a country where the workers are used to dictators, the firm has a choice between adapting or innovating. Whereas participative management may be good for American workers, it may not work in this foreign country. The firm's management could adapt by allowing workers less participation in decision making. If it wished to be innovative, however, it would try to make participative management work there.

Because a firm is always a guest in a host country, it must be careful not to offend the host government. This, however, may lead to problems with the parent country's government. How does a firm with worldwide operations decide on matters of social responsibility? What about an

American-based firm that makes products abroad rather than export them from America? Should it be concerned about the effects this has on employment in the United States and on our balance of payments? Should it set up a foreign subsidiary in a low-tax country into which it can funnel profits to avoid American taxes? In other words, international business is growing faster than international agreement on the rights and responsibilities of global firms to the different countries in which they operate.

Cultural Environment

International business requires people of different cultures to interact. Business transactions involve the written and/or spoken language. Unless the parties really understand each other, there can be no basis for business. This problem exists even when people in different countries use the same language. English and American people speak the same language but the English put "petrol" in their gas tanks instead of "gas."

American Motors ran into trouble in Puerto Rico with the Matador car. Puerto Rico has a very high traffic fatality rate and the name of the car translated as "killer" in Spanish. Pepsi's "Come Alive" ad theme translated as "Come Out of the Grave" in some languages.

Tastes also vary. Suntans are considered unattractive by the Japanese. Nestlé markets light instant coffee for Americans and dark and thick instant coffee for Italians. The English like their beer at room temperature. Americans like it cold. But tastes also can change. Are McDonald's, Dairy Queen, Kentucky Fried Chicken, Shakey's, and Pizza Hut serving as agents of cultural change by operating successfully in Japan?

There also are differences in cultural values. American ideas about getting ahead are rejected in some cultures. Our emphasis on convenience is equated with laziness in some cultures. Although cultural values do change over time, there is cultural resistance to change. For example, Japan accepted a cultural value of fewer children and legalized abortion long before many other cultures accepted family planning. But the Japanese are reluctant to adopt a new alphabet, even though their alphabet contains too many symbols to make use of the typewriter practical.

The religious beliefs of a people influence their ideas of what is ethical behavior. Our affluent society is rejected by devout followers of Buddhism and Hinduism. Employers who favor their relatives in hiring and promotions are frowned on in the United States. Such favored treatment is part of the religious teaching of Hinduism.

Social Environment

There are differences in the social environments as well. In extremely class-conscious societies, a person is born into a particular social class and remains there. Ad campaigns built around the idea of moving up are not effective, nor are personnel policies that encourage employees to move up the job ladder.

Social customs also vary. In Oriental societies extreme politeness and formality are part of doing business, unlike the more informal American way. An American who wants to get down to business without engaging in the proper social behavior is headed for trouble.

Economic Environment

The economic systems of some countries are simple when compared to the American economy. In many, people live at a subsistence level. Perhaps more important to business people is what the country is doing to advance. Some "backward" countries do not appear to want change. This may be because of religious beliefs that look down on material progress.

Underdeveloped countries that are rich in natural resources have the potential to develop faster than those that are poor in natural resources. Valuable natural resources attract foreign investment to a country. This brings its people into closer contact with people from more developed nations, which may encourage them to pursue economic growth. But as the world's supply of natural resources dwindles, many countries that export them want to use them to help industrialize their own countries.

The tax structure affects a country's appeal to the multinational firm. Because most of the people in underdeveloped countries are poor, their governments rely heavily on business taxes. This sometimes discourages foreign business. The same is true of inflation. High rates of inflation are common in many underdeveloped countries.

In recent years the industrialized nations have had difficult problems with inflation. The members of OPEC (Organization of Petroleum Exporting Countries) have, from time to time, raised the price of their oil. One reason for this is that inflation in the industrialized nations means that the OPEC countries must pay more for the products they import. Thus they want more for the oil they export.

Technological Environment

One of the biggest differences between "have" and "have-not" nations is the technology gap. Advanced transportation and communication are taken for granted in the United States. In many underdeveloped nations, they are almost nonexistent. Managers must evaluate the level of technology in those countries where they expect to operate. This may enable them to adapt their operations to the present technology or attempt to import new techniques. NCR, formerly National Cash Register Company, developed crank-operated cash registers to market in some countries where the availability of electricity is limited.

A lot has been said about technology transfer over the years. Some people, for example, believe that the United States is transferring too much computer technology to the Soviet Union. Several proposed sales of computers by American firms to the Soviet Union were held up during 1978 by President Carter because of the military implications of the proposed sales.

TECHNOLOGY TRANSFER

> As Saudi Arabia moves tentatively toward the first stage of its industrialization, the Saudi government's inner circle is debating whether the oil-rich nation should begin to acquire strategic stakes in selected Western companies. The objective: to attract much needed industrial technology and knowhow, without which Saudi industrialization cannot get off the ground.

Source: *Business Week.*

Political and Legal Environment

When a government owns the means of production, foreign firms doing business there must deal with that government. A firm may have to enter into a partnership arrangement with a government before the firm can begin operations there. For example, Dow Chemical Company had to enter into a joint venture with Yugoslavia as a condition of setting up a petrochemical plant in the country. Three years of talks were needed to get the joint venture set up.

An American-based firm that deals with foreign governments and/or businesses gets involved in politics. It's hard to keep sharp dividing lines between politics, economics, business, and ethics. This often poses a dilemma for managers. Should they risk offending some people by doing business with Israel? When Coca-Cola awarded a franchise to an Israeli firm, it was immediately blacklisted in the Arab world. Should a firm pay fake commissions to "sales agents" who really are government officials in order to get government contracts? Even if that is accepted practice in the foreign market, several American-based MNCs have been in trouble under American law for engaging in bribery.

In recent years some American-based multinational firms have been accused of, or have admitted to, engaging in certain acts overseas that are illegal or, at the least, unethical in the United States. Examples of such acts are bribing government officials, illegal "gifts" to foreign government officials, and funneling money into foreign funds for the purpose of making illegal political contributions to politicians in the United States. The Foreign Corrupt Practices Act of 1977 imposes jail terms and fines for overseas payoffs by American-based firms.

Suppose that an American executive in an overseas subsidiary of an American-based firm pays a certain amount of money to a government official there. The payment is for that official's help in closing a sale with the official's government. The American executive calls it a "sales-agent fee." Somebody less kind calls it an illegal bribe. Yet such behavior is considered completely aboveboard in that country. Should the American executive be fined or jailed? YOU BE THE JUDGE!

YOU BE THE JUDGE!

Business Ethics and the Multinational Company

The governments of many of the emerging nations try to instill in their people a strong feeling of nationalism. This sometimes leads them to distrust foreigners. This can hurt multinational business.

Business activity thrives under conditions of political stability. Management should study the past history of political stability and current trends before committing itself to operations in a given country.

Many laws restrict a parent firm's control of its overseas operations. These include laws that require a subsidiary to hire local nationals or restrict how much profit can flow out of the country. A multinational firm takes on a considerable risk, much of which is political. IBM several years ago was forced to leave India. The government wanted the firm to allow Indians to have partial ownership and control of IBM's plants in India. IBM refused to comply. Coca-Cola was willing to share ownership, but it refused the Indian government's request that the firm give it the secret formula for Coke.

A firm operating in different countries is subject to different political and legal systems. Quite often what is legal in one is illegal in another.

The firm is caught in the middle but must be careful not to violate the laws in any country in which it operates.

Summary and Look Ahead

Trade among countries broadens the market and permits greater exchange and specialization. The principles of absolute and comparative advantages show why there is economic benefit in trade. International trade enables each country to use its limited resources to the best advantage in raising its people's standard of living.

Despite the advantages of trade, there are many obstacles, or trade barriers. Distance is a natural barrier. But there also are tariff and nontariff barriers. Examples of nontariff barriers are import quotas, embargoes, exchange control, tax control, government procurement policies, government standards, customs procedures, and subsidies and countervailing duties. As governments recognize the mutual benefits from trade, they want more trade and work to eliminate the tariff and nontariff barriers.

The balance of trade and balance of payments are very important to international business people. In recent years the United States has had trade and payments balance deficits. This has affected the foreign exchange rate of the dollar.

In free economies international trade basically means international business—firms and individuals in different countries buying from and selling to each other. There are, however, some forms of state trading even in free economies. In state-controlled economies, trading is handled through state trading companies.

There are many reasons why firms export and import products, and there are different types of international business involvement. An unintentional exporter is much less committed to international business than is a multinational company. A multinational company is based in a parent country and has production and marketing activities in one or more foreign (host) countries.

A basic understanding of the environments of international business is important to executives in global firms. The surest way to fail in any type of overseas business dealings is to assume that foreigners are all alike.

Just as environmental factors are crucial in international business, they can be crucial at home. In the next chapter we consider the many environmental factors affecting business decisions in the United States.

My name is Melissa M. Lacroix. I serve as section head of market research with Lykes Bros. Steamship Company, Inc.

I graduated from Newcomb College of Tulane University in 1975. My major was economics; other areas of concentration were mathematics and accounting. After studying the theories and applications of international economics, I pursued my interest in this field by researching the fluctuations in the U.S. economy and the effects on the economies of countries with fixed exchange rates to the U.S. dollar. I entered the job market with Lykes immediately following graduation. One of the best preparations for my job with Lykes was working two summers with a major grain exporting company in New Orleans. This exposure to the shipping industry provided a head start in learning shipping terminology, the names of the major operators, and the network of transportation within the U.S., that is, the railroads, trucking, and barge transport.

I am involved in the supervision, delegation, and review of work performed in the market research section as well as the actual performance of the following functions: manipulating, presenting, and analyzing statistics related to commodity flows, shippers and consignees, and Lykes' market share. I also regularly read and monitor selected periodicals and in-house correspondence to stay abreast of market developments and in-house developments so that I can anticipate information that may be needed and help to develop forecasts of Lykes' market share.

Outside contacts on behalf of Lykes are an important aspect of the market research function. These relationships include liaison with the various sources of our data such as the Bureau of the Census, the Maritime Administration, and the *Journal of Commerce.*

The Port of New Orleans is the city's major industry, and the opportunities available to college graduates with a business background are excellent. The intense competition among carriers for U.S. exports and imports opens the door for more sophisticated analysis of statistical data. An analyst is challenged not only from a methodology standpoint but also by the need to acquire new and improved marketing data. This competitive environment among operators and ports has expanded their demand for the most accurate information available on the cargo flows forming the mainstay of their markets.

Pursuing an upper-management position within the steamship

industry requires extensive background training in all aspects of transportation, from rate making, to regulatory compliance, to scheduling of vessels.

My first position with Lykes was as a cost analyst within the finance division. This initial experience with Lykes enabled me to learn the distribution and structure of costs for current and long-range planning. As a cost analyst, I also prepared studies on existing and potential trade areas and on port and commodity profitability. This financial background broadened my perspective as a market research analyst and enhanced my understanding of the market and Lykes' role among its competitors.

As a market research analyst I am now associated with the traffic division, which deploys the fleet and monitors the day-to-day activities of the vessels for each trade area. By performing my functions as a market research analyst, I am expanding my background and opportunities for upward mobility.

Key Concepts

absolute advantage A country has an absolute advantage in producing a product when it is the only country that can produce that product or when it can produce it at a lower cost than any other country.

balance of payments The difference between money flowing into a country and money flowing out of that country as a result of trade and other transactions. An unfavorable balance means more flowing out than flowing in.

balance of trade The difference between the money values of a country's imports and exports. An unfavorable balance means that the money value of imports is greater than the money value of exports.

cartel A group of firms or countries that agrees to operate as a monopoly to regulate prices and production.

combination export manager A person or firm that represents several exporters and handles the task of exporting their products. Helps firms with little knowledge in international business and those with relatively small export volume to become involved in international business.

comparative advantage According to the principle of comparative advantage, the people of a country will enjoy a higher standard of living if the country specializes in producing those products in which it has the greatest comparative advantage or the least comparative disadvantage in relation to other countries. A country's natural resources, labor and capital cost, nearness to markets, labor skills, technological skills, and so on determine where its relative or comparative advantage lies.

contract manufacturing The contracting by a firm in one country with a firm in another country to produce a product intended for sale in that and other countries.

devaluation The reduction by a nation's government of the value of its currency in relation to gold or other currencies.

dumping Shipping substantial quantities of a product to a foreign country at prices that are below either the home-market price of the same product or the full cost (including profit) of producing it.

embargoes Legal prohibitions on the import

and/or export of certain products into or out of a country.

exchange control Government control over access to a country's currency by foreigners.

expropriation In international business expropriation occurs when a government takes over ownership of a foreign-owned subsidiary. The firm may or may not be compensated, and it may be sold to private citizens in the expropriating country.

foreign exchange rate The ratio of one currency to another. It tells how much a unit of one currency is worth in terms of a unit of another.

foreign licensing The licensing of a firm in one country by a licensor in another country to make and sell the licensor's product in the licensee's country. For example, McDonald's in the United States licenses firms in Japan to make and sell McDonald's hamburgers.

General Agreement on Tariffs and Trade (GATT) A treaty among the world's major trading nations that is administered by a permanent secretariat through which member countries act jointly to reduce tariff and nontariff trade barriers.

import quota A limit set by the government on the amount of a product that can enter the country.

international trade Flows of products between or among nations.

joint venture The agreement between a firm in one country that wants to do business in another country with a firm in that foreign country to produce and/or sell a product. There is mutual ownership of the overseas firm. (See Glossary for definition of joint venture in domestic business.)

multinational company (MNC) A firm having production and marketing operations spread over several countries. The ultimate commitment to international business. A global enterprise.

piggyback exporting The use by one firm (the carrier) of its overseas distribution network to sell noncompetitive products made by other firms (riders).

regional trading bloc A group of nations that reduces or eliminates trade barriers among themselves.

state trading company A government-owned operation that handles a country's trade with other governments or firms in other countries.

tariffs Duties or taxes that a country's government imposes on products imported into or exported from that country.

tax control The practice of a country's government of using its taxing authority to control foreign investments in that country. Involves applying discriminatory taxes to foreign-owned firms.

trade barriers Natural and "created" obstacles that restrict trade among countries. Distance is a natural obstacle. Tariffs and nontariff barriers are "created" obstacles.

Webb-Pomerene associations Associations made up of American firms that compete in the U.S. market but work together in expanding their overseas sales. They are not subject to U.S. antitrust laws as long as they do not lead to reduced competition in the United States and they do not engage in unfair methods of competition.

For Review . . .

1. Explain how trade between two countries can benefit their citizens.
2. Do governments engage in international trade? Explain.
3. List the three general types of trade barriers and give an example of each.
4. Are the majority of tariffs on imports into the United States protective tariffs or revenue tariffs? Explain.
5. Does the General Agreement on Tariffs and Trade (GATT) help to restrict or to increase international trade? Explain.

6. Can a nation with a favorable balance of trade have an unfavorable balance of payments? Explain.
7. What effects do fluctuating exchange rates have on international trade?
8. Suppose a country has an unfavorable balance of trade and an unfavorable balance of payments. Will this tend to result in a rise or a decline in the foreign exchange rate of its currency? Explain.
9. Contrast unintentional exporting and intentional exporting.
10. Contrast an exporting company and a multinational company in terms of their commitment to international business.

... For Discussion

1. To which country does the management of a large multinational company owe its primary allegiance?

2. Is it ethical for an American-based company to open a plant in a low-wage country when unemployment in America is at a high level?
3. "Investments made by American-based multinational firms in foreign countries are good for both the United States and the foreign countries." Do you agree?
4. "It is easier for a firm to live up to its social responsibility when its operations are confined to one country than when it engages in international business." Do you agree?
5. Doing business in many countries exposes a firm to many risks that could be avoided by limiting its operations to its home country. What are these risks and how does a firm cope with them?

Incidents

RCA Color TV Sets in Poland

"The color-TV plant being completed at Piaseczno, near Warsaw, last month produced its first 100 sets, using RCA Corp.'s latest designs, technology, and components. The factory, which in the 1980s will have a capacity of 600,000 sets per year, will eventually supply all RCA color TVs for sale in Europe, and will by that time use only Polish components. The $69 million contract between RCA and Poland was signed in June, 1976, and includes the training of Polish foremen in the U.S."

Deere and Company

Although the U.S. government generally favors increasing international business, there are some government-imposed obstacles with which American-based firms must contend.

"This month, Deere & Co., which has sold agricultural tractors to Iraq in the past, ran into an

Questions

1. Is any technology transfer involved in this contract? Explain.
2. How does RCA benefit from this contract?
3. How does Poland benefit from this contract?

Source: *Business Week.*

export barrier embodied in legislation that prohibits U.S. companies from certifying in contracts with Arab countries that the products to be sold are not made in Israel. Deere has no plants in Israel. Nonetheless, Deere had to withdraw from bidding on an $18 million order for 1,500 tractors to Iraq because of the language in the proposed contract."

Questions

1. In your opinion, is this requirement of the U.S. government a type of nontariff trade barrier? Explain.

2. Should political considerations be set aside in shaping the U.S. government's export policy? Why or why not?

Source: *Business Week.*

ROCKETOY COMPANY 8

Last month, Terry got a letter from a toy distributor in Japan indicating an interest in importing several models of Rocketoy's products. The firm wanted to import the toys and sell them through its own distribution outlets in Japan. Terry was somewhat surprised by the letter. He had never really considered selling Rocketoy's products abroad. He called in Julia Rabinovitz, the vice-president of marketing, for her thoughts on the matter.

Julia's first reaction was that Rocketoy should be thinking of moving into new market areas. Competition in the American market had become very intense. Selling in foreign countries would be a logical next step in Rocketoy's development.

Terry decided to talk to the new vice-president of production, Robert Ensminger. (Uncle Joe had resigned a year earlier due to poor health.) Robert was mildly enthusiastic. He said that it made no difference to him where the toys were sold. He had some extra production capacity and he could produce a "reasonable" number of extra toys without any problems.

Based on Julia's and Robert's reactions, Terry wrote a letter to the Japanese firm in which he indicated a willingness to enter into further discussion on the proposal.

Within two weeks the Japanese firm replied. It offered to make an initial cash purchase of 20,000 toys and then negotiate for additional orders if the toys sold well in Japan. Terry, Julia, Robert, and Pam met together to discuss whether or not to accept the proposal. All agreed that this was a golden opportunity to gauge the potential of international marketing for Rocketoy.

Rocketoy, therefore, agreed to supply the initial order of 20,000 toys on the condition that most of the "details" of exporting and importing would be handled by the importing firm. The Japanese firm agreed and a contract was signed between the two parties.

Questions

1. What do you think prompted the Japanese firm to contact Terry about the possibility of importing Rocketoy's products?
2. Why do you think Terry was surprised by the proposal?
3. Compare Julia's and Robert's reactions to the proposal.
4. How would you describe Rocketoy's commitment or involvement in international business after signing the contract with the Japanese firm?
5. Suppose that the market reaction to Rocketoy's products in Japan is very enthusiastic. What advice would you give Terry about further negotiations with the Japanese toy distributor? Explain.

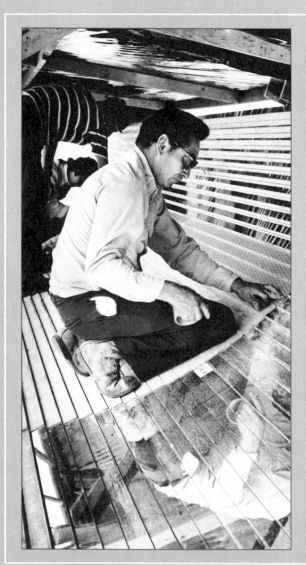

U P TO THIS point we have shown why economic systems exist and why the business firms within them come into being. We have also discussed the motivations of business people in a capitalistic system and have described the production, marketing, and financial functions of business. All of this takes place in an environment that can make the difference between success and failure.

Chapter 17 looks at this environment. It includes cultural, social, ethical, political, legal, economic, and technological dimensions. All are interconnected and change constantly.

A firm makes better decisions if it knows how the environment affects its decisions. Recognizing trends in the environment helps a firm to plan and to understand its customers and employees. Understanding values in the environment also helps a firm to set standards for its own business behavior. This is important because in the long run a firm must behave in a way that is acceptable to the society. What society expects of business usually ends up in the form of laws. Business must understand and comply with the laws.

The economy, its health, and its growth rate have a lot to do with business success, too. Technology often determines the success or failure of an economy and the firms in it. A business must know what is happening in the area of technology as it relates to its products and services.

In Chapter 17 we'll concentrate on the interaction of society and business. After you have read this chapter, you'll have a clearer understanding of how dynamic and interconnected the different aspects of the environment are and how they relate to business success.

Our final chapter could be the most important one for you because the subject is you and your career. You'll be taken through a brief tour of the future business world in the form of some not-so-wild predictions about things that are changing the world you will work in. You'll be shown what the best sources of information are concerning job opportunities by industry and occupation. After that you will be guided through a matching process. This process involves matching you and your talents with the job best suited for you.

Photos: left—Stock, Boston; right—Magnum Photos.

SECTION FIVE

Business, Society, and Your Career

How Business and Society Interact

CHAPTER 17

Objectives: After reading this chapter, you should be able to

1. Show how business creates part of the environment of society.
2. Explain how environmental influences are interdependent.
3. Tell the difference between the way society affects business directly and the way it does so through government.
4. Describe the major projected changes in the United States' birthrate, income distribution, educational attainment, and sex composition of the workforce.
5. Explain why large consumer products firms hire demographers.
6. Give examples of the impact of the changing family on business planning.
7. Illustrate the importance to a food producer of monitoring changing tastes.
8. Give an example of at least three different roles played by government in the environment of business.
9. Name and describe the purpose of several federal administrative and regulatory agencies.
10. Explain the nature of antitrust activity.
11. Differentiate between regressive and progressive taxes.
12. Outline some changes in laws which resulted from actions by the consumer movement since 1965.
13. Evaluate the potential for public-private partnerships in solving social ills.

Key concepts: Look for these terms as you read the chapter

environment
net annual household
formation
multiearner family
zero population growth
administrative law
voluntary compliance
consent order

antitrust laws
progressive tax
regressive tax
traditional business ethic
professional-managerial
ethic
public-private partnership

Just as business decisions affect the society, society affects business. Individuals and groups in the society affect business decisions both directly and indirectly through government. This kind of environmental influence upon business takes many forms. People can tell a business executive something by buying or not buying the firm's product or by electing a person to Congress who opposes monopoly power. They can, in fact, cause the failure of a business by demanding, for example, laws against nuclear waste dumps or against violence on TV. They can influence hiring or product design policies of firms by picketing or by joining consumerist organizations. Business can also be a part of society's environment. As a result, business and society interact.

What Is an Environment?

The environment of something consists of all those things that come in contact with it and influence it. The influence can be direct or indirect. In some simple cases, such as that of the physical environment of a plant, the influences of soil, temperature, and moisture on plant growth are obvious. These environmental influences are independent of the quality of the seed from which the plant grew, but they influence growth at least as much. Obviously the plant has no control over its environment.

environment

Human life and activities occur within a complex environment, most of which is beyond the control of individuals. People, however, *can* interact with their environment and can often modify it. When people in large groups want to bring about changes in the environment, they can do so—especially in the social environment. Society interacts with the business environment, too.

Business as Environment

Business, including the billions of decisions made by millions of firms in the United States, constitutes a big part of the environment of society. The way that society thinks and behaves, the welfare of society, the vigor of society, the opportunities for growth as well as the threats to its growth, and the nuisances it experiences are often a direct function of business decisions. There is a kind of interdependence between business and society as well as further interdependencies involving the sphere of science and technology and the sphere of law and politics. (See Figure 17–1.)

While we will not emphasize the scientific-technological or the legal-political spheres, they cannot be ignored in the discussion of the environmental influences of business on our society and vice versa. All of these influences are interdependent and the relationships are dynamic.

Let's look at some current examples of how interdependent and dy-

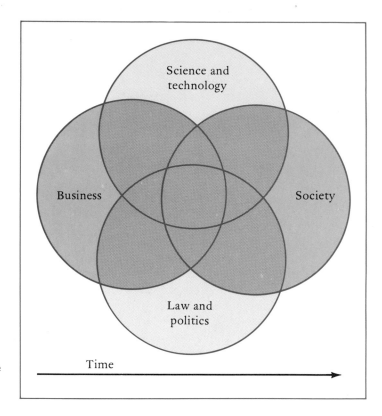

FIGURE 17-1

Interdependency of business, society, science and technology, and law and politics

namic they are. The Crown-Zellerbach Corporation, a large box and paper products manufacturer, made a decision to close two of its plants in the town of Bogalusa, Louisiana in 1976. The people of the town were very much affected when over 1,000 of the town's 18,000 citizens lost their jobs. Naturally, the workers' families, the grocery stores, the movie houses, the banks, the corner drug stores, and the schools—all aspects of the society—were affected by a business decision.

Why was the plant closed? The answer lies partly in the scientific-technological sphere and partly in the legal-political sphere. Crown-Zellerbach management decided that the additional cost of meeting new air pollution standards set by the Environmental Protection Agency (EPA) would be too high for continued operation. Of course, other costs were rising, too, including the cost of labor. Also, some of the plant's production equipment was becoming obsolete. The new EPA requirement was the "straw that broke the camel's back." All of this illustrates how business is an important part of society's environment, and how, in turn, the demands of the larger society (through the legal-political framework) to clean up the air make up an important *societal* environment of business. It is only fair to add that governmental aid (the Economic Development Administration) for construction of an industrial park in Bogalusa has since led to the relocation of several new plants in the town, restoring much of the employment (and the morale) which had been lost.

In the even smaller town of Craig, Colorado, a different tale of environmental dependence was told. The "energy crisis"—partly a function of politics and partly a function of technology—led to the construction of a power plant in the town because coal is available there for fuel. The plant led to a doubling of the population and booming business in general. Unfortunately, according to the news media, the business boom has brought with it many of the ills of big city life, including large increases in alcoholism, drug abuse, and emotional depression. Three new mental health clinics have opened in a very short time. This illustrates that the economic benefit stemming from a business decision may have negative social consequences as well. As we will see, the *positive* consequences for society are also often very great.

Individual and Household Influences

Individuals and the households they form influence business through their role in the political system—electing political leaders and lawmakers. They also influence business by the kinds of lives they lead—their tastes in products and services, their lifestyles, and their attitudes toward work and family.

Society's Influence Through Government

You probably remember the basic facts about our government's structure from your civics or government classes. The people as voters decide who will be president, governor, representative, and senator, and their choices set the tone of government's influence on business. We will return to the roles of government with respect to business later in this chapter. Meanwhile we turn to more direct involvement of society's members in the affairs of business.

Changing Characteristics, Values, and Lifestyles

When Alvin Toffler wrote the book *Future Shock,*[1] he told Americans what they should have been aware of already—that our society is going through a process of change which is ever more rapid. Many of these changes affect even our most fundamental institutions—motherhood, education, the family, work, and religion.

[1] Alvin Toffler, *Future Shock* (New York: Bantam Books, 1971).

net annual household formation

These changing values show up in the statistics which describe the U.S. population. Perhaps the most crucial population characteristic watched by producers of consumer goods and services (especially durable products) is the net household formation rate. **The net annual household formation is the number of new households minus the number of households dissolved during the year.** This number, it is predicted, will decline from its peak of 1.65 million in the latter half of the seventies to 1.55 million in the first half of the eighties. (See Figure 17–2.) This has deep meaning for thousands of business planners because the demand for household products is mainly dependent on the number of households. The size and composition of these households is also vital to planning for production of thousands of products from houses to breakfast cereals. The formation rate is a function of mar-

FIGURE 17-2

Households and household formation

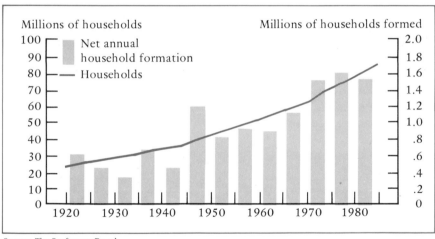

Source: The Conference Board.

FIGURE 17-3

Educational attainment (years of school completed, persons 25 and over)

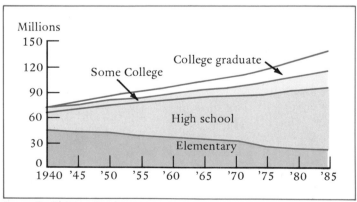

Source: The Conference Board.

riages, divorces, and changing patterns of separate living for young unmarrieds and for widows and widowers.

The level of educational attainment has always been a major factor to consider in business planning. Figure 17–3 shows the numbers of people over 25 who have reached or who are predicted to reach various levels of education. It shows that the number of persons with only an elementary education is declining steadily and is expected to do so through the first half of the eighties. It also shows that the numbers in all three higher educational groups are rising. By 1985, it is predicted, more than 90 million people will have the high school diploma but no college, and there will be between 20 and 25 million persons in the "some college," as well as the "college-graduate," categories. This fact is important for business both in terms of the workforce that will be available and in terms of the tastes of the customers of the future. Notice that the rise in college-educated persons is much more pronounced among women than it is among men.

This gives special meaning to Figure 17–4, which indicates the rising number and share of women in the labor force. By 1985, it is predicted, over 45 million women will be in the labor force, more than double the number 25 years earlier. This, as we will discuss in subsequent sections, has effects on consumption as well as production planning. **With more women working and with more teenagers and college students working, the multiearner family becomes important—families in which two or more members are actively employed for pay.** In 1974, more than half of all families (see Figure 17–5) were multiearner families, and more than 15 percent had three or more earners among their members.

multiearner family

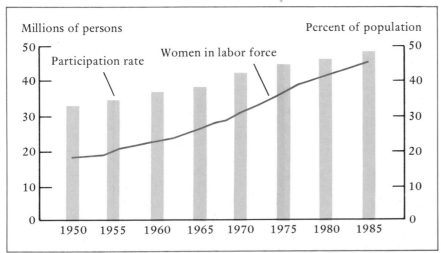

FIGURE 17-4

Women in the labor force

Source: The Conference Board.

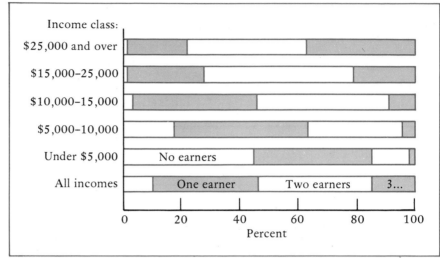

FIGURE 17-5

Multiearner families (total, each income class, 1974 = 100%)

Source: The Conference Board.

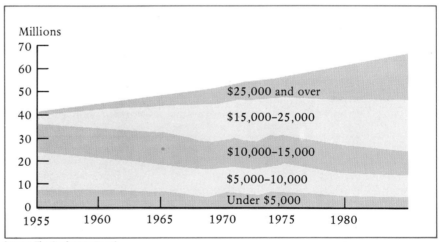

FIGURE 17-6

Families by income class (based on 1975 dollars)

Source: The Conference Board.

The higher-income families are much more likely to contain two or three earners or more. Nearly 40 percent of the families with $25,000 incomes in 1974 had three or more earners and nearly 80 percent had two or more earners.

These facts mean a lot as far as spending patterns of families are concerned, and they have affected the overall family income distribution, as shown in Figure 17–6. In 1980 more than ten million families had incomes of at least $25,000 per year. Think what that means in terms of discretionary buying power, especially as family size decreases!

The dynamics of population change also affect business decisions,

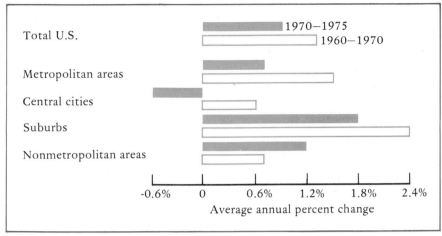

-0.6%   0   0.6%   1.2%   1.8%   2.4%
Average annual percent change

FIGURE 17-7

Population growth by place of residence

Source: The Conference Board.

espccially those changes concerned with the location of potential work-ers and customers. Figure 17–7 shows the overall decline in the popula-tion growth rate in the seventies and the great loss of population in central cities. The big-city suburbs continue to be the fastest-growing areas, but their rate of growth dropped from 2.4 percent a year in the sixties to 1.8 percent in the seventies. It is interesting to see that non-metropolitan areas (areas other than big cities and their suburbs) show a higher growth rate in the seventies than in the previous decade.

Large corporations are now hiring demographers (experts in popula-tion analysis) to make plans for the future in the light of population trends. Public utility firms like the Chesapeake and Potomac Telephone companies and the Pacific Gas and Electric Company have put such experts at work interpreting trends in family formation, births, and other trends relevant to utility demand. General Motors uses such an expert to help find minorities and women to fill professional jobs, and Westinghouse is projecting the need for hospitals, schools, and other facilities. Private decisions by members of the society regarding family size, occupation, and so on, are being monitored by big businesses be-cause they know that these outside decisions are an important part of their environment.

Women, the Birthrate, and Work

Tradition says that motherhood is right up there with God and country and a few notches above baseball, hot dogs, and apple pie. But how strong is that tradition today? For many young women motherhood is not an ideal. For others it still is an important goal, but the nature of its importance has changed. In other words, motherhood is not exactly what it used to be.

Until recently the role that most women played in society was limited to that of mother, homemaker, and occasional part-time contributor to the family's income. Today, many women want to be something else.

The Women's Rights Movement, supported by government action, has opened a variety of careers, once reserved for men, to women. Better education, smaller families, and the greater social acceptability of an active single life make it more likely for women to take part in the worlds of work and politics.

It's okay for women to stay single and enjoy it. Those who marry are having fewer children, and they are spending less time with their children and less time shopping. This means kids learn more (including product preferences and lifestyles) from their friends and from TV. Others (husbands and older children) are doing a greater part of the job of "purchasing agent" for the family. TV advertisers have to think about influencing these husbands and children who share in the shopping chore.

Women, on the other hand, are playing an increasing and more complex role in the labor force and in management. More women are working, and a greater percentage of them are working in managerial and professional jobs. They are also spending a greater part of their lives in the labor force. Women's impact on business from the inside is growing while their impact on household decisions decreases.

The entry of greater and greater numbers of women into the workforce has had some interesting effects. For one thing, it has increased the pressure for more flexible working hours (see Chapter 12) to accommodate women who have family duties as well as their employment to cope with. The states of California and Wisconsin have experimental projects in "job sharing," which allows two workers to share one job, one salary, and one set of benefits. Working wives have led to changes in store hours, lower PTA attendance, and higher family incomes.

What business managers of the future do with the opportunity to bring women more fully into the mainstream of business will have a great and unpredictable impact on the business world and on society itself.

The changing view of women's role means that families are getting smaller. The post–World War II rise in family size lasted well into the 1950s. Thereafter, the birthrate began to decline. This has continued through the 1960s and even more steeply through the 1970s. Most young couples have accepted family planning and have postponed having children. Many have rejected parenthood completely. This is partly a response to the widespread fear of the effects of overpopulation. In fact, "Zero Population Growth," which was only a motto of population control groups in the late sixties, is close to a reality today. **Zero population growth (ZPG) means the population is not growing.**

zero population growth (ZPG)

For the population to remain static (ignoring migration), the number of births must equal the number of deaths. In recent years we have come close to this despite the huge number of women of childbearing age, themselves born in the population boom period of the forties, fifties, and sixties. The number of women of childbearing age is large enough to explain the fact that the number of births is on an upswing from 1975 to 1985. The total fertility rate in 1978 was 1.8 children per woman, compared to the previous low rate of 2.1 children in 1936, the bottom of the Great Depression. So it is the huge number of potential mothers and not the birthrate which is causing the number of births to rise at this time. Should the low birthrate continue until such a time that there are not so many women of childbearing age, then we could easily fall well below the ZPG mark.

What does it mean to a firm to know that the population of the country in which it is located will probably not grow? This depends mostly on what kind of business the firm is in. The demand for some products like hamburger meat, salt, inexpensive clothing, and furniture depends on the number of customers. When the number stops growing, all that the existing producers can hope for is that they will increase their share of sales. Such a situation makes it hard for a new producer to enter competition.

Some markets for products, of course, will not be hurt by zero population growth. These are the markets for luxury products, the products that depend more on the level of family or individual income than on the number of households or individuals. The demand for recreation, new labor-saving devices, and other luxuries will go up as long as a nation increases its productivity and everyone gets a share of buying power out of that productivity.

A dramatic drop in the number of children the average woman has means something besides a possible slowdown in total population growth rates. It also means much smaller families, and it means a changing proportion of the people in different age groups. Both of these changes can mean changes in business decisions. A trend to smaller families means that a house builder must build homes with fewer bedrooms. A breakfast cereal maker must package the product in smaller sizes. Refrigerators, too, must be smaller, as well as dining tables and cars. The volume of products used by babies and children is already stabilizing. Firms producing baby foods, cribs, toys, and school buildings are being affected. Their managers must plan ahead for growth.

Of course, the changed view of motherhood is not the only change affecting family life. There has been a rapid growth of new types of households. Estimates are that there are 4 million unmarried couples, 7 million single parents, 2.5 million married couples involved in "open marriages" or "swinging arrangements," and more than 11 million gay people in the United States. Thus there are other important changes occurring in American lifestyles, changes that affect businesses. For example, the growing number of households headed by women has led to credit reform, with the support of the Women's Rights Movement. The Federal Reserve System outlaws discrimination against borrowers on the basis of sex or marital status. Now a divorced woman has a better chance to get credit at department stores and banks.

Changing Tastes, Spending, and Saving

Despite all the efforts on the part of firms to influence households and individual consumers, the fact is that the American consumer has always been hard to predict. Carefully planned marketing programs have often gone astray. The best-publicized examples of this probably are the failure of the Edsel car and the failure of American women to accept the skirt-length dictates of fashion designers. Besides these, there are thousands of cases that show that consumers can exercise their control over the marketplace. The fact is that many modern businesses are aware of this and monitor the marketplace closely. Close monitoring makes it possible for these firms to react to changes in tastes so quickly that major failures can be avoided.

Good marketing information systems, then, although they are expensive to maintain, often protect the business firm from the serious penalties associated with ignorance of current events in the consumer market. Procter and Gamble, one of the more successful marketers in the world, has been keeping a close eye on its Pringle's Potato Chips. When sales levels did not meet original expectations, P&G did some marketing research and made changes both in product design and in advertising. They had to take steps to overcome a general consumer impression that the product was too uniform and that it was not as "natural" as the traditional potato chip. Advertising for many products now stresses the "natural" characteristics of the products because people today value "natural" qualities in food and personal care products.

Another indication of responsiveness to changing consumer values is Holiday Inns, Inc.'s approval of a proposal to build and operate a $55 million hotel-casino in Atlantic City, New Jersey. Holiday Inns, one of the more successful firms in America, has built its success on the ability to satisfy the tastes of most Americans who travel in the family car. Up to now it has been strictly a family-oriented business. By entering the hotel-casino business, Holiday Inns, Inc. shows it is aware of profound changes in American tastes. They feel Americans are sophisticated enough today to tolerate a casino associated with their familiar brand name. Holiday Inns, in other words, has digested the statistics we have referred to earlier in this chapter regarding family size, income distribution, and changing lifestyles, and has altered its product mix accordingly.

Source: Drawing by D. Fradon; © 1978 The New Yorker Magazine, Inc.

Businesses have also been keeping a close eye on the effects of the recent years of inflation upon spending. Researchers in Norwalk, Ohio in 1978 were asking people in this Ohio town their reactions to inflation. They concluded that inflation was not having much of an effect on the spending habits of the typical family. Instead, they found that it was spurring purchases of appliances and cars as a kind of hedge against inflation. For this reason housing demand also seems to have increased, even in the face of rising interest rates.

Such monitoring of customer reaction to a changing economic environment is an important part of business planning. Businesses must study, for example, how individuals and households behave in the face of growing inflation or the discovery of possible cancer danger in meat preservatives.

Whether and how much consumers save is also important for the business environment. For a healthy economy, a certain amount of sav-

THEN AND NOW

Government Debt

The founders of our nation were dedicated to the ideal of thrift. This was reflected in their approach to managing government. They believed that no government should spend more than it collected in taxes. Government debt, like personal debt, was to be avoided.

Today, our federal government often spends more than it collects in taxes. It has been doing this in almost every year during the past several decades. This apparently doesn't particularly concern the majority of our people as long as the national debt doesn't grow out of proportion to the Gross National Product. The reason is that today the typical American thinks borrowing is all right as long as we can "meet the notes."

There is some evidence of rising concern, however, in the passage of Proposition 13 in California and in the nationwide attempt to call a Constitutional Convention for the purpose of putting a limit on the national debt.

ing is needed. Unfortunately, as we saw in Chapter 10, the trend in the proportion of income which is saved in our country is down, and it has fallen far below that of other nations. The downward pressure on personal savings and the resulting drop in funds available for capital investment can be attributed to the following set of causes:

- the high rate of inflation
- easier consumer credit
- federal limits on interest rates paid by savings institutions
- high taxation of wealthy people who do most of the saving
- government shifts of income to poorer people who are most likely to spend

The capital shortage causes banks to raise interest charges to businesses, and, to some extent, it stimulates the influx of foreign investment in United States businesses and real estate.

Governmental and Group Influences

As individuals act through larger groups and institutions they create another set of pressures and environmental influences on business. The most important of these institutions is government, which "wears many hats" while influencing the environment of business.

Ours is one of the strongest and most flexible governmental systems ever created. Based on the Constitution, our federal government is divided into three branches—the executive, the legislative, and the judicial branches. Laws are passed by the legislative branch—the Senate and House of Representatives. The judicial branch—headed by the Supreme Court and including lower federal courts—interprets the laws in light of the Constitution. It does this to decide whether an act performed by a business or citizen is lawful. The executive branch, headed by the President, provides leadership in government, including the national defense and enforcement of the law. It also introduces legislation to Congress. We call this threefold allocation of authority in government the "separation of powers." Similar separations exist at the state level.

Government serves two primary needs of society. First, it limits individual behavior that is thought to be contrary to the public interest. It does this by passing laws and setting up a system of justice and law enforcement. Second, it provides means of doing certain tasks that people alone or in small groups could not perform very well. These include military defense, basic health and sanitation services, water and recreation systems, schools, and a host of other services desired by the great majority of citizens.

The Roles of Government

The modern roles of government with respect to business are many. Among these are its roles as

- competitor
- economic stabilizer
- regulator

The Role as Competitor

The two major political parties often differ on what government should do—how much it should regulate and how much it should compete with business. When a government "takes over" a service, it removes private business from that area of economic activity. The Tennessee Valley Authority (TVA), a major federal agency that produces electric power, as we have seen in Chapter 1, is an example of this. When the TVA was established (during the depression of the 1930s), private industry was unwilling to risk the investment needed to provide electricity to some rural parts of the South. Today, our railroad system is going through a period of change from a strictly private system to one that is subject to substantial federal support and control because of the inability of private enterprise to operate the railroads (particularly passenger service) at a profitable level.

For some years now the system of the National Railroad Passenger

Corporation (known as Amtrak) has operated most of the railroad passenger services in the United States. Lately it has been strongly criticized. Critics include Trailways and Greyhound, its private competitors, and the National Taxpayers Union, a private lobby against high government spending. The U.S. Department of Transportation has proposed large cutbacks in Amtrak trackage and service because of big deficits in its operation. There is also widespread criticism of the Postal Service; it is frequently compared unfavorably to its private competitors, such as United Parcel Service, Inc.

The government plays many roles with respect to business. As TVA or Amtrak, government is a competitor of private business. As the Small Business Administration, government is a supporter of private business. As a defense system, government is a customer of business. Government is also a regulator of business and a stabilizer of the economic environment of business.

The Role as Economic Stabilizer

Ever since the Great Depression of the 1930s, our government has assumed more responsibility for the nation's economic welfare and stability. President Franklin D. Roosevelt's program of legislation, "the New Deal," reflected a new kind of economic theory developed by John Maynard Keynes, a theory that suggested a strong economic role for government.

Two laws which most clearly reflect the decision to have government play a strong role in the economy are the Employment Act of 1946 and the Humphrey-Hawkins Full Employment Act of 1978. The former declared federal responsibility to promote full employment, maximum economic growth, and price stability. It created the Council of Economic Advisers to help the President reach these goals. The council and the President are required to present an annual economic report to the nation, describing the state of the economy and current government programs to deal with it.

The Humphrey-Hawkins Act declared similar goals concerning employment, growth, and price stability and added goals concerning a balanced federal budget and an improved balance of trade. This act also differed from the 1946 act in terms of emphasis on economy in government and of primary reliance on the private sector. It also required the Federal Reserve Board (see Chapter 10) to report twice a year on its monetary policies and their relationship to the goals of the act.

There are frequent complaints by business people about "undue government regulation and interference." But there is wide public support for a big economic role of the federal government in the business activity of the nation. No one really wants to risk another major depression. In fact, when a President has sponsored a bill to reduce government regulation, there is often as much opposition as support from business itself. The reason is that very often "one firm's regulation is another firm's protection." There has been, for example, strong opposition by truckers and some unions to efforts to reduce regulation of the trucking industry.

The Role as Regulator

Many kinds of business activities are affected by administrative law. Under this body of law, government officials—sometimes elected and sometimes appointed—act both as judges and as legislators. Some of the important administrative and regulatory agencies at the national level are described briefly in Table 17–1.

administrative law

The force of any agency is felt in several ways. Much is done by encouraging voluntary compliance to regulations. **Voluntary compliance means that the firm agrees to do what the agency advises without a hearing.** The Federal Trade Commission (FTC), for example, upon

voluntary compliance

TWO POINTS OF VIEW

The FTC Acts Against State Regulations

Beginning on July 3, when a new trade rule restricting the state regulation of the eyeglass industry takes effect, the FTC will be working to throw aside state laws that the agency feels act to the detriment of consumers.

This action represents an interesting confrontation between two levels of government, state and federal, both of which purport to represent society by placing restrictions upon private business decision-making. In this case, the federal agency is confronting representatives of industry as well as the state government.

In its first trade rule against a restrictive professional practice—the so-called eyeglass rule—the FTC will preempt laws in at least 40 states that prohibit, restrict or place burdensome specifications on the advertising of prescription eyeware or of eye examinations.

Whereas the FTC believes this action will improve the state of competition, it is not strange that private professional groups disagree, nor that state governments resent what they consider to be federal intervention in matters traditionally left to the states.

Source: *Business Week.*

TABLE 17-1

Some important administrative and regulatory agencies

Agency	Major purpose
Interstate Commerce Commission (ICC), created in 1889	Created by the Interstate Commerce Act to regulate railroad rates. ICC jurisdiction extends to all forms of interstate public transportation with the exception of air carriers, pipelines for gas and water, and certain motor and water carriers operating in metropolitan areas.
Federal Trade Commission (FTC), created in 1914	Created by the Federal Trade Commission Act of 1914 to regulate unfair methods of competition and unfair or deceptive practices in interstate commerce, including false advertisements.
Federal Communications Commission (FCC), created in 1939	Created by the Communications Act of 1939 to regulate the broadcast media and communication carriers, including radio stations, telephone and telegraph companies, and, more recently, television broadcasting.
Securities and Exchange Commission (SEC), created in 1934	Created by the Securities Exchange Act of 1934 to oversee the operation of the securities exchanges and the issuance and sale of corporate securities.
Federal Power Commission (FPC), created in 1920	Created by the Federal Water Power Act of 1920, the Federal Power Commission controls the nation's water power resources and regulates interstate electric and natural gas utilities.
Food and Drug Administration (FDA), created in 1938	Created by the Food, Drug, and Cosmetic Act of 1938 to prohibit adulteration and misbranding of foods, drugs, devices, and cosmetics.
Equal Employment Opportunity Commission (EEOC), created in 1965	The Civil Rights Act of 1964 as amended by the Equal Opportunity Act of 1972 is the legal basis for the EEOC. This agency settles complaints of discrimination in employment because of alleged bias in hiring, upgrading, salaries, and other conditions of employment.
Environmental Protection Agency (EPA), created in 1970	Created by the National Environmental Policy Act of 1970 to set standards for and to enforce standards of quality in air, water, and other environmental elements.
National Highway Traffic Safety Administration (NHTSA), created in 1970	Created by the Highway Safety Act to improve the safety performance of motor vehicles, drivers and pedestrians. The Administration also publishes mandatory fuel economy standards for automobiles since the 1978 model year.
Occupational Safety and Health Administration (OSHA), created in 1971	Created by the Occupational Safety and Health Act to assure every working man and woman in the nation as safe and as healthful working conditions as possible.
Consumer Product Safety Commission (CPSC), created in 1972	Created by the Consumer Products Safety Act to protect the public against unreasonable risks of injury from consumer products. It also helps consumers evaluate products for safety, develops uniform safety standards and researches the causes and prevention of product-related deaths, illnesses, and injuries.

request of a firm, provides an advisory opinion on a particular practice. This clarifies for a business whether what it is doing is lawful.

The Federal Trade Commission also issues trade practice rules and trade regulation rules. The former are developed in conference with representatives of an industry and are purely advisory. The latter can be used to bring a case against an alleged violator. The trade regulation rules are published and available to all competitors.

Once cases are instituted, the FTC will often settle informally if a firm agrees to discontinue a practice. If not, the FTC makes a formal complaint about the unfair method of competition or deceptive or monopolistic practice. **The firm may (this occurs in 80 percent of the cases) sign a consent order. This is an agreement to "cease and desist" a practice.** It avoids the need for further action by the commission. If the firm refuses to stop, a public hearing before an FTC examiner is held. The examiner reviews the facts and makes a decision which, in turn, may be reviewed by the full commission.

consent order

Whenever a firm has reason to believe that the agency has issued an erroneous order (one that does not accurately interpret the law under which the agency operates), that firm may bring the case before the appropriate Federal Circuit Court of Appeals and even to the U.S. Supreme Court.

Recently, some agencies have been attacked on the grounds that they are dominated by the industries they are supposed to regulate. The whole system of regulatory agencies has been questioned. Until it is changed, however, it remains an important reality for business managers.

What Does the Law Expect of Business?

There are hundreds of ways in which today's businesses are affected by the law. We'll look at several such areas with an emphasis on law at the national level. We'll see that the law expects firms

- to compete
- to provide tax revenues
- to serve the consumer fairly

The Requirement of Competition

Influenced by the economic theory of Adam Smith, the policy of our nation toward business for more than a century was one of laissez faire, "hands off." Over time, it became obvious that laws were needed to keep business competing. Otherwise, one or several large businesses could take over and ruin competition in an industry. Such laws are called antitrust laws. (See Table 17–2.) **Antitrust laws are laws that try to get**

antitrust laws

firms to compete against each other. Unfortunately, there has never been a very clear agreement in Congress, in the courts, or among business people on how to define competition.

How well antitrust laws work is a tough question to answer. They place a big burden on many firms. This is because firms have to get involved in frequent legal battles. They also often lead to inefficiency. At

TABLE 17-2

Major antitrust laws

Legislation and date	Major purpose
Sherman Antitrust Act of 1890	The first of the general antitrust laws. It prohibits "every contract . . . or conspiracy in restraint of trade or commerce among the several states, or with foreign nations . . ." and names as illegal any act that monopolizes or attempts to monopolize any part of trade or commerce. The Antitrust Division of the U.S. Department of Justice enforces this act. Violation of the major provisions of the Sherman Act is subject to criminal penalties, including fines and prison terms. More common is the use of civil suits and "consent orders."
Clayton Act of 1914	Prohibits price discrimination, specific anticompetitive devices including tying contracts, interlocking directorates, and stock acquisitions that might substantially lessen competition.
Robinson-Patman Act of 1936: An Amendment to the Clayton Act	Updates and makes more explicit the price discrimination portion of the Clayton Act. Makes it illegal in interstate commerce to discriminate in price between different purchasers of commodities of like grade and quality or where the effect is to create a monopoly or injure competition for either the buyer or seller. This act also rules out certain specific forms of price discrimination such as disproportionate allowances for advertising and certain "commissions."
Celler-Kefauver Act of 1950: An Amendment to the Clayton Act	Substantially reduces the likelihood of monopoly in an industry by means of asset-acquisition merger. Since 1950, if the FTC thinks that the acquisition of the stock or assets of one firm by another "may be substantially to lessen competition in any line of commerce in any section of the country," it may exercise its power to prevent it.
Federal Trade Commission Act of 1914	Created a commission to consist of five members appointed by the President with the consent of the Senate. The commission was authorized to prevent persons and corporations, with the exception of banks and common carriers, "from using unfair methods of competition in commerce." If the commission finds after investigation that any person or corporation has engaged in any form of unfair competition prohibited by this act, the commission publishes a report of its findings and orders the offending party "to cease and desist from using such methods of competition."
Wheeler-Lea Act of 1938: An Amendment to the FTC Act	Declares unlawful "unfair methods of competition in commerce, and unfair or deceptive acts or practices in commerce." False advertising is illegal if the article will injure the health when used as advertised or if the advertising was made with the intent to defraud or mislead the purchaser.

the same time, however, many experts agree that they have helped to slow down or avoid the growth of monopoly power in some industries.

An experiment in improving antitrust enforcement has been tried recently in New England and in other areas. Under the New England program residents in five states can use a toll-free telephone number to let Justice Department attorneys know about suspected antitrust violations. Similar hotlines have also been established in Pittsburgh and Denver. The Pittsburgh hotline generated numerous antitrust complaints and led to several criminal and civil investigations into suspected antitrust violations.

THINK ABOUT IT!

Costs of Regulation

> Willard C. Butcher, president of Chase Manhattan Bank, reports the following:
>
> > In 1977 alone, according to our research, government regulation cost us more than $100 billion. In terms everyone can understand, $100 billion equals:
> > - $470 for each person living in the U.S.
> > - 5% of the gross national product.
> > - 25% of the entire federal budget.
> > - Nearly three-quarters of the annual private investment in plant and equipment.
>
> **THINK ABOUT IT!**

Source: *Business Week.*

Business as Taxpayer

Our Constitution gives the federal government taxing power in order to pay debts, provide for defense, and promote the general welfare. These three expense categories still dominate the budget. Figure 17–8 shows average income sources and outlays for the seven-year period from 1970 to 1976 and the estimates of the same data for 1980. National defense has dropped from 32 percent to 24 percent of total outlays, while income security has increased from 29 percent to 31 percent. Health, education, and employment programs have increased from 13 percent to 17 percent, while interest on the national debt is up from 7 percent to 8 percent of all outlays.

In recent decades the major source of federal government revenue has been income tax. The federal income tax generated about 58 percent of the federal government's revenue in 1980, 44 percent from individuals and 14 percent from corporations. The current income tax law provides for progressive rates on the incomes of individuals and corporations. Corporations pay about one-fourth of all federal income tax.

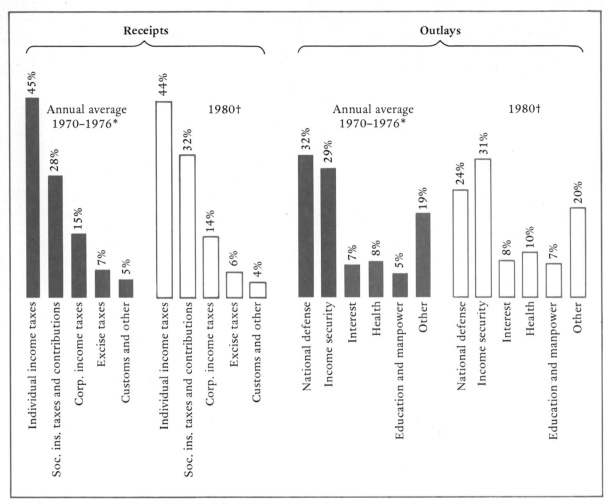

FIGURE 17-8

Source: U.S. Office of Management and Budget.

The annual federal budget, 1970–1976 and 1980

progressive tax

regressive tax

Additional income taxes are also levied by a majority of state governments and an increasing number of cities. **A progressive tax makes richer people pay a higher percent of their income than poorer people. The federal income tax is an example.**

Altogether, state governments rely most on sales taxes and next on gasoline and income taxes for their revenues. Cities most commonly use general property taxes and sales taxes. The latter are regressive. **A regressive tax means that poorer people pay a higher percent of their income than richer people.**

Businesses, labor unions, consumer groups, the poor, and many others demand government services. These services must be paid for with taxes. Taxes are compulsory payments. There is much controversy about their purposes and the best way to levy them.

Rarely does anyone feel happy about taxes. This is especially true of business owners. They spend large sums to find legal ways to avoid taxes and to influence the content and/or the final passage of new tax laws.

In the last few years we have witnessed in some states a large-scale taxpayers' revolt. The strength of the antitax movement was first made known in California with the passage of Proposition 13 in 1978. The proposition to cut back substantially on taxes in that state was overwhelmingly passed in a popular vote. The people were willing to cut back on state and local services in order to get tax relief. This feeling was demonstrated again in other states and in the campaign pledges of candidates for Congress and governor since that time. There is much talk of further tax cuts on a national level. Proposals include substitution of a value-added tax on the production of products for present high social security taxes and for some of the federal income tax.

We will discuss the question of the obligations of business to consumers in the next section of this chapter.

Other Groups and Institutions

Part of the environment of business created by society originates with informal and formal groups who conceive of themselves as spokespersons for society or a large part of it. These pressure groups sometimes deal directly with business and sometimes through government by lobbying. An important part of this effort is the consumer movement.

Consumerism

Concern for consumer welfare has become an important cause several times in American history. It usually developed during economic depressions when people were especially careful about spending. In the past it was never as big a movement in this country as it was in the Scandinavian countries or in Canada. However, in recent years the U.S. consumer movement has become strong.

Whatever the underlying cause, the success of modern consumerism has been sparked most by one man, Ralph Nader. Since his 1965 publication of a carefully researched study on the Corvair automobile, *Unsafe at Any Speed*, Nader has been the best-known consumer crusader. His efforts led to the passage of five consumer protection laws in the period of 1966 to 1968 alone. They are the National Traffic and Motor Vehicle Safety Act of 1966, the Wholesome Meat Act of 1967, and three laws in 1968—The National Gas Pipeline Safety Act, the Radiation Control for Health and Safety Act, and the Wholesome Poultry Products Act.

Nader and other consumer advocates also helped to pass the Fair Packaging and Labeling Act in 1966 and the Consumer Credit Protection Act in 1968. One law sets minimal standards to ensure more accurate labeling and informative packaging of most "kitchen and bathroom" consumer products. The other law requires disclosure of annual rates of finance charges on loans and installment sales in dollars and cents as well as in percentages. It also restricts garnishment of wages by creditors. (Garnishment means a creditor uses the courts to get employers to deduct the indebtedness of an employee from his or her pay and give it to the creditor.)

An important new consumer advocate group, the American Council on Science and Health, has been labeled a rival of Ralph Nader's organization. The new group sees as its purpose the study of controversial health issues independent of political interests. It hopes to provide the public with a balanced view of nutrition and health-hazard questions involving consumer products. Some see the entry of this group into the consumer movement as bringing more conservative thinking into it. It is considered to be somewhat more objective in its view of the food and drug industry than the Nader group has shown itself to be in some instances.

Another experienced consumer group is the Consumers Union. The Consumers Union publishes *Consumer Reports,* a monthly magazine that reports on the quality, safety, and dependability of products and has the power to influence the success or failure of many firms. Readers of this publication, mostly educated middle-class people, are often swayed by it when they make product decisions. A 1978 issue of *Consumer Reports,* for example, appears to have affected sales of two Chrysler Corporation cars, the Omni and the Horizon, by criticizing the steering mechanism of the current models and by describing them as unacceptable. Chrysler Corporation immediately challenged the validity of the Consumers Union tests and findings, pointing out that a federal inspection agency had previously judged the automobiles to be safe. Subsequent review by Consumers Union led to withdrawal of its objections to the steering mechanism.

Two government agencies established in response to consumerist and environmentalist movements in past years are the National Highway Traffic Safety Administration and the Environmental Protection Agency (see Table 17–1). They have been at the heart of a variety of problems recently facing the auto and tire industries because they have pressured these industries to recall millions of products. In the period 1977–1978 these two agencies have been involved in the recall of more than 35 million vehicles (many from all of the major United States car makers) for safety or pollution-related defects. The Firestone Tire and Rubber Company lost millions when it recalled a large percentage of its steel-

"What a clear unspoiled stream! . . . You can read the labels on the beer cans!"

Source: *Dunagin's People*, Field Newspaper Syndicate.

belted radial tires produced in the years 1976–1977. This very expensive kind of government-consumerist pressure is expected to force these industries to adopt stricter in-house product quality and safety standards.

Recent consumer laws differ from earlier laws in that the new laws cover a wider range of industries. The breadth of public support is greater these days, too. It suggests that more and stronger consumer laws are on the way. FTC hearings in the 1970s hinted that stronger control of advertising claims would be adopted. This could have important effects on marketing methods.

The 1975 FTC ruling relating to retailers who sell their accounts or notes receivable to other firms is an important step for consumers. It permits a dissatisfied purchaser to stop payments on a product to force satisfaction of his or her claim even though the note is held by someone other than the original seller.

Other Action Groups

Over the years, special interest groups of all kinds have worked directly and through government to affect the decisions of business. Among these are the National Association for the Advancement of Colored People, the Southern Christian Leadership Conference, and the Urban League in the field of minority rights. They have acted to bring about racial integration of retail stores as well as schools and have pressured for higher proportions of minority employees in all levels of jobs and industries, especially in higher-ranking positions. These efforts, as we saw in Chapter 12, have been backed up by the Equal Employment Opportunity Commission and other federal agencies.

Women's groups, such as the National Organization of Women (NOW), have performed similar functions for women. NOW and other feminist groups are pressing for state endorsement of the Equal Rights Amendment, which would further strengthen the position of women in business as well as in other aspects of American life. Spanish-heritage citizens and American Indians have also formed groups to put pressure on firms to improve employment opportunity for their particular ethnic groups. All of these groups have become instruments by which society can affect business decisions.

How Business Affects Society

The way that business views its responsibility to society is a major factor determining the kind of interaction there is between these two forces. We can distinguish two kinds of ethics for business.

The Traditional Business Ethic

Two of the obvious ways that business has always affected society are by creating employment and by producing useful products and services. Most people agree that these are the basic responsibilities of business to society. Under our modified capitalistic system, as we saw in Chapters 1 and 2, businesses take risks by investing in plants and equipment. They do this mainly to make profit, but in the process they create jobs.

This function of business in society is a basic part of the traditional economic theory of capitalism. Job-creation is an important by-product of the motive for profit which underlines capitalist risk taking. **The traditional business ethic, then, says that business owes it to society only to seek profit. In so doing it creates jobs and produces products and services.** This position has dominated our business climate for many decades. It is still supported widely by associations such as the Chamber of Commerce of the United States, and most small and medium-sized firms still feel pretty much this way. This ethic usually also calls for minimum government control of business, and it serves the interest of the business's owners or stockholders almost exclusively. It also tends to favor protective tariffs for American products. All in all, it is rather conservative and is in sharp contrast to the professional-managerial ethic (see Figure 17–9).

traditional business ethic

Traditional business ethic	Professional-managerial ethic
1. Maximum profits	1. Satisfactory long-term profits; other values are weighed
2. Minimum government control	2. Government-business "partnership"
3. Protectionism	3. Internationalism
4. Stockholder-oriented	4. Serves several masters including stockholders, customers, citizens, and employees

FIGURE 17-9

Comparing the assumptions of two ethics in business

The Professional-Managerial Ethic

professional-managerial ethic

The professional-managerial ethic[2] has become accepted in recent years by an increasing number of the largest corporations. It holds that managers represent the interests of stockholders, customers, employees, and the general public. Decisions are weighed in terms of longer-range company welfare, not immediate profit. Also, it is assumed that usually what is good for the employees and the general public is good for the company. For example, a firm that participates voluntarily in training and hiring the disadvantaged may not expect increased profits to result in the next year or two. However, the firm may expect that such activity will pay off in the long run. The society gains, and a stable, healthy society is presumed to have long-run beneficial effects on the firm. There are also indirect benefits in the form of good public relations from such activities.

Another important part of this ethic is the belief in a cooperative partnership relationship between business and government instead of the traditional hostility. This thinking fosters business participation in solving social problems.

The Changing Responsibility of Business

Business's attitude toward its social responsibility has changed dramatically in recent years. As we saw in the preceding section, the prevailing ethic among large businesses has shifted from the traditional view that the only responsibility to society is that which springs from the profit motive to the broader professional-managerial ethic which recognizes social obligations. One of the more interesting and promising views of the role of today's business as a social problem solver is that of the public-private partnership.

public-private partnership

The Committee for Economic Development (CED) has made a good case for a public-private partnership to attack the problem of finding jobs for the hard-to-employ. This activity can take many forms but it means drawing on the special experience of private businesses, unions, and community organizations to join with government in solving social problems such as finding jobs for the hard-to-employ.[3]

The program for jobs recommended by the CED says that

- the private sector should be involved more than before
- already-working job and training programs in the private sector

---

[2] This professional-managerial ethic is described in a booklet published by the Committee for Economic Development, *Social Responsibility of Business Corporations* (New York: Committee for Economic Development, 1971).

[3] *Jobs for the Hard to Employ: New Directions for a Public-Private Partnership* (New York: Committee for Economic Development, 1978).

should be described and the methods of training made known to all businesses
- tax breaks and other incentives should be given by the government to participating firms
- jobs and training should be stressed rather than pay for not working
- skill upgrading and work sharing should be substituted for outright layoffs in recessions
- management and operations of the U.S. Employment Service and CETA should be improved
- an "in-between" organization to do the paperwork and counseling would make private firms more willing to get involved in training

There are many success stories in such cooperative programs. Chicago United is an organization made up of 20 large firms and 20 minority group firms and organizations formed to handle all on-the-job training programs in Chicago. In Oak Ridge, Tennessee there is a training and technology workshop run by Union Carbide and a group of colleges. The National Manpower Institute in conjunction with major firms has formed a "school-to-work transition network." These examples show that public-private partnerships can work.

Summary and Look Ahead

The impact of society upon business is at least as great as the impact of business upon society. We have seen that this influence is exercised directly by individuals and by groups of individuals as well as through governmental action.

The dynamic changes in the lifestyle, the birthrate, the income distribution, and the tastes of people in the United States have many effects upon decision making in business firms. Firms must respond to the smaller families, working wives, and more outspoken and confident minority workers and customers.

Government acts as a competitor, as a regulator, and as an economic stabilizer. In each case it has important effects on private firms. The federal government through its laws and law enforcement practices expects business to compete, to provide tax revenues, and to serve the consumer fairly. The Federal Trade Commission and newer agencies such as EPA and OSHA lead many firms to complain bitterly of overregulation. Business has also complained about excessive taxation by governments at the federal, state, and local levels.

There are many pressure groups or lobbies which also have an impact on the environment of business. These include consumerist groups, such as those led by Ralph Nader, and special-interest groups in the fields of civil rights and pollution problems.

Business can approach society in two ways. The traditional ethic says it must provide jobs and goods but no more than that. The professional-managerial ethic says it must incorporate social needs into its responsibility. Many feel that the proper solution to social ills is found through a public-private partnership.

In the final chapter we will project some of the environmental trends discussed in this chapter and see how they relate to your future career. We will also give you some tips concerning selecting a career and job-hunting.

YOUR CAREER AND CONTINUING YOUR EDUCATION

No one ever stops learning. There are always higher goals to reach and further education is often the key. If your present plans are to take a full-time job after two years at a community college, give some thought to getting the bachelor's degree. The general rule is, the more formal education you have, the greater your career potential. Even more important is the fact that more education leaves you with more job alternatives to choose from. You are more flexible that way. Talk to your favorite instructor about programs available in nearby four-year colleges.

If you are already in a four-year college, the chances are that your diploma is still a few years away, but it is never too early to think in terms of the master's degree or even the doctorate. There are several colleges and universities in each state that offer the Master of Business Administration (MBA) degree. Thousands of young people and many people of all ages who have returned to school, or who are studying evenings while they work, are getting their MBAs.

The MBA generally gives broad advanced training to students, usually with some quantitative or scientific management component; it usually takes one or two years of college work beyond the bachelor's degree. It leads people into responsible managerial or junior executive positions with excellent chances of advancement.

The doctorate [either a Ph.D. (Doctor of Philosophy) in Business or a DBA (Doctor of Business Administration)] requires two or three additional years of study with some specialization. It generally leads to a teaching position or, sometimes, to a research job in industry. It is not unusual to move from the doctorate to a line executive position in industry.

Even if you don't go for a degree beyond what you are working on now, you should think in terms of continuing your education in some way. Perhaps an occasional evening course on an interesting topic will be sufficient. Continuing to learn means continuing your growth as a human being.

Key Concepts

administrative law A body of law under which administrative officials (for example, the FTC) act as judges and legislators.

antitrust laws Laws designed to maintain competition, including the Sherman Act and the Clayton Act.

consent order An agreement by a firm to stop doing something that a regulatory agency has found to be illegal.

environment All the outside factors that may influence the behavior or success or an organization. In the case of business we include the social, legal, economic, technological, political, and ethical factors influencing business decision making.

multiearner family Families in which two or more persons, usually husband and wife, are regular contributors to family support.

net annual household formation Number of households formed minus the number disbanded or ended by death.

professional-managerial ethic The position that

corporate managers represent the interests of stockholders, employees, and the general public.

progressive tax A tax that taxes higher incomes at a higher rate.

public-private partnership A collaboration between government and business to solve social problems.

regressive tax A tax that places a relatively greater burden on the poor than on the wealthy (like a sales tax).

traditional business ethic The view that decisions depend only on anticipated effects on profit for the owners of the firm and that profitability should be counted in the short run.

voluntary compliance Arrangements by which businesses whose activities conflict with existing regulations agree to change their behavior without the need for formal action by an agency.

zero population growth (ZPG) Stabilized population level. This term also refers to a movement to achieve a stabilized population level.

For Review . . .

1. What is an environment? Give an example.
2. Describe the "separation of powers" in the United States government.
3. What has happened to the number of births in the United States since 1960? What explains the recent rise?
4. What are some of the possible effects of the lower *rate* of births?

5. Give an example of the federal government's role as a competitor of business.
6. What did the Employment Act of 1946 do to the role of government in the economy?
7. Describe the way the FTC deals with an antitrust case.
8. What proportion of total federal tax revenue is paid by corporations? Review from Chapter 3

the tax disadvantages of the corporate form of ownership.

9. What is the significance of Proposition 13 as far as the future of taxation is concerned?

10. Give two examples of consumerist impact on specific corporations in the last eight years.

11. Describe in your own words the traditional business ethic.

12. Can a public-private partnership solve social problems? Give an example.

... For Discussion

1. What are the marketing implications of the multiearner family?

2. If the United States goes below ZPG in 1985, what will happen to the workforce in 2005 and how will this affect personnel policies of that period?

3. Discuss both sides of the argument regarding the regulation of business in regard to pollution control.

4. Should corporate shareholders be subjected to "double" income taxation?

5. Why does consumerism exist at the same time that firms practice the marketing concept (see Chapter 7)?

6. Which of the two business ethics most nearly reflects the "Protestant ethic" and why?

Incidents

Access to Employee Health Records

"The Occupational Safety and Health Administration is proposing a rule that would overturn the widespread industry practice of withholding from employees their medical records and data on their exposure to workplace hazard. The rule's broad language has already aroused concern about protecting the confidentiality of such files and is likely to spur debate over OSHA's authority to insist on worker access to them."

Questions

1. What are the basic rights of the employees here?
2. Do they conflict with the rights of the employer?
3. How could the rule affect the profitability of the employer?

Source: *Business Week.*

More Women As Business Owners?

Fewer than one out of twenty businesses in the United States are owned by women and these represent less than 1 percent of business sales. These facts were discovered in 1978 by a task force reporting to President Carter. The President's task force recommended that the federal government set up programs to encourage women's business ownership, to train women for business management and entrepreneurship, and to make certain that there is no financing discrimination against women owners.

Questions

1. Are such recommendations necessary in today's business environment? Explain.
2. If the recommendations are enacted into law, how will banks be affected? How about corporate board membership?
3. What role can women now pursuing business studies play in seeing that this imbalance is corrected?

Source: *The Wall Street Journal.*

ROCKETOY COMPANY 9

Rocketoy has become a mature firm with nationwide distribution as well as substantial export sales. It has 5 percent of the national toy market and is the third largest producer. Recently it has begun to feel the effects of two major environmental developments.

The legal department has recently received a visit from a federal regulatory agency. The agency claims that laboratory tests have confirmed that six Rocketoy products, representing 20 percent of last year's sales, do not meet newly established safety standards. The agency has asked that Rocketoy voluntarily remove them from the market. Present inventories of these toys are valued at $80,000.

An unrelated but equally disturbing report concerns new technological developments in plastics production. Fibertron Corp. has recently patented a new plastic that makes obsolete the material presently used by Rocketoy in half of its products. It is lighter, more durable, and less expensive. Fibertron is one of Rocketoy's major competitors and is unlikely to lease patent rights.

These two developments have caused serious doubts about Rocketoy's profit performance in the next year. Julia Rabinovitz, still active in management, has plans to bring a major complaint to the next meeting of the board of directors. She will charge that Terry Phillips is not capable of dealing with problems of the type that have come up. She will call for the removal of Phillips on the grounds that he does not seem to understand the importance of a first-class legal staff and a research and development department.

Questions

1. How could Rocketoy have avoided the conflict over product safety?
2. What action do you suggest with respect to the agency request? Why?
3. What kinds of information would you need to evaluate the new plastic's impact on Rocketoy profits next year?
4. What lesson does this episode teach about the relationship between environmental factors and management decisions?
5. Would you support Julia in her effort? Why or why not?

Your Career in Tomorrow's Business

CHAPTER 18

Objectives: After reading this chapter, you should be able to

1. Point out at least two trends that will probably affect the business careers you are thinking of.
2. Distinguish between positive and negative effects of each of these trends.
3. Summarize the general employment outlook for major classes of jobs (blue-collar, white-collar, etc.).
4. Name four industries that are growing.
5. Find two general and two specific sources of job information.
6. Draw up your personal job evaluation formula.
7. Write and evaluate your own personal résumé.
8. Fill out a job application form completely.
9. Write a letter of inquiry for a job.

Key concepts: Look for these terms as you read the chapter

normalization	career values
nationalism	letter of inquiry

We have studied a great deal about today's business world. We have studied management and how managers plan, organize, staff, direct, and control profit-making businesses. We have seen that businesses take resources—materials, machines, money, and, most important of all, men and women—and produce goods and services to sell in a free market. We have also studied the three functional areas of business—production, marketing, and finance. We have seen how they relate to each other in the profit-seeking process of business.

In all of this we tried to show how important the environment is. The social, cultural, economic, technological, and political–legal aspects of the environment all say something to decision makers in business. They affect what can be sold, how it can be produced, and how it can be financed. The manager must be sensitive to the environment in the present and must respond to change in it.

Institutions and people must adapt to new realities. You are no exception. In a few years you may be playing a major role in the business world, possibly as a manager. Your business world will be different from the one described in this book. It will contain many of the same things, but it will also have many new features that will come about during the course of your career. You will grow and change, too. You must grow and change so that you can meet the future on even terms.

It is not easy to predict change, but since your career is in the future, you should start doing some thinking about what the future business world will be like.

Although we can't really predict the future, there are three things this chapter will provide to help you prepare for it. First, we will review some of the most important environmental trends on the assumption that "the seeds of the future lie in the present." Second, we will examine some forecasts of industrial growth and how these affect your prospects for a job in various industries and lines of work. Finally, we'll get down to your encounter with the job market and how to prepare for it.

Some Trends That Will Affect Business and Your Career in It

Seven noticeable trends are having an effect on the business world now, and it seems that they will continue to have an effect in the future. These trends are

1. greater leisure and technology
2. increasing assertion of women's rights
3. longer life spans
4. adjustment to a peacetime economy
5. permanent inflation
6. energy shifts
7. new international realities

Some of our comments are little more than "educated guesses" as far as the future is concerned. You should study them critically.

Leisure and Technology

Advancing technology is cutting down the amount of physical labor and increasing the amount of "brain" labor in the world of work. This is true in business, too. Computers provide the best example. Even a simple mechanical skill such as typing is changing as typewriters become more and more automated. This underlines the need for special training and education in tomorrow's job market. It also suggests that working hours may become shorter and vacations will become longer. The improvements in technology, together with a rising minimum wage, are leading to shorter working hours and slowing the growth in the number of jobs for young people in some industries already, notably in the fast-foods industry. In this $80 billion industry employee hours were going down despite the fact that business was up. These firms compensated for reduced labor input by, for example, substituting individual packets for sugar bowls and pots of liquid creamer or by increasing the use of other self-service features. Further means of reducing labor input can be anticipated.

More leisure, of course, means more jobs in leisure and recreation-oriented businesses. The spectacular rise of discos is an example. This industry is reputed to have grossed $4 billion in 1977 and was growing rapidly. This could mean many new jobs, but the disco business is also a case of substituting technology (stereo systems) for live musicians.

Other leisure-time pursuits involve greater use of human services, such as formal restaurants, hotels, ski lodges, resorts, music or dance lessons, and a wide range of continuing education programs. The growth of these leisure-related industries suggests that this is one of the sectors in the economy in which you may find employment.

A related trend which is progressing slowly is the idea of a four-day work week. A survey by the University of Michigan shows that more than half of manufacturers surveyed think that the four-day work week will be in effect some time in the 1980s. This, of course, could lead to an increase in travel and the travel-related industries. It could also lead more workers to hold two jobs, including one during the "long weekend."

Women's Rights

Especially if you are a woman, today's struggle for women's rights will affect your future in business. This struggle, together with strong government support of equal treatment for the sexes, will mean greater opportunity for women. Higher-paying supervisory and technical jobs, previously thought of as strictly for men, are opening up to women. So are a large number of blue-collar jobs. The United States Labor Department, for example, is setting guidelines for federal contract-holders to encourage an increase in female participation in construction jobs previously held exclusively by men.

Law schools, medical schools, and business schools report a major increase in the percentage of female students. What represents greater opportunity for women may mean tougher competition for men in the job market. It will have a strong effect on family lifestyles and the ways in which some businesses will be conducted. Male secretaries and fe-

Source: Elizabeth Hamlin.

male production supervisors may become commonplace. This takes cultural adjustment, but it is happening.

Longer Lives and Employment

There is a clear trend toward longer lives in America. (See Figure 18–1.) Not only are people living longer but their later years are becoming healthier and more active because of higher incomes and Medicare. The elderly are organizing to put political and economic pressure on businesses. One of their main goals has been to combat the trend toward early retirement. They want to keep their jobs longer. In a sense, then, senior citizens are competing for jobs against you and other younger entrants into the job market. The antidiscrimination movement has already resulted in better treatment for elderly job seekers. Recent changes in the Age Discrimination in Employment Act of 1967 have made it possible for people to postpone retirement past age 65 if they want to do so. The changes prohibit employers of 20 workers or more from forcing workers to retire before age 70 if they are capable of performing their jobs.

There are other by-products of the trend toward longer lives. For example, the construction industry will need to answer the demand for

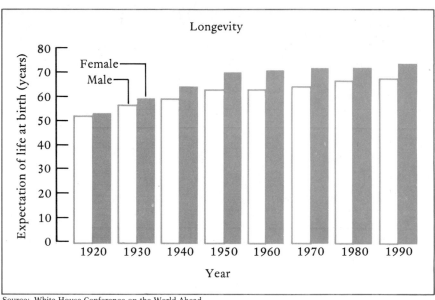

FIGURE 18-1

Longevity of life in the United States

Source: White House Conference on the World Ahead.

new types of housing to meet the needs of older people. Growing elderly markets are already resulting in the use of older persons in ads and more careful marketing treatment of this important group of the population. Anticipating longer retirement periods, workers and their unions will probably emphasize better retirement plans when they negotiate collective bargaining agreements.

Adjustment to a Peacetime Economy

Advances in technology depend to a large extent on development of weapons systems by the Department of Defense. In other words, there is a significant "spill over" of technology—originally made possible by the huge defense budget—into nonmilitary applications by private industry. This, in turn, means that a large part of business in our society has depended on the military for its existence and growth. Peacetime brings demands for reductions in such spending, and defense contractors need to convert to nonmilitary production. An important example is the aerospace industry. Fortunately, American commercial jet producers have profited from the boom in air travel which followed the air travel rate reductions and deregulation of airlines. Jet producers have added to or replaced their military aircraft contracts in this manner, and many new jobs in the aircraft/aerospace industries are the result.

Since the end of the war in Vietnam, there has been a sentiment in the United States against war. In the last 10 years there has also been a "thawing" of the cold war between the United States and both the Soviet Union and the People's Republic of China. There is progress toward normalization of relations with these traditional foes. **Normalization is a process by which two previously hostile nations establish better relations. This includes communications and trade.** This would mean reduced tension and better prospects for trade. The progress in establishing diplomatic relations and business ties with mainland China during 1978 and 1979 is indicative of very important new trade opportunities in the Far East. For those United States industries that produce products needed in China, a period of growth lies ahead.

normalization

This fact, together with the growth of serious problems at home, has led to a shifting of expenditures in the federal budget. A greater part of the talent and physical resources of our nation will be devoted to the solution of domestic problems such as urban blight, the energy shortage, and ecology.

Of course, this means that certain firms will suffer. In fact, some will disappear because of the change in national priorities. It also means that many people will lose their jobs in industries that are downgraded and they will have to find work elsewhere. Many workers will have to be retrained to find employment in a peacetime industry. The most far-sighted producers of military material are already partially shifting into peacetime production. This means some protection for them against further military cutbacks. We are testing the theory that our economy can prosper without war.

Political events are difficult to predict. Despite general improvement in U.S. relations with the Communist powers, there is recurrent evidence of the traditional hostility. Discovery of Soviet troops in Cuba, for example, could easily set back SALT and other hopes for better, more peaceful relations.

Inflation as a Way of Life?

The recent history of prices in our country (see Figure 18–2) shows that since the middle sixties there has been a change in the "typical" annual rate of inflation in prices consumers pay. During the period 1960–1965, inflation rates of 1 to 2 percent prevailed. From 1966 to 1972 the rate of price increase ranged between 3 and 6 percent. Between 1973 and 1978 the rate ranged between 6 and 11 percent, hitting 9 percent or more for three of those years. It was even higher in 1979.

Inflation has become bad enough that Americans rank it as the most serious problem facing the nation, one that just won't seem to go away. What does this mean to business today and tomorrow? It is beginning to have some major effects. One that we have touched upon previously is the tendency to reduce saving which, in turn, presents problems of insufficient capital accumulation for investment. This gets at the very

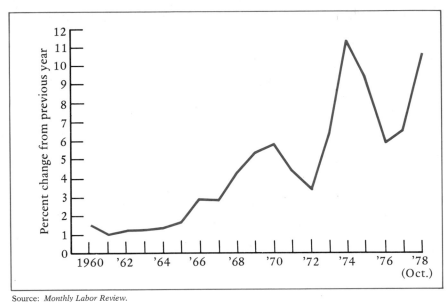

FIGURE 18-2

Percent change in consumer price index, 1960–1978

Source: *Monthly Labor Review.*

"We need some voluntary controls with more force!"

Source: *Dunagin's People,* Field Newspaper Syndicate.

heart of our economic growth rate. The decline in savings, together with skyrocketing real estate prices, threatens the rate of home building and even the very tradition of private home ownership for many young families.

A second effect is a greater strain on labor-management relations. President Carter has attempted to set maximum wage and price increase guidelines, but reports of high profits and continued price rises caused labor to reject the guidelines in the course of collective bargaining. Who will yield first? It's very much like the arms race.

Still another effect relates to accounting processes. What does a balance sheet really mean when it includes some assets bought years ago (at low cost prices) and others bought recently (at high cost prices)? Often, then, the current value of a firm's assets is grossly understated. Profit calculations on the income statement are also distorted under conditions of rapid inflation. Radical changes in traditional accounting are being tried and they may finally alter traditional accounting practice.

Energy Shifts

For the last several years, our newspapers have reported the story of the petroleum shortage. You know of the efforts of this nation to become independent of foreign sources of oil. The most obvious task facing industry is to find new sources of energy to satisfy our needs for industrial growth and for household use.

In the petroleum industry this means expansion of exploration for new oil fields and better ways of getting more oil from existing fields. In the coal mining industry this means a spectacular boom. Our nation has a large part of the world's supply of coal, so it's natural that we should turn to coal to meet our energy needs. Recent federal action requires that many new power plants be fueled by coal and that there be limits placed on natural gas consumption in existing plants. This kind of legal limitation speeds up conversion to coal.

The principal problems with coal usage relate to ecology and the transportation of this heavy, bulky fuel. Burning coal can dump large amounts of poisonous wastes into the air. Some mining techniques create serious health problems for miners, and others are said to threaten the ecology of some western states. The demand for energy is so great that we are tempted to overlook the bad ecological side effects. We are also, of course, working to improve coal burning systems so as to reduce their bad effect on the air. Federal loans for financing coal pollution safeguards are being made to power plants and manufacturing firms that convert to coal. Plants in gas- and oil-producing states are not happy about the conversion, partly because of the high transportation and storage costs involved.

The energy shortage is also creating vast research programs in the field of solar energy, nuclear energy, geothermal energy, and others. In the case of nuclear energy, the possible harmful side effects of disposing

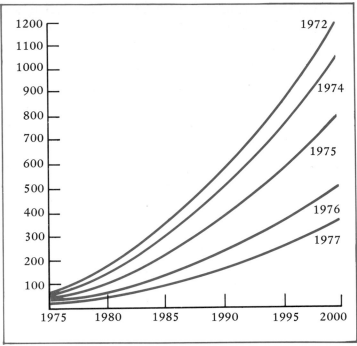

Source: *Congressional Quarterly.*

FIGURE 18-3

Nuclear power growth estimates

of nuclear wastes are slowing down its development. (See Figure 18–3.) Despite this problem, it seems likely that the future will show greater dependence on coal and nuclear fuel and less on petroleum. We are stepping up solar energy research because of its advantages in terms of ecology. California is subsidizing the installation of certain types of solar energy systems. Federal tax advantages may also lead to heavier reliance on the sun for future energy needs. Which way we turn for energy will affect your future in business.

New International Realities

The pressure put on the advanced industrial nations by the small oil-producing nations of the Middle East has started to change the relationship between the advanced and the underdeveloped countries of the world.

Some underdeveloped countries possess large amounts of the world's vital resources. After seeing the success of the Arab oil countries, it is possible that certain Latin American and African nations will threaten to withhold their vital raw materials. They would hope to gain greater political and economic power in the world and a higher standard of living for their people.

Such actions could lead to changes in the way we do business in this country. In the first place, it could lead to efforts to produce substitutes for an increasing number of raw materials. It could eventually mean that many people in these deprived nations will begin to be able to afford to buy manufactured goods from the United States and Europe. This, in turn, could tend to reduce world tension.

For still others of the underdeveloped nations there is little hope of economic improvement. Instead, there is a strong possibility of more hunger and starvation unless rapid progress is made in population control. This will mean the constant need to export agricultural surpluses from the United States and Canada to these sometimes starving nations without any promise of a long-term solution to the food problem. Western businesses and farmers may benefit from exporting goods and medical supplies to these nations, but this may require great amounts of economic aid voted by our Congress.

The growing number and power of small, underdeveloped nations in the United Nations has already led to at least one proposal which will have a direct bearing on corporations doing business in more than one country. The UN's Commission on Transnational Corporations has proposed a plan requiring extensive reporting by such corporations regarding finances, pricing, investment, and other operational facts to the United Nations. There is even a proposal for expanded "social accounting" reports. This "auditing" could lead to slower growth of multinational firms.

There is a growing spirit of nationalism in smaller, less-developed countries. **Nationalism is a strong feeling of pride and independence among the people of a country.** It has sometimes resulted in large-scale takeovers of the American-owned plants and distribution centers in these smaller nations. This movement has caused American firms to be much more cautious about foreign investments. Many such foreign operations today are almost completely staffed by local people rather than by North Americans, and some are co-owned by local governments and investing firms.

Another changing reality lies in the growth of foreign ownership in the United States as we have already seen in Chapter 16. The advanced nations of Europe, the oil-rich Middle-Eastern nations, and Japan have all joined the rush to invest in American industry and land. Many businesspeople are alarmed at the rate of such investment. Japanese firms in the United States (see Figure 18–4) are buying into everything from aircraft to zippers. Locations range from Alaska to Georgia and from New Jersey to California. This new international reality is not strange, considering the "bargains" created by the drop in the value of the dollar and considering the relative stability of the United States as a place to invest. This trend means you may well find a career in a firm

nationalism

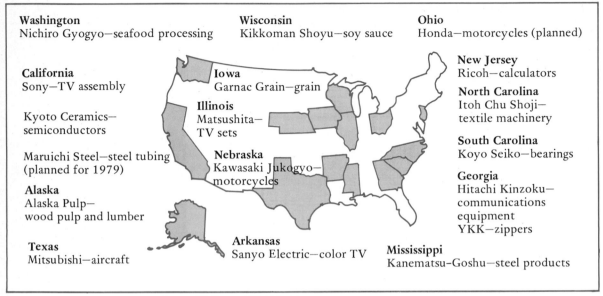

Source: *U.S. News and World Report.*

FIGURE 18-4

Japanese firms in the United States

which is American but which is, at the same time, owned by Japanese or French or Saudi Arabian investors.

From this review of some likely areas of change for business, we turn to the role you will have in the changing business world. We hope the guidance that we offer will help you make some important decisions.

Choosing a Career

As we have just seen, the business world of tomorrow will be vastly different. The pace of change is expected to be rapid. In a matter of decades whole new industries will arise because of new inventions and because of changes in resources and lifestyles. This can be a source of confusion for you, but it has its very definite positive aspect. A dynamic business world is a healthy business world. If nothing were to change, the future world would be a familiar one, but it would also provide very little opportunity. You should be optimistic and you should begin to plan for the business career that lies ahead of you.

What you will be doing in the business world depends on

- job market conditions
- what you have to offer
- how well you present your talents to potential employers

We will examine each of these factors.

The Job Marketplace

There are at least two ways to examine the marketplace for jobs. One way is to look at the market for individual occupations (regardless of the industry in which it is found). Another is to check out the projected growth of whole industries in which jobs may be available. Which way you choose should depend on how clear your ideas are about a career and on the "career values" you have established.

By career values we mean those things that you feel are important in selecting a career. You may, for example, value living in a certain place or dealing with the public or using your artistic talent or having the opportunity to rise rapidly in an organization. It may be that you are excited about working in a particular industry like the communications industry but haven't decided on the specific job you want in that industry. On the other hand, you may have a clear idea about the kind of work you want to do (for example, accounting), but you don't care much about the specific industry.

career values

The Department of Labor is a good source of information about the job market. It makes frequent analyses of the job outlook. Data from a recent study are presented in Figure 18–5. The figure shows expected growth rates of employment in major job classes to 1985. Figure 18–6 shows how many openings are expected to become available in these

FIGURE 18-5

Expected employment growth in the United States, 1976–1985

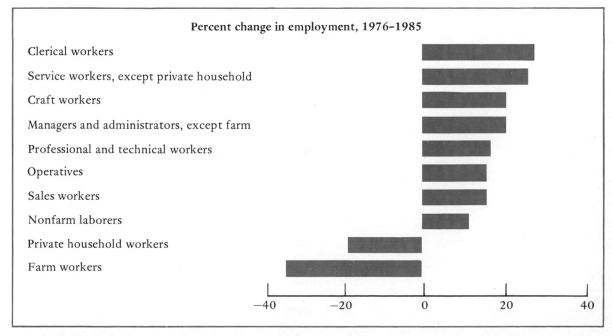

Source: Bureau of Labor Statistics.

TABLE 18-1

Estimated 1974 employment, projected 1985 requirements, and average annual openings, by occupation, 1974–1985

jobs by 1985. This includes new, "growth" jobs and replacements for persons who have left the labor force.

There will be more than 40 million job openings between 1976 and 1985, well over half of which are in white-collar jobs. Of these, 10 million are clerical jobs, 3 million are sales jobs, 5 million are for managers and administrators, and more than 6 million are in professional-technical jobs. Clerical, service, and professional-technical openings are growing at the highest rates. In nearly every job category, the number of new (growth-related) jobs is exceeded by the number of jobs to open because of retirements, etc. (replacements).

Figure 18–6 shows that the greatest growth is expected in white-collar jobs. These jobs are found in all kinds of businesses, but they are especially important in finance, insurance, real estate, service industries, trade, and transportation. These jobs include accountants, salespeople, bank tellers, secretaries, and the various professions.

FIGURE 18-6

Job openings due to replacement and growth, 1976–1985

More specific analysis is provided in Table 18–1. It shows estimated employment in 1974, projected requirements in 1985, and annual average openings in specific jobs for which business education and training

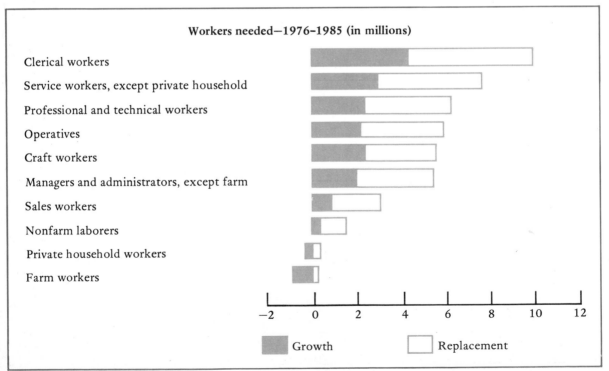

Source: Bureau of Labor Statistics.

Occupation	Estimated employment 1974	Projected requirements 1985	Percent change 1974–1985	Annual average openings 1974–1985		
				Total	Employment change	Replacement needs
Sales occupations						
Automobile parts counterworkers	75,000	96,000	27.5	3,500	1,900	1,600
Automobile salesworkers	130,000	160,000	25.5	5,500	2,900	2,500
Automobile service advisors	20,000	28,000	21.3	800	450	350
Gasoline service station attendants	450,000	525,000	16.3	12,700	6,700	6,000
Insurance agents and brokers	470,000	536,000	15.0	19,400	6,400	13,000
Manufacturers' salesworkers	380,000	387,000	2.4	9,500	800	8,700
Real estate salesworkers and brokers	400,000	480,000	21.8	28,500	7,800	20,700
Retail trade salesworkers	2,800,000	3,175,000	15.1	190,000	38,000	152,000
Route drivers	190,000	200,000	4.1	3,700	700	3,000
Securities salesworkers	100,000	130,000	31.9	6,100	2,900	3,200
Wholesale trade salesworkers	770,000	883,000	15.0	30,000	10,000	20,000
Office occupations						
Clerical occupations						
Bookkeepers	1,700,000	1,875,000	10.9	121,000	17,000	104,000
Cashiers	1,111,000	1,340,000	20.6	97,000	21,000	76,000
File clerks	275,000	320,000	15.9	25,000	4,000	21,000
Hotel front office clerks	54,000	63,000	17.3	4,250	850	3,400
Office machine operators	170,000	190,000	13.1	12,800	2,100	10,700
Postal clerks	293,000	302,000	3.1	9,700	800	8,900
Receptionists	460,000	635,000	38.3	57,500	16,000	41,500
Secretaries and stenographers	3,300,000	4,860,000	47.8	439,000	142,500	296,500
Shipping and receiving clerks	465,000	560,000	20.4	20,500	8,700	11,800
Statistical clerks	325,000	375,000	15.8	23,000	4,500	18,500
Stock clerks	490,000	610,000	25.0	26,000	11,000	15,000
Typists	1,000,000	1,400,000	34.9	125,000	33,000	92,000
Computer and related occupations						
Computer operating personnel	500,000	545,000	10.1	27,500	4,500	23,000
Programers	200,000	285,000	42.5	13,000	7,800	5,200
Systems analysts	115,000	190,000	65.2	9,100	7,000	2,100
Banking occupations						
Bank clerks	517,000	718,000	38.9	54,000	18,000	36,000
Bank officers	240,000	333,000	38.9	16,000	8,500	7,500
Bank tellers	270,000	377,000	38.9	30,000	10,000	20,000
Insurance occupations						
Actuaries	10,700	14,400	34.1	700	350	350
Claim representatives	125,000	152,000	21.8	6,600	2,500	4,100
Insurance agents, brokers and underwriters	470,000	536,000	15.0	19,400	6,400	13,000
Administrative and related occupations						
Accountants	805,000	995,000	23.9	45,500	17,500	28,000
Buyers	110,000	150,000	37.6	9,000	4,000	5,000
City managers	2,900	4,200	47.4	150	100	50
Credit managers	66,000	90,000	36.4	4,500	2,200	2,300
Hotel managers and assistants	120,000	150,000	22.8	6,500	2,500	4,000
Lawyers	342,000	490,000	43.3	26,400	13,500	12,900
Personnel and labor relations workers	320,000	450,000	40.2	23,000	12,000	11,000
Public relations workers	100,000	134,000	28.8	6,500	2,300	4,200
Purchasing agents	189,000	258,000	36.5	11,700	6,300	5,400
Urban planners	13,000	18,000	38.5	700	450	250

Source: Bureau of Labor Statistics.

are needed. For example, it projects an annual demand for more than 45,000 accountants, 13,000 computer programers, and 5,500 automobile salesworkers. What about the demand for the kind of career you have in mind?

From what you have learned about markets you know that future demand is not the only factor to examine. It is also necessary to think about the future supply. These two factors will determine the general level of wages in an occupation and how hard it is to get a certain type of job. The Department of Labor has made projections of the supply of people trained for most occupations. It is a good idea to consult the statistics released by the Labor Department in order to get a feel for the future marketplace for the job or jobs you are interested in.

You may wish to get statistics on a particular job market from trade or professional associations such as the American Marketing Associa-

TABLE 18-2

Business-related occupations

Clerical occupations	Administrative and related occupations
Bookkeepers	Accountants
Cashiers	Advertising workers
Collection workers	Buyers
File clerks	City managers
Hotel front office clerks	College student personnel
Office machine operators	workers
Postal clerks	Credit managers
Receptionists	Hotel managers and assistants
Shipping and receiving clerks	Industrial traffic managers
Statistical clerks	Marketing research workers
Stock clerks	Personnel and labor relations
Stenographers and secretaries	workers
Typists	Public relations workers
	Purchasing agents
Computer and related occupations	Sales occupations
Computer operating personnel	Auto parts counterworkers
Programers	Auto salesworkers
Systems analysts	Auto service advisors
	Gasoline service station
Banking occupations	attendants
Bank clerks	Insurance agents and brokers
Bank officers and managers	Models
Bank tellers	Manufacturers salesworkers
	Real estate agents and brokers
Insurance occupations	Retail trade salesworkers
Actuaries	Route drivers
Claims representatives	Travel agents
Underwriters	Securities salesworkers
	Wholesale trade salesworkers

Source: *Occupational Outlook Handbook.*

tion or the American Bankers Association. Some state departments of labor or state departments of commerce and industry also have current job market statistics.

Of course, statistics don't present a complete picture. You will also want to know something about these jobs—expected earnings, working conditions, advancement, etc. A good start in finding such information is available in another Labor Department publication, the *Occupational Outlook Handbook*. The latest edition of this publication should be available in the library. It provides a comprehensive survey of job opportunities, so it's definitely worth checking out. It reports for each job

- the nature of work
- the places of employment
- advancement, training, and other qualifications needed
- employment outlook
- earnings and working conditions
- additional information sources

Of particular interest to students of business are the listings under the general headings of office occupations and sales occupations. These occupations are listed in Table 18–2 and a complete example of such a listing is shown in Figure 18–7.

FIGURE 18-7

Occupational Outlook Handbook **listing**

CREDIT MANAGERS

(D.O.T. 168.168)

Nature of the Work

Both businesses and individuals may require credit (the postponement of payment until a future date) to meet their daily needs for a variety of goods and services. For most forms of credit, a credit manager has final authority to accept or reject a credit application.

In extending credit to a business (commercial credit), the credit manager, or an assistant, analyzes detailed financial reports submitted by the applicant, interviews a representative of the company about its management, and reviews credit agency reports to determine the firm's record in repaying debts. The manager also checks at banks where the company has deposits or previously was granted credit. In extending credit to individuals (consumer credit), detailed financial reports usually are not available. The credit man-

ager must rely more on personal interviews, credit bureaus, and banks to provide information about the person applying for credit.

Particularly in large organizations, executive level credit managers are responsible for formulating a credit policy. They must establish financial standards to be met by applicants and thereby determine the amount of risk that their company will accept when offering its products or services for sale on credit. Managers usually cooperate with the sales department in developing a credit policy liberal enough to allow the company's sales to increase and yet strict enough to deny credit to customers whose ability to repay their debts is questionable. Many credit managers establish office procedures and supervise workers who gather information, analyze facts, and perform general office duties in a credit department; they include application clerks, collection workers, bookkeepers, and secretaries.

In smaller companies that handle a limited number of accounts, credit managers may do

FIGURE 18-7 (continued)

much of the work of granting credit themselves. They may interview applicants, analyze the information gained in the interview, and make the final approval. They frequently must contact customers who are unable or refuse to pay their debts. They do this through writing, telephoning, or personal contact. If these attempts at collection fail, credit managers may refer the account to a collection agency or assign an attorney to take legal action.

Places of Employment

About 53,000 persons worked as credit managers in 1976. About one-half were employed in wholesale and retail trade, but many others, about one-third of the total, worked for manufacturing firms and financial institutions.

Although credit is granted throughout the United States, most credit managers work in urban areas where many financial and business establishments are located.

Training, Other Qualifications, and Advancement

A college degree is becoming increasingly important for entry level jobs in credit management. Employers usually seek persons who have majored in business administration, economics, or accounting, but may also hire graduates holding liberal arts degrees. Some employers promote high school graduates to credit manager positions if they have experience in credit collection or processing credit information.

Newly hired workers normally begin as management trainees and work under the guidance of more experienced personnel in the credit department. Here they gain a thorough understanding of the company's credit procedures and policies. They may analyze previous credit transactions to learn how to recognize which applicants should prove to be good customers. Trainees also learn to deal with credit bureaus, banks, and other businesses that can provide information on the past credit dealings of their customers.

Many formal training programs are available through the educational branches of the associa-

tions that serve the credit and finance field. This training includes home study, college and university programs, and special instruction to improve beginners' skills and keep experienced credit managers aware of new developments in their field.

A person interested in a career as a credit manager should be able to analyze detailed information and draw valid conclusions based on this analysis. Because it is necessary to maintain good customer relationships, a pleasant personality and the ability to speak and write effectively also are characteristics of the successful credit manager.

The work performed by credit managers allows them to become familiar with almost every phase of their company's business. Highly qualified and experienced managers can advance to top-level executive positions. However, in small and medium-sized companies, such opportunities are limited.

Employment Outlook

Through the mid-1980's employment is expected to grow more slowly than the average for all occupations. Despite this relatively slow growth, many jobs will become available each year due to the need to replace persons who leave the occupation. Although there will be opportunities throughout the country, employment prospects should continue to be best for well-qualified jobseekers in metropolitan areas.

The volume of credit extended rose very rapidly during the past decade. In the years ahead, businesses can be expected to require increasing amounts of credit to secure raw materials for production and obtain finished goods for eventual resale. It is in the area of business credit where demand for credit managers will be strong.

Consumers, whose personal incomes have risen, are expected to finance greater numbers of high-priced items. In addition, the use of credit for everyday purchases is expected to grow as demand increases for recreation and household goods as well as for consumer services. Despite increases in consumer debt, the use of computers

FIGURE 18-7 (continued)

for storing and retrieving information will enable this greater volume of information to be processed more efficiently. The use of telecommunications networks enables retail outlets to have immediate access to a central credit office, regardless of distance.

Another factor that is expected to slow the growth in the number of credit managers is the increased use of bank credit cards. As stores substitute bank credit cards for their own charge accounts, credit departments may be reduced or eliminated.

Earnings and Working Conditions

In 1976, credit manager trainees who had a college degree earned annual salaries that ranged from about $10,000 to $11,000, depending on the type of employer and the geographic location of the job.

Assistant credit managers averaged about $12,000 to $14,000 a year and credit managers had average earnings of about $17,000. Individuals in top-level positions often earn over $40,000 a year.

Credit managers normally work the standard workweek of their company—35–40 hours, but some work longer hours. In wholesale and retail trade, for example, a seasonal increase in credit sales can produce a greater work volume. Some credit managers attend conferences sponsored by industry and professional organizations where managers meet to develop and discuss new techniques for the management of a credit department.

Sources of Additional Information

Information about a career in consumer credit may be obtained from:

International Consumer Credit Association, 375 Jackson Ave., St. Louis, Mo. 63130.
National Consumer Finance Association, 1000 16th St. NW., Washington, D.C. 20036.

For information about training programs available in commercial credit, write:

National Association of Credit Management, 475 Park Ave. South, New York, N.Y. 10016.

Source: *Occupational Outlook Handbook.*

When you refer to the *Occupational Outlook Handbook* or the *Encyclopedia of Careers and Vocational Guidance*[1] you should be careful to note the date of publication. This is important because it does not take long for the supply or the demand to change. Also, it is possible that in the particular city or area you may be looking at, the job market is quite different from the national average. Population growth or new industries could mean that a given city or area has jobs open in most occupations. On the other hand, the recent closing of a large plant or a slump in tourism for a resort city could have the opposite effect.

The Future of Specific Industries

The *Occupational Outlook Handbook* also provides a rather detailed analysis of 37 major industries. For each of the industries listed in Table 18–3 it provides information about the nature and location of each industry, the occupations found in each, employment outlook, and a vari-

[1] William E. Hopke, ed. (Chicago, Illinois: J.G. Ferguson Publishing Company, 1978).

TABLE 18-3

Industries analyzed for opportunity

Agriculture	Textile mill products
Coal mining	Civil aviation
Petroleum and natural gas production*	Electric power
Construction*	Merchant marine
Aircraft, missile, and spacecraft*	Radio-TV broadcasting
Aluminum manufacturing	Railroads
Apparel	Telephone
Baking	Trucking
Drug manufacturing	Restaurants*
Electronics	Retail food stores
Foundries	Banking*
Industrial chemical manufacturing	Insurance
Iron and steel	Hotels
Logging and lumber mills	Laundry and dry cleaning
Motor vehicles and equipment	Federal civilian employment
Nuclear energy*	State and local government*
Office machine and computer*	Armed forces
Petroleum refining	Paper products manufacturing
Printing and publishing	

* Industries expected to have above-average growth into the 1980s.
Source: *Occupational Outlook Handbook.*

ety of job facts similar to those provided for individual occupations. It also gives sources of career information for specific industries. Some of the industries that are expected to have rapid growth into the 1980s are marked in Table 18–3 with a *.

Even more detail concerning prospects for specific industries is available in *U.S. Industrial Outlook,* published annually by the U.S. Department of Commerce. Major corporations and labor unions will also gladly provide you with industry and job information. For a complete list of job information sources, you might consult "Where To Go for Further Information" by Helen K. Wright in the *Encyclopedia of Careers and Vocational Guidance.*

Once you are well informed, you should begin to look at yourself. What kind of job are you best suited for?

You Are the Product

There are several ways of looking at the career selection process. Since we have been studying about markets and prices of products, why not look at yourself as a product that some business firm will "buy"? A good salesperson must know his or her product. You, then, must know your-self.

John W. Loughary and Theresa M. Ripley[2] have developed a very useful, methodical system for self-evaluation and understanding in preparation for job hunting. They recommend that the job-seeker use certain exercises to understand

- his or her evolving values
- abilities and skills
- interests as they relate to careers
- social issue attitudes
- influence of important others
- ability to identify and express feelings

What Do You Really Want Out of a Job?

A job will bring you great unhappiness and little chance for success if it conflicts with what you really are. You must, therefore, explore your own values and interests in life. What are the things that really are important to you? Do you like meeting people? Do you value security or free time or your hometown?

Career values are those things you really want to get out of a job. It may help you to examine the "Career Value Checklist" (Table 18–4). Look over each of these 10 questions carefully. Can you give yourself a pretty clear answer to each question? If so, you know yourself better than most college students do! You are in an excellent position to evaluate a specific job from the "interests" or "values" perspective. If you are

TABLE 18-4

Career value checklist

	YES	NO
1. Do you like meeting people?	☐	☐
2. Do you welcome responsibility?	☐	☐
3. Do you want a flexible work schedule?	☐	☐
4. Do you want to be your own boss?	☐	☐
5. Do you want security in your job?	☐	☐
6. Do you expect high starting pay?	☐	☐
7. Is rapid promotion potential important?	☐	☐
8. Is staying in your hometown important?	☐	☐
9. Do you want public recognition?	☐	☐
10. Do you want to retire before age 60?	☐	☐

[2] John W. Loughary and Theresa M. Ripley, *A Career Planning Program for College Students* (Chicago: Follett Publishing Company, 1978), pp. 9–28.

unsure of some answers, this is typical. You can still use this checklist to clarify your value system for a job choice.

First, try to rank the 10 questions in terms of their importance to you. You should be able to rank at least 6 or 7 of them. Once you've done this, then pick out several jobs you know something about and rate them in terms of the important job values you have chosen.[3] This process should help you to understand what a job means to your life in the ways that are important to you. It will also prepare you to make a final job choice.

Once you have checked this list, read the description of several of the jobs you are most seriously interested in. From the descriptions you should be able to tell which ones match up best with your "career values." Another big question besides your interests and values is your set of skills. How do they match the jobs you are considering?

What Are Your Skills?

Your skills and interests are usually closely related. You are more likely to be interested in those things in which you excel. If you had trouble learning the multiplication tables, you would not be interested in a statistician's job.

While some skills are very specifically related to a job, others are required of most jobs. A skill that is needed in most jobs, particularly as you move up in a company, is the human relations skill—the ability to communicate with others and to listen to and understand what they have to say. Another general skill is skill in organizing. If you have a knack for keeping things in order and putting them in perspective, there are many jobs in which this skill will prove valuable. More specific skills include skill in writing, skill in calculation, mechanical skills such as typing and shorthand, and skills relating to memory and precise observation.

Sometimes your physical characteristics, such as strength and appearance, are an asset or a handicap in getting a job. Consider your physical characteristics. Do they seem appropriate for the job you want? Sometimes a firm sets up physical specifications for a job applicant because of the demands of the position. Check to see if you meet these before you go too far in the job-seeking process. The descriptions in the *Occupational Outlook Handbook* will tell you which skills are needed in various jobs.

As a rough guide to the importance of various skills, traits, interests, values, etc., Figure 18–8 is worth examining. It shows how a group of 87 marketing/sales managers weighted a variety of factors in judging applicants for marketing jobs.

Up to this point we have shown how you can survey the general job

---

[3] The authors are indebted to Professor Robert S. Ristau of Eastern Michigan University for this idea as well as for several useful suggestions on the subject of career development.

Hiring criteria as seen by managers

Rank	Characteristic*	Variable	Mean score
1.	P	Maturity	3.68
2.	M	Personal selling/sales mgmt. skills	3.67
3.	P	Appearance	3.60
4.	P	Cooperativeness	3.54
5.	N	Communications/public speaking	3.45
6.	P	Disposition	3.34
7.	P	Punctuality	3.30
8.	P	Mannerisms	3.28
9.	M	General mktg. skills	3.21
10.	N	English/writing skills	3.14
11.	N	Management skills	2.89
12.	P	Extroversion	2.74
13.	S	Mktg. department reputation	2.60
14.	M	Product development/mgmt. skills	2.59
15.	N	Finance skills	2.55
16.	M	Market research skills	2.51
17.	M	Market logistics skills	2.49
18.	N	Personnel mgmt. skills	2.48
19.	O	Civic functions	2.48
20.	N	Mgmt. science skills	2.47
21.	M	Advertising/advtsg. mgmt. skills	2.45
22.	M	Consumer/industrial buyer behvr. skills	2.38
23.	S	School reputation	2.38
24.	M	Pricing skills	2.36
25.	N	Accounting skills	2.36
26.	S	Internship program	2.34
27.	O	Social functions	2.30
28.	S	Recruiting success w/school	2.21
29.	N	Internship training skills	2.19
30.	O	Sports participation	2.10
31.	M	Retailing/retail mgmt. skills	1.99
32.	O	Home hobbies	1.99
33.	O	Fraternal organizations	1.99
34.	N	Social sciences/arts skills	1.93

* **P**: Personal traits. **M**: Marketing skills. **N**: Nonmarketing skills. **S**: School reputation. **O**: Outside activities.

Source: *Marketing News.*

FIGURE 18-8

Hiring criteria as seen by managers

market to discover the occupations and industries that show promise for you. We have seen the importance of self-evaluation in terms of interest and competence. Now we turn to the process of finding a particular job.

Specific Job Search and Choice

You will probably have lots of advice—some you will ask for and some you will get without asking—about how to get a job. A bit more won't hurt, so we'd like to offer you a few tips about job hunting and the final decision.

Job Hunting

After making a general survey of opportunities and of yourself, you should start to narrow down the field. You must make a decision and carry it out.

Don't waste time with firms or jobs you are not actually interested in! To find out more about specific jobs, you can start by writing to the appropriate firm—either the personnel department or the department in which you want to work. You will be provided with general facts about the firm, job availability, wage scales, union status, how to apply for a job, and so on. You can supplement this by talking to employees in different industries and firms. They can tell you what it's really like to work in a certain job or in a certain firm.

FIGURE 18-9

Time-line for implementation plan

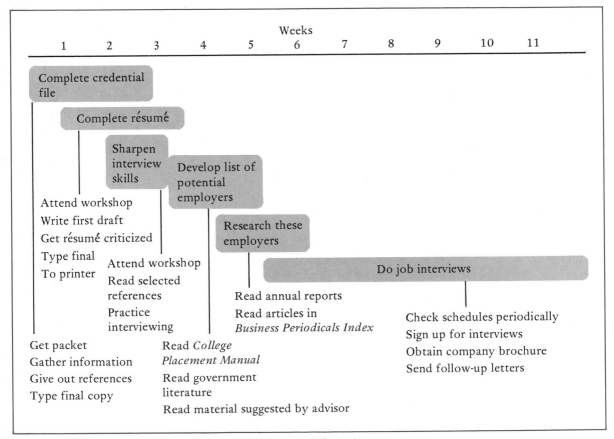

Source: Loughary and Ripley, *A Career Planning Program.*

Next, you should start checking for specific job openings. Your school's placement director will have good information about possible openings. He or she may have a schedule of employers coming to the campus for interviews. You should also visit the nearest state employment office. This agency can give you a quick overview of the job market and probably can give you a specific list of openings. The classified ads are also a good source of information.

The best opportunity may sometimes result from a frank "letter of inquiry." This is a letter you send to a firm asking about the possibility of getting a job. It may be that you already know they are looking for someone with your qualifications. In this case your letter should start with that information. Such a letter is presented in the Appendix. It is also possible to send letters to firms without knowing if they are "looking." In that type of letter you should stress your general interest in working for the firm and how you feel that your talents might best be used. Sometimes this brings surprising results.

letter of inquiry

For a more detailed treatment of the job search process, please examine the Appendix carefully. Loughary and Ripley have also developed a novel "time-line" for implementing the job hunt.[4] (See Figure 18–9.)

Making the Final Choice

If you are in a position to choose between or among job offers, it is wise to set up a practical system to reach a decision. To do this you need a standard, or set of values, to guide your choice. You will also need all the facts about each job. We have already discussed what you "want out of a job." These are the standards, or values. We assume you have gained the facts about each job from the job-search process.

A job-selection formula could look like Table 18–5. Assume that you have three jobs to choose from. These are labeled A, B, and C at the top of the three columns of Table 18–5. Assume further that you have honestly searched your values and that only five factors are important to you in choosing: your level of interest in the job itself; the starting pay; the opportunity for promotion; the prestige of the job; and the location. You have assigned relative importance, or weights, of 5, 3, 4, 2, and 1, respectively, to each of these five factors. This means that, for example, level of interest is five times as important to you as location and that promotion opportunity is twice as important as prestige. Assigning these weights will require some careful thought.

Next, you start to "rate" each job on a 1 to 10 scale according to each of your value factors. Table 18–5 shows your interest level in job A is

---

[4] Loughary and Ripley, *A Career Planning Program*, p. 63.

TABLE 18-5

A job selection formula illustrated

Directions:	Rate each job by each value factor on a 1 to 10 scale. Multiply scores by indicated weights and then total the products for each job.

Value Factors and Weights	Job A	Job B	Job C
Interest × 5 =	3 (15)	5 (25)	8 (40)
Starting pay × 3 =	4 (12)	8 (24)	7 (21)
Promotion opportunity × 4 =	5 (20)	9 (36)	6 (24)
Prestige × 2 =	10 (20)	6 (12)	8 (16)
Location × 1 =	3 (3)	4 (4)	10 (10)
Total score	70	101	111

Note: This concept was developed from suggestions offered by Professor Robert S. Ristau of Eastern Michigan University.

only rated 3, while your interest in job B is rated 5, and your interest in job C is rated 8. Since the weight, or importance, of the factor "interest level" is 5, you multiply the job ratings times 5 and score them 15, 25, and 40 in that order. (These scores are circled.) Next, you do the same in terms of the starting pay. In this case, job A rates a 4, job B an 8, and job C, a 7. Multiply these by 3—your "weight" for starting pay. The scores appear circled below the ratings. They are 12, 24, and 21. You do the same for the other value factors and add up the scores for each job—all the circled values in each column. The total scores in this illustration are 70, 101, and 111.

The results in Table 18–5 indicate that you should choose job C. However, since job B is so close, you might want to go through the process once more for jobs B and C. No formula is perfect, either. There may be something about one of these jobs that attracts you but you can't put your finger on it. It might be enough to make you select the "close second" choice according to the formula.

When You Start to Work

You may have noticed already that a successful career in school requires the ability to discipline yourself. You may sometimes "get by" because of a good memory or because of luck, but you will perform consistently well if you form good study habits, work at your studies on a regular schedule, and take every subject seriously. The payoff will be twofold. You will earn the best grades that your ability will allow. Also, you will be a much better potential employee because of what you have learned and, more important, because you have learned *how* to learn. The discipline, patience, and open-mindedness required to learn things well in school are exactly the same things you will need to learn and to grow in your job.

If you start showing these qualities from the very beginning in your job (by working overtime if necessary, volunteering for assignments, and doing your work thoroughly), your efforts will be rewarded. Patience, too, will help, because any time you go to work for a specific boss there will be occasions when "the boss's way" and the way you learned previously will differ. Personality conflicts, too, will arise. They will require patience and tact, but this does not mean that a new employee must be a doormat. It only means that you must present your views in a polite but confident way. It is wise to assume that when you are new on a job, the "old hand" probably does know more about how things should be done. In the long run, your ability, good judgment, and creativity will become apparent to your employer.

Promotion and Changing Jobs

Sometimes the best way to get a promotion is *not* to seek it. This may sound funny, but it is often true. The worker or manager who concentrates on doing the best possible job with what he or she is assigned doesn't have the time to be looking for a promotion. The football team that looks ahead to next week's big game instead of this week's may get beaten by an underdog team. This is especially true if the other team takes "one game at a time."

Let's assume that you have been doing everything that is expected of you and perhaps a little bit more. If so, the word is likely to spread that you "more than carry your weight." The next time a better job in the organization comes up, the chances are that your name will come up. While obvious attention paid to superiors can backfire, making their acquaintance can help your career. The key ingredient, of course, is doing quality work!

What about changing jobs? Recent estimates predict widespread and frequent occupational shifts for young people now entering the job market. It seems likely that by the year 2000 many of the kinds of jobs done today will no longer even exist!

**WHAT WOULD
YOU DO?**

**Leaving an
Employer for
Another Job**

> John Tatum took his first job with the Booker Company after graduating from college. The Booker Company is in the business of selling office machines.
>
> John is happy with his job. Mr. Booker, the owner of the firm, taught John the business from the ground up. But a big office machine manufacturer recently approached John with a job offer. The opening is in the sales department. The job is very appealing to John, but he feels that leaving Mr. Booker's firm would not be fair to Mr. Booker. WHAT WOULD YOU DO?

There are many reasons why you may need to change jobs during your lifetime. This can be caused by obsolescence, by government contract shifts, by the competition of imports, and by many other things. A wise person keeps a sharp eye for the kinds of events that can force a job change. He or she also keeps an eye out for opportunities. Otherwise, the time spent between jobs can be painful.

Two kinds of preparation for job changing can help. One is to stay as financially prepared as possible—to save something and to think ahead in terms of temporary "back-up" jobs you might take. The second, and more important, is to continue your education and training throughout your lifetime. This has the effect of broadening your skills and increasing your ability to adapt to new and different jobs. In a world of dynamic change, the future belongs to those who remain flexible.

A Final Word

You now have a taste of what the business world is like. It is such a huge and complicated set of industries and firms that it is almost impossible to describe adequately. Even if we could describe it well, you would still have to become a part of it to begin to really appreciate it. And even after you're in it for a while, you'll realize that because it's changing so rapidly, you'll never really learn all there is to know. You'll probably take other business courses in school that will concentrate on specific aspects of operating businesses to prepare you more completely for a specific job. They will also help you in choosing a career.

YOUR CAREER—COPING WITH CHANGE

In the first part of this chapter we outlined some of the important changes we think the future will bring. They suggest strongly that you will probably have more than one kind of job during your lifetime. This could be caused by competition, by new technology, by resource shortages, or by changes in you and your value system. In any case, you must prepare for changing employment.

Job changes can be hard to face unless you convince yourself that you can handle them when they come. Self-confidence, of course, doesn't do it alone. Your self-confidence must be solidly based. You should have trained yourself all along to react positively to change, to view it as an opportunity rather than a threat. Change is an opportunity for the man or woman who has learned how to learn in school and who does not take a narrow view of life. You may have a second and even a third or fourth career in your life. Each one can be more rewarding than the last for the broadly educated, flexible person.

No matter what you choose as a career, the essential ingredients will be flexibility and willingness to learn. At some time in your career, you may have to be completely retrained if your job becomes obsolete. This is one of the bad features of technical advance. This specific kind of insecurity can be overcome if you have the right attitude. Think of your education as a process of learning how to learn, learning to keep an open mind, and learning about the relationships between yourself and your environment.

Such an attitude toward your education will sharpen your appreciation of it. How you approach the rest of your college experience will set a pattern for your lifetime. You should make sure that it is a pattern that includes the appreciation of learning as a continuing and unending process.

Key Concepts

career values   Those factors that have an important effect upon the choice of a career or a job.

letter of inquiry   Letter sent to a possible employer to inquire about a job opportunity.

nationalism   A strong feeling of pride and independence within a nation. It is rising among many of the less-developed nations of the world.

normalization   A process by which two previously hostile nations establish better relations. This includes communications and trade.

For Review . . .

1. Give two examples of the influence of new technology on job availability.
2. Identify five specific jobs that have become available to women for the first time in the last 10 years.
3. How does the rise in mandatory retirement age affect job availability for young people?
4. What economic effects have resulted from the end to the Vietnam war?
5. Describe the major shifts in energy consumption that are occurring.
6. Why have firms from foreign nations invested in the United States?
7. What is meant by a career value? What are your own career values?
8. List your major strengths and weaknesses as they might relate to becoming an accountant. Do the same for what you hope to be five years from now.
9. Prepare a complete résumé for yourself as of today. Do the same for what you hope to be five years from now.
10. Look up in the *Occupational Outlook Handbook* the occupations of systems analyst and bank officer. What are the major differences between these jobs?

. . . For Discussion

1. What might happen to the economies of coal- and oil-producing states if a major shift to nuclear power occurred?
2. What are some of the factors that contribute to inflation? Which are controllable?
3. How can a resource shortage in the United States give political power to an underdeveloped country?
4. Is it logical to think of yourself as a "product" in the job marketplace?
5. Construct your own version of Table 18–5. Develop your own value factors and weights. How do they differ from the text example and why?

Incidents

A New China Trade Picture

One of the most exciting but, in some ways, troublesome events of recent years is the shift in American relations with the "two Chinas." When President Carter announced the shift in foreign policy which opened the door for broadening economic relations with the People's Republic of China (mainland China) and reduced support and recognition of the Chinese government in Taiwan, many new economic currents were set in motion.

For the short term, the decision has a very high risk attached, considering that U.S.–Taiwan trade in 1978 exceeded $7 billion while U.S.–mainland China trade was only about $1.3 billion in that year.

In addition, many large American firms have made heavy capital investments in Taiwan. There were more than 300 firms with over $600 million in plant investments there at the time of the policy change.

Questions

1. What do you think justifies such a great economic risk in the minds of our government leaders?
2. Does the fact that mainland China, despite its low level of economic development, has about one-fourth of the world's population have anything to do with it? Discuss.
3. What U.S. industries are most likely to be affected by this change? Discuss.

Source: *The New York Times.*

Leisa Flynn

Leisa Flynn until recently worked about 25 hours a week as a cashier at a Kentucky Fried Chicken restaurant while she was a student at a community college in Maryland. She just completed a two-year program in restaurant management. Her experience and training point to a career in the fast-food industry. However, a counselor at her college, noting her high IQ and outstanding performance in language classes, has advised her to get a four-year degree in languages and to consider graduate study.

Questions

1. What is the key unanswered question here?
2. What are the pros and cons concerning the counselor's advice to Leisa?
3. What kind of information does Leisa need and where can she get it?

ROCKETOY COMPANY 10

In recent months Rocketoy management began to feel that they were "losing touch" with the market. Even Terry Phillips was now in his fifties, and he was the youngest of the present members of top management. The board of directors had a conference with Terry and convinced him that it was time to find someone from the younger executive ranks to be promoted to a vice-presidency. Their idea was that, if the person chosen for this position were successful, he or she would succeed Terry to the presidency of the company within a year or two.

After an extensive search of all the divisions of Rocketoy, a selection committee decided upon Paula Devine. Paula had come to Rocketoy from a large department store five years ago. She had been a toy buyer for seven years before coming to Rocketoy as chief of product design. In her short career at Rocketoy, Paula had made quite a name for herself as a clever analyst of public taste in toys. She had been particularly successful with an idea for a new line of dolls. Her vision and willingness to experiment had brought in some entirely new market segments, including the teenage market.

Paula was named vice-president for development. She was given the charge to set up a "blue skies committee," which was expected to study changes in society and in technology and to translate such environmental change into new product policy for Rocketoy. Paula, now 33 years old, was ready to assume this challenge. Little did she think thirteen years before, when she graduated from junior college, that she would succeed as well as she had.

Questions

1. Give Paula some advice about choosing members of her "blue skies" team.
2. What changes in the environment do you think should enter into the new committee's planning?
3. Assuming you are a recent graduate of the same junior college Paula attended and you wanted to start a career as a junior designer at Rocketoy, what kind of letter of inquiry would you write to her? Write such a letter.
4. What are the pros and cons of following a career in the toy design department at Rocketoy? Discuss this from the point of view of a 23-year-old male graduate of a midwestern university engineering program and from the point of view of a 20-year-old black female with artistic talent who is just completing a two-year junior college program in art.

Student Data Sheets, Résumés, Letters of Inquiry, and Job Interviews

APPENDIX

In Chapter 18 we gave a general discussion of careers in business. The type of thinking you do about career opportunities is perhaps the most important type of analysis you will ever engage in. It affects your entire future lifestyle. Needless to say, you should approach this with a great deal of careful thought.

But there is a big difference between firming up your ideas about career opportunities and landing a job that is related to your career plans. In this Appendix we narrow our sights. We assume that you have some rather specific career choices in mind and are seeking employment.

Most of you will not be seeking a full-time job until after completing your studies. As a college student, however, you may be looking for a part-time job right now. Our discussion of student data sheets, résumés, letters of inquiry, and job interviews is helpful in getting both part-time and full-time jobs.

The Student Data Sheet

Many schools have on-campus services that can be helpful to you in career preparation. For example, many schools have a student testing and guidance counseling center that can help you formulate more concrete career plans. This can be very helpful in your choice of a major area of study.

The student placement office is another service offered by many schools. Placement office personnel can help you find a job in the career field of your choice. Find out what services are offered. The personnel there are trained to help you make a smooth and productive transition from student to employee.

Your student placement office schedules on-campus interviews with prospective employers. These employers (business firms, government agencies, and other organizations) send campus recruiters to interview students who are about to complete their courses of study. Later in this Appendix we will discuss in detail the mechanics of interviewing. At this point our main concern is the student data sheet.

A student data sheet (sometimes called a college interview form) is a form prepared by the student placement office and filled out by the students who sign up for campus interviews. All students who establish placement files in the placement office fill out this form. A campus interviewer, therefore, can examine this form for each student who signs up for an interview. Figure A–1 shows a student data sheet.

The Résumé

A résumé is a biographical summary of your education, experience, activities, interests, career goals, and so on. It contains much of the same type of data that the student data sheet contains. The major difference is that it is tailor-made by the person who is seeking employment.

Your student data sheet is put into your placement file in your school's placement office for inspection by employers who send campus interviewers to your school. But if you want to apply for a job with employers who do not recruit on your campus, you must prepare a résumé and mail it to them.

Preparing a good résumé takes a lot of effort and care. Personnel departments receive many job application letters and résumés each day from persons seeking jobs. A well-prepared résumé—one that is creative, neat, and complete—overshadows others that are poorly prepared, lacking in creativity, messy, and incomplete.

Usually, you will want to send your résumé to several employers.

COLLEGE / UNIVERSITY INTERVIEW FORM
(Do not include information where prohibited by law.)

UNIVERSITY OF NEW ORLEANS
CAREER PLANNING & PLACEMENT CNTR.
Lakefront, New Orleans, La. 70122

☐ Regular Employment   ☐ Other Employment

Personal Data

Name Last First Middle Initial	Social Security No.

Present Address (Street, City, State, ZIP)	Present Phone, Area Code	Check one: U.S. Citizen ☐
Permanent Address	Perm. Phone, Area Code	Permanent Resident ☐ / Student Visa ☐

Work Preference

Brief Statement of Job Interests and/or Description of Work Desired

Date Available for Employment	Geographical Preference	Geographical Objections

College Information

Name and Location of Colleges Attended	Dates (Mo./Yr.) From	To	Degree Earned or Expected	Grad. Date Month	Year	Academic Major	Other courses studied 15 or more hours.
	/	/					
	/	/					
	/	/					

Honors, Activities and Organizations

Employment Information

Employment and Business Experience (Include Permanent, Cooperative, Intern, Volunteer, Summer work and any prior U.S. military service.)

Work Experience (Name and Address of Employer)	Description of Work (Descriptive Title)	Hours per Week	Dates (Mo. Yr.) From	To
			/	/
			/	/
			/	/
			/	/

General Information

References: such as faculty members who know you well and past supervisors; name, title, business address and telephone number

Other Information: Community Activities, Hobbies, Interests, etc.

THE PLACEMENT CENTER HAS MY PERMISSION TO RELEASE MY PLACEMENT CREDENTIALS IN ENTIRETY TO PROSPECTIVE EMPLOYERS. THE PLACEMENT CENTER SHALL IN NO WAY BE RESPONSIBLE FOR THE CONTENTS OF ANY REFERENCES OR FOR ANY INFORMATION CONTAINED THEREIN.

SIGNATURE	DATE SIGNED

Source: University of New Orleans.

Unless you are going to prepare a different résumé for each employer or if you are going to type each employer's copy of the same résumé separately, you will face the problem of reproducing your résumé. Try to produce copies that are as clean and neat as the original.

Do not send carbon copies or poorly reproduced photocopies. Some methods of photo reproduction are acceptable as are some offset-printed methods. You can get help here from a professional reproduction service either on campus or off campus.

Style and Format

There is no one best style and format for a résumé. If you are interested in several career options, you may want to prepare several different styles and formats for different employers. Each résumé would be tailor-made to best appeal to each employer.

But there are several important guidelines for preparing your résumé. One is the "KISS" rule—keep it short and simple! Unless you have had a great deal of prior work experience, your résumé probably should not be longer than one typewritten page. To keep it short, do not use complete sentences. The reason is simple—personnel departments do not have unlimited time to devote to examining résumés.

Another good rule is to avoid creating a résumé that appears crowded. Don't try to squeeze too much on the page. You've probably seen ads in the classified section of newspapers that have a lot of "white space." The purpose is to draw attention to them. They stand out against a background of ads that are practically all "black space." Skillful use of white space in a résumé enables you to draw attention to important parts of your résumé. It also increases the chance that your résumé will be examined by the person to whom it is sent.

Look at your résumé as a type of promotional effort. Your task is to create interest in you as a prospective employee. Be honest, candid, and to the point.

Contents

Remember, you are working with a limited amount of space. You cannot tell all that you might want to tell. You must concentrate on or highlight your strongest points.

Work Experience

If you think that your major appeal is your previous work experience, then stress that experience. Of course, if you are a typical student, you won't have much to highlight here. But if you are an experienced worker, then highlight your experience.

In covering your work experience, list the last job you held first. Then work backward to your earliest job. If you held summer jobs while in school, list them. If you show that you worked for the same employer for several summers, this tells the person who examines your résumé that you performed well in your job. If you got a promotion, be sure to indicate that.

Extracurricular Activities

By all means, list your extracurricular activities. Membership in a collegiate chapter of a professional association, such as the American Marketing Association, shows that you are seriously interested in professional development. Membership in an honorary organization or society shows that you are a notch above the average. Membership in social organizations shows that you work well with others and are people-oriented. If you held an office in any of these organizations, list that also. This shows leadership ability. The same is true of honors and other types of recognition that you may have earned. In other words, try to give some insight into your interests and show how well rounded you are.

Grades

While your résumé is not the place to list each course you took and each grade you earned, you should give some indication regarding your overall grade-point average. You could do this by stating "average grades in courses outside major; very good grades in courses in major"; or by stating your specific grade point average—"3.2 out of a possible 4.0."

It's hard to say how much importance a given employer will place on grades. Some employers consider grades to be the most objective thing they have to go on in the case of a young prospect with little work experience. Some others, particularly in recent years, discount grades because they believe that grade inflation is widespread.

Your grade-point average, of course, is not the only thing that employers consider. An average grade point might look very impressive if you also were involved in on-campus activities and worked part-time. A high grade-point average might be less impressive if you did nothing else but kept your nose in a book the whole time you were in school.

References

Generally, it's a good idea to include the names, titles, and addresses of persons who are in a position to evaluate your performance as a student and/or employee. Get their permission to list them on your résumé. Do not list relatives or only friends. If you have reference letters in your file in your school's placement office, you might say that your references can be obtained from that source. Figure A–2 is a sample résumé.

FIGURE A-2

A sample résumé

```
                    RESUME FOR ALFRED JOHN POWELL
                   (Date Prepared:  April 15, 1980)


    Address:  3060 Avenue A, Apt. 21-C
              New Orleans, LA  70122 (to June 1, 1980)
    Telephone:  (504) 288-9543
    Home Address:  2106 Myrtle Avenue
                   St. Rose, LA  70090
    Home Telephone:  (504) 721-0810)
    Personal Data:  Age-21; Weight-175 pounds; Height-6'1";
                    Health-excellent

Education:
        B.S., Business Administration, University of New Orleans
        (1980).  Majored in marketing.  Overall grade point average of
        3.2 on 4.0 scale.  In major, 3.5.  Dean's list during my last
        two years.  I received a scholarship that paid 100 percent of
        my tuition during my last two years.  I worked during summer
        vacations and held other part-time jobs to pay 75 percent of
        my total expenses during my college career.
Career Goal:
        Salesperson, with ultimate goal to move into sales management
        or marketing management.
Extracurricular Activities:
        Treasurer, Collegiate Chapter (UNO), American Marketing Assoc.
        Chairperson, Bus. Student Advisory Council (to the Dean,
        College of B.A.)
        Member, Society for Advancement of Management
        Member, Sailing Team
        Representative, College of Business Administration
        Student Government Association
Work Experience:
        June 1, 1978 to present, Zeppo Electronics, Inc., New Orleans,
        LA.  Part-time salesperson.  Received outstanding part-time
        salesperson award for 1979.

        Summers, 1976 & 1977, Beta Retail Stereo Systems, Kenner, LA.
        Stock clerk.  Promoted to salesperson in June, 1977.
References:
        Mr. Donald Sykes, Director of Student Placement, University of
            New Orleans, New Orleans, LA  70122 (for references from my
            college professors).
        Mr. Anthony Pizzo, sales manager, Zeppo Electronics, Inc.,
            2001 Laramie Ave., New Orleans, LA  70111.
        Ms. Vera Callahan, owner, Beta Retail Stereo Systems, 7911
            Marcott St., Kenner, LA.  70031
```

Preparing Your Letter of Inquiry

After preparing your résumé, you should write a letter of inquiry. Both are mailed to employers with whom you are seeking employment.

Purposes

The basic purpose of a letter of inquiry is communication. You are trying to communicate in writing to the employer your interest in working for that employer. You want it to lead to communication from the employer regarding your prospects for a job.

Your letter must first of all get the employer's attention. Second, it should spark the employer's interest in you as a prospective employee. Third, it should motivate the employer to respond to your letter—by sending a job application form and/or contacting you to set up a preliminary employment interview.

When to Send One

There are two situations in which you might write a letter of inquiry. The first is in response to an employer's ad in a newspaper (or any other medium) seeking applicants for a job in which you are interested. In your letter you would refer to the ad and express your desire to apply for that job. In a sense, this type of letter is solicited (or asked for) by the employer.

The second type of situation exists when you want to apply for a job with an employer even though you are unsure whether that employer is seeking job applicants. Your task of creating employer interest in you is tougher in this situation than in the case where an employer asks for such letters.

Contents

In a letter of inquiry written in response to a job ad, you should refer to the ad and where you saw or heard it. This is important because the employer may be advertising for several types of jobs. By referring to the specific ad, you leave no doubt about the job you want.

In an unsolicited letter of inquiry, your task is a little tougher. The task of specifying where you might fit into the employer's organization is entirely yours. Furthermore, the employer may be less interested in receiving such letters. You must overcome this barrier in order to avoid getting a polite rejection letter. You must do an extra good job of motivating the employer to respond.

Regardless of the situation that prompts you to write a letter of inquiry, it must be brief and to the point. Put yourself in the employer's shoes. Write with the "you attitude," the "you" being the employer.

FIGURE A-3

A sample letter of inquiry

```
                                        3060 Avenue A, Apt. 21-C
                                        New Orleans, LA  70122
                                        April 18, 1980


Mr. Charles H. Browning
Personnel Manager
Nationwide Electronics, Inc.
P.O. Box 1475
Dallas, TX  75221

Dear Mr. Browning:

I read your advertisement for sales trainee applicants in the NEW
ORLEANS TIMES, April 17, 1980.

Your company came to my attention during the time I have been
employed as a part-time salesperson with Zeppo Electronics, Inc., in
New Orleans, Louisiana.  Ms. Barbara Robbins handles Zeppo's account
with Nationwide.  We have talked about sales career opportunities
with your firm on several occasions.  Those conversations, along
with some reading I have done on Nationwide in business periodicals,
have made me very interested in working for Nationwide.

Although I have been very satisfied with my part-time position with
Zeppo, I want to relocate with a larger firm after graduating from
college next month.  As you can see on my resume, I majored in
marketing.  I will graduate in the top 15 percent of those students
receiving B.S. degrees in Business Administration at the University
of New Orleans.

A career in selling has been my goal since my sophomore year in
college.  Eventually, I want to be a sales manager or a marketing
manager and am willing to work hard to reach that goal.

Please consider my qualifications for employment with Nationwide.
I am looking forward to hearing from you regarding an interview.

                          Sincerely,



                          Alfred J. Powell
```

Show your interest and qualifications in a manner that motivates the employer to answer your letter favorably.

You indicate your interest by either referring to a specific job ad or to the employer in general. Again, it is easier to show interest when you are applying for a specific job. When sending an unsolicited letter, avoid being too narrow in stating your career goals. That narrows your appeal. But don't be too broad either. Leave some room for the employer to fit you into the organization.

Flexibility is good. It's much easier to fit a promising applicant who states his or her career interest as "bookkeeper" than it is to fit the applicant who states his or her career interest as "accounts payable clerk." If the employer doesn't need an accounts payable clerk, the applicant's letter may be answered with a "sorry, we can't use your talents now" letter. But the applicant for a bookkeeping job may be considered for an opening in the employer's accounts receivable department.

In general, try to communicate your career goals, education, experience, and personal qualifications as briefly as possible. Try to stimulate the employer to at least take the time to review your résumé. Figure A–3 is a sample letter of inquiry.

Preparing for Job Interviews

No matter what career you want, before you can actually land a job you will have to have a job interview. In fact, before landing a job, you will probably have several interviews.

The Preliminaries

A good way of looking at a job interview is to think of it as a sales pitch. You are trying to sell yourself to the interviewer. As any good salesperson knows, you don't go into a selling situation without being prepared.

For campus interviews it's a good idea to start interviewing three or four months before you complete your program of study. Starting too early lessens the interviewer's interest in you since you will not be available for employment in the short run. Few employers can accurately predict their employee needs beyond several months. But don't wait to start interviewing until two weeks before you need a job. That will greatly limit your chances of finding a good job. In fact, you may be so desperate that you will accept a job that is below your skill level.

A campus interview is an ideal opportunity for you. Prospective employers, in effect, come to you. After you leave school, you will have to find them on your own. In other words, the search process is much harder.

But how many interviews should you schedule? In general, it's a good idea to sign up only for those that you are really interested in. If you have never taken an interview, however, you should sign up for two or three to learn what it's all about. Experience is a good teacher of how to interview. But even these practice interviews should be with employers who are looking for people to fill jobs that you are interested in. There is always the chance that you could "pull it off" in your first interview. Your attitude is also better when you are really interested in the job.

Do Your Homework

Above all, an interview is an exercise in face-to-face communication. You are the major communicator. An interviewer is not there to sell you on the employer as much as you are there to sell the interviewer on your value to that employer. It's a good idea to look at it as a buyer's market. Remember, the interviewer is the buyer. You are the seller.

If you have an interviewing opportunity, make the most of it. Jot down the place and time where the interview is to be held. That is basic but often overlooked, forgotten, or incorrectly noted.

Gather some information on the prospective employer. If it's a company, go to the library and check reference works such as *Dun and Bradstreet Reference Book.* If the firm is a corporation, try to locate and to read its recent annual reports to stockholders. Ask your instructors and any others who might be familiar with the firm about its operations. If it's a government agency or nonprofit organization, check the *U.S. Government Organization Manual,* encyclopedias, or other pertinent publications. You'd be surprised how many interviewees don't have the foggiest notion of the type of business or service the prospective employer is engaged in.

After you have a basic knowledge of the employer's operations (products sold, services performed, size, position in its industry, etc.), your next step is to learn something about the employer's representative—in this case, the interviewer. Don't overlook earlier interviewees as a source of information here. Knowing the interviewer's age, sex, hair style, style of dress, mannerisms, types of questions asked, and so on can help you relate better in the interview. Some interviewees will go into an interview and mispronounce the interviewer's name—and, even worse, the company's name. That does little for the interviewer's ego and even less for his or her first impression of you as a person.

Finally, try to anticipate and be prepared for one or more hard questions. Many interviewers ask questions such as "Why do you want to work for _____?" "What can you do for _____?" "Why are you here?" If you walk in cold, chances are that you will "blow it."

Get Your Head on Straight

Don't be nervous. Some people get so uptight about interviews that they fall apart at the seams. Try your best to get the "bugs" out of your stomach before you go into the interview.

But don't be so relaxed that you give the impression of not really caring whether or not you get the job. What is needed is a mild amount of anxiety—enough to keep you alert and responsive during the interview, but not so much as to make you "uptight."

Going to the Interview

Take a note pad and pencil and have questions prepared. An interviewer is always impressed when an interviewee has meaningful questions prepared in advance.

Be careful about your appearance. In recent years, many employers and their interviewers have adjusted to some of the newer clothing styles and have modified or done away with dress codes. But you are wise not to appear in a "way-out" outfit. Cleanliness, neatness, and moderation are very desirable.

Most important, be on time!

The Interview

Your preparation for the interview will pay off once you go through the door to be interviewed. But that was only preparation. You did not rehearse for a part in a play. Interviewers are too diverse a group to permit you to walk in prepared for everything.

Introducing Yourself

By introducing yourself, you avoid the chance that the interviewer will mispronounce your name. Beyond that, it's a good idea to consider yourself a guest. Don't rush to sit down unless you are asked to. Don't walk in with your hand outstretched for a handshake. Let the interviewer make the invitation.

Interviewer-Interviewee Interaction

As we said earlier, an interview is an exercise in face-to-face communication. But who dominates the conversation depends on the interviewer's style of interviewing. Some interviewers like to do most of the talking. Others like the interviewee to do most of the talking. Regardless of how much you did or did not prepare, you will have to play it by ear once you are in the interview room.

If the interviewer asks simple, direct questions, that does not mean that "yes" or "no" answers are all that is expected of you. Elaborate, but not to the point of "running off at the mouth." The interviewer's reactions are your best guide here. They tell you how much to say if you are observant.

If there is a noticeable break in the conversation, it's a good clue that you are slipping. Pick up the ball and run with it! It's a good chance to stress your good points, to reinforce and to elaborate on items in your résumé. But don't "blow your horn" so loud that it forces the interviewer to "tune you out."

Above all, be honest and sincere in answering questions. Be creative in asking them. Don't give the impression that you dropped in because you had nothing better to do.

Things to Avoid

There are several interviewing "don'ts." Don't chew gum, smoke, squirm in your chair, stare at the ceiling, or crack your knuckles. Don't take notes as if you were in a lecture class. Don't try to "butter up" the interviewer. Don't be phoney. Don't give the impression that you believe that the business world has been waiting too long for you to become available. Don't try to pull a "snow job."

Don't try to be a comedian. On the other hand, don't be overly serious and pompous. Don't try to hide the "real you." Don't accept a job or schedule further interviews with higher-ups unless you really want the job. Don't give up if you get the feeling that you aren't making it. That's instant death to your chances of landing the job. Finally, don't emphasize an interest in the firm's retirement plan. That tells a lot about your motivation and enthusiasm—all bad!

Getting to Specifics

There are certain important questions that you will want answered. A major one, of course, is the nature of the job. What does it involve? What about the chances for promotion to higher jobs? What is the starting salary? A discussion of the salary often is the most ticklish part of an interview. You may be asked what you would expect. You should have a floor salary in mind—what you need to get by on, given your personal circumstances. You should also have an idea of what the going rate for that particular job is in the area. But don't give the impression that you're interested only in the salary. Mention the job's challenge to you and your desire to see how you measure up to it. Emphasize that you want to learn.

If asked whether you are willing to relocate, give an honest answer. But you do limit your appeal when you say that you want to stay close to home. If you want to relocate in a city that is very desirable to a lot of interviewees, be prepared for stiffer competition for jobs in that city.

A much-asked question is "Where do you see yourself 10 years from now?" How well you can answer this question depends largely on how well you did your homework on the job and the company. The main thing to get across is that you want to move up in the firm. But be realistic about how far and how fast you expect to go.

When asked what kind of employees they want, many top-level executives answer in very general terms. "I want people who can think" is a typical response. In most cases, however, you are not interviewed by a top-level executive. An interviewer has more specific qualities and skills in mind when looking for prospective employees. This is why it's a good idea to try to learn as much as you can about the interviewer before and during the interview. He or she is a "gate keeper." The "gate" will be closed to you if you do not make a good impression on the interviewer.

Closing the Interview

When you sign up for a campus interview, notice how far apart the interviews are spaced. That gives you an idea about how long a typical interview will last. Make sure you get all your questions answered in the allotted time.

Many people leave interviews in a total state of confusion. Very rarely is a person hired during the first interview. Few are even definitely offered a job. This, of course, is disappointing to many interviewees who expect to "sew it up" during the interview. They often leave feeling frustrated, rejected, or unsure of themselves.

Before leaving, however, you will get some indication as to your status. Usually, you will be told that the interviewer will be in touch with you in a couple of weeks. Thank the interviewer and leave.

After the Interview

Be patient! When the letter arrives, it will be either: (1) an outright rejection; (2) a notice that your skills are not needed now but that your résumé is being placed in the active file; or (3) a letter expressing a desire to arrange another interview with higher-ups.

If, however, you do not hear from the interviewer within a reasonable period after the interview, write a follow-up letter. If you get a letter saying that your résumé is being placed in the active file, write a follow-up after two or three months to keep your résumé active. If you get an outright rejection, do not become discouraged. If you get a letter or phone call for the purpose of setting up another interview, respond tactfully and promptly.

Remember, during your career you will probably work for several employers. Your choice of a first job and employer is not a choice that will commit you to a lifetime with one employer. Approach that first job with a desire to learn all that you can. That increases your mobility and promotability.

Glossary

absenteeism   The failure of workers to report to work.

absentee ownership   A term usually applicable to a corporation owned by a large number of stockholders who do not actively participate in managing its affairs.

absolute advantage   (See page 551.)

acceptance sampling   A procedure to control the quality of purchased items; it involves examining a sample and deciding to accept or reject the shipment based on inspection of the sample.

accessory equipment   A category of industrial goods. Accessory items are less costly than installations (for example, manufacturing equipment) and their useful lives are shorter. Like installations, they do not become a physical part of the goods they are used to produce. Typewriters and fork-lift trucks are examples.

account   (See page 287.)

accountability   (See page 124.)

accounting   (See page 285.)

accounts payable   Money owed to creditors who supplied the firm with goods and services on credit. Listed in the current liabilities section of the balance sheet.

accounts receivable   Money owed to a firm by its customers. Listed in the current assets section of the balance sheet.

accrual   The process of holding over expenses or income to another period.

accrued expense   (See page 293.)

acid-test ratio   A ratio that measures a firm's liquidity. Cash and near-cash items divided by current liabilities.

Active Corps of Executives (ACE)   (See page 536.)

actuary   Loss-predicting expert who helps determine premiums for insurance companies by examining past occurrence of loss.

administered pricing   The process of determining pricing policies that guide the actual setting of prices on a firm's output rather than relying only on the daily market forces of supply and demand to determine prices. Common in market structures other than pure competition.

administrative law   (See page 611.)

advertising   (See page 253.)

advertising agency   (See page 255.)

advertising department   A separate department within a firm that oversees the firm's advertising activities. It may deal with the firm's advertising agency, which is outside the firm.

advertising media   (See page 255.)

affirmative action plan   (See page 401.)

agency-principal relationship   (See page 105.)

agency shop   (See page 448.)

agent middleman   A middleman who does not take title to the goods he or she sells and who earns a commission.

aggregate demand   Overall or total demand for all goods and services in an economic system.

aggregate supply   Overall or total supply of goods and services in an economic system.

AIDA process   (See page 256.)

alien corporation   A corporation that operates in countries in addition to the country in which it was chartered. It is an alien corporation in those foreign countries.

amalgamation   (See page 382.)

AMEX   The American Stock Exchange.

antitrust laws   (See page 613.)

applied research   Research effort that in contrast to basic research has immediate and practical application.

apprenticeship training   Training that occurs when an employee works under the direct supervision of an experienced and skilled worker in order to learn a trade.

aptitude tests   Tests used to tell if a person is likely to do well in a particular kind of work. They estimate the ability to learn a skill.

arithmetic mean   (See page 495.)

array   A list of all values in a statistical series, usually from lowest to highest.

articles of copartnership   A written agreement between or among partners that specifies the rights and duties of each.

assessment center   A systems approach based on the use of group techniques to diagnose and assess individual performance. Useful in determining individual training and development needs of present and potential workers and managers.

assets   (See page 288.)

audit   A periodic check of accounting, financial, or marketing records and/or performance either to verify compliance with generally accepted principles and/or to make recommendations for improving performance.

auditor   An accountant who inspects and reviews accounting records of firms and individuals and verifies the accuracy of the data recorded.

authority   (See page 124.)

autocratic leader   A leader who makes decisions without consulting subordinates or without allowing them to participate in the decision making that affects them.

automatic transfer account   A type of bank account that enables a depositor in a commercial bank to move money automatically from time deposits to demand deposits.

automation   (See page 190.)

background investigation   (See page 410.)

backward vertical integration   A term that describes a firm's integration backward from its present type of operation. Examples are a retailer who goes into wholesaling or an electric utility that goes into coal mining.

bailor-bailee relationship   (See page 106.)

bait and switch advertising   Advertising one inexpensive item that is really not available and then convincing those persons who want to buy it to buy a more expensive substitute.

balance of payments   (See page 564.)

balance of trade   (See page 563.)

balance sheet   (See page 291.)

bankruptcy   (See page 385.)

bargainable issues   (See page 454.)

barter   A simple type of trade or exchange. Trading one kind of good or service for another kind of good or service. Money is not involved in the trade, or exchange.

BASIC   A computer language; a simplified version of FORTRAN.

basic accounting equations   (See page 289.)

basic research   Research effort to study general relationships among phenomena in order to understand them. In contrast to applied research, basic research is conducted with no immediate concern for practical application.

bear market   A market for securities in which prices are falling and investors expect falling prices to continue. There is little buying of securities in a bear market. Investors are pessimistic.

belonging needs   In Maslow's hierarchy of needs they include social belonging, love, affection, affiliation, and membership needs.

Better Business Bureau (BBB)   (See page 524.)

big board   The New York Stock Exchange.

blacklists   (See page 437.)

block diagram   A method of presenting a computer program that shows visually the functions performed and their sequence; a means of documentation.

blue chip stock   Common stock of corporations able to produce profits and pay dividends in both good times and bad.

blue-collar workers   Workers who perform manual labor.

blue-sky laws   State laws that apply mainly to the sale of new securities. Their purpose is to prevent corporations from issuing securities that have nothing of value to offer the buyer.

board of directors   (See page 90.)

board officers   Officers of the board of directors elected by the board. They include a chairperson, vice-chairperson, and a secretary.

bona fide occupational qualification (BFOQ)   (See page 411.)

bond   (See page 338.)

bond indenture   The agreement under which bonds are issued. It designates the trustee.

boom period   That period in the business cycle during which the volume of business activity is at a high level. Consumers and businesses are very confident and optimistic.

boycott   (See page 462.)

brand   (See page 233.)

breakeven analysis   (See page 498.)

breaking down   (See page 189.)

brokerage house   (See page 340.)

budget   (See page 303.)

bull market   A market for securities in which prices are rising and investors expect rising prices to continue. There is a lot of buying of securities in a bull market. Investors are optimistic.

business   (See page 33.)

business cycle   The cyclical changes that occur as the level of economic activity varies over time: boom, decline, recession or depression, and recovery.

business opportunity   (See page 62.)

business trust   (See page 103.)

call provision   A provision sometimes included in preferred stock and bond issues. It permits the corporation to retire preferred stock by paying the stockholder the call price. For bonds, it per-

mits the corporation to redeem the bond before its maturity date.

"canned program"   A computer program that has been placed in storage and is available for use by anyone who so desires.

capital   (See page 17.)

capital budget   (See page 365.)

capital formation   (See page 24.)

capital-intensive   (See page 190.)

capital investment   A firm's financial commitment to buildings, land, machinery, and other productive assets.

capitalism   (See page 19.)

career values   (See page 641.)

cartel   (See page 577.)

cash discount   A discount off list price for prompt payment. Used to speed up collection of accounts receivable.

cash dividend   Cash payments made to a firm's common and preferred stockholders as a return on their investment in the firm.

cashier's check   A check written by a bank's cashier and payable to a specified payee.

cash trading   In the commodities markets, cash trading means the actual buying and selling of commodities for delivery in the cash market. In the securities exchanges, purchases of securities for cash.

caveat emptor   "Let the buyer beware." The philosophy of business during the 1800s. The consumer is responsible for his or her purchase behavior.

cease and desist order   An order handed out by a federal agency that informs a business that it must stop a questionable practice.

CED (Committee for Economic Development)   A national group of representatives of major American corporations. It is concerned with optimum resource allocation and is viewed as a supporter of the professional-managerial ethic for business.

centralization   (See page 125.)

centralized organization   An organization in which decision-making power and authority are concentrated in the hands of a few upper-level managers.

central planning   (See page 21.)

central processing unit (CPU)   (See page 483.)

certificate of deposit (CD) A deposit made for a certain period of time by individuals, business firms, or other organizations. The interest rate is higher than that on regular passbook accounts. There is a penalty for early withdrawal; usually the depositor must forgo 90 days' interest and is paid only the passbook rate on the funds that are not withdrawn.

certified check A check that is stamped "certified" by a bank, which immediately withdraws the amount of the check from the drawer's checking account.

certified public accountant (CPA) (See page 286.)

chain of command The authority relationship that exists between superiors and subordinates. It is a command relationship in which line authority has the right to direct the work of subordinates.

chain store A unit in a group of stores that are centrally owned and managed; each unit is engaged in the same type of business. A&P is a chain store organization. A particular A&P supermarket is a chain store.

Chamber of Commerce of the United States (See page 524.)

channel of distribution (See page 236.)

chattel mortgage bond A bond that is secured by movable property.

checkoff The employer's deduction of the employee's union dues from his or her paycheck to give to the union.

class action suit A lawsuit by a single consumer that may result in recovery by a number of similarly injured parties.

close corporation A corporation owned by only a few stockholders. Its shares are not sold to the public.

closed shop (See page 448.)

COBOL (See page 487.)

coinsurance clause A clause in a fire insurance policy that requires the insured to carry adequate insurance (usually 80 percent) on the market value of the property.

collateral Assets of a borrower pledged as security against the amount of money lent him or her.

collateral trust bond A bond secured by stocks and bonds in other corporations that are owned by the issuing corporation.

collective bargaining (See page 435.)

collective bargaining agreement (See page 435.)

collectivism (See page 20.)

combination (See page 189.)

combination export manager (See page 574.)

commercial bank (See page 315.)

commercial finance company (See page 320.)

commercial paper Promissory notes issued by corporations that are backed only by the firm's promise to pay.

commercial paper house (See page 322.)

committee organization A type of organization structure in which several persons share authority and responsibility for accomplishing an objective. This form of organization, where it does exist, usually exists within the overall line and staff organization. Also called project management, program management, team management, and group management.

commodity exchanges (See page 349.)

common carrier (See page 241.)

common market A term often used for the European Economic Community, which was founded in 1958 by Belgium, France, Italy, Luxembourg, the Netherlands, and West Germany. Denmark, Ireland, and the United Kingdom have since joined. See *regional trading bloc.*

common stock (See page 90.)

communication (See page 164.)

community property Property husbands and wives own together under the laws of community property states.

comparative advantage (See page 553.)

comparative advertising Advertising which makes comparisons of the advertised brand to named competitive brands.

competitive bidding A purchasing department's invitation to sellers to submit bids to fulfill its purchase requirements. It requires the buyer to specify in detail what is needed. A purchase contract will be awarded to the lowest bidder who can meet the specifications.

competitive structures Variations in the market framework that imply variations in the degree and type of competition that the firm must face (for example, oligopoly, monopoly).

component parts and materials A category of industrial goods. They become part of the goods they are used to produce. Examples are car batteries, car tires, and cement.

compulsory arbitration (See page 460.)

computer (See page 477.)

computer program (See page 481.)

computer programer A person who writes programs for computers.

conciliation (See page 459.)

conglomerate A firm involved in a number of noncompetitive industries.

consent order (See page 613.)

consignment Goods bought on consignment by a wholesaler or retailer are not paid for until they are sold.

conspicuous consumption (See page 271.)

Consumer Credit Protection Act The "Truth in Lending Act" of 1968. Requires firms that sell on credit to consumers to state the charges for loans and installment purchases in terms of the annual percentage rate (APR).

consumer finance company (See page 320.)

consumer goods (See page 223.)

consumerism (See page 26.)

consumer power. (See page 25.)

consumer price index A measure of inflation. A figure that measures the change in the dollar value of a selected group of consumer goods from a base period.

Consumer Product Safety Commission A commission created by the Consumer Product Safety Act of 1973. It enforces consumer protection laws. Its main concern is preventing unsafe products from reaching the market.

consumer sovereignty (See *consumer power.*)

containerization (See page 243.)

continuous production (See page 190.)

contract (See page 105.)

contract carrier (See page 242.)

contract manufacturing (See page 580.)

control chart (See page 200.)

controllers (See page 486.)

controlling (See page 170.)

convenience goods (See page 226.)

convertible bond A bond that can be converted to common stock at the bondholder's option.

cooperative advertising The sharing by a manufacturer and middlemen in the channel of distribution, mainly retailers, of the costs of advertising the manufacturer's product.

cooperative association (See page 104.)

corporate charter (See page 89.)

corporate officers The top managers of a corporation who are selected by the board of directors. They usually include the president, vice-president(s), secretary, and treasurer. They are employees of the board.

corporate PAC A political organization composed of the employees of an incorporated firm. It often supports candidates and causes that are thought to be favorable to business.

corporation (See page 82.)

corporation bylaws (See page 94.)

corrective advertising Advertising done by an advertiser to correct previous advertising that is considered deceptive by a regulatory agency such as the Federal Trade Commission.

cost of living A measurement often used to assess the impact of inflation. It compares the prices of goods bought by consumers to their wages.

cost per contact An expression of the cost of reaching a prospective buyer with the advertising message. It is often used in selecting among advertising media.

cost-push inflation An increase in the price level due to increases in the cost of the factors of production.

Council of Economic Advisers A three-member group that advises the President of the United States on economic problems. Established in 1946 to help the President to achieve the goals set out in the Employment Act of 1946.

countervailing power (See page 100.)

coupon bond A bond for which the owner's name is not registered and does not appear on the bond. The owner clips coupons from the bond and presents them to the corporation's bank for payment of interest due.

craft unions (See page 442.)

credit union (See page 319.)

Critical Path Method (CPM) (See page 201.)

culture All those elements of a civilization that give it its distinct character.

cumulative quantity discount A discount on purchases that is figured on the total volume of purchases made during a certain period of time. It encourages buyer loyalty.

cumulative voting   (See page 91.)

current assets   (See page 291.)

current liability   (See page 292.)

current ratio   (See page 299.)

data processing   (See page 481.)

debenture   A corporate bond that is backed only by the general credit and strength of the issuing corporation.

debt capital   Borrowed funds, as distinguished from equity capital or equity financing provided by the owners of the firm.

debt financing   (See page 367.)

decentralization   (See page 125.)

decentralized organization   An organization in which decision-making power and authority are dispersed throughout the organization as a result of the delegation process.

decision-making process   (See page 173.)

delegation   (See page 124.)

demand   (See page 45.)

demand curve   (See page 54.)

demand deposit   (See page 322.)

demand-pull inflation   An increase in the price level due to excess demand for goods and services in relation to their supply.

demarketing   A term referring to a firm's efforts to decrease the demand for its products or services due to supply shortage. An electric utility that urges its customers to "turn off unnecessary lights" is practicing demarketing.

democratic leader   A leader who consults with his or her subordinates and allows them to participate in the decision making that affects them.

demographic   Relating to population size, characteristics, or distribution.

departmentation   (See page 121.)

depreciation   (See page 292.)

depression   That period in the business cycle during which the volume of business activity is at a very low level. Consumers and businesses are extremely pessimistic. Unemployment is high as is the rate of business failures.

devaluation   (See page 564.)

directing   (See page 162.)

discharge   (See page 426.)

disciplinary action   Action which is administered by the worker's supervisor when the worker fails to adhere to employee discipline policy. It ranges from oral reprimands to discharge from the company.

discount rate   The rate at which the Federal Reserve System discounts the notes it buys from member banks that desire to increase their deposits with the system. The higher the rate, the less willing member banks are to borrow.

discouraged workers   The "hidden unemployed." Persons who want jobs but do not seek them because they believe that jobs are not available to them.

discretionary income   (See page 46.)

dismissal   (See page 425.)

disposable personal income (DPI)   (See page 12.)

distribution of income   The way in which the aggregate income of a nation, region, or area is allocated among individuals or families. It determines the number of potential customers for products other than basic necessities and the number of persons eligible for welfare assistance.

diversification   The involvement of a firm in a variety of products or activities at the same time.

documentation   (See page 488.)

domestic corporation   A corporation that operates in the state in which it was chartered.

domestic international sales corporation (DISC)   A tax-shelter subsidiary. By setting up a DISC, an American firm that exports goods can defer some of its taxes on export earnings.

dormant partner   A partner, in a partnership, who does not actively participate in managing the firm and whose identity is not disclosed to the public.

draft   A written order made by one party (the drawer) addressed to a second party (the drawee) ordering the drawee to pay a certain amount of money to a third party (the payee). Examples are ordinary checks drawn on banks, trade acceptances, certified checks, and cashier's checks.

dumping   (See page 560.)

echelons of management   (See page 123.)

ecology movement   A movement for cleaner air,

water, and cities.

economic development   A process by which a nation improves its production per capita. It depends largely upon technology.

economic development council   (See page 524.)

economic freedoms   These include individual initiative and self-interest, private property, profit incentive, consumer power, freedom to compete, occupational freedom, freedom of contract, and limited role of government.

economic problem (the)   (See page 5.)

economies of scale   Savings realized by an increase in the volume of production or size of the productive unit.

egalitarian   Pertaining to the belief that all people are equal and are entitled to the same standard of living. One who holds this belief.

embargoes   (See page 558.)

employee benefits   (See *fringe benefits*.)

employee orientation   (See page 412.)

Employment Act of 1946   This law imposes on the federal government the responsibility to promote full employment, maximum economic growth, and price stability.

encounter groups   (See *T-group training*.)

endowment insurance   A type of insurance that emphasizes savings over protection. It is in effect for a stated number of years. If the insured dies during the period, the face value is paid to the beneficiary. If the insured lives, the insured receives the face value.

entrepreneur   (See page 17.)

entrepreneurship   (See page 17.)

environment   (See page 579.)

equal opportunity employer   An employer who hires, promotes, and pays people without regard to race, sex, or national origin.

equity   (See page 288.)

equity financing   (See page 367.)

equity theory of compensation   Equity is the perceived fairness of what a worker does compared to what he or she receives from the employer. Inequity results when the worker perceives imbalances between the inputs (such as skills) and the outputs (tangible and intangible rewards from the employer).

escalator clause   (See page 457.)

esteem needs   In Maslow's hierarchy of needs they include social-esteem needs such as prestige and include social-esteem needs such as prestige and status, and self-esteem needs such as competence and self-respect.

ethics   A system of "oughts." A way of defining obligations and rights among people.

European Economic Community (EEC)   (See *common market*.)

exchange   (See page 7.)

exchange control   (See page 558.)

exit interview   (See page 425.)

expense   (See page 288.)

exports   Goods produced in country A and sold in country B are an export of country A. The opposite of imports.

expropriation   (See page 578.)

facilitating middleman   One who participates in transporting and storing a product as it moves through its distribution channel, but who does not participate in the actual buying and selling of it. Examples are railroads and public warehouses.

factoring company   (See page 319.)

factors of production   (See page 14.)

Fair Labor Standards Act   (See page 438.)

fashion obsolescence   Obsolescence of a product due to a change in fashion.

featherbedding   Paying for work which workers do not perform or offer to perform.

Federal Advisory Council   A council of 12 members who advise the board of governors of the Federal Reserve System. There is one member from each Federal Reserve Bank.

Federal Communications Commission (FCC)   Established in 1939, this agency regulates the broadcast media and communications carriers.

Federal Deposit Insurance Corporation (FDIC)   An agency of the U.S. government that insures savings accounts in member banks up to $40,000 for each account.

Federal Fair Packaging and Labeling Act of 1966   A law requiring that consumer goods be clearly labeled in order to provide consumers with product-related information.

Federal Open Market Committee (FOMC)   A committee composed of 12 members (7 from the board of governors and 5 from Federal Reserve banks) who set the Federal Reserve's open-market policy. It directs the Federal Reserve banks either to buy or to sell government securities.

Federal Power Commission (FPC) This commission has jurisdiction over interstate electric transmission lines, the sale of electric utilities, and the transmission of natural gas by pipeline; it also regulates interstate electric rates.

Federal Reserve System (See page 327.)

Federal Savings and Loan Insurance Corporation (FSLIC) An agency of the U.S. government that insures savings accounts in member savings and loan associations up to $40,000 for each account.

Federal Trade Commission (FTC) The FTC Act of 1914 created the FTC, which regulates competition and controls unfair or deceptive practices in interstate commerce.

fee simple A person is the owner in fee simple of real property when he or she owns the entire estate.

fidelity bond Insurance that protects, up to the policy limits, the employer from employee theft of company funds.

final selection interview (See page 411.)

financial accounting (See page 285.)

firm's publics Those groups in society that have an interest in the affairs of a firm—its owners, employees, labor unions, suppliers, creditors, government, etc.

fixed asset (See page 292.)

fixed cost Costs that do not vary in total as the volume of business varies (for example, executive salaries and fire insurance premiums).

flex time Flexible, as opposed to fixed, working hours.

floor planning (See page 372.)

Food and Drug Administration (FDA) The federal agency charged with protecting the people from dangerous foods and drugs.

foreign assembly The assembling of a finished product by a subsidiary or licensee in a host country from parts exported to it by a parent firm.

foreign corporation A corporation that operates in states other than the one in which it was chartered.

foreign exchange Money transactions in international trade. International trade requires that firms in different countries transact business in different currencies.

foreign exchange rate (See page 569.)

foreign licensing (See page 580.)

formal leader One who is delegated authority or power over his or her subordinates.

formal organization The structure created by management so that human, financial, and physical resources of the firm can be related to each other. Depicted by the organization chart.

form utility (See page 221.)

FORTRAN (See page 487.)

forward vertical integration A term that describes a firm's integration forward from its present type of operation. Examples are a wholesaler who goes into retailing or a raw-materials supplier who goes into manufacturing.

franchised retailer (See page 238.)

franchisee (See page 526.)

franchiser (See page 525.)

franchising Licensing of a name, design, process, or symbol by its owner for use by others. Also applies to setting up small retail or service firms under such a licensing agreement.

franchising agreement (See page 527.)

frequency distribution (See page 496.)

fringe benefits Paid vacations, retirement plans, sick leave, and so on that accompany the wage or salary the employee receives.

functional authority (See page 127.)

functional discount (See page 264.)

functions of management (See page 156.)

future estate Property owned but that cannot be enjoyed until some future time. A wife owns a future estate in property that her husband owns but that will go to her upon his death.

futures markets The buying and selling of contracts to receive or deliver a certain quantity and grade of commodity at a specified future date. Most futures trading does not result in the physical exchange of goods. Buyers of futures contracts try to protect themselves against adverse future price changes or try to make speculative profits from those price changes.

Gantt Chart A special time map used to schedule production that involves a number of interdependent processes.

General Agreement on Tariffs and Trade

(GATT)   (See page 562.)

general partner   A partner with unlimited liability for the debts of the partnership and who actively participates in the management of the firm.

generic brand   A product identified by the name of the product class to which it belongs rather than by a manufacturer or a middleman brand. For example, "laundry detergent" rather than Tide or Topco.

goal congruence   The coincidence of personal and corporate goals.

grievance   A complaint about the job that is taken up with management. A simple complaint is not a legitimate grievance unless it violates the worker's rights.

grievance procedures   (See page 461.)

gross margin   Total dollar sales minus the cost of goods sold.

gross national product (GNP)   (See page 8.)

gross profit   (See page 294.)

gross working capital   Total current assets.

group norms   Standards of behavior established by groups. An example is an upper limit on production that workers set.

group sanctions   The rewards or punishments that a group confers upon its members for living up to or violating group norms of behavior.

guaranteed annual wage   (See page 448.)

hard-to-employ   A new term which describes persons who, because of education, race, physical handicap, or background, are unemployed.

hardware   (See page 483.)

hierarchy of needs   (See page 134.)

hierarchy of organizational objectives   (See page 121.)

histogram   (See page 497.)

holding company   (See page 382.)

horizontal integration   The buying out by a firm at one level in a distribution system of other firms on that same level. An example is a supermarket chain buying out another supermarket chain.

human resource   (See page 395.)

Humphrey-Hawkins Full Employment Act   A 1978 law that reinforces previous government policy to maintain employment. It includes emphasis on economy in government and greater reliance on the private sector.

imports   Goods produced in country A and bought by people in country B are imports of country B. The opposite of exports.

import quota   (See page 557.)

import surcharge   A tax on goods imported into a country that makes them more expensive to buy. The purpose is to reduce imports.

incentive pay   (See page 417.)

income statement   (See page 293.)

in-depth interview   (See page 410.)

individualism   (See page 22.)

industrial goods   (See page 223.)

industrial services   A category of industrial goods. They are often necessary to support plant or office operations. Examples are maintenance services and food services purchased from other firms.

industrial unions   (See page 442.)

inflation   (See page 9.)

inflationary psychology   A widespread belief among the people in an economic system that prices will rise rapidly, resulting in little incentive to save money rather than spend it.

informal groups   (See page 139.)

informal leader   One who enjoys influence over others because they want and accept him or her as leader.

informal organization   (See page 140.)

informative labeling   The practice of including information on a product's uses, precautions, contents, durability, etc., on the product's label.

injunction   (See page 438.)

input and output (I-O) devices   (See page 485.)

insolvency   A firm or person is insolvent when its debts exceed its ability to pay them off with readily available funds.

installations   A category of industrial goods. They are costly and do not become a physical part of the goods they are used to produce. Major equipment and buildings are examples.

installment credit   A type of credit that involves making regular monthly payments (installments) on credit purchases, usually of durable products such as cars.

institutional advertising   Advertising that is intended to promote the advertiser's organization as a whole rather than one of its products. An example is the slogan "GM Mark of Excellence."

institutional investors Professional investors who invest in the securities of other firms and government securities (for example, mutual funds, pension funds, investment clubs, insurance companies).

insurable interest (See page 378.)

insurable risk (See page 378.)

insurance company A firm that shares pure risk with its policyholders (customers) for the payment of a premium.

insurance premium The price paid for insurance protection.

intangible assets Assets that do not have a tangible form but are still valuable, for example, goodwill.

intelligence tests Tests used to measure a person's general verbal abilities and specific abilities such as reasoning.

interest The amount paid for using borrowed money.

intermittent production (See page 190.)

intermodal service Transportation that uses the facilities of two or more modes of transportation as complements or supplements to one another, for example, piggyback truck/train transportation.

international business The business activities of a firm that involve persons or firms outside the home nation of that firm.

international trade (See page 554.)

interstate commerce Commerce between or among states.

Interstate Commerce Commission (ICC) This agency, created by law in 1889, regulates rates of all forms of interstate public transportation except air carriers, pipeline companies, and certain intrarurban carriers.

intrastate commerce Commerce within a particular state.

inventory Items of value kept in stock for sale (merchandise inventory) or use (supplies or parts inventory). A major type of asset. Also applies to the process of accounting for the level of such assets.

inventory turnover rate (See page 266.)

investment bank (See page 339.)

isolationism Noninvolvement with other countries. An isolationist country limits its social and economic contact with other countries.

job analysis (See page 398.)

job application form (See page 407.)

job description (See page 399.)

job enlargement The addition of new tasks to a worker's job.

job enrichment (See page 168.)

job evaluation A part of wage and salary administration. A method for determining the relationship between pay rates for particular job classifications. Considers factors such as the desirability of the work, amount of skill, and education needed to perform a given job.

job rotation Involves periodically assigning workers to new jobs in order to reduce boredom.

job sharing A new working arrangement to accommodate people who cannot work full time. Two workers share one job, salary, and set of benefits.

job-skill training (See page 413.)

job specification (See page 400.)

Jobs Program A program of the National Alliance of Businessmen that recruits persons who might otherwise be viewed as unemployable and trains them on the job in participating firms. The program is run in cooperation with state employment agencies.

joint liability Liability for debts that exists in a general partnership. Each general partner is responsible for the business debts incurred by the other general partner(s).

joint tenancy The sharing by two or more persons of title to personal or real property. Each has equal rights to use and enjoy the property during their lives. When one owner dies, the entire estate goes to the surviving title holder(s), not to that owner's heirs.

joint venture (See page 103.)

joint venture (in international business) (See page 581.)

journal In accounting, books in which original entries are recorded in chrononological order and then transferred to ledgers.

jurisdictional dispute Controversy between or

among labor unions regarding which union should perform which jobs or which union should represent workers in a given industry or firm.

keypunch machine A machine used to record information on computer punch cards by punching holes in them. Similar to a typewriter.

key ratio (See page 298.)

label That part of the total product which describes the content and other features (durability, precautions, etc.) of the product.

labor (See page 16.)

laboratory training (See *T-group training.*)

labor force Persons able and willing to work and actively seeking jobs or currently employed.

labor-intensive (See page 190.)

labor relations The relationship between management and unionized employees.

labor turnover Employees quitting their jobs.

labor union (See page 435.)

laissez faire (See page 19.)

land (See page 16.)

Landrum-Griffin Act (See page 440.)

law of demand (See page 46.)

law of large numbers (See page 377.)

law of supply (See page 51.)

layoff Temporary separation of an employee from his or her job due to variation in the demand for the products the company markets. Also used to discipline employees.

layout The arrangement of parts in a printed advertisement—illustration, headline, and copy.

leader pricing Pricing a widely bought item at a low price to attract buyers to a retail store.

leadership (See page 168.)

lease (See page 366.)

leasing The act of renting buildings, equipment, etc., rather than buying them. The lessor is the party who rents to the lessee.

ledger Account books of final entry. Each ledger shows a current balance. Examples are cash, accounts receivable, and accounts payable ledgers.

legal reserves The amount of money that member banks of the Federal Reserve System must maintain in the form of cash or deposits with a Federal Reserve Bank.

legal tender Coins and paper money. Creditors must accept them in payment of debts that are expressed in money terms.

letter of inquiry (See page 653.)

leverage Using borrowed funds to earn more than their cost.

liability (See page 288.)

life estate An interest in property that is granted to or willed to a person and that lasts only during the possessor's lifetime.

life insurance (See page 381.)

life insurance company (See page 319.)

lifestyle A pattern of work, leisure, sexual habits, and tastes.

limited liability Stockholders of a corporation enjoy limited liability for debts of the corporation. Unlike proprietors and partners whose personal, and in some cases, real property can be taken to satisfy company debts, the stockholder's liability is limited to the amount he or she paid for the shares of stock. Limited partners also may enjoy limited liability.

limited partner A partner who enjoys limited liability for the debts of the partnership and who does not actively participate in the management of the firm.

limited partnership (See page 103.)

limited payment life insurance Insurance for which the insured pays premiums only for a stated number of years, at the end of which his or her policy is paid up.

line and staff organization A type of organization structure comprised of line managers in the chain of command who are advised and served by staff personnel who are outside the chain of command.

linear programing (See page 501.)

line authority (See page 126.)

line functions (See page 126.)

line of credit (See page 371.)

line organization The oldest and simplest type of organization structure in which a person in the chain of command takes orders from people higher in the chain and gives orders to people lower in the chain.

liquidity (See page 361.)

listed securities Stocks and bonds that are traded

on organized stock exchanges such as the New York Stock Exchange.

load mutual fund   The purchase price of a share that includes a sales commission.

lobbying   (See page 444.)

local development company   A corporation set up by citizens of a community for the purpose of improving their local economy by promoting and assisting the development of small business firms.

local union   (See page 443.)

lockout   (See page 463.)

logistics   (See *physical distribution*.)

long run   Usually a period of time that exceeds one year; equivalent of long term.

long-term capital   (See page 364.)

maintenance factors   In Frederick Herzberg's theory of motivation, maintenance (or hygiene) factors include pay, working conditions, and job security. They are job context, or extrinsic, factors that are not part of the work itself. They tend to be dissatisfiers if they are absent or inadequate.

make-or-buy decision   (See page 193.)

management   (See page 151.)

management by exception   (See page 175.)

management by objectives (MBO)   (See page 157.)

management development   (See page 414.)

management hierarchy   (See *echelons of management.*)

management information system (MIS)   A firm's MIS is made up of people and machines. People feed in data that are deemed necessary for decision-making purposes. These data are processed and fed out as information to decision makers who need it.

management inventory   (See page 398.)

manager   (See page 151.)

managerial accounting   (See page 285.)

managerial approach to marketing   (See page 222.)

managerial skills   (See page 153.)

manufacturer's agent   (See page 238.)

manufacturer's brand   Also called a national brand. A brand owned by a manufacturer as opposed to a middleman.

margin requirement   (See page 330.)

margin trading   (See page 346.)

market economy   (See page 43.)

marketing   (See page 219.)

marketing concept   (See page 222.)

marketing mix   (See page 228.)

marketing research   (See page 269.)

market penetration pricing   (See page 266.)

market segment   A subgroup within a market that is made up of people who have one or more characteristics in common. For example, one segment of the market for motels is made up of young couples who take vacations with children.

market segmentation   (See page 268.)

market share   The proportion of the total market for a type of product held by a given seller.

market system   An economic system in which prices are determined in markets. The market forces of supply and demand determine relative prices.

markup   (See page 262.)

mass production   The application of technology and scientific management to the continuous production of a large volume of goods.

maturity   (See page 367.)

mechanization   Changing from manual operation to machine operation.

median   (See page 496.)

mediation   (See page 459.)

member bank reserves   The basis for commercial bank credit. The extent to which commercial banks can create money depends on the volume of their reserves. Vault cash and deposits with Federal Reserve banks.

mercantilism   (See page 19.)

merchandise inventory   All those items purchased for resale but not yet sold by a firm.

merchant middlemen   Those who actually take title to the merchandise that they resell.

merger   (See page 382.)

merit rating system   (See page 415.)

middlemen   (See page 223.)

military-industrial complex   A network of power and interdependence between large firms and the armed services that appears to direct the use of a very large part of our nation's resources and that may influence both domestic and foreign policy of the nation.

minority enterprise   The ownership of their own

businesses by ethnic or racial minorities.

minority enterprise small business investment company A small business investment company that is created to further minority enterprise. It is privately owned and privately operated and is licensed by the Small Business Administration to provide long-term financing and management assistance to small, minority-owned business firms.

mixed economic system A system that is not purely capitalist or purely collectivist. Such a system has a private and a public sector.

mode (See page 496.)

model building (See page 500.)

modes of transportation Ways of transporting goods and people—air, water, rail, motor carrier, and pipeline.

money (See page 315.)

money center banks Large commercial banks in New York City and Chicago.

monopolistic competition (See page 261.)

monopoly A market condition in which the single producer could theoretically demand as high a price as "the market will bear," or as high a price as buyers will pay before seeking substitutes for the product.

morale Employee attitudes about the work environment.

motivation (See page 165.)

motivational factors In Frederick Herzberg's theory of motivation, motivational factors (motivators) include achievement, recognition, and responsibility. They occur as part of the work itself and are job content, or intrinsic, factors that make work rewarding in and of itself.

multiearner family (See page 601.)

multinational company (MNC) (See page 575.)

mutual company (See page 104.)

mutual fund (See page 347.)

National Alliance of Businessmen (See *Jobs Program.*)

National Credit Union Administration A U.S. government agency that insures savings accounts of member credit unions up to $40,000 per account.

nationalism (See page 639.)

nationalization In international business, nationalization occurs when a government expropriates a foreign-owned firm and the government runs the nationalized firm. The owners of the firm may or may not be compensated.

National Labor Relations Board (NLRB) (See page 438.)

national union (See page 443.)

near cash Assets that can be quickly converted into cash. An example is short-term Treasury bills.

negotiable instruments Checks, promissory notes, etc., the ownership of which may be transferred from one party to another.

net annual household formation (See page 600.)

net working capital Total current assets minus current liabilities.

noise Any barrier that interferes with the communication process.

no-load mutual fund A fund in which the purchase price of a share is net asset value (no sales commission).

nominal partner A person who is not an actual partner in a firm but whose name is identified with the firm. Usually a well-known personality.

noncumulative quantity discount A discount on purchases that is figured on the size of each individual order, not on the total volume purchased during a certain period of time. Encourages the buyer to place larger orders.

noninstallment credit A type of credit that involves paying in full credit purchases at the end of the credit period, usually 30 days.

nonprice competition Competition among firms based upon advertising, product differentiation, service, and so on, rather than price differences.

nonroutine decision (See page 175.)

normalization (See page 635.)

norms Standards of behavior. (See *group norms.*)

Norris-LaGuardia Act (See page 438.)

nutritional labeling The practice of including nutritional information on the label of a food product.

NYSE The New York Stock Exchange; "the big board."

obsolescence (See page 204.)

Occupational Safety and Health Act (OSHA) (See page 422.)

odd lot Less than 100 shares of stock.

oligopoly (See page 261.)

on-line system (See page 485.)

open-book account A type of credit arrangement in which the seller of merchandise bills the buyer when the ordered merchandise is shipped. No credit instruments are involved. The seller includes the bill along with the shipment of merchandise.

open corporation A corporation whose stock is widely held by investors and is actively traded.

open market operations Federal Reserve banks' buying and selling of government securities to control member bank reserves and, consequently, the money supply.

open shop (See page 448.)

operational planning (See page 157.)

operations management (See page 209.)

operations research (OR) (See page 500.)

opportunity costs (See page 364.)

optimum Pertaining to the best result possible under given conditions.

organization (See page 117.)

organizational objectives The goals that the formal organization is structured to accomplish. Examples are "to increase market share" (economic objective) and "to be a good community citizen" (social objective).

organization chart (See page 130.)

organization development (OD) (See page 415.)

organization manual The handbook given to employees that contains information on company policies and procedures.

organized labor That part of the total work force that is unionized.

organizing (See page 161.)

outside data storage systems (See page 484.)

outside directors Members of the board of directors of a corporation who are not corporate officers.

over-the-counter market (OTC) (See page 342.)

owner-managers Persons who own and directly manage their business firms.

owner's equity (See page 288.)

ownership utility (See page 221.)

package An important part of the "total product." The container or wrapper for the physical product. Protects the product, divides it into convenient units, and serves a promotional role.

participative management (See page 162.)

partnership (See page 79.)

partnership agreement (See page 80.)

par value The value printed on the stock certificate. Many stock certificates do not show a par value (no-par value stock). Par value may represent the price of the stock when it was originally issued or it may be a completely arbitrary amount.

patent (See page 235.)

peer group A group composed of one's contemporaries (for example, people of the same age) who interact regularly.

perception How an individual interprets a situation or a message or how he or she "sees" somebody else.

perfect competition A competitive state with many buyers and many sellers, a uniform product, perfect market information, and no excess profit.

performance appraisal system (See page 415.)

performance rating A part of wage and salary administration. Setting a series of rates (steps, or pay ranges) for each job. New employees start at the base rate and advance to higher rates as they gain experience, proficiency, and seniority.

performance tests Tests used to measure a person's proficiency in a given type of work, such as typing.

personal property (See page 106.)

personal selling (See page 258.)

personal staff A staff person who performs duties at the request of his or her line boss. Usually designated by the title "assistant to."

personnel administration (See page 396.)

personnel department (See page 396.)

personnel management (See page 396.)

personnel management information system (PMIS) A computerized system that helps the personnel department to do a more effective job of personnel management by keeping more accurate and timely personnel data.

PERT (Program Evaluation and Review Technique) (See page 201.)

Peter Principle The promotion of a competent

person for good performance until he or she winds up in a position in which he or she is incompetent, because the demands of the position exceed the person's capacities. Developed by J. L. Peter.

physical distribution (See page 240.)

physiological needs The most prepotent needs in Maslow's hierarchy of needs: food, clothing, shelter, and sex.

picketing (See page 461.)

piece rate (See page 417.)

piggyback exporting (See page 574.)

place or distribution (See page 236.)

place utility (See page 221.)

planned obsolescence (See page 231.)

planning (See page 156.)

plant capacity (See page 195.)

plant layout (See page 195.)

pollution and blight Taken together, they constitute any damage to the environment. Pollution refers to the physical environment and blight refers to the social environment.

portfolio The set of securities owned by a person or a firm.

postindustrial society A society that has progressed beyond the industrial society. Instead of manufacturing being the dominant form of business activity, the services industries are predominant.

precedent A previous case decided in the same legal jurisdiction, for which there was no explicit written law or statute and whose circumstances and issues were the same as those in a subsequent case, which will therefore be decided in the same way as the earlier case.

preemptive right The right of old stockholders to buy new shares issued by a corporation before anyone else. It enables a stockholder to maintain his or her same proportionate ownership of the corporation.

preferred stock (See page 90.)

preliminary employment interview (See page 407.)

prepaid expense A current asset representing an expenditure of funds the benefit of which has not yet been realized in the firm's operations.

preventive maintenance (See page 203.)

price (in economics) (See page 44.)

price (in marketing) (See page 261.)

price discrimination Charging different prices to competitive buyers of the same product for reasons not associated with costs.

price/earnings (P/E) ratio The present price of a share of stock divided by the current earnings per share.

price index The ratio of prices in the current period (or year) to prices in a base period (or year); a measure of inflation.

price leadership (See page 261.)

price lining (See page 267.)

price system (See *market economy*.)

pricing model (See page 264.)

primary demand The demand for a product category rather than the demand for a particular brand of product within that category (selective demand). For example, the demand for milk and the demand for Borden's milk.

primary research (See page 270.)

prime rate of interest (See page 326.)

principle of indemnity (See page 379.)

private brand Also called middleman brand or dealer brand. A brand owned by a wholesaler or retailer as opposed to a manufacturer.

private carrier (See page 242.)

private corporation A corporation that is organized, owned, and operated by private investors.

private enterprise (See page 19.)

product (See page 229.)

product cost accounting (See page 304.)

product differentiation (See page 267.)

production (See page 187.)

production management (See page 192.)

production to order Production as required on demand from the firm's customers.

product life cycle (See page 230.)

product mix (See page 232.)

product obsolescence The replacement of one product or product feature by a newer, better, or cheaper one.

product offering The product element of the marketing mix that includes not only the physical product but also the guarantee, service, brand, package, installation, alteration, etc., that accompanies the physical product.

products liability insurance A policy designed to protect a company from claims made by users of its products.

professional-managerial ethic   (See page 622.)

professional managers   (See page 100.)

profit   (See page 33.)

profit sharing   The receipt by an employee of a portion of the profits earned by the employer.

progressive tax   (See page 616.)

promissory note   (See page 333.)

promotion (in marketing)   (See page 253.)

promotion (in personnel administration)   (See page 420.)

property and casualty insurance   (See page 379.)

prospecting   That part of a salesperson's job that involves developing a list of prospective customers.

prospectus   (See page 348.)

protestant ethic   (See page 22.)

proxy   (See page 92.)

public corporation   A corporation organized, owned, and operated by government.

publicity   (See page 260.)

public market   (See page 336.)

public-private partnership   (See page 622.)

public relations   (See page 260.)

punched card   (See page 481.)

pure risk   (See page 376.)

quality control   (See page 202.)

quality of life   A concept used as an indicator of the "real" effects of modern society on human life as opposed to the more narrow, traditional economic indicator such as GNP per capita. The idea is that higher income can be offset by such things as pollution or obsolescence.

quantitative tools   (See page 495.)

quasi-public corporation   A corporation that is organized, owned, and operated jointly by government and private investors.

quick ratio   (See *acid-test ratio*.)

raw materials   A category of industrial goods. They become a physical part of the goods they are used to produce. Examples are farm products such as cotton and natural products such as lumber.

real estate mortgage bond   A bond that is secured by real property.

real income   (See page 46.)

real property   (See page 106.)

recapitalization   (See page 384.)

recession   That period in the business cycle during which the volume of business activity is declining. Consumers and businesses are losing confidence and are becoming pessimistic about the future.

reciprocity   (See page 207.)

recovery   That period in the business cycle during which the volume of business activity is expanding after a recession or depression. Businesses begin investing again and consumers begin buying again. Optimism prevails.

recruiting   (See page 401.)

recycling   Means developed in order to turn pollution sources into economic resources by reusing them.

redeemable bonds   Also referred to as callable bonds. They can be redeemed or called in prior to maturity.

reference groups   Groups that help define a person's place in society, his or her goals, and his or her aspirations.

regional trading bloc   (See page 577.)

registered bond   A bond on which the owner's name appears; his or her name is registered with the issuing corporation.

regression analysis   An estimate, arrived at by use of an equation, of the form of the relationship between a dependent variable and one or more independent variables.

regressive tax   (See page 616.)

reorganization   (See page 385.)

research and development   (R&D) A general category of activities that are intended to produce new products and processes.

reserve requirement   (See page 330.)

resignation   (See page 425.)

responsibility   (See page 124.)

responsibility accounting   (See page 304.)

résumé   A brief statement of a person's qualifications for employment.

retailer   A firm selling goods to households or other ultimate consumers.

retained earnings   Profits that have been held in the business as capital. A major source of funds.

reurbanization   People returning from the suburbs to be nearer to the centers of cities. They do this to avoid the problems of daily commuting and to be near city services.

revenue (See page 288.)

reverse discrimination Discrimination against a nonminority person in favor of a minority person. Claims of such discrimination were made in the Bakke and the Weber cases before the U. S. Supreme Court.

revolving credit (See page 371.)

right-to-work laws (See page 448.)

risk (See page 64.)

Robinson-Patman Act A 1936 federal law designed to curb unfair marketing practices. It outlaws price discrimination and other anti-competitive forms of behavior.

round lot A unit of 100 shares of stock.

routine decision (See page 175.)

safety needs Needs that emerge after the physiological needs in Maslow's hierarchy of needs. They include the need to feel that you will survive and that your physiological needs will continue to be met.

salary (See page 417.)

sales finance company (See page 320.)

sales forecast (See page 303.)

sales promotion (See page 260.)

sales quota The number of units or the dollar sales volume that is set as a target for salespersons. Often, sales above quota result in the salesperson earning a bonus.

sales revenue The total amount of money a firm receives from the sale of its product(s). Price per unit multiplied by the number of units.

sample (See page 497.)

sampling The use of a part (sample) of a larger group (universe or population) to represent that larger group.

savings and loan association (See page 317.)

savings bank (See page 317.)

secondary research (See page 269.)

secret partner In a partnership, a partner who actively participates in managing the firm but whose identity is not disclosed to the public.

secured loans (See page 372.)

Securities and Exchange Commission (SEC) An agency that polices the operation of national exchanges, the over-the-counter market, and cor-

porations whose securities are traded on them.

securities exchanges (See page 340.)

selection tests (See page 407.)

selective demand The demand for a particular brand of product within a product category. For example, the demand for Borden's milk as opposed to the demand for milk in general (primary demand).

self-actualization In Maslow's hierarchy of needs, it is the drive for achievement, creativity, and the need to achieve your potential in life.

self-insurance (See page 375.)

seniority (See page 415.)

sensitivity training (See *T-group training.*)

serial bonds A large issue of bonds with varying maturity dates.

Service Corps of Retired Executives (SCORE) (See page 536.)

services Services are a type of consumer good. They provide consumer satisfactions and benefits but they are not physical objects. Examples are the services of physicians, beauticians, banks, and restaurants.

severance pay A payment to the worker above his or her wage or salary that is due when he or she terminates employment with the employer.

shopping goods (See page 226.)

short run A period of time of one year or less; equivalent of short term.

short selling (See page 346.)

short-term debt Notes issued by a firm or any debt that it has incurred that will require less than one year for repayment.

short-term capital (See *working capital.*)

silent partner In a partnership, a partner who does not actively participate in managing the firm but whose name is identified with the partnership.

sinking fund (See page 373.)

sinking fund bonds The annual deposit of funds by the issuing corporation with a trustee so that those deposits, along with earned interest, will be available to redeem bonds upon maturity.

skimming pricing (See page 266.)

sleeping partner (See *dormant partner.*)

Small Business Administration (SBA) (See page 532.)

Small Business Administration (SBA) direct

loans (See page 534.)

Small Business Administration (SBA) guaranteed loans (See page 534.)

Small Business Administration (SBA) participating loans (See page 534.)

Small Business Institute (SBI) (See page 536.)

Small Business Investment Company (SBIC) (See page 534.)

social cost In pursuing profit expressed in dollars, a firm may incur great social cost in the form of polluted streams, air, or blight of cities.

Social Darwinism The nineteenth-century political and economic philosophy that advocated the survival of the economically fittest in an unregulated competitive environment.

social responsibility of business Refers to the general idea that a business firm has obligations to individuals and groups (its publics) other than its owners.

social stratification Division of members of a society into recognized classes or groups of varying status (that is, upper class, middle class, lower class).

society A large group of people who are bound together by a complex set of relationships.

software (See page 487.)

sole proprietorship (See page 77.)

span of control (See *span of management.*)

span of management (See page 123.)

specialization (See page 6.)

specialized staff Staff personnel who serve the entire firm, not just one line manager. The director of marketing research is an example.

specialty goods (See page 227.)

speculative risks (See page 376.)

speculative trading Buying or selling securities in the hope of profiting from near-term future changes in their selling prices. Common especially in bull markets.

staff (See page 127.)

staff functions (See page 127.)

staffing (See page 162.)

stagflation A peculiar economic condition under which inflation and depressed economic activity occur at the same time.

standard A predetermined level of quality, speed, strength, or size pertaining to some aspect of a firm's operation. Could relate to product or people or finance.

standard metropolitan statistical area (SMSA) An integrated social and economic unit with one city (or twin cities) of 50,000 or more inhabitants. It includes the county of this central city and adjacent counties that are socially and economically integrated with the central city.

standard of living (See page 8.)

state development company A corporation organized by state government to operate statewide in assisting the growth and development of business firms.

statement of financial position (See *balance sheet.*)

state trading company (See page 555.)

statistics (See page 495.)

status A person's rank in a social system as perceived by others.

status symbols Symbols often used to affect how others will perceive a person's status. An executive with a plush carpet on the office floor enjoys more status than another executive with cheap tile on the office floor.

statutory law Written or codified law as developed in city councils, state legislatures, and the Congress of the United States and supported by city charters, state constitutions, and the federal Constitution.

steward A union official selected by the employees in a plant to represent them.

stock and bond averages Indices used to tell what is happening on the securities exchanges, that is, prices advancing or declining.

stockbrokers Middlemen who buy and sell securities for their investor-clients. They work for brokerage houses.

stock dividend A payment to stockholders in additional shares of stock. Enables a corporation to conserve its cash.

stockholders (See page 83.)

stock split An action that gives a shareholder a greater number of shares but maintains his or her same proportionate ownership in the corporation.

straight life insurance A type of insurance for which the insured pays premiums until his or her death, at which time the face value of the policy is paid to the beneficiary. Has savings and protection elements.

strategic planning   (See page 157.)

strike   (See page 461.)

Subchapter S Corporation   (See page 85.)

subculture   A different culture existing among a group within the larger group of people who possess the main culture.

suboptimize   Pertaining to being satisfied with something less than the best. In trying to integrate personal and organizational objectives, management frequently must suboptimize.

subsidiary   A company owned by a parent company.

subsistence economy   A nation or region in which the people have a very low standard of living, barely enough to survive.

Sunbelt   A popular term used to describe states in the South and Southwest.

supplemental unemployment benefits (SUB)   (See page 453.)

supplies   A category of industrial goods. They are relatively inexpensive items that do not become a physical part of the goods they are used to produce. Examples are light bulbs, nuts and bolts, and paper clips.

supply   (See page 51.)

supply curve   (See page 54.)

surety bond   A bond that insures a person or firm against loss if the other party to a contract does not fulfill a contractual obligation.

surrender value   The amount the insured gets back from the insurance company if the insured cancels his or her life insurance policy. Not applicable to term life insurance policies.

systems concept   (See page 161.)

Taft-Hartley Act   (See page 440.)

tangible net worth   (See page 299.)

target market   (See page 222.)

tariffs   (See page 555.)

tax control   (See page 558.)

taxpayers' revolt   A widespread movement of the late seventies for tax reduction. The most dramatic example was the passage of Proposition 13 in California.

technological obsolescence   The obsolescence of a product or production process because of technological progress. The alternator made the generator technologically obsolete for cars.

technology   The application of science to do new things or to do old things in a better way.

tenancy in common   The sharing by two or more persons of title to real property. Each tenant's share passes to his or her heirs at the tenant's death.

tenants by the entirety   A form of joint tenancy of real property. It can be ended only by death of one party. The other partner becomes sole owner.

term life insurance   A type of insurance written to cover a certain number of years. If the insured dies during that period, the beneficiary receives the face value of the policy. If not, all premiums paid belong to the insurance company. It is pure protection.

T-group training   A T-group is a laboratory where trainees come together in small discussion groups to deal with real (not simulated) problems that exist within the training group itself. Rather than only teaching skills, the purpose is to help trainees learn about their individual weaknesses, how groups work, and how to behave more effectively in interpersonal relations. Also called sensitivity training, laboratory training, or encounter groups.

theory X manager   A term developed by Douglas McGregor to describe a manager who assumes that the average person inherently dislikes work and is, by nature, lazy, irresponsible, self-centered, security oriented, indifferent to the needs of the organization, and unambitious, and wants to avoid responsibility.

theory Y manager   A term developed by Douglas McGregor to describe a manager who assumes that the average person is capable of developing interest in his or her work, committing himself or herself to working to reach company goals, and working productively with a minimum of control and threat of punishment.

time deposit   (See page 322.)

time sharing   (See page 486.)

time utility   (See page 221.)

total cost concept   (See page 241.)

trade acceptance   (See page 334.)

trade barriers   (See page 555.)

trade credit   (See page 369.)

trade draft   (See page 334.)

trademark   (See page 235.)

trade position discount   (See page 264.)

traditional business ethic   (See page 620.)

transaction   (See page 288.)

transfer   Shifting an employee from one job to another that does not require the employee to possess greater skills or assume more duties.

transfer agents   Agents who record changes in stock ownership of the corporations that they represent. Usually they are trust companies.

Treasury bills   Short-term debt issue of the U.S. government. A highly liquid investment or asset in a portfolio or on a balance sheet.

treasury stock   Stock issued by a corporation and subsequently repurchased by it.

treatment   (See page 189.)

trust company   (See page 318.)

trustee   Usually a trust company. A corporation selling bonds to a large number of investors appoints a trustee to protect the bondholders' interests.

underdeveloped nations   Nations in which the bulk of the people live in poverty. Per capita GNP is low in comparison to other countries. Also called less-developed countries.

underemployment   working at jobs below the skill level of the worker.

unfair labor practices   Illegal actions by management or labor related to employment.

unfair lists   (See page 437.)

Uniform Commercial Code (UCC)   (See page 108.)

union federation   (See page 443.)

union shop   (See page 448.)

unit pricing   The expression of the price of a product in cost per ounce or some other standard measure. That information is posted on or near the product on the retailer's shelf.

unlimited liability   (See page 78.)

unlisted securities   Securities not listed on any of the organized securities exchanges. They are traded in the over-the-counter market.

unsecured loan   A loan that is not backed by collateral. It is backed by the borrower's promise to repay it.

urban blight   Deterioration of central cities, seriously reducing the quality of life therein.

usury   Interest in excess of the legal rate.

utility   (See page 13.)

value-added tax   A tax applied each time a good changes hands based on the difference between the buying and the selling price. Used in Europe and under discussion in the United States.

value analysis   (See page 208.)

value in exchange   (See page 14.)

variable cost   A cost that increases as the number of units of output produced increases. Materials cost is an example.

vendor analysis   (See page 208.)

venture capitalists   Persons who provide equity or debt financing to new and/or risky businesses in the hope of making a profit.

voluntary arbitration   (See page 460.)

voluntary compliance   (See page 611.)

wage   (See page 417.)

wage and salary administration   (See page 416.)

wage and salary surveys   That part of wage and salary administration that involves conducting surveys to determine the general pay level in the firm's community and industry.

wage-push inflation   An increase in the price level due to increases in wages that are greater than gains in labor productivity.

Wagner Act   (See page 438.)

warranty   (See page 106.)

Webb-Pomerene Associations   (See page 574.)

wholesaler   A vendor who sells goods for resale by other merchants or for use in other businesses.

working capital   (See page 359.)

yellow-dog contract   The requirement as a precondition of employment that the worker sign a contract in which he or she agrees not to join a union. Outlawed by the Norris-LaGuardia Act of 1932.

zero population growth (ZPG)   (See page 604.)

Index

This page continues p. iv credit list.

Opposing Farm Mechanization," *Time*, January 29, 1979, p. 45. Reprinted by permission from *Time*, The Weekly Newsmagazine; Copyright Time Inc. 1979. p. 20—"Cambodia: Silence, Subterfuge and Surveillance," *Time*, January 8, 1979, pp. 30–31. Reprinted by permission from *Time*, The Weekly Newsmagazine; Copyright Time Inc. 1979. p. 25—"GM Tests Arbitration to Quell Buyer Unrest," *Business Week*, October 2, 1978, pp. 34, 36. Reprinted from the October 2, 1978 issue of BusinessWeek by special permission, © 1978 by McGraw-Hill, Inc., New York, NY 10020. All rights reserved. p. 29—"Socialism: Trials and Errors," *Time*, March 13, 1978, pp. 24–27, 29–30, 35–36. Reprinted by permission from *Time*, The Weekly Newsmagazine; Copyright Time Inc. 1978. p. 31—*Dunagin's People* by Ralph Dunagin. Courtesy Field Newspaper Syndicate. p. 37—"Mexico, the Quandary: How to Invest Oil Riches," *Business Week*, June 5, 1978, pp. 69, 72. Reprinted from the June 5, 1978 issue of BusinessWeek by special permission, © 1978 by McGraw-Hill, Inc., New York, NY 10020. All rights reserved. p. 38—"Black Market Cosmetics Big in Russia," *The Times-Picayune*, December 11, 1978, sec. 3, p. 6.
Chapter 2: p. 40, 41—Daniel S. Brody/Stock, Boston. p. 45—*Dunagin's People* by Ralph Dunagin. Courtesy Field Newspaper Syndicate. p. 47—*Time*, January 15, 1979, p. 58. Reprinted by permission from *Time*, The Weekly Newsmagazine; Copyright Time Inc. 1979. p. 48—"Using IOUs to Fight Inflation," *Business Week*, October 16, 1978, pp. 88–89. p. 50—*The Better Half* by Barnes, reprinted courtesy the Register and Tribune Syndicate, Inc. p. 60—*Statistical Abstract of the United States, 1978*, 99th ed. (Washington, D.C.: U. S. Bureau of the Census, 1978), p. 579. p. 62—"Refinery Waste Conversion: Balanced Transport Makes It Possible," *Traffic Management*, May 1978, pp. 62–65. p. 67—"Hy-Gain Loses," *Time*, January 23, 1978, p. 66. Reprinted by permission from *Time*, The Weekly Newsmagazine; Copyright Time Inc. 1978. p. 68—"Why Furniture Makers Feel So Comfortable," *Business Week*, July 30, 1979, pp. 75–76. Reprinted from the July 30, 1979 issue of BusinessWeek by special permission, © 1979 by McGraw-Hill, Inc., New York, NY 10020. All rights reserved.
Section Two: p. 70 (top left)—Joseph Schuyler/Stock, Boston. p. 70 (bottom left) Jean Boughton/The Picture Cube. p. 70 (right)—© Donald Dietz, 1976.
Chapter 3: p. 72, 73—Jean Boughton/The Picture Cube. p. 77—"Conrail's Troubles Grow Even Worse," *Business Week*, July

10, 1978, p. 25. p. 84—Courtesy General Motors Corporation, Detroit, MI 48202. p. 88—Articles of Incorporation for the State of Mississippi reproduced by permission. p. 92—James C. Furlong, *Labor in the Boardroom: The Peaceful Revolution* (Princeton, N.J.: Dow Jones & Company, 1977), pp. 1, 5–7. p. 93—Courtesy Jaclyn, Inc., 635 59th St., West New York, NJ. p. 94—*Agatha Crumm*, © King Features Syndicate, Inc., 1979. p. 95—*Statistical Abstract of the United States, 1978*, 99th ed. (Washington, D.C.: U.S. Bureau of the Census, 1978), p. 561. p. 96—*Statistical Abstract of the United States, 1977*, 98th ed. (Washington, D.C.: U.S. Bureau of the Census, 1977), p. 550. p. 97—*Fortune*, May 7, 1979, pp. 270–71. 1979 *Fortune* Directory; © 1979 Time Inc. p. 99—Reprinted with permission of the Warner & Swasey Company, Cleveland, Ohio, © 1979. p. 111—"His Name Meant Hotel," *Time*, January 15, 1979, p. 65. Reprinted by permission from *Time*, The Weekly Newsmagazine; Copyright Time Inc. 1979. p. 112—"SBA Steps Up Aid to Exporters," *Business America*, June 4, 1979, pp. 9–11.
Chapter 4: p. 114, 115—Joseph Schuyler/Stock, Boston. p. 129—C. Northcote Parkinson, *Parkinson's Law and Other Studies in Administration* (Boston: Houghton Mifflin, 1957). p. 134—Rensis Likert, *New Patterns of Management* (New York: McGraw-Hill, 1961), p. 113. p. 136—*Peanuts* by Schulz, © 1979 United Feature Syndicate, Inc. p. 146—"Last Chance for Leyland," *Time*, November 14, 1977, p. 82. Reprinted by permission from *Time*, The Weekly Newsmagazine; Copyright Time Inc. 1977. p. 147—"Chrysler Gets Some 'Firepower,'" *Time*, November 13, 1978, p. 94. Reprinted by permission from *Time*, The Weekly Newsmagazine; Copyright Time Inc. 1978.
Chapter 5: p. 148, 149—© Donald Dietz, 1976. p. 158—"The New Planning," *Business Week*, December 18, 1978, pp. 62–66, 68. p. 162—*Selling Short*. Copyright 1978, Universal Press Syndicate. p. 165—*B.C.* by permission of Johnny Hart and Field Enterprises, Inc. p. 169—Robert Tannenbaum and Warren H. Schmidt, "How to Choose a Leadership Pattern," *Harvard Business Review*, May-June 1973, p. 164. p. 174—*Beetle Bailey*, © King Features Syndicate, Inc., 1979. p. 179—"Deep Sensing: A Pipeline to Employee Morale," *Business Week*, January 29, 1979, pp. 124, 126, 218. Reprinted from the January 29, 1979 issue of Business-Week by special permission, © 1979 by McGraw-Hill, Inc., New York, NY 10020. All rights reserved. p. 180—"An Executive Crash Course in Liberal Arts," *Busi-*

ness Week, August 14, 1978, p. 58. Reprinted from the August 14, 1978 issue of BusinessWeek by special permission, © 1979 by McGraw-Hill, Inc., New York, NY 10020. All rights reserved.
Section Three: p. 182 (left)—Chris Maynard Photography. p. 182 (top right)—© George W. Gardner, 1973. p. 182 (bottom right)—Hirohito Kubota/© Magnum Photos, Inc.
Chapter 6: p. 184, 185—Chris Maynard Photography. p. 188—Board of Governors of the Federal Reserve System. p. 191—Steven Lewis/The Picture Cube. p. 193—"Broader Procter & Gamble Distribution Slated for Large Number of New Products," *The Wall Street Journal*, September 7, 1978, p. 4. Reprinted by permission of *The Wall Street Journal*, © Dow Jones & Company, Inc., 1978. All rights reserved. p. 204—Chris Maynard Photography. p. 210—Richard Chase and Nicholas Aquilano, *Production and Operations Management*, rev. ed. (Homewood, Ill.: Richard D. Irwin, 1977), p. 14. © 1977 by Richard D. Irwin, Inc. p. 214 (top)—Daniel Machalaba, "Movable Feasts," *The Wall Street Journal*, July 13, 1978, p. 1. Reprinted by permission of *The Wall Street Journal*, © Dow Jones & Company, Inc., 1978. All rights reserved. p. 214 (bottom)—"Ford Is Recalling Some 1.5 Million Pintos, Bobcats," *The Wall Street Journal*, June 12, 1978, p. 2. Reprinted by permission of *The Wall Street Journal*, © Dow Jones & Company, Inc., 1978. All rights reserved.
Chapter 7: p. 216, 217—© Donald Dietz, 1975. p. 223—Cartoon by Henry Martin. Reprinted by permission of the Chicago Tribune-New York News Syndicate, Inc. p. 232—Both photos courtesy of Burroughs Corporation, Detroit, MI 48232. p. 234—*Pepper . . . and Salt* courtesy of Cartoon Features Syndicate. p. 242—*Yearbook of Railroad Facts* (Washington, D.C.: Association of American Railroads, 1979), p. 36. p. 248—David McClintock, "Spurred by Rise in Postal Rates, Publishers Expand Use of Private Delivery Services," *The Wall Street Journal*, August 9, 1978, p. 36. Reprinted by permission of *The Wall Street Journal*, © Dow Jones & Company, 1978. All rights reserved.
Chapter 8: p. 250, 251—© George W. Gardner, 1973. p. 254—Prepared by Robert J. Coen, McCann-Erickson, Inc. 1968 data reported in *Marketing/Communications*, February 1969, p. 60; 1978 data (preliminary) reported in *Advertising Age*, January 8, 1979, pp. 5–9. p. 256—"Ads Start to Take Hold in the Professions," *Business Week*, July 24, 1978, pp. 122–123. p. 259—*Marketing molehills*. Reprinted from *Marketing News*, June

Goell/The Picture Cube. p. 480—Courtesy of Xerox Corporation, 280 Park Avenue, New York, NY.; and of Needham, Harper & Steers, Inc., 909 Third Avenue, New York, NY 10022. p. 482—Courtesy of International Business Machines Corporation, Chicago, IL 60611. p. 484—All photos courtesy of International Business Machines Corporation, Chicago, IL 60611. p. 486—*Pepper . . . and Salt* courtesy of Cartoon Features Syndicate. p. 490—*Pepper . . . and Salt* courtesy of Cartoon Features Syndicate. p. 491—Adapted from Barry Render and Ralph M. Stair, Jr., "How to Evaluate Computer Systems," *Louisiana Business Survey,* October 1977, pp. 14–15. p. 493—Courtesy of International Business Machines Corporation, Chicago, IL 60611. p. 505 (top)—Roger B. May, "As Costs Fall and Incentives Rise, Supermarkets Begin to Install Computer Checkouts on Counters," *The Wall Street Journal,* June 13, 1978, p. 40. Reprinted by permission of *The Wall Street Journal,* © Dow Jones & Company, 1978. All rights reserved. p. 505 (bottom)—June Kromholz, "Bottom Line Ranch," *The Wall Street Journal,* September 1, 1978, p. 1. Reprinted by permission of the *Wall Street Journal,* © Dow Jones & Company, 1978. All rights reserved. **Section Four:** p. 506 (left)—Terry McKoy/The Picture Cube. p. 506 (right)—© Donald Dietz, 1974. **Chapter 15:** p. 508, 509—© Donald Dietz, 1974. p. 511—*SBA Business Loans* (Washington, D.C.: U.S. Small Business Administration, 1975), p. 3. p. 513—Courtesy of Collin Street Bakery, Corsicana, TX 75110. p. 516—Rebecca Morehouse, "$5,000 to $20 Million in Five Years," *The* (New Orleans) *Times-Picayune,* December 10, 1978, sec. 4, p. 18. p. 519—*The Business Failure Record, 1977* (New York: Dun & Bradstreet, 1977), p. 12. By permission of Dun & Bradstreet. p. 520—"The Combleat Mower," *Time,* May 24, 1976, p. 64. Reprinted by permission from *Time,* The Weekly Newsmagazine; Copyright Time Inc. 1976. p. 525—"Supermarketing Legal Services," *Time,* October 9, 1978, p. 116. Reprinted by permission from *Time,* The Weekly Newsmagazine; Copyright Time Inc. 1978. p. 526—Courtesy of Wendy's International, Inc., P.O. Box 256, 4288 W. Dublin Granville Rd., Dublin, OH 43017. p. 527—*Funky Winkerbean* by Tom Batiuk. © Field Enterprises, Inc., 1979. Courtesy Field Newspaper Syndicate. p. 533—U.S. Small Business Administration, "Small Business Loans" (Issued by the Office of Public Information, February 1975, OPI-18). p. 539—*The Business Failure Record, 1977* (New York: Dun &

Bradstreet, Inc., 1977), pp. 3, 15. By permission of Dun & Bradstreet, Inc. pp. 545–546—Allan J. Mayer with William J. Cook, "Computers: Taking on IBM," *Newsweek,* December 6, 1976, pp. 84, 86. Copyright 1976 by Newsweek, Inc. All rights reserved. Reprinted by permission. p. 546—"How the Classroom Turns Out Entrepreneurs," *Business Week,* June 18, 1979, pp. 86, 90. **Chapter 16:** p. 548, 549—Terry McKoy/The Picture Cube. p. 553—*Survey of Current Business,* January 1979, pp. S-22, S-23, S-24. p. 554—*Survey of Current Business,* January 1979, pp. S-22, S-23. p. 559—"World Roundup," *Business Week,* October 9, 1978, p. 62. p. 563—*Survey of Current Business,* selected years. p. 565—"Europe's New Money Union," *Time,* December 18, 1978, p. 69. Reprinted by permission from *Time,* The Weekly Newsmagazine; Copyright Time Inc. 1978. p. 566—*Business Week,* March 12, 1979, p. 67. Reprinted from the March 12, 1979 issue of BusinessWeek by special permission, © 1979 by McGraw-Hill, Inc., New York, NY 10020. All rights reserved. p. 569—*Dunagin's People* by Ralph Dunagin. Courtesy Field Newspaper Syndicate. p. 571—"The Price of Stormy Petrol," *Time,* February 26, 1979, p. 60. Reprinted by permission from *Time,* The Weekly Newsmagazine; Copyright Time Inc. 1979. p. 573—"The Reluctant Exporter," *Business Week,* April 10, 1978, p. 65. Reprinted from the April 10, 1978 issue of BusinessWeek by special permission, © 1978 by McGraw-Hill, Inc., New York, NY 10020. All rights reserved. p. 575—"To a Global Car," *Business Week,* November 20, 1978, p. 102. p. 576—*Business Week,* July 24, 1978, p. 82. Reprinted from the July 24, 1978 issue of BusinessWeek by special permission, © 1978 by McGraw-Hill, Inc., New York, NY 10020. All rights reserved. p. 578—*Survey of Current Business,* August 1978, p. 17. p. 579—*Survey of Current Business,* August 1978, p. 39. p. 580—"High Interest," *Time,* September 11, 1978, p. 52. Reprinted by permission from *Time,* The Weekly Newsmagazine; Copyright Time Inc. 1979. p. 584—"Saudi Arabia: Luring Technology by Equity Investment," *Business Week,* July 10, 1978, p. 38. p. 590—"World Roundup," *Business Week,* October 16, 1978, p. 72. pp. 590–591—"The Reluctant Exporter," *Business Week,* April 10, 1978, p. 60. **Section Five:** p. 592 (left)—Antman/Stock, Boston p. 592 (right)—Godfrey/© Magnum Photos, Inc. **Chapter 17:** p. 594, 595—Godfrey/© Magnum Photos, Inc. p. 600 (top)—*The Consumer: A Graphic Profile* (New York: The Conference Board). p. 600 (bot-

tom)—*The Consumer: A Graphic Profile* (New York: The Conference Board). p. 601—*The Consumer: A Graphic Profile* (New York: The Conference Board). p. 602 (top)—*The Consumer: A Graphic Profile* (New York: The Conference Board). p. 602 (bottom)—*The Consumer: A Graphic Profile* (New York: The Conference Board). p. 603—*The Consumer: A Graphic Profile* (New York: The Conference Board). p. 607—*The New Yorker,* October 23, 1978. Drawing by D. Fradon; © 1978 The New Yorker Magazine, Inc. p. 611—"The FTC's Move to Dump State Regulations," *Business Week,* July 10, 1978, p. 74. p. 615—Willard C. Butcher, "The Stifling Costs of Regulation," *Business Week,* November 6, 1978, p. 22. p. 616—Data from the U.S. Office of Management and Budget. p. 619—*Dunagin's People* by Ralph Dunagin. Courtesy Field Newspaper Syndicate. p. 621—*The New Yorker,* September 17, 1978. Drawing by Dana Fradon; © 1978 The New Yorker Magazine, Inc. p. 626 (top)—"OSHA Tries to Expose On-job Medical Files," *Business Week,* August 7, 1978, pp. 28–29. p. 626 (bottom)—"Report Urges U.S. Help Women to Be Business Owners," *The Wall Street Journal,* June 29, 1978, p. 12. Reprinted by permission of *The Wall Street Journal,* © Dow Jones & Company, Inc., 1978. All rights reserved. **Chapter 18:** p. 629, 630—Antman/The Picture Cube. p. 633—© Elizabeth Hamlin, 1976. p. 634—White House Conference on the World Ahead, Washington, D.C., 1973. p. 636 (top)—*Monthly Labor Review,* 91 (January 1979): 110. p. 636 (bottom)—*Dunagin's People* by Ralph Dunagin. Courtesy Field Newspaper Syndicate. p. 638—*Congressional Quarterly Weekly Reports,* March 11, 1978, p. 626. p. 640—Reprinted from *U. S. News & World Report,* December 11, 1978, p. 57. Copyright 1978 U. S. News & World Report, Inc. p. 641—U.S. Bureau of Labor Statistics, Department of Labor, Washington, D.C. p. 642—U.S. Bureau of Labor Statistics, Department of Labor, Washington, D.C. p. 643—*Occupational Manpower and Training Needs* (Washington, D.C.: U.S. Department of Labor, Bureau of Labor Statistics, bulletin 1918; revised 1976), Appendix B. p. 644—*Occupational Outlook Handbook, 1978–1979* (Washington, D.C.: U.S. Department of Labor). pp. 645–647—*Occupational Outlook Handbook, 1978–1979* (Washington, D.C. U.S. Department of Labor), pp. 141–142. p. 648—*Occupational Outlook Handbook, 1978–1979* (Washington, D.C. U.S. Department of Labor). p. 649 (top)—Indirectly quoted from *A Career Planning*